From Bill
May 22, 1994

AMERICAN INDIAN ALMANAC

by John Upton Terrell

BARNES
& NOBLE
BOOKS
NEW YORK

The author and publisher gratefully acknowledge permission to quote from the following works:

Harold E. Driver, *Indians of North America,* © 1961 by the University of Chicago. Published 1961.

Mark Raymond Harrington and Ruth D. Simpson, *Tule Springs, Nevada, with Other Evidence of Pleistocene Man in North America,* Southwest Museum Papers, No. 18, Los Angeles, 1961.

Royal B. Hassrick, *The Sioux: Life and Customs of a Warrior Society.* Copyright 1964 by the University of Oklahoma Press.

Theodora Kroeber, *Ishi in Two Worlds,* originally published by the University of California Press; reprinted by permission of The Regents of the University of California.

H. M. Wormington, *Ancient Man in North America,* Denver Museum of Natural History, 1941, 1957.

This edition published by Barnes & Noble, Inc., by arrangement with Nina Terrell

1994 Barnes and Noble Books

ISBN 1-56619-457-1

Printed and bound in the United States of America

M 9 8 7 6 5 4 3 2 1

Contents

PART TWO

Gulf Coasts and Tidal Swamps   68

PART THREE

Southeastern Woodlands   117

CONTENTS

PART SIX

Northern Great Plains   252

CONTENTS

PART NINE

The Great Basin   365

PART TEN

The Pacific Coast   396

CONTENTS

Foreword

This book is written for readers who are interested in gaining more knowledge than they may possess about prehistoric American Indians.

Most persons tend to shy away from archeological, anthropological, ethnological, and geological papers, and with good reason. As they must be, they are highly technical, replete with equations, postulations, charts, graphs, and language enlightening and comprehensible only to men and women thoroughly trained in these sciences. That is a distinction to which I make no claim.

I am a writer, specifically a historian. That is a field—speaking with proper modesty, of course—in which I have been granted by good fortune a certain measure of achievement. I do not believe that I have overplayed the role in which I have been cast for many years.

The goal I set for myself in writing this book really may be simply explained. It was to tell, in what may be termed everyday language, as much as I could, within an allotted number of pages, about the peoples who inhabited the region of the United States up to the beginning of the historical period. As the bibliographical notes will attest, I have sought to glean from a mass of sources, both scientific and historical, material that, when presented in orderly form, would comprise an interesting, informative, colorful, and dramatic story.

I have divided the United States into ten geographical regions. While they are arbitrarily delineated, they conform generally to prehistoric cultural areas. Although there was through the millennia widespread diffusion of customs and beliefs, the people in each region differed in marked respects from the peoples in the other regions. Ecological patterns differed. Climatic conditions, for example, influenced and shaped economies, just as did supply and demand. Social structures were greatly varied, as were physical characteristics, mores, arts and crafts, political systems, and religious ritual. Intertribal warfare, incessant in all regions, caused countless migrations and resulted in the extinction of some tribes.

Each part of the book concludes shortly after the historical period began in the region of which it treats. The time of man's arrival in the Western Hemisphere cannot yet be accurately stated. The hands of the archeological clock are being turned steadily backward. Therefore, although the book can have an ending, actually it cannot have a beginning.

JOHN UPTON TERRELL

Southwestern Deserts and Mesa Lands

Spring in Dead Horse Gulch

A Negro cowhand, George McJunkin, in 1926 was patrolling the greening range in northeastern New Mexico. About eight miles west of the little town of Folsom, he turned into an arroyo called Dead Horse Gulch, through which flowed a tiny intermittent tributary of the Cimarron River. Passing around a bend of the rivulet, his eyes were attracted by several large and peculiar animal bones protruding from a bank that had begun to disintegrate.

After briefly observing them, he went on, completely unaware that in a few moments he had ridden back some ten or eleven thousand years into the Pleistocene Age.

Word of the incident was disseminated through the channels of casual neighborhood gossip. Two residents of Raton, New Mexico, thirty miles to the west, thought the discovery might be of some interest to scientists, and sent word of it to the Colorado Museum of Natural History.

When summer came, several paleontologists were at work in the gulch excavating at varying depths the bones of a bison species known to have been extinct for thousands of years. In loose dirt thrown from the diggings they came upon two fragments of flaked and grooved flint. Their curiosity was profoundly stirred, but the find they made a short time later electrified them.

Embedded in clay between two ribs of a Pleistocene bison, which may have weighed nearly a ton when alive, was another piece of flint, not only flaked and grooved but pointed. Obviously it was the man-made tip of a projectile that had been broken.

Carefully a large block of matrix, containing both the bones and the flint point as they had been found, was extracted and taken back to the museum laboratory in Denver. There it was cleaned and thoroughly studied. The geology of the formation and the identity of the bison species were established beyond question. Excitement rose when archeologists found that one of the flint fragments obtained from the loose dirt fitted to the projectile point which had been embedded between the ribs.

It was a discovery of transcending significance. For the first time there was incontrovertible evidence to show that man had been hunting in the area of the United States when animals of the Ice Age were alive. For the first time there was proof that man's antiquity in the Western Hemisphere was far greater than scientists had believed was possible.[1] *

And in 1926, when the director of the Denver museum, Dr. J. D. Figgins, notified the scientific world of the New Mexico findings, few archeologists were willing to acknowledge their validity. Many of them expressed the opinion that, somehow, the flints and the ancient bones had become mixed. More proof that the artifacts and the long extinct bison were contemporaneous was needed. Dr. Figgins, convinced of the accuracy of the museum's report, was determined to obtain it.

A second expedition was sent to the Folsom site in the summer of 1927. Several more broken points were found, but unfortunately were in loose dirt. At last another point was uncovered in matrix in unmistakable association with bison bones. All work was stopped. Telegrams were sent to a number of scientific institutions, reporting the new discovery, but only three noted archeologists appeared on the scene in response to the messages. They, however, fully supported the contentions of the Denver museum scientists.[2]

Still, the majority of leading specialists remained skeptical. The excavating was continued in 1928.[3] More projectile points were found among bison bones. More telegraphic invitations were sent, requesting authorities to view the finds *in situ.* Now the little town of Folsom experienced an uncommon influx of celebrated archeologists, paleontologists, and geologists. All doubts were dispelled from their minds. Homo sapiens unquestionably had lived in America at least as early as the period when the great glaciers, which at times had covered nearly a sixth of the earth's land surface, were in the process of their final retreat.

Folsom is still a little crossroads farming town, but in the annals of archeology its name is famous. The projectile flints found in Dead Horse Gulch became known around the world as Folsom points.

They would not long hold the distinction of being the oldest man-

---

* The superscript numerals refer to the notes appearing at the end of the book.

made hunting artifacts discovered in America—far from it. Within a short time other implements and tools of much greater age would be unearthed. But the Folsom points were the first to be recognized, and it would become the custom of scientists to think of them as a kind of time reference. A spear point would be described as being either pre-Folsom or post-Folsom.[4]

Unbroken Records in Arizona

A family tree cannot be drawn for early American Indians. For example, the Folsom people were nomadic hunters, and the weapons and tools they used have been found in widely separated sites not only in the West but throughout the eastern two thirds of the United States, and even in Mexico and Canada. The same thing may be said of others living before and after them—they moved with the animals, remaining in an area while the hunting was good, and moving to greener fields if it declined.

And there is another fundamental reason why it is impossible to trace with accuracy the ancestry of Indians of historic times back into the dark vaults of prehistory. Migrations from Siberia by way of the Bering (Strait) Land Bridge continued for an indeterminable number of millennia.[5] And migrations continued within the Western Hemisphere long after people had occupied every part of North and South America. Culture after culture arose and was superseded or merged with other cultures. Wide gaps exist between early and late cultures that scientists have not yet been able to bridge. Of course, in the sense that Indians have lived in America since the first of the migrants reached it, there is no real hiatus between cultures. But where or how long a certain people or group occupied a certain location are mysteries that may remain unsolved.

However, two places in the Southwest have provided incomparable exceptions to these puzzles, and have rewarded scientists with records of the people who occupied them for at least thirteen thousand, and perhaps fifteen thousand years. They are the Ventana Cave, in the Castle Mountains west of Tucson, and several sites called the Cochise Complex in southeastern Arizona and southwestern New Mexico.[6]

Oddly enough, it was in 1926, the year of the first Folsom point discovery, that archeologist Byron Cummings came upon the skull of a mammoth in clear association with crude stone tools and the bones of other ancient animals, twelve miles west of Douglas, Arizona. It soon became apparent, as other scientists excavated in the region, that although Dead Horse Gulch and Cochise Indians were contemporaries they represented different cultures. Yet they had been separated by no more than five hundred airline miles.

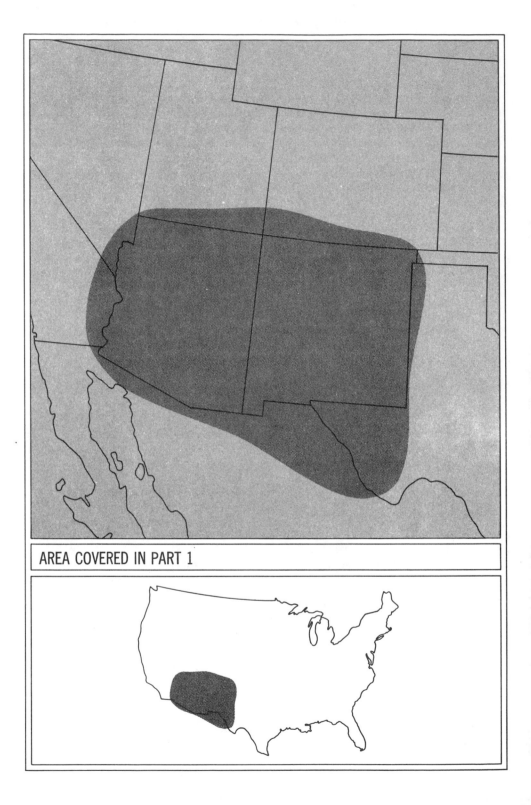

AREA COVERED IN PART 1

In the Cochise sites were found a great many metates, or grinding stones, stone hammers, and manos, which are stones small enough to be used by one hand in milling seeds. But the only points recovered, after years of excavating, were too small to have been used for killing the immense Pleistocene mammals. However, that these animals had been killed and butchered by Cochise men at the time was clear, for their bones had been charred and split, apparently for the purpose of extracting marrow. If the earliest Cochise Indians had large spear points, they must have made them of some perishable material, such as wood. Hearths, hearthstones, and charcoal were found in numerous campsites.

Here, for the first time, was unmistakable evidence of an early people who followed a sedentary way of life. They hunted, but they were largely dependent upon wild plant foods, such as seeds, berries, edible roots, and tubers and nuts.

Scientists E. B. Sayles and Ernst Antevs recognized three distinct stages of the culture which showed a continuous occupancy of the sites from 13,000 to 500 B.C. They grouped them under the overall name Cochise, the Arizona county in which many of the finds were made.*

The earliest stage, which lasted from 13,000 to 8000 B.C., was called Sulphur Spring, for it was at Double Adobe in Sulphur Spring Valley that the oldest artifacts were found. There was no evidence of pottery, basketry, or ornaments. Nor could anything be learned of the social customs of the Sulphur Spring Indians or the type of shelters in which they lived. The workmanship of their stone tools and implements was extremely crude. Many of them were discovered in the sheer walls of arroyos where they had been exposed by comparatively recent erosion.

The geology of the area, especially in the places of the deepest erosion, told a fascinating story. At the time of the Sulphur Spring Period a cool and moist climate prevailed in the region. There were rich grasslands and running streams. A section that is now a desert *playa* was then a large lake covering some 120 square miles. Along the creeks and bodies of water stood groves of cottonwoods and hickory trees. Today there are no living hickory trees closer than seven hundred miles to the area. But hickory charcoal was found in Sulphur Spring campsites. Thus, the Sulphur Spring people lived in the Pluvial Period that existed at the end of the Ice Age in some regions that are now arid.

The second stage of the Cochise Complex was named Chiricahua, for the mountain range in the area, and continued from 8000 to 3000 B.C.

The people of this period still depended largely on food-gathering.

---

* The county was named for the great leader of the Chiricahua Apaches, who migrated to the area probably in the seventeenth century and who still live there.

5

Grinding stones and stone tools predominated among the recovered artifacts. However, the milling metates were larger than those of the preceding period and had shallow basins, probably intentionally shaped.

There was evidence to indicate that these people were in contact with other cultures, for flaked projectile points, similar in some respects to Folsom spearheads, were found. They were made of fine-grained quartzite, a material alien to the location. In some Chiricahua sites implements flaked on both sides and points with broad lateral notches and indented bases were recovered.[7] The presence of antler fragments and bone splints indicated that doubtlessly bone tools were made, but only one complete bone awl was found.[8]

Geologists have determined that the region was considerably drier than it had been during the Sulphur Spring stage, so the beds in which Chiricahua artifacts were found have been placed in the post-Pluvial Period.

The San Pedro Period of the Cochise Complex, named for the San Pedro River, along which many of the sites were discovered, continued from 3000 B.C. to within a few centuries of the beginning of the Christian Era. The finds made in the sites of this period were highly informative and exciting.

Large pits that obviously had been houses were excavated at campsites in association with smaller pits that had been used for cooking and storage. Nothing could be learned of the kind of roofs constructed over the house pits, but it was apparent that their inhabitants entered them through a side aperture, stepping down to their floors from the outside ground surface.

The dryness of the climate continued to increase in this period. The desert of the present day was forming.

There were fewer milling stones, and many pressure-flaked implements, showing that the San Pedro Period people were depending more for their survival on hunting than on food-gathering. There were large projectile points and chipped knives, scrapers, and choppers made of fine-grained igneous stone, quartz, chert, and obsidian.

Now for the first time in the Cochise Complex were found fragments of shell and mica that may have been used as ornaments. The shell fragments were an extremely important discovery, for they indicated that the people of the San Pedro Period were either in contact with coastal areas, the Pacific, and the Gulf of California, or had received shells over trading routes.[9]

And now for the first time, corn pollen was found in some of the San Pedro sites. Here was evidence that agriculture had reached the Southwest well in advance of horizons previously hypothecated.[10] Now there was good reason to believe that the Cochise people were the forerunners of the Mogollon and Hohokam peoples, who are known to have been agriculturists.

The man-made artifacts recovered in the sites of the Cochise Complex bridged the cultural gap between hunters and sedentary peoples. The materials charted the cultural evolution that occurred gradually over many thousands of years, and showed that changes took place in an orderly normal manner. The end of the Cochise sequence came with the advent of the era of pottery-making. And pottery-making was not an invention of Indians living in the area of the United States. It came north to them from South America and Mexico, and it was an art already well-developed when it arrived.

The story of Ventana Cave is much like that of the Cochise Complex. It was occupied by Indians for at least thirteen thousand years. Indeed, debris on its floor when the first excavations were made in 1941 showed that Indians had used it as late as 1800 A.D. This work was undertaken by the University of Arizona and the Arizona State Museum under the direction of Dr. Emil W. Haury.[11]

Here in one place were uncovered cultural sequences that were major contributions to American archeology. Down the diggers went through modern-day cultures, through the Hohokam to the Cochise and the Folsom. But, beside pulling together the evidence of various cultural stages, Ventana Cave yielded other noteworthy evidence and materials.

Tools and points were found with an apparent relationship to types found in Lake Mojave, the Pinto Basin, and among early San Dieguito people of southern California, and in Gypsum Cave, Nevada. The stratified deposits of Ventana Cave yielded artifacts which indicated that cultural relationships and interchanges were in progress even in this ancient time. Ventana Cave underscored the concept of a cultural continuum in western America.[12]

Marine shells from the Pacific also were recovered, and it is believed that since they showed no signs of human workmanship they were not ornaments but were used as containers, probably for liquids.

The Cochise Complex and Ventana Cave may, and probably do, represent the cultural history of all American Indians, for not only do the artifacts found in them show connections with those recovered in other distant western sites, but the food-gathering habits and the tools of the early peoples who inhabited them are characteristic of the earliest known cultures of the eastern United States.

Visitors at Blackwater Draw

Near the Texas–New Mexico border, on the flat, windy, dry Llano Estacado, is an area containing more than twenty arid basins that once were beautiful lakes. Scientists speak of them as blowouts which the winds of ages cut into the dry earth after the lakes had vanished. In 1932 a gravel pit was opened by road builders in Blackwater Draw, a few miles from the town of Clovis, New Mexico. Ancient artifacts and mammoth teeth were uncovered. In the same year expeditions from the Philadelphia Academy of Natural Sciences and the University of Pennsylvania Museum began excavations. Soon flake knives and scrapers, projectile points, and other artifacts were found among burned bones of Pleistocene animals.

The story of Blackwater Draw and the entire Clovis Complex is similar to reports of archeological discoveries at numerous other southwestern sites, except in a few respects. A new type of projectile point, comparable in age to the Folsom, was found among mammoth remains. Measuring three to four inches in length and grooved halfway up the face, they were given the name of Clovis fluted.[13]

Two polished, tapering, cylindrical bone shafts with beveled ends were found in the remains of two mammoths. These were undoubtedly projectile points, but what makes them extremley important is that points of a similar type have been recovered in Pleistocene muck in Alaska, lower Klamath Lake, California, Lind Coulee, Washington, and in the bed of the Itchtucknee River in Florida—from one extremity of the United States to the other.

Another unique feature of the blowouts poses a problem that has not been resolved to the satisfaction of all the scientists who have worked at Blackwater and other sites of the Clovis Complex. It is the disconformities between the various strata of the ancient lake beds. Some geologists believe that these disconformities were caused by periods of high aridity occurring when there was extensive wind action. The eminent geologist Ernst Antevs vigorously disagrees. He does not believe there were dry periods during the Pluvial, and he has proffered an astonishing theory, applicable, at least in his opinion, to the lake at the gravel pit, called Blackwater Number One. It is that the depression containing the lake was closed by an artificial dam built by man, and that three times the dam was destroyed and rebuilt after the location had been subject to stream erosion.

Dam builders in the Pleistocene—a somewhat startling thought.[14]

Sandia Points in Las Huertas Canyon

A group of archeologists from the University of New Mexico, directed by Dr. Frank C. Hibben, in 1936 began excavating in a long and narrow cave of the Sandia Mountains, not far from Albuquerque. On the cave floor was bat guano, pack rat dung, horns and bones of modern-day animals. Digging through a crust of calcium carbonate, they came upon Folsom artifacts and charcoal of ancient campfires. This was an interesting but not exciting discovery, for since the original finds in Dead Horse Gulch, literally thousands of Folsom points had been recovered in various places throughout North America.

They continued to dig, passing through a layer of sterile yellow ocher to a stratum that contained the remains of several species of Pleistocene animals, and stone and bone implements and weapons, one of which turned out to be made of tusk ivory.[15]

And there they found a previously unknown type of projectile point.

Only nineteen specimens were recovered during the summer's work, but analysis of these showed that they had been made by man to kill Ice Age animals at least eighteen (and more probably twenty) thousand years before the beginning of the Christian Era. The name Sandia was given to them.

As old as were the projectiles found in Las Huertas Canyon of the Sandia range, it would soon be learned that they were not as old as other man-made weapons and implements which were being discovered each year in numerous parts of the United States. The hands of time were being turned backward steadily, and there was no longer any question that before man had learned to flake sharp spear points, knives, and scrapers, earlier men had hunted and performed other functions with crude and blunt stone weapons and tools. Within a short time, archeologists were becoming convinced that evidence would be unearthed to prove that man had reached the Western Hemisphere forty thousand years ago. What a great change had occurred in little more than a decade in scientific thinking! Now the eminent scholars were talking of an indefinite period which they called a Pre-Projectile Point State.[16]

Some Facts and Fancies

Of particular interest here are the people who made the Folsom, Clovis, and Sandia artifacts, their southwestern environment, and the mammals they hunted and on which they depended for their survival.

The most certain things that may be said of them are two in number: (1) They came originally from the north, and (2) almost all of them for thousands of years lived by hunting and the gathering of native plant foods. Here an impenetrable curtain falls to conceal further knowledge. Nothing can be learned of the clothing, the social customs, the religious ceremonials, the houses, the languages of these early wanderers.

Some of them remained in the Southwest for long periods. Others passed through the region to the east, to the south. Some undoubtedly returned, bringing with them articles and customs and ideas of other cultures. Always there was shifting, an advancing and retreating.

9

They did not live in large towns, as did later peoples of the Southwest, although they may have established villages in places where game
was plentiful and remained in them for a few years. This possibility is
indicated by the recent discovery of what appears to be "a more than
transient occupation site of Folsom Culture hunters near Albuquerque." [17] There more than eight thousand Folsom spear points and
other relics were found among circular depressions which were evidently lodges and may have been covered with poles, brush, and skins.
The place may prove to be the oldest village site to be discovered in
the Western Hemisphere, but it was a small town, in all probability
housing no more than twenty families.

That the men who made Sandia, Folsom, and other types of early
points were incredibly daring and competent hunters cannot be questioned. Conjectures are never acceptable as evidence to scientists, yet
they cannot refuse to consider them, for it often happens that imagina-
tion and theory open gates to the discovery of indisputable facts. The
eminent Dr. Hibben, discoverer of the Sandia points and other ancient
artifacts, does not hesitate to write such imaginary scenes as this: [18]

"The elephant whirled and trumpeted shrilly as he sighted the men
beyond the burning grass. One of the hunters fitted a long spear to his
spear-thrower. Swinging his body into the cast, the man hurled the
javelin. It struck high behind the mammoth's foreleg. The flint point
ripped through the inch-thick skin, shattering a rib, and bit deep into
the lungs. A spout of blood blew out of the mammoth's trunk. The
other men shouted, and rushed in for the kill.

"The beast whirled to face them. His 10-foot-long tusks swept around.
As a man closed to launch another spear, one tusk struck him on his
side. In the same instant, the mammoth's trunk lashed at the man's
head. His body broke like a shattered reed.

"The animal thrust his tusks again and again into the shapeless mass
that had been a human, but now other spears thudded into his chest.
One flint point, striking low behind the foreleg, pierced the great heart.
Blood pumped out of the gash. The mammoth swayed. He trumpeted
once again, blowing a plume of blood above his back. Then, with a
crash that shook the ground, the elephant fell on his side and died.

"Now women who had been standing behind a line of bushes came
forward. Some carried long flint knives. The men and the women
together began to hack through the tough hide and butcher the car-
cass . . . they did not go near what was left of the hunter's body. . . .
Death was a normal hazard of the hunt in America of 10,000 B.C."

Few hunters of today would attack an elephant with nothing more
than a flint-tipped spear. The Ice Age hunters did it without hesitation.
Indeed, they were mass killers of mammoths, camels, horses, giant
ground sloths, and other animals. The truth of this assertion is amply

illustrated. Sites have been found that are littered with the bones of thousands of Pleistocene mammals.[19]

And this fact leads to another conjecture, or theory, that is finding growing favor among archeologists.

Near the end of the Ice Age, the American Southwest was a hunters' paradise. Lush grasslands, dotted with lakes, reached away to every horizon. Immense numbers of animals of more than fifty species grazed on the luxuriant endless ranges.

By the end of the Ice Age almost all of them had disappeared. It has long been suggested that their extinction was caused by the change of climate which followed the melting of the great glaciers. But this explanation is no longer put forward as conclusive. Even after the Ice Age there remained vast regions covered with rich grasses and forests, and containing bodies of water and rivers. Now it is suggested that Sandia-Folsom-Clovis hunters hastened the extinction of Ice Age animals by slaughtering millions of them. Unlike later Indian hunters who generally killed only as much game as they required for food, clothing, and shelter, the Ice Age hunters killed wantonly, perhaps as much for sport as for necessity. The many sites of "mass kills" give support to this contention. Conservation is a practice developed within the memory of the living. The idea, if it was broached at all, was ignored by Americans pushing the frontier of civilization westward. Hunting laws limiting kills were invoked too late to prevent the extinction of some animals and fowls—the buffalo and the passenger pigeon are good examples. Many other species are nearing extinction, for man's mad passion for killing continues today to be one of his most discreditable attributes.

Bat Cave: the Farmers' Clock

Between the towns of Magdalena and Datil, New Mexico, are the plains of San Augustin. Near the southwestern end of this rough grasslands area is Bat Cave. In 1948 archeologists excavating in this large rock shelter made a discovery which forced the revision of all dates relating to prehistoric American agriculture.

They found ears of maize. That in itself might not have been considered an unexpected discovery. But laboratory analysis disclosed that the Bat Cave corn was probably five thousand years old.

Botanists Paul S. Mangelsdorf and C. Earle Smith, Jr., two authorities in this field of science who made the unprecedented finding, reported that it was by far the most primitive type of this invaluable grain recovered.[20] It was both a pop corn and a pod corn. The ears were not enclosed in husks. After the initial discovery, a much newer type of maize was found in Bat Cave. The cobs and kernels were larger, and it had a husk similar to modern corn. It was given a date at about A.D. 1. Here was evidence of long cross-breeding to improve yield.

There is no doubt that domestic corn was developed in South America. The oldest Bat Cave ears have characteristics similar to those of an ancient variety found in Paraguay. The newer Bat Cave ears show hybridization with Mexican plants. The question remaining to be answered is how and when domestic maize reached American territory. However, at least in part it has been answered. For in Bat Cave archeologists also found projectile points as old as any yet discovered in the United States.

Other finds indicate that probably between 600 and 500 B.C. another variety of maize reached the Southwest, and botanists think it may have come from a more eastern region. Strangely, when it was crossed with strains from Mexico a corn with greater drought-resistant capabilities resulted. This made the new hybrid particularly adaptable to the arid southwestern region, and crop production was increased.

It has been established that beans reached the Southwest from Mexico as early as 3000 B.C. Other agricultural products were being grown by numerous peoples in scattered areas several centuries at least before the beginning of the Christian Era, but it was after that time when cultivation had reached the stage where peoples became largely dependent on it.

Imported Ceramics

The Cochise people of the late San Pedro Period knew about pottery. It had come north from Mexico, probably between 400 and 300 B.C.[21] Not until two centuries later, however, had they acquired the ability to make pottery.

The importation of agricultural products and ceramics into the Southwest not only led to the rising of great new cultures but brought about drastic changes in the economy of southwestern Indians. As the time sequence of the region is continued, these changes and their significance will be remarked upon in an appropriate place.

Mogollon: Change of Identity

The people were the same, the descendants of the Cochise–San Pedro people. Their name was changed to Mogollon, not by them, but by scientists who found the evidence of their way of life in this century, more than eight hundred years after their culture had been dissipated and they had been absorbed by other bloods.

The rise of the Mogollon Culture, which largely existed in the adjoining southern corners of Arizona and New Mexico, can be associated with the arrival of agriculture and pottery. But the earliest Mogollons did little farming, and derived their sustenance mainly from wild plant foods, small game, and fowls, including the turkey. They were probably not greatly dependent on hunting, as few arrowheads had been found. They made undecorated brown and red pottery. Many of their stone tools and implements were crude. They were not expert flakers, and for cutting used pieces of stone which had been sharpened by nature. They interred the dead in flexed positions, sometimes beneath the floors of their pit houses. They smoked wild tobacco, possessed dogs, and wore shells as ornaments.

Thus, except for pottery and perhaps a small amount of cultivated agricultural products, they were not much different from their immediate predecessors.

Changes and improvements came slowly, in some respects hardly noticeable, as the centuries passed. Agriculture increased, and such implements as hoes came into use. Houses became larger and better. A form of matting was adopted. Ornaments remained the same. Pottery remained largely the same. Tools were little improved. The dead were still buried in sitting positions.

The lack of progress and development of the Mogollons unavoidably leads to conjectures. They obviously had few enemies, for no evidence of defense works has been found in their small villages. Some archeologists believe that besides being relatively well isolated they were naturally timid, retiring, and homogeneous.[22] Perhaps they made little effort to learn from others. Perhaps they avoided others as much as possible.

At any rate, they appeared to resist innovations, and if the reasons for their attitudes cannot be determined with certainty, there is no doubt what happened to them. The influences, ideas, and customs of a far more powerful and far more energetic and progressive civilization, known as the Anasazi Culture, spread southward from northern Arizona and New Mexico to overwhelm them. Among the most notable Anasazi practices they adopted were these three: (1) geometric designs on pottery; (2) masonry (with stones, mud plaster, and posts they built houses above ground, grouped and with common walls—pueblos); (3) there were large ceremonial houses, the lower levels below ground, the roofs supported by massive posts, the walls of masonry, and these structures resembled in many respects the sacred kivas of the Anasazi civilization.

By the year A.D. 1100 few remnants of the Mogollon Culture were distinguishable from the Anasazi way of life.

Strange Exodus

The final stage of the Mogollon Culture is known as the Mimbres Period, named for the Mimbres River in southwestern New Mexico, and the people are known as Mimbreños.[23] They lived in one-story pueblos with masonry walls, built entirely above ground around a plaza, and sometimes containing rooms for fifty families.

The Anasazi Culture predominated. The Mimbreños had subterranean kivas, with fire pits and ventilator shafts. Maize was the most important crop cultivated, and large amounts were grown, but they also depended on hunting and wild plant foods. The mountainous country in southeastern Arizona and southwestern New Mexico in which they dwelt was highly productive. It received considerable precipitation during several months of the year. The Mimbreños could gather mesquite beans, seeds, acorns, walnuts, roots and leaves of yucca and century plants. In the highlands and on the great grass-covered mesas they could kill deer, antelope, and numerous other kinds of game. They developed skills as artisans, making excellent pottery in many shapes and sizes, decorating it with figures of human forms, animals, birds, and with a great variety of designs. They possessed shells and turquoise, and made beads, bracelets, pendants, and rings of them. Like the people of older Mogollon periods, they interred the dead beneath the floors of their houses, sealing the remains in a heavy adobe coating. Tools, jewelry, and pottery were placed in the graves. The pottery was "killed," that is, in each piece used as a burial offering a hole was drilled.

They lived a good life in a beautiful and bountiful country, but about A.D. 1200 they began to abandon it. Why they left remains a mystery, but where many of them—and probably most of them—went has been determined. They went south into the area that is today the Mexican state of Chihuahua.*

That people of the Mogollon–Mimbres Culture merged with the less advanced culture in northern Mexico is unquestionable. For the artifacts, the houses, the pottery types and designs, and even the burial customs of the Chihuahua people of the time show the Mogollon–Mimbres influence. That is where the Mimbreños went, but no one can say why they went.[24]

---

* People of another culture, the Salado, also migrated to the same area from farther north, and their story will be considered in pages ahead.

Hohokam: Those Who Have Gone

The subtitle above is an English translation of the Pima word *Hohokam,* and that is the name scientists have given to the culture which flourished in the deserts of central and southern Arizona from several centuries before the beginning of the Christian Era until historical times. Indeed, in a sense it has not ended, for the direct descendants of the Hohokam people still live in the same area, now called Pimas.

The Hohokam people left a dramatic, colorful, and in some respects extraordinary, social and economic record. Their earliest culture can be linked to the San Pedro Cochise Period and the cultures of other desert peoples who dwelt along the lower Colorado River, more than two hundred miles to the west. However, there were notable differences. They had their own peculiar ways and skills. They cremated their dead with burial offerings, and placed the ashes in a specially prepared pit.* They were good potters, and their skill would rise through the years to a high degree of excellence. From the beginning of their known existence in the area they made clay figurines, and these, too, would develop into remarkable works of art.

It was about the year A.D. 600 that a truly distinct Hohokam Culture began to emerge, and it was during the next five centuries that most of the great dramatic episodes and developments of their civilization took place.

They were the first people to practice canal irrigation in prehistoric America. With stone and wooden implements and their bare hands they built ditches to carry water from the Salt and Gila rivers—then permanent streams—to their fields of corn, cotton, and other products. At least one of these canals was sixteen miles in length. Numerous others were from three to ten miles long. One network is believed to have covered a hundred and fifty miles.[25]

They played a game of ball on smooth, hard-packed courts that were almost identical to those used by the Mayans in Central America. The courts varied in size, the largest measuring about 61 by 180 feet. The Mayans used a rubber ball in their game. A rubber ball was recovered from a Hohokam archeological site.[26]

They did not smoke tobacco in pipes like most early (and late) Indians, but it is believed that in ceremonies they smoked cane cigarettes.

They had small copper bells. They knew nothing of casting metal. The bells came from Mexico.

They had a great variety of ornaments and decorations—beads of

---

* In later centuries the ashes were given a final resting place in pottery urns.

shell, turquoise, steatite, and argillite; shell and stone rings; bracelets and pendants bearing intricate carvings of turtles, frogs, snakes, and birds; carved shell hair ornaments; and mosaics, the bases encrusted with pyrites held in place by an adhesive.

They made what were probably the first etchings in the world—on shells. Their acid was fermented juice from the fruit of the saguaro cactus. The resist they used to protect the parts of the design that were not to be etched was made of gum and pitch. The art died out with their culture, and was never revived by later peoples in the Western Hemisphere.[27]

They were great traders, and Hohokam artifacts have been found in distant regions.

Many of the Hohokam traits and ideas originated in central and southern Mexico. Scientists are not in accord on how they came north. There was contact of some kind between the two widely separated regions, but whether the customs and developments which made the Hohokams different from other southwestern peoples reached them through a process of diffusions or by migrations remains a puzzle to be solved.[28]

If one notes the great difference between the earliest Hohokams, say before A.D. 500, and the Hohokams of a later period, after A.D. 500, one might be inclined to give serious consideration to a recently advanced theory. It suggests that the later Hohokams "were colonists or invaders from Mexico, who either overwhelmed the earlier settlers or drove them to the western and northern fringes of the southwest area." [29]

This may or may not prove to be the solution to the puzzle.

Rare Coexistence: Salado and Hohokam

Between A.D. 1150 and 1300 two events took place in the Hohokam region that were not only without precedent at the time but have no counterpart in later periods of prehistoric man's long history in America. The peoples of three different contemporaneous cultures were able to do what modern-day men appear unable to accomplish. That is, they were able to affiliate and live in peace.

Shortly before A.D. 1150 Hohokams pushed north to the vicinity of the present Flagstaff, Arizona, a high plateau and mountain country, occupied by the Sinagua people. The Sinagua were agriculturists and their culture was a mixture of influences which had reached them by diffusion from surrounding environments. Later in the twelfth century, pressures from the great Anasazi Culture, which was spread over a vast territory from the Colorado River on the west to the Pecos River in New Mexico, and in southern Utah and southern Colorado, caused the Sinagua to move south. They pushed back the expanding Hohokams and brought their traits, many of which were Anasazi, into the main Hohokam region. This shift was completed without armed conflict, and the two cultures were blended.

In the spectacular mountain country bordering east-central Arizona and west-central New Mexico lived the Saladoans. The Salado Culture, which was flourishing as early as A.D. 700, compounded traits of both the Anasazi and Mogollon civilizations. By A.D. 1200 the Mogollon influences had all but vanished, and Anasazi ways predominated. The Saladoans followed a sedentary way of life, farming and dwelling in multi-storied apartments built around plazas and surrounded by protective walls.

About the year A.D. 1300 a great shifting of peoples occurred, causing a widespread imbalance of populations throughout the Southwest.* It is believed that the movement southward of many Pueblo Indians from their large towns in the San Juan River drainage area forced the Saladoans to leave their homeland, through which the Little Colorado River—then a dependable and invaluable stream—flowed.

The Saladoans moved toward the southwest, into south-central Arizona, and established themselves among the Hohokams.

For many reasons it was the most extraordinary union of two peoples on record in the Western Hemisphere. The most remarkable thing about it was that although the Saladoan and the Hohokam amalgamated, each maintained their own culture. Each pursued their own way of life. No hybrid civilization emerged. They existed together in harmony and peace. Neither dominated nor even sought to dominate the other.

The years between A.D. 1100 and 1400 are designated as the Classic Period of the Hohokam civilization. Even before the Saladoans had joined them, the Hohokams had adopted the Anasazi custom of building their villages—containing either pit houses or contiguous one-story structures of many rooms—in compounds. Some of the compound walls were seven feet thick and twelve feet high. A compound at the Los Muertos archeological site measured 200 by 320 feet, and contained several small plazas on which houses faced.

Adjacent to the low Hohokam villages the Saladoans built great houses, two, three, and four stories in height. Around these large structures were clustered one-story dwellings. Their villages also were surrounded by thick and high walls. The famous ruin at Casa Grande, which thousands of touring Americans go to see each year, was built by the Saladoans. It stood beside a Hohokam village. Forty feet in width and sixty feet in length, its thick walls, laboriously constructed layer by layer of adobe, rose forty feet. Originally it contained sixteen

---

* See below, in the section *Silent Towns.*

17

rooms. Surrounding the town in which the Casa Grande house stood was a wall seven feet in height. The wall has long been gone, and the magnificent structure itself would have vanished were it not for a protective cover built by the National Park Service.

The Saladoans cooperated with the Hohokams in building and maintaining larger canals than previously had existed. One near Los Muertos was thirty feet wide and seven feet deep. So excellent was the engineering of these ancient ditches that some of them were cleaned out and incorporated into modern irrigation systems.

The two peoples continued to make their own types of pottery, to use their own types of implements and tools, to follow their burial customs, the Saladoans by inhumation, the Hohokams by cremation. For more than a century each was aware of the techniques and customs of the other, yet each preserved their own way of life.

Between A.D. 1400 and 1450 the Saladoans moved away. Internal friction appears to be the most unlikely reason for the separation. More plausible are the conjectures that the cultivated soil was becoming exhausted or covered by silt from the canals, that water supplies failed for successive years, that the water became alkaline—these and other undetermined factors may have combined to an extent that made the arable area incapable of supporting so many people.

But if the reason or reasons for the Saladoan exodus may not be stated with certainty, there is strong evidence to indicate where they went. It seems most probable that they followed the Mimbreños southward into Chihuahua. In that area archeologists have found traits and influences of both the Mogollon–Mimbres and the Salado cultures. Notable are pottery types, the custom of early Chihuahua Indians of burying their dead beneath the floors of their houses, and, most indicative of all, the ruins of multi-storied adobe houses, similar in many respects to the great houses built by the Saladoans at Casa Grande and Los Muertos.[30]

The Hohokams remained where they had lived for so many centuries. Their culture died away, and finally vanished. But their descendants, the Indians now called Pimas and Papagos, still live in southern Arizona, and they call the Hohokams their ancestors—"those who have gone."

Anasazi: the Old Ones

The Anasazi Culture, the most influential and most enduring of all southwestern civilizations, but not the oldest, still flourishes in many respects today. Oddly, *Anasazi* is an anglicized form of a Navajo word meaning "the old ones" which scientists adopted as an inclusive term for the older Basketmaker–Pueblo periods. But the Navajos, whose tongue derived from the Athapascan language of the Canadian Northwest, were not present in the American Southwest until at least a thousand years after the Anasazi Culture had begun to emerge.

The Anasazi people were spread over an immense region several hundred miles in width in the high plateau and mountain country of northern Arizona, southern Utah, southwestern Colorado, and northern New Mexico. Their culture is dated by archeologists as beginning about A.D. 1. It was then and for several centuries afterward largely a conglomeration of cultures, for traits of various desert peoples were manifest in it. However, at the crest of its development, in its "Golden Age," which came after A.D. 1000, it represented an extraordinarily high type of civilization, and its religious and social structures and its economic systems exerted powerful influences in all parts of the Southwest.

To recount the story of the earliest Anasazi people would be, with one outstanding exception, repetitious of the history of other early southwestern cultures. The exception is their skill in weaving vegetable fibers. They did not know how to make pottery, and they possessed none, but they developed the weaving of baskets, foot-coverings, and clothing to a high art. They wove utensils, transport equipment, and storage containers in many sizes and for special needs. So fine and so expert was their work that they could use baskets for cooking and carrying water. Quite appropriately the years A.D. 1 to 400 are designated as the Basketmaker Period, and the years A.D. 400 to 700 as the Modified Basketmaker Period.

The Basketmakers were food-gatherers, hunters, and farmers. They built their shelters both in caves and in the open. Some of their villages had contiguous rooms of pit houses, the roofs made of poles and mud. Adjacent to them were pit storage bins. Two significant transitions occurred in the Modified Basketmaker Period. Social organizations and religious ceremonials began to evolve that would last for more than a thousand years. And the Basketmakers began to make pottery. Quite understandably the first pottery was constructed in basket molds. But they were capable learners, adapters, and they were ingenious. Not many years had passed before they fired their ceramics and tempered the walls with sand and crushed stones. In time the Anasazi people produced some of the finest pottery in the Southwest, some of it unequaled by any others in quality, finish, and design.

Transition in architecture and construction methods steadily evolved, and skills as artisans steadily developed, during the periods known as Pueblo I, A.D. 700–900, and Pueblo II, A.D. 900–1050. Pit houses were abandoned. Dwellings were built aboveground, the walls constructed of horizontally laid stones. They stood in single and double rows, and the roofs of wooden beams were supported by stone pillars. In each town were underground kivas, entered by ladder from a smoke hole in the roof, and used by men for ceremonial rites and social or political meetings.

Then came the "Golden Age," dated A.D. 1100–1300. It was the age of great houses, built in the open, on the tops of mesas, and in recesses of towering canyon walls. The remains of these immense dwellings may be seen today in such places as Mesa Verde National Park, Chaco Canyon, Bandelier National Monument, Canyon de Chelly, and scores of other places—some still isolated and difficult to reach—throughout the vast region of which the center is the common corner of New Mexico, Colorado, Utah, and Arizona.

Silent Towns

Before the Pueblos built the big cliff houses and towns, they had lived in small independent villages, each perhaps containing no more than several score persons, and each dominated by a social clan, all members of which were blood relatives. There are several theories as to why they saw advantages in amalgamating and building large urban-type communities: easier defense, pooling of agricultural labor, development of water supplies, manufacture of improved types of utensils and tools by the application of various skills. The caves were desirable locations; facing south they were warm and sunny in winter, and protected from rains and snows.

At the beginning of the fourteenth century, or shortly thereafter, the cliff houses and big communities had been abandoned. They stood silent and crumbling in the winds that swept through the great canyons. The Indians who had occupied them moved southward and eastward in clans, and had resumed their former way of life in small independent and scattered villages of their own or had found homes among other peoples.

It is improbable that any single force brought the end of this amazing human experiment. Attack by raiders was the least of the pressures which caused the abandonment. There were no Indian adversaries in the region strong enough to sack and destroy the easily defended big towns. Small bands of raiders, drifting in from the mountains to the north and the plains to the east, might have made incursions, pilfering corn and carrying off unguarded women and children. That such raids took place in this period against small pueblos there is no question. The ruins of isolated villages show that they were destroyed by fire, and in some of them arrowheads have been found in skeletons, both male and female, indicating that these persons died defending their homes.

This was not the case in the great cliff dwellings and the large pueblos. Yet it seems illogical to think that people would construct these strong buildings halfway up immense precipices, necessitating the toting of water and provisions up a series of ladders, if not to safeguard themselves. The fear of invaders must have had some influence on their actions, but the fact remains that the cliff buildings and the big urban pueblos were not overthrown and destroyed by attackers, and the inhabitants were not involved in large-scale warfare. Some burned rooms have been found in them, but doubtless these fires were accidental. In a few places charred bones and mashed skulls have been discovered, but it would be unreasonable to assume that violent rows, especially between members of different clans, and with visitors, had not occurred with tragic results.

The main causes of the mass exodus from the big towns appear to be two in number—drought and internal dissension.

The science of dendrochronology (dating wood by growth rings) provides support for the first.[31] It has shown that a severe drought persisted in the region of the Anasazi civilization from A.D. 1276 to 1299. Faced with repeated crop failures, the absence of game, and inadequate water supplies, the only alternative for the people of the stricken land would have been to leave and rejoin relatives or find places to live among friendly tribes where water was available. Members of a clan would have remained together, and, therefore, the united peoples of the "great houses" once more would have been separated.[32]

The science of ethnology provides support for the second most likely cause of the extensive movement. The people who built the large towns came from many small pueblos, each one with its own social mores and religious rites. While the material aspects of their culture, and they themselves in a physical sense, were adjusted to existence in the big communities, they refused to abandon their respective social and religious practices.

Four towns, for example, each containing fifty people related to each other, gathered together and built a big cliff house.[33] The four groups helped each other in various ways, but each group insisted on maintaining its social and ceremonial structures, which were well adapted to a small town but not to a large one. Therefore, mores, marriage regulations, methods of reckoning blood descent, and various ceremonies prevented the development of a strong central administration to act for the whole group. Actually, the big town consisted of four independent towns, each functioning differently from the others. The result was that the big town was constantly disturbed by internal feuds. Amicable relationships between clans were impossible. Big Town was a sociological disaster. Finally it collapsed. The clans moved out, going their separate ways, and eventually Big Town was left to the ghosts.

More than drought, this analysis appears to present the most logical reason for the migrations. The Pueblos had been through severe droughts before, and they understood that the "weather wheel" always turned. Moreover, in temperament, attitude, and character, the people of 1300 were no different than people of 1970—getting along with each other was one of the biggest problems they faced, the same as it is for the city dwellers of today.

The exodus of the Pueblos affected the lives of all peoples of the Southwest, forcing many of them to shift to new locations. For longer than a quarter of a century the Pueblos moved at various times, and in varying numbers, into the valleys of the Rio Grande, Little Colorado, Puerco, Verde, San Francisco, Pecos, Salt, Gila.

By A.D. 1500, the only areas of the Southwest in which people of the Anasazi civilization lived (where they still live today) were in and near the valley of the upper Rio Grande, Acoma, Zuñi, and the Hopi Country.

Their Golden Age had ended.[34]

Chemehuevi: Swift of Foot

In ancient times—no one can say how long ago—the Chemehuevi inhabited the eastern half of the Mohave Desert in southern California. They were a small offshoot of the Paiute, who lived farther north and east in the Great Basin, and probably at no time did they number more than eight hundred men, women, and children.[35]

When or how they occupied lands inhabited by Yuman tribes along the Colorado River is not known. Yet before the beginning of the historical period in this region they dwelt along the river between the Bill Williams Fork and The Needles.[36] They were physically inferior to the Mohave Indians, their neighbors with whom they maintained friendly relations, and with whom they allied themselves in times of both peace and war. However, the Chemehuevi possessed great endurance, were exceptionally fleet of foot, and traveled long distances on hunting and predatory excursions.[37] They cultivated some fields in the valley that bears their name and in other locations, using water from the Colorado River, but mostly they depended upon hunting and gathering of wild plant foods for their existence. In addition to lances and bows and arrows they used a crook-stick to pull gophers, rabbits, and other small animals from their burrows. They wove baskets in which to store and carry food and possessions, and, like other Colorado River tribes, they had no canoes, but used rafts made of bundles of reeds to cross the stream. Ethnologists have been unable to learn anything significant of their social or political structures.

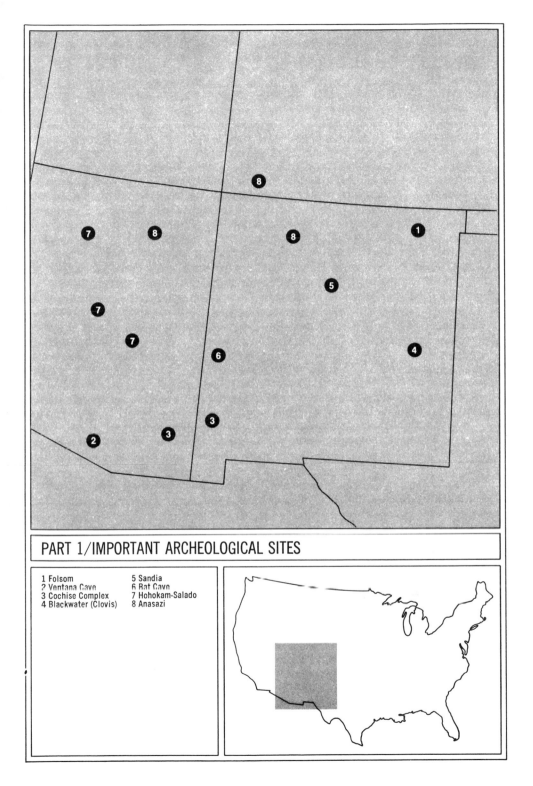

PART 1/IMPORTANT ARCHEOLOGICAL SITES

1 Folsom
2 Ventana Cave
3 Cochise Complex
4 Blackwater (Clovis)

5 Sandia
6 Bat Cave
7 Hohokam-Salado
8 Anasazi

Cocopa of the Desert Coast

The Cocopa lived where the raging Colorado River collided with the great tidal bores of the Gulf of California. They were handsome and well-proportioned, although not physically superior to other tribes of the Yuman family, of which they were a division. Nor were they as hostile as some of the people to whom they were related, and who took advantage of their peaceful nature to raid their villages. Yet they were not cowardly, and when sufficiently aroused and angered by predators they would strike back with telling effect. It is believed they numbered as many as three thousand persons at the beginning of the historic period, and could send at least three hundred capable warriors into the field of combat.

They cremated their dead, and one wonders if this practice was adopted after contacts with the Hohokam (q.v.), for some archeologists think that some of the Hohokam migrated to the lower Colorado River area in the declining years of their civilization.

During the burning summer months the Cocopa lived in brush arbors, and during the winter in wattled huts plastered inside and out with mud. There was little game to be found in the forbidding country of the Colorado delta, and without irrigated farming they could not have existed in their homeland. They cultivated corn, melons, pumpkins, and beans, supplementing this diet with fish caught in the river and the Gulf of California, and wild seeds, roots, and mesquite beans gathered in season in the surrounding desert.* [38]

Yuma: Son of the Captain

The people to whom history would give the name Yuma (Yahmayo—Son of the Captain) called themselves *Kwichan*ᵃ. In prehistoric times they dwelt (as some of them do at present) on the Colorado River above the Cocopa. They were in several ways a remarkable people, and their name has been given by scientists to the large Yuman linguistic family, which contains many tribes of the far Southwest and in both southern and Baja California. The present city of Yuma, Arizona, stands approximately at the northern border of their prehistoric homeland. This was the place where the main trade trail from the San Diego area on the Pacific crossed the Colorado River. The Yuma themselves were a sedentary tribe, but engaged in trade, perhaps as a kind of forwarding agent or "middleman," for through their hands passed shells from the

---

* A Yuman tribe, the Halyikwamai, also called Quigyuma, living on the Colorado River below the mouth of the Gila in early historical times are believed to have been absorbed by the Cocopa, and thereafter dwelt below the present international border.

Pacific and the Gulf of California, and pottery and other products from tribes living to the east.

The Yuma were physically superior to most of their congeners. They were brave and able defenders of their country, and although not overly hostile, as were some of their neighbors, they were not fearful of war nor did they refrain from launching an attack if they deemed it necessary. Otherwise they seldom left their villages. They were competent farmers, watering by hand their fields of maize, beans, pumpkins, and melons. The name Yuma has been given to a distinct type of projectile point which they fashioned. It was long and narrow, with parallel sides and parallel flaking across the blade at a slight angle and no fluting.[39]

Like other tribes who lived in the fiercely hot country, the Yuma wore little or no clothing during the larger part of the year. Customarily the men were totally nude. The women wore only a short and scanty covering made of tree bark about the waist.[40] Sandals were donned on war excursions, otherwise all persons went barefoot. In the winter months they slept in rabbit skin robes. They had few hides, for large game animals were extremely scarce, and most of the skins they possessed, such as those of the deer and antelope, were obtained in trade from peoples living in the forested and higher regions to the northeast. The most common hairdress of both men and women included bangs in the front. The men twisted their hair into strands at the back, and the women let it hang long.[41] For hair dressing certain plant gums and a type of sticky mud were used. Both sexes painted their faces and bodies, some with black, some with red, and some with a variety of colors.

To the Yuma, and several of the tribes with whom they were consanguineous or otherwise affiliated, dreams were of the greatest importance. Men who had unusual dreams told of them in the minutest detail at campfire gatherings, and it was believed that dreams both foretold events and endowed those receiving them with extraordinary powers. Bands of raiders and larger war parties were usually led by men who were thought to have received supernatural powers in dreams. The Yuma also cremated their dead. They practiced a loose form of government, each band or *rancheria* having a chief who was more an advisor than a commander or ruler.

Only a small number of full-blooded descendants of this once fine and strong people are alive today.

Havasupai: People of the Blue-Green Water

For several reasons, the Havasupai are one of the most unusual tribes of the Southwest.

Their origin can be traced far back into prehistoric times. It is believed that at one period they dwelt in caves on the Verde River near the northern edge of the Tonto Basin, in central Arizona. For a reason unknown they moved northward and probably affiliated with a clan or tribe of Pueblo people. On the Colorado Chiquito, east of the San Francisco Mountains, they dwelt in pueblo-type permanent villages. The Havasupai have always claimed that ruins in this area are sites of their early homes.

Forced to abandon these prehistoric towns by warring tribes from the east, they took refuge in the San Francisco Mountains for a time, and then vanished into one of the most remote and inaccessible regions of the Southwest, a place now known as Cataract Canyon, a branch of the great Grand Canyon. There the blue-green waters of Cataract Creek tumble down in lovely cascades and make possible the isolated existence they have enjoyed for an indeterminable number of years.

The migrations of the Havasupai give strength to the theory that some tribes of the Hokan linguistic group, to which the Yuman people belong, moved westward to the Colorado River region before and early in the Christian Era. A factor that makes the Havasupai especially interesting, however, is that of all the Yuman tribes they are the only one that borrowed—perhaps adopted is a better word—a culture similar in some respects, but not as far advanced, to that of early Pueblo people.

Some Havasupai dances and religious rituals may be likened to those of the Hopi, with whom they have always maintained a close and friendly relationship. And like the Hopis they were skilled in preparing raw material, such as the dressing and tanning of buckskin. Deer and other animals were plentiful in the immense forests of the high canyon country, and the Havasupai men were expert hunters. The women were not especially good potters, but they wove excellent baskets. Pottery could be obtained in trade, and they had something of value to trade. It was the fine red ocher which they mined in the Grand Canyon, and for which there was a wide and constant demand. From the ocher could be made a superior grade of red paint, especially preferred by women and by both male and female participants in certain ceremonials and dances. The Havasupai bartered the red ocher to the Hopis, who traded it to the Pueblo peoples of the Rio Grande and as far east as Santa Fe and Taos.

In their beautiful hidden canyon the Havasupai practiced irrigation, ditching water to their little fields of corn, calabashes, sunflowers (for seeds to eat), and melons. In their hunting they used a variety of weapons—slings, clubs, pikes, and bows and arrows.

Consanguineally their society was patriarchal, and in this respect they differed from many other tribes of the Southwest. They were polygamists. A Havasupai man could have as many wives as he could support—if he could find them. Betrothals were arranged by purchase, but divorces were granted only on one ground, infidelity.

The Havasupai were always a small tribe, perhaps never numbering more than three hundred. Throughout all the centuries their population remained close to this level. Because of their isolation they were one of the last, if not the last, Indians to be encountered by white men. And that is still all right with them, although today they will escort visitors on horseback into their canyon of the blue-green water, but only for a fee.[42]

SOUTHWESTERN DESERTS AND MESA LANDS

Earliest Population Estimates*

Apache (1680)	5,000		Cocopa (1776)	3,000
Navajo (1680)	8,000		Halchidhoma (1680)	3,000
Chemehuevi (ancient)	800		Halyikwamai (1680)	2,000
Hopi (1680)	2,800		Havasupai (1680)	300
Jumano (1572)	10,000(?)		Kamia (ancient)	400
Papago (1680)	6,000		Kohuana (1680)	3,000
Pima (1680)	4,000		Maricopa (1680)	2,000
Sobaipuri (1680)	600		Mohave (1680)	3,000
Piro Pueblos			Walapai (1680)	700
(16th. Century)	9,000		Yavapai (1680)	600
Tiwa Pueblos (1680)	12,200		Yuma (1776)	3,000
Pecos (1540)	2,500		Keresan Pueblos	
Jemez (1680)	2,500		(1760)	4,000
Tewa Pueblos			Zuñi (1680)	2,500
Northern (1680)	2,200			
Southern (1630)	4,000		TOTAL	98,100
Manso (1668)	1,000			

* It is not possible, of course, to determine with any degree of accuracy whatsoever the population of prehistoric peoples. The earliest information available is contained in documents prepared in the first years of the historical period, such as the accounts of explorers and missionaries, statements of traders, church records, and reports of military and civil officials. For the figures presented here I have relied mainly on three authorities who have made studies of the subject, Drs. James Mooney and John R. Swanson, of the Bureau of American Ethnology, and A. L. Kroeber of the University of California.

Maricopa and Yuma: Blood Enemies

The Maricopa were kin of the Yuma, and they lived in prehistoric times at various places along the lower Colorado River. In the eighteenth century—a historical period, although very few white men had encountered them—a political fight over the election of headmen resulted in an incurable break between the two tribes.

The Maricopa moved north to the Gila River, and found a haven among the Pima. Although neither one of these peoples could understand the language of the other, they lived in harmony, each maintaining their own ways and religious rituals. The Gila was a living stream, in certain seasons carrying large amounts of water, which made it possible to grow adequate crops. The Maricopas called themselves *Pipatsje.* The Pima gave them the name Maricopa, by which they would be known in history.

As the years passed, the animosity between the Maricopa and the Yuma developed into burning hatred and clashes frequently occurred. It is known that in 1775 the two tribes were engaged in open warfare, and not until 1857 did the conflict end. In that year ninety-three Yuma warriors launched an attack. The Pima came to the aid of their friends. Only three Yuma fighting men escaped alive. After that disaster the Yuma never again ventured up the Gila.*

Mohave: Residents of Three Mountains

Hamakhava was a Mohave word that meant "three mountains," but it referred specifically to The Needles that rise in the valley of the Colorado River. The Mohave lived from this point northward along the stream to the great Black Canyon, the magnificent and forboding chasm of purple walls that tower sheer for a quarter of a mile above the racing foaming waters.† But the Mohave also had another name for themselves. It was *Tzi-na-ma-a,* and they said they were known by it "before they came to the Colorado River." How far back in the dim ages of prehistory that was could not be reckoned by time. Nor could they say whence or by what route they came, but archeologists would find clues to indicate that they probably migrated westward, descending from a people of great antiquity.

They were perhaps the most populous of the Yuman tribes, and certainly the most hostile. War was a way of life, especially for the young

---

* The population of the Maricopa was sharply increased when, in early historical times, two other Yuman tribes, the Halchidhoma and the Kohuana, were absorbed by them.

† The site of Hoover Dam.

men who sought to achieve prestige and honor on the field of battle and in raids upon kinsmen as well as enemies.

Mohave women were among the most attractive of all the Colorado River tribes, and Mohave men were strong, well-proportioned, athletic, and handsome. Both sexes painted their bodies with unexcelled artistry. Peculiarly the decorations on their pottery were crude. Just as the Hohokam passed on shells from the Gulf of California and the San Diego area, the Mohave acted as middlemen on the trade route from the Pacific that crossed the Mohave Desert to northern Arizona. But the Mohave themselves also journeyed to the coast to obtain shells, shell beads, and fishhook blanks manufactured by the coastal Indians. They traded these objects to the Pueblos for pottery and textiles.[43]

The Mohave did not live in large villages. Their low mud, pole, and brush houses were widely scattered over a long area bordering each side of the river. They were neither expert farmers nor skilled artisans. They grew corn, beans, melons, and other crops on bottomlands, but they were not irrigators. They depended on floodwaters, and when the river did not rise sufficiently to overflow their fields their crops failed. Although they manufactured some pottery, they did not weave baskets but obtained them in trade from other tribes.

The Mohave system of identifying individuals was one of the strangest and most confusing on record. The authority, A. L. Kroeber, explains it this way: "Certain men, and all their ancestors and descendants in the male line, have only one name for all their female relatives. Thus, if the female name hereditary in my family be Maha, my father's sister, my own sisters, my daughters (no matter how great their number), and my son's daughters will all be called Maha. There are about twenty such women's names, or virtual gentes, among the Mohave. None of these names seems to have any signification. But according to the myths of the tribe, certain numbers of men originally had, or were given, such names as Sun, Moon, Tobacco, Fire, Cloud, Coyote, Deer, Wind, Beaver, Owl and others, which correspond exactly to totemic clan names; then these men were instructed by Mastamho, the chief mythological being, to call all their daughters and female descendants in the male line by certain names, corresponding to these clan names.[44]

An example: *Hipa* means "coyote." Therefore the male ancestors of all women bearing the name *Hipa* are believed to have been originally named Coyote.

Somewhat less confusing perhaps are the facts that the Mohave form of political and social organizations remained quite distinct from other tribes to whom they were related, and that their chieftainship was hereditary in the male line.

Walapai and Yavapai:
Pine Tree and Crooked Mouth People

These Yuman tribes were, respectively, the Walapai and the Yavapai.

The Walapai—*Xawalapaiy*, meaning "pine tree folk"—were closely related to the Havasupai of the blue-green water, but they were not as sedentary in nature, and they roamed over an immense area north of the Mohave people, from the Colorado River well into the interior of Arizona, in the present Hualapi, Yavapai, and Sacramento valleys and southward almost to Bill Williams Fork. Nor were they as progressive as their kinfolk in Cataract Canyon. They subsisted mainly on hunting and by gathering roots and seeds, appearing to have an intense dislike for farming. Even in early historic times they cultivated few crops, but displayed a liking for stock-raising, and sought to acquire a large number of horses. After becoming mounted Indians they extended their hunting excursions far into the magnificent high forested country that swept away to the north and east, bordering the Grand Canyon.*

Not all of the Yavapai gave the same meaning to the name *Enyaeva* by which they called themselves. Some said it meant "people of the sun," but others interpreted it as "crooked mouth people" who were sulky and hostile and had many troubles with other tribes. This latter interpretation appears to have prevailed, for the Yavapai came into history known as Apache Mohaves, or Mohave Apaches, and *apachu* is a word of the Zuñi language meaning "enemy." †

The Yavapai also ranged over a great area of Arizona. At one period they had *rancherias* on the Colorado River in the country occupied by the Halchidhoma (q.v.) and the Chemehuevis. But they were chiefly an interior tribe, their territory extending from the Bill Williams and Santa Maria rivers southward as far as the Gila.

They, too, were a small tribe, comparable in size to the Walapai. The white man's gift to them, as it was to so many tribes, was tuberculosis, which almost wiped them out. Only a few score remain alive today, although their tribal name, whatever its correct meaning, is perpetuated in the name of an Arizona county.

---

* Only a few days before writing these words I bought gas for my car at a Walapai filling station and ate a sandwich at a Walapai restaurant. The Walapai appear to be far more enterprising and progressive today than in the past, and their population is continuing to increase.

† The early Spaniards pronounced it *Apache*, but the meaning remained the same.

The Ancient Inland Sea

On cliffs and mountainsides bordering the low valleys called Coachella and Imperial one may still see the marks of the beach line of the waters that once filled them, the waters of the Gulf of California. Then a general uplift occurred, and the sea withdrew, and the delta of the Colorado became a barrier that cut off the area which would become known as the Salton Sink. With the uplift the cutting power of the river was increased and it formed the terraces that now border it.[45]

Geologists believe these drastic changes occurred no more than a thousand years ago. Indians were living in the region long before that time. In the area of the Imperial Valley and the so-called Salton Sea of today were the Kamia, a small Yuman tribe, perhaps numbering no more than two or three hundred persons.[46]

They long ago became extinct, probably through absorption by other tribes, but they were worthy of being remembered if for no other reason than that they were a kind of link between the large and powerful tribes of the Colorado River, only a few miles to the east, and the Diegueño to the west, to whom they were also related. Through their land ran the great prehistoric trade trail that crossed southern California from San Diego to Yuma. It might also be mentioned that they were undoubtedly the dirtiest and most degraded tribe in the Southwest. The people of the main river tribes bathed and soaped themselves regularly throughout the year, but to overcome vermin the Kamia coated their hair with mud. On hot days they weltered in mudholes like pigs. They sold their children. As there were few animals in their tortured land, they subsisted on fish, seeds, and roots. Many were dreadfully scorbutic.

Pima: the No People

There is a story that the early missionaries in northern Mexico heard the word *pima* so often from a certain tribe that they thought it was their name. That may be apocryphal. In any case, *pima* signifies "no" in the language of the Nevome Indians of Sonora, and they became mistakenly called Pima. Later, when it was learned that the same people also inhabited the region to the north that is now Arizona they were called Pima Alta, and the Nevome were identified as Pima Baja. The whole immense area in which both the Upper and Lower Pima lived was given the name of Pimeria.

The Pima who roamed through the valleys of Arizona's Salt and Gila rivers had a name for themselves. It was *A-a'tam*, meaning simply "people," and to distinguish themselves from their close relatives, the Papago, who dwelt farther south in the Arizona desert, they used the name *A-a'tam kimult,* signifying "river people." One may understand why the missionaries preferred "no," and why the true name of the Pima was ignored.

The Pima preserve a story of their origin and history that archeologists recognize as probably being more accurate and truthful than most native traditions. Their tribe, say the Pima, had its genesis in the Salt River Valley, and they are direct descendants of the great people, the Hohokam (q.v.). They maintain that the many ruined adobe towns, including the large Casa Grande, found in their country were built and occupied by their progenitors, and the prehistoric Pima Culture gives strong support to the claim. The early Pima lived in houses similar to those of the Hohokam, made pottery decorated with Hohokam designs, and, perhaps most important of all, like the Hohokam they constructed irrigation works—dams, reservoirs, and canals—and cultivated extensive fields.

Raiders, states the Pima's own history, swept down upon them in three successive waves from the east, destroyed their homes and fields, and killed and enslaved many of them. They fled their homeland, and when at last they returned they did not rebuild their substantial adobe towns or large irrigation systems. They lived a precarious existence in mud and thatch houses, growing crops as they were able with flood and hand-watering, and always ready to flee. For by this time, the seventeenth century, the Apache had moved westward from the Great Plains and had begun their long history of terrorizing, stealing, destroying, and killing. The historical period began later for the Pima than for most southwestern Indians.

The Pima were polygamists, and the number of wives a man took was governed only by his ability to support them. Husband and wife could separate with no more effort than moving apart. The life of Pima women was hard. They performed most of the labor. When traveling on a trading mission, the man might carry no more than his bow and arrows, while behind him came the women burdened not only with children but with heavy baskets containing the goods that would be traded, usually for articles the husband desired for his personal adornment.

In the Pima belief an owl carried the soul of a dead person off to another world, and the hooting of an owl was thought to be a premonition of an impending death.[47]

Papago: the Bean People

The Papago lived to the south of their kinsmen, the Pima, in one of the hottest and most barren deserts of the United States. Known as the Papagueria, it spread from the Santa Cruz River Valley westward and southward into Sonora, Mexico. The word *papago* derives from two words of the Piman dialect they spoke, *papah* meaning "beans," and *ootam*, signifying "people." The name "bean people" undoubtedly was given to them because, although they grew some maize, they depended in large part, when water was available, on cultivated beans, and in time of drought (a frequent occurrence) on the beans of wild plants, such as the mesquite. The Papago's own name for themselves was *Tono-oohtam*, signifying "people of the desert." And they were that.[48]

Because there were no dependable streams in their land, they were forced to follow a nomadic way of life, constantly shifting to obtain sufficient water to nourish their little fields. This was the greatest difference between them and the Pima. Otherwise, their traditions, their customs, their religious beliefs, and their language were almost identical to those of their more affluent relatives of the Salt and Gila valleys.

The Papago were a frugal and peaceful people, but they did not hesitate to go into battle against raiders, and in their fighting they displayed great courage. Because of their isolation and the forbidding character of their homeland they were among the last people to come in contact with Europeans.[49]

The People Called Pueblos

It is not an Indian name. It does not signify a linguistic family. It is not a tribal name. *Pueblo* is a Spanish word meaning "town." It came into usage in early historical times as a convenient general term to designate Indians who dwelt in permanent stone buildings. Tribes who lived in more fragile structures, such as those made of brush and mud, who were less sedentary in nature, who moved with the seasons or roamed widely in their foraging and hunting, who engaged in long-range excursions of war, were called by individual names.

Although they always had many customs in common, deriving mainly from their way of living in what may be termed urban communities, or apartments, their methods of subsisting as horticulturalists, and their overall economy, they were not the same people. Indeed, they belonged to four distinctive linguistic stocks.[50]

The Pueblos were descendants of the people who built the great cliff dwellings and large mesa towns which were abandoned in the thirteenth and early fourteenth centuries. While their material, social, and spiritual customs are sufficiently homogeneous to warrant the name Pueblo Culture, there are innumerable local differences in their architecture, farming methods, living habits, rituals, ceremonials, and religious beliefs.

There were literally hundreds of small and large pueblos built during the prehistoric centuries over an immense area of the Southwest. Warfare, drought, internal dissensions caused frequent shiftings. Towns were destroyed or abandoned, and new ones were built in locations more favorable to defense or where water was available. Political and social conflicts resulted in countless group movements.

If generalities are not favored by scientists, in the case of the Pueblo people they provide an enlightening picture.[51] In the northern parts of the Pueblo area the houses were usually built of sandstone, readily quarried near at hand. In some places blocks of lava or tufa were used. The groups of dwellings were compact structures of several stories, with many small rooms. The villages were often rectangular, with open courts, but usually there was little fixed plan of outline, new dwellings being added wherever and whenever need demanded. The result was groups of community houses forming irregularly oblong, square, semicircular, circular, and elliptical ground plans, with wings and minor projections. The pueblos were built in terrace fashion, with the upper tiers set back of those next below, so that the roofs of the lower stories formed a kind of front yard for those next above. The lower stories were without doors, and were entered from the roofs by means of hatches and ladders. The upper houses were reached on movable ladders, or by masonry steps built against the outer walls. In the ancient pueblos the fireplace was a pit in the floor, the smoke escaping through a roof hatchway. Floors were paved with stone slabs or plastered smooth with adobe mortar. Adjacent to or in each pueblo was at least one kiva, usually beneath the surface of the ground, and used by men for political meetings, religious rites, and proceedings of secret societies.

As potters and weavers the Pueblos were never excelled by other Indians north of Mexico. Their earthenware vessels consisted of practically every form known to prehistoric peoples, ranging from large rough cooking and storage vessels to delicately molded and beautifully painted and decorated jars, bowls, platters, bottles, ladles, and box-shaped utensils.

The small fields of the Pueblos were irrigated from living streams or from storage reservoirs. They grew corn, beans, pumpkins, melons, and cotton. The cotton was woven into clothing, cloaks, kilts, and leggings, and these were extensively traded to other tribes. The Pueblos hunted large game animals, those living in the eastern part of their country journeying to the plains to kill buffalo. Additional meat was obtained from small mammals, wild birds—the eagle was especially prized for its feathers—and large flocks of domesticated turkeys, but fish were never eaten.

The ancient clothing of Pueblo men consisted typically of a short tunic and knee-length trousers made of deerskin, or skin or cotton leggings held in place at the knee with a decorated garter, and moccasins of deerskin with rawhide soles neatly sewn with sinew.

The typical dress of the women was sleeveless, and fastened over the right shoulder, leaving the left one exposed. They wore embroidered sashes, long robes of rabbit fur or of feathers, cotton, and deerskin mantles, and undyed white leggings and moccasins or sandals.

Both sexes adorned themselves with a large variety of ornaments of shell, bone, turquoise, and other colored stones in the form of necklaces, beads, bracelets, and rings.

Every Pueblo tribe was composed of a number of clans or gentes. Most of the clans took their names from natural objects or elements, especially animals and plants. Each society had its own series of rites and ceremonies, some of which were performed in secret, while others, in the form of outdoor public dances, were elaborate and impressive.

All the Pueblos were monogamists. The status of women was much higher than among many other peoples. The Pueblos reckoned descent through the mother, and the home was the property of the woman. They had no colorful or elaborate marriage ceremony, and a divorce was quickly and easily effected. A wife had it in her power to dismiss a husband, even for a trifling reason, and he was obliged to return to the home of his parents. Divorced people were free to remarry. Many Pueblos, however, married only once and lived harmonious and happy lives. Unlike many other Indian tribes, Pueblo men and women shared the necessary daily labors. They worked together in house-building, gathering fuel, planting and harvesting, and men wove blankets and made moccasins for their families.

The government of the Pueblos was controlled by the priesthood. The representatives of various societies met to make decisions on issues of vital importance to the tribe.

Hopi: the Peaceful Ones

Hopi is a contraction of the word *Hopitu*, meaning "the peaceful ones." The Hopi were unique in that they spoke a dialect of the Shoshonean language and they were the only Shoshonean people who adopted an Anasazi (Pueblo) Culture.*

The Hopi country may be likened to the hub of a great wheel, a center, to which they migrated in prehistoric times from several directions. Therefore, the Hopi and their culture are composites, composed

---

* One is obliged to write of some Indian peoples (i.e., Hopi, Navajo, Apache, Pueblo, and others in the western region) in both the present and the past tense, for they still live in their ancient homelands, and some are thriving and increasing in population.

Language Groups in Part One

SOUTHWESTERN DESERTS AND MESA LANDS

Na-Dene Group:	Athapascan:	Apache
		Navajo
Uto-Aztecan-Tanoan Group:	Utaztecan:	Chemehuevi
		Hopi Pueblos
		Jumano
		Papago
		Pima
		Opata
		Sobaipuri
	Tanoan:	Piro Pueblos
		Tiwa Pueblos
		Pecos Pueblos
		Jemez Pueblos
		Tewa Pueblos
		Manso
Hokan-Coahuiltecan Group:	Hokan:	Cocopa
		Halchidhoma
		Halyikwamai
		Havasupai
		Kamia
		Kohuana
		Maricopa
		Mohave
		Walapai
		Yavapai
		Yuma
Keres Group:	Keresan Pueblos	
Zuñi Group:	Zuñi Pueblos	

of accretions from widely divergent sources and from people of different linguistic stocks. Obviously, however, the tongue of the Shoshonean family predominated, but the dialect that evolved contained many archaic words not found in other dialects of the same language, and which were of Keresan, Tewa, Pima, Zuñi, Ute, Navajo, and Apache derivation.

Ruins of ancient villages in which the Hopi say their ancestors lived have been discovered as far north as the Colorado River, as far west as Flagstaff, Arizona, as far south as the Verde Valley in the Tonto Basin and the Gila River, and as far east as the Rio Grande in northern New

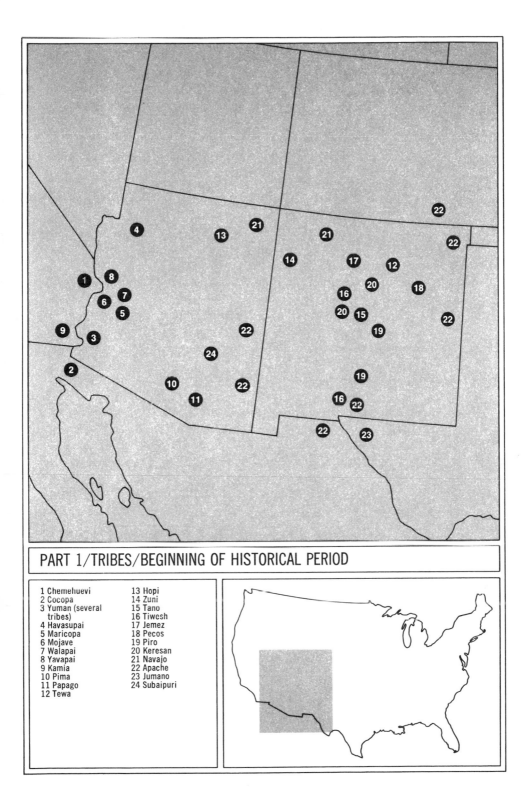

PART 1/TRIBES/BEGINNING OF HISTORICAL PERIOD

1 Chemehuevi
2 Cocopa
3 Yuman (several tribes)
4 Havasupai
5 Maricopa
6 Mojave
7 Walapai
8 Yavapai
9 Kamia
10 Pima
11 Papago
12 Tewa
13 Hopi
14 Zuni
15 Tano
16 Tiwesh
17 Jemez
18 Pecos
19 Piro
20 Keresan
21 Navajo
22 Apache
23 Jumano
24 Subaipuri

Mexico. There are, as well, numerous ruins of pueblos in the Hopi Country, for there was much shifting of the early people. Towns were abandoned and new ones were constructed as the result of cleavages between phratries, each of which always adhered (and still does) to its own customs, dances, and religious ceremonials. There were many phratries, each composed of numerous clans, among the Hopi at the beginning of the historical period. Most of them still exist, and while some clans have become extinct in certain towns, in others they continue to exert powerful political and religious influence.

The seven principal Hopi pueblos stand on three enormous mesas, between which flow ephemeral streams. On the Third Mesa, counting from east to west, is Oraibi. It was built about A.D. 1150, and is believed to be the oldest continuously occupied town in the United States.* But Hopis were living in the area long before that year. In adjacent ruins archeologists have found Hopi pottery types which were manufactured as early as A.D. 500. Thus, it is clear that the Hopi were present during the Modified Basketmaker Period, to which science ascribes the date A.D. 500–700.[52]

From earliest times the Hopi have been outstanding weavers and artisans. Hopi textiles, made from a native cotton which they cultivated, were unexcelled and were in great demand throughout the prehistoric Southwest and northern Mexico. Some of their early pottery was the finest ware ever manufactured by Indians in the region of the western United States. They were expert at dyeing and embroidering blankets, belts, kilts, and sashes. They were noted agriculturalists and hunters, growing maize, beans, pumpkins, onions, chili, and sunflowers, and they traveled to the mountains and forested canyon country north and west to kill antelope, elk, and deer. They hunted with bows and arrows, but they were also clever at catching game animals in pitfalls or driving them into concealed corrals. They were thrifty and frugal, whenever possible storing at least a third of their produce to prevent want in the event of a crop failure. They had flocks of domesticated turkeys. All small animals were cooked in their pots. Rabbits were killed with boomerangs, prairie dogs and other rodents were drowned out of their burrows, and birds were caught in snares.

The Hopis' affluence and the great variety and value of their manufactured products attracted raiders from near and far. They were forced to maintain strong and extensive defenses. As their name indicates, they were the "peaceful ones," but they were brave and fierce fighters against invaders.

No people possessed a richer mythology, were more religious, nor

---

* The pueblo of Acoma may be as old or nearly as old.

devoted more time to ceremonials, rites, and dances, each of which had a peculiar spiritual significance. They were monogamists, and a marital scandal was a rarity. They maintained law and order, more with intelligent reasoning than with force. Murder was unknown, thefts seldom occurred, and liars were condemned and ostracized.

Yet they were not excessively sober and serious. Indeed, they were merry, full of laughter, and greatly appreciative of practical jokes. They manufactured toys, dolls, masks, and made kachinas carved, painted, and adorned with great artistry. Many of the kachinas were personifications of ancestors, for ancestral worship was predominant in the ceremonies of every Hopi clan.

Twelve Hopi towns, some destroyed and some, of course, still occupied, are in and close to the present Hopi Country, but there were others, some far distant, that once were occupied by their ancestors.

The Hopi were not monotheists. They recognized many supernatural beings, but their greatest deities were the Sky Father and the Earth Mother. They believed that the human race was created in the earth, and emerged through an opening called *sipapu*. They knew the place of mankind's emergence. It is now called the Grand Canyon.[53]

Zuñi: the Flesh

Zuñi is a popular name, adapted by early Spaniards from *Sunyitsi*, a Keresan word of unknown meaning. It is not the name by which the Zuñi people called themselves. That was *A'shiwi*, meaning "the flesh," and the name of their tribal range was *Shi'wona*, meaning "the land that produces flesh."

The Zuñi spoke a language all their own. Therefore, they have been given the status of a distinct linguistic family.

Archeologists and ethnologists have determined that the Zuñi are descended from two main parental stocks. One migrated to the area from somewhere in the north. The other can be more clearly identified. It came from the region of the lower Colorado River, joining the first group in the Zuñi River Valley of far western New Mexico, and its culture resembled those of Yuman and Piman peoples. These two stocks were the nucleus of the Zuñi tribe, but how long ago the first group settled on the Zuñi River, or how long ago it was joined by the people from the west, is not known. Zuñi traditions say it was a very long time before the historical period. At least it may be stated that the Anasazi Culture, to which the Zuñi belonged, began to emerge about two thousand years ago. Ancestors of the Zuñi may have been in their homeland long before that time. After the merger of the two parental stocks there were numerous other accretions from other tribes, and there were numerous desertions. The Zuñi, therefore, were a composite Pueblo people, but the mingling of bloods did not have a deleterious effect. Indeed, it made them strong and highly intelligent.

The big main pueblo of the Zuñi stands on the bank of the river named for them, not far from the Arizona border, but during the summer many of them live in adjacent farming communities of their own. The ruins of sixteen pueblos formerly inhabited by the Zuñi have been located within a radius of a few miles of their main town.

In character and customs the Zuñi generally resemble the Pueblo tribes (q.v.). They were progressive, quiet, and industrious, but their good nature vanished when they were menaced by raiders, and they were daring and unrelenting fighters.

They would, unfortunately for them, play a prominent but tragic role when the drama of the historical period opened in the Southwest.[54]

Tewa: Moccasins

That is the meaning of the word *Tewa*, but it applies chiefly to the northern division of the tribe. The southern division is known as Tano, and it is this name that linguists have adopted to designate the linguistic family—the Tanoan—which also includes the Tiwa, Piro, Pecos, and Jemez peoples.

The Tewa, as they were always popularly known, comprise a major division of this stock. In prehistoric times, these people separated into two groups in the ancient town of Tjeuingge Ouiping, which was located on the southern slope of the hills along the Rio Grande where the pueblo of San Juan now stands. Several pages would be required to enumerate and locate the villages that the Northern Tewa and the Southern Tewa (Tano) occupied at various times through many centuries. There may have been more than a hundred of them. The ruins of some four score have been found. Interestingly enough, however, each of these many villages was divided into two sections, known as the Winter People and the Summer People, and each group was headed by a cacique. The Summer Cacique served from the vernal equinox to the autumnal, and the Winter Cacique from the autumnal to the vernal equinox. Perhaps because the events of the cold months were not as important in the lives of the people, the Winter Cacique was inferior to his summer counterpart.

At one time towns of the Northern Tewa were spread from near Santa Fe northward to the mouth of the Rio Chama, and the Tano towns were scattered southward from Santa Fe to the vicinity of Golden, and were back from the Rio Grande. Countless thousands of New Mexico residents and tourists each year speed along freeways that pass close to old towns in which descendants of the Northern Tewa still live—Nambe, sixteen miles north of Santa Fe on the Nambe River;

San Ildefonso, near the Rio Grande about eighteen miles northwest of Santa Fe; San Juan, northwest of Santa Fe about twenty-five miles, near the Rio Grande; Santa Clara, thirty miles above Sante Fe on the Rio Grande; and Tesuque, eight miles north of Santa Fe. The ancient towns of the Southern Tewa are crumbling in dust, the people vanished. Many were slain in the late prehistoric period by Apaches from the southern plains, and warfare, revolts, and disease of historical times destroyed all but a very few of the survivors, who found havens among friends and kin to the north and west.[55]

Taos: the Best-Known Pueblo

Other Indians always spoke of the Tiwa, as they are known today, by their own name, which was Tiwan, the plural being Tiwesh. The first Spaniards to find their land would twist it to Tigua and Tiguex, but if the *conquistadores* could not pronounce their name they could never forget the bravery and stubbornness of the Tiwan in battle. The Spaniards robbed them, tortured them, slaughtered them, burned them at the stake and raped the women, but they did not destroy them.

However, that tragic tale belongs to the historical period. In prehistoric times the Tiwan were divided into three divisions. On the north stood (and still stands) the best-known pueblo in the United States—Taos. Not far away was Picuris. The middle group of Tiwan lived (and still do) in Sandia and Isleta, near Albuquerque. The southern Tiwan established towns near El Paso. Scattered throughout these three areas were nearly two score other Tiwan pueblos. The sites of some have been established but others are known to have existed only through tradition, and if they can be named they have not been located.

The Tiwan were good farmers and lived well, possessing many articles they obtained in trade. The northern region of the Tiwan was well-watered, and the people not only cultivated extensive fields, but hunted in the high forested mountains and journeyed through the passes to the plains for buffalo. In both prehistoric and historic times Taos was an important trade center, especially for the valuable furs and hides which Indians dwelling in more arid sections could not obtain.[56]

Jemez: Valley of Tiny Farms

The name Jemez is derived from the word *Ha-mish* (or *Hae-mish*), a sandy valley about twenty miles northwest of the present Bernallilo, New Mexico. The Jemez people did not always live there. According to their tradition they emerged from a lagoon, somewhere in the north, and slowly drifted southward to the upper tributaries of the Rio

Jemez. There they lived in a number of villages—and there are ruins to support their story—at last settling in the main valley of the Jemez.

With good reason, the Jemez did not build and occupy large towns. The cultivable areas of their valley were small and widely scattered. The Jemez would not be easily subjugated by the Spanish. They were strong and determined fighters against all foes. Several times they were allies of the Navajo and joined in raids on the towns of other Pueblo peoples and against the first settlements of the white invaders. In the face of adversities they would take refuge in the unknown Navajo Country to the west of their homeland.

Big Towns of the Pecos

The Pecos were kin of the Jemez, but they did not live with them, nor did they live in the same way. Nearly a hundred miles separated the Jemez, to the west of Santa Fe, and the Pecos, to the southeast of the old New Mexico capital. Yet, together they constituted a distinct group of the Tanoan linguistic family.

At the beginning of the historic period the Pecos towns were the largest and most populous of the Pueblo people. In prehistoric times the Pecos lived in numerous pueblos each containing from two hundred to three hundred rooms, and they also occupied many compactly built single-story house groups each comprised of ten to fifty rooms. These villages stood for some forty miles along the beautiful mountain valley of the upper Pecos River.

Probably because of an increasing number of attacks by raiders who could reach the Pecos Valley with ease from the plains of eastern New Mexico, the Pecos built two immense towns that could be more easily defended. Constructed on the terrace plan, each was four stories in height. One contained nearly six hundred rooms, the other a slightly lesser number.

Like the Jemez, the Pecos believed they had their origin somewhere in the north, but, unlike the Jemez, they reached their homeland in a long circular route, coming into it from the southeast. They, too, fought long and courageously against invaders, but within two centuries after the discovery by white men of the Southwest there were few of them left. The last survivors, a mere handful, went to live with their relatives, the Jemez. The Pecos tribe was soon extinct, and their big towns vanished into dust.

The Piro of New Mexico

The meaning of the word *piro* remains a mystery, but when the valley of the Rio Grande first became known to the outside world, the people bearing this name dwelt in and near it in two main divisions. The towns of the northern Piro stretched along the river from Socorro County northward to within fifty miles of Albuquerque. The southern Piro inhabited an area east of the Rio Grande in the vicinity of the salinas, and they were also called Salineros.

They were a large tribe. The names of nearly a hundred towns believed to have been occupied by the Piro have come down in history, although the ruins of all of them have not been found.

The Apache of the plains was the first insuperable destroyer of the Piro. The second was the Spanish. Town after town was sacked by the red raiders, until the survivors of the southern Piro were forced to abandon their homeland of the salinas. So great became the Piro's fear of the early Spaniards—the main road from Mexico to Santa Fe passed through their country—that many joined them. Others fled to live with various tribes, some into Chihuahua, below El Paso del Norte. That is a chapter that belongs in the record of historical warfare, and not in this work. It may be mentioned, however, that in less than two centuries following the advent of white men the Piro blood had become largely absorbed by the bloods of other peoples, both Mexican and Indian, and the Piro were forever lost.

Keresan of Bean Creek

Today Bean Creek is called Rito de los Frijoles, but it once had an Indian name—*Tyuonyi*. Coursing down from high mountains, Bean Creek and other streams cut deep canyons in the Pajarito Plateau. In those well-watered canyons, in the twelfth and thirteenth centuries, the Keresan built both large and small towns. But long before the beginning of the historical period these cliff dwellings had been abandoned, and the Keresan had moved farther southward and had separated into a number of autonomous communities.

Like so many other Pueblo tribes, the Keresan believe they emerged from the earth far to the north through the great aperture of Sipapu. At least, the direction whence they came is scientifically correct, and there is no doubt that eventually they settled along the Rito de los Frijoles. There today may be seen the ruins of the great structures they built.

Although they were beset by enemies through the centuries, and they occupied numerous towns, the Keresan did not become extinct. Indeed, their population now is increasing. Their present towns are known throughout the world, and annually are visited by thousands of tourists. They still are excellent farmers and craftsmen, and some of their pottery is still rated as among the best of all Pueblo earthenware. It brings them a good income.

On the Rio Grande between Santa Fe and Albuquerque stand the famous old Keresan pueblos of Cochiti, San Felipe, and Santo Domingo. On the Rio Jemez are Santa Ana and Sia. On the San Jose River is Laguna. And on a great rock mesa, three hundred and fifty-seven feet in height, about sixty miles west of the Rio Grande, is the celebrated old town of Acoma, standing majestically on its *penol* against the blue southwestern sky.

Wide freeways sweep near these ancient villages, and one wonders how long it will be before the dissolving force of American civilization will swallow them and they will forever vanish.[57]

Navajo: the Newcomers

The Navajos speak of it as *Dinetah*—"old Navajo land." It is a region of pastel canyons, juniper-covered mesas, and saffron washes in northwestern New Mexico. East and south of it high hogbacks jag the Continental Divide. To the north of it, in southwestern Colorado, rise the peaks of the San Juan and La Plata mountains. And to the west the Carrizo, Lukachukai, and Chuska ranges lift blue pine-clad barriers against the Arizona sky. The San Juan River enters Dinetah in the northeast, transects it in a slow southerly bend, and leaves it near the guarding sentinel of Winged Rock (Shiprock to Americans) beyond its northwest corner.

The Navajo call themselves *Dineh*—"the people." In their language the name Navajo is not to be found. It was given to them by early Spaniards and adopted by Americans. Before the time of written history they did not know it.

For the Navajos the primal levels in the theory of evolution take the forms of four underworlds through which they rose to reach the surface of the earth. Their Origin Myths relate that most of them were created somewhere in the mountains of southern Colorado. Other Dineh emerged into life somewhere beside the western sea. And all of them moved to live together in Dinetah.

Archeology, ethnology, and linguistics, of course, provide a different account of Navajo beginnings. The directions of their migrations as given in the Origin Myths are correct, that is, southward from Colorado and eastward from the Pacific, and the evidence is clear that the first permanent homeland of the Navajos in the Southwest was Dinetah.

However, the Navajos came into the region of the United States from northern Canada. Their tongue unmistakably belongs to the Athapascan linguistic family, one of the largest and most widely distributed in North America. The languages of peoples who now live, or formerly lived, in Alberta, British Columbia, Alaska, and along the

Pacific in Oregon and northern California are similar in innumerable respects to the tongue of the Navajos. The great question that remains unanswered is when the Navajos, as well as the Apaches, who belong to the same family, first reached the Southwest.

If the pace of the southward movement of Athapascans is not known, some other facts about them may be stated with certainty. They were hunters, trappers, fishermen, and wild-food-gatherers. They brought with them to the vast Southwest the culture of a northern forest people. The bounties of nature guided their individual or group movements. Adverse weather and scarcities forced them to take meandering routes—their lives were an eternal search for sustenance. In areas where food supplies were stable, bands may have remained for several generations.

Scientists believe that most Navajos came southward along the western edge of the Great Plains. (Certainly the Athapascan Apaches came that way.) Some of the first Navajos may have lived for a time among plains buffalo-hunting peoples, or circled into the high mountains and lived among Paiutes, but there is no archeological proof that the bulk of them migrated by way of the Great Basin.

However, wherever they wandered, whatever circuitous routes some of them took, they found that other peoples had preceded them. A number of important cultures had flourished in the Southwest before the Navajos penetrated the region, but it was the Anasazi, or Basketmaker-Pueblo civilization that more than any other influenced the lives of the Navajos and shaped their history.*

Most of the great Anasazi pueblos probably were inhabited only by ghosts when the Navajos reached the Southwest. Into the abandoned land of spectacular cliff-houses, multi-storied mesa-top towns, and sprawling communal dwellings in the deep canyons moved the Navajos. And it became their country. And there they stayed.

The Navajos did not take over the deserted big towns. They built their homes as they had built them from time immemorial, hogans constructed of mud, of logs, of brush, the roofs supported by poles or forked sticks. Some hogan-type ruins found in western Colorado appear to date from A.D. 1000, and may have been Navajo dwellings. The ruins of other hogans with walls of stone have been found in the same general area and are believed to have been constructed as early as A.D. 1100. People were living in the Largo and Galina canyons of New Mexico between the years A.D. 1100 and 1250 who had pottery very similar to the gray pointed type known to have been made by early Navajos. This evidence is insufficient to be accepted as conclusive, but

---

* See *Anasazi: the Old Ones,* in this part.

that is not the case with three sites found in the Gobernador Canyon of Dinetah. They are unquestionably early Navajo, and they range in date—determined by tree rings—from A.D. 1491 to 1521.

In the Southwest the Navajos found something they had never known. Having always lived at best a step ahead of hunger as hunters and food-gatherers, the life of the Pueblo peoples represented security and plenty inconceivable to them. In amazement they gazed upon patches of corn, pumpkins, beans, gourds, and a wonderful fiber—cotton. They saw fine pottery bowls, jars, pitchers, mugs, ladles, and plates decorated in geometric designs of numerous colors. They saw beautifully woven baskets. They saw stone hoes and axes and broad flint knives and many other ingenious tools, such as polishers and scrapers. They saw feather robes, and blankets and garments and bags of woven cotton. They saw mosaics and ornaments, pendants and beads of turquoise and other bright stones. And they saw astonishingly lovely articles made of shells from the Pacific and the Gulf of California.

And they saw only one way to acquire for themselves the comforts, the security, the luxuries of the Pueblos, and that was to take them.

The Navajos settled in the Southwest, spreading out over an immense territory, and became bandits. Banditry was the cornerstone of their economy, and on it a new culture was born. It was a blend of many ingredients. Something of the far northern woodlands, something of the plains, something of the mountains, and a great deal of the Pueblo civilization would be preserved in it. But the Navajos would give it more than these things, more than the brutality and cunning of wild animals, more than the basic characteristics which all men possess—greed, jealousy, and desire—more than the common instinct of self-protection and self-aggrandizement. They would contribute qualities which not only distinguished them but graded them above many other peoples of their race—superior intellect, extraordinary perspicacity, consuming ambition, and inexhaustible enterprise.

And woven into the new Navajo culture—vital strands in its texture—would be many of the customs, practices, mores, and beliefs of the town dwellers, whose wealth, sophistication, and complicated, beautiful, stirring religious ceremonials so greatly excited the wanderers, the newcomers, from the north.

Banditry was the original form of the Navajo economy, but they did not depend upon it alone. They were the great adapters, the great learners, the great developers. Steal and capture. Steal not only material things, but capture male craftsmen and artisans. Capture young female potters, weavers, cultivators, but not to serve only as slaves. Respect them and marry them and give them children to whom they could pass on their skills. Adoption of agriculture modeled after that of the Pueblos was the initial significant transition in the primitive Navajo way of life, but with it the Navajos also adopted Pueblo agricultural ritual, although with some loss of form and much loss of meaning, for the Navajos were neither peaceful nor sedentary by character or by tradition. They were wild, dangerous, and unpredictable. It was in keeping with their nature to want immediately both the freedom of the wind and the rewards of the patient laborer and saver, to want and to revere their own gods and still be willing to pay obeisance to the gods of others, if by so doing they might gain benefits for themselves.

And the Navajos did, and their culture flourished. Largely through accretions their population soared, and through their extensive intellectual capacity, their boundless energy, their cleverness and daring as thieves, their hard labor, their shrewdness and discernment in practical matters, they soon became the dominant and most affluent tribe in the Southwest.

Yet, oddly, the greatest and most significant period of Navajo acculturation came not in the early years of their contacts with the Pueblos but in historical times, after the arrival of white men in their country.[58]

Apache: the Enemy

Apache is an American Indian name better known around the world than any other. It has been taken into literature to indicate fierce and ruthless individuals, as well as criminals. Yet it is not the Apaches' name for themselves. Like their kinsmen, the Navajos, they call themselves simply *Dineh*, "the people." Nor does the word "apache" come from their own language, which belongs to the Athapascan family of the Na-Dene linguistic group. It comes from an entirely different tongue, the Zuñi, and is derived from the Zuñi word *apachu*, meaning "enemy." A most appropriate name for them it was, indeed, for from prehistoric times until within the memory of the living the Apaches were universally feared by all men who encountered them, both red and white. They were incomparable and incorrigible raiders, cunning and daring fighters, and no Indian people made a more determined and courageous struggle to hold their homelands against the inroads of civilization. To the early Spaniards, *apachu* became *apache*, and they learned the true definition of the word in a most realistic and unforgettable manner.*

At some time, perhaps half a millennium before the beginning of the historical period in the Southwest, the southward route of the

---

* This was the case also of the Spaniards' encounters with the Navajo, whom they called *Apaches de Navaju*, interpreted as signifying "Apaches of cultivated lands, or wide fields." *Navaju* was the name of an ancient Tewa pueblo adjacent to an extensive agricultural area.

Athapascans migrating from the far north branched near the southern end of the Rocky Mountains, in Colorado or northeastern New Mexico. One fork turned southwestward, and over it went the people who would become known as Navajos. The other fork continued on southward, and over it traveled the Apaches to find their first permanent home in southeastern New Mexico and western Texas.

But unlike their Navajo relatives, who became a single tribe, the Apaches developed into several divisions, or tribal groups, and they steadily spread out until they dominated and terrorized enormous parts of Texas, New Mexico, Arizona, and northern Mexico. They rejected the cultures of the sedentary peoples they overwhelmed, and maintained (even well into the American period) a hunting, food-gathering, raiding way of life.

The Apaches grew few crops. One of their principal staples was the maguey plant. Both fish and bear were taboo as food. They had little artistic skill, although the women were expert at weaving baskets. Being nomadic, they had few permanent homes, and lived mostly in easily erected brush shelters. It is not believed there were many of them in the beginning, but they increased rapidly in population as a result of their custom of taking women captives for wives from other tribes, notably the Pueblo, Pima, and Papago.

Even today there is doubt as to which Apache subdivisions should be given tribal status, if any at all. A popular name of a group may have been derived from some local or temporary habitat, or may have been first applied by early white men on account of some characteristic. Thus, because the Apache groups almost constantly shifted in their enormous territory, numerous names may be synonymous. At last, the Apache were conquered, but they have not ceased to create confusion, nor because of their subjugation have they deteriorated. There are more of them today than there were before the time of written history.[59]

Four Strangers

The significance of the name *Jumano* is not known, but the people who bore it lived in prehistoric times mainly along the Rio Grande between the mouth of the Concho and the site of El Paso del Norte. They belonged to the Uto-Aztecan-Tanoan linguistic group. Usually each year they trekked northward, east of the Pecos River, to hunt buffalo on the plains, and they traded with other Pueblo people who lived farther north in the Rio Grande Valley, especially with the Piros (q.v.). The Jumanos lived in permanent villages. Most of their houses were built of adobe and had flat pole roofs covered with sod and grass. They cultivated maize, beans, and pumpkins.

About the beginning of the year A.D. 1536, four strange men, accompanied by a large group of west Texas Indians, came out of the east into the valley of the Rio Grande. Three of them were heavily bearded. Their long hair was held by thongs of deerhide. Except for skin breechclouts, they were naked. Their bodies were lean, hard, lithe, and deeply burned by years of exposure. About their necks crudely carved wooden crosses were suspended on cords of woven animal hair.

The fourth man was even more startling to behold. He was the color of ebony, and he towered above the other three and the Indians who swarmed about him. He had a great head of kinky black hair adorned with bright feathers. His powerful muscles rippled, his white teeth gleamed, and he strode in a regal manner.

The first Europeans had reached the perimeter of the Southwest.

The leader of the four strangers was Álvar Núñez Cabeza de Vaca. His two Spanish companions were Andrés Dorantes de Carranca and Alonzo del Castillo Maldonado. The fourth man was a blackamoor from Morocco, the slave of Dorantes, called simply Estevanico the Black. They were the only survivors of more than two hundred men of the Narváez expedition wrecked on the Texas coast seven years earlier, in November, 1528.

In his famous *Relación*, Núñez Cabeza de Vaca would write of the Jumanos: "They gave us beans and many squashes to eat, gourds to carry water in, blankets of cowhide [bison] and other things . . . great festivities were made over us. . . . They took us to the settled habitations of others, who lived upon the same food. . . . Those who knew of our approach did not come out to receive us . . . but we found them in their houses. . . . They were all seated with their faces turned to the wall, their heads down, the hair brought before their eyes, and their property placed in a heap in the middle of the house . . . they had nothing they did not bestow. They have the finest persons of any people we saw, of the greatest activity and strength, who best understood us and intelligently answered our inquiries. . . . The women are dressed in deerskin, and some few men, mostly the aged. . . . The country is very populous."

For two years there had been no rain. Moles had eaten the corn which had been planted. Yet the Jumanos had corn stored in jars, and the visitors were informed that it had been obtained from other people far to the north where rain had fallen. Núñez Cabeza de Vaca thought their method of cooking "so new that for its strangeness I desire to speak of it; thus it may be seen and remarked how curious and diversified are the contrivances and ingenuity of the human family. Not having discovered the use of pipkins, to boil what they would eat, they fill the half of a large calabash with water, and throw on the fire many stones of such as are most convenient and readily take the heat. When hot, they are taken up with tongs of sticks and dropped into the calabash until the water in it boils from the fervor of the stones. Then whatever is to be cooked is put in, and until it is done they continue taking out cooled stones and throwing in hot ones. Thus they boil their food."

The three Spaniards and the black were the first men of the Old World to see Indians of the southwestern United States, and the *Relación* was the first account to contain information about them.

Early in the year 1537 Núñez Cabeza de Vaca and his companions left the valley of the Rio Grande, turning westward near a village known today as San Augustine, about twenty miles south of El Paso del Norte. They went on across the great Sierra Madre to Spanish settlements on the Gulf of California, and were taken as heroes to Mexico City.

They were first to cross the continent north of Mexico, and their feat, which took eight years to complete, is the most remarkable in the long record of American exploration.

Núñez Cabeza de Vaca's *Relación* is an invaluable contribution to history, and as a narrative of suffering and privation it has no equal. He will never be forgotten. Yet, of the four men who made the miraculous journey into darkness, Estevanico the Black would win the greatest fame as the true discoverer of the Southwest.[60]

The Death Rattle

The people of Mexico City were in a state of feverish excitement. Reports had spread like wildfire through dry grass that on their epic journey Núñez Cabeza de Vaca and his companions had heard of the long-lost Seven Cities of Cibola. If they had had means of transport they would have brought with them an inconceivable fortune. They had crossed streams that flowed in beds of solid gold. They had seen Indian children playing with diamonds, pearls, and emeralds which had been cast away as worthless. They had passed hills of silver and one mountain which contained so many jewels of all kinds that they dared not look at it in the sunlight for fear of being blinded. They had seen buildings several stories in height, and had met people who ate from golden dishes.

Neither Núñez Cabeza de Vaca nor the others had made any such claims. When they repeated stories heard from Indians they had not failed to add that the information had been given to them in the sign language and they could not vouch for its accuracy. They had seen no great cities nor tall buildings, and the only evidence they had that the unknown land along their route contained any mineral resources at all consisted of some scoria of iron, some small bits of mica, some galena with which the Indians painted themselves, some pieces of turquoise, and five arrowheads made of some semiprecious stone.

The people of Mexico City suspected that for obvious reasons they were not telling all they knew. Plans to send out a strong expedition to reap the harvest began to take shape. It would cost a great deal of money, and the Viceroy Don Antonio de Mendoza, although he was deeply stirred by the fanciful tales, did not abandon the cautiousness he customarily exhibited in disbursing funds of the New Spain treasury. It would be wise, he decided, first to dispatch a relatively small scouting expedition to the mysterious north for the purpose of obtaining possible verification of the fabulous reports. In turn, he asked Núñez Cabeza de Vaca, Dorantes, and Castillo to lead it, but they had had enough of the wilderness and declined.

His next choice was a remarkable and adventurous priest, Fray Marcos of Nice, who had been gallivanting about the New World for seven years. With Fray Marcos would go another priest, Fray Onarato, and a group of Indian slaves. Their guide would be Estevanico the Black.* Meanwhile, plans would be carried forward for an immense expedition to follow their trail of discovery, and it would be led by a young nobleman, only twenty-eight years of age, who recently had been appointed governor of the Province of Nueva Galicia—Don Francisco Vásquez de Coronado.

The spring of 1539 was in full glory along the Pacific coast when the little advance party turned northward on their great adventure. "I command him to obey you . . ." Mendoza had written of Estevanico to Fray Marcos. Estevanico had no intention of obeying anyone. He fully understood that once they were in the wilderness, beyond the reach of the military, Fray Marcos would be completely dependent upon him for his survival. He would be the one who would make decisions, and he relished the idea of being in such an influential position.

If the attention and respect paid to him in Mexico City had inflated his ego, it would not have been an unusual reaction. What other slave had been given such consideration, and called *intelligent* by a viceroy? He had been over the trail as far as Pueblo de los Corazones, in the Opata Country of upper Sonora, where the unknown northern lands began. He was the man the Indians knew, and their faith would be in him. No longer would he be only an assistant shaman overshadowed by the great Núñez Cabeza de Vaca. Now he would be a god in his own right.

---

* Fray Onarato would not make the trip because of illness.

Estevanico the Black had acquired numerous personal belongings—baggage, clothing, and ornaments. Among his most prized possessions were a shelter tent, sleeping robes, two greyhounds, and four large green dinner plates, his *servicio de mesa,* on which he was served his meals. No one else was permitted to use them.

In one of his packs was a sacred gourd rattle, acquired from Indians in Texas. It had been the custom of Núñez Cabeza de Vaca to send a similar medicine rattle ahead, to signify his power as a god, when approaching a strange village. Estevanico carried on the custom. The story of his life might well have had a different ending if he had left the rattle behind him.

On the trail to the north, he acquired a harem, Indian girls he found especially pleasing, and they straggled along in his wake, much to the consternation and disapproval of Fray Marcos.

In March, 1539, Fray Marcos, profoundly aggravated by Estevanico's immorality, ordered him to go ahead in the hope that he would not spend so much time carousing. Despite Fray Marcos' scoldings, Estevanico swaggered through medicine ceremonies, made the sign of the cross over the sick, and performed religious rites in emulation of Núñez Cabeza de Vaca and the other two Spaniards on the previous journey. He ignored the priest's demand that he reject the women offered him, and he saw no reason to refuse the turquoise and coral and feathers and countless other gifts made to him by Indians. In fact, he had no hesitancy in asking for any article which attracted his eye, and his acquisitions were, in Fray Marcos' view, reaching vulgar proportions.

Fray Marcos gave the irrepressible Moor orders. If in going ahead he should discover something "of moderate importance" he was to send back a white cross a span in size. If he came upon something of "greater importance" he should send back a cross two spans in size. If he discovered something "greater and better than New Spain" he was to send Indians back with a large cross.

Crosses came back to Fray Marco at intervals—always large ones—but he never was able to overtake Estevanico. He never saw him again.

North of Pueblo de los Corazones, Estevanico the Black went into a land that was a blank space on the maps of the world.

It was a wild and colorful pageant that crawled northward through the fearsome *despoblado,* across the angular tilted mesas, up the hot valleys, over ridge and sweeping plain, through the canyons. Followed by more than three hundred Indians from Mexico, steadily onward went the intrepid and fearless Moor, the greyhounds panting at his side, feather plumes answering the moving desert airs, strings of turquoise and coral dripping over his big chest, *cascabelles* tinkling on his ankles, sweat gleaming on his powerful ebony limbs. With each stride he wrote history in the dust.

On a May day in the year 1539, Estevanico the Black unlocked the gateway to the Southwest of the future United States. From a high ridge in the Huachuca Mountains, where the air is thin and sweet with the perfume of evergreens and flowers, the place where he crossed the present international border may be seen in a magnificent panoramic view.

His trail into Arizona went down the San Pedro River. In the vicinity of Benson, his guides led him to the northeast, across Arivipai Valley, to Eagle Pass. From Chichilticale (Red House) the trail swung northward to the Gila River and went on across high plateau country to the Little Colorado, near St. Johns. Turning northeasterly again, it crossed Carrizo Creek and reached the Zuñi River.

The end came at the Zuñi pueblo at Hawikuh.

Following his custom, Estevanico had sent the colored sacred gourd ahead with Indian emissaries to inform the Zuñis that he was approaching. He had decorated it with a string of little bells, and two feathers, one white and the other red.

The headman to whom the gourd was delivered examined it briefly and then wrathfully hurled it to the ground and ordered Estevanico's messengers to leave at once. They obeyed. When Estevanico heard their report, he laughed, and told his followers that the same thing had happened more than once to Núñez Cabeza de Vaca, and on each occasion Indians who had been suspicious or unfriendly at first always had been humble and hospitable in the end.

Estevanico went on, but matters did not turn out as he had expected. The people of Hawikuh refused to allow him to enter the town. They lodged him in a small house on the outskirts, took from him all his possessions, and held him prisoner.

For three days the Zuñi leaders questioned him, seeking to "find out the reason he had come to their country. . . . The story which the Negro gave them of . . . white men who were following him, sent by a great lord, who knew about the things in the sky, and how these were coming to instruct them in divine matters, made them think he must be a spy or a guide from some nations who wished to come and conquer them, *because it seemed to them unreasonable to say that the people were white in the country from which he came and that he was sent by them, he being black.* Besides these other reasons, they thought it was hard of him to ask them for turquoises and women, and so they decided to kill him." [61]

To prove that Estevanico was not a god, but an ordinary human being, they cut him up in little pieces and distributed them widely among neighboring tribes with a warning to kill any other strange men, black or white, who appeared. His executioners kept his turquoises, his corals, his feathers and his *cascabelles,* his greyhounds and his green dinner plates. They threw away the sacred gourd rattle.

Fray Marcos received the news of Estevanico's death far back down the trail, perhaps south of the Gila River, and fled "with more fear than food" back to Mexico. He told the Viceroy Mendoza and Coronado, however, that after hearing that Estevanico had been slain at Cibola (Zuñi) he had gone on until he could see Hawikuh from a high hill and that the pueblo was "larger than the city of Mexico."

Fray Marcos would be proven to be an unmitigated liar. He did not see Zuñi.

It was Estevanico the Black who discovered Arizona and New Mexico, who was the first man of the Old World to enter them. It was he who found out that the vaunted Seven Cities of Cibola were nothing more than ancient Zuñi pueblos, although he paid with his life for the discovery.[62]

A Strange Kind of Thunder

Although the Coronado expedition had been organized, and the Viceroy Mendoza fully intended to send it north, he could not overcome his feeling that more cautiousness was required. It may have been that, recognizing the imaginative powers of Fray Marcos and knowing the friar's talent for dramatizing commonplace incidents, he suspected him of fabricating fine tales.

Mendoza ordered the veteran frontiersman Melchior Díaz to take a small company of horsemen and check on Fray Marcos' report. Captain Díaz was alcalde mayor of Culiacán. As Mendoza well knew, he was a man of unquestionable integrity, and a realist, who would not be taken in by wild stories. Díaz would report the truth and nothing but the truth.

It was mid-November of 1539, a poor time of the year to be starting north, when Díaz, his mounted soldiers and Indians, perhaps forty-five in all, left Culiacán.

This is a most important chapter in the history of American exploration, important not because of Díaz's discoveries, for he made none on this journey, nor because of his daring adventure, but important because he and his men rode the first horses to tread the soil of the country that would become the western United States.

If the Indians of northern Sonora and Arizona had heard of horses—and they probably had heard of them from people living farther to the south who had encountered Spanish slave-hunters—they had never seen one.

Now they heard a strange kind of thunder on the old Indian trade trail running from tropical Mexico to Zuñi, a rhythmic beating on the earth in tempos they had never known. Now there were nights when the lights of campfires caught on the sides of the great beasts tethered about the tents of Díaz's company, and there were new sounds in the shadows, the sounds of fodder being munched, the sounds of stamping, and there were the strange smells of an unknown kind of sweat and an unknown kind of manure.

A new age and a new way of life had come to the West.

Díaz learned what he could from Indians along the trail. He confirmed Estevanico's death. He gathered articles which the people said had come from Zuñi, but he could learn nothing of great cities, nothing of such desirable things as jewels and gold.

Díaz did not reach Zuñi, however, for winter defeated him. Several of his men died of exposure. At the ancient ruin of Chichilticale, in southeastern Arizona, his journey was halted by snow and low temperatures. Returning in the spring of 1540 he met the expedition of Coronado advancing northward on the coastal road at Chimetla.[63]

Shattered Dreams and Bloody Deaths

The color of the pageantry rivaled the glory of the dream. An army was marching northward to Cibola, and ahead, in the visions of officers, soldiers, gentlemen adventurers, and red and black slaves alike, lay another Peru. Under the supreme command of Coronado were two hundred and fifty mounted men, some eighty foot soldiers—a few accompanied by their wives and children—and perhaps as many as a thousand servants. At least half a dozen padres, led by the redoubtable Fray Marcos, padded along in their robes and sandals. At the rear came droves of cattle, sheep, oxen, and swine, heavily loaded packmules, and a herd of a thousand horses.

When Coronado and his men, weary, bruised, and hungry, came at last in sight of the Zuñi pueblo of Hawikuh ". . . such were the curses that some hurled at Fray Marcos," said Castañeda,[64] "that I pray God may protect him from them. It is a little crowded village looking as if it had been crumpled all up together. There are haciendas in New Spain that make a better appearance at a distance."

In July, 1540, Coronado fought the Zuñi and captured the pueblo. He sent a detachment, led by Don Pedro de Tovar, to look into an Indian province called Tusayan. These were the first white men to meet the Hopis, who told them of a great river that lay several days to the northwest. Coronado sent Don García López de Cárdenas and twelve soldiers to visit the river. Hopis guided them to the Grand Canyon of the Colorado.[65]

The Southwest Gate was being opened wider. From Zuñi, Coronado went on across totally undiscovered lands, across New Mexico to the valley of the Rio Grande, and on to the Great Plains, leaving in his wake a trail of blood and death, of destroyed towns and slain Pueblos.

He and his men were the first to meet the Tewa, the Tigua, the Jemez, the Piro, the Keresan, the Pecos, and the Apaches. There is nothing of record to show that he encountered Navajos, although he passed through a part of the country inhabited by them, but neither is there a record to show that they did not see him. The chroniclers of the Coronado expedition wrote the first descriptions of the Pueblo towns and the people who inhabited them, and who were robbed, abused, tortured, and slain by the invaders. That is a tragic tale, however, that has no fitting place in an Indian almanac of prehistoric times.

But the writings of Castañeda, a soldier in Coronado's army, may be legitimately excerpted in this work, for his accounts stand as memorials marking the beginning of the period of written history.

Of Cibola, the country of the Zuñi: [66]

"It has seven villages. . . . The houses are ordinarily three or four stories high, but in Macaque [the largest village] there are houses with four and seven stories. These people are very intelligent. They cover their privy parts with cloths made like a sort of table napkin. . . . They wear long robes of feathers and the skins of hares, and cotton blankets. The women wear blankets, which they tie or knot over the left shoulder, leaving the right arm out. They wear a neat well-shaped outer garment of skin. They gather their hair over the two ears, making a frame which looks like an old-fashioned headdress. . . . They plant in holes. Maize does not grow high. . . . There are large numbers of bears . . . and lions, wildcats, deer, and otter. There are very fine turquoises, although not so many as was reported. They collect the pine nuts [piñón] each year and store them. . . . A man does not have more than one wife. . . . They do not have chiefs . . . but are ruled by a council of the oldest men. They have priests who preach to them. . . . There is no drunkenness among them nor sodomy nor sacrifices, neither do they eat human flesh nor steal. . . . They burn their dead. . . ."

Of the upper Rio Grande pueblos:

"In general, these villages all have the same habits and customs, although some have some things in particular which the others have not [such as ceremonials and religious rites]. They are governed by the opinions of the elders. They all work together to build the villages, the women being engaged in making the mixture and the walls, while the men bring the wood and put it in place. They have no lime, but they make a mixture of ashes, coals, and dirt which is almost as good as mortar. . . . They have a hearth made like the binnacle or a compass box of a ship, in which they burn a handful of thyme [sagebrush] at a time to keep up the heat. . . . When a man wishes to marry, it has to be arranged by those who govern. The man has to spin and weave a blanket and place it before the woman, who covers herself with it and becomes his wife. The houses [kivas] belong to the men. . . . The country is so fertile that they do not have to break up the ground the year around, but only have to sow the seed, which is presently covered by the fall of snow, and the ears come up under the snow. In one year they gather enough for seven. . . . There are a great many native fowl. . . . When dead, these keep for sixty days . . . and without any bad smell, and the same is true of dead men. . . . The villages are free of nuisances, because they go outside to excrete, and they pass their water into clay vessels, which they empty at a distance from the village. They keep the separate houses, where they prepare the food for eating and where they grind the meal, very clean. . . . A man sits at the door playing a fife while they grind, moving the stones to the music and singing together. . . . The people are not cruel. . . . I found out several things about them from one of our Indians. . . . I asked him especially for the reason why the young women in that province went entirely naked, however cold it might be, and he told me that the virgins had to go around this way until they took a husband, and that they covered themselves after they had known man. The men here wear little shirts of tanned deerskin and their long robes over this. In all these provinces they have earthenware glazed with antimony and jars of extraordinary labor and workmanship, which are worth seeing."

The Colorado River: Unfailing Guide

In August, 1540, three small Spanish vessels reached the head of the Gulf of California. They were supply ships for the Coronado expedition, and were commanded by Hernando de Alarcón, a young, ambitious, and adventurous captain in the service of the Viceroy Mendoza. As they had sailed northward for weeks from Acapulco and Culiacán, keeping close to the eastern shore of the Gulf, lookouts had watched night and day in vain for some signal from Coronado.

Now Alarcón found himself confronted on three sides by rugged desert coasts that swept against the sky in weird formations, and the waters immediately ahead were laced by a seemingly impassable network of frothing shoals guarding the mouth of a great river.

The pilots and seamen of the little flotilla wanted to turn homeward, but Alarcón closed his ears to their pleas. It was his hope, if not his conviction, that the river might lead to the Province of Cibola, Coronado's destination, and he intended to go on at all costs, in an attempt to fulfill his mission.

Alarcón was the first European explorer to enter the mouth of the Colorado River, to which he gave the name *Buena Guia*—Unfailing Guide. After anchoring the vessels in a protected channel, he equipped two launches with food, supplies, and arms, and taking the most experienced crewmen to man them, he pushed up the raging waters of the Colorado's delta. Although, through no fault of his own, he would fail to reach Coronado, his daring feat would comprise the first chapter in the history of a land which at the time was totally unknown to the civilized world.

In the launches Alarcón would make two ascents of the Colorado, on the second journey passing (probably by only a short distance) the site of the present town of Yuma, Arizona.

On the west bank was a land that one day would be known as the state of California, and Alarcón and his crew were the first white men to set foot upon it.

Alarcón met Indians who not only had visited the Province of Cibola—probably going to Zuñi on trading expeditions—but knew that Estevanico the Black had been killed there and that Coronado had captured the pueblos and had slain many of their inhabitants. News of such importance was carried rapidly across the immense deserts of the Southwest.

For days Alarcón sought to induce the Indians to guide him to Coronado, but they coldly refused. More men calling themselves Christians, they declared, would not be welcome in Cibola, and Indians accompanying them could expect only death at the hands of the Zuñi. Indeed, after hearing of the events which had transpired in Cibola, Alarcón's own men rejected his proposal that they go on without guides.

Alarcón discovered the people of the Yuman tribes, the Cocopa, Mojave, Maricopa, Walapai, Halchidhoma, Halyikwamai, Kohuana, Yuma, and perhaps others, people of whose existence nothing was known.

He wrote the first reports of them, describing some as "large and well-formed without being corpulent. Some have their noses pierced, and from them hang pendants, while others wear shells. They also have their ears pierced with many holes, in which they place shells and beads. All of them [the males], big and little, wear a multicolored sash about the waist; and, tied in the middle, a round bundle of feathers hanging down behind like a tail. Likewise, on their biceps, they wear a narrow band, wound around so many times that it had the width of a hand. They carry small blades of deer bones tied around one arm, with which they scrape off sweat, and from the other arm reed canes are hung. They have also a kind of sack tied to the left arm . . . and it is filled with seeds from which they make a sort of beverage. Their bodies are branded by fire; their hair is banged in front, but in the back it hangs to the waist. The women go about naked, except that, tied in front and behind, they wear large bunches of feathers, colored and glued. They wear their hair like the men."

He told of Indians whose homes were in mountains to the west but who came to the river each spring to plant crops where there was adequate water to nourish them during the hot growing season. These people may have been the Yuman Kamia and the Shoshonean Chemehuevis. The tribes who lived permanently along the river grew maize, melons, and squashes, and they had cotton plants but did not harvest the fiber, "for there was no one who knew how to weave." With signs and drawings in sand, an elder portrayed for Alarcón a big animal that was unmistakably the buffalo, yet the nearest buffalo range was a thousand miles to the east. It is possible that the old man was attempting to tell Alarcón of products made from buffalo hide which were obtained in trade, for it is extremely doubtful that the people of the lower Colorado River traveled the great distance to the plains to hunt.

Dejected and dispirited, in the early fall Alarcón gave up hope of reaching Coronado, and returned to his ships in the delta. Someplace along the river he blazed a tree, carved words on it, and buried letters in a jar beneath the trunk—a message to tell whoever might follow him that he had been there and had done his best to complete the mission on which the Viceroy Mendoza had sent him. Then he sailed for Mexico.

Death on the Colorado

By the late summer of 1540, Coronado's army in Cibola was becoming badly in need of food supplies and equipment. No news had come of the fate of Alarcón's relief ships. Perhaps, Coronado reasoned, Alarcón was waiting for some word from him at the head of the Gulf of California. He decided that someone must be sent to make a thorough search for the vessels.

The man he selected for the dangerous assignment was the reliable and experienced Captain Melchior Díaz. Returning from Cibola, Díaz set out for the Colorado River late in September, 1540, from San Gerónimo de los Corazones, Sonora, on the quest that would enshrine his name on the roster of great discoverers of the southwestern region —a quest from which he would not return.

Díaz took with him twenty-five *mounted* Spaniards, a contingent of Opata Indians from the Sonora Valley, and a band of sheep to provide a supply of fresh meat. The word "mounted" is significant. Díaz had taken the first horses into the western United States in the fall of 1539 on his journey to investigate the reports of Fray Marcos and the death of Estevanico the Black. Now, a year later, he would take not only the first horses but the first sheep into the future American California.

One other animal with the expedition deserves special mention. It was a greyhound, owned by one of the soldiers, and it would play an important role in history.

Díaz's Opata guides led him through a country never before entered by white men. The route they followed ran from the vicinity of Ures, Sonora, northwest to Magdalena, westward to Caborca, and northwestward again to Sonoita. Thence it twisted along the present international border, skirting around the northern end of the great Pincate lava bed. This was the most difficult part of the journey, a section of burning desert that would come to be known much later as the *Camino del Diablo*—the Devil's Highway. On it, in years to come, countless men and animals would perish. Near the Tinajas Alta Mountains the trail swung northward, probably following the Coyote Wash, until reaching the Gila River near where the town of Wellton now stands. Descending the Gila along the well-traveled ancient Indian trade trail that came from the Pacific Coast, Díaz reached the Yuma Crossing of the Colorado.

He had passed through lands inhabited by both Pima and Papago never encountered by white men, and he must, therefore, be credited with being the discoverer of these tribes.

Alarcón had arrived by water in the area and he had convinced the river Indians that he was a man of peace. Díaz and his men had come by land, mounted on prancing animals like those which Coronado and his soldiers had ridden when they conquered and killed the Cibolans. The Indians could draw only one conclusion: Díaz had come to subdue them. Their fears were not alleviated when they learned from the Opatas that Díaz had been with Coronado in the attack on the Zuñi.

Like Alarcón, Díaz and his men were astonished at the size and strength of some of the Indians. Many of them stood well over six feet and were extraordinarily powerful. One of them easily picked up a log which six Spaniards were unable to lift. Speaking of them as giants, one early account of the Díaz journey stated that they "are naked and live in large straw cabins built underground like smokehouses, with only the straw roof aboveground. They enter these at one end and come out the other. More than a hundred persons, old and young, sleep in one cabin. When they carry anything, they can take a load of three or four hundredweight." They "carry a firebrand with which they warm their hands and body, changing it from one hand to the other as they travel along."

Alarcón had been on the river during the terrible heat of summer, but Díaz was there in the winter, and he saw the people following customs and a manner of living which Alarcón had not witnessed. Unaware that Alarcón had called the Colorado *Buena Guía*, Díaz appropriately christened it *Río del Tizón*—Firebrand River—and long thereafter it would be popularly known by that name.

Díaz found Alarcón's letters beneath the blazed tree, and he learned from them "how long Alarcón had waited for news from Coronado's army," and it was explained in the letters that the peninsula called California was not an island but an extension of the mainland forming the western side of the gulf. This was geographical knowledge never before disseminated, and, incidentally, it would soon be forgotten or ignored. For decades to come, Baja California would continue to be shown on maps as a long narrow island.

Deeply disappointed at finding that Alarcón had departed, Díaz turned back up the river. Now his actions become mysterious. Instead of setting out homeward to report to Coronado, he elected to cross the Colorado in the vicinity of the point where the Gila flows into it.

It was at this crossing that the first warfare between the river people and white men occurred. The Indians—perhaps the warlike Maricopas—attacked at dawn, but they were no match for the firearms of the Spaniards, and a number were killed before they retreated.

Díaz led his men into American California. One early report states that after crossing the river on rafts—the horses swam and the sheep were ferried—Díaz and his men "continued their search for the other coast." It is not illogical to think that Díaz had heard from Indians that the Pacific was not a great distance to the west, and had in mind going to the coast. There are suggestions in old documents to indicate that he may have circled north in American California. One account says that he "passed on from the Firebrand River fifty leagues to where he found the country very sandy, windy, and filled with large and high dunes . . . which grow, diminish, or move depending on the strongness of the wind." If he had traveled that distance on the west side of the river he would have reached a point above the town of Blythe. There are large dunes in this area.

The only other place in the present southern California where immense blowing dunes are to be found is between Yuma and the Imperial Valley. That Díaz skirted them in his wandering appears to be an indisputable fact, for Castañeda would write that traveling toward the southwest "they came upon some beds of burning lava. No one could cross them, for it would be like going into the sea to drown. The ground upon which the Spaniards walked resounded like a kettle-drum, as if there were lakes underneath. It was amazing to see the cinders boil in some places, for it looked like something infernal. They turned away from this place because it seemed to be dangerous and also because of a lack of water."

This part of Díaz's route can be accurately delineated. Passing along the edge of the sand hills that rise about fifteen miles west of the Colorado, he had swung southwestward, had crossed the boundary between American California and Baja California, and had continued until he came to the Cerro Prieto (Dark Hill). The place that "looked like something infernal" is Volcano Lake, at the foot of Cerro Prieto, about twenty miles southeast of the city of Mexicali. There hot mud bubbles up from ground pots, steam and acrid fumes arise, and reaches known as "rubber meadows" tremble and resound as a man walks on them.

Díaz's own journey ended a short distance from Cerro Prieto. After surviving the perils and ordeals of living for years in the wilderness, Fate decreed that he die the victim of a freakish accident.

On a day late in December, 1540—either the 29th or 30th—the soldier's greyhound, perhaps being in a playful mood, began to annoy the little band of sheep. Angered by this threat to the rapidly diminishing supply of fresh meat, Díaz charged after the dog on his horse and threw his lance at it. He missed his target. The lance stuck in the ground immediately before him, and being unable to stop his horse quickly enough "he went over the lance so that it nailed him through the thighs and the iron came out behind, rupturing his bladder."

He fell from his saddle, lay writhing and groaning in terrible agony, and then lapsed into unconsciousness. The men knelt beside him believing him dead.

He was not dead, and when he came to, he himself extracted the iron lance. The flow of blood was stanched and the wound bound with cloths. "If I only had a silver tube I could get along," he said.

There in the unknown Baja California desert, as the year 1540 neared an end, began one of the most remarkable displays of loyalty and devotion in the long story of American exploration. Díaz's men constructed a litter, placed him gently upon it, lifted it to their shoulders, and started on the homeward journey, by the route they were required to take, some five hundred miles in length.

Indians attacked them again at the Colorado River, but the harquebusiers drove them off, while others got Díaz across on a reed raft. On they marched, hour after hour, day after day, taking turns under the litter, across the *Camino del Diablo*, every moment hoping that "they would reach the settlements in time for Díaz to be confessed, for there was a priest at San Gerónimo de los Corazones."

They lost the race.

Díaz lived "for about twenty days." The date of his death was January 18, 1541, and "the soldiers with great sorrow buried him on a little hill and there erected a cross, covering him with a large mound of earth and stones."

The grave has never been found.[67]

Dates to Remember

They had opened the gates: Núñez Cabeza de Vaca and his three companions in 1536; Estevanico the Black in 1539; and in the memorable year 1540, Alarcón, Coronado, and Díaz.

Much of the northern mystery had been solved. The old civilizations, the ancient peoples, and the unknown land had been made known to the Old World beyond the seas, and together they comprised a picture that shattered illusions and dreams long held.

The historical period had begun in the Southwest.

SOME INDIAN PLACE NAMES*

Arizona

Maricopa, county, town
Mohave, county
Pima, county, town
Cosnino, caves
Yavapai, county
Arizona, state
Yuma, county, town, desert
Apache, county, town, peak, creek
Navajo, county, town, creek, mountain
Zuñi, river
Mobile, town
Mohawk, town
Miami, town

New Mexico

Jemez, river, mountains
Cochiti, town
Acoma, town
Pecos, town, river
Nambe, town
Tesuque, town
Taos, town
Zuñi, town, river, mountains
Seneca, town
Miami, town
Jicarilla, town, mountains
Ute Park, town

* Tribes and tribal subdivisions.

Scientific Note—Origin of Indians

They were predominantly Mongoloid, and they reached North America from Siberia.

They crossed the present Bering Strait when it was dry land.

That a land bridge (or bridges) between Asia and North America existed for thousands of years during the Pleistocene Glacial Age has been indisputably proven by both zoological and geological evidence. The same animals lived in both regions. During the Ice Age sea levels were much lower than at present, because a large part of the world's water was locked in great glaciers. The water that made the glaciers came from the sea in the form of fog and clouds. It fell as snow. The glaciated regions were so intensely cold that annual summer melting was less than winter precipitation. The glaciers continued to build up. Over enormous areas the ice cap was a mile high, but in some localities it reached a height of nine thousand feet.

The Bering Strait is shallow. If the present water level fell only one hundred and twenty feet, the Strait would not exist. It would once more be a land bridge between the two continents. Moreover, it is only fifty-six miles in width, and this distance is broken by islands. The widest expanse of open sea is only twenty-five miles, and on a clear day people on one side can see the opposite coast. A land bridge would have provided grass for grazing animals. And men followed the animals, living both with them and on them. For these men were first hunters and second food-gatherers.[68]

Never was all of northern North America covered by ice at one time. Through countless millennia, as climatological metamorphoses occurred, glaciers advanced and retreated, reaching deep into the continent and withdrawing, scarring the earth and changing its contours. In their wakes they left warmth, and great lakes, and even deserts. Important, as far as the migrant from Asia is concerned, is the geological knowledge that for long periods there were ice-free corridors through which both animals and men could have lived and passed. As an example, consider the last major glacial period of some twenty-five thousand years ago. Its center was in the vicinity of Hudson Bay. Far to the west there was considerably less ice, and there were ice-free corridors opening the way to the south. However, there were known to be what geologists call interstadials, periods when ice would not have confronted man with impassable barriers. And that man had reached the region of the United States several thousand years before the last major glaciation can no longer be disputed. For unmistakable evidence of his presence as much as thirty-seven thousand years ago has been reclaimed from the dust.

Man did not originate in the New World. He evolved from brute ancestry in the Old World, and reached North America, by way of the Bering Land Bridge only, as Driver [69] succinctly states, "after he had become modern physically and a member of the single species of modern man called *Homo sapiens,* wise man. Man's nearest animal relatives, the anthropoid apes, are all found in the Old World today: the chimpanzee and gorilla in Africa, the orang and gibbon in Southeast Asia and the neighboring continental islands. Man's next nearest animal relatives, the catarrhine monkeys, are likewise all confined to the Old World. The platyrrhine monkeys of the New World (South and Central America) share classification with man in the order of primates, but they are more distant than the Old World monkeys and apes and could not possibly have been the direct ancestors of the Indians. More important, there is a total absence in the New World of missing links and other intermediate fossil forms in man's family tree. In the Old World, on the other hand, some hundreds of skeletons of individuals intermediate in physical type between men and apes have been discovered by the spades of archeologists and paleontologists."

It is in the shifting of animals that much of the answer as to why people came to North America is to be found. When northern Europe was glaciated, as Coon [70] explains, the animals moved southward and eastward, reaching southern Europe and north-central Asia, both of which were free of ice. The people depended upon these animals for their existence. And when, in time, it was learned that the northern part of the Asiatic continent was richer in game, they drifted toward it.

The animals moved north and east as the glacial ice retreated. And the people followed them in order to secure a steady supply of meat and furs. They followed them into Siberia. And then they went across into Alaska. Gradually—actually very slowly, for it is doubtful that any band shifted farther in a day than was necessary in their hunting— they moved on southward. And they found the climate better, and the game even more plentiful.

Coon suggests that two main avenues of travel were open to them. One ran along the Pacific Coast. The other ran along the eastern slope of the Rocky Mountains. Over these two great natural thoroughfares the people moved. Over them passed culture after culture. And each culture in turn distributed its own peculiar mores and systems of economics and industry and religious ritual.

Wormington,[71] an extremely conservative scientist, thinks that during one or more of the interstadials that preceded the last phase of the final major glacial period, "as well as in post-glacial times, the Mackenzie Valley was probably free of ice. Those who reached it by moving along the low northern coastline of Alaska could have followed the valley and gained access to the northern plains. People who moved up the Missouri could have reached the Snake River Plain and the Great Basin."

The analysis is undoubtedly correct, but Indians were far down in North America long before the last phase of the final major glaciation. They had not moved in a mass migration. They had traveled in small bands, or family groups, stopping wherever they found an adequate supply of game. People, as Wormington points out, who are totally dependent on hunting and food-gathering are prevented from traveling together in large numbers.

But there are other reasons why they pushed onward in small contingents. They were not all the same in character, color, or physique. They had come from many places, from many climates, from many kinds of country. They spoke many tongues and countless dialects. They had many ways and many habits. They told many legends and they held many spiritual beliefs, worshipping many gods.

They had no racial unity. For peoples of different bloods had moved through the land mass of Asia long before any peoples moved into the land mass of the Western Hemisphere. Perhaps not very many had moved into Asia proper from Africa and the eastern Mediterranean—that cannot be said—but even a few would have been enough to leave telltale marks of their different bloods. Although they would be predominantly Mongoloid, the people who moved on to North America would bear those telltale marks.[72]

Driver sums up information on the subject, gathered from numerous authorities, in these words: [73] "The physical type of the Paleo-Indian shows some differences from that of contemporary Indians, who are classed as Mongoloids by all anthropologists today. On the whole the earliest Indians had longer and narrower skulls, with heavier jaws and teeth. Muscle attachments on the bones of the limbs as well as on the skull were heavier, indicating a more heavily muscled individual. The longitudinal crests of some of these early skulls tend to form a sort of ridge, with the skull bones sloping away somewhat like the two-pitched roof of a house from the ridge pole. This is a primitive characteristic found in pre-*sapiens* species of fossil men.

"However, all bones of Paleo-Indians so far discovered are unquestionably *Homo-sapiens,* and some individuals fail to exhibit any of the primitive features and could even pass for contemporary Indians. On the whole, however, the Paleo-Indian is less Mongoloid than contemporary Indians, although the latter show variation in this respect.

"It therefore appears that the first immigrants to America from northeast Asia date from a time when the European (Caucasoid) and Asiatic (Mongoloid) races were less differentiated than at the present time. The Paleo-Indian belongs to a more generalized type of Caucasoid-Mongoloid race with a slight bias in favor of the Mongoloid. As time went by and the Mongoloid race became more and more dominant in northeast Asia, successive waves of immigrants [to North America] became more and more Mongoloid."

To which Martin, Quimby, and Collier add: [74] ". . . it is impossible to characterize an 'Indian' in any brief, general manner. The Indian as we know him today is not pure Mongoloid or pure anything else." The successive waves of Asiatic migrant "represented a composite of several racial strains, some bearing Mediterranean strains, some bearing Oceanic Negroid strains, and most of them bearing Mongoloid strains . . . the primary divergencies of physical types, now observable in the American Indians, first appeared in Asia and then were perpetuated in the New World."

The Paleo-Indian met little resistance in the region of the United States as he drifted southward. There were no established tribal territories. The people moved with the game, going where it was most plentiful, and always seeking better hunting. None of them had a destination. They knew nothing of what lay ahead. A dependable food supply was far more important than looking into the unknown beyond the horizon.

Yet it is known that they moved steadily on, always southward, and if a band had traveled only three miles a week the southernmost tip of South America could have been reached in about seventy years. Such a journey, of course, undoubtedly never took place, but, as Martin remarks, "it is unnecessary to postulate thousands of years of moving and multiplying to account for the peopling of the New World."

Artifacts which have been recovered in Central and South America are as old as those found in archeological sites of the United States. And Indian agriculture developed first in the southern regions of the hemisphere. Domestication of root crops originated in the upland region of Mexico and Guatemala. Indian agriculture spread north, not south.

With regard to subsistence patterns of American Indians, three major stages may be recorded. They are: (1) The earliest people lived mainly by hunting, their diet supplemented only to a small extent by nuts, berries, and fruits; (2) about twelve thousand to eleven thousand years ago, with big Pleistocene mammals rapidly diminishing in number, wild vegetable foods became vital to existence; and (3) the domestication of nourishing and staple food plants—which may have been achieved as early as nine thousand years ago—permitted the Indian to become a farmer, to live in permanent villages, while continuing to hunt game edible and useful in other ways as his needs and his desires dictated.

Authorities estimate that when Columbus made his first New World landfall, between a million and a million and a half Indians were living in the third stage in the region of North America that would become the United States.

PART TWO

Gulf Coasts and Tidal Swamps

A Long-Forgotten Pelvis

Dr. M. W. Dickeson, a physician, knew a human pelvis when he saw one. If they were all pretty much alike, what made the pelvis he found near Natchez, Mississippi, of particular interest was its location. He came upon it among bones of sloth, mastodon, horse, and big-horned bison, long-extinct animals of the Pleistocene Age. It and the other bones lay in a bed of blue clay that was covered with loess, a yellowish, fine-grained deposit of windblown dust.

The year was 1846. At the time, if there was some curiosity about the antiquity of man in America there was little knowledge of the subject. Anthropology, archeology, and ethnology were professions still in their cribs in the United States.

The method of dating ancient bones by testing their fluorine content is not new. Several years before the beginning of this century archeologists employing this method had determined that the Natchez pelvis and at least one of the sloth bones found in association with it were substantially the same age.[1]

That they were very old, there was no doubt, but an impenetrable barrier remained to prevent a conclusion as to their exact age. It was the lack of knowledge as to when the Pleistocene animals had become extinct in the region where Dr. Dickeson had found the human pelvis.

And this is a question that is still far from being answered. Certainly such mammals as the sloth, the horse, the big-horned bison, and the mammoth have been extinct for millennia in the area of the

United States, but it is equally certain that they did not become extinct in all sections of the United States at the same time. Scientists are convinced that they survived in some parts long after they had vanished in other regions. However, it is believed that few, if any, of them existed anywhere in this country later than seven thousand years ago. That is, therefore, the minimal age which may be assigned to the Natchez pelvis, but it may be much older.

Strangely, from about the beginning of this century until 1951 the Natchez pelvis was all but forgotten. Then archeologist T. D. Stewart brought it once more to the attention of the scientific world.[2] In 1956, another archeologist, George I. Quimby, published a paper recounting his efforts to find the place where Dr. Dickeson, more than a hundred years before, had made his discovery. It was too late. Quimby found that erosion had destroyed the locus of the site.

But the search goes on, and it is the hope of investigators that they still may come upon more human bones and artifacts in the area.

Mysterious Texas Sculptors

Geology has revealed that at times in the past the valley of the Trinity River, on the coastal plain of Texas, was lowered. Three major terraces were formed. Thus, the oldest is on top, and its level is some seventy feet above the present flood plain of the river. It is composed largely of gravel, a most useful material in many types of construction, and numerous pits have been opened. It was in 1929 that men working for a gravel contractor launched a mystery that is yet to be solved.

Sixteen feet below the surface of a pit five miles west of the town of Malakoff they came upon a carved stone head. Weighing about a hundred pounds, it measured approximately sixteen inches high and fourteen inches in width. It was a sandstone concretion, and on one side were carved eyes, nose, ears, and mouth. Bore holes had been made to depict teeth.

In 1935 another gravel pit was opened a thousand feet away, and another carved head was found. It was similar to the first, but smaller, weighing a little more than sixty pounds.

In the pits of this ancient terrace also were found remains of various extinct Pleistocene species, among them elephant, mastodon, horse, camel, and ground sloth.

The Texas Memorial Museum sent an expedition under E. H. Sellards to the site in 1939. During the course of the excavations in 1940 a third image was uncovered more than twenty feet below the surface in the pit in which the first had been found. It was the most baffling of all. Considerably larger than the other two, it weighed about a hundred and thirty-five pounds. Crudely executed on it were carvings that may have been intended to represent two likenesses, one human and one animal.

Sellards has given the opinion that the terrace from which both the heads and the ancient mammal bones were recovered was formed a considerable time before the close of the Pleistocene period, but there all explanations come to a halt. No human bones, tools, or other artifacts have been found in the sites. No cultural affiliation may be assigned to the heads. There is no question but that they are of great antiquity, but who sculptured them remains an unfathomed, and perhaps unfathomable, mystery.[3]

Controversy in Florida

One would not expect anything not made of metal or stone to survive the destructive forces of the wet Gulf Coast climate for many years. But that was not the case in several places in Florida, and ancient discoveries made in them have given rise to a conflict of opinion that most probably will long continue.

The events, in all of which eminent scientists had prominent roles, may best be recounted in chronological order.

In 1916, near Vero, Florida, E. H. Sellards came upon human skeletons and artifacts in association with extinct Pleistocene mammoth and mastodon. The remains lay under undisturbed deposits, which, in Sellards' opinion, precluded the possibility they had been carried to their positions by floods or some other means, nor could the human bones have been intentionally buried in the deep sand stratum. Moreover, although the human bones were broken, most of them were complete, and he maintained that they were too fragile to have been moved by any force without receiving greater damage. He believed both animal and human bones were of the same age.[4]

A few years later, in similar strata, below undisturbed deposits, more skeletal remains, including a crushed skull, were found with mammoth and mastodon bones near Melbourne, a few miles from Vero.

In 1926, James W. Gidley and Frederick B. Loomis agreed with Sellards that Vero Man and Melbourne Man lived at the same time as the ancient mammals.[5] However, that did not mean that Gidley and Loomis were in agreement with Sellards as to the age of the discoveries. It was their contention that the mammoth, mastodon, and other contemporary animals had not become extinct in the area until the end of the Pleistocene.

Investigations continued on the Florida scene. In 1951, Irving Rouse issued a "cultural and chronological interpretation." [6] An excellent nontechnical analysis of Rouse's findings was made by Wormington: [7]

"Rouse does not believe that the human bones were deposited at the

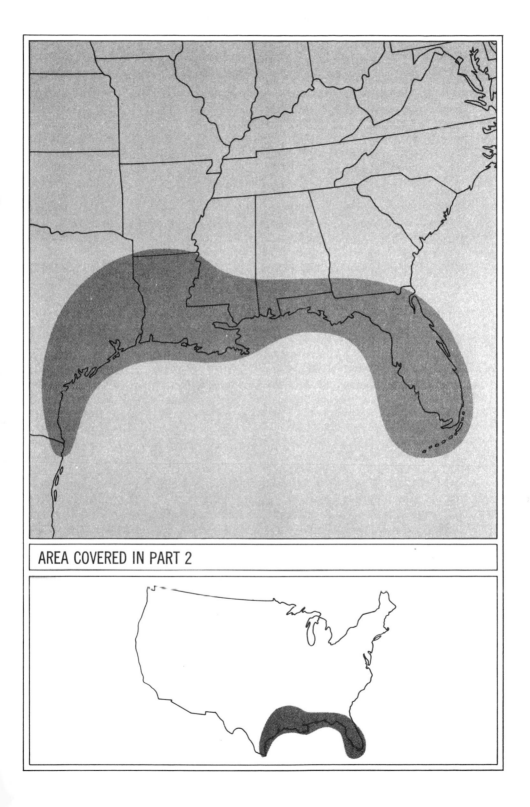

AREA COVERED IN PART 2

same time as the extinct fauna. He notes that . . . the [skeletal] bones did not lie in anatomical order but were broken and scattered in such a way as to suggest that they had been dug out of the ground. Since Sellards' cross-sections show a hole in the top of the . . . stratum [in which Sellards found the bones] at this point, Rouse suggests that Indians lived at the site while the stratum was at the surface, dug a pit into it, encountered a primary burial while so doing, and scattered the bones around the edges of their excavation. This would account for the fact that Sellards found most of the human bones on rather than in the . . . stratum and that the bones were disturbed but not water-worn. . . . Since the stone and bone artifacts found with the human bones are typical Archaic forms and the custom of digging 'wells' is also known from the nearby Archaic site of South Indian Field, he concludes that the burial dates from the Archaic period." *

Chemical tests tended to support Sellards' belief that the human bones could be as old as those of the extinct animals. But more disagreements were created by another phase of the studies. The eminent Ales Hrdlicka was always an implacable foe of all claims for the antiquity of man in North America.[8] He was the first anthropologist to examine the Vero and Melbourne skulls, and he failed to find primitive features which he maintained must be present in cranial remains of great age. Many noted scientists disagreed with Hrdlicka's theories, and still do. As Wormington points out: [9] "These skulls are comparable to those found in Archaic sites in the area, but are quite unlike those found in later sites. . . . They do not have any distinguishing features that provide proof of great age, but neither do they have any characteristics that would prevent their placement in the Paleo-Indian category." †

There is one thing, however, on which everyone is agreed. It is that man lived in Florida a very long time ago, and probably inhabited the Gulf Coast region as early as he did many other areas of the United States. There is evidence to substantiate this assertion, even if the ages of the human bones remain questionable. Man-made stone spear points, which have been given the name of Suwanee, were found in the Indian River area which resemble other very old points found on the high dry plains several hundred miles to the northwest.

Changing Cultures

No geographical area of America was affected more by foreign influences than the Gulf Coast South. None saw more social, economic,

---

* The Archaic Period began later than ten thousand years ago.
† The Paleo-Indian State is dated before ten thousand years ago.

and religious structures. None saw more drastic cultural changes.

It was through prehistoric ages an incredibly bountiful country, a country of immense river-bottom trees, of swamps, of pine and hardwood forests, of grasslands, and dissected by endless networks of navigable rivers and bayous. It was inconceivably rich in game, fowl, and fish.

As was the case in other regions, the first inhabitants were small nomadic bands who lived by hunting and food-gathering. But unlike other regions, it did not suffer from ruinous climatic changes. There were no prolonged periods of drought during which vegetation was destroyed, animals and birds vanished, and streams dwindled and died. Nature never forced people to abandon it. When the Ice Age animals disappeared, probably about ten to eight thousand years ago, smaller animals were hunted and the gathering of natural bounties, such as vegetal plants and shellfish, was increased. The economies were amply sustained. Always the people of the Gulf Coast could live well and comfortably.

For an unknown number of millennia the hunting–food-gathering way of life endured. Perhaps because of the plentiful supplies of various types of natural foodstuffs, farming appears to have diffused slowly through the area. There is no evidence that it was practiced to any appreciable extent until several centuries after the beginning of the Christian Era.

Intertribal trade was extensive, diffusing techniques and knowledge, and, thus, bringing cultural changes. Most commercial centers today— this is true of all regions—stand between contrasting geographical environments, and the situation was not different in prehistoric times. Tribes of the lowlands traded with tribes of the uplands, those of the coast with those of the interior. The rivers were the main arteries of commerce. Markets were maintained, and trade fairs were held.

Among the products bartered were "dried or smoked fish, corn, beans, fruit, coontie flour, dried meat, flint, stone beads, pearls, pieces of crystal, shell beads, shark teeth, hides and furs, feathers, bills of the ivory-billed woodpecker, bow wood, mats, baskets, pottery, canoes, wooden platters and bowls, paint pigments, angelica root, and the famous plant *Ilex vomitoria* used in the emetic called the Black Drink. . . . Perhaps the most important single trade item was salt, which was peddled by itinerant merchants throughout the area but especially in the Mississippi drainage. Most of it was made by evaporating saturated solutions of salt, obtained at salt licks, in shallow pottery pans set over a fire. West of the Mississippi, at least, salt was made into cakes of two or three pounds each, as in Meso-America." [10]

Some products moved great distances. Copper reached the Gulf region from the Appalachians and even from Lake Superior. Bow wood went out to the Southwest to be exchanged for cotton cloth and turquoise. Gourd rattles made on the lower Mississippi passed through trade channels to the Great Lakes and the upper Missouri River regions.

The people learned from each other, and the lives of all were benefited and changed as a result of far-reaching commerce based entirely on barter.

Among most tribes of the coastal region attitudes about sex were especially liberal. According to anthropologists Driver and Massey: [11]

"Both young men and women were allowed premarital sexual experience, which was taken for granted and was nothing to be ashamed of or kept secret. . . . It was even legitimate for unmarried young women to sell themselves for a price . . . and this was carefully distinguished from professional prostitution on the part of adulteresses who had been cast off by offended husbands. Prostitutes were looked down on but were tolerated. Premarital pregnancies were fairly common, the children being reared by the mother's family, extended, or sib as a matter of course. While the child was apparently always kept within its mother's sib, it might be adopted by some family other than the mother's; or, if the unwed mother preferred, she had a right to put her infant to death soon after birth."

Unknown Voyagers

The first drastic cultural transition that archeologists have been able to record in the region of the southeastern coasts began about 2700 B.C. Then, and within the span of a few years thereafter, pottery appeared at various places. Of the greatest significance is the fact that it was also the first pottery known to have reached the area of the continental United States.

It has been given the name Stallings Island, the site in Georgia where the oldest examples have been found. For years the origin and development of the type puzzled scientists, but at last some of them believe the mystery has been solved. Stallings Island pottery undoubtedly came from South America. This conclusion makes mandatory the consideration of what anthropologist Carleton S. Coon appropriately terms "the transpacific problem." [12]

For, in the opinion of James A. Ford and other archeologists, Stallings Island ware is similar in some traits to ancient Japanese pottery. And this particular type of ceramics—called Valdivia—apparently was first introduced on the coast of Ecuador some five thousand years ago.[13]

The possibility that voyagers from Japan reached North and South America as early as 3000 B.C. seems remote, but it cannot be ignored. The prevailing winds sweep in a great arc eastward across the northern

Pacific. The voyage westward would have been even easier. In a daring adventure, Thor Heyerdahl proved that men sailing on a raft of the type used by Peruvian Indians could reach the Polynesian Islands. Moreover, he found ancient Peruvian pottery on Easter Island, where it was pre-Polynesian.

Prehistoric South American and Caribbean Indians made long voyages on trading missions to Cuba, Haiti, Jamaica, many other islands, and along the coasts of Colombia, Panama, Guatemala, and Mexico. They could easily have reached the mainland of the southern United States from many of these places. Evidently their pottery did reach it, if not on direct voyages then by transfer from people to people along the way.

Two types of decorated pottery soon emerged in Florida from the first undecorated Stallings Island ware.[14] Called Tick Island and Orange Incised, they have traits indicating their derivation from pottery found in northern South America, which in turn has traits found in Ecuador's Valdivia pottery. Thus, if Ford is correct in his postulations, an unbroken chain of diffusion is established, indeed a very old and very long chain running from Japan, across the Pacific to Ecuador, and up the coasts to the southernmost area of the United States.[15]

Patterns of Migration

There were no great migrations to the area of the Mississippi River delta. Groups of people drifted over a long period northward from Mexico, eastward from Texas, southward from Ohio and Illinois, southeastward from tidewater Virginia and the Carolinas.

Influences of migrants from middle America can be traced back at least thirty-five hundred years in Louisiana. A new culture, called Poverty Point, began to emerge. In the land of the hunting–food-gathering people who had long been there, earthworks, some very extensive, arose. Utensils, tools, and ornaments showing able craftsmanship and artistic skill appeared. Not only economic structures changed, due to the introduction of agriculture, but definite forms of government and new religious systems evolved. Leaders arose who were capable and powerful enough to devise and direct developments, to enforce their decrees, to control and instruct large labor forces.

Another significant influence began to manifest itself as early as three thousand years ago in the same region. It was the appearance of burial mounds, reflective of cultures, such as the Adena and the Hopewell, of the Northeast. During the cultural period that followed, population showed a marked increase, large settlements were established, villages were built on top of shell heaps, intertribal trade expanded, and a widespread diffusion of ideas, customs, and manufacturing techniques occurred.

Through the centuries culture after culture moved across the southern coastal stage, each in turn undergoing changes, each at last being absorbed by new imported and local customs. The most significant development of all, however, was the appearance, about A.D. 700, of temple mounds.

The Temple Mound Culture is believed to have begun almost a thousand miles north of the Mississippi delta, along the Ohio, Illinois, and middle Mississippi River. Traits of the northeastern Hopewell Culture were pronounced in it, but in time became submerged in other and stronger systems that probably were locally created. The development of agriculture changed its structure. As it spread southward, it became infused by southern Mexico traits which appear to have reached the lower Mississippi through the Caddoan area of Texas.

The Temple Mound Culture brought developments which in many respects were more complicated, and certainly were more dramatic and more ostentatious, than any others in the United States. On flat-topped pyramidal mounds, some of which were forty feet high and two hundred feet square at the base, were built large ceremonial temples and houses for ruling dignitaries. In the temples burned eternal fires. Around the pyramids large settlements spread out, some of them being strongly fortified. In the political and social structures were to be found rulers believed to be divinely guided, laboring and upper classes, and professional specialists. Beyond the villages were large communal farms. In some areas leaders holding the power of life and death directed and controlled all affairs.

The Temple Mound Culture was the most advanced—economically, socially, politically, and spiritually—of all the cultures of the Gulf Coast region. It was also the last of the prehistoric cultures in the area, reaching its climax in the sixteenth century.

The decline was brought about by the same forces that marked the deterioration of previous cultures—changing religious and political systems, the advent of new ways of life and transitions in economic and social patterns. Yet it survived until well after the beginning of the historical period, and, at least in some places, its collapse was caused by a death blow delivered by Europeans. The colonizers of the Gulf Coast introduced diseases that in a few years wiped out immense numbers of Indians.

The Long-Nosed God

It was a small mask with the nose extended out of proportion to the other features, and it symbolized what archeologists have named the Southern Death Cult.

The Death Cult did not arise until after A.D. 1200 in the Gulf coastal region. It was compounded largely of foreign elements, but it was not a crystallization of ideas recently introduced to the coastal peoples. In some aspects it resembled older cultures, notably the Hopewellian of the Northeast. In others it reflected unmistakable Middle-American influences, especially paraphernalia, adornments, ceremonies, and various objects and symbols from the Huastec region of Mexico. In the later years of its existence, after the beginning of the historical period, the Death Cult spread rapidly and took the nature of a religious revival. This was also a time when southern coastal cultures reached their peaks, an unprecedented but short-lived flowering.[16]

The age of metal, at least in the form of ornaments and decorations, reached the Gulf region from Mexico during the time of the Death Cult. Religious paraphernalia included copper pendants, and copper plates on which were depicted dancing eagle warriors, some carrying a human trophy head and a baton. Archeologists also have recovered numerous other objects representative of the Death Cult in its Mexicanized aspects, such as monolithic axes of stone; ceremonial clubs of stone; shell pendants, conch shell masks; pottery engraved with crosses, hands, rattlesnakes, and horned and feathered serpents; stone figures with Negroid faces; shell gorgets; and various vestments made of feathers; beaded belts; heart-shaped pouches; breechclouts with fringed sashes; beaded arm, leg, and neck bands; necklaces and moccasins, some with representations of animal and bird claws on the heels.[17] All costumes of priests and warriors were extremely lavish.

In the period of the Death Cult, human sacrifices were made, as they were in the Huastec area of eastern Mexico. According to anthropologist Harold E. Driver: [18] "Along the Gulf from Louisiana to Florida . . . chiefs had absolute authority over their subjects, including the power of life and death.* In this area men were compelled to serve in the armed forces; they had no choice in the matter. . . . Scalps or heads taken in battle were treated primarily as sacrificial offerings by the tribe to the supernatural rather than as appeasers of individual grief or as symbols of individual war achievement. . . . It also seems likely that true slavery existed in this area, that war prisoners were sometimes kept as slaves for the remainder of their lives. The tendons in the feet of captives were sometimes cut so that they could not run fast enough to escape.

"Human sacrifice as members of the in-group, as well as the sacrifice of war prisoners, has also been reported for this region. Wives and slaves were also killed at the death of a chief so that they might accompany him to the afterworld. Such sacrifice was also thought to

---

* This was also true of some coastal tribes as far north as Virginia.

appease the wrath of powerful spirits. Men sacrificed their own children at public spectacles to gain favor of the chief and be raised to the rank of nobility. These sacrifices were generally independent of the fortunes of war; they were held annually by some tribes but only when catastrophe struck among others. They were more closely associated with religion than with war, although the two were interrelated. Sacrificial victims were not tortured, but were killed quickly and efficiently; nor was cannibalism practiced on their remains."

Some archeologists believe that the religious revival which swept through the tribes during the latter years of the Death Cult's existence was born out of chaos and despair. For it occurred after A.D. 1500. Assuredly with the passage of a few decades early in the sixteenth century, the people of the Gulf Coast region knew of the conquest of the Aztec Empire by the Spanish. Undoubtedly they had heard tales of the plundering, treachery, and slaughtering. Indeed, Spanish ships had passed along the coast. Spaniards had fought Indians in Florida, and in other Deep South areas. Soldiers had left a river of blood in their wake across much of the southern United States.

The Indians sensed the impending destruction of their way of life and the approach of their own doom. Fear, despair, uncertainty, and social and economic disruptions are conditions which create an atmosphere conducive to a surging of religious fervor.[19]

In any case, whatever causes were responsible for it, it occurred. And it was the final chapter in the history of Gulf Coast cultures. Long before the end of the seventeenth century the Death Cult had disappeared, and the civilization of the region in which it had flourished was being systematically destroyed by Europeans.

People of the Everglades

Among the most remarkable prehistoric Indian artists were the Calusa, who ranged over most of the southern half of the Florida peninsula, including the Keys. Even their spear-throwers were beautifully carved, and spears, clubs, and swords had closely spaced shark teeth glued into slots in precise rows. They made a large variety of tools—adzes, scrapers, hoes, hammers, knives, saws, rasps, awls—of antlers, shells, shark teeth, fish jaws, bones, coral, and sandstone, usually artistically decorated and carved. They made beads of deer horns and shells, wooden brooches inlaid with tortoise shell, ornaments such as earrings and pendants of shells, inlaid and colored. They sculpted superb animal heads, some with movable ears attached to them with leather; carved images half-animal and half-human, and painted wildlife on wooden tablets.

Their name has never been interpreted with certainty. An early

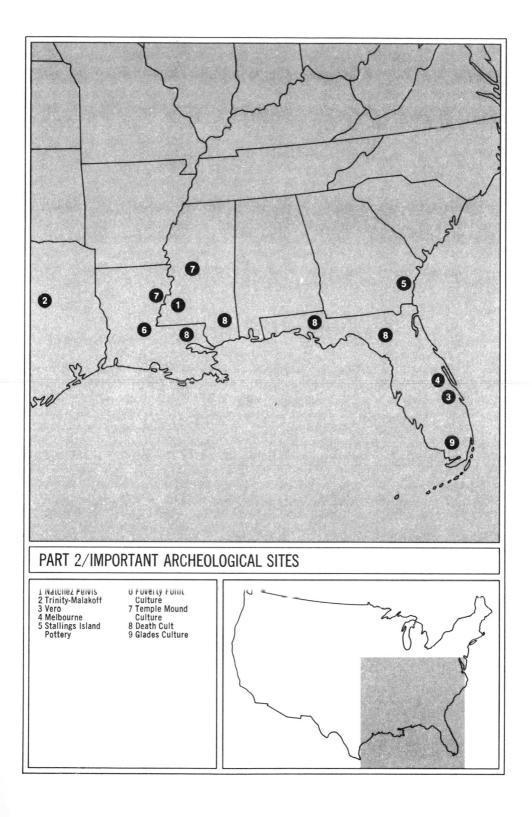

PART 2/IMPORTANT ARCHEOLOGICAL SITES

1 Natchez Pelvis
2 Trinity-Malakoff
3 Vero
4 Melbourne
5 Stallings Island
  Pottery
6 Poverty Point
7 Temple Mound
  Culture
8 Death Cult
9 Glades Culture

Spaniard who was a captive among them said it means "fierce people." That would have been an appropriate name for them, but there is no means of determining its accuracy, for only a few words of their language have survived, and even these are of doubtful origin. Some of the first accounts gave them the name of Carlos, but it is believed to have been adopted by a Calusa chief after he had heard of the greatness of Emperor Charles V from Spanish captives. Other accounts speak of them as Caloosa, and that identification has been preserved in Caloosa Village and Caloosahatchie River.

The Calusa lived in thatched wooden houses built on piles along the myriad of bayous and rivers that laced their country. Their sacred buildings were erected on flat-topped mounds, some of which were faced with conch shells. In late prehistoric times they apparently were influenced by the Southern Death Cult. They sacrificed captives from other tribes to their gods, and in warfare habitually scalped and dismembered the bodies of wounded enemies, and sometimes ate human flesh.

Besides being fine artists and craftsmen—they made furniture with cushions of woven mats—and fierce fighters, they were daring seamen. In their dugout canoes they sailed and paddled to Cuba and other islands of the Caribbean. They also traveled by water far up the coasts of Florida on raids and trading missions. It is believed that at one period they occupied nearly threescore widely scattered towns. One of them, perhaps the most northern, was called Tampa.

No tribe stood more determinedly before white invaders than the Calusa. They became feared not only as defenders of their homeland but as murderous brigands. They came into possession of veritable fortunes in gold and silver. The treasures were obtained from ships wrecked on the south Florida coast, the crews of which they cruelly killed. But the riches benefited them not at all, for they knew nothing of metallurgy, and disposing of them was impossible.

Under the pressures of repeated invasions by Indians from the north and white men of several nations from the sea they steadily decreased in number. At last most of those surviving fled to Cuba and other islands, but some remained hidden in the wilderness of the Everglades, and eventually their descendants would ally themselves with fleeing Seminoles and fight American soldiers.* [20]

---

* Although popularly thought of as a Florida tribe, the Seminole were not in the area of the present state in prehistoric times. They were Creek (Muskogee) who migrated southward from Georgia into northern Florida in the first half of the eighteenth century. After years of prolonged warfare with whites most of them were forcibly removed to Oklahoma. Some avoided capture and took refuge in the Everglades. Their struggle against American forces, ending in 1842, comprised a notable example of the possibilities of guerrilla warfare carried on by a small number of men in a semitropical, swampy country. Seminoles still live in the Everglades.

Calusa Cousins

These were the Ais and the Takesta. Both tribes dwelt along the southeast coast of Florida. Both were under the domination of the stronger Calusa, and, like the Calusa, both vanished from their respective homelands, in all probability also migrating to live with Cuban peoples.

But the Ais and the Takesta each have their own place in history. The Spanish had little success in subduing them, and neither they nor the Calusa were converted to Christianity. If not for those events, then they may be remembered for other facts. The Ais were at one period the most important tribe on the southeastern Florida coast, and the name of Indian River was given to the stream on which their villages stood. The Takesta were the earliest known people to dwell on the site of the city of Miami.

Natchesan Culture: Children of the Sun

In the lower Mississippi Valley were a people who spoke a tongue so unique in its dialectal forms that at one time it was thought to comprise a distinct language, but later scientists were able to establish a remote connection with the great Muskhogean linguistic family. They were divided into three divisions. The largest was the Natchez. Their earliest known homeland was on St. Catherine's Creek, east of the Mississippi city that bears their name. But the meaning of the word *natchez* is unknown.

The other two divisions were the Avoyel and the Taensa.

The Avoyel dwelt in the vicinity of the present Marksville, Louisiana. Their name signifies "people of the rocks," probably referring specifically to flint, for the Avoyel were long established as middlemen in supplying tribes of the Gulf Coast with that valuable commodity.

The meaning of the word *taensa* also is a mystery. It was the name of one of their main towns, in Tensas Parish, Louisiana. A distinguished linguist, Albert S. Gatschet, suggests that it may have derived from the Taensa word for corn, but the interpretation remains doubtful.

The three related groups were descended from ancient people of the area, but became notable in their own right. Probably about the beginning of the Christian Era they began to develop religious and social structures so different from those of surrounding tribes that they have been awarded an identity of their own, called the Natchesan Culture. Fortunately, it reached its zenith shortly after the beginning of the historical period, and therefore, the first explorers to enter the country of the Natchez people had the opportunity to write accounts about them of inestimable value to historians and scientists.

81

The Natchez were sedentary, living in permanent villages. They were advanced agriculturists, but also depended on hunting, fishing, and food-gathering for their subsistence. They were skilled as artisans, expert at weaving a textile fabric from the inner bark of the mulberry tree, and made excellent pottery.

The outstanding characteristics of their culture, however, were an extreme form of sun worship, a highly complicated ritual, and the division of their society into two exogamic classes, nobles and commoners.

The great chief of the Natchez held absolute power over the property and lives of his subjects. He maintained a large harem. When he died, his wives and his servants were put to death so that they might serve him in the afterlife. Children were sacrificed by fearful parents in the hope of appeasing the wrath of the powerful supernatural spirit who had taken away their leader. The body of the deceased chief, who was regarded as a descendant of the sun, was disemboweled and laid to rest in a temple beside the remains of his predecessors.[21]

In the case of nobles who died, the procedure was somewhat different. Their bodies were placed on raised platforms. Involved rituals took place. After decomposition the bodies were dissected, and the bones were placed in chests of wood or cane in various temples. Commoners were interred in graves near the village in which they lived.

No tribe of the Gulf Coast region maintained a social class system that may be compared to that of the Natchez. In the Natchez society there were three ranks of nobility and one group of commoners.* These are identifiable by name, but there was also an additional group not even remotely consanguineous to royalty—most probably largely composed of persons captured in warfare or who had sought sanctum among the Natchez—that was accorded no rank at all.

Omitting the unranked fourth group, this was the Natchez social structure:

1. Suns: Children of Sun mothers and Stinkard (Commoner) fathers.
2. Nobles: Children of Noble mothers and Stinkard fathers, or of Sun fathers and Stinkard mothers.
3. Honored People: Children of Honored mothers and Stinkard fathers, or Noble fathers and Stinkard mothers.
4. Stinkards: Children of Stinkard mothers and Honored fathers, or of Stinkard fathers and Stinkard mothers.[22]

---

* In the Chitimacha tribe, which lived in the vicinity of Grand Lake, Louisiana, the chief and his descendants were regarded as nobles and were addressed with special terms of respect by other tribal members. However, there is doubt about the accuracy of the few reports available on this system, and it certainly could not be compared with the Natchez system in scope, nor was it as complicated.

Thus, it will be seen that all members of the nobility groups were obliged to marry a Stinkard, and only Stinkards could marry within their own group.

The Suns were looked upon as royalty, and they were the supreme rulers. War chiefs and other officials were chosen from the ranks of Nobles.

Because little was known, and less was understood, of the Natchez before 1682, in order to get a picture of them as they were in prehistoric times it is necessary to rely on the accounts of early explorers who encountered them.* It was in the spring of 1682 that the greatest of all the explorers and conquerors of North America, Robert Cavelier, Sieur de La Salle, on his way down the Mississippi to found the Province of Louisiana in the name of the King of France, met the Taensa.

La Salle was ill at the time, and was unable to accept an invitation to visit the Son of the Sun. He assigned in his place his distinguished and loyal lieutenant, Henri de Tonty, and a priest, Zenobe Membre.[23]

The town in which the great chief resided was on a lake (in Tensas Parish, Louisiana) that had once been adjoined to the main Mississippi but which had been isolated when the river changed its course. A canoe was carried by Taensa on a foot trail through a swamp to a lagoon, and Tonty and Membre were paddled to the village. They were astonished at the size and structure of the buildings, which were square, built of sun-baked mud mixed with straw, covered with arched roofs of cane, and stood in precise rows about a large rectangular area. The visitors were escorted to the dwelling of the chief. It was forty feet square, its walls ten feet in height and a foot in thickness, and the roof, which was a dome, was fifteen feet high. Nearby was another equally large building, the Temple of the Sun. Tonty described it as being surrounded by strong mud walls in which spikes were fixed, from which hung the heads of enemies who had been sacrificed to the sun god.

The chief was waiting for his guests. He sat on a raised platform that resembled a divan, and he was wrapped in a splendrous white cloak woven of mulberry bark. Beside him were three of his wives, and assembled nearby were a group of sixty elders, the council of the tribes.

Tonty and Membre were graciously made welcome, and the chief appeared to be greatly pleased with the trinkets Tonty placed before him. His wives howled and swayed as he spoke his appreciation of them.

Tonty and Membre were next taken into the Temple of the Sun God. "In construction it was much like the royal dwelling. Over it were

---

* This is the case with numerous other tribes who existed after the arrival of the white man.

rude wooden figures, representing three eagles turned to the east . . . before the door was a block of wood, on which lay a large shell surrounded with the braided hair of victims who had been sacrificed. The interior was rude as a barn, dimly lighted from the doorway, and full of smoke." [24] Membre thought a structure in the middle was a kind of altar, and ". . . before it burned a perpetual fire, fed with three logs laid end to end, and watched by two old men devoted to this sacred office."

Tonty and Membre were astonished at the sight of pieces of metal breastplates, knives, sabers, and several guns, all of which were heavily coated and made useless by rust. These, said the Taensa, had been found in their country, but in the memory of the oldest of them no white man had entered it. However, it had come down to them in legend that at one time a grand army in armor and plumes and mounted on horses had passed over the Mississippi and disappeared in the sky.

This was not a legend. They were speaking of the De Soto expedition which had passed through the region a century and a half before La Salle. Where the Taensa found the relics is not known, but it is improbable they recovered them in one place. Nor is it known that De Soto encountered Taensa. If he did not, then La Salle and his men were the first to meet them, and, certainly, Tonty and Membre were the first to write of them.

If because of illness, said the Taensa chief, La Salle was prevented from coming to his house, he would honor him with a visit the following day.

Preceding the chief into La Salle's camp the next morning were two men bearing white plumes. Next appeared a warrior carrying a disk of burnished copper, a symbol of the chief's ancestor, the sun. When the chief arrived he was accompanied by tambourine players, a group of women singing his glories, and a throng of naked warriors waving white fans. A cane mat was placed on the ground for him. La Salle "received him with much politeness, and gave him some presents." The chief reciprocated with "plenty of provisions and some of their robes." It was Membre's impression that while the chief "maintained a very grave demeanor" his visit was "full of confidence and marks of friendship."

The Mississippi gateway to America had been opened, and would never again be closed. La Salle and his small company went on down the great river, meeting (or hearing of) other Natchesans, and people of which little is known—the Koroa, Houma, Tiou, Quinipissa. In one place, a short distance below the Quinipissa, they came upon a village which appeared to be deserted. A landing was made. It was then discovered that only a few days before, the village had been sacked and plundered. In three huts were bodies stacked like cordwood. This was probably a town which had been occupied by Tangipahoa. Little was heard of this tribe in ensuing years, and it is believed that the survivors of the tribal wars were absorbed by their nearest relatives, the Acolapissa.*

As La Salle and his company neared the end of their epic journey, the last of their staples was consumed, and hunting in the seemingly endless swamps was difficult and unproductive. They welcomed the discovery by one of the scouts in a deserted cabin of what appeared to be a quantity of venison. It had been dried and smoked in thin strips and was well preserved. As he nibbled on it, Father Membre pronounced it "good and delicate." Nodding in agreement, an Abnaki member of the expedition informed him that he was eating human flesh. "We left the rest to the Indians," wrote the priest, "and lived on wild potatoes and alligators."

Atakapa: Man-Eaters

As the Gulf of Mexico coast curved southwestward to the land that would become Texas, it was occupied by the Akokisa, a division of the Atakapa of Louisiana. The word *akokisa* may signify river people,[26] but of this there is no certainty. They dwelt on the lower Trinity and San Jacinto rivers and along the shores of Galveston Bay.

Something more can be said of the Atakapa as a whole. They belonged to the Tunican stock, and were closely related to their eastern neighbors, the Chitimacha. Their own name for themselves was *Yuk'-hiti ishak,* but, as is so often the case, they would become known to history as the Atakapa, a word coming from a Muskohegan dialect and meaning "man-eater."[27] There was a good reason why this identity, applied by other Indians, should prevail: in their rituals they ate the flesh of captured enemies.

The coast of Texas has been a poor orchard for scientists, but diligent research and accounts by early Spanish and French explorers compose a picture which, if vague and incomplete in many respects, gives an indication of Indians and their life in the region as it was in late prehistoric times.

The evidence shows that the various bands of the Atakapa differed not at all in character or custom. They were "dark skinned, with dirty-short, coarse black matted hair; their bodies stout, stature short, and

---

* Other tribes of the lower Mississippi and the adjacent Gulf area would become first known to history through early French authorities, notably Iberville and Jean Baptiste le Moyne Bienville, among them the Biloxi, Pascagoula, Adai, Avoyel, Chitimacha, Acolapissa, Bayogoula, and Opelousa.[25]

heads of large size. . . . The ears were very large, as were the mouths, and the cheek bones and nose prominent. . . . Their teeth were stained from the various leaf substitutes they used for tobacco. Head deformation, cuts on the nose and chin, and tattooing were noticeable, especially in the elder members." [28] They wore few clothes, although in the winter garbed themselves in various hides. They made periodic journeys to the interior plains to hunt buffalo. Some of the Atakapa bands grew maize, but all of them subsisted chiefly on fish, shellfish, and wild plant foods. They were very skillful at killing fish, small game, and fowls with light spears.

Karankawa: People Walking in the Water

The Karankawa, who inhabited the Gulf Coast to the south of the Atakapa, were called "people walking in the water" by the Lipan Apaches of the inland Texas plains. The meaning of *karankawa* is unknown. It is merely the name of one of five related tribes who ranged the low country of inlets and river mouths between Trinity and Aransas bays. The other four groups were known as the Coapite, the Coaque, the Kohani, and the Kopano.

There are striking differences between the Karankawa and their neighbors to the north. Many of the Karankawa were tall and well-formed, although most of the women were heavy. They did not cut their hair, and on some men it hung down the back to the waist. Like most of the peoples of the long Texas coast, they were cannibals, but the eating of human flesh may have been limited to special religious ceremonies.

If they were tall and muscular, they were far from handsome. The bodies of the men were made hideous by a mixture of alligator grease and dirt, which was applied as a defense against mosquitoes. On the warpath each man painted half his face red and the other half black, and wore a breechclout with a sash bordered with tassels. Pieces of cane were thrust through the nipples of the breast and the lower lip.

The garb of the women consisted mainly of an apron made of grass. Married women and prostitutes painted their bodies in stripes and figures of birds, flowers, and animals. Maidens adorned themselves with only a single stripe running from the forehead, down the nose, and through the middle of the lips.

The diet of the Karankawa was varied and seasonal. They depended for their food largely on shellfish and wildfowl, which could be obtained only at certain times of the year. They journeyed inland to hunt and to harvest wild plants, roots, and fruits. Thus, their life was perforce nomadic, an uninterrupted program of moving from one place to another in order to survive, for no one type of food was continuously plentiful. They were not agriculturists, and stored little of the wild food they gathered. They lived from day to day, stuffing themselves with whatever they found. Big game was scarce, and they considered themselves most fortunate when they killed a bear, deer, javelina, or a wandering buffalo. Often they ate wild meat raw, and consumed quantities of bear fat, and in times of dire want made a gruel of locusts, lice, or any insect available.

They were unusually skillful handlers of dugout canoes, and expert archers. Their bows were five to six feet in length. The arrows were propelled with tremendous force, and would pass through a young bear or a large deer. They made crude pottery and wove baskets, manufactured knives and other tools from shells and stones, used weirs to trap fish, and ground seeds on small milling stones.

All possessions of the Karankawa, even their pole huts, were portable. When the time came to leave a fishing ground or oyster bed, a village and all it contained could be quickly loaded into canoes, and as quickly reestablished at some other place where sustenance was to be obtained. The Karankawa lived in small groups, sometimes consisting of only a single family, and although they had leaders who usually gained their powers through acts of courage or prowess as warriors, each group was independently governed. They had no all-powerful tribal chief.[29]

Tonkawa: They All Stay Together

In this way other tribes characterized the Tonkawa. Yet, at the beginning of the historic period they were a people divided into at least a score of autonomous bands, and they roamed over an immense area of central and eastern Texas, from the Edwards Plateau to the Brazos Bottoms and within a few miles of the Trinity River.

They constituted a distinct linguistic family, although their language had affinities for other tongues, the Coahuiltecan, the Karankawan, and the Tunican. Tonkawa was a Waco word, and as in the case of the Karankawa, it was the name of one of the principal tribes, but has been applied to the entire family. The Tonkawa tribes called themselves *Titska watitch,* which may be loosely translated to mean "the most human of people," but doubt remains about that interpretation.

The mode of life of the Tonkawa was more like that of plains Indians than of coastal peoples. They were warlike wanderers, living almost entirely on game, especially the deer, bear, and buffalo, and herbs, roots, seeds, and nuts, especially the wild pecan, acorns, and tunas of the prickly pear. But unlike typical plains people, they also ate fish and shellfish. Rattlesnake meat was considered a great delicacy. For religious reasons they would not touch the flesh of wolves or coyotes. The names by which other tribes called them indicate that they practiced cannibalism, at least on certain occasions.

They were constantly at war with the Apaches who dwelt to the west and north of them, but they had numerous other enemies, and Indian stories suggest that they were despised by other tribes, were ill-natured, and were clever thieves. They lived in "scattered villages of skin tipis, which they moved according to the caprice of the chiefs or the demands of the chase." [30]

They were unsurpassed as runners, and were expert bowmen. Their dress and manner of decorating themselves were as unique as their language. The principal garment of the women was a short skin skirt, but the men wore an extremely long breechclout. Both sexes painted and tattooed their bodies, both were adorned with earrings, pendants, and other ornaments, and both parted their hair in the middle. While women cut their hair short, men let it hang far down the back and braided it with buckskin. Women painted black stripes on their face, back, and breasts. In warfare the men wore protective hide vests, feathered and horned headdresses, and painted themselves red, yellow, green, and black.

Archeological research pictures the Tonkawa as a people whose culture belonged to both the central Texas plains and the Gulf Coast, a people divided in their religious beliefs, worshipping numerous deities, and without the social and political cohesiveness that would have precluded their early destruction and ultimate extinction. "They all stay together" was hardly an appropriate name for them.[31]

Coahuiltecan: Curious, Confusing

This subtitle describes the Coahuiltecan better than the name by which they are known in history. For the name derives from that of a Mexican state, Coahuila, and the Coahuiltecans were living in it, and in southern Texas, for thousands of years before Europeans reached either place.

They are accorded the distinction of being a linguistic family, but no one knows where they came from, when they arrived, or what forces brought them together, and even their tongue, which has many dialects, gives rise to mysteries that may never be solved.

Archeological and ethnological evidence gives south Texas "the appearance of a relict region, an isolated backwash in which cultures remained virtually unchanged for long periods." [32] Here, keeping that assertion in mind, appears one of the baffling mysteries. Other evidence suggests that the "Coahuiltecan-speaking peoples were related to the Hokan group of languages of California." [33] Indeed, some linguists term Coahuiltecan a Hokan language, but others connect it with the

Karankawan and Tonkawan groups. Whatever the case, Newcomb [34] points out that while between the Hokan-speaking peoples of the Pacific Coast and the Coahuiltecan of the western Gulf region there is a tremendous gap, "there are several ways in which the Hokan-Coahuiltecans could have become separated from one another in some dim, prehistoric era." Perhaps the most logical hypothesis is that thousands of years ago the Hokan-Coahuiltecans were a single people, and were forced apart by waves of peoples speaking other languages, who drove the two groups to the areas in which they were found at the beginning of the historical period. Swanton [35] puts the conjecture in the form of a question: May it not be that the aboriginal Californians and south Texans represented remnants of earlier waves, split in two by these late-comers and driven west and east respectively?"

However the catastrophe may have occurred, the south Texans got the worst of it. They came to live in a barren and forbidding land of great dry reaches, immense sweeps of stunted growth and thorny shrubs. They were hunters and food-gatherers, not farmers, and knew nothing of growing crops by irrigation, as did some of the early peoples of the western deserts.* Large game animals were extremely scarce on the arid plains of south Texas, and even small animals were not plentiful. Perhaps the prehistoric Coahuiltecans killed a few buffalo in the winter. There were some deer, antelope, and javelina, and there were rabbits, reptiles, birds, and various insects. But there were not enough of any species of animal to provide them with adequate and assured supplies of meat. They lived largely on wild plant foods, and they were no less than ingenious in making good use of cacti, mesquite beans, nuts, sotol, agave, and other vegetable growths.

That primitive people could survive for thousands of years in this poor country is remarkable, but that they could increase as the Coahuiltecans did is almost inconceivable. Archeologists have composed a list of more than two hundred Coahuiltecan bands.

A Haunting Caribbean Myth

It said that either on the mainland or on one of the islands adjacent to it was a magic spring, and perhaps a beautiful stream, and those who drank of the waters would be eternally youthful.

This was not a white man's story. It was an ancient Indian legend, and it had passed from generation to generation among the Arawak and the Carib, who inhabited the many islands, large and small, that would come to be called the West Indies.

There was continual communication between the prehistoric peoples

---

* See Part One—*Hohokam: Those Who Have Gone.*

of the Caribbean Islands and the Florida peninsula, and it is believed that many searches were made for the wondrous fountain of youth. Supporting this assertion is the indisputable fact that a group of Arawak from Cuba, attempting to discover the spring, reached the southwest coast of Florida about the time Columbus made his first landfall in the Western Hemisphere. They were held prisoners by the Calusa (q.v.), but were allowed to live, and they established a colony and maintained their identity for at least a century, well into the historical period, before they vanished. In all probability they returned to their former homeland.

The cinnamon-colored Arawak—at least a few of them—therefore properly belong in the American scene. They were, as well, the first native people Columbus encountered in the islands, and he reported of them that they "all go naked, men and women, just as their mothers bring them forth, though some women cover one part with a leaf of a plant. . . . They have no iron . . . nor any weapons other than the stems of reeds . . . on the end of which they fix little sharpened stakes . . . they are most wondrously timorous."

They came out of the dank green forests to greet the astonishing bearded strangers with gifts of value and gestures of friendship. They were cannibals. Their faces were gross and hideous, their nostrils large and distended, their foreheads low, their teeth dirty and black, their eyes fierce and protruding. So thick were their skulls that often Spanish swords broke over them.

Greatly in contrast were the Carib. They were travelers and raiders who had migrated northward from South America and had captured islands in the Lesser Antilles. Although no less primitive than the Arawak, and following similar customs, they were better physical specimens, handsome and given to habitual smiling. Their skin was an olive shade, and many of them displayed extremely white teeth. They were devoted to cleanliness, and bathed each day. The Carib men shaved parts of their heads, and in preparing for feasts or dances both men and women painted themselves in weird and colorful patterns.

It was from the Arawak that the Spanish heard the legend of the fountain of youth, and it haunted them and they dreamed of finding it. The first organized attempt was made early in the second decade after the beginning of the sixteenth century, and it marked the beginning of the Spanish conquest of territory that would become the United States. In 1513, a true blueblood, Juan Ponce de León, set out from Puerto Rico, which he had conquered by the simple means of killing and enslaving hundreds of helpless Indians. Wishful thinking of the Spanish by this time had provided the old legend with embellishments particularly attractive to them. The fountain of youth, they believed, was on an island called Bimini that was not constructed of the usual coral, sand, and palms but of almost pure gold.

This was a part of the country dominated by a group of cognate tribes that would come to be known by two names, Utina and Timucua. The first means "powerful," and may have derived from the word *uti*, signifying "earth." The second is the name of one of the principal groups, and it is used to identify the linguistic family of all the Utina.

They dwelt in several score towns spread over a large part of northern Florida, on the east coast from south of Cape Canaveral to Georgia, on the west coast from Tampa Bay to the Ocilla River, and inland along numerous streams and on the shores of many freshwater lakes. Timucuan men were generally tall, and both men and women had excellent physiques. Except for a breechclout, both sexes were usually naked, and their bodies were elaborately tattooed. They farmed only to a very limited extent, depending almost entirely for their subsistence on hunting and fishing, gathering shellfish and wild plant foods, especially the nourishing coontie root, from which they made a kind of bread. Their towns were surrounded by strong stockades. The houses were circular, constructed of poles, had roofs thatched with palmetto palm leaves, and stood around a public square, in the center of which was a larger building used for ceremonies and council meetings.

Their social structure was based on the clan system. Some of the chieftainships were hereditary. In warfare captives were scalped and mutilated. Their religious ritual included human sacrifices.

Although the Timucuan tribes were scattered over a large area, it appears obvious that they maintained some type of a military organization that could be brought into operation in times of emergency, for they cooperated with each other in harassing Ponce de León with running attacks wherever he went. It seems improbable that they had ever seen a white man, but there is evidence to substantiate the belief that they were well informed of the slaughter and the slave trade taking place in the West Indies.

Menaced constantly by superior forces of Timucuans, Ponce de León shortly abandoned his search for treasure and the fountain of youth, and departed. But he did not forget the land he had discovered.

As the years passed, Ponce de León became increasingly fearful that usurpers would steal from him the Florida which he considered his by right of discovery. Obtaining a new royal patent to settle it and the fabled fountain of youth island—if he could find it—he sailed again with two ships. This time he went to the west coast and made a landing at Charlotte Harbor. Now it was the Calusa who were ready for him. They boldly attacked. Suffering from a severe arrow wound, Ponce de León fled back to Cuba and died.[36]

Pinpoints of Light

The curtain had risen on the American mainland. After Ponce de León's disappointing expedition—and perhaps even before it—daring Spanish pilots had taken their little ships into the Gulf of Mexico. Who they were, how far they went, what Indians they encountered, or what, if any, landings they made, are not matters of dependable record.

But of one voyage factual information has been preserved. In 1519 a competent and courageous mariner, Alonso Álvarez de Piñeda, sailed close to the Gulf Coast from Florida to Vera Cruz, Mexico. The identities of any Indians he may have seen are not known, although it seems reasonable to assume that he saw some, and certainly his ship was sighted, probably in numerous places, by Indians on shore.

However, one event makes his long sea journey historically important. About midway along the coast he crossed the mouth of a great unknown river flowing from the north. He had discovered the Mississippi, and it would be thereafter noted, although not by that name and not always in its correct location, on maritime charts.*

Álvarez de Piñeda and other pilots had lighted flickering tapers, mere pinpoints of light along the Gulf Coast, but behind them the vast state and all the peoples on it remained in total darkness.[37]

The Search for Apalachen

In Holy Week of 1528 four small caravels and one brigantine dropped their anchors at St. John's Point, near the entrance to Tampa Bay. Crowded into the vessels were four hundred and eighty men, a number of wives, and eighty horses.

Commander of the expedition was the newly appointed governor of Florida, a tall, courtly, veteran soldier with a silk patch over an empty eye-socket, a beard that resembled curled copper wire, and a voice that sounded as if it came out of a cave. He had lost his eye in a fight with Cortez in Mexico, and after that misfortune the surviving orb had developed a fierce and penetrating gleam. In conquering Jamaica and Cuba he had won acclaim as one of the most proficient butchers of natives among the many *conquistadores* who possessed outstanding talent in this field of endeavor. His name was Pánfilo de Narváez.

Treasurer of the expedition, and Narváez's most able and conscientious aide, was a young officer named Álvar Núñez Cabeza de Vaca.

---

* This was twenty-two years before the expedition of De Soto, who was not the discoverer of the river, as so many histories erroneously state. He was the first to cross it north of its delta.

GULF COASTS AND TIDAL SWAMPS

Earliest Population Estimates*

Coahuiltecan (1690)	15,000	Acolapissa and Tangi-pahoa (1698)	1,500
Karankawa (1690)	2,800	Bayogoula and Quini-pissa (1650)	1,500
Tonkawa (1690)	1,600	Avoyel (1698)	280
Acuera (In Timucua)		Washa, Opelousa, Oke-lousa, and Cha-washa (1698)	1,000(?)
Ais (1650)	400(?)		
Apalachee (1650)	7,000		
Calusa (1650)	3,000	Taensa (1650)	500(?)
Chatot (1674)	1,500	Biloxi (1650)	540
Mococo (In Timucua)		Atakapa (1650)	2,000
Pensacola (1726)	160(?)	Chitimacha (1650)	3,000
Seminole (1800)	2,000	Koroa (1650 with three other small tribes)	2,000
Pohoy (1680)	300		
Potano (1650)	3,000		
Tekesta (1650)	1,000(?)	Adai (1698)	400
Tacobaga (In Timucua)		Eyish (1779)	300
Timucua (1650)	13,000	Natchitoches Confederacy	1,000
Mobile (1650)	2,000		
Houma (1650)	1,000		
Natchez (1650)	4,500	TOTAL	72,740
Pascagoula (1698)	460		

* See Note, Population Table, Part One.

The landing had been made in Calusa Country, but no Indians were seen, and the little villages in the area were deserted. It seems logical to surmise that upon observing the great strength and firepower of the expedition the Calusa had withdrawn to await reinforcements before attacking.

They never got a chance to attempt to drive the invaders out, as they had done only seven years earlier to Ponce de León. On May 1, 1528, only a few days after landing, Narváez started north from Old Tampa Bay. With him he took two hundred and sixty men on foot and forty on horses. This was the first overland expedition on American soil.

Cabeza de Vaca and others had vehemently protested the precipitant departure on a journey for which they thought preparations were inadequate, but Narváez closed his ears to them. Crazed by a craving for fortune that would surpass that acquired by Cortez in Mexico, which he had seen with his one good eye, Narváez began his march into a totally unknown wilderness without any form of plan. Not only was he unaware of the type of country which lay ahead or what Indian forces he would face, but his stores permitted the distribution to each man of only two pounds of biscuit and half a pound of bacon. They would live off the country, he said in blind confidence, which was certain to be not only rich in treasure but bountiful.

The Indians watched. A few were sighted at a distance now and then, but they made no assault. The Calusa saw the column move slowly and laboriously through the dismal swamps and palmetto wastelands, and pass out of their territory, into the land of the Timucua.

The first skirmish occurred on the Withlacoochee River. A small band of Timucua quickly retreated under gunfire, but horsemen captured several warriors who, to save their lives, offered to serve as guides.

Presumably they were the first Indians to tell Narváez of a kingdom called Apalachen, far to the north, in which there was a city marvelously rich in jewels. This was one of the earliest occasions on which Indians were known to fabricate a tale they understood their white captors wanted to hear. Apalachen became Narváez's goal.

The guides eventually were able to slip away, and like the Calusa, the Timucua were relieved to see the expedition pass northwestward out of their territory and into the country dominated by one of the most warlike tribes of the Gulf Coast region, the Apalachee.

The name correctly spelled is A'palachi. It comes from the language of the Choctaws, who dwelt in Mississippi and to whom the Apalachee were closely related, and it means "people on the other side."

They were a large tribe, perhaps in late prehistoric times numbering between eight and ten thousand. Besides being noted far and wide for their cunning and courage as fighters, they were excellent agriculturalists, and were industrious and prosperous. The center of their homeland was above the great bay of the gulf that is named for them.

The Apalachee also watched in silence as the Narváez column moved into their country, but they were carefully formulating their plans to repel them. In their observations they were learning a great deal about the first white men they had ever seen. They saw that the Spaniards were without food supplies, were suffering from hunger, and were subsisting almost entirely on maize and fish confiscated in small villages which the inhabitants had deserted. They saw that the Spaniards were poor woodsmen and poor hunters. They did not know, of course, that most of the soldiers had never seen a jungle or a great forest before reaching the Indies from Spain only a short time earlier. In a land abounding in wild game, the invaders were unable to provide themselves with sufficient meat; they could not get close enough to a deer to shoot it, and even rabbits, squirrels, and game birds eluded them, for they traveled with a great commotion and noise; they had brought no fish nets with them.

The Spaniards staggered on, fighting terrible summer heat and unmerciful insects, searching vainly for Indians they seldom saw and who occasionally sniped at them from dense undergrowth, and constantly hungry. The Apalachee may have asked themselves why the suffering white men did not turn back, but an explanation was not forthcoming. The Apalachee could not have understood that unquenchable self-esteem, irrepressible confidence, and indestructible visions of glories to come provided the strength to carry on—until they came in sight of the "great city" of Apalachen. It consisted of forty low thatched huts on the shore of Lake Miccosukee. It was dilapidated, dirty, deserted, and devoid of anything of value, except a quantity of maize and dried fish.*

The dream was shattered with heart-sickening reality, and the Apalachee, seeming to sense the despondency of the Spaniards, struck at them in a series of furious attacks.

Scientists have learned much about the Apalachee, and a parade of historians have written about them, but no one ever provided a better description of them as they were at the dawn of the historic period than Cabeza de Vaca. After all, he was there at the time.

The prolonged fighting between the Narváez expedition and the Apalachee was the first major Indian and white conflict within the area of the United States, and in it the Apalachee proved they were far superior to their adversaries on the field of battle.

Harquebuses, Cabeza de Vaca explained, were of small benefit in fighting enemies who did not remain longer than a moment in one place, who slipped through the thickets with the quietness of rabbits and the speed of deer, who could conceal themselves like burrowing rodents. Clumsy matchlocks which had to be supported for firing by a hook were virtually useless against running targets. Even the vaunted crossbows were ineffective against shadows which appeared from behind trees only long enough to discharge an arrow or throw a lance and then vanish.

The Apalachee, he said, were so "effectual in their maneuvering that they can receive very little injury." If they feared anything, it was not the guns, not even the Spaniards, but the horse. The sight of the great snorting animals seemed to fill them with awe, and they were struck with terror when the monsters charged upon them. This advantage, however, was not held long by the riders. The Apalachee soon learned that the horse, too, was mortal, that it bled and died, and with that

---

* This town of the Apalachee was in Jefferson County, northern Florida, a few miles from Tallahassee.

realization their superstition and awe decreased with equal rapidity.

Cabeza de Vaca believed the Apalachee were aware of the despondency and alarm of the Spaniards. "Whoever would fight them," he wrote, "must be cautious to show no fear, or desire to have anything that is theirs; while war exists they must be treated with the utmost rigor; for if they discover any timidity or covetousness, they are a race that will discern the opportunities for vengeance, and gather strength from any weakness of their adversaries." They possessed not only the cunning of animals, but the endurance and hardness. "Oftentimes," he said, "the body of an Indian is traversed by the arrow; yet unless the entrails or the heart be struck, he does not die but recovers from the wound."

From the time Narváez and his men were first attacked by the Apalachee the disintegration and destruction of the expedition advanced with increasing speed. Their retreat became a rout. The Apalachee maintained an incessant assault, striking suddenly from the front, from the flanks, from the rear, and always disappearing into the forest and tall grass as swiftly as they had come.

Early in July another deserted Apalachee town, Aute, was reached. It stood near the head of St. Marks Bay. The supplies of maize, squash, roots, and fish found there would not long meet the needs of the expedition. Seventeen men and a dozen horses had been killed. More than a score of soldiers were wounded.

Cabeza de Vaca thought it ". . . piteous and painful to witness our perplexity and strength . . . there was not anywhere to go."

Worse conditions were to come. Fever and dysentery struck. Men lay writhing in agony on the ground. Narváez, his one eagle eye glazed by sickness, his arrogance gone, ordered that all who were able gather about his bed. Piteously he asked for advice. Out of the conference came a decision. The only means of escape was by the sea. Somehow boats must be constructed.

The American wilderness never saw a stranger sight than that which took place on September 22, 1528, on St. Marks Bay. Five of the most peculiar craft ever built pushed out of the shallow waters toward the Gulf of Mexico. Each was about thirty-three feet in length, a weird conglomeration of rough pine planks, crudely hewn stays and ribs, horsehides and palm leaves. The masts were debarked trees, the fittings of silver, gold, and brass, the rigging of horsehair, the sails odd pieces of clothing and blankets, the anchors stones. Crowded into them, crushed together in an almost helpless condition, were two hundred and forty-two men, many of them dangerously ill. Overloaded beyond the most remote degree of safety, the gunwales were no more than a foot above water.

Now the most disastrous mistake of the entire expedition was made. It was believed that they were closer to Panuco, a little Spanish slaving station on the central coast of Mexico, than to Bahia de la Cruz, Tampa Bay. If they had sailed down the west coast of Florida on a fairly straight course they would have reached their starting place, where the ships still waited for them, after a voyage of no more than two hundred miles. Panuco was six times as far away, and they set out for it.

They had escaped from the country of the Apalachee, but they were on a course to complete disaster and death.[38]

Keeper of the Morgue

Narváez's ships waited a year at Tampa Bay. Then they sailed for Mexico, the men in them, and especially the wives, still harboring a faint hope that there they would learn some word of the fate of the land expedition. They were to hear nothing of it.

One gentleman who had remained with the ships was Juan Ortiz, a native of Seville. From Mexico he made his way back to Cuba. For the purpose of personally expressing his condolences, he called on the widow of Narváez. It was a great mistake. The wily woman induced him to return to Florida to make another search for her husband.

The only boat Ortiz was able to secure at the moment was a pinnace, hardly adequate for the voyage, but with twenty hired crewmen he bravely set sail in it. Skirting the southwestern coast of Florida, he entered Charlotte Harbor, the scene of the Ponce de León debacle.

The Calusa were waiting for him. As he anchored, several Indian men appeared on shore. One of them held up a piece of paper. Thinking it might be a letter left by Narváez, Ortiz and a seaman landed. They were immediately taken prisoners. When Ortiz's companion resisted, he was killed. Ortiz was taken to a nearby town. A chief, whose name has come down through history as Ucita, commanded that Ortiz be burned to death. Ortiz was bound to a scaffold and a fire was kindled.

The chronicler of the De Soto expedition, who signed himself simply as the Gentleman of Elvas,[39] would be the first to publish an account of Ortiz's grueling experience. He would record that "a daughter of the chief entreated that he might be spared."

This is the first known appearance of the story, which was to be repeated many times and become universally popular, about a white man being saved by an Indian princess. The narrative of the Gentleman of Elvas was published in Portugal in 1557. This was thirty-eight years before Pocahontas, who allegedly saved the Englishman John Smith in a similar manner, was born.

Pleaded Ucita's daughter, according to the Gentleman of Elvas: "Though one Christian might do no good, certainly he could do no harm, and it would be an honor to have one for a captive; to which the father acceded, directing the injuries to be healed."

Ortiz had suffered some burns, but when he recovered Ucita gave

Language Groups in Part Two

GULF COASTS AND TIDAL SWAMPS

Hokan-Coahuiltecan Group:	Coahuiltecan:	Coahuiltecan
		Karankawa
		Tonkawa
Muskogean Group:	Timucua	Acuera
	Mobile	Ais
	Houma	Apalachee
	Natchez	Calusa
	Pascagoula	Chatot
	Acolapissa	Mococo
	Avoyel	Pensacola
	Bayogoula	Seminole
	Okelousa	Pohay
	Quinipissa	Potano
	Taensa	Tekesta
	Tangipahoa	Tacobaga
Siouan-Yuki Group:	Siouan:	Biloxi
Tunican Group:		Atakapa
		Chawasha
		Chitimacha
		Opelousa
		Washa
		Koroa
Iroquois-Caddoan Group:	Caddoan:	Adai
		Eyeish
		Natchotoches Confederacy

him a job. He was obliged to work at night. The duty assigned to him was to keep voracious wolves from eating the bodies in a Calusa cemetery.

For almost ten years Ortiz lived in various Calusa towns. He learned their tongue, and became thoroughly familiar with their spiritual beliefs. By the end of nine years he had abandoned all hope of being rescued. Then suddenly the ships of the great De Soto expedition appeared on the blue horizon, and "great was the joy of Ortiz."

Ortiz became De Soto's principal interpreter and scout. He went happily north with the Spaniards, but he would not see civilization again. In an Indian town called by the Gentleman of Elvas Autiamque, and located on the Arkansas River, he lost his life, "a loss De Soto greatly regretted."

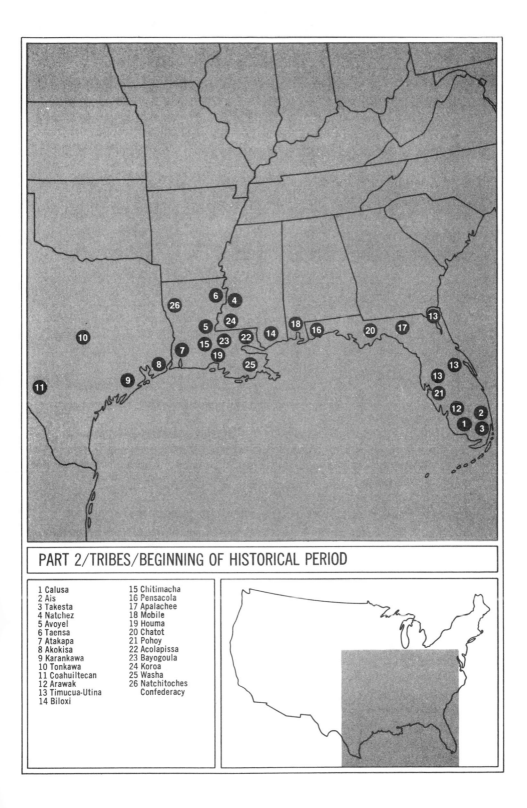

PART 2/TRIBES/BEGINNING OF HISTORICAL PERIOD

1 Calusa
2 Ais
3 Takesta
4 Natchez
5 Avoyel
6 Taensa
7 Atakapa
8 Akokisa
9 Karankawa
10 Tonkawa
11 Coahuiltecan
12 Arawak
13 Timucua-Utina
14 Biloxi

15 Chitimacha
16 Pensacola
17 Apalachee
18 Mobile
19 Houma
20 Chatot
21 Pohoy
22 Acolapissa
23 Bayogoula
24 Koroa
25 Washa
26 Natchitoches
   Confederacy

Pensacola: Hair People

Pensacola, meaning "hair people," is the name of the Indians who lived about the bay and city that would be named for them. They were a small and unimportant group related to the Choctaws, and they were driven from their territory in tribal conflicts early in the historical period. Their only claim to distinction is that they engaged in a fight with Narváez.

That the flimsy, awkward boats of the Narváez expedition stayed afloat long enough to pass along the Gulf Coast of Florida is truly remarkable. That any of the men in them survived the ordeals of storms, heavy seas, thirst, and hunger is nothing less than miraculous. A number did perish, succumbing to sickness, wounds, and malnutrition. Most of the food that kept the remainder alive was obtained in small Indian villages, from which the inhabitants fled at the sight of the unbelievable flotilla.

As the boats entered Pensacola Bay, on a day in mid-October, 1528, several canoes came out to meet them. The paddlers were large and well-formed men. They called out unintelligible words, and then turned back toward a village on the shore. The Spaniards followed. On landing, a chief appeared and made signs of welcome. A number of clay pots before the houses contained fresh water, and the half-crazed men madly drank it. Savagely they consumed some cooked fish found about the campfires of the settlement.*

As darkness fell over the village on the shore of Pensacola Bay, the campfires revealed the forms of exhausted men sleeping on the ground, their thirst temporarily quenched, their bellies momentarily pacified. Not a few of them had been only half conscious when they landed, and they slept in the crumpled positions in which they had fallen after eating.

The friendliness exhibited by the Pensacola had deceived them into dropping their guard. Narváez, Cabeza de Vaca, and some other officers had willingly accepted an invitation to spend the night in the house of the chief.

The unexpected attack came sometime after midnight. Falling suddenly upon the men sleeping along the shore, the Indians killed three

---

* A critical footnote seems appropriate at this point. Only a few times in his *Relación* does Cabeza de Vaca state that fish and other seafood were caught. In his account of the difficult journey along the Florida coast he makes no mention of catching fish or gathering crustaceans. These types of food were obtained only in Indian villages. Yet they were in waters rich in seafood. Redfish, sea trout, flounder, drum, grouper, and mullet, to name only a few species, abound in the area. The shallow bays and inlets, especially in the vicinity of Apalachicola, provide three quarters of the large annual Florida oyster harvest.

soldiers before any effective resistance could be accomplished. A group assaulted the men in the chief's house. Narváez was struck in the head by a stone and went down. Only quick action by Cabeza de Vaca and the others saved him from being killed. They seized the Indian chief, but in a wild struggle he was liberated by warriors. In the melee his royal robe of civet-marten was torn from his body. Cabeza de Vaca kept it, and thought the skins "the best that can be found; they have a fragrance that can be equaled by amber and musk alone . . ."

The unconscious Narváez was carried to his boat, and the Spaniards formed to make a stand at the water's edge. They were barely successful in repulsing three ensuing attacks. Cabeza de Vaca was wounded in the face, and rocks and arrows inflicted severe injuries on others. An encircling tactic, executed by fifteen men, prevented a disaster. The contingent slipped away in the darkness and struck the Indians from the rear. Under pressure from two sides, they broke and fled.

The expedition went on the next day, taking along the clay pots filled with fresh water, as well as the food remaining in the village.

Mobilian Trade Language

De Soto is credited with being the discoverer of the Mobile Indians, but there is evidence to indicate that the Narváez expedition encountered them several years earlier. Not only is their name, which may have derived from a Choctaw word, *moeli,* meaning "to paddle," perpetuated in a large bay, a large river, and a large city, but a strange form of communication was known by it throughout much of the region of the southern states.

The so-called Mobilian trade language was a corrupted Choctaw jargon. It was used by Indians from Florida to Louisiana, and by tribes of the Mississippi River as far north as the mouth of the Ohio, to communicate with each other in intertribal trade.

The month of October was drawing to a close as the boats of the Narváez expedition entered Mobile Bay and were met by Indians in canoes. Here two men, unable to stand the hardships of the voyage any longer, deserted. A soldier of Greek descent, called Teodoro, and a half-breed Arawak Indian seaman, whose name is not known to history, leaped from their boat into one of the Indian canoes, and were taken ashore.

Cabeza de Vaca seized two Indians as hostages, and announced by signs that they would be returned only when Teodoro and the seaman were released. A running fight followed, and for the first time Cabeza de Vaca tells of the use of slingshots. A number of the Indians were armed with them, and flung stones with telling effect at the Spaniards. The Mobile warriors encircled the boats in their canoes, raining clubs, stones, and arrows on them, and attempting to recover the hostages. A freshening wind gave the Spaniards an advantage. The water soon became rough, and the Mobile were forced to make for shore.

Twelve years later, De Soto's men heard from some Indians how the vessels of Narváez had arrived in Mobile Bay "in want of water, and how a Christian named Teodoro and another man had left them." The bearers of this information produced a dagger which they said had belonged to Teodoro, but they professed to know nothing of the fate of the deserters.

Nor is anything known of what happened to the two Mobile men carried off by the Spaniards, for Cabeza de Vaca made no further reference to them after the departure from Mobile Bay.*

Malhado Island

Early in November, 1528, the boats of the Narváez expedition were wrecked at various places, between Galveston Island and Lavaca Bay, on the coast of Texas.

Three Spanish officers and a blackamoor would survive the disaster, only four men of the three hundred who had set out the previous spring, dreaming of treasure and glory, from Tampa Bay. They were Cabeza de Vaca, Dorantes, Castillo, and Estevanico the Black.†

The first men of the Old World to enter the western Gulf of Mexico region that would become a part of the United States, they would spend almost six miserable years among various tribes of coastal Indians before making their escape. Between September, 1534, and July, 1536, they would make the first crossing of the continent north of Mexico, a journey without counterpart in the annals of North American exploration but a story that belongs to the historical period and not in this work.

What properly belongs here, however, are Cabeza de Vaca's accounts of the Indians of the coastal area and the interior plains of south Texas. He was the first to write of peoples whose existence was unknown to the civilized world, peoples still living in the shadows of the Stone Age, whose farthest cultural advances were crude pottery and the bow and

---

* The Biloxi, whose name is so well known today, are not believed to have been on the Gulf Coast in prehistoric times. It is possible they are the Capitanesses, located west of the Susquehanna River on early Dutch charts, who migrated southward in the early historical period. They belonged to the Siouan linguistic family. The first known historical record of them is the account of Pierre le Moyne d'Iberville, who reported meeting them on his first expedition to Louisiana in 1699. They moved frequently afterward, and early in the nineteenth century some were living in Louisiana and in Texas. A few years later the Texas group moved to Oklahoma. Their identity as a tribe has long been lost.

† See Part One—*Four Strangers.*

arrow, who had never heard of white or black men—unless some of them, by chance, had seen a Spanish ship passing along the low swampy shore—and who ate human flesh.*

Cabeza de Vaca's boat and one other were destroyed on the long sand spit known today as the Velasco Peninsula. His description shows that it was then an island. He gave it the name Malhado—Island of Ill-Fate. In the immediate area were two tribes speaking different languages. He called them *Cahoques* and *Hans*. They were, respectively, Karankawa and Akokisa (q.v.), and both groups customarily spent the winter in the vicinity.

The Karankawa appear to be the Indians who gave the wrecked Spaniards fish and roots to eat and took them to their homes on Malhado Island. Of them Cabeza de Vaca wrote:

"The people we found there are large and well-formed; they have no other arms than bows and arrows, in the use of which they are very dextrous. The men have one of their nipples bored from side to side, and some have both, wearing a cane in each, the length of two palms and a half, and the thickness of two fingers. They have the under lip also bored, and wear in it a piece of cane the breadth of half a finger. Their women are accustomed to great toil. The stay they make on the island is from October to the end of February. Their subsistence then is the root I have spoken of, got from under the water in November and December. They have weirs of cane and take fish only in this season; afterwards they live on the roots. At the end of February, they go into other parts to seek food; for then the root is beginning to grow and is not food.

"Those people love their offspring the most of any in the world, and treat them with the greatest mildness. When it occurs that a son dies, the parents and kindred weep as does everybody; the wailing continuing for him a whole year. They begin before dawn every day, the parents first and after them the whole town. They do the same at noon and at sunset. After a year of mourning has passed, the rites of the dead are performed; then they wash and purify themselves from the stain of smoke. They lament all the deceased in this manner, except the aged, for whom they show no regret, as they say that their season has passed, they having no enjoyment, and that living they would occupy the earth

---

* The cannibalism of the coastal Indians was practiced only to a limited extent, and, it is believed, was confined to slain enemies. This assumption is given some support by tragic events. Many of the wrecked Spaniards died of starvation, and others attempted to sustain life by eating their comrades. The Karankawa appeared to be deeply disturbed when they heard that the white men had eaten the flesh of their own kind, and condemned them. It is the opinion of this author that although Cabeza de Vaca and his companions were held as prisoner-slaves they were not looked upon as enemies, and that this fact alone may have saved them from becoming victims of cannibalism.

and take aliment from the young. Their custom is to bury the dead, unless it be those among them who have been physicians. These they burn. While the fire kindles they are all dancing and making high festivity, until the bones become powder. After the lapse of a year the funeral honors [for medicine men] are celebrated, everyone taking part in them, when that dust is presented in water for the relatives to drink.

"Every man has an acknowledged wife. The physicians are allowed more freedom; they may have two or three wives, among whom exist the greatest friendship and harmony. From the time a daughter marries, all that he who takes her to wife kills in hunting or catches in fishing, the woman brings to the house of her father, without daring to eat or take any part of it, and thence victuals are taken to the husband. From that time neither her father nor mother enters his house, nor can he enter theirs, nor the houses of their children; and if by chance they are in the direction of meeting, they turn aside, and pass the distance of a crossbow shot from each other, carrying the head low the while, the eyes cast on the ground; for they hold it improper to see or speak to each other. But the woman has liberty to converse and communicate with the parents and relatives of her husband. The custom exists from this island the distance of more than fifty leagues inland.

"There is another custom, which is, when a son or brother dies, at the house where the death takes place they do not go after food for three months, but sooner famish, their relatives and neighbors providing what they eat. As in the time we were there a great number of the natives died, in most houses there was very great hunger, because of the keeping of this their custom and observance; for although they who sought after food worked hard, yet from the severity of the season they could get but little; in consequence, the Indians who kept me, left the island, and passed over in canoes to the main, into some bays where are many oysters. For three months in the year they eat nothing besides these, and drink very bad water. There is great want of wood; mosquitoes are in great plenty. The houses are of mats, set up on masses of oyster shells, which they sleep upon, and in skins, should they accidentally possess them."

Cabeza de Vaca wrote little that may definitely be applied to the people he called Han, except to remark that they held some of the Spaniards, "were of different tongue and ancestry," and that they "went to the opposite shore of the main to eat oysters, where they stayed until the first day of April [1529], when they returned. The distance is two leagues in the widest part. The island is half a league in breadth and five leagues in length."

However, the following statement appears to apply to both the

Akokisa and the Karankawa: "The inhabitants of all this region go naked. The women alone have any part of their persons covered, and it is with a wool that grows on trees [Spanish moss]. The damsels dress themselves in deerskin. The people are generous to each other of what they possess. They have no chief. All of a lineage keep together. . . . They have a custom when they meet, or from time to time when they visit, of remaining half an hour before they speak, weeping; * and, this over, he that is visited first rises and gives the other all he has, which is received, and after a little while he carries it away, and often goes without saying a word."

Cabeza de Vaca: *El Vendador Primero*

In the summer of 1530 a bearded Spaniard bearing a pack on his back traveled from tribe to tribe along the coastal plain of Texas. His gaunt, sun-blackened body was only partially covered by a filthy, worn deerskin.[40]

Scheming to free himself from the endless toil of his enslavement, and to find a means of escaping to civilization, Cabeza de Vaca had hit upon an ingenious idea. He had persuaded his brutal captors to let him become a trader—the first European to engage in commerce with Indians in the territory of the United States.

Gathering a stock of goods, he set out. At each opportunity he went into the interior, trading his wares and at the same time learning the country, the ways of rivers, and the length and breadth of each arm of the sea.

On three sides of him was wilderness. The people told him it was endless. His intelligence told him that was not true. Somewhere, in each of the three directions, there was an end. There had to be an end.

Indians gave him orders for a variety of articles, and he gave to the world an invaluable glance at the primitive prehistoric commerce. For if the occupation was new to him, it was not to his customers. Indeed, it had been carried on in much the same manner for millennia. During those millennia only the products of the trade had changed—and many of them had not changed at all—and there had been no changes in man's common needs, his needs for food and fibers, his needs for protection, for medicines, and his desires for things which pleased his eye and stirred his heart, things that brought comfort and pleasure and affluence.

And so Cabeza de Vaca wrote:

"I set to trafficking, and strove to make my employment profitable in the ways I could best contrive, and by that means I got food and

---

* This custom of weeping was common among a number of tribes.

good treatment. The Indians would beg me to go from one quarter to another for things of which they have need; for in consequence of incessant hostilities, they cannot traverse the country, nor make many exchanges.*

"With my merchandise and trade I went into the interior as far as I pleased, and traveled along the coast forty or fifty leagues.† The principal wares were cones and other pieces of sea-snail, conchs used for cutting, and fruit like a bean of the highest value among them, which they use as a medicine and employ in their dances and festivities. Among other matters were sea-beads. Such were what I carried into the interior; and in barter I got and brought back skins, ocher with which they rub and color the face, hard canes of which to make arrows, sinews, cement, and flint for the heads, and tassels of the hair of deer that by dyeing they make red. The occupation suited me well; for the travel allowed me liberty to go where I wished, and I was not obliged to work, and was not a slave. Wherever I went I received fair treatment, and Indians gave me to eat. . . . I became well-known. The inhabitants were pleased when they saw me, and I had brought them what they wanted; and those who did not know me sought and desired the acquaintance. . . ." [41]

A Matter of Identity

Of more than a score of tribes named by Cabeza de Vaca in the accounts of his trading ventures and the journey across Texas as he and his three companions escaped, ethnologists have been able to identify only six with any degree of certainty. They are:

His Name	Correct Name and Probable Affiliation
Atayos	Adai of Caddoan stock
Quevenes	Kohani of the Karankawa
Quilotes	A Karankawa tribe
Mariames	Muruam group of Tonkawa
Han	Akokisa tribe of Atakapa
Coaques	A Karankawa tribe

Regrettable as this is, his writing of peoples whose tribal connections cannot be established still stands as a valuable contribution to prehistoric knowledge.‡

---

* See *Scientific Note,* Part Four.
† The Spanish judicial league equaled 2.634 English miles.
‡ The following tribes to which he gave names have not been identified with people known to have lived in the western Gulf region at the beginning of the historical period: Doguenes, Cuthalchuches, Malicones, Coayos, Susolas, Chorruco, Mendica,

The Mariames killed a survivor of the Narváez expedition who attempted to escape from them after a squaw had a bad dream in which he appeared. Telling of this slaying, Cabeza de Vaca said:

"Thus in obedience to their custom they take life, destroying even their male children on account of dreams. They cast away their daughters at birth, and cause them to be eaten by dogs. The reason of their doing this, as they state, is because all nations of the country are their foes; and as they have unceasing war with them, if they were to marry away their daughters, they would so greatly multiply their enemies that they must be overcome and made slaves; thus they prefer to destroy all, rather than that from them should come a single enemy. We asked why they did not themselves marry them; and they said it would be a disgustful thing to marry among relatives, and far better to kill than to give them either to their kindred or to their foes.

"This is likewise the practice of their neighbors the Yguazes, but of no other people in that country. When the men would marry, they buy the women of their enemies: the price paid for a wife is a bow, the best that can be got, with two arrows: if it happens that the suitor should have no bow, then a net a fathom in length and another in breadth. . . . The marriage state continues no longer than while the parties are satisfied, and they separate for the slightest cause. . . ."

Presumably still writing about the Mariames, Cabeza de Vaca stated that they "are universally good archers and of a fine symmetry. . . . They have a nipple and a lip bored. Their support is principally roots, of two or three kinds, and they look for them over all the face of the country. The food is poor and gripes the persons who eat it. The roots require roasting two days: many are very bitter, and withal difficult to be dug . . . so great is the want these people experience that they cannot get through the year without them. Occasionally they kill deer, and at times take fish; but the quantity is so small and the famine so great that they eat spiders and the eggs of ants, worms, lizards, salamanders, snakes, and vipers that kill whom they strike; and they eat earth and wood, and all there is, the dung of deer, and other things. . . . They save the bones of the fishes they consume, of snakes and other animals, that they may afterwards beat them together and eat the powder. The men bear no burdens, nor carry anything of weight; such are borne by women and old men who are of the least esteem. . . . Some among them are accustomed to sin against nature. . . . The majority of the people are great thieves; for though they are free to divide with each other, on turning the head, even a son or a father will take what

---

Guaycones, Yguazes, Acubadoes, Quitoks, Chavavares, Comos, Camoles, People of the Figs, Lanegados. He obviously passed through country occupied by the Emet and Cava, two Tonkawa tribes, but does not identify them by those names.

he can. They are great liars, and also great drunkards, which they become from the use of a certain liquor.*

"These Indians are so accustomed to running that without rest or fatigue they follow a deer from morning to night. . . . They pursue them until tired down, and sometimes overtake them in the race. Their houses are matting, placed upon four hoops. They carry them on the back, and remove every two or three days in search of food. Nothing is planted for support. They are a merry people, considering the hunger they suffer; for they never cease, notwithstanding, to observe their festivities. . . . To them the happiest part of the year is the season of eating prickly pears; they have hunger then no longer, pass all the time in dancing, and eat day and night. While these last, they squeeze out the juice, open and set them to dry, and when dry they are put in hampers like figs. . . . The peel is beaten to powder."

Life at Home Along the Coast

Speaking of Coahuiltecan tribes he did not name, Cabeza de Vaca noted that "they have the custom from the time in which their wives find themselves pregnant, of not sleeping with them until two years after they have given birth. The children are suckled until the age of twelve years [probably the age of puberty], when they are old enough to get support for themselves. We asked why they reared them in this manner; and they said because of the great poverty of the land it happened many times, as we witnessed, that they were two or three days without eating, sometimes four, and consequently, in seasons of scarcity, the children were allowed to suckle, that they might not famish; otherwise those who lived would be delicate, having little strength.

"It is common among them all to leave their wives when there is no conformity, and directly they connect themselves with whom they please. This is the course of the men who are childless; those who have children remain with their wives. . . .

"When they dispute and quarrel in their towns, they strike each other with the fists, fighting until exhausted, and then separate. Sometimes they are parted by the women going between them; the men never interfere. For no disaffection that arises do they resort to bows and arrows. After they have fought, or had out their dispute, they take their dwelling and go into the woods, living apart from each other until their heat has subsided. When no longer offended and their anger is gone, they return. From that time they are friends as if nothing had happened. . . ."

---

* The drink probably was made from the peyote, or mescal, button. It is still used by some Indians, and produces visions and stupefaction.

Of some unidentifiable people:

"Everywhere they produce stupefaction with a smoke, and for that they will give whatever they possess.

"They drink a tea made from the leaves of a tree like those of the oak, which they toast in a pot; and after these are parched, the vessel, still remaining on the fire, is filled with water. When the liquor has twice boiled, they pour it into a jar, and in cooling it use the half of a gourd. So soon as it is covered thickly with froth, it is drunk as warm as can be supported. . . .*

"When the women have their indisposition, they seek food only for themselves, as no one else will eat of what they bring.

"I witnessed a diabolical practice; a man living with another, one of those who are emasculate and impotent. These go habited like women, and perform their duties, use the bow, and carry heavy loads. Among them we saw many mutilated in the way I describe. They are more muscular than other men, and taller. . . ."

In one place, after starting on their westward journey, the three Spaniards and the blackamoor were given "a great quantity of the flour of mezquiquez [mesquite]. The fruit while hanging on the tree is very bitter and like unto the carob; when eaten with earth it is sweet and wholesome. The method they have of preparing it is this: they make a hole of requisite depth in the ground, and throwing in the fruit, pound it with a club the size of a leg, a fathom and a half in length, until it is well mashed. Besides the earth that comes from the hole, they bring and add some handfuls, then returning to beat it a little while longer. Afterward it is thrown into a jar, like a basket, upon which water is poured until it rises above and covers the mixture.

"He that eats it, tastes it, and if it appears to him not sweet, he asks for earth to stir in, which is added until he finds it sweet. Then all sit around, and each putting in a hand, takes out as much as he can. The pits and hulls are thrown upon a skin, whence they are taken by him who does the pounding, and put into the jar whereon water is poured as at first, whence having expressed the froth and juice, again the pits and husks are thrown upon the skin. This they do three or four times to each pounding.

"Those present, for whom this is a great banquet, have their stomachs greatly distended by the earth and water they swallow."

---

* This was the first notice of the so-called black drink, which is made from ilex leaves and was brewed by tribes of the American South and the Gulf Coast region as an intoxicant. Among some people the drink was taken in religious ceremonies.

The First American Indian Folk Tale

As Cabeza de Vaca, Dorantes, Castillo, and Estevanico the Black slowly made their way westward from the coast to the higher plains they became famous as medicine men. Crowds of Indians appealed to them to cure the sick and to drive off evil spirits.* One people whom Cabeza de Vaca called both Chavavares and Avavares made a plea he never forgot. He recorded it in this way:

"They said that a man wandered through the country whom they called Badthing; he was small of body and wore beard, and they never distinctly saw his features. When he came to the house where they lived, their hair stood up and they trembled. Presently a blazing torch shone at the door, when he entered and seized whom he chose, and giving him three great gashes in the side with a very sharp flint, the width of the hand and two palms in length, he put his hand through them, drawing forth the entrails, from one of which he would cut off a portion more or less the length of a palm, and throw it on the embers. Then he would give three gashes to an arm, the second cut on the inside of an elbow, and would sever the limb. A little after this, he would begin to unite it, and putting his hands on the wounds, these would instantly become healed.

"They said that frequently in the dance he appeared among them, sometimes in the dress of a woman, at others in that of a man; that when it pleased him he would take a *buhio*, or house, and lifting it high, after a little he would come down with it in a heavy fall.

"They also stated that many times they offered him victuals, but that he never ate: they asked him whence he came and where was his abiding place, and he showed them a fissure in the earth and said that his house was there below."

So Cabeza de Vaca heard of the Chavavares' "devil" and "hell." He and his companions laughed and ridiculed the tale, and the Chavavares, "seeing our incredulity, brought to us many of those they said he had seized; and we saw the marks of the gashes made in the places according to the manner they had described."

Agreeing that Badthing was certainly "an evil one," the Spaniards told the Chavavares "that if they would believe in God our Lord, and become Christians like us, they need have no fear of him, nor would he dare to come and inflict those injuries, and they might be certain he would not venture to appear while we remained in the land. At this they were delighted and lost much of their dread."

---

* They were miraculously successful as shamans.

SOME INDIAN PLACE NAMES*

Louisiana

Avoyelles, parish
Goula, bayou
Houma, town
Natchitoches, parish, town
Opelousas, town
Tensas, parish, river, bayou
Tangipahoa, parish, town, river
Washa, lake
Natchez, town
Tunica, town
Coushatla, town
Powhatan, town
Tioga, town
Caddo, parish

Florida

Indian, river
Apalachee, river, bay
Apalachicola, town, river, bay
Tallahassee, town
Caloosahatchee, river
Choctawhatchie, river, bay
Miccosuki, lake, town
Ocala, town
Pensacola, town, river
Alachua, county, town
Seminole, county, town
Tomoka, creek
Oklawaha, town
Okeechobee, county, lake
Muskogee, town
Lacota, town

Mississippi

Biloxi, town, river, bay
Mississippi, state, river
Natchez, town
Pascagoula, town, river, bay
Yalobusha, county, river
Chickasaw, county
Chickasawhay, river
Choctaw, county
Tunica, county
Yazoo, county, town, river
Cayuga, town

Alabama

Alabama, state, river, town
Natchez, town
Mobile, city
Apalachee, river
Choctaw, point
Tensaw, river
Chewacla, town
Seminole, town
Chickasaw, town
Choctaw, town, county
Chehaw, town
Cherokee, county, town
Shawnee, town
Covsada, town
Eufaula, town
Tuskegee, town
Powhatan, town
Appalachian, mountains
Tennessee, river
Kansas, town

* Tribes and tribal subdivisions.

Dates to Remember

1519—The prehistoric period came to an end in the American Gulf Coast region when the first Spanish pilot took his little ship close enough to make out Indians on the low swampy shores. Who that pilot was is not known to history, and it seems quite probable that several may have touched along the northern and western Gulf coasts before Piñeda sailed in 1519 from Florida to Panuco. The voyage of Piñeda, however, is recorded in authentic documents.

1521—Ponce de León attempted to land at Charlotte Harbor, was wounded by Indians, and withdrew to Cuba, where he died. He had previously reached Florida on the Atlantic side in 1513, had sailed along the coast, and had rounded the Keys before returning to Puerto Rico.

1528—Narváez landed near Tampa Bay. This was the first overland expedition on American soil. After being disastrously defeated by Indians in northern Florida, the company embarked in boats and sailed westward in the hope of reaching Panuco. The boats were wrecked on the coast of Texas, and only four men survived the catastrophe.

1539—Hernando de Soto landed on the Gulf coast of Florida, marched northward and then westward, traversing the southeastern United States. In 1543, survivors of the expedition, led by Luis Moscoso de Alvarado, sailed down the Mississippi from the mouth of the Arkansas to the Gulf, and reached Panuco.

Of all the explorers who participated in opening the Gulf Coast region of the United States, the greatest honor must go to Cabeza de Vaca. His *Relación,* first published at Zamora in 1542, not only recounted his incredible journey with three companions across the continent but gave the world the first knowledge of prehistoric Indians who dwelt along their route between Tampa Bay and the Gulf of California.

Scientific Note—Chronology and the Indian

When an archeologist finds a projectile point embedded in the bones of a long extinct animal he is both gratified and happy. A date has been established. True, it cannot be a very exact date, but there are general maximum and minimum limits between which it can be placed.

In a hypothetical case, these facts are indisputable: (a) the flint projectile was made by a Paleo-Indian, who flaked it to the desired shape; (b) it was driven into the quarry as a spearhead, probably with the aid of an atlatl, or spear-thrower; (c) the slain animal belonged to a species that lived in the Pleistocene Age.

These problems remain to be resolved: (a) the animal, say it was a Pleistocene bison, did not become extinct in all parts of the United States at the same time; (b) when did it disappear from the area in which its bones and the *in situ* projectile were discovered? (c) what kind of climate existed when it lived in this particular place? and (d) what does the geological record of the region reveal?

Since World War II scientists have achieved remarkable progress in discovering reliable methods by which the chronology of ancient artifacts, bones, and other physical properties can be established. For example, long years of study have resulted in the conclusion that no Pleistocene animals survived, at least north of the tropical regions, longer than seven thousand years ago. That is a minimal date. Thus, the projectile point being considered is no less old. Helpful knowledge, indeed, but far from being satisfactory. The projectile may be much older, for some species of Pleistocene mammals became extinct in certain areas ten or twelve thousand years ago.

Here research on elements and chemistry takes over the problem.

It has been known for some years that buried bones "receive free fluorine ions from the ground water. The fluorine combines with hydroapatite, which is present in all bones, and forms a mineral called fluorapatite. The older the bone, the more fluorapatite will be present." [42] But this method of dating, helpful as it has been, is not adequate, for some ground waters contain larger amounts of fluorine than others, which precludes the comparison of bones found in different locations.

In some sites archeologists have been successful in determining relative chronology by means of stratigraphy, the position and sequence of layers in which artifacts have been discovered. Remains found in the lowest layer, of course, will be older than those in higher layers. Geologists can supply relatively accurate dates for soil strata, and artifacts may be assigned to a culture or period. This is a sound system, but unfortunately can be employed only in a few places, where the strata have not been disturbed by natural forces. However, some of the oldest Indian sites in North America have been dated by what may be termed geologic chronology, that is, by associating them with deposits known to have been laid down during or shortly after the last glacial period. The Southwest serves as an outstanding example of the application of this method, for in that region at the time of the last glaciation there prevailed "a cool and wet, or pluvial, period lasting from about 35,000 to 10,000 years ago. The subsequent warmer and drier postpluvial period lasted from 10,000 to about 4,000 years ago. There followed a minor wet period of about 1,000 years' duration, and, finally, modern climatic conditions prevailed." [43] The age of Indian tools or weapons found on an ancient lake beach or in some other deposits can be judged with fair accuracy.

One of the most notable contributions to archeology was made not by an archeologist, geologist, paleontologist, or paleobotanist, but by an astronomer. While engaged in a study of sunspots, Dr. A. E. Douglas reached the conclusion that disturbances in the sun affect weather. With the hope of obtaining long-range weather records, he began an exhaustive examination of pines in his native Southwest. The reward was even greater than he had anticipated. He discovered that variations in rainfall were reflected in the width of the annual growth rings of trees.

Now he felt that he was on the track of his goal, and further studies proved him correct. He found that almost all trees in a given area displayed the same pattern of narrow and wide rings. From hundreds of trunks studied in various southwestern regions and altitudes he developed a master chart that went back some two thousand years. No section of this tree ring calendar was the same as another section.

Dr. Douglas had demonstrated that, at least for this length of time, tree rings were weather records. But he had achieved more than that. He had devised a means of dating logs and beams in prehistoric Indian ruins, such as cliff houses and other buildings in the western regions.

Archeologists had been given a new method of dating, and it was used, as Martin (1947) explains, "by overlapping the ring patterns of old living trees with those of still older logs found as beams in old houses and mission churches, and these in turn with the ring patterns of beams and charred posts from prehistoric Indian ruins. For example, a large pine tree cut in 1920 had 300 annual rings; therefore, it had begun to grow in the year 1620. The pattern of wide and narrow rings yielded a record of wet and dry years during this period of 300 years. In an old church was found a large beam with 150 rings. The pattern of the thirty outermost rings of this beam matched perfectly that of the 30 innermost rings of the tree that had begun to grow in 1620. Therefore, the church beam had been cut in 1650 and had begun to grow in the year 1500. By finding still older timbers, the ring patterns of which successively matched and overlapped backward in time, the chronology was carried still further back."

However, dendrochronology, the scientific name for tree-ring dating, has a major drawback in the field of archeology: a time limit. For wood is perishable. While trees more than three thousand years old—notably the giant sequoia—are living, only under the most beneficial conditions will a cut log or beam remain intact as long as three hundred years. This occurs only in the arid Southwest. In more moist climates disintegration rapidly takes place.

Dr. Douglas had made a great contribution, but something more was needed, some method by which archeologists could extend accurate chronological dating back into the most remote periods of man's habitation in America.

It was found.

By 1955, Dr. W. F. Libby and his co-workers at the University of Chicago—site of the great discoveries in nuclear fission—had developed the most remarkable and sensational method of determining the age of ancient materials ever known in the field of chronology.

It is called radiocarbon-14 dating. For those readers who are in the dark as to the exact meaning of the term—and I feel certain there are a few—I shall let two highly qualified—and happy—scientists explain.

Driver: [44] "Radiocarbon dating is based on measurement of radiation. Ordinary carbon has an atomic weight of 12, but radioactive carbon has an atomic weight of 14. Radiocarbon is present in very small quantities in every living thing, plant or animal. In living wood, for example, only one out of every trillion carbon atoms is radioactive. That is enough, however, for the physicist to measure the radioactivity of a piece of wood.

"Radiocarbon is produced by cosmic rays which bombard the upper atmosphere of the earth, producing fast-moving neutrons. These neutrons combine with nitrogen atoms to produce hydrogen and carbon-14. All vegetation absorbs carbon dioxide containing carbon-14 from the air and animals obtain the radioactive carbon by eating the plants or other animals which are plant eaters. When a plant or animal dies, its supply of carbon-14 is not renewed but gradually becomes less and less. At any time after death the amount of carbon-14 left in a portion of the remains of plants and animals may be measured by the amount of radiation still emanating from it.

"It has been found that when an organism has been dead for 5,760 years, its rate of radiation is half that of a living organism, and the amount of carbon-14 remaining is, therefore, half the original amount. After 11,520 years the rate of radiation is one-fourth of the original amount, and after 17,280 years only one-eighth."

Wormington: [45] "The basic step in radiocarbon dating is to reduce the material to be dated to pure elemental carbon or a pure compound of carbon. Next, it is necessary to determine what percentage of carbon is Carbon-14. When the quantity of Carbon-14 has been reduced beyond a certain point, it is not possible to determine the exact amount which remains.* Using the first technique that was employed, the solid carbon counting method, it was impossible to date samples that were much more than 20,000 years old. New techniques utilizing various gases and liquids have made it possible to date samples more than 30,000 years old, and the dating of 50,000-year-old samples is now believed possible. The use of gas also permits the use of smaller samples."

Contamination of samples to be tested can create difficulties. If newer organic material was introduced into them while they were still in the ground the dates obtained would be too recent. This can happen in a number of ways, as Wormington notes, "through root penetration, micro-organisms, fungal action, or the activity of burrowing animals.

---

* But long before that point was reached dates that would delight any archeologist would have been established.

. . . Some errors may occur through the addition of dead carbon or inorganic carbonates, or through the exchange of Carbon-14 for Carbon-12. This will make the dates too old.

"There is also danger of contamination after excavation. There have been times when laboratories using the solid carbon method have had to interrupt their activities because of the 'fall out' of radioactive material following explosions set off in the course of testing fissionable materials many thousands of miles away. The use of gas counters has done much to minimize these difficulties in the laboratory, but stored samples, unless they are properly protected, may be exposed to various airborne contaminants."

Radiocarbon 14 dating may be a delicate and difficult method requiring exactitude, technique, and knowledge that only the most expert physicists can supply, but the fact remains that it works, it is successful.

"In spite of certain sources of error," says Driver, "which are gradually becoming recognized, the radiocarbon method is the most accurate so far devised by science for dating within the period from about 70,000 to 2,000 years ago."

The most reliable material for determining the date of an ancient site is charcoal, although shells, animal horns, and bones can be used. Since Dr. Libby's great discovery, archeologists diligently search for ancient hearths. For pieces of charcoal can tell—at least within the span of a few centuries—when a Paleo-Indian hunter cooked a mastodon steak for himself and his family over a campfire.

And if this date can be established, then the true ages of the stone implements and utensils and weapons found at the site of the campfire also can be determined.

Southeastern Woodlands

Stories in the Earth

They were small bands wandering through the forests of uplands and valleys and even into the mountains in their eternal search for food. They were there in the region that would become the southeastern United States when great mammals of the Pleistocene Age were alive, and they hunted them in the manner of their contemporaries who lived in the Southwest, that is, with similar fluted stone points and spears and atlatls. But there was one notable difference in the hunting methods of the two widely separated peoples. At various sites in the Southeast where archeologists have found bones of Ice Age animals and man-made artifacts, large numbers of stones also have been found. In the Southeast there were many bogs, especially in the lowlands bordering the streams. It is believed the stones were used as missiles thrown to frighten the immense animals and stampede them into swampy places where they would become mired and could be slain with comparative ease.

The dust confesses to science, but does not reveal all its secrets. Always mysteries remain to be solved. It cannot be said when Homo sapiens first reached the Southeast. Men may have been hunting there as early as they were in the Far West. Nor can it be told by what routes they crossed the Mississippi and spread out through the rich country until they were halted by the Atlantic Ocean. Probably they moved into the Southeast over many courses, but even the main trails of their migrations cannot be established, for countless ways were open to them.

It can be said that they were there at least ten thousand years ago, but if that is a safe assertion it must be considered a minimal date. For if human beings dwelt in other parts of the continent three, four, and perhaps five times as long ago as that, there seems to be no reason to think they were not in Tennessee, Alabama, Mississippi, Georgia, the Carolinas, and the Virginias at the same time.

Perhaps the dust will surrender more of its secrets in the future. Meanwhile the scientifically established facts at hand must suffice.

Projectile points which radiocarbon dating shows are more than eight thousand years old have been recovered in Russell Cave, near Bridgeport, Alabama.[1] Some other artifacts found there may be as much as two thousand years older. The bones of a man who stood only five feet two inches in height were discovered beside a grinding stone on what is believed to be a level of the Archaic Age. Among the most surprising Russell Cave finds, however, according to Baity,[2] were "a hinged fishhook, and an animal-fat wick lamp made from a bear's foreleg hollowed out and packed with fat. Both were found in an eight-thousand-year-old layer. . . . These artifacts are like those used much later by Eskimos and other circum-polar people, explain it how you will. . . . Dr. J. L. Coe of the University of North Carolina has located in the Carolina Piedmont a series of small sites where projectile point forms are found which resemble those in Russell Cave."

Stone tools, atlatl weights, and points almost as old as those taken from Russell Cave have been found at the Eva Site in Tennessee. Mussels that lived in southern rivers were a staple of the Eva people. They interred the dead in flexed positions. Dogs also were buried, a custom that may have been followed for various reasons. If it may not be definitely explained in this case, it is understood in the case of later peoples who performed it.[3]

The stage called Paleo-Indian by archeologists is generally dated from twenty thousand to ten thousand years ago. In 1951, Frank J. Soday discovered a Paleo-Indian site near Decatur, Alabama.[4] Nearly a thousand artifacts belonging to a fluted point complex were recovered. Most of the points were made of a blue chert that is also found in New York and Pennsylvania, but not in this part of Alabama. A site of the Archaic stage—after ten thousand years ago—was uncovered at the Decatur find, which is named the Quad Site. It was learned that the later peoples did not manufacture their tools from the same chert, perhaps because it was no longer available to them, or perhaps because they found other materials better suited to their needs. Sites in two Kentucky counties, Butler and Hopkins, produced Paleo-Indian points, as well as Archaic artifacts. William S. Webb, who investigated both sites, attributed some of the tools to early hunters.[5] A later investigator, Raymond H. Thompson, suggested that the Hopkins discovery may

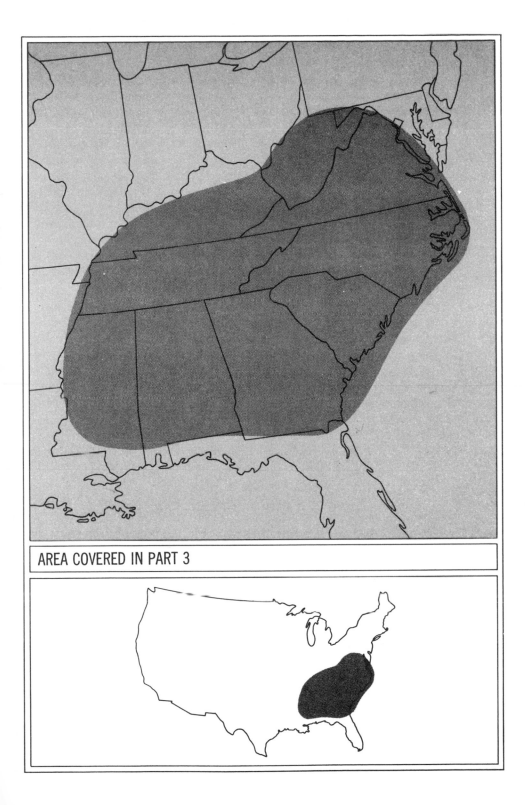

AREA COVERED IN PART 3

represent a period of transition between the Paleo-Indian and the Archaic stages, and that the collection was basically homogeneous.[6]

Especially in the last decade the evidence to show man's early presence in the Southeast has piled up. I quote from a letter written to me by Robert L. Stephenson, state archeologist of South Carolina: "There has been but very little done in the archeology of South Carolina. I came here about a year ago to remedy this situation and we are making great progress. . . . We know we have early man sites going back to eight thousand to twelve thousand years ago, from surface indications, yet we have none of these excavated and reported. . . . In short, we have the whole time-sequence of more than ten thousand years. . . . At least five hundred good sites are presently known to me. . . . See me in about five years and I will tell you a lot about these."

Some other southern states have not been as neglectful in their digging as South Carolina. Tennessee excavators have made notable discoveries of prehistoric peoples at Moccasin Bend, Nickjack Reservoir, Tims Ford Reservoir, and Lake Chickamauga.[7] Members of the Archeological Society of Virginia spent nine years on a survey of fluted eastern points found in that commonwealth. Nearly three hundred have been located on maps.[8] Joffre Coe, investigating various sites in North Carolina, has recognized eight pre-ceramic complexes.[9] At the Hardaway Site on the Yadkin River, Paleo-Indian points have been uncovered. Points similar to ancient types of the Far West have been found in Alabama. In Mississippi the Womack Mound is an important site. Indeed, in every southern state there are Paleo-Indian sites in which points called eastern fluted have been discovered. The people were there. The chief question to be answered is: How long?

The Old Stone Fort: Perhaps a Sacred Place

It has long been called the Old Stone Fort, but there is ample evidence to suggest that this is a misnomer, that it was a great ceremonial complex and was not constructed to protect its prehistoric occupants against invaders. It stands between the forks of Duck River, near the town of Manchester, in Coffee County, Tennessee, and the known ages of the artifacts and the charcoal of cooking fires found in it proclaim that it was built near the beginning of the Christian Era. In archeological terms, that is not very long ago, yet scientists have not been able to establish the identity of the Indians who were its builders.

The walls encircle an area of fifty acres in extent and if they were continuous they would have a total length of forty-six hundred feet. However, the walls were only constructed where the stream bluffs were not precipitous. This would lead to the belief that they were erected only in areas vulnerable to intrusion or attack.[10] That very well could be an erroneous belief. The walls were too low to be an effective barrier, and no indication of palisade posts was found. Rotting posts most probably would have left some evidence of molds.

The scarcity of cultural material in the wall fill was a factor given careful consideration by excavators. Only seven projectile points, identifiable with cultures which existed in the centuries of the early Christian Era, were found, and archeologist Charles H. Faulkner reported that "all except one occurred near the edge of the embankment and could not be definitely associated with the erection of the wall. Besides scattered charcoal and a few random chert flakes and chunks, no definite artifacts were found deep within the walls."

In the entire Old Stone Fort site, besides the seven identifiable projectile points, more than twelve hundred artifacts were recovered from trenches and test pits. These included unidentifiable broken projectile points, scrapers, stone cores, chert hammerstones, flakes, and worked and unworked pieces of flint. Two tools discovered, a uniface end scraper and a large flake with a longitudinal working edge, may be of Paleo-Indian origin. Especially perplexing to the diggers was the fact that no pottery was found. The absence or paucity of certain utilitarian items indicates the site was never used intensively for habitation or that these things were deliberately removed.

The oldest date, established by the radiocarbon method, was obtained from charcoal that was removed from slightly more than four feet below the surface. It was approximately A.D. 30. The Old Stone Fort was built by prehistoric Indians who, at least, were living then in Tennessee, but who most probably had dwelt in the area for centuries before that time.

Until recently the theory that the Old Stone Fort was built for defensive purposes prevailed, but it is no longer acceptable. One fact alone, determined by scientific analysis, defeats it. The Old Stone Fort was not erected in a short time. Indeed, it was under construction for many decades, perhaps for several generations, and this factor, if nothing else, removes it from the category of a defensive works.

The Old Stone Fort is no longer called a "fort" by many archeologists. They use the term "enclosure," and think of it as a sacred place, renovated and repaired through the years, to be sure, but intended chiefly as a place in which the builders, and after them their descendants, gathered to worship, to perform religious rituals, to appease their gods.

The Old Stone Fort of Tennessee had an elaborate entrance between large pillars. Its walls would have been ineffective against a strong force of raiders, for they were low and encompassed an extensive area. Even if the enclosure had been palisaded, it would have taken a large force of defenders to man the walls. The eminent

Driver [11] maintains that "fights between whole tribes seem to have been rare before White contact." The typical prehistoric Indian war party was relatively small.

As Faulkner (1967) points out, "if one can interpret the walls and the entrance complex as having a sacred as opposed to secular function . . . walls cease to be barricades to prevent the incursion of enemies, but become markers to enclose the sacred area. They could provide a 'no trespassing' symbol to the uninvited or the uninitiated. The entrance complex becomes a device to not only deter intrusion during solemn ceremonies, but also to provide an ostentatious setting for a spectacular entrance ceremony.

"Although it is evident a large force of laborers built the structure and presumably used it at least periodically, thus far it seems they left no prosaic articles within the walls. It is almost as though an effort was made not to profane this sacred place with mundane things."

There is other evidence to support such a contention. It has been well established that many tribes of the Southeast kept their ceremonial areas meticulously clean. The Old Stone Fort unquestionably was not only thoroughly cleaned, and probably with an accompanying and appropriate ritual, but was renovated from time to time as rites increased in importance over a period of several centuries.

One of the most baffling questions remaining to plague archeologists is the type of ceremonial ritualism that was performed. If the motivations of these prehistoric people could be determined, it probably would be possible to learn much about their social and religious systems, and what inspired them to expend a great amount of toil and time to build and maintain this immense structure high on a Tennessee bluff.

The Cultural Zenith: Middle Mississippi

With the single exception of the Southwest, nowhere in the area of the United States was there a prehistoric civilization which spread with such vigor and rapidity as that which is called the Middle Mississippi Culture. It extended over the larger part of the Southeast, and was characterized by intensive agriculture, by temple and burial mounds, by immense ceremonial centers, by "states" whose rulers controlled the society and the economy of satellite towns, by complex social systems, and by unprecedented artistic achievements.

The Middle Mississippi Culture had its roots in numerous older cultures, some as far distant as southern Mexico and the Great Lakes region. It began to emerge as early as the eighth century A.D., not among a single tribe, not among a linguistic group, but from a profusion of peoples who spoke different tongues and followed different customs. The causes of its emergence are unknown. Archeologists presume its development began in various localities of the middle southern area by the compounding of mores of previous cultures which had existed in the same region,* and the infusion of ideas and customs of the Hopewell Culture of Ohio, Illinois, and the Northeast, and the introduction of social and economic systems from Meso-America. Out of all these blended ingredients arose a civilization that continued to develop and expand for several centuries, that reached its greatest intensification after A.D. 1200, and that flourished well into the beginning of the historical period.

There are many archeological sites of the Middle Mississippi Culture, scattered over half a dozen states. However, one of the largest and in several respects one of the most uncommon is on the Warrior River a few miles south of Tuscaloosa, Alabama. There stand a group of thirty-five mounds, roughly arranged in a square, and forming one of the largest prehistoric cultural centers in the Southeast. The name of the nearest town, of course, is Moundville.[12]

The mounds cover approximately one hundred and sixty acres, and the largest, occupying a central position, rises more than fifty-eight feet. Most of them are pyramids with flat tops. They were constructed as raised bases for the domiciles of important persons, sacred temples, and council buildings.

Houses of the villagers were scattered throughout the area surrounding the mounds. These dwellings were twenty to thirty feet square. The walls were built of small poles interwoven with matting and plastered with mud. The roofs were thatched. Storage and garbage pits were dug both inside and outside the houses. Dead were interred in shallow graves at various places throughout the village, and some were buried under house floors, a custom that was still followed by some southern Indians in historic times. Burial offerings, such as pottery vessels, stone and bone implements, beads and copper and shell ornaments have been found in the graves. In all, more than three thousand burials, a thousand unbroken pottery vessels, and thousands of implements and ornaments have been found at Moundville.

Excavations at stratified sites in the region have placed Moundville in its proper chronological position in the archeology of the Southeast. Evidence has been found to show the presence of a hunting people belonging to the Paleo-Indian Period. One bluff shelter examined by the University of Alabama provided a radiocarbon date of 9,640 years for the deepest level. Surface finds have been made of fluted projectile points similar to those used more than ten thousand years ago

---

* Perhaps the cultures known as Alexander, Candy Creek, Hamilton, Early Macon, Savannah River, Deptford, and others.

by hunters in New Mexico and Colorado. In stratified sites along the Tennessee River archeologists have recovered artifacts of a hunting–food-gathering people who built their homes on huge shell mounds, whose implements were crudely made, whose cooking vessels were cut from stone, and who had no knowledge of pottery. Superimposed on the remains left by these earliest people were village layers containing evidence indicating that agriculture had been practiced and that a more sedentary way of life was followed.

On top of these primary and intermediate levels are the remains of a highly developed cultural era, an era in which aboriginal art attained its zenith, and handsomely executed pottery as well as bone, stone, and shell work illustrate the presence of a highly artistic and imaginative people. These are artifacts of the Middle Mississippi Period to which Moundville belongs.

The Middle Mississippi Indians were probably the best potters in eastern North America. Countless types of vessels were made, ranging from utilitarian bowls, to shallow plates, to high-necked water bottles. Painted ware was not uncommon, but the finest designs were made by engraving. Many attractive conventionalized designs symbolizing the sun and wind, and drawings of feathered serpents, eagles, fish, frogs, animal and human forms were portrayed by this method. Depictions of the human hand and eye, as well as skulls and arm bones, were engraved on some of the vessels.

Comparable representations of southeastern Indian art have been found at few other places. Types that are rare in many areas are common at Moundville, and even a few pottery forms and designs that have not been recovered elsewhere have been found there. It would not be a careless deduction to assert that Moundville was an outstanding cultural center, and that outlying tribes and groups borrowed Moundvillian techniques or made trades for Moundville products.

Throughout much of the Southeast during the time the Middle Mississippi Culture flourished—probably in its later stages—individual tribes and affiliated groups maintained agricultural projects termed "chief's fields." Unlike the Natchez, however, the chiefs of these peoples did not wield absolute authority. They were more like elected officials and could be removed from office by popular mandate. Driver [13] states that either a chief or his lieutenants "gave orders for all able-bodied men and women to work in the public (or chief's) fields, and criers walked through the towns and villages to call out the man and woman power. The produce from these fields did not become the personal property of the chief, but was stored in a public granary. While the chief's immediate family subsisted on the results of this community enterprise and did no physical labor themselves, they were also obligated to feed foreign guests as well as needy local families from public stores. Food for public ceremonies also came from the same store-houses. The role of the chief, then, was that of a custodian of a public reserve of food."

Tobacco played an important part in the culture. Every medicine bundle contained a sacred pipe and tobacco. The bundle's custodian, a shaman or priest, taught the rituals in which it was used to a neo-phyte, who eventually would succeed him. Pipes were smoked on nu-merous other occasions, such as council meetings, and were a vital part of peace-pact negotiations.

Stone sculpture was a highly developed art of the Middle Mississippi Culture. Pipe bowls were decorated with sculpted animals and humans, beautifully wrought and polished. Archeologists have recovered stone statuettes of human figures two feet in height. Meso-American influ-ence is apparent in stone carvings, in engraved shell decorations, and in ornaments made from sheets of copper and mica. The copper was cold-hammered, and the craftsmanship demonstrated had no equal north of southern Mexico.

A table of the prehistoric cultures of Georgia, the Carolinas, Vir-ginia, Kentucky, and Tennessee would show a chronology similar to those of Alabama, as well as some areas to the north and west. A single exception, however, should be noted. In a shell midden of the Savan-nah River swamp in southeastern South Carolina archeologists discov-ered the oldest pottery yet to be found in the area of the United States.* It was given the name of Stallings Island, and was approximately four thousand five hundred years old. Other discoveries of the same type of pottery have been made at other places in the Savannah River drainage region and along the coast of Georgia.

The people were there, throughout the entire Southeast, from the dim ages of the Pleistocene until the white man destroyed both their cultures and them. They progressed from hunters using the crudest stone weapons to outstanding craftsmen and artists, from wandering bands with loose social customs and no form of organized government to people ruled by highly sophisticated economic and political systems.

As for Moundville itself, it was not the scene of this extended cul-tural evolution, but it was the scene of a perpetuation of the highest stage of the Middle Mississippi Culture.

It was uninhabited when the first white settlers appeared in the area. What caused the abandonment of this magnificent cultural center is not known, and unless future archeological work unearths some clues to the mystery, the last chapter of its long history cannot be written.

---

* See *Unknown Voyagers* in Part Two.

Sioux: a Broken Family

Most people undoubtedly think of the Sioux as a large and warlike western tribe. They were that, but not until the period of recorded history had begun in several parts of North America. And many of them never saw the northern plains and mountains which became the final homeland of this great people before Americans, with unconscionable deceit, greed, and brutality, finally crushed them.

With the exception of the Algonquian, the Siouan tribes at one time comprised the largest linguistic family in the region of the United States. The name Sioux, by which they have become known in history, was not a name by which any of the numerous branches of this immense family identified itself. The word is an abbreviation of *Nadowessioux,* which in turn is a French corruption of *Nadowe-is-iw,* a name by which the Cheyenne called a western group of tribes and which means "snake" or "adder," and, by metaphor, "enemy" in the peculiar Algonquian dialect which the Cheyenne spoke.

The prehistoric migrations of the Siouan people, which resulted in numerous separations, remain for the most part unsolved, and probably insoluble, mysteries. Numerous conflicting theories have been advanced by ethnologists. Some students think that in a remote period various sections of the stock dispersed from the region inhabited by the Winnebago (also a Siouan tribe), near Green Bay, Wisconsin. Others believe the separation occurred at some point north of the Great Lakes. Still others hold the opinion that the primitive home of the Sioux was on the Atlantic Seaboard, whence they spread outward, some going to the Ozarks, some down the Ohio to cross the Mississippi and settle in the middle plains, some to Wisconsin and Minnesota.

Traditions recorded by early investigators give a measure of support to these theories, but the evidence is circumstantial, and the best that can be said of it is that Siouan tribes are known to have been living in these places when the historical curtain was first raised to reveal them.

How or when the Sioux entered the Southeast—or if it was their original homeland—are facts that scientific endeavor has been unable to ascertain. Yet it has been established that when the earliest Europeans touched along the Atlantic coastline Siouan tribes comprised one of the most powerful groups in the entire region between Florida and Virginia.

If it cannot be stated how many centuries, or millennia, they had inhabited this territory, it can be said that there were at least twenty-

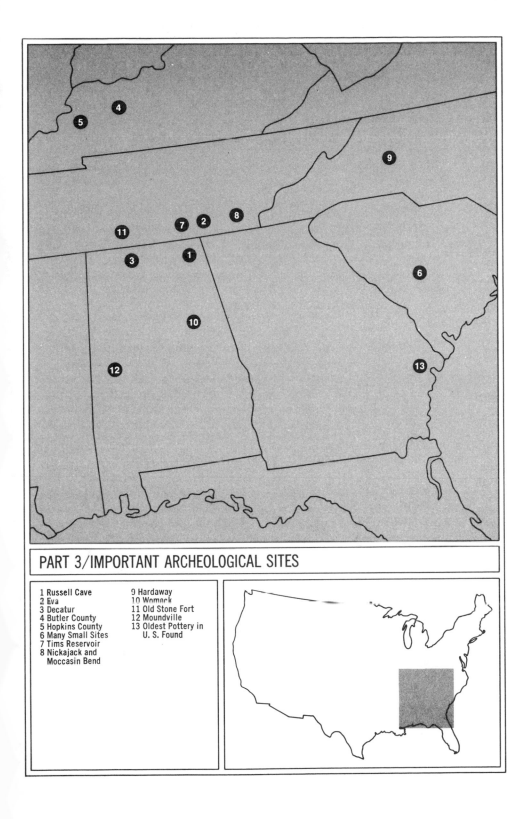

PART 3/IMPORTANT ARCHEOLOGICAL SITES

1 Russell Cave
2 Eva
3 Decatur
4 Butler County
5 Hopkins County
6 Many Small Sites
7 Tims Reservoir
8 Nickajack and
  Moccasin Bend

9 Hardaway
10 Womack
11 Old Stone Fort
12 Moundville
13 Oldest Pottery in
   U. S. Found

five identifiable Siouan tribes scattered through the area of four south-eastern states.*

These were:

South Carolina: Catawba, Congaree, Peedee, Santee, Sewee, Sugaree, Waccamaw, Wateree, Waxhaw, Winyaw.

West Virginia: Moneton.

North Carolina: Cape Fear Indians, Cheraw, Eno, Keyauwee, Sha-kori, Sissipahaw, Woccon, Yadkin.

Virginia: Manahoac, Monacan, Nahyssan, Occaneechi, Saponi, Tu-telo.

The story of the southeastern Sioux, as it has come down through tribal traditions and reports of the first white men to know them, is one of endless setbacks and tragedies that brought inescapable amal-gamations, expulsions, and defeats, and resulted in the early extinction of some of the tribes. Later peoples who rose to power in the South, and whose cultures were radically different from that of the Sioux, re-garded them "not with routine intertribal animosity, but with a loath-ing not to be appeased short of extermination." [14] Incessant attacks were conducted against both them and their Algonquian neighbors by Muskhogean and Iroquoian tribes. Under these unrelenting pressures, to which must be added diseases introduced by Europeans, they rap-idly decreased in numbers. Some fled to unknown destinations. Some united with relatives. Some found havens among enemy tribes, even as far north as Canada. Some stood their ground to the end and were destroyed.

The southeastern Siouan tribes were organized internally into clans with maternal descent. They practiced head-flattening and tattooing, wore their hair long, and permitted professional prostitution, all cus-toms which at least some of their enemies abhorred. Both the Sioux and the Algonquians conducted extremely harsh initiation ceremonies for young persons. According to Driver,[15] no other ceremonies of this extreme character have been reported anywhere else in Anglo-America east of the Pueblos in New Mexico. He states that the Siouans had a separate tribal initiation for adolescent girls, and that the Algon-quians of Virginia kept their males of ten to fifteen years of age iso-lated in a specially constructed wilderness structure for nine months, not permitting them to speak with anyone during the entire period, although they were instructed in religious lore during their confine-ment.

An Englishman who lived among eastern Siouan tribes at the period

---

* On the Pascagoula and lower Yazoo rivers in the Gulf Coast region (Part Two) were two other isolated Siouan tribes, the Biloxi and the Ofo, or Mosopelea, which may have migrated southward respectively from Ohio and Pennsylvania.

of their decline (1701–1710) wrote this account of the initiation ceremonies to which all their young men were subjected: [16]

". . . once a year, at farthest, once in two years, these people take up so many of their young men as they think are able to undergo it, and husquenaugh them, which is to make them obedient and respective to their superiors, and as they say, is the same to them as it is to us to send our children to school, to be taught good breeding and letters. This house of correction is a large, strong cabin, made on purpose for the reception of the young men and boys that have not passed the graduation already; and it is always at Christmas that they husquenaugh their youth, which is by bringing them into this house and keeping them dark all the time, where they more than half starve them. Besides, they give them pellitory bark, and several intoxicating plants, that make them go raving mad as ever were any people in the world, and you may hear them make the most dismal and hellish cries and howlings that ever human creatures expressed; all which continues about five or six weeks, and the little meat they eat is the nastiest, loathsome stuff, and mixt with all manner of filth it is possible to get. After the time is expired, they are brought out of the cabin. . . . Now when they first come out, they are as poor as ever any creatures were; for you must know that several die under the diabolical purgation. Moreover, they either really are, or pretend to be dumb, and do not speak for several days; I think, twenty or thirty, and look so ghastly, and are so changed that it is next to an impossibility to know them again, although you were ever so well acquainted with them before. . . . They play this prank with girls as well as boys, and I believe it a miserable life they endure, because I have known several of them run away at that time to avoid it. Now the savages say if it were not for this, they could not keep their youth in subjection, besides that it hardens them ever after to the fatigues of war, hunting, and all manner of hardship . . . they add that it carries off those infirm weak bodies that would have been only a burden and disgrace to their nation, and saves the victuals and clothing for better people that would have been expended on such useless creatures."

Remnants of the Eastern Sioux

The fate of some of the eastern Siouan tribes has been partially established.

The last that is definitely known of the Manahoac, who had migrated from Virginia to Ohio, is that in 1608 they were at war with the Powhatan and the Susquehanna. Thereafter they disappeared from history under their own name, but they may have lived for some years with the Monacan on the upper James River.

Both the remnants of the Manahoac and Monacan ultimately may have been absorbed by the Saponi and Tutelo. This also may be true of the Nahyssan and Occaneechi tribes, which were driven from their ancient homes by the Iroquois.

The Saponi and Tutelo tribes were forced by enemies to move several times. After attempting to live in numerous places in North and South Carolina and Virginia, they straggled north. It is believed that they separated at Niagara Falls, New York, the Saponi being absorbed by the Cayuga, and the Tutelo going on to oblivion in Canada.

Some of the Cape Fear Sioux were captured and sent to Europe under the pretext that they would be given a Christian education. A remnant of this tribe and of the Peedee were last known to be living in South Carolina.

The Cheraw, suffering attacks from the powerful Iroquois, fled their South Carolina home and took refuge among the Catawba. The Eno of North Carolina also were last heard of among the Catawba, as were the Keyauwee, the Shakori, the Sissipahaw, and the Woccon. However, some members of all these destroyed tribes may have fled to other places.

The fate of the Yadkin is not known.

The Catawba became widely scattered. Some still live in South Carolina. Some intermarried with the Cherokee. Some went with the Choctaw to Oklahoma. The earthly trail of others ended in Arkansas and Colorado.

Over half of the Congaree were sent to the West Indies as slaves, and some of the remainder are believed to have joined fleeing bands of Catawba and other tribes.

The fate of the Santee was similar to that of the Congaree.

The Sewee became victims of the white man's smallpox and alcohol, and vanished.

Warfare all but wiped out the Sugaree.

The last of the Waccamaw, who were decimated by attacks on them, may have been absorbed by Indians of mixed blood mistakenly called Croatan. There was no tribe with that name.

The Wateree were another tribe that may have fused with a branch of the Catawba.

Most of the Waxhaw died on the battlefield, but some of them fled to Florida, where historical mention of them is made as late as 1720. Thereafter they vanished.

It is believed that the Winyaw united with the Waxhaw, but there is no acceptable evidence of this.

The Moneton of West Virginia were last heard of in 1674, when they were visited by a trader. Where they went has not been determined.[17]

When Columbus made his first great voyage of discovery, the warfare that ultimately would destroy the eastern Sioux had begun. It would continue for more than two centuries, for they were courageous and not easily subdued. After the establishment of colonial settlements along the southeastern seaboard the rapidity of their decline quickened. But even before that time they were in reality a beaten people. Before the historical period was very old the Southeast was dominated by tribes and confederacies whose populations and military powers were swiftly increasing—the Iroquoian Cherokee and the Muskhogean Chickasaw, Creek, and Choctaw.

Cherokee: Sturdy Mountaineers

The Cherokee occupied the highest region of the Southeast, the thickly forested Appalachian ranges that rise in southwest Virginia, western North and South Carolina, eastern Tennessee, northern Georgia, and northeastern Alabama.[18] They were an immense tribe. The names of nearly two hundred Cherokee towns have been preserved, and although not all of them have been precisely located, it has been learned that they were spread over an enormous area, probably embracing more than forty thousand square miles.

Scientists shake their heads to indicate their perplexity if they are questioned about the origin of the Cherokee. Not even the meaning of the name is known. Yet there are theories about both subjects, and most of them are given credence by Indian traditions and some, if not a desirable amount, of factual evidence.

The tongue of the Cherokee is the most aberrant form of speech of the Iroquoian linguistic family, and thereby hangs a tale.

If the Cherokee language, peculiar as it is, derived from the Iroquois, then logic dictates that at some remote prehistoric period they lived in the region of the Great Lakes. That appears to be an indisputable fact, and it is substantiated not only by language similarities but by tradition perpetuated by countless generations of Delaware Indian historians who recounted tales of their ancestors during the long winter nights of the northern woodlands.

The Delaware was a large and powerful Algonquian tribe. Their ancient homeland was in New York, New Jersey, eastern Pennsylvania, and the state named for them. In times long gone, they say, they fought the Cherokee—their name for them was Talligewi—and defeated them. The warfare lasted through the reigns of three Delaware chieftains before a final victory was achieved. Then Iroquois warriors united with the Delaware to drive the Cherokee south of the Ohio River.[19]

The accuracy of this tradition is indicated by physical evidence. In Ohio, Illinois, Virginia, and Tennessee archeologists have found deposits from which they recovered pipes and other artifacts similar to those used by later southern Allegheny Cherokee, and it is believed that these remains were left by ancient Cherokee retreating slowly southward after their disastrous defeat by the Delaware and Iroquois.[20]

These revelations most probably account for the final migration of the Cherokee, but obviously there were prior migrations, for there is no information suggesting that they were more than temporary residents—that is, perhaps for no longer than a few hundred years—of the northern region. There are some clues, however, which throw small beams of light into the darkness.

More than a dozen names applied to the Cherokee by other tribes have been recorded.[21] Most of them are significantly connotative.

The Tonkawa called them *Tcalke,* and the Tonkawa lived in eastern and central Texas.

The Caddo called them *Shanaki,* and the Caddo lived in northern Texas.

The Wichita called them *Tcerokieco,* and the Wichita lived on the Canadian River in the southern Great Plains.

The Arapaho called them *Baniatho,* and the Arapaho lived on the northern Great Plains.

The Fox called them *Shannakiak,* and the Fox lived on the west side of Lake Michigan.

The Wyandot called them *Ochie'tari-ronnon,* and the Wyandot (Hurons) lived north of the Great Lakes and in the St. Lawrence Valley. It is interesting to note, as well, that the Wyandot, who belonged to the Iroquoian linguistic family, also had two other names for the Cherokee, *Uwatayo-rono* and *Entari ronnon,* which mean, respectively, "cave people" and "mountain people." These appellations provoke the suggestion that they may have come into usage after the Cherokee had gone into the southern Alleghenies.

The Delaware called them *Talligewi,* as mentioned above.

The Catawba (Siouan) called them *Mantera,* and the Catawba lived in South Carolina, North Carolina, and Tennessee.

Another Iroquois name for them was *Oyata'ge'ronon,* and it signified "inhabitants of the cave country."

A line drawn through the prehistoric homelands of these tribes appears to point to only one conclusion: At some very remote period, and perhaps over a very long time, the Cherokee migrated from Mexico northward through the eastern edge of the Great Plains to the region of the Great Lakes, and then eventually were driven back southward and finally ended their long trek in the southern mountains, where they lived at the beginning of historical times.

The eminent archeologist Frank G. Speck [22] believed the great migration of the Cherokee was much longer than I have suggested in my own analysis. He advanced the startling theory that the Cherokee originated in the basins of the Orinoco and Amazon rivers in South America. It was Speck's contention that none of the southeastern tribes, except the Cherokee and possibly their neighbors, the Catawbas, "rimmed their baskets with a thin oak loop bound fast with a hickory fiber withe, a characteristic of baskets made by natives of the Orinoco and Amazon basins." [23] Also, both the Cherokee and the South American Indians employed the double-weave and the chain-and-diagonal pattern.

Speck's theory has not been accepted by many archeologists, and, indeed, his evidence is insufficient to prove his case beyond a shadow of doubt. Yet there are other good reasons why Speck's contentions may not be completely disregarded. Not only people came northward from tropical regions into the area of the United States, but ideas, manufacturing techniques, religious rituals, social and political systems also came north through Mexico. Of that there is ample proof.

As for the name by which the prehistoric Cherokee identified themselves, it was *Ani'Yun'-wiya*. Its meaning: "real people." [24]

SOUTHEASTERN WOODLANDS

Earliest Population Estimates*

Siouan tribes (1600)	22,300	Yuchi (1650)	2,500
Chakchiuma (1650)	1,200	Chowanoc (1650)	1,500
Chickasaw (1600)	8,000	Tuscarora (1600)	5,000
Choctaw (1761)	20,000	Cusabo (1600)	2,800
Tunica (1650)	2,000	Meherrin (1600)	700
Yazoo (in Tunica)		Nottaway (1600)	1,500
Creek Confed. (1700)	22,500	Shawnee (1650)	3,000
Cherokee (1650)	22,000		
Guale (1650)	4,000	TOTAL	119,000

* See Note, Population Table, Part One.

Powhatan: Falls in a Current of Water

Powhatan was the name of a small Algonquian tribe, but more significantly, as far as history is concerned, it was the name of an Indian village that once stood at the falls of the James River, in the present metropolitan area of Richmond, Virginia.

How long the town of Powhatan was inhabited in prehistoric times is not known—probably a great many years, for it occupied an ideal location on the north bank of the river—but that is not a factor important to its story.

The event that would give it prominence in American Indian history, and bring fame to the name Powhatan, did not take place until the year 1607, when the first permanent English settlement in North America was established at Jamestown.

The village of Powhatan was at the time the favorite residence of a powerful chieftain, Wahunsonacock, who ruled a confederacy of some thirty tribes. Most of them were small, probably altogether numbering no more than ten thousand persons, but under normal circumstances a population of this size would include at least fifteen hundred, and possibly two thousand, warriors, a formidable fighting force.

The English settlers were soon made aware that Wahunsonacock was the military, economic, and political lord of a large territory embracing most of tidewater Virginia and the eastern shore of the Chesapeake Bay. It was to their best interests to establish amicable relations with him, and this, at least for a time, they were able to achieve. For convenience they called him Powhatan—it was, of course, easier to say than Wahunsonacock—and in this way all the people subject to him became known as Powhatans.

A member of the Jamestown colony, John Rolfe, had a reason more personal than economic or political for maintaining friendly relations with Powhatan. One of the chief's daughters deeply stirred his emotions. Her name was Pocahontas.

Almost nothing of the origin or early history of the so-called Powhatan Indians has come to light. It is believed they were more closely related to the Delaware, who lived along the coast north of them, than to any of the more northern and western tribes, and they may have derived either directly from them or from the same stem of the linguistic family. The opinion has been expressed that the various tribes which ultimately were drawn into the Powhatan Confederacy, as well as the Algonquian Pamlico, may have migrated individually southward into Virginia, the Pamlico continuing on to the Pamlico River in North Carolina, where they first became known to Europeans.

Knowledge of Powhatan customs, mode of living, and religious ritual, therefore, comes in large part from men who saw them at the beginning of the historical period. One of these was an Englishman, Henry Spelman, who was for a time a prisoner of them. Another is the famous explorer Captain John Smith who, according to legend, was saved from execution by Pocahontas.

Spelman [25] recounted that Powhatan priests shaved the right side of the head, leaving a little lock at the ear, and some of them wore beards.

The other men pulled out facial hairs as fast as they grew. Most men kept the hair on the right side of the head cut short, "that it might not hinder them by flapping about their bowstrings when they draw it to shoott; but on ye other side they let grow and haue a long locke hanginge doune ther shoulder."

From Spelman also comes the information that tattooing was practiced to some extent, especially by the women. Among the "better sort" it was the custom when eating for the men to sit on mats round about the house, to each of whom the women brought a dish, as they did not eat together out of one dish. Regarding their marriage customs, "ye man goes not unto any place to be married, but ye woman is brought unto him wher he dwelleth." If the presents of a young warrior were accepted by his mistress, it was considered that she had agreed to become his wife, and, without any further explanation to her family, she went to his house, which became her home, and the ceremony was ended.

Polygamy, Spelman asserts, was the custom among the Powhatan. A man could have as many wives as he desired, if he could support them. Burial customs varied according to the rank of the deceased. The flesh of dead chiefs was removed and dried, then was wrapped with the bones in a mat, and the bundle placed on a scaffold. The remains of ordinary people were wrapped in skins and interred in deep graves.

The Powhatan believed in a multitude of minor deities, paying worship to any power that was able to harm them beyond their prevention, such as fire, water, lightning, and thunder. They believed in immortality, and also paid obeisance to a kind of chief deity called Okee and carved images of him which were usually used as burial offerings.

Smith, who recorded the names of more than a hundred and sixty Powhatan villages,[26] wrote that "their houses are built like our arbors, of small young sprigs, bowed and tied, and so close covered with mats or the bark of trees very handsomely, that not withstanding wind, rain, or weather they are as warm as stoves, but very smoky, yet at the top of the house there is a hole made for the smoke to go into right over the fire." The houses varied in length from twelve to twenty-four yards, and some were as much as thirty-six yards long, although not of great width. Many of their towns were enclosed in palisades ten to twelve feet in height. Where great security was required, a triple stockade was erected. The Powhatan were competent farmers, cultivating two or three varieties of maize, beans, melons, root vegetables, and several kinds of fruit trees.

The ethnologist Mooney [27] states that the Powhatan computed by the decimal system, and their years "were reckoned by winters, cohonks, as they called them, in imitation of the note of the wild geese, which came to them every winter. They divided the year into five seasons, viz., the budding or blossoming of spring; earing of corn, or roasting-ear time; the summer, or highest sun; the corn harvest, or fall of the leaf; and the winter, or cohonk. Months were counted as moons, without relation to the number in a year; but they arranged them so that they returned under the same names, as the moon of stags, the corn moon, first and second moon of cohonks." The Powhatan divided the day into three parts, "the rise, power, and lowering of the sun." They kept their accounts by knots on strings or by notches on a stick.

John R. Swanton of the Bureau of American Ethnology identified the thirty tribes of the Powhatan Confederacy, some of which are perpetuated in American place names. The tribes were: [28]

Accohanoc	Moraughtacund	Potomac
Accomac	Mummapacune	Powhatan
Appomattoc	Nansemond	Rappahannock
Arrohattoc	Nantaughacund	Secacawoni
Chesapeake	Onawmanient	Tauxenent
Chickahominy	Pamunkey	Warrasqueoc
Chiskiac	Paspahegh	Weanoc
Cuttatawomen	Pataunck	Werowocomoco
Kecoughtan	Piankatank	Wicocomoco
Mattapony	Pissasec	Youghtanund

Some descendants of the Powhatan still survive in or near their ancestral homes, but their story, the recounting of the forces that destroyed their once powerful confederacy, as well as the adventures and romances of Pocahontas, belong entirely to the period of recorded history.

Shawnee: Wanderers

It is improbable that in either prehistoric or historic times any tribe moved, divided, and were reunited more than the Shawnee. They were not an exceptionally large tribe, yet they had a strong influence on the history of eastern and midwestern Indians.

Their movements have been traced to areas of fifteen states of the Union. Except, possibly, in some remote period, they made no mass migration. Groups and subtribes of Shawnee filtered through the midwestern prairies and southeastern mountains for centuries, joining, separating, and rejoining, and living in widely separated locations for long periods.

The earliest Shawnee home that archeologists have discovered—and it is not believed to have been their habitat until relatively late in the prehistoric period—was in Ohio. They seem to have drifted slowly southward over a number of years. When French traders, breaking wilderness trails of the Great Lakes region, first heard of them, the larger part of the Shawnee were living in the Cumberland basin of Tennessee. However, there was also at the same time, in the seventeenth century, a strong colony of them on the middle Savannah River in South Carolina. The intervening country was occupied by the Cherokee, and Mooney [29] thinks it possible that "the Cherokee invited the Shawnee to settle upon their eastern frontier in order to serve as a barrier against the attacks of the Catawba and other enemies in that direction. No such necessity existed for protection on their northwestern frontier." The Catawba were one of the most powerful and hostile of the eastern Siouan tribes. They long engaged in warfare with the Iroquois, Cherokee, Shawnee, and other peoples.

From the Cumberland and Savannah rivers Shawnee trails go out in countless directions—to Alabama, Georgia, Illinois, Indiana, Kentucky, Maryland, Pennsylvania, Missouri, Texas, Virginia, back to Ohio—until the last one came to an end in the mid-nineteenth century in Oklahoma.

There were no better woodsmen, no better hunters, no better fighters, no more intelligent Indians, than the Shawnee.* From the earliest time of which there is an authentic record of them they were feared as warriors by Indians and white men alike. No people struggled with greater ferocity and courage to halt the forces of civilization that were driving the Indians from their ancient homelands.

Of the origin of the Shawnee there is no certain knowledge. Linguistically they belong to the Algonquian family, and their tongue is closely related to the dialects of the Sauk, Fox, and Kickapoo. Shawnee means "southerners." There is no proof, however, that they migrated southward from the Wisconsin region. The branch of the Shawnee who once lived in South Carolina were called Savanna, and the city of Savannah, Georgia, and the Savannah River are named for them.

A tradition of the Delaware may have its roots in truth. According to it, the Delaware, the Shawnee, and the Nanticoke were originally one people. They separated in a remote period, after the traditional expulsion of the Cherokee from their prehistoric homeland. The tradition adds only that the Shawnee "went south." [30]

---

* Some of their leaders, notably Catahecassa (Blackhoof), Tenskwatawa (the Open Door), better known as the Prophet, and his brother, the great Tecumseh (Springs), stand high on the roster of famous American Indians. A Shawnee, Nika, guided La Salle to the discovery of the Ohio River, was a loyal companion and aide of the great explorer on his later journeys of discovery, and made several trips to France with him. Nika was slain by La Salle's murderers in Texas. Shawnee served as guides and hunters with many other early exploring expeditions.

League of Nations

A tradition of the Muskogee indicated that they came into the South-east from the Northwest. It is not a unique tradition, for it appears in the tribal lore of other southeastern peoples, notably the Choctaw and Chickasaw. They and the Muskogee are the three main members of the large Muskhogean linguistic family who inhabited the Deep South of the United States region.

The meaning of the word *muskogee* is as unknown as the origin of the people to whom it was applied as a name. Undoubtedly, as is so often the case, it was given to them by other Indians—perhaps the Shawnee—who spoke a different tongue, for it is not a Muskhogean word.

The Muskogee are better known as Creek, and there are some pos-sible clues to the source of that name. Customarily their villages were built at desirable locations, adjacent to rich agricultural lands, along southern rivers and creeks. There the first white traders found them, and perhaps lacking a tribal name applicable to all of them came to speak of them as "Creeks." That is conjecture, yet it seems to be par-ticularly true of the Muskogee towns that stood along Ochesee Creek (Ocmulgee River) in Georgia. This was one of the first areas in which English traders established contact with them.

However, they were there and in other southern localities centuries before that time. It is not improbable that they migrated in some re-mote period from northern woodlands that became dominated by Al-gonquian peoples. That cannot be proven, but archeologists have de-termined that the culture of the Creeks, as we shall call them hence-forth, belongs to the late Mississippian, or Temple Mound, stage. They were among the last people to maintain their temple mound structures into the historical period.

Long before the coming of the Spaniards, who were the first Euro-peans to enter their country, Creek towns were spread all the way from the Atlantic coast of Georgia and the vicinity of the Savannah River to central Alabama.[31] The Muskogee group seem to have been gifted with an inherent genius for organization. By persuasion and political guile, if not by military prowess, they created a nucleus of tribes out of which ultimately evolved the large and powerful "league of na-tions" known as the Creek Confederacy.

The dominant Muskogee gradually brought into amalgamation the Apalachicola, Hitchiti, Okmulgee, Sawokli, Chiaha, Asochi, Yuchi, Alabama, Tawasa, Pawotke, Muklasa, Koasati, Tuskegee, and sections of the Shawnee, Guale, and Yamasee. In addition, numerous broken bands and family groups from various parts of the South were drawn into the confederation. Any estimate of the population of the prehistoric Creek Confederacy would be worthless.*

The Creek Confederacy was not ruled by a permanent central government. Its structure was a combination of both democratic and communistic principles. Several of the main southern tribes, as Cotterill notes,[32] managed "to reconcile a system of economic communism with a retention of individual liberty—a combination that no modern society has been able to effect. They did this by reducing their government so nearly to anarchy that it operated only by practically unanimous consent, and, consequently, had no dissident minorities to restrain." Each town—and there may have been in excess of three hundred Creek towns when the confederacy was at the height of its power—had its civil and war leaders, but they were elective and could be removed. Among the Creeks, as among the Choctaw and Chickasaw, "the unit of government was the town with its elective, permanent civil chief and elective, temporary war chief. The town chiefs composed the national council, which met generally twice a year, in May (when vegetables were plentiful) and in September (when the grain was harvested). Then, with elaborate ceremony and prolific oratory, it declared the national policy and occasionally made a law. There is little evidence that prior to contact with the Europeans any southern Indian tribes had a head chief or even regional chiefs. . . . The decisions of the national council did not bind any town which chose to dissent; even the decrees of the town council bound no individual who wished to disobey. Notwithstanding this virtual absence of authority, life among the Indians was perhaps as tranquil as among the white people. Civil wars were almost unknown; the abnormality of murder is shown by the horror in which it was held; civil disputes were settled by arbitration. . . . The paradox of anarchy and order is, of course, to be explained by the strength of custom which regulated conduct and disregard of which made the Indian a pariah." [33]

Under this political system Creek lands belonged to the tribe as a whole. There was no such thing as private ownership of land.† Private ownership of crops, however, was permitted, but each owner was re-

---

* The Indians who would be called Seminole left the lower Creek towns and migrated southward into Florida in historical times. The word "seminole" has been variously interpreted as "one who has camped out from the regular towns," as "runaway," and as "pioneers." In Florida these Creeks were united with the Oconee, who also had come south from Geogia. The Oconee became the nucleus of the Seminole Nation, for which they furnished strong leaders. Later the Seminole were joined by Muskogee, Alabama, Yamasee, and Yuchi people. All eventually lost their individual identity and became mixed bloods under the name Seminole. These events do not belong to the prehistoric period.

† True of most tribes in the United States.

quired to contribute to a reserve for public use. The individual was assured of his civil rights by a peculiar form of democracy, and "freed by communism from ambition to acquire wealth as anarchy freed him from temptation to seek power." [34]

The average Creek woman was short of stature, but well-formed. Many of the men stood over six feet in height, were slender, lithe, erect, and graceful in their movements. "They were proud, haughty, and arrogant; brave and valiant in war." [35] The customary prehistoric dress consisted chiefly of blankets and skins. The blankets were "like shawls, some of them made from the inner bark of trees, and others of grass resembling nettles, which, by treading out, becomes flax. The women use them for covering, wearing one about the body from the waist downward and another over the shoulder with the right arm left free . . . the men wear but one, which they carry over the shoulder in the same way, the loins being covered with a braguerire of deer skin. . . . The skins are well dressed the colour being given them that is wished, and in such perfection, that when of vermillion, they look like very fine red broad cloth, and when black, the sort in use for shoes, they are of the purest. The same hues are given to blankets." [36]

Another early visitor of the Creek wrote that both men and women wore "match coats" made of hair, furs, feathers, and cloth that "are very pretty, especially some of them, which are made extraordinarily charming, containing several pretty figures wrought in feathers, making them seem like a fine flower silk shag; and when new and fresh, they become a bed very well, instead of a quilt. Some of another sort are made of hair, raccoon, beaver, or squirrel skins, which are very warm. Others are made of the green part of the skin of mallard's head, which they sew perfectly well together. . . ." [37]

Tattooing was widely practiced, but one of the first white men to encounter the Creek thought that "the most beautiful painting . . . is on the skin and bodies of their ancient chiefs and micos, which is of a bluish, lead, or indigo, color." Often every part of the body from head to foot was "beautifully depicted or written over with hieroglyphics: commonly the sun, moon, and planets occupy the breast; zones or belts, or beautiful fanciful scrolls, wind round the trunk of the body, thighs, arms, legs, dividing the body into many fields or tablets, which are ornamented or filled up with innumerable figures, as representations of animals or battle with their enemy . . . and a thousand other fancies. These paintings are admirably well executed, and seem to be inimitable. They are performed by exceedingly fine punctures, and seem like mezzotinto, or very ingeneous impressions from the best executed engravings." [38]

Creek villages varied in size from twenty to a hundred houses erected about a public square. Each town had a meeting house, a ceremonial center, and a public playground. The dwellings were "covered with dry grass; then upward they are roofed with cane after the fashion of tiles. They are kept very clean: some have their sides so made of clay that they look like tapia . . . every Indian has a winter house [room section] plastered inside and out, with a very small opening. . . . He has likewise a house for summer and near it a kitchen, where fire is made and bread baked. Maize is kept in barbacoas, which is a house with wooden sides like a room, or raised aloft on four posts and has a floor of canes . . ." [39]

Driver [40] states that the Creeks had a "tendency to rank lineages and sibs, but it was not carried far enough to produce social classes. Warriors were divided into three grades, but these statuses were based entirely on war record, not on heredity." The high rank of the ceremonial leaders "was achieved only after learning the long and complex rituals of the tribe. War prisoners were taken, but the men were generally tortured to death [*] and the women and children assimilated. Prostitutes were known in historic times, at least, and formed a low-ranking group, but hardly a social class. Therefore, the Creeks had a rather well-defined system of rank, based primarily on achievement and only secondarily on heredity, but there were no definite social classes."

Certain aspects of Creek religious ritual may be likened to those of two widely separated regions, leaving ethnologists with questions that keep them awake nights. Each summer the Creek held their greatest annual ceremony, the Green Corn Dance. An immense fire was built in each village, and from it every housewife took coals for her hearth. This is reminiscent of Meso-American customs. And like the Navajo of the Southwest, Creek religious specialists "performed fixed rituals and uttered verbatim prayers at public ceremonies in the temples . . ." [41]

Perhaps the most extraordinary feature of the Creek religion, however, was the absolution granted wrongdoers during the Green Corn Dance. Every past offense except murder was forgiven, and all offenders —some of whom concealed themselves in the woods until time for the ceremony—were reinstated in the good graces of the tribe and their sins were thereafter no longer of concern to others. Here, as Driver so appropriately remarks, was "a remarkable concession for people steeped in a tradition of blood feuds and 'eye for an eye and tooth for a tooth' notions of justice. It meant that a measure of internal peace had been brought to irritable, vengeful personalities."

It meant, also, that tribal unity, communal solidarity, and internal harmony were paramount in the reasoning of the remarkable Creek, for they were not a single tribe ruled by a despot whose word was law, but a group of many small tribes who needed each other to survive. [42]

---

[*] This was true of the Shawnees and other southern tribes.

Chickasaw: the Fierce Independents

They were the Chickasaw, but the significance of their name, or how they acquired it, are questions for which there are no answers. Language and customs indicate that they and the Choctaw are one people, and although this probability is not without legendary support it is without confirmation by indisputable evidence. Traditions of both tribes maintain that they migrated together to the Southeast from the West at some remote prehistoric period, but at this point their history becomes concealed in the vault of ignorance. They have no knowledge, nor even a belief, as to where or when they crossed the Mississippi River, and they can proffer no clues that might possibly point to the region of their origin.

At some time after they had reached the Southeast a quarrel took place which resulted in their division, and of the factuality of this tradition there can be no doubt. While the nature of the dispute may not be stated with certainty, there are factors which strongly suggest the causes that gave rise to it. These factors are to be found in the conflicting characteristics and qualities which smoldered in the Choctaw-Chickasaw people—whether they were one tribe or not does not matter—and at last burst into unquenchable fires of dissent and enmity.

Those who would come to be known as Choctaw were influenced by customs of older inhabitants of the southern forests, the Siouan people, the customs of wearing the hair long, flattening the heads of infants, picking flesh from the bodies of the dead.[43] Also, they preferred a semi-sedentary life and were pre-eminently agriculturalists.

Those who would come to be known as Chickasaws looked with scorn and contempt on these ways of life, and would tolerate none of them. They demanded complete freedom to roam and hunt at will through the immense trackless woodlands, mountains, and prairies. Their restlessness was uncontrollable. They were wild, intractable warriors possessed of an intense dislike for an orderly life within the confines of towns. They were fighters, not hoe farmers. They were raiders living with an enduring dream of new conquests and battlefield victories.

The schism occurred, and as the years passed it steadily widened, the Chickasaw pervaded by burning hatred and inane spitefulness, until at last they became the implacable and deadly foe of the Choctaw.*

---

* The Chakchiuma were a division of the Chickasaw-Choctaw people, and migrated to the Southeast with them. After the split they sided with the Chickasaw. Their villages were on the Yalobusha and Yazoo rivers in Mississippi and reached eastward between the territories of the Choctaw and Chickasaw as far as West Point. Treacherous warriors, they plotted at one time to join other Indians and French

It is doubtful that the Chickasaw ever knew peace after reaching the Southeast, not because it was not attainable but because they did not want it. They claimed an immense territory and sought to defend it. One of the earliest homes for at least a part of the tribe was along the Tennessee River in northern Alabama. Some of them lived in northern Mississippi. They attempted for a time to maintain an outlying colony on the Savannah River in Georgia, but Creeks succeeded in driving them back westward. On the north their territorial claims extended to the confluence of the Tennessee and Ohio rivers, on the northeast into the Cumberland, on the south deep into Alabama and Mississippi, on the west to the Mississippi River. Their main landing place on the Mississippi was at the bluffs that would be named for them, the site of Memphis, Tennessee. From there a trail more than a hundred and sixty miles long led to their villages.

Chickasaw towns grew without a semblance of order. In some places they were strung out for several miles, always along a stream. Any form of urban living was not for them. They wanted space between their dwellings. Their independence extended into every phase of their daily lives.

Although they established territorial boundaries that other tribes were forbidden to cross, the Chickasaw did not confine their own activities within them. Indeed, the opposite was true. They were aggressors incapable of being satisfied. Raiding was a way of life, and conquering was the greatest achievement of which a man was capable. They were almost constantly involved in conflicts with their congeners, the Choctaw, and their neighbors, the Creek, the Cherokee, and the Shawnee. If they were not at war with one or more of these tribes they went farther afield, making long incursions to the north and across the Mississippi to plunder the Illinois, the Kickapoo, the Osage, the Quapaw, and others.

Although they were intrepid, clever, and vicious fighters, they sustained serious losses in battle. Yet their number is believed to have remained almost at a constant level. This was accomplished by the assimilation of numerous small tribes they subdued. The result was that early in the historical period they became a people of greatly mixed blood. At the beginning of colonial times scarcely a person of pure Chickasaw blood could be found, and traders had given them the nickname of the Breeds.

The decline of the Chickasaw can be traced to the beginning of the great conflict for control of interior North America. Probably because English traders had established themselves in their country before the

---

in an attack on their own people. Forewarned of the diabolical scheme, the Chickasaw all but exterminated them, and the tribe soon lost its identity.

settlement of Louisiana, the Chickasaw sided with Great Britain. Attempts by the French to make peace with them were futile. As practically all of the tribes surrounding them were devoted to the French, the Chickasaw suffered severely in consequence of the final English victory.

Following the Revolutionary War, the Chickasaw sought to maintain amicable relations with the newly created nation. But that is a story belonging to the history of America's westward expansion.[44]

Tunica: Those Who Are the People

Several small tribes who spoke dialects of the peculiar Tunican language dwelt on the lower Yazoo River and at various times on both sides of the Mississippi, in the state of that name as well, and in the extreme northeastern part of Louisiana.* Their origin is unknown, and it may be that they had inhabited this region since the Archaic Period, or even earlier in prehistoric times.

The main tribe of this group was the Tunica, after which the linguistic family has been named. Affiliated with them were the Yazoo and the Koroa, and there may have been other bands which do not merit tribal distinction. The story of the Tunica, as it unfolded in the early historical period, differs from that of the Yazoo and the Koroa, who shared a common fate.

If the Tunican language was known to scientists before late in the nineteenth century, no words of it had been recorded. In 1886 the distinguished linguist Albert S. Gatchet of the Bureau of American Ethnology made the initial study of it, fortunately being able to interview some descendants of Tunican stock who knew something of their native tongue. As he reported,[45] the Tunican language "is vocalic and harmonious, rich in verbal forms and possessing also a declension of the noun, and, what is more remarkable, nominal and pronominal gender. It appears to have no genetic connection with any other family of languages."

The word *tunica* means "those who are the people," but the significance of the words *koroa* and *yazoo* has never been discovered.

When European explorers first heard of the Tunica they were living on the west bank of the Mississippi, although there is reason to believe that at an earlier time their villages were on the other side of the river, in Tunica County, Mississippi. They were industrious, specializing in making salt, which they traded to surrounding tribes. One of the first accounts of them stated that Tunica women "made an excellent fabric

---

* See Part Two, Language Groups Box, for names of other Tunican tribes.

of mulberry cloth; there was a fair division of labor between the sexes; the men cultivated the soil, planted and harvested the crops, cut the wood and brought it to the cabin, and dressed the deer and buffalo skins; the women performed the indoor work and made pottery and clothing; polygamy was rare among them." [46]

If the Tunica were hard workers and tillers of the soil, their nature was unpredictable and they showed themselves to be totally untrustworthy as friends. In the early historical period, for an unknown reason, but perhaps because of pressure from stronger people, not improbably the Chickasaw, they abandoned their villages on the Yazoo River near the present Vicksburg. As refugees they were received by the Houma, who then resided on the Mississippi opposite the mouth of Red River in northern Louisiana.

The Tunica repaid this kindness by falling upon the Houma and killing half of them. They then appropriated the Houma town and occupied the region for some years.

Strong supporters of the French, the Tunica suffered heavy losses in the colonial wars from tribes friendly to the English. Thereafter they gradually scattered, a few continuing to live in Louisiana, a few in Texas, a few in Oklahoma, a broken and nearly extinct tribe.

The earliest known home of the Koroa was in the interior of northeastern Louisiana. They also lived on the lower Yazoo and on the Mississippi. No geographical feature commemorates their existence. In this respect, if not in destiny, the Yazoo fared somewhat better.

Unlike the Tunica, the Koroa and the Yazoo elected to cast their fortunes with the Natchez in an attack on a French fort on the Yazoo. This unwise choice resulted in bringing tribes allied with the French down upon them, and they suffered disastrous losses. The survivors found a haven with the Choctaw, and vanished from history.[47]

Tuscarora: They Could Go Home Again

When the curtain went up on the drama of North Carolina's bloody history the Tuscarora were found living on the Roanoke, Tar, Pamlico, and Neuse rivers. How many centuries they had occupied this wide region probably will always remain a secret. Not even they themselves were able to offer a tribal tradition to the first Europeans who encountered them that would suggest a possible solution.

But of one thing they were certain: the Southeast was not the land of their origin. If they had no knowledge as to when they had reached it, they knew the direction from which they had come. It was north.

And of this there can be no doubt. For their language belongs to the Iroquoian linguistic family. But when they separated from the Iroquois of New York and the Great Lakes region, or why, remains a mystery scientists have never been able to unravel.*

The word *tuscarora* only further obscures the question. It derives from *ska-ru-re^n*, by which they identify themselves, and it means "hemp-gatherers." Obviously, Tuscarora is a name they acquired by an unknown means *after* their towns stood along the North Carolina rivers. This seems to be made apparent by the fact that they were celebrated far and wide among other peoples for their skillful and numerous uses of the *Apocynum cannabinum*, the genus of the dogbane family better known as Indian hemp. From it they obtained fibers for clothing, bases for medicinal and narcotic compounds, emetics, and cathartics. It appears unquestionable that the Tuscarora had another name when they lived in the North, but they had long forgotten it by the time the first white men encountered them.

The story of the Tuscarora comprises one of the great tragedies of American Indian history. A recounting of it will not be undertaken here, for it is beyond the scope of this work. However, a note about it may be in order. Enslaved, robbed, deceived, cheated of their possessions, denied their civil rights, kidnapped, imprisoned, and wantonly slain, first by the British and then by Americans, they became the instigators of two bloody wars against unconscionable white colonists that raged for years throughout the Carolinas. Defeated and facing annihilation, they made futile pleas to authorities for mercy.

When all hope of survival was gone, they turned their faces toward the north. Through Virginia, through Pennsylvania, they straggled in ragged starving bands, constantly harassed and brutally driven on by white men, denied any degree of kindness, compassion, or protection. At last they reached the country of their ancient kinsmen, the Iroquoian Seneca and Oneida, and they were made welcome as long lost brothers.

They could go home again.

Choctaw: Long Hair and Flat Heads

A tradition of the Choctaw relates that they migrated to the Southeast from the Far West when they and the Chickasaw were one tribe. That much of it is in accord with the origin myth of the Chickasaw, but the Choctaw embellish their story with factors that suggest Christian influence. The infiltration of this doctrine may be explained initially in the fact that the first white men to live among the Choctaw were missionaries; second, in the reasoning that dramatic biblical tales

---

* Two other smaller Iroquoian tribes were found living in Virginia at the beginning of the historical period. They were the Meherrin and the Nottaway, who occupied lands on the rivers of the same name.

would have a strong appeal to the fanciful and quixotic Choctaw mind; and, third, in the knowledge that Choctaw legends were not collected and analyzed until late in the nineteenth century.[48]

The odd mixture of biblical and Indian legends provides no clue to possible reality. Some Choctaw told white investigators that on their great migration they were "miraculously guided by a sacred pole, which was carried by their leader during the day and planted by night in their place of encampment. Every morning it was found to be leaning toward the east as a signal for them to continue their journey. . . ." When at last they came to a place called Nanih Waya, the sacred pole "remained in an upright position. In consequence they settled there, built mounds and ramparts, and made it the ceremonial center of their Nation." [49]

Into their versions of the "exodus," and the "pillar of cloud and fire," and the "great flood," and the "reappearance of dry land," the Choctaw blend ingredients compounded of their own fancies. The Choctaw Noah, Oklatabashih, for example, "sent a dove to see if any dry land could be found. She returned with her beak full of grass, which she had gathered from a desert island. Oklatabashih, to reward her for her discovery, mingled a little salt in her food. Soon after this the waters subsided and the dry land appeared; then the inmates of the great boat went forth to repeople another earth. But the dove, having acquired a taste for salt during her stay in the boat, continued its use by finding it in the saltlicks that then abounded in many places. . . ." [50] One day, after having eaten some grass, the dove "unfortunately forgot to eat a little salt as usual. For this neglect the Great Spirit punished her and her descendants by forbidding them forever the use of salt. . . ." Thereafter, each spring the doves continued their sad cooing.

The Choctaw tradition of the ceremonial center of Nanih Waya, however, is less burdened by Christian myths. Moreover, it proffers more credibility, for it existed on headwaters of the Pearl River in Mississippi. Originally it consisted of an immense oblong mound, perhaps fifty feet in height and covering an acre. Surrounding the central structure were smaller mounds, at least one of them used for burials, and the entire complex, which spread over an area of a square mile, was enclosed by strong ramparts ten feet in height and as much as forty feet in width.

Two factors appear to be obvious. The Choctaw were present in the Southeast when the Mississippian Culture developed there, perhaps as early as the eighth or ninth century of the Christian Era. The great compound was not only built as a religious center but was a defensive works to protect the Choctaw against raids upon them by their blood brothers, the Chickasaw, from whom they had separated.

Because of their custom of artificially flattening the heads of infants, the Choctaw were called *têtes plates,* or Flatheads, by early French *voyageurs.* However, they had an older name, unknowingly discovered by the first Spaniards to meet them. The Choctaw wore their hair long. In Spanish documents of the sixteenth century the words *Pafallaya* and *Apafalaya* were applied to a Choctaw "province." They undoubtedly derived from the Choctaw word *pansfalaya,* which means "long hairs."

The Choctaw were not people of large stature, as were some southeastern tribes. Both men and women were handsome and graceful, although the women usually became stout in middle life. While moral standards could not be termed strict, male deviates were held in contempt, and adulterous wives often suffered for their indiscretions. A husband might drive a wayward wife from his home, or he might take her to the public square of the village and there she would be forced to yield in public to any man who chose to have intercourse with her. According to Swanton,[51] an early French visitor who witnessed such a scene was informed that "the way to disgust lewd women is to give them at once what they so constantly and eagerly pursue."

The Choctaw believed in the immortality of the soul, and that the spirit of the deceased lingered near the remains for some days after death. The body of a dead person was wrapped in skins and bark and placed on a scaffold near his or her former home, and beside the corpse "were placed food and drink, a change of clothing, and favorite utensils and ornaments which would be needed by the spirit in its long journey to the other world. A dog was killed to provide the deceased with a companion. . . ."[52] While a similar custom was practiced by numerous Indian peoples, the Choctaw performed an additional rite that was found in the burial ceremonies of few other tribes. It is best described as "bone-picking."

There were among the Choctaw professional male and female bonepickers who were distinctly tattooed, and who "allowed their fingernails to grow long for their revolting occupation."[53]

Debo[54] relates that a body remained upon a scaffold for a fixed period, varying in length from one to six months, and during this time the "relatives frequently resorted to the foot of the platform to wail and mourn, although in warm weather the stench from the decomposing body became so intolerable that the women sometimes fainted. . . ." Swanton[55] states that the Choctaw also followed the "custom of setting up poles around the new graves, on which they hung hoops, wreaths, etc., to aid the spirit in its ascent."

And Debo adds that when the body "had remained upon the scaffold the specified time, a bone-picker was summoned, and all the relatives and friends were invited for the last rites. These mourners surrounded the scaffold, wailing and weeping, while the grisly undertaker ascended the platform, and with his long fingernails thoroughly cleansed the bones of the putrefied flesh. The bones were then passed down to the waiting relatives, the skull was painted with vermillion, and they were carefully placed in a coffin. . . . The flesh was left on the platform, which was set on fire; or it was carried away and buried. The hamper of bones was borne with much ceremonial wailing to the village bone house. . . . There it was placed in a row with other coffins, and the mourners all returned to the house [of the dead person's family], where all participated in a feast over which the bone-picker presided (without having washed his hands, as shocked white observers were wont to state)." [56]

The Choctaw were the most competent farmers in the Southeast. Their economy was based on agriculture, supplemented by fishing and hunting. Their society was divided into two phratries, each of which contained several gentes. While members of moieties did not live separately, marriage of a man and a woman belonging to the same moiety was forbidden. Oddly, a father had no authority over his own children, who were under the control of their oldest maternal uncle. Descent was in the female line, and the chieftainships that were hereditary passed from uncle to nephew rather than from father to son. The names of some hundred Choctaw villages have been preserved, although the exact location of some of them has not been established.

The Choctaw were by nature probably the most peaceful Indians in the Southeast, yet they were almost constantly involved in defensive wars. Their most persistent attackers were the Chickasaw and the Creek. If they were not aggressive, however, they were not timid. When war was forced upon them they were capable fighters.

The Choctaw could not escape becoming involved in the struggles between the European powers, and they suffered greatly as a result. The Americans completed the destruction begun by the Spanish, British, and French. Another historical note seems to be appropriate. After being forced to cede their lands in Mississippi and Alabama and to move to Oklahoma, the Choctaw established their own government. Modeled after that of the United States, and termed a "republic," it endured until early in the present century, when it and the similar political organizations of the other four so-called civilized tribes—the Cherokee, Chickasaw, Creek, and Seminole—were absorbed by the state of Oklahoma.[57]

Chowanoc: Mistaken Trust

The story of the Chowanoc can be briefly told. They belonged to the Algonquian linguistic family, but their origin is unknown. Their name means "people at the south," and when they were first met by white men, about 1584, they lived on the Chowan River in North Carolina. At the time they were the most powerful Algonquian tribe south of the Powhatan.

About a century later, in 1663, they entered into a treaty under which they submitted to the English Crown. The document marked the beginning of their decline. In less than a decade they were forced by the unjust treatment inflicted upon them by colonists to take to the warpath. Defeated after a year of fighting, they were allotted twelve square miles of land, but greedy whites soon managed to take half of it away from them.

Still hoping for justice, they sided with the colonists in the war against the Tuscarora. For this assistance they were rewarded by being forced to live with the Tuscarora on a small reservation, and they saw no alternative but to incorporate with their former enemy. The merger took place in 1773. Twenty-two years later the governor of North Carolina reported that only five Chowanoc, two men and three women, were known to be alive.[58]

Claims to Distinction

Cusabo may mean "Coosawhatchie River people," the stream on which some of them lived, but it also may be a collective term used to designate a group of small tribes of the Muskhogean linguistic family who dwelt in prehistoric times along the South Carolina coast between Charleston Harbor and the Savannah River, as well as for some distance inland in the Ashley, Edisto, Ashepoo, Combahee, Salkehatchie, and Coosawhatchie valleys.

These peoples were, besides the Cusabo, the Coosa, Etiwa, Wando, Kiawa, Stono, Edisto, Ashepoo, Combahee, Wimbee, and Escamacu. They may have been offshoots of the great Muskhogean tribes of the Southeast, and may have come from the West with them or may have migrated eastward at an earlier or later period. However, there is no evidence, not even a tradition, to substantiate either of these theories. Indeed, there is nothing but their language to suggest their possible origin.

Although earlier navigators had sailed along the South Carolina coast and may have seen some Cusabo—as I shall call the group—it was not until 1521 that they made their first appearance in history. In that year Lucas Vázquez de Ayllón anchored his ship in a harbor in Cusabo territory. He was given a friendly welcome, and "introduced the blessings of White civilization to the unsuspecting natives by carrying away about seventy of them." [59] He returned happily to Cuba with the captives and sold them profitably as slaves.

Four years later Ayllón sent a second successful slaving expedition to the same area. Meanwhile, living with the dream of finding great treasurers that all *conquistadores* harbored, Ayllón had returned to Spain in quest of a royal patent that would permit him to establish a colony on the southeastern coast. He took with him one of his captives, called Chicora, the name that also had been given to the region he had been the first to enter.

Chicora, a prehistoric Indian until his capture, obviously was gifted with a somewhat remarkable mentality. He not only furnished Spanish historians with considerable factual information about the geography and climate of his country, but he captivated the Spanish Court with glowing fables of the splendors and riches to be found in it.

The land of Chicora, said Chicora, was inhabited by men with long hard tails like alligators. Gold and all manner of precious stones littered the earth. All one had to do to become fabulously wealthy was to gather them in baskets. He would be pleased to furnish the baskets.

If not the first, this was one of the earliest known occasions when an American Indian engaged in a practice that would be used many times later to good advantage. It was that of fabricating tales of a kind they understood white explorers most wanted to hear.

With the aid of Chicora, who wanted nothing as much as to go home, Ayllón got the patent he sought, and he left Spain with a strong expedition of six vessels and five hundred colonists.

The venture was a complete disaster. Chicora's fabulous homeland turned out to be nothing but a forbidding wilderness. In a few cabins thrown up on the Pee Dee or in the neighborhood of the Savannah River, Ayllón and his settlers rapidly fell victims of malnutrition and disease. In the early spring of 1527, only a hundred and fifty were still alive, and these starving human wrecks managed to sail to Haiti, leaving their leader in a Chicora grave.*

Through the gate Ayllón had opened came other slaving expeditions, and within a few years some of the Chicora tribes had all but vanished.

The Cusabo have two claims to distinction. They were the first Indians in the southeastern region to be slaughtered and enslaved, and they were the first among whom European settlements were begun.[60]

---

* Close relatives of the Cusabo were the Guale who dwelt on the Georgia coast between St. Andrews Sound and the Savannah River. Part of them were probably true Creek or Muskogee. The last Ayllón expedition, or at least a part of it, was in or near Guale Country. Eventually most of the Guale became scattered, some fleeing to the Creek, others to the Yamasee, others to Florida. A few continued to live on the coastal islands near St. Augustine until early in the eighteenth century, when they were virtually extinct. If any Guale survived longer in other places, they lost their identity through absorption by other tribes.

Language Groups in Part Three

SOUTHEASTERN WOODLANDS

Muskogean:	Chakchiuma	Tunican:	Tunica
	Chickasaw		Yazoo
	Choctaw		
	Alabama	Iroquoian:	Cherokee
	Creek Confederacy		Tuscarora
	(Muskogee)		Meherrin
	Tuskegee		Nottaway
	Apalachicola		
	Chiaha		
	Guale	Algonquian:	Shawnee
	Hitchiti		Chowanoc
	Cusabo		Powhatan

For Siouan tribes in the Southeast,
see **Sioux: A Broken Family,** this part.

Trail of Blood and Death

Hernando de Soto landed his great expedition on the west coast of Florida in May, 1539. The winter was spent in Apalachee, the region in which Narváez had met disaster. As he marched northward with his powerful army of six hundred soldiers and scores of Indian burden-bearers chained to each other in the following spring, De Soto entered country never before known to white men.

Like *conquistadores* before him in the New World, and like others who followed him, De Soto knew a fierce conflict within himself. Discouragement and suspicion lost to unquenchable faith and naïveté. Reality lost to dreams.

When Indians told him of a kingdom farther north that was ruled by a woman of astonishing proportions and incalculable wealth, the place became his immediate goal. The kingdom consisted of a few huts on the Savannah River, and its only wealth was a few freshwater pearls of no value. Moreover, the queen wasn't very large and she was exceedingly unkempt and unattractive.

It was a story repeated over and over again, differing only in locale and minor details. Always great treasures awaited the taking just ahead, sometimes in the very next village. Always the honey was around the next bend of the river. Always paradise lay beyond the next hill. Always tomorrow would bring fulfillment of the white man's dream.

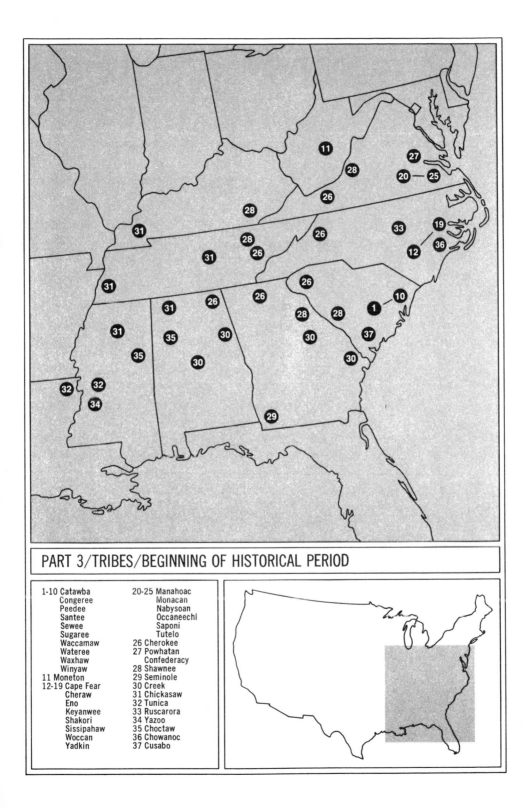

PART 3/TRIBES/BEGINNING OF HISTORICAL PERIOD

1-10 Catawba
    Congeree
    Peedee
    Santee
    Sewee
    Sugaree
    Waccamaw
    Wateree
    Waxhaw
    Winyaw
11 Moneton
12-19 Cape Fear
    Cheraw
    Eno
    Keyanwee
    Shakori
    Sissipahaw
    Woccan
    Yadkin

20-25 Manahoac
    Monacan
    Nabysoan
    Occaneechi
    Saponi
    Tutelo
26 Cherokee
27 Powhatan
    Confederacy
28 Shawnee
29 Seminole
30 Creek
31 Chickasaw
32 Tunica
33 Ruscarora
34 Yazoo
35 Choctaw
36 Chowanoc
37 Cusabo

In the last three years of his life, held in the vise of this irresistible opiate of indestructible hope, De Soto plunged on through the vast expanses of wilderness, on through Georgia, Alabama, Mississippi, Tennessee, crossing the great river he called Rio Grande a short distance below the site of Memphis, on through Arkansas, into Oklahoma, and back again to the Mississippi, to which his body was quietly given. The survivors, led by Luis Moscoso de Alvarado, attempted to escape from the country by land, then turned back to the Mississippi near the mouth of the Arkansas. Descending the river in boats in the summer of 1543, and skirting the Gulf shore of Texas, they reached Panuco, Mexico, in September.

De Soto brought an end to the prehistoric period in the Southeastern Woodlands, encountering many tribes not known to exist. Clashes with determined Indian defenders followed one upon another across the entire southern region of the United States. It was a moving fight of attrition, not of the red peoples but of the invaders. In a rich land the Spaniards lived poorly, but they suffered not only for food of the kinds they knew and craved. They suffered from a steady depletion of spirit, from constantly growing dejection and despondency. Several times they came perilously close to being annihilated by courageous and skillful warriors.

Of a Creek chief, called Tastaluca by a De Soto chronicler,* to whom Moscoso, with a guard of fifteen cavalrymen, was sent to announce the approach of the great white conqueror:

"The cacique [chief] was at home, in a piazza. Before his dwelling on a high place, was spread a mat for him, upon which two cushions were placed, one above another, to which he went and sat down, his men placing themselves around, some way removed, so that an open circle was formed about him, the Indians of the highest rank being nearest to his person. One of them shaded him from the sun with a circular umbrella, spread wide, the size of a target, with a small stem, and having deerskin extended over cross-sticks, quartered with red and white, which at a distance made it look of taffeta, the colors were so very perfect. It formed the standard of the chief, which he carried into battle.

"His appearance was full of dignity: he was tall of person, muscular, lean, and symmetrical. He was the suzerain of many territories, and of a numerous people, being equally feared by his vassals and the neighboring nations. The master of the camp [Moscoso], after he had spoken to him, advanced with his company, the steeds leaping from side to side, and at times towards the chief, when he, with great gravity, and seem-

---

* A misspelling. Tascaluca in the Creek tongue, meaning Black Warrior.

ingly with indifference, now and then would raise his eyes, and look on as in contempt."

Here we have an excellent picture of an Indian leader who a few hours before this scene took place was a prehistoric man, a graphic description of him and his people as they were at the very beginning of the historic period in this section of America. Black Warrior did not rise as Moscoso approached him. After calmly informing the Spaniards that they were welcome, he said curtly:

"It is idle to use many words here, as it is not well to speak at length where a few may suffice. The greater the will the more estimable the deed; and acts are the living witness of truth. You shall learn how strong and positive is my will, and how disinterested my inclination to serve you. . . ." [61]

As De Soto continued to cut his trail of blood and death through the Southeastern Woodlands, the same chronicler—the Gentleman of Elvas, as he signed his account—left other invaluable word pictures.

In 1540 the Mobile, close relatives of the Choctaw, dwelt between the Alabama and Tombigbee rivers. Their leader of the time, Tuscaloosa, who held great influence throughout a large area, inspired the people to attack the Spaniards. A fierce battle for the fortified town of Mabila,* that brought the invaders to the brink of disaster, took place in mid-October.

De Soto dispersed his cavalry at strategic points about the town, ". . . and into each squadron of foot he put a soldier with a brand, to set fire to the houses, that the Indians might have no shelter. His men being placed in full concert, he ordered an arquebuse to be shot off; at the signal the four squadrons, at their proper points, commenced a furious onset. . . . The Indians fought with so great spirit [with spears and arrows against guns] that they many times drove our people back out of the town. The struggle lasted so long that many Christians, weary and very thirsty, went to drink at a pond near by, tinged with the blood of the killed, and returned to combat." De Soto charged into the town on horseback, the buildings were fired, and ". . . then breaking in upon the Indians and beating them down, they fled out of the place, the cavalry and infantry driving them back through the gates, where, losing the hope of escape, they fought valiantly; and the Christians getting among them with cutlasses, they found themselves met on all sides by their strokes, when many, dashing headlong into the flaming houses, were smothered, and, heaped one upon another, burned to death."

An estimated two thousand, five hundred Indian men, women, and children were slaughtered in this fight.

---

* In Greene County, Alabama.

As De Soto was preparing to cross the Mississippi River ". . . the cacique arrived, with two hundred canoes filled with men, having weapons. They were painted with ochre, wearing great bunches of white and other plumes of many colors, having feathered shields in their hands, with which they sheltered the oarsmen on either side, the warriors standing erect from bow to stern, holding bows and arrows. The barge in which the cacique came had an awning at the poop, under which he sate. . . . All came down together. . . ."

Standing on the riverbank, De Soto invited the cacique to land, but without reply he sent three barges containing fish and other foods to the Spaniards. The gifts delivered, the barges moved away, and "the cacique began to draw off from the shore, when the cross-bowmen, who were in readiness, with loud cries shot at the Indians, and struck down five or six of them."

The Indians "retired with great order, not one leaving the oar, even though the one next to him might have fallen, and covering themselves, they withdrew. . . . These were fine-looking men, very large and well formed; and what with the awnings, the plumes, and the shields, the pennons, and the great number of people in the fleet, it appeared like a famous armada of galleys." *

West of the great river, billeted in a walled Indian town called Guachoya,† De Soto "sank into a deep despondency at sight of the difficulties that presented themselves to his reaching the sea; and, what was worse, from the way in which the men and horses were diminishing in numbers, he could not sustain himself in the country without succor. Of that reflection he pined. . . ."

Hoping to obtain the desperately needed supplies, De Soto sent a messenger to another town, Quigaltam, to inform the cacique there that "he was the child of the Sun, and whence he came all obeyed him, rendering their tribute. . . ." The reply he received did nothing to bolster his fading spirits. It was:

"As to what you say of your being the son of the Sun, if you will cause him to dry up the great river, I will believe you: as to the rest, it is not my custom to visit with anyone. . . . If you desire to see me, come where I am; if for peace, I will receive you with special goodwill; if for war, I will await you in my town; but neither for you, nor for any man, will I step back one foot." [63]

A few days later, in the dawn, a contingent of cavalry and infantry

---

* The identity of these superbly disciplined Indians has not been established with certainty. It is not unlikely, however, that they were Kaskinampo, related to the Koasati, the Alabama, the Choctaw, and other Muskhogean people. Swanton thinks they dwelt in the area which De Soto called "Casqui Province," and which he entered immediately after crossing the Mississippi.[62]

† Believed to have stood at a large prehistoric Indian mound near Arkansas City.

swept upon Quigaltam with such swiftness ". . . that they were upon the inhabitants before they could all get out of town. The ground was open field; the part of it covered by the houses, which might be a quarter of a league in extent, contained five or six thousand souls.* Coming out of them, the Indians ran from one to another habitation, numbers collecting in all parts, so that there was not a man [Spaniard] on horseback who did not find himself amidst many; and when the captain ordered that the life of no male should be spared, the surprise was such, that there was not a man among them in readiness to draw a bow.

"The cries of the women and children were such as to deafen those who pursued them. About one hundred men were slain; many were allowed to get away badly wounded, that they might strike terror into those who were absent."

Some Spaniards "were so cruel and butcher-like that they killed all before them, young and old, not one having resisted little or much. . . ." The Indians of the town, "being ferocious and bloodthirsty, God permitted that their sin should rise up against them in the presence of all. . . ."

So began the historical period in the Southeastern Woodlands region of the United States.

Dates to Remember

1521—Lucas Vázquez de Ayllón's first slaving expedition to South Carolina. He discovered the Cusabo tribes and the Guale. Francisco de Gordillo passed along the coast from Florida to South Carolina.

1523—Giovanni da Verrazano, under the French flag, crossed the Atlantic to Carolina, went a short distance south, then turned north.

1524—Esteban Gómez, a Spaniard, sailed southward along the Atlantic coast.

1525—Ayllón's second slaving expedition touched along Georgia and South Carolina coast.

1526—Ayllón attempted to establish settlement in vicinity of Pee Dee or Savannah rivers.

1527—British ship *Mary Guildford* explored southeast coast, reached West Indies.

1539—Hernando de Soto began his treasure search through southeastern wilderness. He was the first to encounter the following tribes: Hitchiti, Creek, Chakchiuma, Chickasaw, Choctaw, Alabama, Mobile, Tuskegee, Chiaha, Yuchi, Cherokee, Tunica, Kaskinampo.

---

* Undoubtedly an excessive number.

1559—Tristán de Luna y Arellano attempted to establish a Spanish colony at Pensacola.

1566—Expedition under Juan Pardo explored Southeast.

1584—Sir Walter Raleigh's first colonizing expedition landed in July on Roanoke Island, North Carolina.

1606—Jamestown, Virginia, founded.

1673—Père Jacques Marquette and Louis Joliet descended Mississippi River to mouth of the Arkansas.

1682—René Robert Cavelier, Sieur de La Salle, descended Mississippi River to Gulf of Mexico, and in April formally established the Province of Louisiana in the name of the King of France.

Scientific Note—Projectile Point Distribution

When ancient projectile points of the same size and construction, or even points bearing strong similarities, are found in widely separated areas, three conclusions may be drawn:

(1) The people who made them were wanderers, or,

(2) Individual craftsmen changed their places of abode for some reason, or,

(3) The points were exchanged and distributed in trade.

It cannot be said of any particular type of point how it was dispersed, but the fact remains that all of them were moved from place to place by one or more of the means cited. This is indisputable evidence that even in the most remote periods of man's existence in the United States region not only were groups in contact but they exchanged both products and technical skills.

Many types of projectile points have similarities, but the following have features (shape, size, fluting, lack of fluting, weight, etc.) which qualify them for individual identity: Folsom, Sandia, Clovis, Eden, Pinto Basin, Gypsum Cave, Midland, Plainview, Meserve, Milnesand, Cody, Scottsbluff, Angostura, Browns Valley, Lake Mohave, Silver Lake, Yuma. There may be others.

The Folsom point was undoubtedly the most widely distributed. True Folsoms, ore types bearing Folsom features, have been found in almost every state of the Union. Notable finds of Clovis points have been made in New Mexico, Arizona, Texas, Nevada, Washington, Oregon, California, Missouri, Massachusetts, Pennsylvania, Ohio, Alabama, Tennessee, and New York, as well as other locations. Angostura points reached Wyoming and Texas from South Dakota. Browns Valley points have been recovered in Minnesota, Wyoming, and Missouri. Sandia points have appeared in New Mexico, Oregon, and Vermont, indicating national distribution.

As far as known, Gypsum Cave, Lake Mohave, Silver Lake, Yuma,

SOME INDIAN PLACE NAMES*

Georgia

Apalachee, river, town
Seminole, town
Chattahoochee, river
Okefenokee, swamp
Cherokee, county
Savannah, city, river
Muscogee, town
Appalachian, mountains
Omaha, town

Tennessee

Yuma, town
Cherokee, lake
Tennessee, state, river
Appalachian, mountains
Shawanee, town
Tuskegee, town
Mississippi, river
Oneida, town
Erie, town
Huron, town

Virginia

Piankatank, river
Chincoteague, town
Wicomico, town
Rappahannock, county, river
Powhatan, county, town
Pamunkey, river
Mattapony, river
Appomattox, county, town, river
Appalachia, town
Appalachian, mountains
Chickahominy, river
Nottoway, county, town, river
Meherrin, town, river
Saluda, town
Zuñi, town
Catawba, town
Chesapeake, bay
Ottawa, town
Lakota, town
Omaha, town

North Carolina

Pensacola, town
Appalachian, mountains
Cherokee, county, town

Tuskegee, town
Catawba, county, town, river
Saluda, town
Chowan, county, river
Eno, river
Hatteras, cape
Neuse, river
Pamlico, county, sound
Haw, river
Saxapahaw, river
Tuscarora, town
Yadkin, county, river
Yadkinville, town
Sioux, town
Arapaho, town

South Carolina

Tucapan, town
Appalachian, mountains
Cherokee, town, county
Catawba, town
Congaree, river
Coosawhatchee, river
Pee Dee, town, river
Saluda, river
Santee, river
Cheraw, town
Enno, town
Enoree, town
Seneca, town

Kentucky

Yuma, town
Appalachian, mountains
Ocala, town
Onelda, town
Mississippi, river
Ohio, river
Omaha, town
Texas, town

West Virginia

Catawba, town
Appalachian, mountains
Powhatan, town
Tioga, town
Miami, county
Kanawha, river
Chesapeake, town
Osage, town

* Tribes and tribal subdivisions.

and Pinto Basin points achieved distribution mainly throughout the Rocky Mountain region, the Southwest, and California. Other types were less widely distributed, but have been found in locations hundreds of miles apart.

These early projectile points should not be called arrowheads, for they were affixed to spears. The spear might have been propelled with the aid of an atlatl, a spear- or javelin-thrower, attached to the hunter's arm. The bow and arrow was not a weapon known to America's first hunting peoples, and did not come into use until a much later period.

Northeastern Woodlands

Ipswich B.C.

On a spring day in 1951 William C. Eldridge, a spare-time collector of Indian relics, arrived at the Peabody Foundation in Andover, Massachusetts, with several projectile points and other stone artifacts. He and his friend, Joseph Vaccaro, had picked them up not far away in a gravel pit near Ipswich.

As archeologists Douglas S. Byers and Fred Johnson examined the collection they were surprised to find some pieces that looked quite different from the usual run of material found in eastern Massachusetts. One in particular, as Byers wrote,[1] caught their attention. It was "a point about two and a half inches long, shaped like a Gothic arch. Not only was it made from stone of a kind such as we had never seen before, but its entire form differed from that of points usually found in New England. Its base was concave, and from it, on either face of the point, a long thin chip led towards the tip."

Eldridge had recovered points known as Clovis fluted,* a type used by hunters of Pleistocene Age mammals more than ten thousand years ago in the southwestern region of the United States. For example, Dr. Emil W. Haury of the University of Arizona informed Byers that if the Ipswich finds and Clovis fluted points recovered among ancient mammoth bones near Naco, Arizona, were mixed together it would not be possible to distinguish them from each other.[2]

Hopes soared in Ipswich. No discovery of fluted points in association with the bones of mammoths, mastodons, giant bison, or other long

---

* See *Visitors at Blackwater Draw*, Part One.

extinct species had been made in the Northeast. Numerous kinds of projectile points had been found in states east of the Mississippi, but most of them had been picked up on the surface. Now one had been exposed by a bulldozer in a gravel pit. It began to look, as Byers said, as if there might be something worthwhile at Ipswich.

His hopes were dashed as swiftly as they had risen. When he and his colleagues surveyed the gravel pit—given the name of the Bull Brook Site because of the proximity of that stream—the geology of the area gave them good cause to be discouraged. The gravel and sand had been carried by water flowing from a melting glacier.

"To our disappointment," Byers recounted, "we found no sign of a buried soil—no darker streak in the sand below the loam and turf, to mark a surface on which the makers of the fluted points could have lived. We made tests of our own; we probed the walls of the pits, and still found no reason to believe that anything more would be found so deep beneath the loam. At any site in the West where such finds have been made, there always seemed to be either traces of a buried land surface, camp refuse and rubbish trodden into a surface on which people had lived, or bones of animals which had been killed. No such signs appeared in these pits, and so we gave it as our considered opinion that although we might have luck enough to find one or two more things, we saw no reason to believe that there had ever been any consistent occupation of the area by people who made fluted points. Never did words return to haunt so thoroughly!"

The digging and trenching was carried on spasmodically, however, as the bulldozers of the gravel company relentlessly destroyed the site, and persistence was rewarded. Between 1951 and 1957, an area of some ten acres yielded more than three thousand artifacts, more than one hundred of which were fluted points and fragments. They were made of materials for which no local sources have yet been found.[3]

About the confusing factor that no evidence of an old land surface was found, Dr. Marie Wormington notes: [4] "The later excavations, however, indicated that there had been a good bit of disturbance and that this zone had been unstable for a long time. . . . There was probably some trampling of the sand by the makers of the implements and later disturbance by frost action and wind throw of trees. Such a site is not suitable for geological dating, and no material [such as charcoal from ancient campfires] has been obtained which could be utilized for radiocarbon dating."

The implements recovered were not spread evenly over the site. Most of them were found in so-called hot spots that were arranged in a rough semicircle, suggesting a camp circle. Because the sand did not tread in "floors," there was no way of telling whether the "hot spots" were simultaneously occupied. Byers thinks it more likely that they were occupied at different times, "for to have them simultaneously occupied would bring together more people than ordinarily assemble among contemporary hunting peoples except in times of great abundance of food." [5]

No bones of prehistoric Indians or animals were found at Bull Brook, thus there is no knowledge of what the early Bull Brookers ate or what game they sought. Archeologists hold no hope of ever finding any skeletons of the fluted point hunters in the Northeast nor any contemporary animal bones. The sands of New England produce a notoriously acid soil, and the chances of bones or bone implements being preserved under such conditions are practically nil.

Clovis fluted points are at least ten thousand, and perhaps twelve thousand, years old. That people using them dwelt at Ipswich there can be no doubt. Speaking in archeological terms, they may have lived there until comparatively recent times, perhaps until four or five thousand years before Christ. But as Byers remarks: "Until we can find something that will enable us to date an eastern site we cannot be sure that these early hunters developed their industry in the East and moved west . . . or whether they were the forerunners of the invasion of the eastern states by people who could no longer stand the great open spaces of the Southwest." [6]

They Went the *Other* Way

From the time the first colonists landed on the Atlantic coast until well into the last century white men pushed westward. Throughout this period there was always a "frontier." The constant westward expansion created new customs, new needs, and new institutions, under varying environmental pressures that shaped and directed the development of the unique American culture.[7]

There was an earlier period, however, when Americans went the other way. The movement did not begin at the same time in all geographical regions of the West. But generally it may be dated, as far as the Eastern Woodlands are concerned, between eighteen thousand and twelve thousand years ago, the end of the last major glacial stage.

At some time between these two dates, probably closer to the latter than the former, small bands of hunting people moved eastward from the ice-free region of the Southwest. The traditions of some southeastern Indians tell of such migrations, and they undoubtedly took place in the Southeast before any people found it possible to live in the Northeast, for the great glaciers did not reach into the southern United States.*

---

* See Part Two.

The "frontier" for these people, therefore, lay to the east, and westward migrations by northeastern and southeastern Indians did not occur to any appreciable extent until late prehistoric times.

The prehistoric cultures of the Northeast Woodlands—Michigan to the Atlantic Seaboard, Canada to southern Pennsylvania and the Ohio River—are divided into three stages:

Paleo-Indian, eighteen thousand to eight thousand years ago.

Archaic, eight thousand to three thousand years ago.

Woodland, three thousand to four hundred years ago.

Stone artifacts of Paleo-Indians have been found scattered throughout this wide region, but neither their skeletal remains nor bones of the great Ice Age animals they must have hunted have been discovered. However, this regrettable fact does not mean that nothing is known of them. Quite to the contrary, archeologists have been able to learn much about their way of life. Not only the forms and the materials of their tools and weapons indicate customs and their competence as craftsmen, but the locations of these artifacts tell significant stories.

The Shoop Site near Enterline, Pennsylvania, has furnished the best evidence of an occupation comparable to the Clovis point level of the Southern Great Plains. This Paleo-Indian site was first discovered by a private collector who kept it a secret for more than fifteen years. When at last he told qualified scientists about his find he had removed more than twoscore Clovis fluted points and several hundred other artifacts. Further excavations by experts resulted in the recovery of several hundred more tools and weapons which were scattered over an area some twenty acres in extent. So great was the assemblage of finished and unfinished products that archeologist John Witthoft [8] gave it the name of the Enterline Chert Industry. Most of the fluted points that are found in Pennsylvania are made of local jasper or a fine-grained black flint, but only a few of these types were found at Enterline. More than eight hundred specimens collected were made of a material called Onondaga chert. The nearest source of this stone is in western New York, some two hundred miles away.[9]

Paleo-Indian fluted points have been recovered in dozens of sites throughout Ohio, New York, Pennsylvania, and the New England States. An especially important complex was discovered six miles south of the Canadian border, near Shawville, Vermont. Called the Reagan Site, it has yielded nearly two hundred artifacts that were spread over an area of two miles. They were made of a variety of materials, most of which were not locally available. The abundance of flint debris present indicated that some were manufactured on the site, although made of material the sources of which were hundreds of miles distant.[10]

Of special significance were a few points similar to those known as Sandia, used some twenty thousand years ago by New Mexico hunters,

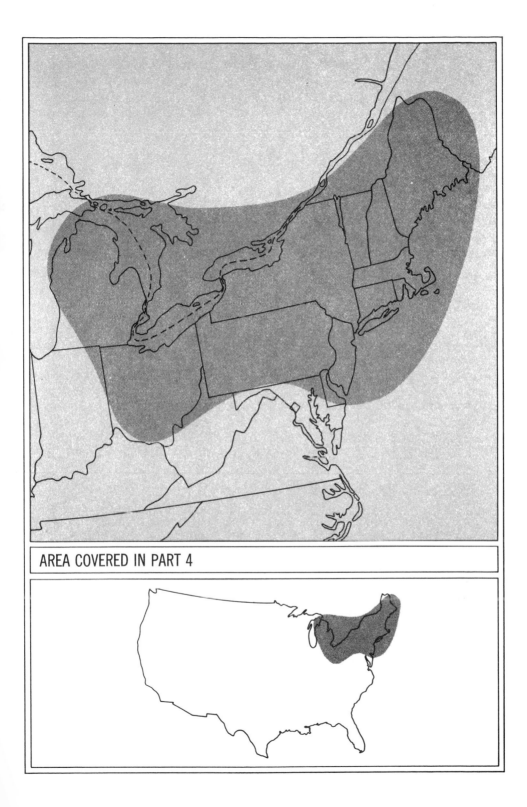

AREA COVERED IN PART 4

and other points resembling unfluted Folsom points found in Texas.

The distribution of Paleo-Indian artifacts, as archeologist William A. Ritchie points out, leads to the conclusion that the first inhabitants of the Northeastern Woodlands "comprised a wide scattering of tiny bands, in all likelihood limited to a few families, of great mobility and primarily dependent for sustenance on large game mammals." [11] Extensive parts of the New World were pioneered on this level of culture.[12] Investigations indicate that the Northeast was totally unoccupied when the early migrants from the West reached it, and they enjoyed a freedom to wander in search of food as great as any known in the history of man.

As to how the Paleo-Indians came into the Northeast, Ritchie has this to say: [13] "The thin scatter of fluted points in the Northeast follows the principal river systems, and it would appear that the primary movements had originated to the south and southwest of the area. Thus a trail of fluted point users seems to ascend along the Ohio and Allegheny rivers into southwestern New York; another to follow the Susquehanna and Delaware systems from Pennsylvania into central New York; while yet another to lead northward through the Hudson Valley. The Long Island Sound coastline of southern New England appears to have provided a fourth route from which entry was effected into river valleys like the Connecticut and as far north along the coast as Mount Desert Island, Maine."

The finding of two fluted points at different locations on eastern Long Island indicated that some of these prehistoric people were able to get across the lower Hudson. They are not known to have possessed tools, such as adzes, celts, and gouges, necessary in the work of felling trees and shaping dugout canoes. Most of the eastern rivers, however, might have been crossed on rafts made of driftwood. The wide and deep lower Hudson would have presented a difficult problem, but perhaps in those remote times passage was possible on the ice. In the immediate post-glacial period the Northeast was an extremely cold region. Forests and grasslands may have been in existence more than fifteen thousand years ago, but the final glacial bodies of water did not disappear until seven thousand years ago.

Much more can be told of the descendants of the Paleo-Indians, the people who lived in the Northeastern Woodlands in the epoch known as Archaic, for their skeletal remains have been found, and, as any anthropologist will state, Indian man himself can be known best from the grave where his family laid him to rest.

For the Pennsylvania Historical and Museum Commission, John Witthoft prepared this description of the Archaic Age Indian who dwelt in the forests of the Northeast: [14] ". . . a small man, rarely more than five feet, five inches tall. He was of very slight build, and probably weighed no more than 130 pounds. His bones were especially light and delicate as compared with almost all other human types. Delicate modeling of the facial bones and thinness of the skull bones is conspicuous in Indian skeletons. Despite this, he was almost always an exceedingly muscular man, as is indicated by the form of those parts of his bones which were at the ends of muscle bundles.

"All evidence from the skeletons suggests that the Indian was wiry, strong and extremely tough. He had a strongly sculptured face as compared to the Caucasian, with jutting cheek bones and a large, well-developed palate and dental arch. Despite this, his teeth were subject to the same decay and diseases as ours, and to much more wear; he had ordinarily lost all but a few of them before he was thirty-five years old. He did not chew the way we do, but bit his tough food with his incisors edge-to-edge, grinding with both his front teeth and molars.

"The Indian of the forest seldom lived to his fortieth birthday, usually dying before he was thirty-five. His diseased teeth and the infections they caused were probably a prelude to death. Hunger, exposure and hunting accidents were probably the other major causes of early death. Various arthritic and rheumatoid diseases were remarkably frequent and often severe, judging by evidence from the skeletons.

"The Indian was a tough, wiry little man who carried many physical defects and who was constantly exposed to the worst rigors of our climate. He slept curled into a ball, with his knees under his chin, a habit acquired during a lifelong struggle against a cold and brutal natural world. He was a man who lived very hard and died young. This is not the Indian of our romantic literature, but it is most certainly the Indian whose bones we study."

Numerous early white explorers and settlers thought of themselves as the first human beings to enter the wilderness of the Northeastern Woodlands. Perhaps they didn't consider the Indian human. In any case, this attitude of conceit bespeaks their ignorance. Indians were hunting in the Eastern Woodlands region of the United States when Europeans were living in the early New Stone Age, very long before the idea of building great pyramids had been conceived by the Egyptians. And they had lived for millennia before that time in other parts of North America.

Riches of the Past

Until about thirty-five hundred years ago—give or take a few centuries—the hunting–food-gathering way of life endured in the Eastern Woodlands. A long procession of cultures, stemming from a vague beginning, can be traced through the region, from Ohio to New England —cultures known to archeologists as the Lamoka, the Frontenac, the

Laurentian, the Indian Knoll, the Glacial Kame, the Early Coastal, to name a few of the earliest. The people belonging to these cultures lived in much the same way as did their ancestors. Their implements and utensils were still reflective of earlier far western cultures, especially the Folsom and the Cochise,* and had undergone few changes in thousands of years. They used spear-throwers, lived in caves and crude bark and brush dwellings, and made projectile points, knives, scrapers, mortars for grinding wild seeds such as acorns, bowls, digging sticks of flint, other types of stone, wood, horn, and bone.

Significant cultural changes took place about four thousand years ago in some areas, and at later times in other regions of the Eastern Woodlands. One of the earliest involved burial customs. Greater emphasis was placed on ritual, ceremonies became complex, cremation and the use of burial offerings increased, and, in some parts, the custom of interring the dead in flexed positions in pits and mounds began to evolve.

Sometime after three thousand years ago, simple forms of agriculture began to reach the Eastern Woodlands. It came north from Mexico by way of the Mississippi and Ohio valleys and slowly spread over the Appalachians to the seaboard. For many years thereafter, however, the people continued to depend for the most part on wild foods. Quite logically, the development of farming came soonest in the southern sections of the region. In one area of Kentucky, archeological investigations have shown that the people living there depended upon some cultivated plants for almost half of their subsistence shortly before 1000 B.C.

The first pottery seems to have appeared in the Eastern Woodlands about three thousand years ago, but how it reached the region is not known. Pottery was used on the southeastern coast a thousand years earlier. It had been brought there from southern Mexico, and the assumption that it was gradually transported to Ohio, Pennsylvania, New York, and New England seems reasonable. Yet this contention, as Josephy notes,[15] is disputed, and it has been "suggested by some persons that its distinctive cord-marked style resembled ceramic work done by people of the forest zones of Europe and Asia, and that it was introduced in the Northeast at this time by migrants who had come originally from Siberia. Others theorize, instead, that it developed independently within the area." Still others think it came to the Northeast more or less directly from Mexico, but this supposition is weakened by the fact that the oldest pottery of the Eastern Woodlands has been found near the Atlantic coast.

Following the introduction of agriculture and pottery, cultures re-

* See Part One.

flecting a more sedentary way of life—notably the Adena—began to evolve. These cultures were characterized by larger burial and temple mounds, by tools made of copper, by improved ceramics, by ornaments and decorations designed and constructed in ways illustrative of considerable artistic ability, by engraved tablets, and by woven articles displaying distinctive weaves.

In the Ohio Valley by the early centuries of the Christian Era the Adena Culture had reached its zenith and had begun to give way to one of the greatest and richest cultures that developed in prehistoric times north of Mexico. It has been called the Hopewell, after the owner of one of the sites where its treasures were unearthed.[16]

The influences of the Hopewell Culture, spreading with remarkable rapidity, were greater and more widely diffused than those of any other American Indian culture. Besides the Ohio Valley, other centers of its development have been discovered in Michigan, Pennsylvania, New York, Tennessee, Indiana, Illinois, Iowa, Kansas, and far down the Mississippi River.

It seems that one of the major forces giving impetus to the rise of the Hopewell Culture was created by the establishment of trade channels that ran from the Atlantic coast to the Rocky Mountains, and from the Great Lakes to Mexico. The Hopewellians themselves may have been the instigators in the development of these routes, but certainly they welcomed the trade and the traders, and they sent contingents on round-trip journeys of hundreds and even thousands of miles to procure articles. Their primary purpose was to obtain raw materials and manufactured objects to place with the dead in the immense burial mounds they constructed. Religious beliefs and ceremonials, therefore, stimulated an economic development that was unprecedented in prehistoric America. It also effectively diffused Hopewellian traits over the greater parts of the eastern, middle, and southern regions of the continent. A case in point is the notable Marksville Culture of the Florida Keys, which unmistakably reflected Hopewellian influences.*

From the Gulf region—either carried by Hopewell traveling salesmen or by traders from other peoples—into Ohio and other parts of the Eastern Woodlands were brought conch shells, alligator teeth, pottery, sharkskins and sharks' teeth, and the plumes and feathers of beautiful semitropical fowls. From the region bordering the Atlantic coast were brought mica, shells, wampum beads, and various types of chert. From the upper Mississippi Valley and the region of Lake Superior were brought lead and copper. From the Rocky Mountains were brought grizzly bear teeth and obsidian.

---

* See Part Two.

One of the most elaborate and complicated of all known earthworks was on Raccoon Creek in Licking County, Ohio. They were built on a level area rising thirty to fifty feet above the bottomlands bordering the stream. Spread over nearly four square miles, they included a series of square, circular, and octagonal enclosures, numerous mounds and other structures, all connected with avenues. Moats ran along the interior side of an extensive network of embankments. Unfortunately many of the works were leveled and the artifacts they contained were destroyed or scattered by plows of farmers before archeological investigations were conducted at the invaluable site.

The Hopewell people excelled all other prehistoric Indians as craftsmen and artists. A large part of their manufactured products had some form of religious significance. The immense earthworks with which they enclosed their mounds and their towns had a sacred function. They made excellent decorated pottery for ceremonial use. No people buried their dead with greater care and ceremony, nor with more lavish contributions of burial offerings. Some graves were lined with sheets of mica, with stones, or with finely woven mats. Beside the bodies were placed exquisitely carved bone, wood, and metal figures and scrolls, mosaics made of mineral paints, and necklaces, beads, pendants, earrings, and other ornaments of metal, shell, and bone. Some of the skeletons recovered by archeologists bore bone lesions indicating the presence of syphilis. No earlier appearance of this disease in the Eastern Woodlands is known.

The Hopewellians were the finest metalworkers of all prehistoric Indians, and they made their magnificent ornaments and decorations long before casting was known to any people of the Western Hemisphere. By beating and annealing, and with the aid of delicate tools they invented, they produced an incredible variety of articles out of copper and meteoric iron. Occasionally they used silver and gold in small amounts, but where they obtained these precious ores is not known. It was the white man who taught the Indian the value of silver and gold, and destroyed him if he happened to be in the way of their mad searches for them.

But for all their incomparable artistry, the Hopewellians were a remarkably practical people, and the welfare and happiness of the living were of great concern to them. They made beautiful things to please the eye and satisfy the ego. They garbed themselves in fine furs and robes, well-tanned skins, and woven cloth. They decorated themselves with a large variety of copper, mica, shell, bone, and wood ornaments. Both men and women wore copper and silver earspools and necklaces of pearls and animal teeth and bone beads. They were competent farmers and hunters, and courageous warriors.

They had a highly developed social structure. Their activities were well organized and directed by able leaders who were probably members of an elite class. They had special guilds composed of metalworkers, carvers, woodworkers, and traders—the first craft unions of America. Obviously they were ingenious organizers. Their society was divided into classes, yet there were no social cleavages to disrupt progress. Their great earthworks and mounds were built by community labor, and all of them, regardless of rank and position, were imbued with ideals and desires that contributed to common advancement and affluence.

They were bound together in what might be termed a loose confederacy. It extended from the Atlantic to the plains of Kansas, and from northern Wisconsin to the Gulf of Mexico, but not all of its segments followed precisely similar patterns. On the contrary, in each region the Hopewellian culture was modified by local traditions and environmental differences. Archeologists have discovered no evidence to indicate that the Hopewellians of Ohio, the center of the culture, attempted to force others to accept without any deviation their customs, beliefs, and ceremonials. It was a free society.

The Hopewell culture probably reached its zenith shortly before A.D. 500. It descended more rapidly than it had ascended. What brought about its end is a question for which archeologists long have sought an answer. One of the best guesses is that the far-reaching network of trade routes they had built collapsed. There are probably other explanations, but whatever they may be, the fact remains that after A.D. 500, fewer mounds were built and artistic ability and craftsmanship began to decline. Other cultures infiltrated the Hopewell regions, and the most remarkable prehistoric Indian civilization that ever existed north of Mexico vanished forever from the sites on which it had arisen.

Abnaki: Those Living at the Sunrise

They lived mainly along the coast and in the river valleys of Maine, but some of their villages were in New Hampshire, and at least one group dwelt in northwestern Vermont. The French gave them the name Abnaki, and so they became known to history, but properly it should be Wabanaki, a word that refers to morning and the east, and may be interpreted as those "living at the sunrise."

Although they were among the first northeastern Indians to meet Europeans, almost nothing is known of them as a prehistoric people. They told the earliest white men who encountered them—as did other New England tribes—that they were created far to the southwest and at some very remote period migrated to the rocky woodlands touching the sea. That is probably the truth, but there is nothing to indicate when they made the great journey and the route they followed on it.

They belong to the immense Algonquian linguistic family that reached in a wide belt across the northern part of North America in prehistoric times. This is the family of all the tribes of the most northeastern part of the United States region, but tongue is not an indication of time of arrival. Some may have arrived soon after the end of the glacial age, others at any time in later millennia, but stone artifacts recovered in archeological sites do prove that some of them were there for several thousand years before the beginning of the Christian Era. Where the Abnakis stand on this prehistorical roster can no more be determined than can the position of their relatives, the Passamaquoddy, the Penobscot, the Pennacook, and other tribes.

They can be seen only as the first white invaders of their homelands saw them, and that is not a very satisfactory picture, but it does tell something. For logically, the way they were then was the way they had been for countless centuries.

The Abnakis were said to have been more docile and gentler than some of their neighbors, but when attacked they became revengeful and implacable enemies. They tortured male foes unfortunate enough to be taken alive, although they were kind to captured women and children, and absorbed them.

They wore sewn fur clothing and lived in conical houses constructed of bark and woven mats. Several families occupied a single dwelling. They grew maize, fertilizing the hillocks with fish—and this was a custom of most tribes of the northeast coast—but they relied mainly for their subsistence on hunting and fishing. The ethnologist James Mooney wrote that at least some of their towns were enclosed in palisades, and each contained a "council house of considerable size, oblong in form and roofed with bark; and similar structures were used by the males of the village who preferred to club together in social fellowship." [17]

A grand council, consisting of the chiefs and two men from each family, determined matters of great importance to the tribe, and possessed the power to sentence persons guilty of serious crimes to death. A so-called general council was in reality the entire tribe, and dealt mainly with questions relating to warfare.

Bloody conflicts with encroaching British colonists so depleted the Abnaki that early in the historical period the survivors withdrew to Canada. Accorded protection by the French, with whom they had always maintained friendly relations, they settled at Becancour, Sillery, and St. Francis, among other refugee tribes from the south, and so vanished forever from the New England scene.

Passamaquoddy signifies "pollock-plenty-place," and the place was the bay which bears their name. This tribe had the distinction of being

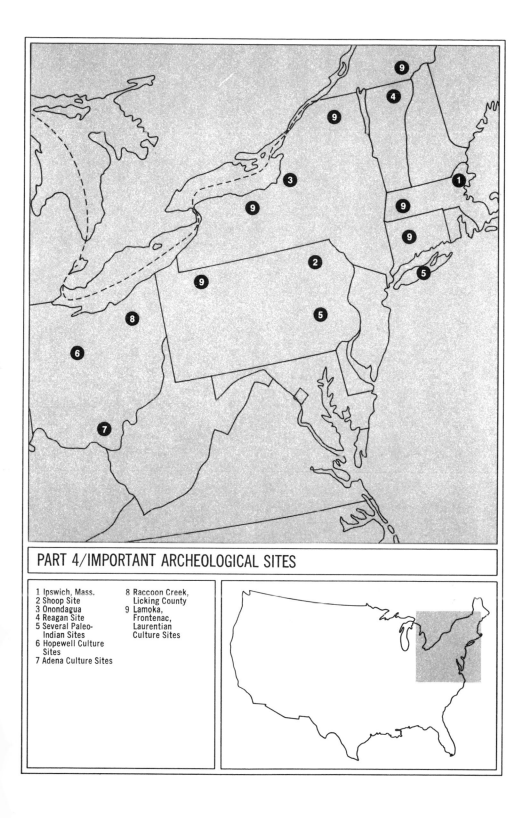

PART 4/IMPORTANT ARCHEOLOGICAL SITES

1 Ipswich, Mass.
2 Shoop Site
3 Onondagua
4 Reagan Site
5 Several Paleo-
  Indian Sites
6 Hopewell Culture
  Sites
7 Adena Culture Sites
8 Raccoon Creek,
  Licking County
9 Lamoka,
  Frontenac,
  Laurentian
  Culture Sites

the easternmost body of Indians in the region of the United States, but that was a fact which brought them no escape from colonists who did not practice what they preached.

Pennacook means "down hill," an appropriate name for this tribe after the colonization of New England. They lived in southern New Hampshire, northeastern Massachusetts and the southernmost part of Maine. Their history is almost identical with that of the Abnaki, except that their destruction by New Englanders began at an earlier time. Suffering brutal pressure from the settlements on Massachusetts Bay, they, too, fled to their final haven at St. Francis.

A bay and a river preserve the name *Penobscot,* which means "the rocky place," specifically the falls between Oldtown and Bangor. But the Penobscot deserve to be remembered in more important ways. After a long period of warfare against the English colonists, they were smart enough to effect a lasting peace which let them retain part of their homeland. They still live in it. And they were the creators of a fabulous tale that excited all Europe.

By some unknown medium—although its origin would not be difficult to guess—early French and British explorers heard that on the banks of the Penobscot River stood an immense city containing miles of buildings, large plazas, and wide avenues, and inhabited by Indians who enjoyed great affluence. Its name was Norumbega.

The word *nolembeka* in the Abnaki tongue, of which the Penobscot spoke a dialect, means "a succession of falls and still water," and it was used by the Penobscot to designate a certain part of the Penobscot River, but not the river itself. This was probably the word the explorers heard and twisted to Norumbega.

Whether that is true or not is of small matter. The news stirred fever in European courts. The splendors of Norumbega grew steadily greater with each repeating of the report. Cartographers seized on the name, and perhaps believing they spoke better Abnaki than the discoverers, gave it new spellings. It appeared on the map of Hieronimus Verrazano in 1529 as Aranbega, and as Auorobagra on a Jomard map issued a few years later. The Gastaldi map of 1550 carried it as Nurumbega. The great city not only became more splendrous and larger, but it was soon expanding into a fabulous "province," or "kingdom," that eventually included the whole coast from Nova Scotia to Virginia.

Disillusionment, needless to say, came with subsequent investigations, and not many more years passed before the name Norumbega on a chart of New England indicated a cluster of bark wigwams on the Penobscot River near Bangor. There is some doubt that this was the correct location, for the site was called Agguncia by the Penobscot, and there is some question about the specific significance of that word.

That was not, however, all that was heard of Norumbega. Linguists and ethnologists, coming into their own in America, waged bitter arguments not only over the meaning and correct spelling of Norumbega, but over its location. A religious who wrote an Abnaki dictionary maintained that it should be spelled Aranmbegik, translated into French as *"au fond de l'eau,"* from *aranm,* *"au fond."* Another authority thought the meaning was "at the clay inlet." Another opined that the Penobscot word *nalambigi* and the Passamaquoddy word *nalabegik* refer to the still, quiet stretch of a river between two riffles, or rapids.

Other interpretations and spellings were rendered as more years passed, but one scientist disputed the authenticity of all of them. It was his claim that the word had a European origin, could be attributed to the Vikings, and derived from Norroembygda, meaning "Norway Country." A colleague improved on this theory by declaring that Norumbega came from Norbega, an ancient name for Norway, and he identified the stream in question as the Charles River of Massachusetts, and the location of Norumbega as the site of the present Watertown in the same state.

All these learned men seem to have overlooked the fact that Norumbega never existed. But, should one have the desire, one could still get an argument about it.

Cousins in the Woodlands

If the historical period of the Northeast is marked by the transatlantic voyages of the Vikings in the decade A.D. 1000–1010, then a story may be told of fifteen prehistoric tribes who dwelt north and east of Maryland, who spoke dialects of the Algonquian language, who were consanguineous in varying degrees, and who followed a similar way of life.* They had dwelt there for millennia, but they can be truly known only as they were when the first vessels of Europeans dropped anchor in the bays and inlets of the northeastern shore.

Most of their names are connotative of a geographical feature, as illustrated by the following: [18]

Massachuset, *at the range of hills,* and these were the hills of Milton. They dwelt from Salem on the north, around Boston Bay, and as far south as Brockton.

Nauset, meaning unknown, but they occupied most of Cape Cod and came to be called Cape Indians.

Nipmuc, *freshwater fishing place.* They lived in southern Massachusetts and northern Rhode Island and Connecticut.

---

* There were other tribes in the Eastern Woodlands region that, for various reasons, warrant individual consideration.

Pocomtuc, meaning unknown. They lived in western Massachusetts, and adjoining parts of Connecticut and Vermont.

Wampanoag, *eastern people*. They lived in parts of Massachusetts, Rhode Island, on Martha's Vineyard and adjacent islands.

Narragansett, *people of the small point*. They lived in Rhode Island west of Narragansett Bay.

Niantic (Eastern), *at a point of land on an estuary*. They lived on the coasts of Rhode Island and Connecticut.

Mohegan, *wolf*, but they were also called *River People*. They lived in the upper valley of the Thames River in Connecticut.

Niantic (Western), meaning same as Niantic (Eastern). They lived on the coast between Niantic Bay and the Connecticut River. These two branches of the Niantic were separated by the Pequot.

Pequot, *destroyers*. They lived on the coast of New London County, Connecticut.

Mahican also means *wolf*, and the Mohegan may have parted from the Mahican in some remote period, but each thought of themselves as a distinct tribe. The Mahican lived on both sides of the upper Hudson River, as far north as Lake Champlain and as far east as the valley of the Housatonic River.

Montauk means *uncertain*. They lived in the eastern and central areas of Long Island.

Wappinger, *easterners*, living northward from Manhattan Island, along the east side of the Hudson to Poughkeepsie and eastward to the lower Connecticut River Valley.

Conoy, meaning unknown, but they also were called Piscataway, the name of a creek on which their main village stood. They lived between the Potomac River (vicinity of Washington, D.C.) and Chesapeake Bay.

Nanticoke, *tidewater people*. They lived on the eastern shore of Chesapeake Bay and in southern Delaware.

Descriptions of the appearances, customs, mores, and ritual of the members of any one of these tribes would be applicable, except in minor details, to the members of all of them. The main differences would be attributable to local environments, as for example, those living on the coast would depend more on fish and crustaceans for their subsistence than did the interior tribes. All of them dwelt in permanent villages, and all were agriculturalists, growing maize, beans, pumpkins, and tobacco.

American wives may get some ideas for new dishes to serve their husbands from the following early culinary notice. One of the main foods of these tribes was boiled maize, sometimes mixed with kidney beans, and they "frequently boil in this pottage fish and flesh of all sorts, either new taken or dried, as shad, eels, alewives, or a kind of herring, or any other sort of fish. . . . These they cut in pieces, bones and all. . . .

I have wondered many times that they were not in danger of being choked with fish bones; but they are so dexterous in separating the bones from the fish in their eating thereof that they are in no hazard. Also, they boil in this frumenty all sorts of flesh they take in hunting, as venison, beaver, bear's flesh, moose, otters, raccoons, etc., cutting this flesh in small pieces. . . . Also, they mix with the said pottage several sorts of roots, as Jerusalem artichokes, and groundnuts, and pompions, and squashes, and also several sorts of nuts or masts, as oak acorns, chestnuts, and walnuts; these husked and dried and powdered, they thicken their pottage therewith. Also, sometimes they beat their maize into meal and sift it through a basket made for that purpose. With this meal they make bread, baking it in the ashes, covering the dough with leaves. Sometimes they make of their meal a small sort of cakes and boil them." [19]

Most of the pots used by these people were made of clay. Dishes, spoons, and ladles were manufactured from wood. They made four-cornered water pails of bark and attached handles. Provisions were stored and transported in baskets made of rushes, stalks, corn husks, grass, and bark, and were ornamented with colored figures of animals. Early explorers mentioned seeing woven mats, beautifully dressed deerskins, feather garments, utensils and tools of stone and horn, and finely woven nets used for catching small fish, as well as large and extremely strong nets with which heavy ocean fish were taken. The people of the coasts and offshore islands were expert canoeists.[20]

Most of their clothing, made of animal skins, was soft and pliable and often colored with paint and decorated with beads made from shells. On special occasions they donned mantles of feathers sewn together so that they overlapped as on the back of a fowl. The dress of the women consisted usually of two articles, a leather shirt ornamented with fringe, and a skin skirt fastened around the waist with a belt and reaching nearly to the ankles. Men covered the lower part of the body with a breechclout and wore a skin mantle. In winter both men and women protected themselves with leggings and leather moccasins decorated with wampum. Hair styles were greatly varied. Women adorned their hair with ornaments and wore bands decorated with beads and wampum. Men went bareheaded, their hair fantastically trimmed, each according to his own fancy. Some shaved one side of the head and allowed the hair to grow long on the other side. Some shaved both sides of the head but left a strip of hair two or three inches in width running from the forehead to the nape of the neck.[21]

Clans and gentes maintained their own cemeteries, but burial customs were similar in each tribe. Immediately after death the corpse was dressed in the deceased's best clothing "and decked with the chief ornaments worn in life, sometimes having the face and shirt painted red, then laid on a mat in the middle of the hut, and personal effects were placed about it. The grave was dug generally by old women. . . . It was the custom of probably most of the tribes to light fires on the grave for four nights after burial." [22] The Nanticoke, however, adhered to a custom followed by some tribes living farther to the south, that of placing the bodies temporarily on scaffolds, later removing the flesh and reinterring the skeletons.

These were the Indians who invented *wampumpeage*, which white men shortened to "wampum." It was their "money," or their "measure of value," and was made mostly from the *poquauhaug*—which became "quahog" in the English tongue—the common round or hardshell clam. Some wampum also was made from the periwinkle, the whelk, and freshwater shells of the genus *Unio*. The value of these strings of beads was determined largely by two factors, color and finish. Wampum of the Northeastern Seaboard was chiefly white and violet, the darker shells ranging in shade from pale or pink violet to rich purple. The deep purple beads were the most valuable.

Wampum beads were cylindrical in form, varying in length from one eighth to seven sixteenths of an inch. Manufacturing them required patient labor and a high degree of skill. Yet, as the scientist J. N. B. Hewitt laments: [23] "Notwithstanding the abundant literature concerning the multifarious uses of these shell beads in trade, the embroidering of articles of dress, the making of objects of personal adornment and badges of rank and official dignity, and in the fiducial transactions of private and public life, no technical statement of the exact methods employed by the natives in their manufacture is available."

He is speaking of prehistoric beads. White colonists soon flooded the country with counterfeit wampum for the purpose of cheating the Indians. However, the Indians were not easily fooled, and the ultimate result was that the value of wampum as trade currency was destroyed.

The northeastern Algonquian tribes were the equal of any Indians in bravery, intelligence, and physical prowess, but they possessed a major weakness which contributed significantly to their early destruction. They engaged in devastating tribal wars. Some tribes were almost completely annihilated by relatives. They seemed to lack the ability to organize, nor did they seem to understand the power and influence they might have wielded by combining their forces and submitting to discipline. The alliances that were effected between tribes were generally temporary and were without real cohesion. There was an element in their character which made them incapable of combining in large bodies, even against a common enemy. Some of their noted chieftains made attempts to unite them to halt the advance of the colonists, and achieved some success for short periods, but a battle loss seemed to bring complete discouragement to all contingents, and the structure of the alliance collapsed.[24]

The northeastern Algonquians could fight each other, and they could fight as tribal units against an aggressor, but they could not fight together.

Delaware: Algonquian Grandfathers

They were the only large and important American Indian tribe to become known to history by an English name—Delaware.* It was not only a corruption but was a misnomer. They called themselves Lenni Lenape, which is variously interpreted by linguists as "true men," "real men," "standard men," and "native, genuine men," all of which are translations with similar connotations.

From the time of their earliest encounters with Europeans they maintained that they had reached their eastern home from a land far to the northwest. More than two centuries later physical evidence supporting this tradition would be discovered.

Noteworthy is the geographical location of their homeland when white men found them. It embraced Manhattan and Staten islands, all of the state of New Jersey, the western end of Long Island, portions of New York west of the Hudson, and parts of eastern Pennsylvania and northern Delaware.[25]

They had lived there a very long time, probably for several millennia, before the beginning of the Christian Era. And long before the earliest explorations of America (including the voyages of the Vikings, although the Norsemen probably did not sail far enough south to see Delaware territory) they had evolved into a loose confederacy. Generally scholars divide it into three major divisions—the Munsee, the Unalachtigo, and the Unami—each of which contained a great many minor subdivisions, but there may have been a fourth division, comprised of groups in New Jersey, for which no name has been established. So long had these affiliated bands occupied their respective territories that dialects of their common basic tongue had developed. In particular, the speech of the Munsee, the northernmost of the major branches, differed so greatly from the other dialects that they were erroneously considered in colonial times to be an independent tribe.

The people calling themselves Lenni Lenape occupied the central part of the northeastern area inhabited by Algonquian tribes. From this territory most of the cognate tribes had diverged. The Delaware, therefore, were looked upon as the "trunk" of the family tree, and

---

* From Lord De la Warr, the title of Thomas West, governor of the colony of Virginia.

were accorded by the many branches the respectful title of "grandfather."

The prehistoric period came to a close for the Delaware at the beginning of the seventeenth century, when Henry Hudson entered the river that would be given his name, although earlier voyagers had touched in the vicinity. From that time forward they were implacable foes of the encroaching white man, but, as was the case with all Algonquian tribes, they were unable to unite in a military force that effectively could withstand the onslaughts. Moreover, unscrupulous colonists were not their only enemies. At one period the Iroquois won domination over them, and allowed settlers to defraud them of their land claims. It is to the credit of the Delaware that for two and a half centuries, although a broken and scattered people, they were in the forefront of virtually every important battle waged between retreating Indians and white settlers moving westward. The annals of American Indians contain no better example of a timetable to oblivion than that which portrays the slow and bloody withdrawal of the Delaware toward the land from which they had come in some remote age.

But if they were destroyed as a people, they were not to be forgotten.

In 1836, Constantine Samuel Raffinesque, a French scholar who spent a number of years in the United States, published a work entitled *The American Nations*. In it was printed for the first time the famous Walum Olum, assertedly a history of the Delaware. Raffinesque stated that the Walum Olum was a translation of an account written in the Delaware tongue. There was doubt as to the author of the original manuscript, but according to Raffinesque it was an interpretation of ancient sacred metrical legends, recorded in pictographs on bark sheets and sticks, which had been obtained by a Dr. Ward in 1820 from some refugee Delaware in Indiana.

In the Delaware tongue, Walum Olum signifies "painted tally" or "red score," from *walam,* meaning "painted," particularly "red painted," and *olum,* indicating "score or tally." [26]

What happened to the bark and sticks on which the legends of the Delaware had been preserved in pictographic chronology—symbols, diagrams, and series of notches indicating change and other statistical information—is not known. Raffinesque was considered a somewhat erratic student, and for some years the authenticity of the Walum Olum remained in question. He died in 1840, and his papers became scattered, but the documents pertaining to the Walum Olum were found by E. G. Squier,[27] a contributor to the publications of the Smithsonian Institution. Squier brought the Walum Olum once more to public attention in an address before the New York Historical Society in 1848.

Squier considered the Walum Olum an authentic depiction of Delaware migrations and changes, but not until 1882 was this opinion given the support required to make it acceptable to scientists. Then the noted ethnologist Daniel G. Brinton, after a careful and critical investigation of the whole subject, published the complete pictography, text of the early manuscripts, and the Delaware tradition, accompanied by notes, in his distinguished work *The Lenape and Their Legends*.[28] In the project Dr. Brinton had the assistance of Lenape scholars, which left no doubt as to the accuracy of his interpretations.

The Walum Olum, wrote Brinton, "is a genuine native production, which was repeated orally to someone indifferently conversant with the Delaware language, who wrote it down to the best of his ability. In its present form it can, as a whole, lay no claim either to antiquity or to purity of linguistic form. Yet, as an authentic modern version, slightly colored by European teachings, of the ancient tribal traditions, it is well worth preservation and will repay more study in the future. . . . The narrator was probably one of the native chiefs or priests, who had spent his life in the Ohio and Indiana towns of the Lenape, and who, though with some knowledge of Christian instruction, preferred the pagan rites, legends, and myths of his ancestors. Probably certain lines and passages were repeated in the archaic form in which they had been handed down for generations."

The pioneer physician Dr. Ward, whose first name and lifetime activities are unknown, it seems, must be credited with making one of the most remarkable American archeological discoveries, the pictographic bark and sticks of the Walum Olum.

In one other unusual way the story of the Delaware is indelibly imprinted on the pages of American history. In 1682 their council fire was at Shackamaxon (the site of Germantown), Pennsylvania. There they signed a treaty with William Penn, which the celebrated Quaker attempted to honor to the best of his ability. At the time, one of the great Delaware chiefs was Tamanend, a name adopted by a famous, or infamous if one prefers, political organization in the form of Tammany.

Mosopelea: Dog People

They were never a large tribe. Indeed, if ever there were more than three hundred of them the proof is lacking. Why they were called Dog People by numerous other Indians is not known. Perhaps they owned a large number of dogs, and considered them a delicacy in the stew pot. In any case, more properly they should have been called Stray Dog People, for ever since they were discovered they were itinerants, wandering over zigzag routes throughout the Middle West and the South.

Apparently the first white men to know of them also were wanderers of a kind, the earliest French fur traders who broke trails beyond the

Great Lakes. These *voyageurs* knew them as Mosopelea, a name of uncertain significance, although it probably derived from an Algonquian dialect. But they were not Algonquians. They were the only Sioux people living in the Ohio Valley, or anywhere near it, and how they came to be there when the French first heard of them—a little island widely separated from their people in the Southeast and in the northern prairies—is not known.

It cannot even be said where they lived before they came onto the historical stage in Ohio. Their story, therefore, belongs entirely to the historical period, for nothing can be told of them as they were in prehistoric times. As will be seen, no one deserves more the right to tell that story than the noted ethnologist John R. Swanton, and this is his account: [29]

"After abandoning southwestern Ohio sometime before 1673, the Mosopelea appear to have settled on the Cumberland, driven thither probably by the Iroquois, and to have given it the name it bears on Coxe's map (1741), Ouesperie, a corruption of Mosopelea. By 1673 they had descended to the Mississippi and established themselves on its western side below the mouth of the Ohio. Later they appear to have stopped for a time among the Quapaw, but before 1686 at least part of them had sought refuge among the Taensa. Their reason for leaving the latter tribe is unknown, but Iberville found them on the lower Yazoo River, close to the Yazoo and Koroa Indians. [Now they were known as Ofo, an abbreviation of the Mobilian term Ofogoula, which may be interpreted as Dog People.] When their neighbors, the Yazoo and Koroa, joined in the Natchez uprising, the Ofo refused to side with them and went to live with the Tunica, who were French allies. Shortly before 1739 they had settled close to Fort Rosalie, where they remained until 1758. In 1784 their village was on the western bank of the Mississippi 8 miles above Point Coupee.

"*But nothing more was heard of them until 1908, when I found a single survivor living among the Tunica just out of Marksville, La., and was able to establish their linguistic connections.*"

Honniasont: Black Badge Wearers

Native Iroquois tale-tellers said that the Honniasont lived on the upper waters of the "Beautiful River" of the Senecas, the Ohio. Their name, in the Iroquoian language, means "wearing something around the neck." They were also known as the Black Minqua, a name with a dual significance. The "black" referred to a black badge the warriors wore on the chest, and the "Minqua" indicated their relationship to the White Minqua, or Susquehanna, tribe. It was a relationship they were to regret.

Language Groups in Part Four

EASTERN WOODLANDS

Algonquian:	Abnakl	Nlantlc	Delaware
	Nauset	Massachuset	Mahican
	Mohegan	Passamaquoddy	Nanticoke
	Pocomtuc	Narrangansett	Montauk
	Nipmuc	Noquet	Pennacook
	Ottawa	Penobscot	Potawatomi
	Pequot	Wampanoag	Wappinger
	Conoy		
Iroquoian:	Erie	Mohawk	Susquehanna
	Cayuga	Seneca	Oneida
	Onandaga	Wenrohronon	Neutrals
	Wyandot (Huron)		Honniasont
Siouan:	Mosopelea		

When the Honniasont first became known to white men—probably the early Dutch traders—they were allies of the Susquehanna in intertribal wars. Perhaps they sought to gain trade advantages that interfered with the ambitions of relatives and friends. Near the end of the seventeenth century they all but vanished. Reports spread through the wilderness that they had been destroyed by the Susquehanna and the Seneca. A few survivors were said to have been absorbed by the Seneca. The Honniasont were never heard of again.

Susquehanna: Stealthy or Treacherous

Minqua was the Algonquian name for the Susquehanna, who belonged to the Iroquoian linguistic family. The meaning of Susquehanna is not known, but it was not a name given to them in the historical period. Captain John Smith,[30] exploring the upper reaches of Chesapeake Bay in 1608, was the first white man to write of them. He spelled the name Sasqueshannock and Sasquesahanough, and recorded: "Such great and well-proportioned men are seldom seen, for they seemed like giants to the English, yea to their neighbors."

In Smith's time, the Susquehanna lived mainly along the river named for them. Hewitt [31] quoted a seventeenth-century source as saying that the settlers of Maryland "regard the Susquehanna as the most noble and heroic nation of Indians, and other Indians, by a submissive and tributary acknowledgment, hold them in like esteem . . . being for the most part great warriors, they seldom sleep one summer in the quiet

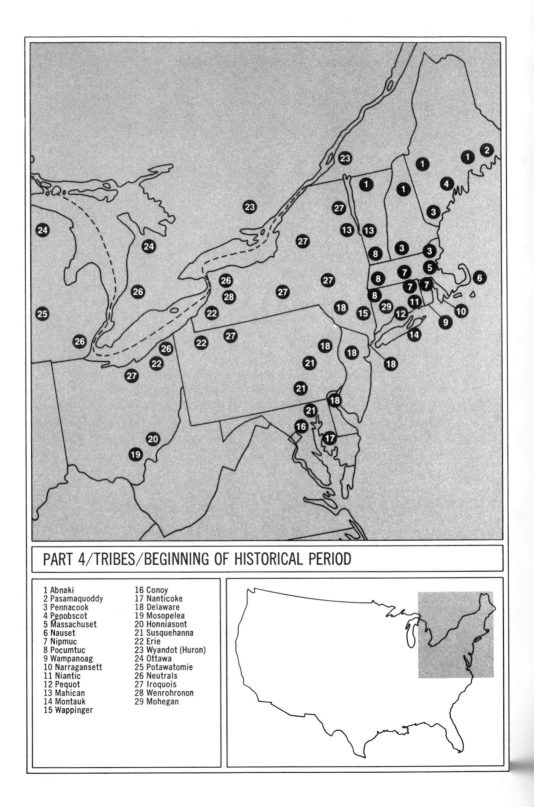

PART 4/TRIBES/BEGINNING OF HISTORICAL PERIOD

1 Abnaki
2 Pasamaquoddy
3 Pennacook
4 Penobscot
5 Massachuset
6 Nauset
7 Nipmuc
8 Pocumtuc
9 Wampanoag
10 Narragansett
11 Niantic
12 Pequot
13 Mahican
14 Montauk
15 Wappinger
16 Conoy
17 Nanticoke
18 Delaware
19 Mosopelea
20 Honniasont
21 Susquehanna
22 Erie
23 Wyandot (Huron)
24 Ottawa
25 Potawatomie
26 Neutrals
27 Iroquois
28 Wenrohronon
29 Mohegan

arms of a peaceful rest, but keep, by their present power, as well as by their former conquest, the several nations of Indians round about them, in a forceable obedience and subjection."

Men, women, and children, in both summer and winter, went almost naked. They painted their faces in red, green, black, and white stripes. Their skins were naturally light in color, but were changed to a dark cinnamon hue by dyeing. Their head hair was worn long, but hair on other parts of the body was removed by extracting each single hair with tweezers. Their bodies, especially the breasts and arms, were tattooed with figures of animals and other objects.

At one time, Susquehanna may have been the name of a group of tribes. When discovered they were thought to have been divided into several subtribes and clans, but little is known of their political structure.[*] Strong and warlike as they were, they were conquered by other Iroquoian tribes early in the historical period. For many years the survivors lived with the Oneida in New York State, but at last were permitted to return to their former homeland along the Susquehanna River, where remnants of other tribes subdued by the Iroquois of New York were living. Epidemics decreased their numbers rapidly, and two decades before the beginning of the American Revolution only a few were alive. In 1763 the last twenty Susquehanna were murdered in cold blood by white men seeking revenge for atrocities committed by other Indians several hundred miles away in the west.

Erie: the Cat People

In the Iroquois tongue the word *erie* means "long tail," and refers specifically to the puma. The Erie, therefore, were popularly referred to as the Cat Nation.

Although they comprised one of the largest tribes of the Eastern Woodlands, and were daring, brave, and skilled fighters, the Erie were among the many losers of one of the greatest family fights in American Indian history.

When early French fur traders and missionaries first encountered them they occupied almost all of northern Ohio and adjacent parts of Pennsylvania and New York State. Every tradition that has been preserved tells of the many wars in which they were engaged since archaic times, but relates nothing of their origin or their social and political history. The earliest accounts in the *Jesuit Relations*, undoubtedly written several years before 1640, state that the Erie had numerous

---

[*] A widely used type of wagon would be called Conestoga, for a Susquehanna sub-tribe, and another branch, the Wyoming, would be remembered in the name of a Pennsylvania valley.

permanent, stockaded towns, that they were composed of several divisions or subtribes, that their language was similar to that of the Hurons, and that they cultivated the soil.

As was the case of so many tribes of the Iroquoian linguistic family, the Erie's greatest enemies were their own people, the tribes comprising the powerful organization known as the Five Nations.

The Erie were formidable bowmen and used poisoned arrows. About 1650 a conflict between them and the Seneca (Iroquois) had concluded with a peace agreement. About 1652, as was the custom, thirty Erie leaders went eastward to the Seneca capital to negotiate for a renewal of the pact. An Erie accidentally killed a Seneca. Convinced this was not an accident but a deliberate act of aggression, the incensed Seneca promptly executed twenty-five of the Cat Nation ambassadors.

Peace was no longer possible, and both tribes took to the warpath. The *Jesuit Relations* recount the final struggle, which continued from 1653 to 1656. Ultimately the Erie were forced to capitulate because they were unable to stand before the guns which the Iroquois had obtained from Dutch and English traders. Before their defeat, however, they won several battles and took a heavy toll of Iroquois warriors.

Paraphrasing the accounts written by the Black Robes, Hewitt [32] wrote that the Erie "fight like Frenchmen, bravely sustaining the first charge of the Iroquois, who are armed with our muskets, and then falling upon them with a hailstorm of poisoned arrows," discharging eight or ten before a musket could be reloaded. In one engagement the Erie assaulted and burned a Seneca town. Other Erie pursued an Iroquois war party returning from the region of the Great Lakes, and cut to pieces its rear guard of eighty picked men. Meanwhile a contingent of Erie scouts had reached "the very gate of one of the Iroquois palisaded towns and had seized and carried into captivity one of the greatest Iroquois captains."

To avenge these losses the Iroquois sent eighteen hundred veteran warriors against the Erie. At the head of this powerful force were two chiefs "dressed as Frenchmen, in order to frighten the Erie by the novelty of their garments." When the Iroquois invaders reached an Erie stronghold, identified as Rique, one of the disguised chiefs, taking a leaf from Jesuit doctrine, asked the Erie to surrender before they were destroyed, telling them that "The Master of Life fights for us. You will be ruined if you resist him." The Erie replied that the only "master of life" they recognized was their weapons.

The battle began with no quarter being asked and none given. Launching a fierce assault, the Iroquois finally were able to overcome the stubborn resistance of the defenders, and "entered the fort and there wrought such carnage among the women and children that blood was knee-deep in some places."

The Erie were a broken people, but the battle at Rique "was won at great loss to the Iroquois, who were compelled to remain in the enemy's country two months to care for the wounded." Some Erie fled to other tribes, but most of those still living were led into captivity "to be adopted as one of the constituent people of the Iroquois tribes."

Wyandot: the Islanders

At the beginning of the historic period the Wyandot had two major enemies, the Iroquois and the fur traders who opened the routes from the St. Lawrence Valley to the Great Lakes.

They had long suffered at the hands of the Iroquois when the first white men reached the sites of Quebec and Montreal, for they bitterly complained to them of the cruel attacks by foes who came from the south, the Cayuga, the Seneca, and the Onondaga. The French increased their woes, their physical sufferings, and their mental confusion by introducing among them alcohol, venereal diseases, and the Christian gospel.

The Wyandot belong to the Iroquoian linguistic family. When discovered they were comprised of four main divisions, at least two of which occupied towns spread along the St. Lawrence Valley from the Saugenay River on the north to the Ottawa River on the south. Others lived farther west in the present Province of Ontario.

They clung to their St. Lawrence territory at least as late as 1544. In the years immediately following they were driven from it by the relentless Iroquois. Fur traders arriving in the area in the early sixteen hundreds found the area deserted, except for a few wandering Algonquian hunters and war parties. The languages recorded by the first explorers were no longer heard, and one *voyageur* attributed their disappearance to "a destruction of people . . . for the Iroquois did assemble themselves to the number of 8,000 men, and discomfited all their enemies, whom they surprised in their enclosures," and they "have heretofore exterminated the Algoumequins [Algonquians], them of Hochelaga [the Wyandot in the vicinity of Montreal], and others bordering upon the great river."

The Wyandot were not exterminated. In 1603 the survivors of the St. Lawrence Valley were living with kinsmen south of Georgian Bay. There the fur traders found them, and by 1615 missionaries were attempting to convert them. Relations between the Wyandot and the French remained amicable for a time, but the Iroquois were not satisfied with the destruction they had wrought.

The meaning of the word *wyandot* is uncertain. As well as "islanders," the interpretation of "dwellers on a peninsula" has been suggested. It was the French who called the Wyandot "Huron," the name by which they would be best known. There are conflicting reasons why this designation was chosen. It stems from the French *hure*, indicating "rugged" or "rough," and the deprecating suffix *-on.* It was applied in France as early as 1358 to rebelling peasants, was expressive of contumely and contempt, and, besides "rough," signified "unkempt lout and wretch."

A missionary to the Wyandot in New France supplied what is perhaps a true explanation of how the term "Huron" came to be applied to them. He maintained that about 1600 a French soldier seeing some of these Indians wearing their hair cropped and roached in a barbaric style, and being very unkempt, gave them the name Hurons, "their heads suggesting those of wild boars."

Samuel de Champlain reported that the palisades of Huron towns stood thirty-five feet in height. Adjacent to their settlements they cultivated several kinds of corn, squashes, tobacco, several varieties of beans, and sunflowers from the seeds of which they extracted oil, using it to anoint their heads and for other purposes. Women were uniquely influential in the political affairs of the tribe, and leaders were chosen by the suffrage of mothers.

The Huron worshipped all material objects, natural elements, animals, and many creatures of a teeming fancy, which in their view directly or remotely affected or controlled their well-being. Ethics and morals as such received only a secondary, if any, consideration. They believed in a kinship system for the persons in their pantheon patterned after that of themselves. Public religious worship took place in elaborate ceremonies performed at fixed times, usually coinciding with the change of seasons.

According to Hewitt,[33] the bodies of the dead were wrapped in furs, neatly covered with flexible bark, and then placed on a platform. Some bodies were similarly prepared and then placed in a grave and covered with timber, bark, and earth. At a "great feast of the dead," celebrated at intervals of eight or ten years, the bodies of persons who had died in the interim were brought together and buried in a common grave with solemn ceremonies.

The Iroquois always have been condemned as the most diabolic and sadistic torturers of enemies. However, the evil reputation was gained not because they excelled in fiendishness, for they did not, but for two other reasons, (1) more priests and more fur traders were among them, therefore, more was written about them, and (2) in their many successful forays and their victories in sustained warfare they took more captives than any other people. Although there are numerous records to substantiate this assertion, one of the most detailed and hideous is contained in the *Jesuit Relations* of 1637. Written by Father Paul Le

Jeune, it tells of the terrible tortures inflicted on a captured Iroquois warrior by the Huron. The missionary reported: [34]

"Towards 8 o'clock in the evening, eleven fires were lighted along the cabin, about one brass distant from each other. The people gathered immediately, the old men taking places above, upon a sort of platform, which extends, on both sides, the entire length of the cabin. The young men were below, but were so crowded that they were almost piled upon one another, so that there was hardly a passage along the fires. Cries of joy resounded on all sides; each provided himself, one with a firebrand, another with a piece of bark, to burn the victim. Before he was brought in, the Captain Aenons encouraged all to do their duty, representing to them the importance of this act, which was viewed, he said, by the Sun and by the God of war. He ordered that at first they should burn only his legs, so that he might hold out until daybreak; also for that night they were not to go and amuse themselves in the woods. He had hardly finished when the victim entered. I leave you to imagine the terror that seized him at the sight of these preparations. The cries redoubled at his arrival; he is made to sit down upon a mat, his hands are bound, then he rises and makes a tour of the cabin singing and dancing; no one burns him this time, but also this is the limit of his rest—one can hardly tell what he will endure up to the time when they cut off his head. He had no sooner returned to his place when the war Captain took his robe and said, 'Oteiondi'—speaking of a Captain—'will despoil him of the robe which I hold'; and added, 'The Atachonchronons will cut off his head, which will be given to Ondessone, with one arm and the liver to make a feast.' Behold his sentence thus pronounced. After this each one armed himself with a brand, or a piece of burning bark, and he began to walk, or rather to run, around the fires; each one struggled to burn him as he passed. Meanwhile, he shrieked like a lost soul; the whole crowd imitated his cries, or rather smothered them with horrible shouts. One must be there, to see a living picture of Hell. The whole cabin appeared as if on fire; and, althwart [sic] the flames and dense smoke that issued therefrom, these barbarians—crowding one upon the other, howling at the top of their voices with firebrands in their hands, their eyes flashing with rage and fury—seemed like so many demons who would give no respite to this poor wretch. They often stopped him at the other end of the cabin, some of them taking his hands and breaking the bones thereof by sheer force; others pierced his ears with sticks which they left in them; others bound his wrists with cords which they tied roughly, pulling at each end of the cord with all their might. Did he make the round and pause for a little breath, he was made to repose upon hot ashes and burning coals. . . . But God permitted that on the seventh round of the cabin his strength should fail him. After he had reposed a short time upon the embers, they tried to make him rise as usual, but he did not stir; and one of these butchers having applied a brand to his loins, he was seized with a fainting fit, and would never have risen again if the young men had been permitted to have their way, for they had already begun to stir up the fire about him, as if to burn him. But the Captains prevented them from going any further, and ordered them to cease tormenting him, saying it was important that he should see the daylight. They had him lifted upon a mat, most of the fires were extinguished, and many of the people went away. Now there was a little respite for our sufferer, and some consolation for us. . . . While he was in this condition, their only thought was to make him return to his senses, giving him many drinks composed of pure water only. At the end of an hour he began to revive a little, and to open his eyes; he was forthwith commanded to sing. He did this at first in a broken and, as it were, dying voice; but finally he sang so loud that he could be heard outside the cabin. The youth assembled again; they talk to him, they make him sit up—in a word they begin to act worse than before. For me to describe in detail all he endured during the rest of the night would be almost impossible; we suffered enough in forcing ourselves to see a part of it. . . .

"As soon as day began to dawn, they lighted fires outside the village, to display there the excess of their cruelty, to the sight of the Sun. The victim was led thither. . . . Meanwhile, two of them took hold of him and made him mount a scaffold 6 or 7 feet high; 3 or 4 of these barbarians followed him. They tied him to a tree which passed across it, but in such a way he was free to turn around. There they began to burn him more cruelly than ever, leaving no part of his body to which fire was not applied at intervals. When one of these butchers began to burn him and to crowd him closely, in trying to escape him, he fell into the hands of another who gave him no better reception. From time to time they were supplied with new brands, which they thrust, all aflame, down his throat, even forcing them into his fundament. They burned his eyes; they applied red-hot hatchets to his shoulders; they hung some around his neck, which they turned now upon his back, now upon his breast, according to the position he took in order to avoid the weight of this burden. If he attempted to sit or crouch down, someone thrust a brand from under the scaffolding which soon caused him to arise. . . . They so harassed him upon all sides that they finally put him out of breath; they poured water into his mouth to strengthen his heart, and the Captains called out to him that he should take a little breath. But he remained still, his mouth open, and almost motionless. Therefore, fearing that he would die otherwise than by the knife, one cut off a foot, another a hand, and almost at the same time a third severed the head from the shoulders, throwing it into the crowd, where someone caught it to carry it to the Captain Ondessone, for whom it had been reserved, in order to make a feast therewith. As for the trunk, it remained at Arontaen, where a feast was made of it the same day. . . ."

By the late sixteen forties the Iroquois were extending their conquests in force to the west and northwest. Armed with some four hundred guns which they had obtained from Dutch traders, in 1648 they swept upon the Hurons, and a year later had completed their work of destruction. Whole Huron settlements had been wiped out, and hundreds had been taken into captivity, with no alternative but to accept adoption and become Iroquois or die.

As a tribe the Wyandot now had been destroyed. Some found haven among the Erie and suffered their fate. Others fled to live among the Tionontati,* who dwelt along the shores of Lake Huron, and the tribe known as Neutrals (q.v.), harbors which provided them with no more than brief safety, for both of these peoples also were driven from their homelands by the Iroquois.

Striving to remain together, the majority of the Huron survivors reached Michilimackinac, in Michigan, where they found good farming lands, and abundant game and fish, but the Iroquois would not permit them to rest, and they were forced to flee westward. Their wandering course took them through the next several decades from Manitoulan Island to Green Bay to temporary residence among the Potawatomi, the Illinois, to the Ottawa on the south shore of Lake Superior, and back to Michilimackinac.

But if they were greatly depleted in numbers—it is doubtful that at any time the Huron still free could boast of more than five or six hundred warriors—they were not lacking in bravery, spirit, or their determination to recover the affluence and power they once enjoyed. By the latter part of the seventeenth century they were settled in the Detroit area and in northern Ohio. Gradually during the next sixty to seventy years, after suffering several setbacks, they acquired a paramount influence in Ohio, and it was by their permission that fleeing bands of Shawnee from the south and Delaware from the east settled north of the Ohio River.

The Huron claimed all of Ohio between the river and northward beyond the western end of Lake Erie, and they "exercised the right to light the council fire at all intertribal councils, and although few in number they joined all the Indian movements in the Ohio Valley and the lake region and supported the British against the Americans." [35]

The Americans finished the job the Iroquois had begun in prehistoric

---

* Called the Tobacco Nation by the English, because of the large amount of tobacco they cultivated.

times, forcing them to sell their Ohio and Michigan lands and migrate to Kansas. The final home of the Huron—or Wyandot—was in Indian Territory, later to be the state of Oklahoma.*

Ottawa: Shrewd Businessmen

The Algonquian word *adawe* signifies "to trade," and from it comes the name Ottawa. The traditions of numerous tribes speak of the Ottawa as the great traders and barterers of the Great Lakes region. Until well into the historic period they dwelt throughout a large territory embracing part of the Ottawa River, the French River, Georgian Bay, northern Michigan, and adjacent areas. These locations put them in a position to become middlemen in intertribal commerce, and they took good advantage of their opportunities, dealing extensively in corn, meal, furs, sunflower oil, mats, tobacco, and a large variety of medicinal herbs. Like the earlier Hopewellians, they sent salesmen and buyers great distances, sometimes, according to Champlain, who was one of the first white men to know them, journeying on their business trips more than a thousand miles (presumably round trips).

In prehistoric times, as well as in later years, the Ottawa men appeared without breechclouts, their bodies richly tattooed in various colors and designs, their faces painted many colors. The women were partly covered, and were also tattooed and painted. Both men and women pierced their noses and decorated their ears with ornaments. Early explorers described them as extremely crude, cold-blooded, shrewd, and practical in business matters, cruel and barbarous in the extreme. Some accused them of cannibalism. All, however, spoke in admiration of them as incomparable woodsmen, hunters, and canoeists.

At least some of their leaders possessed lively imaginations, as is indicated by the account of their origin they told to an early French missionary. These tale-tellers declared the Ottawa had been created out of three families. The first was the family of the Great Hare, a man so gigantic that when he laid nets eighteen fathoms deep the water reached only to his armpits. The Great Hare was born on Michilimackinac Island, and he formed the earth. An ingenious ancestor, he invented fish nets after watching a spider weaving a web with which

---

* In order to give as complete an account as possible of some tribes it is necessary to mention tribal wars and other events which took place in the early colonial period. One must rely almost entirely on reports of the first missionaries and explorers, for by no other means may a true picture be obtained of the various peoples as they were before the arrival of Europeans. However, details of conflicts between Indians and white men are beyond the scope of this work, and are, therefore, studiously omitted. I have made every attempt to conclude the histories of all tribes as closely as possible to the termination of the prehistoric period, but certain exceptions are unavoidable.

to catch flies. The Great Hare also decreed that his descendants should cremate their dead and scatter the ashes in the air, for if they failed to follow this custom snow would remain continuously on the ground and the lakes would remain frozen throughout the year. The second of the three families was that of the Carp. When the sun cast its warm rays on the eggs which the Carp had laid in a stream, a woman was formed. The third family was that of the Bear. While the yarn-spinners had forgotten the manner in which the Bear's genesis had taken place, it represented a very important deity in the Ottawa pantheon. According to the missionary, whenever a bear was killed, a feast was held in its honor and the following plea was uttered: "Have thou no thoughts against us, because we have killed thee; thou has sense and courage; thou seest that our children are suffering from hunger; they love thee, and so wish to cause thee to enter their bodies, and is it not a glorious thing to be eaten by the children of captains?"

More seriously the Ottawa claimed that they, the Potawatomi, and the Chippewa of the Algonquian family were originally one people. They migrated to the Great Lakes region from far to the northwest, and separated at Mackinaw, Michigan. The earliest known home of the Ottawa was on Manitoulin Island.

After the Iroquois had destroyed the Huron in 1648–1649 they turned their Dutch guns on the Ottawa. Together remnants of the Huron and the Ottawa fled to Green Bay, Wisconsin, where the Potawatomi lived. Some of them continued on to the Mississippi River in the vicinity of Lake Pepin. Here they came in contact with the Dakota (Sioux), who permitted no incursions in their own territory. Constantly harassed by the Dakota, they turned back to northern lakes Michigan and Huron. Thereafter, the Ottawa had no tribal homeland, being scattered throughout the lower peninsula of Michigan, Wisconsin, and northeastern Illinois.*

The descendants of the great prehistoric traders are still widely scattered, only a few living in or near the vast territory over which they once ruled.

Potawatomi: the Fire Nation

In the Algonquian language Potawatomi signifies "people of the place of the fire," and early Jesuits spoke of them as the Fire Nation, but there is no explanation as to the origin of the name. Both the Caddo and the Creek called them "watermelon people," and the Fox

---

* The famous chief Pontiac was an Ottawa, but his story belongs to the period of the wars for control of the American interior.

called them "grouse people," and other tribes had other names for them, the sources of which are unknown.

The Potawatomi also maintained that they, the Chippewa, and the Ottawa were originally one people, but their traditions are silent upon the question of when or why they divided. As ethnologists understand, human characteristics often throw light on the causes of such separations, and that may be true in this case.

The predominant nature of the Potawatomi differed significantly in several respects from that of the tribes with which they claimed to be consanguineous. Their earliest known home—which they probably occupied for a great many centuries—was the lower peninsula of Michigan, and the first French missionaries and explorers to meet them there described them as being more docile than other Indians of midwestern America. Subsequent reports about them were consistent, characterizing them as more humane and civilized than their neighbors, describing the women as reserved and showing some tendency toward refinement in their manners, and painting the Potawatomi in general as friendly, kindly disposed, intelligent, and inclined to take life easy, to fish and hunt and gamble at various games rather than to cultivate crops or engage in other laborious pursuits, such as winter trapping, to maintain a stable economy. They enjoyed life to the fullest extent possible, practiced polygamy, danced and sang and caroused in prolonged debauches, and appeared to have few cares. The white man, of course, brought an end to that way of life.

The Potawatomi were sun worshippers, offered sacrifices to the sun, ruler of all the world, with pleas to heal the sick, protect them from their enemies, and provide them with adequate sustenance. One of their great annual events was called the Feast of Dreams, at which dog meat was the chief food consumed, and individuals paid obeisance to private manitos, presumably as directed by their dreams.

Although the Potawatomi were neither as enterprising nor as aggressive as other tribes of the Great Lakes region, they were courageous fighters under attack and were not infrequently victorious on the battlefield. However, by early historic times they had been driven from their ancestral homeland and across Lake Michigan to the vicinity of Green Bay. From there they gradually moved southward and established themselves in the area about the southern end of the lake, maintaining villages on the Milwaukee, Chicago, and St. Joseph rivers.

Thereafter their history is much the same as other peoples of the Midwest. The wars created by white men forced them to part into bands, and the advance of settlers drove them ever westward. Some fled to Canada, but most of the Potawatomi moved from southern Michigan, northern Illinois, and Wisconsin toward the west, crossing the Mississippi, their course to oblivion taking them always toward the setting sun, until it ended on the prairies of Kansas and the Indian Territory.

The Neutrals

This was the name given to several tribes by the early French *voyageurs* because they took no part in the known wars between the Iroquois and the Huron. They dwelt in prehistoric times in southern Ontario, far western New York State, northeastern Ohio, and southeastern Michigan. Although connected to the Iroquoian linguistic family, their speech differed greatly from that language. Other tribes of the region called them *Attiwandaronk,* signifying "those whose speech is awry."

One of the first authentic accounts of the Neutrals came from Champlain, who encountered them in 1616. He reported that they were a powerful people and could muster a formidable force of four thousand warriors. They raised a "great quantity of good tobacco, the surplus of which was traded for furs and porcupine quillwork to northern Algonquian peoples . . . they cleared the land with great pains, though they had no proper instruments to do this. They trimmed all the limbs from the trees, which they burned at the foot of the trees to cause them to die. Then they thoroughly prepared the ground between the trees and planted their grain from step to step, putting in each hill about ten grains, and so continued planting until they had enough for three or four years' provisions, lest a bad year, sterile and fruitless, befall them." [36]

One of the first missionaries to reach the Neutrals, Father Daillon, related that their country contained an incredible number of deer which they slaughtered in large numbers by driving them into enclosures made of hedges. The Neutrals, he declared, believed they must kill all animals "they might find, whether required or not, lest those which were not taken would tell the other beasts that they themselves had been pursued, and that these latter in time of need would not permit themselves to be taken." [37] In addition to the great numbers of deer, the country swarmed with elk, beaver, wildcats, black squirrels, bustards, turkeys, cranes, and other birds and animals, ". . . most of which were there all winter, the rivers and lakes were abundantly supplied with fish, and the land produced good maize, much more than the people required; there were also squashes, beans, and other vegetables in season. They made oil from the seeds of the sunflower, which the girls reduced to meal and then placed in boiling water which caused the oil to float; it was then skimmed with wooden spoons. The mush was afterward made into cakes and formed a very palatable food." [38]

If the Neutrals were sedentary, enterprising, and refused to participate in the conflicts between the Iroquois and Huron, they were far from being a peaceful people. Their head chief at the time of their discovery had won his position and political power as a result of his bravery in seventeen wars between the Neutrals and other tribes. He had returned from each conflict with numerous scalps and prisoners, attesting to his prowess as a warrior. In the early sixteen hundreds the Neutrals were waging vigorous warfare against tribes to the west. In 1643 they sent a force of two thousand warriors against a strongly palisaded town of the Mascouten (prairie band of Potawatomi), took it after a ten-day siege, killed several hundred defenders who had surrendered, and took nearly a thousand men, women, and children captives. After torturing to death several score of Mascouten warriors, they put out the eyes of the old men and abandoned them to starve to death.

It was not so much their "neutrality" as it was their numerical strength and their fighting ability that for years kept the Iroquois from launching a full-scale attack on the Neutrals. This situation was reversed after the Iroquois had destroyed the Huron in 1648–1649. Aware that the Iroquois no longer feared them, or any other tribe, the Neutrals sought to prevent a major conflict with their relatives by themselves turning on the helpless Huron. Many desperate Huron sought asylum among the Neutrals in the belief that their policy of neutrality would afford them protection. Instead of protecting them, the Neutrals seized them as prisoners, and also took other Huron hiding in their own country as captives, thereby sealing the doom of all refugees encountered.

The strategy did them no good. Within a year after their successful conquest of the Huron the Iroquois swept down upon the Neutrals. It took them less than two summers of fighting to destroy them. A few hundred managed to flee to the west and were reported living in the vicinity of Detroit in the winter of 1653, but after that date nothing more is known of them. All others were either slain or absorbed by the Iroquois.

The Neutrals lost their identity as an independent people, but they are commemorated in a magnificent natural monument. The name of one of their divisions was Ongniaahra, pronounced Niagara by white men.

Iroquois: People of the Long House

The ancestors of the people who would come to be known to the world as Iroquois had been in the Mohawk Valley and the lake region of New York State for an indeterminable number of millennia before white men first penetrated the Northeastern Woodlands of America. What these Paleo-Indians called themselves more than ten thousand years ago can never be known. Not even as late as five hundred years ago can they be identified by a name, for language, needless to say, can survive only if it is recorded. But some material things—shaped pieces of stone and charcoal and bones—do survive, each in their own individual longevity, without the aid of man. If they cannot tell when people reached a certain place they can tell when people were there. And they can tell a great deal more than that.

Indians who lived by hunting and gathering wild foods were in the Iroquois Country, as geological evidence reckons time, at least as early as a few thousand years after the last remnants of the final glacial period had wasted away. Forests of mixed evergreens and hardwoods covered most of the land when they reached it, and present-day species of birds, fish, and mammals thrived in large numbers. A distinguished geologist, William A. Ritchie,[39] states that at the time "Many existing mucklands and swamps were then shallow lakes and the streams must have flowed clearer, deeper and certainly more constantly than now due to the thick spongy covering of the forest floor. Studies of fossil pollens from bogs . . . have indicated the prevalence of relatively warm and humid conditions favorable to hunting, fishing and the gathering of wild food plants, especially nuts and fruits."

The Paleo-Indian Period was followed by the culture which archeologists term Archaic. They set the beginning of the Archaic Period in New York State about six thousand years ago. It prevailed until about a thousand years before the beginning of the Christian Era, and during this time the way of life of the people underwent few significant changes.

Two predominant cultures divide the New York Archaic Period. The earliest, called Lamoka, is named for a key archeological site discovered at Lamoka Lake in Schuyler County. The Lamoka people had narrow skulls, faces, and noses, and were clearly related to the early Shell Mound people of the Southeast. It would appear, therefore, that they migrated northward as early as five or six thousand years ago.

This was not the case, however, of the people belonging to the later culture of the New York Archaic Period, which is known as Laurentian. They were bands of hunters who came south from the St. Lawrence Valley, and they were evidently descendants of another early wave of migrants who had come across the Bering Land Bridge from Asia, gradually moved southeastward to the Great Lakes and on into eastern Canada. Their skeletons show that the Laurentians differed drastically in physique from the Lamokans. The Laurentians were a people of stocky build with broad heads, faces, and noses.

Here in this ancient age occurred a blending of two distinct physical types of Homo sapiens, and a blending of cultures, out of which evolved new manufacturing techniques, new and improved weapons, new customs. The Laurentians, for example, had developed a stone gouge, unknown to the Lamokans, with which they could excavate dugout canoes and wooden receptacles. And they had musical flutes fashioned of hollow bird bones.

The Lamoka and Laurentian cultures clashed. The older people resented the intrusions by the nomadic hunters from the north. This hostility is indicated by the arrow wounds on their bones. Eventually the two groups overcame their enmity. Ritchie notes that some of the "skull forms as well as the mixed assemblages of grave goods suggest an eventual peaceful intermarriage. Perhaps in this fashion the Lamoka folk and their culture were gradually absorbed by the dominant Laurentians. At any rate, about this time they disappear from view." [40]

Numerous Laurentian archeological sites have produced rich rewards. The presence of adzes, axes, awls, and other tools made of native copper indicate contact with people of the Lake Superior region who mined and worked this metal. Marine shell pendants came to the Laurentians in trade from the Atlantic coast. Other Laurentian body adornments which have been recovered include perforated canine teeth of bear, wolf, and elk, and beautifully engraved combs of antler. Apparently the Laurentians were emotionally attached to dogs, for skeletons of this animal have been found in individual graves and beside human remains. At one place an infant had been interred with a puppy close against its body.

The Lamokans vanished but the Laurentians remained. Changes, however, came steadily through the ensuing millennia as the result of movements of other peoples into the area and increasing contacts with more advanced cultures in the South and Midwest. In the late Laurentian Period the first crude pottery and the first smoking pipes appeared. Then came farming, and with it a new pattern of economy.

In the period of the culture called Woodland, which began about 1000 B.C., development of agriculture steadily increased until hunting had become a secondary source of subsistence. Settlements became more permanent, and the Woodland people moved only when farming lands became exhausted. Storable crops, such as maize and beans, provided security and gave the people more leisure, allowing them to expend energy in the development of a more sophisticated culture. High artistic achievements and complex ritualism, reflective of the Ohio Hopewell Culture, followed. The flow of ideas, products, and techniques into the New York area rose until the ways of life known in the Laurentian Period disappeared. Trade was extensive and far-reaching. Articles such as shells and shark teeth reached the Iroquois Country from the Gulf of Mexico, copper for tools and personal adornments came from Lake Superior, chalcedony for knives and projectiles came from the Licking quarries of Ohio, and from various other interior areas came steatite, freshwater pearls, and jasper. The "cult of the dead" and mound building, which characterized the Hopewell Culture, became predominant in New York in the Middle Woodland Period.

In the late Woodland Culture Period the white man reached the forests and lakes and river valleys of the New York region. The culture that existed at the beginning of the historical period—called the Old Iroquois—had evolved from cultural streams that one after the other had passed through the land for at least a dozen millennia. The people whom the first explorers encountered were not an original type who had migrated from Asia, but an amalgamation of many types, carrying in their veins blended blood, a mixture derived from successive waves of Asiatic migrants and from the shiftings of peoples who themselves had dwelt from paleolithic times in southern, northern, and western regions of America.

The word *iroquois* does not belong to the language called Iroquoian. Its derivation is to be found in the Algonquian word *iri^nakhoiw,* which signifies "real adders," and to which was appended the French suffix *-ois.* The Ottawa, who belong to the Algonquian linguistic family, called the Iroquois *Mat-che-naw-to-waig,* which may be translated to "bad snakes," and other northwestern Algonquian people called them *Nadowa,* which also means "adders." The Algonquian had good reason to use these names, for the Iroquois were their deadliest enemies and eventually destroyed them.

The Iroquois had a name for themselves which the early European intruders heard. It was *Ongwano^nsionni,* and it meant "we are of the extended lodge." It was beyond the capability of the tongue of most white men, but from it came the popular designation "people of the long house."

The incomparable political organization for which the Iroquois were famed did not exist in 1534 when Jacques Cartier opened the Gaspé Basin to European exploitation. Tribes of the Iroquoian linguistic stock then were politically independent, were almost constantly at war with each other, and were spread over an enormous area, extending from the St. Lawrence Valley and lakes Ontario and Erie to the Deep South and on the east to North Carolina and Virginia.

The center of Iroquoian domination in Cartier's time, however, embraced central and western New York State, western Pennsylvania, and Ohio bordering Lake Erie. In this rich and fertile region dwelt the five main tribes of the family, the Mohawk, the Cayuga, the Oneida, the Onondaga, and the Seneca. They were relatives but not friends, and were almost constantly engaged in feudal bloodlettings. Yet it was these five tribes that within a few years created a federal union that not only brought peace between them but demonstrated that they were without

EASTERN WOODLANDS

Earliest Population Estimates*

Abnaki, Passamaquoddy, and Penobscot (1600)	3,000	Mosopelea (1700) (?)	200
Nauset (1600)	1,200	Massachuset (1600)	3,000
Pocomtuc (1600)	1,200	Nipmuc (1600)	500
Narragansett and Niantic, Eastern (1600)	4,000	Wampanoag (1600)	2,400
		Delaware (1600)	8,000
		Mohegan (1600)	2,200
Pennacook (1600)	2,000	Pequot (1600)	2,200
Niantic, Western (1600)	600	Mahican (1600)	3,000
		Montauk (1600)	6,000
		Wappinger (1600)	4,750
Iroquois (Cayuga, Mohawk, Oneida, Onandaga, and Seneca) (1670)	16,000	Honniasont (1638)	4,000
		Ottawa (in U.S.) (1600)	3,500
Neutrals (1600)	10,000	Conoy (1600)	2,000
Wenrohronon (1600)	2,000	Erie (1650)	14,500
Susquehanna (1600)	5,000	Wyandot (Huron) (1600)	18,000
Potawatomi (1600)	4,000		
Nanticoke (1600)	2,700	TOTAL	105,950

* See Note, Population Table, Part One.

peers among all Indians of the United States region for political sagacity, statesmanship, and military prowess.

The famed organization that would come to be known as the League of the Five Nations was born about 1570.* It was largely the work of two men, Dekanawida, who, according to legend, was a Huron refugee, and a powerful Mohawk medicine man, Hiawatha.† These two remarkable leaders preached that political and military unity would not only bring an end to costly wars of revenge but would bring about a peace based upon equality and brotherhood among all Indians.[41] Their pleas were successful, but besides bringing peace among the five nations the

---

* Sometimes called the Six Nations after the Tuscarora fled from the South to New York in the early eighteenth century.
† Longfellow gave the name Hiawatha to the hero of his epic poem, but erroneously set the scene of his story among the Chippewa of the northern Great Lakes region.

way was paved for the organization of the most formidable Indian military machine ever created.

During the ensuing century Iroquois legions swept repeatedly upon weaker peoples, extending their destruction and devastation as far west as Illinois, far up the St. Lawrence, south through Pennsylvania and into southern areas. After they had been supplied with firearms by the Dutch traders along the Hudson River their domination was acknowledged from the Ottawa River in Canada to the Tennessee River, and from the Kennebeck River to the Illinois River and Lake Michigan. Further westward advance by them was stopped by the Chippewa. The Cherokee and the Catawba were able to establish a barrier against them in the South. The French were able to stand against them in the St. Lawrence Valley. In between these widely separated boundaries, however, no force could repel them.

Their wars were waged primarily to secure and perpetuate their political superiority and independence, with economic gain a close but secondary consideration. They practiced ferocious cruelty toward their prisoners, burning even their unadopted women and children captives. Yet they were not only unrelenting barbarians. Hewitt,[42] a noted authority on the Iroquois, stated that for all their savagery, "they were a kindly and affectionate people, full of keen sympathy for kin and friends in distress, kind and deferential to their women, exceedingly fond of their children, anxiously striving for peace and good will among men, and profoundly imbued with a just reverence for the constitution of their commonwealth and for its founders. . . . The fundamental principles of their confederation . . . were based primarily on blood relationship and they shaped and directed their foreign and internal polity in consonance with these principles. The underlying motive for the institution of the Iroquois league was to secure universal peace and welfare among men by the recognition and enforcement of the forms of civil government through the direction and regulation of personal and public conduct and thought in accordance with beneficent customs and council decrees; by the stopping of bloodshed in the bloodfeud through the tender of a prescribed price for the killing of a co-tribesman; by abstaining from eating human flesh; and, lastly, through the maintenance and necessary exercise of power, not only military but also magic power believed to be embodied in the forms of their ceremonial activities."

While scientists may be able to explain, and sometimes reconcile, the presence of diametrically opposed characteristics in a people, the average person would have great difficulty in such a task. This is made abundantly clear by the accounts of early explorers, fur traders, and missionaries, the only sources from which may be obtained pictures of the Iroquois as they were at the end of the prehistoric period.

Father Jogues, who was adopted by a Mohawk clan and then beheaded in 1646 when he was suspected of being a sorcerer, told of witnessing the death by torture of a woman prisoner who was "burned all over her body by torches, and afterwards thrown into a huge pyre. . . . Her body was cut up and sent to the various villages, and devoured. . . . The common people eat the arms, buttocks and trunk, but the chiefs eat the head and the heart." [43] The *Jesuit Relations* contain innumerable accounts of inconceivable tortures which missionaries were forced to watch, although they were no more fiendish than those practiced by some other tribes, notably the Huron.*

One of the best illustrations of the savagery practiced by the Iroquois in their wars of aggression is to be found in the accounts of La Salle's explorations. In the winter of 1680–1681 La Salle with a small contingent of men pushed ahead of his company and descended the Illinois River. He was anxious to reach his lieutenant, Tonty, who with two priests and several *voyageurs* had been left to construct a fort in the Illinois Country the previous year.[44]

An immense town of the Illinois tribe had stood near the mouth of the Vermilion River. It was inhabited mainly in the summer months when corn was grown in large quantities on the rich bottomlands. As La Salle and his little group passed Starved Rock, an area normally inhabited, they saw no smoke, no sign of human life.

Shortly they reached the site of the great town. It had vanished. Not a mat house stood. The ground was blackened by fire as far as the high bluffs that rose above the valley. They stepped ashore to stand with white faces before a scene of unbelievable desolation. On the charred poles of houses were human skulls which had been picked clean by birds. Wolves ran from them dragging parts of human bodies. Buzzards rose from a large cemetery. Every grave had been rifled and the remains they contained had been scattered, providing a hideous feast for the birds of prey and the animals. The caches of the Illinois had been broken open and the stores they had held had been destroyed. The cornfields had been burned when they were ripening in the early autumn sun.

Searching frantically for some clue that would tell them of the fate of Tonty and the others, La Salle went to a crude defensive works which the Iroquois had erected. More skulls had been mounted on its logs and protruding poles. He came upon several fragments of French cloth —nothing more. He examined innumerable skulls, but the bits of hair remaining on them showed that they were Indian.

"I spent the night in a distress which you can imagine better than I can write it," La Salle said in a letter to a friend,[45] "and I did not

---

* See *Wyandot: the Islanders*, this part.

sleep a moment with trying to make up my mind as to what I ought to do. My ignorance as to the position of those I was looking for, and my uncertainty as to what would become of the men who would follow me . . . made me apprehend every sort of trouble and disaster."

He decided at last to leave three men to await the others, and to continue with four men down the river until he had satisfied himself that Tonty had not gone that way.

He and his companions had not traveled far before they understood that the Illinois had attempted to escape from the Iroquois by fleeing down the river, and had been systematically slaughtered. They passed campgrounds that were littered with bodies, some of which had been hacked to pieces.

Near the confluence of the Illinois and the Mississippi they saw ahead another campground and were startled by the sight of several human figures standing erect and motionless. As they landed they were revolted by the scene which met their eyes.

The erect figures were the partially eaten bodies of women, still hanging from stakes on which they had been tortured to death. About the campground were the corpses of scores of women and children, mutilated masses of rotted flesh. Eyes had been gouged out. Limbs and breasts and vital organs had been torn from them.

Here was the site on which the Iroquois had held their final orgy, a mass torture of women and children. Here they had turned back, their ferocity and demonic passions sated at last in a bloody bath and a feast of human flesh.*

The enmity which the Iroquois always held for the French may be traced to a single event. At the beginning of the seventeenth century in Canada, Champlain had laid the groundwork on which the fur trade eventually would attain an invulnerable healthiness. The Iroquois, and especially the Mohawk, had long been invading the St. Lawrence Valley, wreaking havoc on the tribes who occupied it and the lands to the west. These insatiable aggressors, the Canadian Indians told Champlain, were incomparable warriors who approached like foxes, fought like lions, and flew away like birds. Their homeland was to the south, in a beautiful land of fine forests, lakes, streams, and lush valleys, and which was incredibly rich in furs. Unless their murderous incursions were halted, the St. Lawrence fur trade from the west to Montreal and Quebec could not be profitably conducted.

Champlain understood that it was vitally necessary for the French to hold the friendship and the trade of the Huron, Algonquian, and Montagnais people, and in 1609 he agreed to aid them in delivering a

---

* Tonty and the men with him had escaped the Iroquois and had made their way north to friendly Indians in Wisconsin.

blow that might strike fear in the hearts of the Iroquois. He led a motley force of French and Canadian Indians eastward from the St. Lawrence. On the long lake that would be given his name a war party of two hundred Mohawk, led by three chiefs, was encountered. Champlain ordered an attack. In the short battle that followed he shot two of the chiefs dead and wounded a third. The guns of the other Frenchmen swiftly dispatched several more Mohawk.

This was the first time the Iroquois had come up against the firearms of white men. Completely dismayed and terrorized by the deadliness of the missiles which came out of the noise and belching smoke and fire, they quickly broke and fled. Champlain did not pursue them, but far from achieving its intended purpose the clash marked the beginning of a hundred years of vicious warfare between the French and the Five Nations, and it made the Iroquois friends of both the Dutch and the English.

In the later conflicts between the French and English the Iroquois took the side of the English and were in a large part responsible for their final victory. Subsequently all but one of the Five Nations, the Oneida, fought against the American colonists, and in 1779 met their final defeat at the hands of the new nation's frontier troops.

Wenrohronon: People of the Place of Floating Scum

From time immemorial near the present little western New York town of Cuba a yellowish-brown, foul-smelling liquid had bubbled slowly from the earth and created a filthy stagnant pool. The people who lived there did not speak of the slimy scum as oil, but they, and others, knew that it had some therapeutic value. It softened dry skin, soothed burns, and it had a salutary effect, when compounded with other medicines, on such disorders as stomach pains and constipation.

They were the Wenrohronon, who belonged to the Iroquoian linguistic family, and their name meant "the people of the place of floating scum."

East of them lived the Five Nations, but if these people were their relatives they were not their friends. West of them, however, they had strong allies, the Neutrals, and it was due to this friendly alliance that they were able to maintain themselves until well into the seventeenth century.

In 1639 their doom was sealed. The Neutrals withdrew their guarantee of protection, and the Wenrohronon were left a prey to the Iroquois legions. They sent emissaries to the Huron, asking for asylum, and it was granted to them. Some six hundred, mainly the elderly and women and children, fled to the Huron Country, but many died of hunger, exposure, and exhaustion before they reached it.

The remainder—perhaps as many as fifteen hundred persons—elected to cast their lot with their former protectors, and when the Iroquois destroyed the Neutrals they suffered the same fate.

The People of the Place of Floating Scum vanished, and the Seneca, who had always coveted the famous smelly spring, claimed it. Until long after the Iroquois themselves had been destroyed, and the Americans had taken possession of their country, the floating scum was known as Seneca Oil.

Dates to Remember

1000–1010—In the Sagas it is said that red cloth was offered to the natives for the furs of animals. These Indians were probably Abnaki. During the bartering, violent arguments took place. There was at least one bloody battle in which both Norsemen and natives were slain. Under such circumstances was the wall of mystery which shut out the west, beyond the northern sea, penetrated for the first time.

The aperture, to be sure, was very small, and when the last Vikings vanished into the mists whence they had come, it was again tightly closed. For nearly five centuries the seal of time remained unbroken upon it.

Except for these inconsequential incidents, the history of North America had no dawn. Then suddenly the New World was there, standing in the blaze of a sun fully risen above a horizon that a few moments earlier had separated the fanciful from the real.

1492—At the time Columbus aroused Europe with his southern discoveries, more than a thousand sea miles north of San Salvador Island, along the bleak and rocky coasts of the lands that would be called Canada and New England, men harboring not a dream of reaching India but a more prosaic hope of finding new fishing grounds also were making discoveries of surpassing importance.

Bretons, Normans, and Englishmen, miraculously navigating their staunch little boats on circular courses westward and southwestward from Iceland, had come upon the rugged shores of Labrador and Newfoundland. They had steered into the Strait of Belle Isle, touched at Bonavista, beaten their way around Cape Race into the great Gulf of the St. Lawrence, and some of them had sailed on southward, quartering the headlands of Nova Scotia, standing off bays and river mouths of Maine and avoiding the treacherous sand spits of a queer hook of land that would one day be known as Cape Cod.

They, too, traded with people on the shores, but there are no records to show where they landed to dry their fish and nets and to trade, no records to tell the identities of the people they met. The fishermen of northern Europe were not geographers, not cartographers, not sophisticated explorers, not slavers, and, above all, they were not communicative about the locations of fishing grounds that brought them unexpected rewards. Nor were they talkative about red people who willingly traded valuable furs for worthless trinkets. Not Oriental silks and spices, not gold and silver, not captives, not a passage to China, but fish and furs dominated the reasoning of their practical minds.

They made no statements, wrote no reports, but gossip and words dropped in waterfront taverns of British and French ports leaked out to stir the blood of navigators, to whet the appetites of enterprising merchants, and even to attract ears in high places. While the source of a fish might easily be concealed, the source of a particular kind of luxurious fur, and the location of an immense untouched land inhabited by savages, could not for long be kept secret.

Even as the great Genoese had watched the Azores fade over the stern of the *Santa Maria,* British shipmasters had been poking out into the North Atlantic. They had been looking for islands which the rumors attributed to the fishermen—ignorant fellows with no knowledge of science—indicated lay to the westward.

1497–1498—It was not, however, until five years after the first voyage of Columbus that one of the educated captains succeeded in recording a previously unknown landfall. John Cabot, sailing under royal orders and financed by Bristol merchants, reached the south shore of Newfoundland and went on southwestward to Cape Breton Island before turning homeward. He was back again the next summer, reportedly sailing far enough south along the American coast to alarm the Spanish in the Caribbean. He found people who would be called Massachuset.

1499—Joao Fernandez, a Portuguese from the Azores, saw much more of the coast.

1500–1501—Gaspar Corte-Real reached various localities. He sent sixty Indian captives back to Europe, but the vessel he commanded disappeared at sea. Other explorers passed along the northeastern shores, and although some of them took slaves, they saw nothing of commercial value in the savage culture of the natives. Of course, all of them were blinded by a dream of finding a passage to India, and little else mattered to them.

1523–1524—Giovanni da Verrazano, a Florentine engaged by Francis I of France to find a short northern route to Asia, thought he saw the Pacific on the other side of a narrow peninsula. He was looking into either Chesapeake or Delaware Bay. Turning north he entered New York harbor and Narragansett Bay and sailed along the Maine coast. He encountered numerous natives, probably Delaware, Narragansett, Wampanoag, Penobscot, and others. His experiences with them indicated that all of them were well aware of the slave raids which were taking place along the north Atlantic coast, and were prepared to fight to protect themselves. The Indians were, he said, "so rude and barbarous that we were unable, by any signs we could make, to hold communications with them. They clothe themselves in the skins of bears, lynxes, seals, and other animals."

1524–1525—Close behind Verrazano came Esteban Gómez, voyaging on behalf of the Council of the Indies. He systematically explored the coast from Nova Scotia to Florida. Besides a shipload of Indians, he brought back glowing reports of the "agreeable and useful countries" he had seen. Gómez's voyage made it virtually certain that no waterway led from the North Atlantic to the Kingdom of the Grand Khan, but no one believed him.

1534–1535—Jacques Cartier, on his second voyage to North America, sailed up the St. Lawrence to the site of Quebec, left his ships and continued in small craft as far up the immense river as Hochelaga (Montreal), meeting many Algonquian people. The great waterway to the interior had been opened.

1603—Samuel de Champlain, on his first trip to Canada, ascended the St. Lawrence to Lachine Rapids.

1605—Champlain sailed south from Nova Scotia to Nauset Harbor on Cape Cod.

1606—Champlain reached Vineyard Sound.

1608—Captain John Smith began his exploration of the Chesapeake Bay region and adjacent areas.

1608–1609—Champlain built a fort at Quebec, then passed up Richelieu River to Lake Champlain. Led first attack by white men on Iroquois in their own country.

1609—Henry Hudson sailed up the river named for him as far as Albany.

1610–1611—Champlain developed fur trade on St. Lawrence.

1613—Champlain explored Ottawa River, hoping to reach Hudson's Bay.

1615–1616—Champlain reached Georgian Bay. He joined the Hurons in raiding the Iroquois, crossing Lake Ontario and reaching lakes Oneida and Onondaga. Men Champlain sent out were the first to explore the western Great Lakes region.

1669—Near the Niagara portage La Salle met Louis Joliet, who was returning from a trip in search of copper mines at Lake Superior. La Salle went southward and in the fall discovered the Ohio River near the rapids at Louisville, Kentucky.

SOME INDIAN PLACE NAMES*

Maine

Passamaquoddy, bay
Penobscot, county, bay, river
Appalachian, mountains
Norridgewock, town
Kennebec, county, river
Kennebago, lake
Kennebunk, town
Pemaquid, town

New Hampshire

Mohawk, river
Appalachian, mountains
Ossipee, town, lake, river,
   mountains
Merrimack, county, river
Nashua, town, river
Winnipesauki, lake
Pennacook, town, lake

Vermont

Missisquoi, river
Winooski, river

Massachusetts

Massachusetts, state, bay
Nauset, town
Nantucket, county, town,
   sound
Neponset, river

Connecticut

Connecticut, state, river
Mohegan, town
Willamantic, town
Yantic, river
Niantic, river
Shetucket, river

Rhode Island

Niantic, town
Narragansett, town, bay

New York

Tuscarora, town
Susquehanna, river
Montauk, town, point
Saratoga, town
Oneida, county, town, lake
Onondaga, county, town
Canondaigua, town
Huron, town
Seneca, county
Cayuga, county, lake
Mohegan, town
Montawk, town, point
Niagara, falls, town
Catskill, mountains
Wappingers, falls
Nyack, town
Tioga, county
Nanticoke, town
Erie, county
Ontario, lake
Appalachian, mountains
Carnarsee, town

New Jersey

Raritan, town, bay

Delaware

Tioga, town
Delaware is not an Indian name, and
the state has almost no Indian place
names.

Maryland

Tuscarora, town
Chesapeake, bay
Potomac, river, town
Wicomico, county, river
Seneca, town
Nanticoke, river
Appalachian, mountains
Texas, town

* Tribes and tribal subdivisions.

Pennsylvania

Shawnee-on-Delaware, town
Shawnee, town
Tuscarora, town, mountains,
    creek
Appalachian, mountains
Niantic, town
Susquehanna, county, town,
    river
Erie, lake, city, county
Seneca, town
Tioga, county, river
Conestoga, town
Conoy, town
Nanticoke, town
Wyoming, county, town

Michigan

Mohawk, town
Michigan, state, lake
Huron, lake, county, town,
    river
Noquet, bay
Ottawa, town
Erie, town
Yuma, town
Wyandot, town
Menominee, county, town
Chippewa, river, county
Lacota, town

Ohio

Chickasaw, town
Ohio, state, river
Catawba, town
Chesapeake, town
Oneida, town
Erie, lake
Mohican, town
Coshocton, town
Muskingum, river
Ottawa, town
Erie, county
Miami, county, river
Huron, county, town, river
Wyandot, county, town
Maumee, river
Piqua, town
Chillicothe, town
Shawnee, town
Seneca, county
Chippewa, river
Kansas, town
Spokane, town

Scientific Note: Springs of Commerce

Three specks appear on a distant rise. The sentries of the town give the alarm and watch them. Always the sentries are squinting into distance. Not animals this time, but men. The children are gathered. The women, in preparation for an attack or a siege, see that the water jars are filled and the food stores are covered to conceal them. The men look to their weapons. The dogs have sighted the strangers and with growls retreat to their hiding places or circle about nervously, barking and whining.

The three men approach slowly, pausing now and then and giving signs. They are signs of peace, of friendship. But the people of the town remain alert, on guard, ready.

The three men hold up pieces of colored cloth, or furs, or painted gourds, or bits of stone that catch the sunlight and throw it out.

From the town, some men cautiously walk out. And seeing them, the three strangers sit down.

Traders.

There is some talking by signs. And then all go to the town. There are exclamations of welcome. The trading blankets are spread. A pipe is passed about. There is laughter and banter. The women and children watch in sheer pleasure. There may be new things to gaze at in admiration and wonder. There may be new ideas to talk about.

For a brief time the isolation is interrupted. Then the hills, or the deserts, or the surrounding woodlands are empty again, and the sentries squint once more into distance.[46]

That is an imaginary scene, but there is ample evidence to show that similar events frequently took place in every part of the region of the United States. There is indisputable proof that far back in prehistoric times—no one may say how far—a network of Indian trade trails reached from ocean to ocean. In mid-continent archeological sites artifacts have been recovered that came from the Eastern and Southeastern Woodlands, from the Gulf of Mexico, from the Pacific Coast, from the Gulf of California, from the Rocky Mountains, from Canada.[47]

Prehistoric trade was affected and shaped by conditions, both natural and man-made. And trade was influenced by geography and climate, just as it is today. For the Indians there would have been few vital changes—either social, intellectual, or economic—before the arrival of Europeans without a steadily increasing diffusion of ideas, customs, and products through a constantly enlarging primitive commerce. Trade spread knowledge and awakened minds. It gave to one man the opportunity to learn from another. Trade distributed materials—animal, vegetable, and mineral, in raw form and as manufactured goods—to raise standards of living, to increase comfort, and to improve health. These materials inspired refinements and led to inventions.

The prehistoric Indian's intellect was limited by his way of life and his environment, not by his mental capacities. He was eager to learn and to improve himself. And there were two ways in which he could accomplish these things—by observation and by social intercourse.

Intertribal combat interrupted trade, but chiefly by causing people to be occupied by it instead of engaging in commerce. Yet, most of the time, as Cabeza de Vaca made clear, traders could go with comparative safety where war parties dared not venture. So it seems apparent that in prehistoric centuries there were intertribal laws of commerce. Perhaps they should not be called *laws*. They were not rigid nor were they universal in character. In fact, nothing was universal—neither customs, nor religion, nor any way of life among aboriginal peoples.

Not international *laws* of commerce, then, but *general understandings, general attitudes*. And these understandings and attitudes had for their bases the realization that traders brought benefits and opportunities, not perils and warfare. So it was that bona fide traders in almost every place had well-defined immunities and privileges accorded to no one else. The prehistoric Indian was as commercial-minded as he was artistic and superstitious.

It might be said that prehistoric traders were looked upon as neutrals, but once again it should be noted that there were exceptions. Prehistoric Indians were like all other peoples on earth, in that among them were outlaws, thieves, and irresponsible persons of every conceivable type who had little respect for laws, for established customs and general understandings, or for any form of authority. Trade goods were stolen and traders were injured and slain. But these crimes were not commonplace. In most cases traders were able to complete their missions without undue suffering at the hands of bandits. And there is evidence to show that in historical times goods stolen from traders were paid for in kind or returned. It was undoubtedly the same in earlier times. This was not true, however, of goods taken in warfare. They were considered legitimate spoils, and the losers were accorded no sympathy. Nor did they have any recourse. Only by more fighting, and by being victorious, could a loser recoup his losses.

The world of prehistoric Indian commerce was, in most respects, a world of its own.

All trade routes followed water. However, in some regions the routes were on the water rather than beside it.

In the East, the South, and the Midwest the main arteries of commerce were rivers and lakes, and for the most part goods were transported in canoes. This was true in the far Northwest, on the Columbia and its lower tributaries, where some Indian craft were very large and could carry a number of persons and heavy cargoes. And canoes and rafts, none of them very large, were used on some of the California bays and rivers, but not for great distances. The Missouri River was a water highway from the Mississippi to the northern Rocky Mountains, but Indian travel on it was not extensive before the arrival of the French *voyageurs*. The Mississippi and its many immense tributaries below the mouth of the Missouri, of course, formed the greatest of all trade route networks.

All of these waterways were on the periphery of the West, and between them, in a gigantic region of plains, mountains, forests, and deserts, most of the streams were too shallow, too swift, or too often interrupted by impassable rapids and falls to be useful for transport. In the great West the traders went on foot, bearing their goods in packs.

Yet if the western streams were not usable for travel they were vital to the success of a trading venture. In every part of the West the land trails paralleled the water courses. In areas where there were no living streams the trails ran from waterhole to waterhole. In areas where either streams or waterholes were too widely separated to permit overland travel by foot between them, there could be no trade trails, but that was not the case in most of the West, not even in the worst deserts.

To survive, prehistoric travelers had to have water available at short intervals, for they could not carry much with them. But the water courses were the best routes for another reason—in every region. They were the lines of least resistance, found and carved by the forces of the elements and of the earth.

And so the trade trails found natural crossroads, the crossroads of geography. And from these junctions they ran out like twisting threads until they came to other crossroads, all together forming an irregular woven pattern that was shaped to the contours of the land. Most of the junctions were of little or no consequence in the lives of the people or the journeys of the traders, but some were of great importance and vitally influenced the lives of people. Some had a bearing on the progress and development of society, on economics, on the entire culture of immense regions. Attesting to that fact are the locations of the present-day trade centers of the United States. They invariably arose where geography changed, at the confluences of rivers or where the plains met the mountains or where rivers entered the sea.

Of course, it was the animals which made the first land trails. Demonstrating the superbness of their inherent engineering ability, the animals, for mile after mile, marked out passable courses through the roughest of country. Of all the ridges, they ascended the gentlest. They moved back from a stream only when forced to do it by impassable uplifts, but seldom were the ways they went beyond easy reach of grass and water and shelter. And men followed the animals, rarely being able to improve the courses their hooves had charted.

By necessity, when they hunted or went on raids, the prehistoric peoples carried a minimum amount of baggage. Food, clothing, cover, utensils, tools, religious articles, ornaments, and souvenirs generally were considered in that order in preparing for a journey. This was not the case on trading missions. The products to be bartered were given the highest priority. The largest amount of trade goods that could be borne on human backs—in some areas dogs were used—would be taken along.

Intertribal trade increased demands for luxuries. It inspired higher grades of industry. And Indians in every region sought to fulfill these demands and to produce not only new products but improved ones. Until the coming of the white man, Indian artisans of both sexes gave free rein to aesthetic impulses.

It should not be forgotten that in Pre-Columbian times neither beast nor wind nor water turned a wheel in America. Yet the ingenuity of the prehistoric Indian is made apparent by certain factors, and it cannot be justly contended that had the arrival of Europeans been delayed for only a short time the Indians would not have discovered the wheel. Indeed, wheeled pottery toys were made by prehistoric Indians in Mexico.

In the fifteenth century American Indians were on the border of machinery. They had discovered the reciprocating two-hand drill, the bow and strap drill, and the continuous-motion spindle. Some tribes produced marvelously fine and elegant woven robes of native fibers, of goat and dog hair, of rabbit skin strips, of feathers, and of the skins of birds. Eastern and midwestern craftsmen specialized in quill work, in wood and stone carvings, in metal ornaments and plaques, in decorated costumes. The peoples of the Pacific Coast made matchless basketry. The Indians of the Southwest manufactured and decorated incomparable pottery in an endless variety of shapes and sizes. The tanned animal garments of the Great Plains tribes were far superior to all others.

Nor can the economy of this American wilderness justly be termed simple. It was simple only in the sense that it was founded on barter. There were too many products and too many varieties of them, and they represented too many cultures, and they were transported over distances too great, to permit usage of the words *a simple economy*.

There were five kinds of industrial activities which contributed to the advancement of prehistoric commerce and to the spreading of knowledge:

1. The primary or exploiting arts and industries; that is, the seeking and acquiring of nature's bounties.

2. The shaping and manufacturing of raw materials, the secondary arts and industries.

3. The use of traveling and transportation devices.

4. The development of the mechanism of exchange.

5. The ultimate arts and industries, the using or enjoyment of finished products, or consumption.

Quality, good craftsmanship, and artistry were potent stimulants to prehistoric trade. The people of one region sought the superior products they knew were to be found in another region, and it was not unusual for them to travel hundreds of miles, if necessary, to obtain what they wanted. And if people were unable to go directly to the source, the point of origin, for the things they wanted, they knew how to get them through the channels of intertribal trade.

Central Prairies
and Woodlands

Miss Minnesota

An ornament she had worn was found first. It had tumbled out of a road cut being excavated through a gravel deposit, some ten feet below ground surface, in 1930. A grader operator, attracted by the shiny white object, had climbed off his machine and picked it up. It appeared to be part of a shell. Then he saw that nearby some bones were exposed.

Their curiosity stirred, the highway workers had paused in their duties to do a little digging by hand. They soon came upon a human skull and part of a skeleton. As they removed these remains they found among them a knife about nine inches in length which had been made from an elk antler, and a conch shell with two perforations. The conch shell lay among the ribs and vertebrae of the abdominal area.

Word of the discovery, which was made near Pelican Rapids in western Minnesota, was sent to the University of Minnesota, and the eminent archeologist A. E. Jenks hurried to the scene. He must have felt like crying when he saw the damage that had been done, for he realized at once that a find of transcending importance had been made.

While the workmen had handled the skull with care, their act of removing it from the gravel had prevented trained observers from viewing it *in situ*. Jenks and several aides, however, began a careful excavation of the site, and they recovered *in situ* other bone fragments, some of which could be fitted to those found by the road builders.

It was not so much the finding of the bones as it was the location in which they had been found that caused excitement in the scientific world. The gravel through which the cut was being made was the bed of an ancient lake—known as Glacial Lake Pelican—which had formed shortly after the retreat of the last continental ice sheet, perhaps some twenty thousand years ago, and several millennia later had become extinct. The varved clays in which the remains and the artifacts had been discovered belonged to the Pleistocene, and had been laid down some eleven thousand years ago.

The skeleton was thought at first to be that of a young male, and was given the name Minnesota Man. Later examinations left no doubt that it was that of a girl, probably no more than fifteen years of age.

It seems unlikely that Miss Minnesota would have won any beauty contests, even if they had been held—and perhaps they were held—in the Pleistocene. As Professor Jenks described her, among the most important primitive morphological characteristics of her skull "was the lack of reduction of the jaw and teeth," and archeologist Wormington [1] noted that the "teeth are, in fact, extraordinarily large, even larger than those of certain Paleolithic men. The cusp pattern of the molars is of a primitive type. The upper incisors are shovel-shaped, a trait ordinarily associated with Mongoloids. There is a marked protrusion of the portions of the upper and lower jaws which contain the front teeth and a pronounced backward extension of the skull which is narrow relative to its length."

To most scientists, however, Miss Minnesota is utterly beautiful, and no skeleton has been the cause of more professional squabbling. If she is as old as the glacial deposits in which she was buried, her age outranks that of any other American female whose remains have been discovered. Not a small distinction, to be sure, but after forty years of arguing and discussion anthropologists have failed to resolve the question of whether or not she deserves it. Perhaps it will never be answered to the satisfaction of all of them.

Nevertheless, certain factors of the case are beyond dispute. The perforated shell found in her rib cage, which she probably wore as a pendant on a thong, has been identified as a marine shell of a species found on the Gulf of Mexico. Obviously, since she had it in her possession, there must have been contact between Paleo-Indians of Minnesota and people living farther south. The most reasonable assumption is that it reached Minnesota through trade channels, and, as she was very young, was given to her by a relative or perhaps a young swain who enjoyed her charms. Probably the elk horn knife she carried was suspended from a girdle.

The depth at which Miss Minnesota was found strongly supports the contention of anthropologists and geologists that she lived in the Pleistocene. It seems illogical to think that she would have been interred in a grave ten feet deep. The suggestion that she was buried in a landslide is not substantiated by the geology of the site. Even if she had fallen or had been buried in an open pit ten feet deep, it would be necessary to assume, as some archeologists point out, that the crack had closed over again without crushing or disturbing the bones, a most unlikely occurrence. Even if that had happened, the girl's skeleton still would belong to the Pleistocene, for, according to Wormington, the special climatic and topographic "conditions necessary to induce landsliding would be associated with a period almost as remote as the [clay] varve formation" in which her bones were found.

Most of the many prominent scientists who have studied the case of Miss Minnesota lean toward at least one conclusion. It is that she fell into Glacial Lake Pelican and drowned.[2]

Miss Minnesota's Contemporaries

They lived throughout the entire region of the Central Prairies and Woodlands, from Minnesota to Arkansas, from Indiana to Missouri and Iowa. These Paleo-Indians were there soon after the end of the Ice Age. They lived on the sites of the sprawling midwestern cities, Chicago, Minneapolis, St. Paul, Kansas City, Omaha, St. Louis. That they had been, or were, in contact with people of the Great Plains, the Southwest, and the Rocky Mountains is beyond question. This is made clear by the type of projectiles which have been unearthed in midwestern archeological sites and have been recovered in surface finds. They hunted the great animals of the Pleistocene, such as the woolly mammoth, the mastodon, and the giant bison, with spears tipped with flaked points like those which have been found on the sites of animal kills in Nebraska, Wyoming, and New Mexico. Other artifacts, tools and utensils and ornaments, indicate a previous relationship with other peoples in far-distant environments to the north, to the west, and to the south. This is all that can be told of them, except that their features were Mongoloid, and they were unquestionably descendants of earlier peoples who through millennia had drifted slowly from the Bering Land Bridge southward and eastward to the interior of the continent. Of their social customs, their religious beliefs, their languages, nothing is known. They were hunters and gatherers of wild plant foods—period.

Just when the immense Pleistocene mammals became extinct in this region cannot be determined. It is, of course, unlikely that they disappeared at the same time in all areas. Some may have existed for longer periods than others, and those of one species may have been present longer in some sections than in others. But it is known when they were there, if not when they vanished.

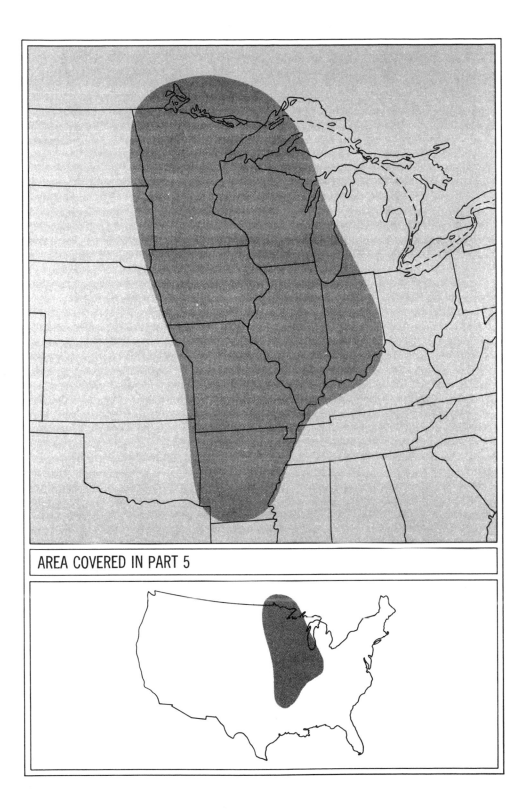

AREA COVERED IN PART 5

Wood, not their bones, has been one important source of definite dates. The Carbon-14 method of dating showed that charcoal found under and beside mastodon bones near Cromwell, Indiana, was more than ten thousand years old. In numerous other localities, charcoal associated with ancient bones has yielded comparable dates.

Missouri has been one of the richest fields in which discoveries have been made that show man in association with Pleistocene mammals. The first important find of record occurred in 1838, when Albert C. Koch, a dealer in fossils, unearthed charred mastodon bones and stone artifacts on the Bourbeuse River in Gasconade County. Two years later, on the Pomme de Terre River in Benton County, he found a mastodon skeleton that was almost complete, and near it three ancient projectile points. He sold some of the bones and the points to the University of Berlin Museum.[3] Although Koch had published papers on his findings, there was some doubt for many years in the minds of anthropologists as to the correctness of his postulations. Records were incomplete and some had been mislaid. However, after World War II, nearly a century after Koch's reports had been written, some of the bones and spearheads were located in the Berlin Museum, and proof of their antiquity was confirmed.

The form of a Pleistocene elephant was carved on a deer shoulder bone that was found in Jacob's Cavern in southwestern Missouri. Physiochemical studies indicated that both the bone and the carving were fourteen thousand years old, but some archeologists do not accept this conclusion.[4]

Thousands of well-flaked, long, narrow, and thick projectile points with straight bases have been recovered on ground surface in the regions of Sedalia and Kansas City, Missouri. They are different enough to merit an identity of their own, and archeologist J. M. Shippee gave them the name Nebo Hill.[5] They were perhaps the forerunners of similar points called Guilford, which are more than six thousand years old and have been recovered in North Carolina. Other types of points have been found in the same areas of Missouri, and some of them may be two or three thousand years older than the North Carolina points. There seems to be little doubt that man hunted in the southern sections of the Central Prairie and Woodland region long before he reached the Northeast.

Another Missouri cave, Graham, near the confluence of the Loutre and Missouri rivers, has produced man-made stone implements which have turned the archeological clock back nearly ten thousand years.[6] Drills, scrapers, knives, and mortars were recovered, as well as several types of points. Of special interest were projectiles resembling the Clovis found in New Mexico, and others similar to points found in Nebraska, Texas, Oklahoma, Arkansas, Iowa, Illinois, and Canada.

The inference seems clear that the Paleo-Indians who occupied Graham Cave, and other adjacent caves, either had wandered over great distances or had acquired different point-making techniques from other wanderers.

In 1900 a Mississippi River flood destroyed part of an island that lay in the main river channel near the northern border of Arkansas. The receding floodwater exposed the skeleton of a mastodon. Some of the bones were carried away by local residents before scientists reached the scene, but some remained in position when Dr. James K. Hampson excavated them. Beneath the pelvis of the immense skeleton he found a broken projectile point. It was similar to those found by Koch more than half a century earlier in Gasconade and Benton counties, Missouri.[7]

One of the most important discoveries in the central region was accidentally made in 1933 near Brown's Valley, Minnesota, by an amateur archeologist, William H. Jensen. According to Elden Johnson, Minnesota state archeologist, Jensen happened to notice fragments of human bones and a flaked projectile point in a load of gravel brought to his place of business from the Brown's Valley municipal gravel pit.[8] He went immediately to the pit where he found other bone fragments and points. Recognizing their importance, he reported the discovery to Professor Jenks of Minnesota University. Jenks wasted no time getting to the site.

The investigation resulted in the finding of more points in association with the skeleton of an adult male who had been interred in a grave dug into gravel at the outlet of Glacial Lake Agassiz. Knives made of brown chalcedony also were found with the human bones.

"Geological evidence," states Johnson,[9] "suggests that the burial was placed in the gravel ridge after the termination of the southern Glacial Lake Agassiz drainage, but before there had been an appreciable soil formation on the gravel surface. No firm date can be assigned to Brown's Valley man, but similar projectile points uncovered in a Wyoming site date to almost eight thousand years ago."

One wonders if Mr. Brown's Valley knew Miss Minnesota or Mr. Sauk Valley, whose remains also were found by gravel pit operators in 1935 near West Union, Minnesota.[10] Johnson reports that the Sauk Valley man's skeleton "appeared to lie deep in a gravel deposit below undisturbed and well-bedded gravels, and the brain case was packed with sand from the deposit. No artifacts were found with the burial. From these observations, the men who studied the site and the find concluded that the skeleton was not a late burial intruded into the gravel deposit, but an accidental entombment dating from the time when the upper gravels were deposited. Such remains of early man are rare in North America, and Minnesota certainly has more than its share of the finds made to date." [11]

Some further clues as to the age of the Minnesota skeletons are to be found in an analysis by Wormington: [12] "Geological evidence, as interpreted by Frank Leverett and Frederick W. Sardeson (1932), indicated that the gravel ridge in which the [Brown's Valley] burial was found had been formed as a gravel bar by water flowing from Glacial Lake Agassiz through an ancient river. The period when water flowed through this river channel was correlated with a beach level known as the Tintah. Leverett and Sardeson, who considered Lake Agassiz to mark the retreat of the Mankato ice, gave a date of eighteen thousand years ago for the beginning of the lake. They dated the beginning of the Tintah stage at about twelve thousand years ago, and the end at between eight thousand and nine thousand years ago. Since the skeleton and the artifacts were intrusive into the gravels, they could not be the same age as the deposits; but the fact that the top of the burial was level with the gravel, and the absence of humus in the burial pit, suggested to Jenks that it was dug soon after the formation of the gravel ridge, before vegetation was abundant."

Worthy of note is the fact that some Carbon-14 dates suggest that Glacial Lake Agassiz began to form *before* the last major advance of the ice. It would appear, therefore, that Mr. Brown's Valley may have been living some twelve thousand years ago, in the Tintah Beach stage, which has been correlated with the gravel ridge in which he was laid to rest, and which was formed by the ancient river. However, that is a postulation that may never be adequately substantiated. The most conclusive evidence of his age is the established antiquity of the projectile points, which make him at least eight, and perhaps ten, thousand years old. They have been named Brown's Valley points, and there is no question as to their similarity to the Eden Valley points found in Wyoming.

Digging in 1952 and 1953 in a rock shelter near Modoc, Illinois, archeologists Melvin L. Fowler and Howard Winters found themselves faced with a mystery. They excavated to a depth of nearly thirty feet. Five distinct zones were uncovered. The upper three zones produced artifacts associated with late prehistoric times. Below these zones they encountered the mystery.

In Zone One, the deepest, they recovered a stone scraper, a pointed bone tool, numerous stone flakes from projectile points, and one projectile point with a contracting stem, a polished bone rod, and a perforated pebble that probably had been part of a pendant. From the material found in this zone they obtained Carbon-14 dates of about nine thousand and ten thousand years of age. [13]

Strangely, similar artifacts found above Zone One, in Zone Two, produced Carbon-14 dates ranging from about eight thousand to more than eleven thousand years ago. Two of the Zone Two dates were older than the oldest date of the Zone One material.

How the oldest artifacts got on top of the deepest part of the excavation is a problem that has not, and may never be, satisfactorily resolved.

A few years ago Iowa became a contender of Minnesota for the distinction of producing the most skeletons of Pleistocene man. As has happened so many times in various localities, it was a gravel pit operator who put Iowa in the running. Near Turin, Iowa, in 1955, Asa Johnson was using a bulldozer to remove loess from a gravel deposit when he saw a human skull roll down a slope. Examining the bank, he came upon other parts of a skeleton. Hearing of the discovery, an eager-beaver county coroner hurried to the site and removed the bones, thinking they might be those of a Turin man who had mysteriously disappeared some years earlier. The obvious great age of the remains precluded that possibility, and a call was put in to the State University. Archeologist Reynold J. Ruppe and paleontologist Weldon D. Frankforter responded. They pronounced the bones to be of great antiquity, and visited the site of the discovery, but no more bones were visible.

Asa Johnson went back to work with his bulldozer, soon unearthed another skull, and notified Frankforter. He brought several other scientists to the site, and a second adult skeleton was discovered. Once more Johnson went back to work. Within a week he had come upon a third skull *in situ*.

Now the scene was reminiscent of the first discovery of Folsom points in New Mexico. In response to telegrams from Ruppe and Frankforter, archeologists, paleontologists, and geologists came from numerous midwestern institutions. Newspapermen also were on hand to give the story to the world. Neither before nor since has the little town of Turin known such excitement nor entertained so many distinguished visitors.

Expert excavators began a systematic investigation of the gravel deposit. A third skeleton, that of an adolescent who had been buried in a flexed position, was removed under what archeologists call *optimum conditions*. Red ocher had been placed in the grave. The digging had reached a depth of approximately fifteen feet when the skeleton of an infant, also buried in a flexed position, was found.

The gravels beneath the loess contained bone fragments of Pleistocene mammals, including mammoth, horse, and camel. No attempt was made to clean any bones on the site. While still in matrix they were wrapped in burlap and plaster and sent to the University of Iowa laboratory. Among the bones of the infant was found a large notched projectile point that resembled types used by early hunters. Whether the infant had been killed by it or it had been placed in the grave as a burial offering could not be determined.[14]

The discoveries placed Turin on the map of Paleo-Indian sites in the central region, for the gravel beds were created by flowage from glaciers. Asa Johnson went back to work removing the loess from them with his bulldozer.

The Rich Land

The great variety of tools, weapons, utensils, and other artifacts recovered are evidence that in the period which archeologists call Archaic —beginning about ten thousand years ago—the northern midlands of the United States region was one of the most bountiful lands on earth.* Many species of game grazed on the lush grasses that in summer waved waist-high on the prairies. Wild fowl in countless millions darkened the sky. Rivers large and small formed a network which permitted travel by canoes from one part to others. Almost every section was suitable for agriculture. Woodlands stood like islands in the rolling prairie sea. Winters in the northern area were usually quite cold and snows were deep, but the length of the growing season, the plentifulness of fuel, and the presence of many kinds of fur-bearing animals prevented economic want. The peoples of the Archaic Period lived well. By far the greater part of their sufferings and privations were of their own making, caused by such things as tribal wars and the greed and jealousy always inherent in man.

Culture after culture came and went through the millennia until the arrival of the white man doomed all Indian culture to extinction. For the Midwest was the crossroads of North America. Waves of different kinds of peoples passed into it and through it from every direction. Archeologists enumerate more than a score of cultures, each of which is characterized by technical changes, by the introduction of different artifacts, and by advancements and developments in customs and economies. Many of them were reflective of cultures in other parts of the United States region—the Hopewell and Middle Mississippi, for example, which have been previously discussed—but some of them had their origin in the Midwest.[15]

The Copper Pounders

The identity of the discoverers of the strange substance cannot be stated. They may have come into the northern Great Lakes area from

---

* See Box *Area Covered,* this part.

the north or northwest. It was copper they found. In surface nuggets and exposed deposits it lay in almost pure form near the shores of Lake Superior. The richest veins were on the Keweenaw Peninsula of northern Michigan and on Isle Royale.

They became the first metalworkers of North America, possibly the first in the world.[16]

At first they worked with the copper as they had worked with the stones from which they made their projectile points and their tools, that is, they pecked it and flaked it. Soon, however, the peculiar qualities of the metal impressed their acute minds, and they found that they could shape it by pounding.

The Old Copper Culture was born, and its influences and products rapidly spread throughout the eastern United States and southward into Mexico.

Copper was not mined in the true sense. Workable chunks could be extracted from the fabulous Lake Superior veins by heating any rock that was found around the ore, and then cracking the hot rock by dashing water on it. Stone mauls were used to knock off any rock adhering to the metal.

Tools, ornaments, and utensils made of Lake Superior copper have been recovered in Florida, Alabama, Louisiana, New York, New England, and on the Great Plains. It was enduring and had a beauty value. Therefore it was in great demand, and traders often traveled long distances to obtain it, either in raw form or in finished products. Most Indians wanted it for ornaments, but it was utilized for many other purposes. From it were made celts, picks, gouges, wedges, awls, fishhooks, knives, drills, projectile points, breastplates, finger rings, earrings, pendants, headplates, beads, and coverings for wooden effigies.

The copper ornaments, utensils, and tools were fashioned in two ways: by cold hammering and by heating. Sheets were made, and birds and other designs were drawn on them. A tool, such as a buckhorn, was used to indent the decorations, and articles were cut from sheets by bending and breaking.

Archeologists are unable to explain the decline of the Old Copper Culture. The most logical explanation seems to be that its end was brought about by changing religious ritual and burial customs, that is, by the rise of other cultures, such as that of the effigy mound builders. In any case, long before the beginning of the historical period it had all but vanished.

American Pyramids

The burial mound custom began to evolve in the latter part of the eighth century A.D. Midwestern cultures characterized by it were the

Red Ocher, Morton, Hopewell, Effigy Mound, Laurel, and others, spread throughout the region from Ohio to Iowa, from Minnesota to Missouri. Hundreds of mounds have been located, and dates of human bones and artifacts assign them to this period. It endured for approximately three hundred years.

Then came the Temple Mound Period,* reaching its most spectacular development in the twelfth and thirteenth centuries. The temple mounds were built, as the name implies, as foundations for ceremonial temples and the expansive dwellings of the highest ranking leaders and priests. There were many of them, but the greatest of all, the Cahokia, rises in the American Bottom, on the Illinois side of the Mississippi River about six miles east of St. Louis.

The Cahokia Mound is the largest prehistoric artificial earthwork in the world.

When built, its greatest height was approximately one hundred feet, its east-west width was seven hundred and ten feet, and its north-south length was about eleven hundred feet. A truncated pyramid, rectangular in form, it covered about sixteen acres.

Construction of the Cahokia Mound probably began between A.D. 1200 and 1300. Archeologists estimate that, considering the means available to prehistoric Indians, more than a thousand workers labored about five years, moving some twenty-three million cubic feet of earth in building it.

At one time more than three hundred lesser mounds spread out in the shape of a fan from the Cahokia Mound for seven or eight miles along two creeks, but scientists were able to save less than a hundred of them. The others were destroyed by white settlers and farmers before legislation creating a state park was enacted.

The Cahokia Mound group is associated with the great Middle Mississippi Culture. The builders, many of whose remains have been unearthed, were superb artisans. Numerous of the thousands of artifacts recovered reflect a strong southern influence.

The Middle Mississippi Culture still flourished when the first Europeans reached the southern area of the United States. The people who built the temple mounds of the Midwest were the immediate ancestors of the Indians whom the first explorers and missionaries encountered along the rivers of the Mississippi system. After that time the Temple Mound Culture swiftly declined and it had vanished before the first plows turned the earth of midwestern bottomlands.[17]

---

* See Part Three.

Early Hillbillies

They lived mainly in the countless caves and rock shelters of the Ozark Plateau for an unknown number of millennia before the beginning of the Christian Era. And they were still there at the beginning of the historical period.

The record of their long existence is exceptionally clear, for in the dry caves their possessions, such perishable articles as wooden utensils, fabrics, and basketry—as well as their bones—which would have decayed in more open deposits have been preserved.

In the beginning, their culture was much the same as contemporaries who dwelt in Kentucky, Tennessee, and other highland areas in which caves are found. They were hunters, living on wild game and fowl, the native vegetable plants, and the nuts and fruits of the region.

But artifacts associated with the earliest years of the Christian Era reflect notable cultural changes. They wove baskets similar to those made by Indians who lived in the Basketmaker Period in New Mexico and Arizona.* Obviously there had been contact with people living in the Southwest. It is not improbable that about A.D. 100–200 Indians of the Basketmaker Culture migrated to the Midwest region. In any case, not only their techniques of basket weaving were obtained by the Ozark cave dwellers, but in the early centuries of the Christian Era farming began to develop along the river bottoms of these Missouri and northern Arkansas areas. The people of the Southwest Basketmaker Period were competent farmers.

That the Ozark bluff dwellers had contacts with other peoples living to the south and southeast is also apparent. The fact is revealed in the ceramics they acquired sometime after the year A.D. 500. They are similar to the pottery used by the Indians of cultures of the lower Mississippi Valley region.

Thus are more threads added to the great pattern of prehistoric cultural diffusions.[18]

Indian Knoll Shell Mounds

People belonging to the Algonquian linguistic family dominated the midwestern region covered in this part. This, of course, is a fact determined after the first French *voyageurs* penetrated the area. However, if nothing can be known of their prehistoric tongues, archeology has established the identity of their immediate ancestors, for various cultures—such as the Middle Mississippi, Tampico, Fisher, Kashena,

---

* See Part Two.

Azatlan, Oneota—endured well into historic times. The Algonquians were direct descendants of the people who belonged to these cultures.

The next largest group of the Central Prairies and Woodlands in the late prehistoric period were people of the Siouan linguistic family. The several Siouan tribes found at the beginning of historic times in the Midwest probably had not been there as long as the Algonquians. At least, some archeologists contend that they migrated northward from Kentucky and adjacent areas, and associate them with the culture called Indian Knoll,[19] which is given a late date of A.D. 500. The name Indian Knoll was applied to this culture because people belonging to it established their villages on shell middens along rivers. Shellfish were a main staple of their diet, and some of the shell middens they created were twelve feet in height.

The Indian Knoll people, however, did not migrate only to the north. According to Hyde:[20] "What makes these Kentucky Indian Knoll folk peculiarly interesting is the fact that they are the earliest Indian group whose movements can be followed with any degree of certainty. They migrated slowly toward the south, southwest, north, northeast, northwest, and, perhaps, the west, taking their type of crude culture with them. To the historians this situation strongly suggests that these Indians were a homogeneous stock, speaking one language, and that as their population increased, they spread in every direction from their old central area."

Not all archeologists accept such a postulation. Yet Siouan peoples did reach the Southeast, South, and the northern Midwest in early times, although their place of origin has not been determined with indisputable evidence.*

Regarding the Indian Knoll Culture, Martin[21] states that it "probably was the end product of a long tradition of hunting, fishing, and food-gathering. In a broad sense the culture is analogous to Cochise and Folsom,† and in its earliest stages, perhaps prior to 500 B.C., there is some suggestion of a relationship to Folsom. Some midden sites of cultures related to Indian Knoll, but probably earlier, produce several varieties of Folsom-like points and scrapers. The grinding stones of Indian Knoll, and, for that matter, of almost all Archaic cultures, are like those of Cochise."

Still the fact remains that Siouan tribes held large parts of the American Midwest, and especially its northern region, when the first white men reached it.

For a single reason only, a small tribe belonging to the great Muskho-

---

* See Part Three.
† See Part One.

gean family, the Kaskinampo, will be included in this section on the Central Prairies and Woodlands.

Miami: Cry of a Crane

Some linguists think the name *Miami* is derived from the Chippewa word *omaumeg*, which signifies "people on a peninsula," but the people called Miami say that is not correct. They maintain in their tribal traditions that it is a derivative of the word "pigeon." Moreover, when Europeans first heard of this Algonquian tribe, their name for themselves was something like Twightwees, meaning "cry of a crane."

They no longer adhered to the culture of their immediate ancestors, the Temple Mound Builders, at the beginning of the historic period. They were, and had been for some time, divided into at least five bands, two of which, the Piankashaw and the Wea, would be recognized as independent tribes. The others would be absorbed by the larger divisions, and nothing may be told of them.

Strangely, although the Miami lived in a country of many rivers and lakes they were land travelers rather than canoemen. A sober and serious people, they were, nevertheless, neither gloomy nor withdrawn. Characteristically roundheaded, they generally exhibited agreeable countenances. In manner they were friendly, affable, and polite. The men were of medium height, the women only slightly shorter. They were devoted to sports, especially to foot racing, in which they excelled. Unlike most Algonquian tribes, the Miami leaders held great power and were highly respected and strictly obeyed by their followers. The strength of the social and political structures, their unity and willing acceptance of leadership, contributed toward making them formidable adversaries in battle. Industrious and enterprising, they were shrewd traders, good trappers, and competent farmers. They grew a type of maize considered by other Indians to be the most delectable in the country. It had a finer skin and its meal was much whiter than most types of Indian corn, and they were credited with having developed it by cross-breeding over a long period of time.

Miami traditions indicated that late in the prehistoric period they began to migrate southward from their homes about Green Bay, Wisconsin, although some of them were still living in that area and on the Fox River as late as 1670. Before that time, however, they had established settlements about the southern end of Lake Michigan, in both northeastern Illinois and northwestern Indiana. Their villages stood on the Chicago River and the St. Joseph River, in southern Michigan, when white men first heard of them.

They continued to expand, going as far as the Detroit area and into Ohio. A noted Miami leader, Little Turtle, would state later: "My

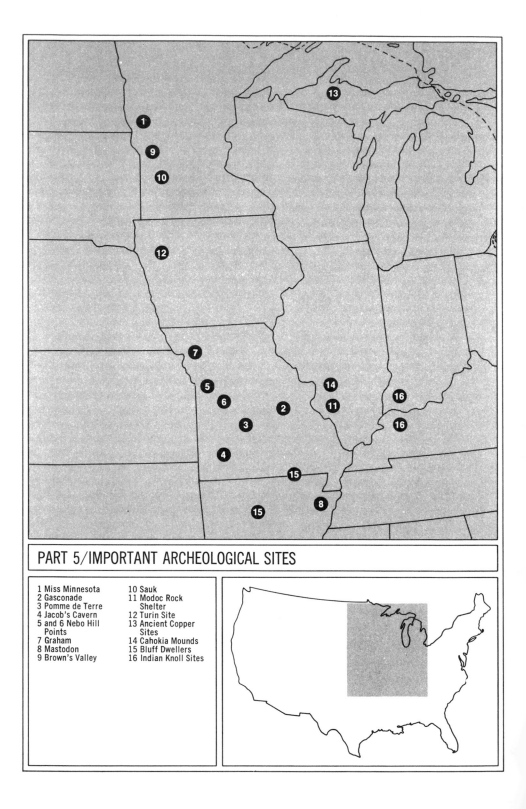

PART 5/IMPORTANT ARCHEOLOGICAL SITES

1 Miss Minnesota
2 Gasconade
3 Pomme de Terre
4 Jacob's Cavern
5 and 6 Nebo Hill
  Points
7 Graham
8 Mastodon
9 Brown's Valley
10 Sauk
11 Modoc Rock
  Shelter
12 Turin Site
13 Ancient Copper
  Sites
14 Cahokia Mounds
15 Bluff Dwellers
16 Indian Knoll Sites

fathers kindled the first fire at Detroit; thence they extended their lines to the headwaters of the Scioto [Ohio]; thence to its mouth; thence down the Ohio to the mouth of the Wabash, and then to Chicago over Lake Michigan." Their main villages, however, stood on the St. Joseph River, in both southern Michigan and northern Indiana, until after 1700.

Shortly thereafter they were driven from the St. Joseph and the area northwest of the Wabash by an alliance of Kickapoo, Potawatomi, and other tribes. They established themselves along the Miami River, in Ohio, and as far east as the Scioto, holding this area until after the middle of the seventeenth century. Their movements after that belong to the history of the colonial wars.

Early *voyageurs* noted that the Miami hunted buffalo by firing the prairie grass on three sides of a herd. When the animals sought to escape through the passageway on the side that had not been fired, the hunters shot them down in large numbers. Miami women were expert at spinning thread from buffalo hair, from which they made bags for the transporting and storing of dried meat.

The Miami sought to keep their religion as orderly and as simple as their daily lives. They worshipped the sun and the thunder, but paid no obeisance to a host of other deities, as did the Huron and the Ottawa. They made coffins by splitting large trees and hollowing out each side to the required depths, but the dead were also interred in graves dug in the earth and in small tightly sealed log cabins especially built for the purpose. Their villages were sometimes enclosed in high palisades. The houses, constructed of logs, were roofed with rush mats. An unfaithful wife was punished by clipping off the end of her nose.[22]

Illinois: the Men

The Illinois, with the exception of the Chippewa, the largest tribe of the Central Prairies and Woodlands region, was one of the weakest. Their name was *Iliniwek,* the plural deriving from the word *ilini,* which signifies "man." The French changed it to Illinois. By that time they were already well along the road to oblivion.

Actually, the Illinois were a confederation of minor Algonquian tribes spread over a large area. The identities and locations of the best known were: [23]

Cahokia, near Cahokia Mound (q.v), Illinois.

Kaskaskia, before 1700 in the present La Salle County, later at the town named for them.

Michigamea, between the St. Francis and Mississippi rivers, Arkansas.

Peoria, in late prehistoric times in northeastern Iowa, later near Peoria, Illinois.

Tamaroa, on the Mississippi about the mouths of the Missouri and Illinois rivers.

Nothing very complimentary was said of the Illinois either by other Indians or by the first white men to encounter them. They were good bowmen, but poor fighters. Inability to coordinate and control their military forces resulted in numerous defeats on the battlefield. Yet they were given to unrestrained bragging about their prowess as warriors, and lying about the great victories they had achieved in intertribal conflicts. Their neighbors saw through their propaganda and understood the emptiness of their claims. Probably only their numerical superiority saved them from being obliterated before any white man saw them. As it was, they were virtually destroyed early in the historic period.

By the middle of the seventeenth century most of the Illinois were concentrated along the river to be given their name, their villages scattered along the banks from the vicinity of Starved Rock to the Mississippi. Almost invariably the first French *voyageurs* and priests to meet them reiterated the opinions other Indians held, describing them as deceitful, timid, boastful, arrogant, fickle, and treacherous. They were easily frightened from their homes, and the main body of them had moved to the Illinois River largely because of harassment by the Sac, Fox, and other tribes living to the north.

A description of the Illinois, written by one of the first missionaries among them, is generally substantiated by reports of other early traders and priests. Wrote Father Membre in 1680: [24] "They are tall of stature, strong and robust, and good archers; they had as yet no firearms; we gave them some. They are wandering, idle, fearful, and desolate, almost without respect for their chiefs, irritable and thievish. Their villages are not enclosed with palisades, and, being too cowardly to defend them, they take to flight at the first news of a hostile army. The richness and fertility of the country gives them fields everywhere.

"Hermaphrodites are numerous. They have many wives, and often take several sisters that they may agree better; and yet they are so jealous that they cut off their noses on the slightest suspicion.* They are lewd, and even unnaturally so, having boys dressed as women, destined for infamous purposes. These boys are employed only in women's work, without taking part in the chase or war. They are very superstitious, although they have no religious worship. They are, besides, much given to play. . . ."

---

* Besides the Miami and Illinois, the Sioux, Apache, and some other tribes inflicted this punishment on unfaithful wives.

The introduction of liquor by French traders turned the Illinois into a virtual tribe of drunkards. It and their inherent weaknesses in combination created a degrading, ruinous force that made them unable to maintain any form of effective political structure or efficient military organization. The frightful slaughter inflicted on them by the Iroquois has been recounted.* The great La Salle sought unsuccessfully to form a league of midwestern tribes and refugee Indians from the East, but the Illinois showed themselves to be untrustworthy, plotted against him, and destroyed the defense works he attempted to construct and which would have given them protection.

The famous Ottawa chief Pontiac was killed by a drunken Illinois at Cahokia. This murder turned several northern Algonquian tribes against them. In the ensuing wars the Illinois were reduced to a fraction of their former strength. The Sauk, Fox, Kickapoo, and Potawatomi easily dispossessed them of their homeland.

Probably no more than two hundred Illinois men, women, and children were alive at the end of the American Revolution.[25]

Language Groups in Part Five

CENTRAL PRAIRIES AND WOODLANDS

Algonquian:	Illinois	Siouan:	Winnebago
	Kickapoo		Iowa
	Menominee		Missouri
	Miami		Quapaw
	Chippewa		Osage
	Sauk		
	Fox	Muskogean:	Kaskinampo

Quapaw: Going with the Current

A social subdivision of the Quapaw was called Arkansas, but they did not dwell in prehistoric times on the river or in the state that would be given that name. Their earliest known homeland was on the Ohio River near the mouth of the Wabash, and it was because of them that the Illinois called this part of the Ohio the Arkansas.

The Quapaw belonged to the Siouan linguistic family. They were mound builders, and were probably descendants of the people of the Indian Knoll Culture.† Other Siouan tribes closely related to them

---

* See *Iroquois: People of the Long House*, Part Four.
† See *Indian Knoll Shell Mounds*, this part.

residing at the same period in the Kentucky-Ohio-Wabash-Mississippi region were the Omaha, Kansa, Ponca, and Osage. Perhaps less than a century before the beginning of the historical period in the Middle West these tribes separated. The date of the separation is not known, but how they divided and where they went are established facts.

The name Quapaw signifies "downstream people," or "those going with the current." They went down the Ohio and on down the Mississippi. The name Arkansas, by which only a part of them called themselves, became the name of all of them. Quapaw was all but forgotten, and Arkansas was applied to the river near the mouth of which they reestablished themselves. The name Omaha signifies "people going against the current," and the Ponca, Kansa, and Osage followed the Omaha up the Mississippi and on up the Missouri River.

The first white men known to meet the Quapaw were Marquette and Joliet and their four companions. They found them in 1673 in villages near the conjunction of the Arkansas and Mississippi rivers, and it was there they halted their descent of the Mississippi and turned back for fear of falling into the hands of the Spanish who held the mouth of the great river.*

Marquette's notice of them, therefore, marks the beginning of the historic period for these people. In his account of the meeting, the priest makes it clear that they lived in dire fear of surrounding tribes and were prevented from trading directly with the Spaniards by enemies living lower down the river. He found them "very courteous and liberal of what they have, but they are very poorly off for food, not daring to go and hunt the wild-cattle [buffalo on the plains to the west and north]. . . . It is true they have Indian corn in abundance, which they sow at all seasons; we saw some ripe; more just sprouting, and more just in the ear, so that they sow three crops in a year. They cook it in large earthen pots, which are very well made; they also have plates of baked earth, which they employ for various purposes.

"The men go naked, and wear their hair short; they have the nose and ears pierced, and beads hanging from them. The women are dressed in wretched skins; they braid their hair in two plaits, which falls behind their ears; they have no ornaments to decorate their persons.

"Their banquets are without any ceremonies; they serve their meat in large dishes, and everyone eats as much as he pleases, and they give the rest to one another. Their language is extremely difficult. . . . Their cabins, which are long and wide, are made of bark; they sleep at the two extremities, which are raised about two feet from the ground.

"They keep their corn in large baskets, made of cane, or in gourds,

---

* The Quapaw had not yet left the Ohio River when De Soto crossed the Mississippi, 130 years before the voyage of Marquette.

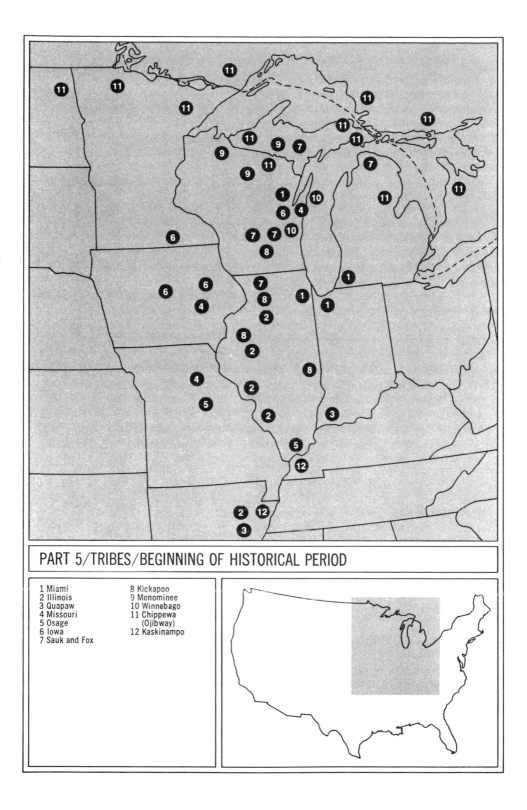

PART 5/TRIBES/BEGINNING OF HISTORICAL PERIOD

1 Miami
2 Illinois
3 Quapaw
4 Missouri
5 Osage
6 Iowa
7 Sauk and Fox

8 Kickapoo
9 Menominee
10 Winnebago
11 Chippewa
   (Ojibway)
12 Kaskinampo

as large as half barrels. They do not know what a beaver is; their riches consisting in the hides of wild cattle.* They never see snow, and know the winter only by the rain which falls oftener than in summer. We ate no fruit there but watermelons. . . .

"In the evening the sachems held a secret council on the design of some to kill us for plunder, but the chief broke up all these schemes, and sending for us, danced the calumet in our presence . . . as a mark of perfect assurance; and then, to remove all fears, presented it to me." [26]

The Quapaw became strong allies of the French. In subsequent years, because of their location, they were visited by numerous explorers, and trading posts were established near their villages. But they were always called by the name the Illinois had given them—Arkansas.

Missouri: Big Muddy

Inappropriately, to say the least, one of the great rivers of America and a state of the Union bear the name of a small, unimportant, and undistinguished Siouan tribe—the Missouri.

The word *missouri* has been interpreted as meaning "big" or "great muddy." It means "people having dugout canoes." Moreover, the word is not Siouan, but in its earliest forms derives from the Illinois dialect of the Algonquian language.

If Indian traditions speak the truth (and often they do), the people who would be called Missouri belonged to the Winnebago and lived in the vicinity of Green Bay, Wisconsin. At some indefinite prehistoric time, political and social squabbles caused them to leave Green Bay. Two other groups, the Iowa and the Oto, joined them in a migration toward the southwest. They crossed the Mississippi and reached the Iowa River.

The Iowa elected to remain on the river, and the Missouri and the Oto continued on until they had reached the Missouri near the mouth of the Grand River. There they, too, had a falling out, the result of which was that the Oto moved farther up the Missouri River.

The Missouri remained in the vicinity of The Pinnacles, in the present Saline County, Missouri, until 1798, when they were all but destroyed by the Sauk and Fox. The few survivors scattered to live among the Osage, Kansa, and Oto.[27]

---

* The Arkansas could obtain robes and various products of the buffalo from other tribes and from traders. Both the lower Mississippi and the Arkansas rivers were always major trade waterways. Besides being good farmers, they were excellent hunters. Game was plentiful in their country, and the rivers and lakes supplied them with all the fish they could consume. Marquette's statement that they were "poorly off for food" seems questionable.

Osage: Children of the Middle Waters

No biblical fantasies are more beautiful than the creation myths of the Osage. They came of the stars, and when they reached the earth neither it nor anything upon it had a name. And they gave names to the sky and the earth and the animals and the waters and to everything else. And to themselves they gave the name Ni-U-Ko'n-Ska, Children of the Middle Waters.[28]

The name Osage would be given to them by white men. It is a corruption of Wazhazhe, the name of one of the three bands of which the tribe was composed.[29]

"The Children of the Middle Waters," writes an Osage, John Joseph Mathews,[30] "had begun to reason long before they came to build fantasies upon the foundations of their biological instincts and upon their mysterious urges. They had begun long before to fumble toward the Light which their mental development would demand that they recognize. They felt more now than the urges of food-getting and mating; there was the third urge that came with thought. This was Wah'Kon, the Mystery Force, and in their urgency to come to some understanding of this life-force, they knew great fear and confusion, and they could only build their own framework into which they would try to fit this Wah'Kon and therefore bring it within the boundaries of their conceptions. They had been busy for perhaps centuries building a ritualistic cage for this Wah'Kon, the Mystery Force, that they might have it under control, materialize it out of the world of abstractions, so that they might know relief or protection from their own fears and uncertainties." Long before Europeans found them, they had not only given names to everything on the earth, but they "also knew how they got there and why they were there, and they also had fumbled toward an understanding of the Wah'Kon, and had a very comforting interpretation under which they dwelt."

The eminent ethnologist J. O. Dorsey [31] ranked the Osage as the most important tribe of the Dhegiha division of the Siouan linguistic family, which also included the Omaha, Ponca, Kansa, and Quapaw. They were divided, he reported, "into two sections, the Tsishu, or peace people, who kept to the left, living on roots, etc.; and the Wazhazhe (true Osage), or war people, who kept to the right and killed animals for their food. Later these two divisions exchanged commodities, and after some time the Tsishu people came into possession of four kinds of corn and four kinds of pumpkins, which fell from the left hind legs of as many different buffaloes. Still later the tribe came upon a very warlike people called Hangka-utadhantes, who lived on animals, and after a time the Tsishu people succeeded in making peace with them, when they were taken into the nation on the war side."

Originally there were seven gentes in each of these prehistoric divisions, but this number was reduced to create more equilibrium between the war and peace sections of the tribe. In the remarkable social organization of the Osage, however, seven remained a sacred number, but, as Dorsey notes, "from the war and other customs of the tribe it appears that the sacred ceremonial number was usually four."

The earliest known prehistoric home of the Osage was on the lower Ohio River, but they had migrated from that area perhaps centuries before white men heard of them. On his map of 1673, Father Marquette located them—although he did not meet them—in the vicinity of the Osage River in Missouri. While the larger part of the tribe, called the Great Osage, was found in this location by the early French *voyageurs*, another group, known as the Little Osage, dwelt on the Missouri River, not far from the main town of the Missouri Indians, which was near the mouth of Grand River.

The Osage were formidable warriors. Indeed, war was a way of life, and they ranged far on their forays. They were almost constantly in conflict with tribes on both sides of the Mississippi. They invaded the territories occupied by tribes of the Plains, and the Caddoan people especially were terrorized by them. To numerous tribes their name was a synonym for the word "enemy."

About the year 1802, as the pressures of settlement enclosed upon them, most of the tribe, led by a chief, Big Track, migrated southward to the Arkansas River. In 1808, the Osage signed a treaty at Fort Clark, near Kansas City, ceding all their lands west of the Missouri River. These comprised virtually the entire state of Missouri and the northern part of Arkansas. The agreement marked the beginning of a tragic ending for the Osage.[32]

Iowa: Dusty Noses

Like the Missouri, their close relatives, the Iowa were an insignificant and inconspicuous tribe. The preservation of their name in a state of the Union, as well as in towns, rivers, a county, and other places, seems unwarranted. They distinguished themselves not at all in prehistoric times, and played no important part in the history of the American Midwest.

The Iowa, Oto, and Missouri traditionally belonged to the Winnebago stock and the three small tribes comprised the Chiwere subdivision of the Siouan linguistic family.*

After crossing the Mississippi in late prehistoric times, they are be-

* See *Missouri: Big Muddy*, this part.

lieved to have settled along the Iowa River, and later to have lived about the Okoboji Lakes. After that they moved frequently, but usually stayed within the confines of the state of Iowa.

They called themselves Pahodja, which signifies "dusty noses." The Dakota called them Ayuhwa, a name the French borrowed and twisted to Iowa. It indicates "sleepy ones," a somewhat fitting description, for they were unenterprising and indifferent as hunters and cultivators, usually exerting themselves no more than necessary.[33]

Sauk and Fox: Yellow Earth and Red Earth

The Sauk and the Fox are generally thought of as neighbors and allies living in Wisconsin. That is because white men first found them there, but long before that time their campfires burned in the lower peninsula of Michigan. The name Saginaw Bay is derived from the Algonquian word *sagina'we*, which signifies "the country or place of the Sauk." In late prehistoric times, the Sauk were driven from their Michigan homeland by the Ottawa and the Neutrals. They retreated through Mackinaw and the upper peninsula of Michigan, finally establishing themselves in the region of Green Bay and the Fox River in Wisconsin. Whether the Fox preceded them or migrated with them is not known. The main Fox villages were in the vicinity of Lake Winnebago, and there is a tradition that they were driven southward from northern Wisconsin by the Chippewa.[34] This suggests that they had left the lower peninsula of Michigan before the Sauk. While there is no certainty about such a conjecture, it should be noted that the Chippewa name for the Fox was *O-dug-am-eeg*, signifying "people of the other shore," that is, the eastern side of Lake Michigan.

The Fox received their name by accident in the historic period. According to the story, a group of them were hunting when they met some French fur traders. Asked who they were, they gave the name of their clan, the Fox. Thereafter the entire tribe was called Fox. Their true name is *Meshkwakihug*. It means "red earth people," the kind of earth from which they believed they were created.

Presumably the Sauk believed they had been created from earth of another color. Sauk derived from their correct name, *Osa'kiwug*, which means "people of the yellow earth."

Although they were closely related, spoke the same tongue, and lived together or near each other for an unknown number of centuries, there were several sharp differences in the characters of the Sauk and Fox.*

---

* The Sauk, Fox, and Kickapoo comprised a subdivision of the Algonquian linguistic family.

These varying qualities are made evident in the descriptions of them written by early Europeans who encountered them in their Wisconsin homeland.

Wrote a fur trader: [35]

"These People are Cald Saukeas. They are of a Good Sise and Well Disposed—Les inclind to trick and Bad manners than thare Nighbers. Thay will take of the Goods on Creadit in the fall for thare youse. In Winter and Except for Axedant thay Pay the Deapt Verey Well for Indians I mite have sade Inlitend or Sivelised Indians which are in General made worse by the Operation.

"Sum of thare Huts are Sixtey feet Long and Contanes Several fammalayes.

"In the fall of ye Year thay Leave thare Huts and Go into the Woods in Quest of Game and Return in the Spring to thare Huts before Planting time. The Women Rase Grate Crops of Corn, Been, Punkens, Potatoes, Millens, and artikels—the Land is Exaleant—and Clear of Wood Sum Distans from the Villeag.

"Thare amusements are Singing, Dancing, Smoking Matcheis, Gaming, Feasting, Drinking, Playing the Slite of Hand, Hunting and thay are famas in Mageack. Thay are Not Verey Gellas of thare Women. In General the Women find meanes to Grattafy them Selves without Consent of the Men."

The Sauk were enterprising farmers and dwelt in permanent towns, but they cannot be called sedentary people, for they spent many months of the year hunting and raiding. They were daring adventurers in the sense that they traveled long distances, hunting buffalo on the Great Plains and undertaking forays far across the Mississippi and to the south. The early Spanish in the Southwest knew them and sought to hold their favor.

According to Hewitt,[36] the social organization of the Sauk contained numerous gentes and its structure was complex. Marriage was restricted to men and women of different gentes, and in the case of death "a man might marry the sister of his deceased wife, or a widow might become the wife of the brother of her dead husband. . . . A child followed the gens of the father, but it frequently happened that the mother was given the right to name; in that case the child took a name peculiar to the gens of the mother but was yet in the gens of the father. . . . The Sauk never developed a soldier society with the same degree of success as did the Foxes. . . . There was a chief and a council. . . . Politically the chief was little more than a figurehead, but socially he occupied first place in the tribe."

The culture of the Sauk was that of the Eastern Woodland area. They made extensive use of both birchbark and dugout canoes. In their religion they looked upon the world as being inhabited by beings possessing magic force that could be either malicious or beneficent. The manitos of Sauk mythology were represented in all nature. Their ghost world was beyond the setting sun, and there went to dwell the spirits of the dead.

In contrast to the Sauk, the Fox were hostile, thoroughly untrustworthy, and avaricious. They were on the warpath a large part of every year. Mooney and Thomas of the Bureau of American Ethnology [37] wrote that neighboring tribes feared and hated the Fox, describing them as stingy, thieving, and quarrelsome. From the beginning of the historic period they were deadly enemies of the white man.* They were constantly at war with the Chippewa on the north and the tribes of the Illinois confederation on the south. They were never successful in their conflicts with the Chippewa, and the Sauk did not join them in all their aggressions. However, as allies the Sauk and Fox inflicted heavy damage on the Illinois, drove them from a part of their country, and took possession of it.

Their location on the Fox River put them in position to act as extortionists and blackmailers, for the river was part of the main fur trade route from Green Bay to the Mississippi. Scouts watched for the canoes of traders. When they approached, a flaming torch was put on the bank. It was a signal to the traders to stop and pay tribute or suffer the consequences. Robbery was the mildest penalty traders would suffer for refusing to heed the demand.

Charlevoix declared the Fox "infested with their robberies and filled with murders not only the neighborhood of Green Bay, their natural territory, but almost all the routes communicating with the remote colonial posts, as well as those leading from Canada to Louisiana . . . all the nations in alliance with us suffered greatly from these hostilities." [38]

Despite their affiliation with the Sauk, the Fox remained one of the most primitive people in the American Midwest. They were not only fierce warriors but were incomparably brave—on that their many enemies and victims were in agreement. They were as well extraordinarily colorful warriors. On a foray they wore headdresses made of animal hair dyed red and tied to a scalp lock in a manner that resembled a Roman helmet. The rest of the head was completely shaved and painted. They wore breechclouts, leggings, and moccasins, and, unless the weather was extremely cold, the upper part of the body was naked and brightly painted. Often men had the print of a human hand on the back or on a shoulder made with white clay.

---

* The Fox were the only Algonquian tribe to engage the early French in serious warfare. At one time the French were considering organizing a force to exterminate them.

The Fox carried flags made of feathers. They displayed a "coat of arms" on shields and skins. Described in heraldic terms, it was a "meadow sinople, crossed by a winding pale, with two foxes' gules at the two extremities of the river, in chief and point." [39] In more common language: an oblique mark representing a stream, with a fox at each end on opposite sides. After a successful raid the Fox would paint the "coat of arms" on a tree in the territory of their victims.

The famous war leader, Black Hawk, was a Sauk. It was the conflict with American troops, to which history has given his name, that brought final destruction and near extinction to both his own people and the Fox.

Kickapoo: the Unconquered

The name *Kickapoo* is one of the best known of all Indians who dwelt in the region of the United States. In the Algonquian language it means "he moves about, standing now here, now there." It would be difficult to conceive of an identity more suitable to them.

CENTRAL PRAIRIES AND WOODLANDS

Earliest Population Estimates*

Miami (1650)	4,500	Kickapoo (1650)	2,000
Quapaw (1650)	2,500	Menominee (1650)	3,000
Kaskinampo (1699)	500	Sauk (1650)	3,500
Illinois (1650)	8,000	Winnebago (1650)	3,800
Missouri (1780)	1,000	Chippewa (Ojibway)	
Osage (1780)	6,200	(1650)	35,000
Iowa (1780)	1,200		
Fox (1650)	3,000	TOTAL	74,200

* See Note, *Population Estimates*, Part One.

The Kickapoo were closely related to the Sauk and Fox, and at some remote prehistoric period may have lived with them, or near them, in the lower peninsula of Michigan. That is an assumption, without either tradition or archeological evidence to indicate that it might be correct. When they first entered upon the state of history, about 1658, at least some of them were living at the portage between the Wisconsin and Fox rivers in Wisconsin.

There was no more warlike people as a whole, and no greater warriors as individuals, in all America. Perhaps only the Navajo and the

Apache can share their distinction as raiders, but no people surpassed them as fighters, and no people were more cunning, more deadly, more formidable, in conflict. Their military organization, if comparatively small, had no equal, and was so well-trained and disciplined that it frequently routed or destroyed forces of much greater size.

It is doubtful if any people—and certainly no tribe of the Central Prairies and Woodlands—ranged over a greater territory in either prehistoric or historic times. Their forays took them over a region now encompassed by a score of states. They ravaged and plundered from the Great Lakes to Georgia and Alabama, into Texas and Mexico, from the Great Plains to New York and Pennsylvania.

In his fine study of the Kickapoo, A. M. Gibson [40] remarks that probably no Indian tribal name has been used as often for non-Indian purposes, having been appropriated by geographers, white Civil War border raiders, recalcitrant political factions, and makers of patent medicines. He notes that Kickapoo became a common household word in the nineteenth century with the organization in Connecticut of the Kickapoo Medicine Company which "peddled Kickapoo Indian Cough Cure, Kickapoo Indian Salve, and Kickapoo Indian Sagway (a panacea guaranteed to cure symptoms of dyspepsia including neuralgia, headache, constipation, kidney disease, various stomach and liver ailments, and female disorders) through the peripatetic medicine show."

However, long before this time the Kickapoo themselves had provided strong doses of their own bad medicine to both red and white victims. Few of the patients who had it forced upon them recovered, and most of them succumbed to afflictions from which they had not previously suffered.

The culture of the Kickapoo was essentially the same as that of the Sauk and Fox, but there all similarity between them and their relatives ends. From the moment the first French adventurers and priests reached their country they became implacable and vindictive enemies of all white men. All efforts to convert them to Christianity were miserable failures. All attempts to induce them to adopt the customs of civilization, to remain peaceful, to halt their raiding, to settle on a reservation, were to no avail.

When the pressures of settlement became too great the Kickapoo moved. They won their notoriety as bandits and destroyers in prehistoric times, but it diminished not at all after the beginning of written history. Swanton records [41] that "Early in the eighteenth century a part of them settled somewhere near Milwaukee River, and after the destruction of the Illinois about 1765, they moved still farther south and lived about Peoria. One portion then pushed down the Sangamon, while another worked east to the Wabash, and made their headquarters on Vermilion River."

As they had fought Indians from time immemorial, and then the early colonials, so the Kickapoo continued to fight Americans moving westward. When the rope of American settlement began to tighten about them, they gave up their midwestern lands and turned toward the setting sun. Unable to escape from the path of the onrushing white steamroller, most of them retreated from Missouri and Kansas toward the Southwest. Joined by a number of Potawatomi, a large number of them continued on through Texas until they found sanctuary in the wild country of the Mexican province of Chihuahua. There, known as the Mexican Kickapoo, they live today.

The Kickapoo were broken as a tribe and split into bands by insuperable white forces, both political and military, but they never accepted the white man's God, they never forsook their own manitos, they never surrendered. Always they were—man, woman, and child—the unconquered and the unconquerable.

Menominee: Reapers but Not Sowers

Indian traditions relate that in prehistoric intertribal warfare the Menominee were driven from their ancient homeland in the vicinity of Michilimackinac. In this same area, at a remote period, also dwelt a tribe called Noquet, a name meaning "bear foot." The fate of the Noquet is not known. They had vanished as a tribe by the time the first white men reached the upper Great Lakes, although a few individuals claimed to be their descendants early in the historical period and the first missionaries heard the name. There is good reason to believe that the Noquet were related to the Menominee. Indeed, they may have been the Menominee, or at least one band of them that was absorbed either by the Menominee or the Chippewa.

Whatever the case, it seems apparent that the Menominee became known by this name after they had settled on the Menominee River in northern Wisconsin and the upper peninsula of Michigan. There was a great abundance of wild rice in this region, and it was the main vegetable staple of the refugees from Michilimackinac. In the Algonquian tongue, Menominee means "wild rice men." They would not have been identified by that term in their former homeland, where there was insufficient wild rice, if any at all, to comprise an important part of their diet.

The Menominee continued to live for two centuries where they were found by the first French fur traders to enter the country—on the river named for them. They still live on Wolf River, not far away in Wisconsin.

The Menominee were not known as aggressors, but they were enemies of numerous tribes around them, and were frequently at war.

Ethnologists Mooney and Thomas [42] wrote of them that although they were "comparatively indolent, they are described as generally honest, theft being less common than among many other tribes. Drunkenness was their most serious fault, but even this did not prevail to the same extent as among some other Indians. Their beliefs and rituals are substantially the same as those of the Chippewa. They have usually been peaceful in character."

Although the Menominee depended largely on wild rice for their subsistence, they steadfastly refused to sow it, contending that to do so would "wound their mother, the earth." [43]

Winnebago: People in the Middle

In the general prehistoric western movement of the Sioux, the Winnebago, for a reason unknown, were left behind. They settled in remote times on the south side of Green Bay, in Wisconsin. The date is uncertain, but it has been determined that they were there when the Potawatomi and the Ottawa were driven from their ancestral homelands to the east by the Iroquois, and they were there, and in league with the Menominee, when the Sauk and Fox were forced to abandon their lower Michigan locations. The Menominee and the Winnebago gave sanctuary to the refugee Sauk and Fox.

Here is a unique situation in prehistoric Indian history. The Winnebago belong to the Siouan linguistic family. In Wisconsin they were surrounded by Algonquian tribes, yet they managed to maintain generally friendly relations with them, even with the warlike Fox and Kickapoo. Such an achievement demonstrated their unusual diplomatic ability. It also reflected their innate tolerance, and a willingness to adopt customs of their neighbors in order to keep peace with them.

Yet they were not weak, not easily dominated, and they displayed courage in conflict. Perhaps the words "intelligent" and "smart" are applicable in describing them. They never abandoned their ancient religious beliefs and ceremonies, but their culture is characterized by both Siouan and Algonquian influences. They sought to live and to let live.

The first French explorers in the region found their villages extended between Green Bay and the big lake that would be given their name.[44] One early traveler reported they were ruled by a "queen." [45] They maintained amicable trade relations with the French. When the French fell from power they were slow to transfer their allegiance to the British, but when they did they remained firm allies, and in the War of 1812 fought bravely for England.

Their name for themselves was Hotcangara, signifying "people of the real or big speech." Winnebago is an Algonquian word of the Sauk and Fox dialects. It means "people of the filthy water." How they acquired it is not certainly known, but both the French and English used it, calling them, respectively, Puants and Stinkards. Assuredly it was not descriptive of the beautiful, clear, blue-green waters of their homeland.

The brutal treatment inflicted upon the Winnebago by Americans comprises one of the most tragic chapters of the history of American-Indian relations.[46]

Chippewa: the Big People

They are called by two names, Chippewa and Ojibway. They are best known by the first, largely due to the works of American writers and poets,* but it is from the second, which most of them preferred to use, that the significance of their name is derived. In the Algonquian dialect they spoke, *ojib* means "to pucker up," and *ub-way* means "to roast." Thus, the name Ojibway is interpreted as "to roast until puckered up." It does not refer to meat or any method of cooking, as might be thought. It refers to a peculiar type of moccasin they made, which had a "puckered" seam.

In prehistoric times the Chippewa was probably the largest individual tribe north of Mexico. Unsubstantiated tradition relates that they migrated from Canada southwestward to the vicinity of Mackinaw. They dwelt in this region for an unknown number of years, although some of them had moved on, and about the time of the discovery of America were established in a large town at La Pointe, Wisconsin. An early *Jesuit Relation* states that a few years after 1600, the Chippewa at La Pointe moved to live at the Sault. Meanwhile, others were pushing westward on both shores of Lake Superior. They drove the Dakota (Sioux) from Mille Lacs, and continued to spread westward. In early historic times the Chippewa occupied an enormous territory, from the Sault on the east, through the upper peninsula of Michigan, across northern Minnesota and southern Manitoba, and as far west as the Turtle Mountains of North Dakota. Some of them also flowed southward around Lake Huron, driving the Iroquois from territory which the Five Nations had long claimed by right of conquest.[47]

The Chippewa were as barbarous as any Indians. They inflicted extreme tortures on prisoners of war. Several branches were long known as cannibals, and even as late as the early twentieth century at least one band living in Canada reportedly ate human flesh in certain cere-

---

* Notably Henry R. Schoolcraft, who married a Chippewa, and Henry W. Longfellow, who took the name of an Iroquois leader, Hiawatha, for the hero of a story set in Chippewa Country.

monies. According to Mooney and Thomas,[48] it was the custom of the Chippewa in southern Manitoba "to allow a warrior who scalped an enemy to wear on his head two eagle feathers, and the act of capturing a wounded prisoner on the battlefield earned the distinction of wearing five." The same authorities assert that the Chippewa "imagined that the shade, after the death of the body, followed a wide beaten path, leading toward the west, finally arriving in a country abounding in everything the Indian desires. It is a general belief among the northern Chippewa that the spirit often returns to visit the grave, so long as the body is not reduced to dust. . . . Like most other tribes they believe that a mysterious power dwells in all objects, animate and inanimate."

Chippewa medicine men, possessing great influence, prevented early missionaries from winning converts. The Chippewa *Medewiwin,* or Grand Medicine Society, was a powerful organization which controlled the movements of the tribe and was a formidable obstacle to the introduction of Christianity.

Although the Chippewa were one of the largest tribes and dominated an immense territory, because of their remoteness from the path of settlement and the arenas of the colonial wars they were never prominent in history.

Kaskinampo: the Unlucky

Except for one event, almost nothing certain is known of the Kaskinampo. A small tribe, they may have lived two thousand years ago somewhere along the Cumberland River, later moving to the mouth of the Tennessee River. Both of these streams at one time bore their name. They were probably closely related to the Koasati, therefore belonged to the Muskhogean linguistic family, but the significance of their name is unknown.

They are included among the tribes of the Central Prairies and Woodlands because traditional evidence indicates that they moved, apparently in the late prehistoric period, down the Ohio and Mississippi rivers and settled in the vicinity of the present Phillips County, Arkansas.

The one event: When De Soto crossed the Mississippi he entered an Indian "province" to which his chroniclers gave the names of Casqui, Icasqui, or Casquin. Unfortunately for the Kaskinampo, they were the people of this "province."

Those who survived the murderous onslaughts of De Soto's army—and there could have been but a few—are believed to have gone to live with remnants of the Koasati in Alabama, where they vanished from history.[49]

SOME INDIAN PLACE NAMES*

Minnesota

Minnesota, state, river
Pequot, town
Osage, town
Sauk, river, town
Winnebago, town
Chippewa, river, county
Dakota, county, town
Sioux, town

Wisconsin

Shawano, county, town
Catawba, town
Seneca, town
Oneida, county, town
Ottawa, town
Wisconsin, state, river
Iowa, town
Fox, river
Kickapoo, river
Menomonee, river
Menomonie, town
Sauk, county, town
Winnebago, county, lake
Chippewa, river, county
Ojibwa, town
Dakota, town

Iowa

Chickasaw, county
Cherokee, county, town
Oneida, town
Potawatomi, county
Iowa, state, town, river
Conoy, town
Osage, town
Sac, county, town
Winnebago, county
Dakota, town
Sioux City
Sioux, county, town
Lakota, town

Missouri

Seneca, town
Missouri, state, river
Montawk, town
Miami, town

Osage, river, county
Sac, river
Kansas, city
Spokane, town

Illinois

Shawnee, town
Potomac, town
Niantic, town
Illinois, state, river, town
Iroquois, county
Seneca, town
Oneida, town
Ottawa, town
Erie, town
Chicago, city, river
Cahokia, town
Kaskaskia, town
Peoria, town
Mississippi, river
Osage, town
Fox, river
Winnebago, county
Dakota, town
Omaha, town
Pawnee, town
Kansas, town

Arkansas

Arkansas, state, river, city,
    county
Alabam, town
Powhatan, town
Oneida, town
Illinois, river
Mississippi, river
Osage, town
Omaha, town
Ponca, town
Texarkana, town

Indiana

Natchez, town
Cayuga, town
Kokomo, town
Miami, county, town
Huron, town
Wyandot, town
Pawnee, town

* Tribes and subdivisions.

Dates to Remember

1610—At the age of eighteen, Etienne Brule, perhaps the most enterprising and energetic of the several young men sent out by Champlain to open the western wilderness for France, and, hopefully, to discover a waterway to the Western Sea, made his first journey of exploration. Brule never returned to live in civilization. He adopted Indian dress, learned several languages, fought in tribal wars, engaged in the fur trade, and made discoveries of surpassing importance. In his explorations he was the first of the *voyageurs* to ascend the Ottawa, first to reach the Great Lakes, Ontario and Huron, first to open for French fur traders a short route from the American Midwest to the Atlantic. He and a companion discovered the source of Great Lakes copper. Traveling along the north shore of Lake Huron, above Manitoulin Island, they passed through the Sault St. Marie to Lake Superior, encountered the Chippewa, found the Indian mines, and brought back a quantity of the metal.

1634—Not all of Champlain's young men can be identified, but others were pushing into the West during the years of Brule's career. Champlain never ceased to believe that a water passage from Georgian Bay to the Pacific existed. One of the last acts of his life was to send the great Jean Nicolet on a new search for it. Nicolet passed through the Straits of Mackinac and discovered Lake Michigan. So confident was he that he could reach the Orient that he took with him a ceremonial robe made of "China damask." He kept it handy in his canoe as he and his companions made their way down the west shore of Lake Michigan, where no white man had ever gone, and paddled up Green Bay. The Indians told him of a "people of the South Sea." He found the Winnebagos, and entered their village wearing the damask robe and carrying a pistol in each hand. From Green Bay he ascended the Fox River. When he decided to turn back, Indians told him that he was only three days from water that emptied into the sea. He had heard of the Mississippi, and he returned convinced that he had learned of a waterway that reached Spanish Mexico. More important, as far as French traders were concerned, he had discovered numerous Indian people not known to exist and a land inconceivably rich in furs.

1654–1656—Medard Chouart, Sieur de Grosseilliers, one of the greatest of early *voyageurs*, further explored the Great Lakes and Wisconsin region, reporting that he had met thousands of Indians who would give a beaver skin for a rusty nail.

1659–1660—Grosseilliers and his intrepid brother-in-law, Pierre-Esprit Radisson, opened trading routes to the Sioux on the upper waters of the Mississippi and the western shore of Lake Superior, and they conceived the idea of establishing a post on Hudson Bay to which ships might sail directly from Europe. However, the plan would be carried out by the English.

1671–1672—Ascending the Chicago River from Lake Michigan, La Salle portaged to the Des Plaines, descended the Illinois, and reached the Mississippi, to which he gave the name Rivière Colbert, in honor of the famous French statesman.

1673—Father Jacques Marquette and the famed explorer Louis Joliet left Mackinac in May, voyaged down Lake Michigan and into Green Bay, ascended the Fox River, portaged to the Wisconsin, and reached the Mississippi. They traveled down the great river as far as the mouth of the Arkansas, before turning homeward.

Scientific Note—Trade Goods

It would be quite impossible to list all the products that entered into intertribal and interregional prehistoric Indian trade. That would mean listing every kind and color of paint, every kind of stone used in ornaments, utensils, and implements, every kind of wood used, every kind of feather, and every kind of shell out of which jewelry and other decorations were made. The inventory would be endless. For example, over prehistoric trade trails in the Southwest alone went at least nine species of shells from the Pacific Ocean, thirty-eight species from the Gulf of California, and ten species which may have come from either sea.

However, for the purpose of showing that the economy of prehistoric Indians was anything but simple, and the number of products in trade was anything but small, a carefully selected list has been compiled of nearly two hundred and fifty manufactured articles and commodities that moved, either short or long distances, in prehistoric Indian commerce.[50]

UTENSILS AND OTHER HOUSEHOLD ARTICLES

Skin bags	Sheep skins	Hoof bowls
Shell dishes	Fox skins	Beaver skins
Gourd dishes	Needle boxes	Coyote skins
Bone spoons	Skin cases	Rabbit skins
Clay jars	Woven boxes	Marmot skins
Bone scrapers	Clay dishes	Goat skins
Shell scrapers	Stone dishes	Badger skins
Pottery trays	Gourd spoons	Medicine pouches
Stone pots	Bone knives	Skin boxes
Pottery bowls	Horn jars	Fur blankets
Woven platters	Stone scrapers	Horn dishes

Hide trunks	Shell ladles	Woven dishes
Grass mats	Woven trays	Gourd ladles
Pounding stones	Basket pots	Flint knives
Buffalo robes	Woven bowls	Bone jars
Wolf skins	Skin baskets	Bone forks
Antelope skins	Textile mats	Shell spoons
Skunk skins	Grinding stones	Pottery pots
Stone bowls	Hoof dishes	Mink skins
Pottery platters	Lynx skins	Pin pouches
Woven baskets	Deer skins	Hide chests
Reed mats	Otter skins	Reed cases
Grass sieves	Marten skins	Textile blankets

ORNAMENTATION AND CLOTHING

Feather robes	Bone beads	Shell bracelets
Cosmetic cases	Copper rings	Bells
Jewelry boxes	Antler headpieces	Bird beaks
Horn ornaments	Quill decorations	Stone beads
Feather cloaks	Cotton garments	Copper decorations
Headdress feathers	Scent pouches	Stone rings
Teeth jewelry	Clothing bags	Coral beads
Animal scents	Wooden ornaments	Shell mosaics
Plummets	Pottery jewelry	Skin garments
Teeth pendants	Armlets	Paint pouches
Face paint	Skin belts	Fur garments
Nose plugs	Moccasins	Bone ornaments
Teeth necklaces	Pigment cases	Headdress horns
Quill headbands	Shell pendants	Wallets
Feather headbands	Body paint	Seed scents
Shell earrings	Lip plugs	Purses
Turquoise jewelry	Stone necklaces	Claw pendants
Pottery disks	Woven headbands	Bird feathers
Buckles	Garters	Hair paint
Copper breastplates	Metal earrings	Claw necklaces
Bone jewelry	Clothing dyes	Shell necklaces
Shell beads	Bird claws	Leather headbands
Hair headbands	Copper bracelets	Bone rings
Bone earrings	Copper earrings	Horn rings
Shell disks	Bone necklaces	Coral necklaces
Clasps	Wooden beads	Turquoise mosaics

IMPLEMENTS

Stone axes	Stone awls	Bone awls
Arrow straighteners	Abraders	Abrasives
Stone clubs	Bone clubs	Drills
Stone fleshers	Bone fleshers	Shell fleshers
Stone hammers	Bone and stone hoes	Bone rakes
Bone fishhooks	Shell fishhooks	Reed nets
Reed weirs	Sinew lines	Polishers
Horn awls	Bone knives	Stone knives
Bone scrapers	Stone scrapers	Shell scrapers
Bone needles	Vegetal fish-lines	Sinew fish-lines

CEREMONIAL AND RELIGIOUS ARTICLES

Bowls	Plates	Boxes
Tobacco	Tobacco pouches	Medicines
Medicine bags	Gourd rattles	Turtle rattles
Seeds	Flutes	Bells
Feathers	Calumets	Bone images
Wooden images	Drums	Prayer sticks

FOODS IN TRADE

Dried fruits	Animal grease	Jerky
Maize	Nuts	Animal oils
Vegetable oils	Pemmican	Salt
Seeds	Gourds	Peas
Beans	Dried berries	Acorns

TRAVEL ARTICLES

Boxes	Skin cases	Woven cases
Skin bags	Fur bags	Leather straps
Dog saddles	Fur robes	Parfleches
Sinew ropes	Hair ropes	Fire drills

WEAPONS

Arrow points	Arrow shafts	Arrow feathers
Bows	Bow sinews	Daggers
Knives	Quivers	Scabbards
Shields	Spear heads	Lances
Tomahawks	Hammers	War clubs

And utensils, ornaments, jewelry, and implements were made, among other materials, of basalt, argillite, Catlinite, diorite, flint, jasper, anthophylite, agate, lac, lignite, nephrite, obsidian, quartz, and steatite.

And not to be forgotten as articles of trade are such things as dolls and other toys, dice made of bone and beaver teeth, snake oil, liniments, tonics, laxatives, and skunk perfume.

Northern Great Plains

Home on the Range

The 1926 discoveries at Folsom, New Mexico, of projectile points among the bones of long extinct animals * had convinced scientists that man had hunted in the Pleistocene Age on the Great Plains at least eleven thousand years ago. Immediately thereafter it became the hope of archeologists to find a site where ancient Folsom man not only had killed the great mammals but also had lived and had manufactured his weapons and tools and utensils.

The search was concentrated largely on the high plains that wash against the frontal ranges of the Rocky Mountains. Within a period of eight years archeological sites of later dates were located, but the main goal remained elusive. Then suddenly in 1934 it was reached.

In northeastern Colorado, not far from the Wyoming state line, three men of a local family named Coffin rode across the rough dry range of the Lindenmeier Ranch.[1] Under a cliff along a wash they came upon a number of partially exposed animal bones. Being educated men, they did not disturb them, but reported the discovery to the Smithsonian Institution in Washington and the Denver Museum of Natural History. Investigations soon revealed that the Lindenmeier Site was one of the richest of the Folsom Complex.[2]

It is in a "vestigial valley above a little stream which is an ephemeral tributary of the Cache La Poudre River. A deep arroyo or gully cuts

---

* See Part One.

through the terrace. Artifacts, charcoal and ash, and animal remains occurred in a dark soil zone overlain by some two to seventeen feet of alluvial material. Many specimens came from the deepest part of the site in an area believed to represent the edge of a shallow pond or marsh." [3]

Here was a place where Folsom people had lived and worked. Unfortunately no human remains were found. Although the hunting band may have occupied it for some time, apparently they had moved on in their eternal hunt for game before deaths had occurred there.

Between 1934 and 1938 excavations were conducted for the Smithsonian Institution by Dr. Frank H. H. Roberts, Jr. The Denver Museum participated in the 1935 investigations. Partially uncovered by erosion and partially still buried, the Lindenmeier Site could be studied by geologists. Findings of the various scientists participating showed "that the camp had been occupied near the terminal phase of the Wisconsin Glaciation—the last state of the Pleistocene or Ice Age." [4] Besides Folsom points, the diggers recovered "other implements used by the Folsom people: knives, pieces of hematite, some carved bone ornaments—all associated with the bones of an extinct species of bison and other paleontological material." [5] Wormington notes that among the "most important finds of bone artifacts were three disks, two whole and one fragmentary, which were characterized by small incised lines around the edges, such as might have been produced by a graver. Since these objects were not perforated, it seems unlikely that they were ornaments, and it has been suggested that they may represent markers or counters used in some type of game." [6]

The Folsom people lived, hunted, worked, and played at the famous Lindenmeier Site, but evidently they didn't die there.

Giants of the High Plains

In 1932 heavy rains fell in northeastern Colorado, and wild floods roared down washes and stream beds that normally carried little water. About five hundred feet south of the railroad station of the hamlet of Dent, a Union Pacific employee, Frank Garner, came upon a mass of extremely large bones partially exposed in the bank of a gully. He told a friend, Father Conrad Bilgery of Regis College, Denver, about the find. With some of his students, Father Bilgery began excavations at the site. Under the pelvis of one of the skeletons they came upon a large grooved projectile point.

This was the first discovery fully acceptable to scientists showing beyond a doubt that man hunted elephants of the Pleistocene Age. For the bones at Dent were those of mammoths.

The next year, Father Bilgery turned the excavating over to the

Denver Museum of Natural History. Extracting from reports, H. M. Wormington of the Denver institution wrote: [7] "The bones of a dozen mammoths were removed from the quarry. One was a large individual, presumably a male, and the others were females and immature individuals. A second point, clearly associated with articulated mammoth bones, was found. This specimen, which is more markedly fluted than the first, was noted while it was still embedded in the matrix surrounding the bones . . . a great many large stones were found with the mammoth remains, although boulders of comparable size are extremely rare elsewhere in the vicinity."

While the floodwaters may be thanked for exposing the giants of the Great Plains, they also did science a disfavor by destroying the stratigraphy of the Dent Site. However, enough evidence remained to convince some geologists that the bones and artifacts were "emplaced during a glacial phase, possibly the Mankato, or an early phase of glacial recessional time." [8]

Eden of the West

Not a very good story—at least, not one satisfactory to scientists—is told by artifacts found on the surface or even in isolation in blowouts. This was the case of a long, narrow, flaked point first recovered in Yuma County, Colorado, and tentatively named for the place of its discovery. Although it was unquestionably very old, and differed in several respects from other points, it could not be dated for the simple reason that it could not be definitely associated with other ancient materials.

In the spring of 1940, archeologist Harold J. Cook was digging near the town of Eden, Wyoming, when he came upon several of the strange Yuma points. This was the first time they had been found *in situ*. The site was given the name of O. M. Finley, who had discovered it, but the projectile points were called Eden.

The find was extremely important, and an expedition from the University of Pennsylvania Museum, headed by Linton Satterthwaite, Jr., was soon on the job. In the following summer a group directed by Edgar B. Howard from the Nebraska State Museum joined forces with the other Eden diggers.

Twenty-four points were recovered in association with Pleistocene mammal bones, but they were not all Edens. Among them were several of a type first found *in situ* near Scottsbluff, Nebraska, six years earlier.

The geologists got busy. Although they wrangled and disagreed on some postulations, it seems apparent that the artifacts and the ancient bison bones found at Eden belonged to the late Ice Age. [9]

Not many more years would pass before it would become apparent that Eden points were used almost entirely by people who hunted in the late Pleistocene on the high plains and in the far north. This was a comparatively narrow area of distribution, but it was very long. For Eden points have been recovered in Alberta and Alaska. Therefore, a hypothesis seems justified. Eden points may have been brought south into the United States region by early bands of hunting peoples migrating from Siberia or from northern Canada.

They Must Have Liked Nebraska

Scottsbluff is a prominent name in the history of the Oregon Trail, but people were living there ten thousand years, and probably earlier, before wagon trains paused at the famous landmark. If the emigrants had done a bit of digging in the vicinity—or at numerous other places along their westward route—they might well have come upon the ancient projectile points and the bones of Pleistocene mammals that were found by archeologists C. Bertrand Schultz and E. H. Barbour nearly three quarters of a century after the last prairie schooner had creaked its way across Nebraska.[10]

Like the Eden, the projectile point that would be called Scottsbluff was picked up first in Yuma County, Colorado. It was found in association with ancient bison bones in 1932 near Scottsbluff, hence its official identity. It is wider than the Eden, was distributed over an enormous area, extending from Canada to Texas and the Deep South.

Of all the states of the Northern Great Plains, Nebraska comes closest to being an archeologist's paradise. A most intriguing situation was created by the finding, associated with both Eden and Scottsbluff points, of other points known as Plainview, the place in Texas which gave them their type name. Hundreds of artifacts which have been dated by the Carbon-14 method as being ten and eleven thousand years old have been recovered from one end of Nebraska to the other. Three principal sites of recovery are Lime Creek and Red Smoke in the Medicine Creek Dam area, and Meserve, near Grand Island.

Obviously this area of the Northern Great Plains must have been for thousands of years a happy hunting ground for Paleo-Indian bands, just as it would continue to be in later prehistoric times, and, indeed, until the white man destroyed the great game herds on which the plains people depended for their existence.

Wyoming Family Tragedy

In 1938, a crew of road builders was blasting rock near Torrington. Following a detonation the workers saw human bones protruding from a crevice. They had blown open the graves of one of Wyoming's first families. With their explosions they also had destroyed the stratigraphy and other geological evidence scientists require to establish the antiquity of a site. Members of the road gang made off with numerous artifacts found in association with the bones, and archeologists were unable to recover them.

Hearing of the discovery, paleontologists hurried to the scene and did the best they could with what was left. The remains of four persons were recovered, an adult male, a middle-aged female, a young female, and a small child—perhaps papa, mama, and two children.

Thorough study of the crania and other features by W. W. Howells and colleagues resulted in a sensational conclusion.[11] There seemed little doubt that the Wyoming people were contemporaries of Miss Minnesota.*

The belief was given additional support by the finding of projectile points at another Wyoming site which were similar to those found with the Brown's Valley and Lake Pelican skeletons of Minnesota.

At least, as the ever-cautious and suspicious archeologists state, it is "suggested" that there may have been some connection between the Pleistocene inhabitants of Minnesota and Wyoming, and as the eminent and conservative Wormington admits, the Wyoming people "were somewhat more long-headed than the Minnesota girl and their jaws were slightly more protruding but, in general, they appear to be representatives of the same racial group and all seem to be of a slightly more primitive type than recent Indians." [12]

Projectile Points: a Matter of Choice

Some hunters of historical times on the Great Plains liked Winchesters, some preferred Remingtons or Sharps. Nine or ten thousand years earlier, some hunters in the same region liked Folsom points, some liked the Eden, the Clovis, the Scottsbluff. Methods of hunting differed, but selection of a weapon in both eras was a matter of individual preference.

There were well-made and poorly made projectile points, just as some guns were products of superior craftsmen while others were less skillfully made. There were, as well, what might be termed *projectile point production centers,* just as there were gun factories. Archeological investigations have shown that at some sites a great many points had been made. However, although points from different localities may be identified as a type, some were obviously manufactured by experts and others were extremely crude. The talents of the men who killed Pleistocene animals greatly varied in degree.

---

* See Part Five.

In 1948 archeologist Jack T. Hughes found some points that were markedly different from other types a few miles south of Hot Springs, South Dakota.[13] With them were a number of artifacts, including cutting, scraping, and perforating tools. Of special significance was a thin stone slab with an oval depression, and several small handstones with smooth surfaces. Here was unusual evidence showing that these early people of the Great Plains supplemented their predominantly meat diet with ground plant seeds. Hughes had come upon what archeologists term an "occupation horizon." [14] That is, people had lived on the site, and Carbon-14 dating of charcoal from their campfires showed the time of their residence to be at least nine thousand years ago. No animal bones were found, but it is believed that soil conditions were unfavorable to their preservation.

The site is gone now, covered by the waters of Angostura Reservoir, and the thin, finely flaked points have been given the name Angostura.

In eastern Wyoming, not far away from the Angostura Reservoir, projectile points with distinct features had been found in 1943 on a site where prehistoric bison had been slaughtered. They had been given the name Agate Basin. However, when they were compared with the Angostura projectiles it was seen that the two were generally similar. Yet there were enough differences to warrant awarding each an individual identity. Here was another example of how craftsmen gave a "personal touch" to points with basic similarities, and of how there were hunters who preferred one or the other for their own use.

Either the makers of Angostura and Agate Basin points traveled far or the products they made were transported great distances. For projectiles bearing characteristics of Angostura points have been found on the Firth River, only sixteen miles from the Arctic Ocean, and on the Seward Peninsula of Alaska. And Agate Basin type points have been discovered in Saskatchewan.[15]

If an amateur may be permitted an observation, it would appear that the locations of projectile points bearing similarities indicate routes of migration.

Buffalo Bill's Complex

The famous scout didn't live long enough to know that an archeological complex had been named for him. In 1949 scientists began excavating on a terrace along the Shoshone River, a few miles from the town of Cody, Wyoming. For several years the digging was continued by groups from Princeton University and the Smithsonian Institution.[16]

The rewards were both rich and numerous. The site produced the remains of nearly two hundred Pleistocene bison, and associated with the bones were some of the "most magnificent specimens of Scottsbluff and Eden points that have been found. The men who made them were truly great craftsmen." [17] Also recovered were scores of tools used for flaking, engraving, chopping, perforating, and rubbing. One of the most valuable artifacts was a distinct type of knife, appropriately called the Cody Knife.

Carbon-14 dates show that the site was occupied at least seven thousand years ago, but geological data indicate that this date possibly should be moved backward another two thousand years.

Regrettably the species of bison which these Cody people butchered may never be identified certainly, for they practiced a peculiar and mysterious custom. As Wormington notes: [18] "The tops of the skulls were removed by the hunters in all but two instances. This can scarcely have been done in order to obtain the edible brains, for in that case the bony portions which were removed would have been left nearby. Perhaps the top of the skulls and horns were taken elsewhere to be used in some ceremony."

Artifacts both identical and bearing similarities to those found near Cody, including the unique Cody Knife, and points of the Scottsbluff and Eden types, have been recovered at widely separated locations, notably at a site in Washington County, Colorado, and in Saskatchewan and Alberta. But nowhere have as many been found *in situ* as at the site on the Shoshone River in Wyoming. Hence the name Cody Complex.

Arteries of Life on Earth

There, on the Plains, were the great routes of travel from north to south. There, from the time—perhaps more than forty thousand years ago—when the first Mongolians pushed out of Alaska and Canada until the last of them crossed Bering Strait from Siberia—an unknown date— the major paths of migration were east of the Rocky Mountains. These were the ways of least resistance, through the tilting levels of grass reaching from horizon to horizon and seemingly endless, along the network of rivulets and streams and big rivers running always southward and eastward in search of a common oblivion.

The shifting of the people was constant. They went on to create the cultures of the South, of Mexico, of South America. Yet there is evidence to indicate that many of them remained in the region of the Northern Great Plains, undoubtedly shifting in pursuit of the game herds, but in reality moving more in circles than in straight lines. The culture called Old Signal Butte, for example, is given a terminal date of A.D. 500 but no date of beginning, for there is geological and archeological evidence to suggest that it may have risen ten thousand years ago. Undoubtedly there were people dwelling on the High Plains long

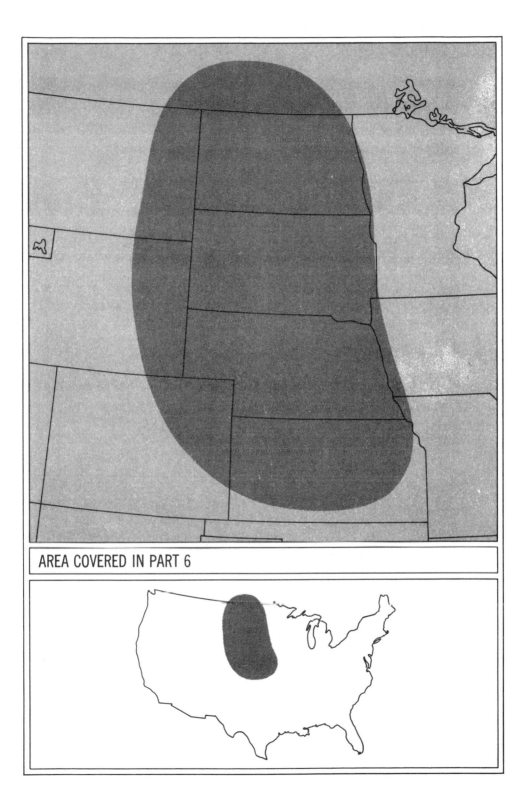

AREA COVERED IN PART 6

before that, and they were there in all the subsequent millennia, there always. And undoubtedly the descendants of people who had passed through the Great Plains came back to them from the south and from the east, and always they continued to come to the Great Plains from the north and the northeast. Archeology has found their trails. In the cultures of the High Plains have been found influences and characteristics that came from the Northeastern Woodlands, from Ohio, and other areas of the Midwest of America.

There were drastic climatic changes which affected the lives of both men and animals of the High Plains. In much of the area following the end of the Ice Age there was a long Pluvial Period, during which rivers were large and lakes and swamplands existed. The people of this period hunted the great Pleistocene mammals. About seven thousand years ago the climate of the High Plains began to be hotter and drier, and apparently the hunters shifted to mountainous areas farther west and to eastern woodland and prairie regions that received more precipitation. The dry period is believed to have peaked between six and five thousand years ago, but it persisted in mild form for at least half of another millennium.

Undoubtedly the aridity had much to do with the disappearance of the Pleistocene mammals, such as the giant bison, the mastodon, the camel, and the great sloth. It is believed that they became extinct on the Northern Great Plains before seven thousand years ago.

The Paleo-Indians were forced to change their way of life. They became hunters of small game and gatherers of wild foods. As the climate grew relatively more moist, the deer, the buffalo, the elk, the antelope increased enormously in numbers, thriving on the seas of grass. Especially in the eastern part of the Northern Plains there was a great variety of wild nuts and fruits and roots and berries and other vegetable foods. It was a rich land, and the people moved there to enjoy its bounties. Archeological discoveries show that about three thousand years ago the human population of the Northern Plains began a rapid rise. Newcomers brought new skills and new tools and new customs to the region. Pottery and rude farming methods were present in the early centuries of the Christian Era. Villages became more permanent. A combined agriculture and hunting economy arose. Contacts with people of regions far removed increased and trade developed.

For at least a thousand years the Indians of the Northern Plains lived the way they did when the first white men reached them.

Arikara: the Corn Eaters

When a Plains Indian talking in the sign language imitates the gnawing of kernels from a cob of corn it means he is speaking of the

Arikara. In the Caddoan tongue, however, Arikara has an entirely different meaning. It derives from *ariki,* signifying "horn" or "elk," and "ra" is the plural ending. Yet, when the name Arikara is spoken it refers specifically to the ancient hairdress of these people. It was the custom of both men and women to wear two pieces of bone in their hair, one standing up on each side of the crest.

Wherever maize could be grown, Indians ate it, and even Indians who lived where it would not grow traveled far to obtain it by barter. In this respect they were all corn eaters, but the name has come down through countless centuries as a special description of the Arikara. There is a reason.

The origin of the Arikara can be traced back to an indefinite period when their home was on the Southwestern Plains. They were then a division of the Skidi Pawnee. At some remote time these people parted. The Skidi settled on the Loup River in Nebraska, but the Arikara pushed on toward the northeast until they had reached the Missouri River. Their villages stood thereafter at various places along the Missouri, at first not far above Omaha, and later in the vicinity of the Cheyenne, Grand, and Cannonball rivers. They became the most northern tribe of the Caddoan linguistic family.

The Arikara were influential in spreading agricultural knowledge among the prehistoric peoples of the upper Missouri. Their oldest traditions relate that they were farmers as well as hunters. Maize always held a vitally important place in both their economy and their religion. They addressed it as "Mother," and they paid it reverence in numerous ceremonies. Obviously corn had reached them from southern tribes, for it was developed in South America and Mexico. And, incidentally, they wove baskets in a manner typical of Indians who dwelt along the Gulf of Mexico.

To the upper Missouri they brought a peculiar kind of corn. The ears were small, and it was exceptionally nutritious. They preserved the seed to be used for spring planting in skins hung near the fireplaces of their houses. When the time for planting came, the seeds were carefully sorted, and only those which showed signs of germinating were used. Some of the finest ears were saved for ceremonial purposes. After usage in rituals they were considered "holy." Medicine men possessed ears that had been preserved for generations, and it was believed that within them dwelt the spirit of the "Mother." Arikara corn had great trade value, and other tribes of the Plains came each year to exchange buffalo robes and fine furs for it.

The Arikara were themselves good hunters. In the winter they engaged in buffalo hunts, but after the crops had been planted they generally remained in their villages to nurture and guard them. They made remarkable round boats of buffalo hides lashed over a framework of willows. Expert swimmers, men, women, and young persons would plunge into the swift muddy waters of the great river to drag floating trees ashore. In this way, and by gathering bank driftwood, they obtained adequate supplies of wood in a land in which such fuel was scarce.

The Arikara constructed lodges of earth and willow work. Each was occupied by several families, and they were usually grouped closely together about an open square. In each town a large community house was erected in which festivities and council meetings were held, especially during the long and very cold winters. They were noted as jugglers and for their feats of magic, and they engaged in a variety of games of skill. Entertaining children and building toys for them was a popular pastime. They were unusually clever at making whistles with which they could imitate the calls of various animals and birds.

Attacks by tribes, notably the Sioux, who considered the Arikara invaders, frequently forced them to abandon their towns and fields in prehistoric times and to reestablish themselves in new locations. The ruins of old Arikara villages have been found from the Platte along the river to North Dakota. When the first French traders established relations with them they were living near the mouth of the Cannonball River. After the United States purchased the Louisiana Territory, besides continuing to suffer from aggressive tribes, the Arikara were victims of rivalries between trading groups. They became deadly enemies of Americans, and warfare, smallpox, and other diseases introduced by white men brought them to the verge of extinction.

Hidatsa: They Crossed the Water

The tribe that became known to history as Hidatsa were closely related to the Crow. They say that when they lived with the Crow on the upper Missouri—probably early in the historical period—the two tribes engaged in a head-breaking row over the results of a sporting event. When it was over they separated from their Siouan relatives, never again to reestablish amicable relations. The Crow moved to the west. Eventually the Hidatsa established themselves close to the Mandan and the Arikara.

From their neighbors they learned to farm, and they became sedentary people, dwelling in earth lodges. Their own traditions name as their earliest home Devil's Lake, North Dakota. Although they belonged to the Siouan linguistic family, they suffered greatly from attacks by Siouan tribes. After their affiliation with the Mandan, they gradually adopted many customs and religious beliefs of that tribe.*

---

* See *Mandan: the White Indians*, this part.

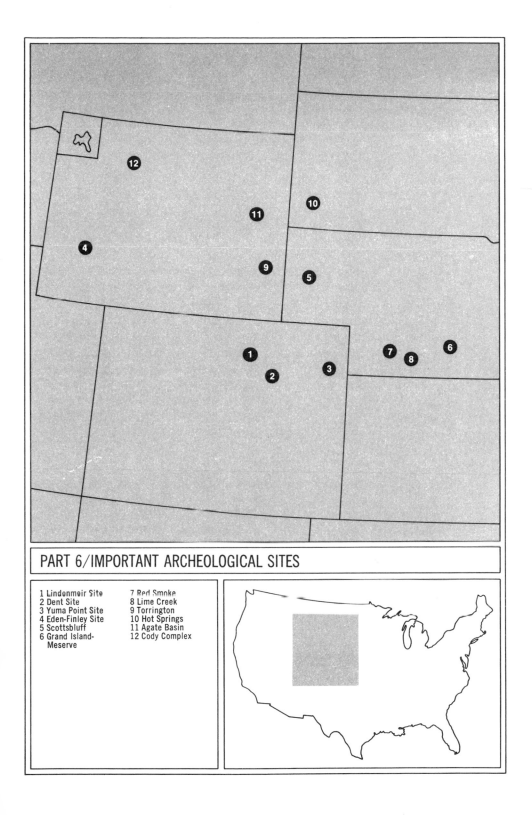

PART 6/IMPORTANT ARCHEOLOGICAL SITES

1 Lindenmeir Site
2 Dent Site
3 Yuma Point Site
4 Eden-Finley Site
5 Scottsbluff
6 Grand Island-
   Meserve

7 Red Smoke
8 Lime Creek
9 Torrington
10 Hot Springs
11 Agate Basin
12 Cody Complex

The tribal name by which they called themselves is not known. The Mandan called them *Minitari*, meaning "they crossed the water." It is said that this identity was applied at their first meeting with the Mandan, at which the Hidatsa crossed the Missouri River. The Arapaho and Cheyenne called them by names signifying that on hunting trips their tepees were erected in a row.

By any name, their fate would have been no less tragic than it was. They were almost exterminated by smallpox spread among them by Americans. The few survivors gathered in a small village. Its name was Hidatsa.

Mandan: the White Indians

When the origin of a people is doubtful, one may safely wager that someone will concoct a genesis for them that has no foundation whatsoever in fact. Dreamers may have enriched American literature with their fanciful tales, but they have served historians and scientists only in the respect that they have kept them busy exposing their fables.

The Indians, according to one fantastic tale, reached America by the continent of Atlantis, long disappeared in the Atlantic Ocean. This myth can be traced back to the ancient Greeks, and there is not a shred of scientific evidence to show that it ever existed. Another fantasy contends that a similar lost continent, called Mu, once existed in the Pacific. Others relate that Indians crossed the oceans in boats, conveniently forgetting that twenty thousand years ago, or even ten thousand years ago, there were no boats capable of making voyages of such length.

As the distinguished anthropologist Harold E. Driver notes: "A more tenable theory involving continents in places where oceans exist today is that of continental drift. This theory holds that North and South America were once joined to Europe and Africa and formed a solid land mass. Then, as the earth's crust cooled and shrunk, a cleavage appeared and the two portions gradually drifted apart. Although this theory may explain certain facts of geology, geography, and prehuman biology, it cannot account for man's presence in the New World because the separation, if it actually occurred, took place hundreds of millions of years before any form of man had evolved anywhere on the face of the earth." [19]

Ever since the time of Columbus, religious groups have maintained that American Indians are the descendants of the Ten Lost Tribes of Israel. This, of course, is ridiculous, because even if some people from Israel had reached America in Old Testament times, they would have found that the Western Hemisphere had been inhabited by Homo sapiens for a great many millennia.

And here the Indians known to history as the Mandan take their places on the mythological stage. Their skin was fairer than that of other Indians. The noses of many of them were thin and not so long and arched as those of other Plains tribes; some were aquiline or slightly curved, some short and straight, but none were broad. The men were tall, well-proportioned, broad-shouldered, muscular, and vigorous. Some of the women were tall and robust, although most of them were short and heavy.

So the dreamers and the religious fanatics contrived a genesis for them. The Mandan were Spaniards. No, they were Welshmen. No, they were the lost people of Israel. In any case, they were white Indians.

As sensible is the story which the Mandan themselves told of their origin. This tradition related: [20] "The whole nation resided in one large village underground near a subterraneous lake; a grapevine extended its roots down to their habitation and gave them a view of the light; some of the most adventurous climbed up the vine and were delighted with the sight of the earth, which they found covered with buffalo and rich with every kind of fruit; returning with the grapes they had gathered, their countrymen were so pleased with the taste of them that the whole nation resolved to leave their dull residence for the charms of the upper region; men, women, and children ascended by means of the vine; but when about half the nation had reached the surface of the earth, a corpulent woman who was clambering up the vine broke it with her weight, and closed upon herself and the rest of the nation the light of the sun. Those who were left on the earth made a village . . . and when the Mandans die they expect to return to the original seats of their forefathers, the good reaching the ancient village by means of the lake, which the burden of the sins of the wicked will not enable them to cross."

Archeology and ethnology tell a different story.

Their earliest identifiable home is in the region of the upper Great Lakes. Their language is closely related to both the Winnebago and the Tutelo. This relationship suggests that even before they lived in northern Wisconsin they may have inhabited the Ohio-Kentucky region. For the Tutelo and other eastern Siouan tribes are believed to have migrated from the Ohio River and its tributaries to the Atlantic Seaboard.

According to their own beliefs, the Mandan went from the upper Great Lakes region to Minnesota and the headwaters of the Mississippi. At some remote time they descended the Mississippi for some distance, then moved overland to the Missouri. At the beginning of the historical period they were established near the mouth of Heart River, North Dakota. A few years later, greatly reduced in number by smallpox, they were located in two villages, one on each side of the Missouri where it is joined by Knife River.

The social structures of the Mandan, Arikara, and Hidatsa were similar in many respects. The economy was virtually identical, based on hunting, farming, and intertribal trading. Matrilocal families were dominant, and their permanent houses were large enough to accommodate an extended family. In addition to the dwelling, the family owned farm plots, household chattels, and dogs. Polygamy was practiced, but it was principally, if not wholly, sororal, therefore fitting into the matrilocal structure.[21] There were clans, moieties, phratries, military and other types of societies. Among the Hidatsa and Mandan certain moieties owned game fields and divided the products of communal hunts. A system of age-societies was maintained by the Mandan, Arikara, and Hidatsa. Lowie [22] states that "an age-classification by the male population is divided into approximately ten classes of successively higher degree, each with its distinctive dance, songs, paraphernalia and privileges." There also were women's societies. According to Driver: [23] "One such group, called the Goose Women, performed ceremonies to insure a good corn crop and also to attract the buffalo. Another women's club, called the White Buffalo Cow Women, also had a ritual to lure a buffalo herd within range of the hunters."

While all tribes owned dogs, the permanent villages on the Upper Missouri swarmed with them. Some families, it is believed, owned as many as forty. On hunting excursions travois pulled by the larger dogs were used to transport tepees, utensils, robes, and meat. In times of want, dogs were eaten, and puppy stew was a delicacy served on special occasions.

More than the white man himself, the greatest enemy of the sedentary tribes of the upper Missouri was the disease which the white man brought to them, and which they had no means of combating. Near the end of the great fur trade era only thirty-one Mandan were alive in their two main villages. All the others had died terrible deaths, victims of the smallpox.[24]

Cheyenne: They Lost the Corn

The Cheyenne say they had been living in southern Minnesota a very long time before the Sioux came to the upper Mississippi region. Their culture and their economy were similar to those of other peoples who inhabited the Central Prairies and Woodlands. They were hunters and farmers living in permanent villages. The women made pottery and were expert at decorating skins with porcupine quills.

In late prehistoric times, under strong pressure from the Sioux, the Cheyenne were forced from their ancestral homeland. They moved gradually westward, for a time establishing themselves on the Sheyenne * River not far from its confluence with the Red River in North Dakota. That they were still attempting to grow maize is indicated by the name which the pursuing Sioux gave to the Sheyenne River. It was "the place where the Cheyenne plant."

There, say the Cheyenne, they "lost the corn."

And there began one of the most romantic, dramatic, and tragic tales to be found in the history of all the Indians of the Great Plains.

The Cheyenne belong to the Algonquian linguistic family. The name by which they call themselves is *Dzitsi'stas*. It means simply "people alike," or "our people." However, by changing inflection it could be given the meaning of "gashed ones." This does not signify gashes on their persons. As Mooney [25] explains, in the sign language the Cheyenne "are indicated by a gesture which has often been interpreted to mean 'cut arms' or 'cut fingers'—being made by drawing the right index finger several times rapidly across the left—but which appears really to indicate 'striped arrows,' by which name they are known to the Hidatsa, Shoshoni, Comanche, Caddo, and probably other tribes, in allusion to their old-time preference for [striped] turkey feathers for winging arrows."

The Sioux gave them the name Cheyenne. In the Siouan language it means "people who speak a strange tongue." It was an appropriate designation, for the Cheyenne dialect was one of the most aberrant of the Algonquian language. The speech of only one other cognate tribe, the Sutaio, shared its peculiarities.

Driven from their settlements in eastern North Dakota by the Assiniboine and other Sioux, the Cheyenne continued to move westward. They reached the Missouri River. Now they were in the heart of the Northern Great Plains, and they were forced to adopt a new way of life. The transition of the Cheyenne from a sedentary agricultural people to nomadic buffalo hunters is one of the most remarkable on record. It was accomplished within a relatively few years, and they became not only fully adjusted to a wandering existence but one of the most formidable tribes of warriors in all the immense Plains region.

According to George Bird Grinnell, an authority on this tribe: [26] "After the question of providing subsistence for himself and his family, the main thing that occupied the mind of the Cheyenne was the protection of his people from the attacks of enemies and the effort to reduce the power of these enemies by attacks on them.

"The fighting spirit was encouraged. In no way could a young man gain so much credit as by the exhibition of courage. Boys and youths were trained to feel that the most important thing in life was to be

---

* As incorrectly spelled by North Dakotans.

brave; that death was not a thing to be avoided; that, in fact, it was better for a man to be killed while in his full vigor rather than to wait until his prime was past, his powers were failing, and he could no longer achieve those feats which to all seemed so desirable."

The historical period opened nearly two centuries later in the northern part than it did in the southern part of the Great Plains. The eastern and southern parts of the United States region were well colonized long before the prehistoric age had ended on the Great Plains north of the Platte River. But even after traders had reached the upper Missouri and had begun to push westward toward the mountains the Northern Plains were the scene of fierce and constant intertribal warfare, and the philosophy of late prehistoric times prevailed well into the period of recorded history.

The rigors of war and hunting and long marches could not be endured by the aged, and, as Grinnell states,[27] "How much better, therefore, to struggle and fight, to be brave and accomplish great things, to receive the respect and applause of everyone in the camp, and finally to die gloriously at the hands of the enemy!

"Among the Cheyennes, as among other Plains tribes, this feeling was very strong. They fought not only to gain the approval of their fellow tribesmen but for pure enjoyment of the struggle—real *gaudium certaminis*. The spirit of the camp was such that young men going into battle thought of it as the beginning of a good time they were to have. To them fighting was a real joy."

Whether at some remote time the Sutaio and the Cheyenne lived close to each other is not known. There is circumstantial evidence suggesting that the two closely related tribes were together east of the Missouri River. In any case, the Sutaio had preceded the Cheyenne to the west. They encountered each other when the Cheyenne pushed on toward the Black Hills. Traditions relate that at first the two tribes were disposed to keep apart and were not on good terms, but eventually became strong allies. In the end the Sutaio would lose their identity as a tribe and become known as Cheyenne.

However, it was the Sutaio who gave the Sun Dance to the Cheyenne after they had united on the Western Plains, and it became thereafter their greatest tribal ceremony. The Sun Dance was an annual summer ritual confined to Plains tribes, and was of great religious significance.* Directed by a self-perpetuating priesthood, it might be performed for a number of reasons: the overcoming of certain cosmic elements, such as to avert lightning; to gain new strength, health, and courage; to purify the heart; to win rebirth. Generally the dramas of the Sun Dance con-

---

* It was also held by the Arapaho, Sitsika, Cree, Dakota, Assiniboine, Mandan, Crow, Ponca, Omaha, Pawnee, Kiowa, Shoshoni, and Ute.

tinued for eight days and nights. The lodge in which it was held usually was a roofless enclosure, perhaps a hundred feet in length, with an opening always on the east side. A tall center pole represented the sun. Voluntary self-laceration or torture took place, the most common form being to insert in one breast a skewer attached to a thong. The thong was fastened to a buffalo skull, and the performer, always a man, dragged the skull around the lodge, giving no indication of the pain he was suffering. Vomiting and sweating were employed as purification rites.[28]

The Cheyenne might be likened in some respects to a military organization. The perilous life they led demanded strict obedience to rules. Violations could bring danger or even disaster to many persons. The will of the leaders was enforced by a police organization. Standards of behavior were established, and extended into the private lives of individuals. For example, while premarital mating was condoned by most Plains tribes, Cheyenne families sought to instill standards of virtue in their daughters.

The political structure of the Cheyenne, although complicated, was based upon rigid regulations. The tribe was governed by a council of forty-four elective chiefs, of whom five were priests and held the power to elect one of their own number head chief. The council was symbolized by two "bundles," one of forty-four "invitation sticks," and one by four sacred "medicine arrows." According to Cheyenne tradition, the four sacred "medicine arrows," each of a different color, constituted the tribal palladium, and had existed "since the beginning of the world." [29]

The priestly body of five chiefs conducted tribal rituals, such as the Sun Dance. The head chief, who was called the Prophet and represented the mythical and cultural hero, presided at the council meetings and controlled manipulations of the sacred "medicine bundles." Driver states [30] that when one of the five priestly chiefs retired, he chose his successor from the remaining thirty-nine members of the group, or, if he died so suddenly that he could not choose his successor, the surviving four priestly chiefs chose one for him. A priestly chief, on retirement, did not leave the council but stepped down only to the rank of the undifferentiated chiefs. "If an undifferentiated chief died without choosing his successor," Driver writes, "the entire council chose one for him. Each ordinary chief could serve only ten years, which explains why the rules of succession are so complicated. New chiefs were chosen on the basis of merit, and it was considered bad taste for a man to choose his son. The personal qualities which constituted merit were control of temper and generosity. None of the forty-four chiefs ever exerted any force to carry out the will of the civil council."

Four ranking members of six men's societies composed a council of twenty-four war chiefs. A man could not be both a civil chief and a war chief. One of the war chiefs was appointed to lead each raid, and when it was over, his authority terminated. The council of war chiefs also named commanders with coercive powers on two other important occasions: moving camp and the tribal buffalo hunt. Moving camp was in fact always a military venture because of the ever-present danger of encountering an enemy, while a tribal buffalo hunt was a vitally important economic undertaking, and teamwork was required to make it successful.[31] It should not be forgotten that these hunts were conducted on foot. A stampeding herd could not very well be pursued any great distance, and the strategy of ambushing the animals and killing the greatest number in the shortest possible time had to be devised and directed by skillful leaders. A Great Plains tribe like the Cheyenne, with no permanent abodes, depended upon the buffalo for its existence. Women participated in all hunts, playing important roles, such as driving the animals within range of the hunters. While to the squaws fell most of the work of butchering slain animals, preserving the meat, and dressing the skins, there was an exclusive buffalo society in which women sought to attain membership. The goal was not easily reached. Only women who had embroidered at least thirty buffalo robes with porcupine quills were eligible. Such an achievement might require several years of patient and painstaking work in spare time, but Cheyenne women looked upon the honor as worth the long struggle.

At the time of the acquisition of the Louisiana Territory by the United States the Cheyenne were living on the headwaters of the Platte River. In the period when the American fur trade was at its height in the Far West they divided. A large number moved south to the upper Arkansas, and the others remained in the north, ranging between the North Platte and the Yellowstone rivers. Thereafter, the two groups were distinguished as the Southern and Northern Cheyenne.

The remainder of the Cheyenne story belongs to the history of western settlement and wars with the American army. It is doubtful if any Indians of the Great Plains suffered more at the hands of greedy and fiendish American settlers, brutal soldiers, and unconscionable politicians and grafters. The name "Cheyenne" is preserved in numerous places. The Americans who gave the name to towns and various geographical features can make no claim to honoring a great people, but the Cheyenne can take just pride in the punishment they inflicted on their persecutors.

Sioux: Seven Council Fires

The Dakota of the Northern Great Plains always have been, and always will be, the "picture Indian" of western history. They fully deserve the honor. For they rank physically, mentally, and morally among the highest type of American aborigines, and they are superior in these qualities to many, if not most, tribes. As a warrior society they may be compared to the Navajo. As to courage and bravery they have no peers. As to color in their regalia and drama in their social, military, and religious rites they are unsurpassed. As to cohesiveness and unity as a people, and as to faith in themselves as individuals and as a "nation," as to confidence in their capabilities to overcome all obstacles, all adversities, all enemies, and as egotists, they are incomparable.

That is, they were all of these things long before, and even for a century after, the first white men came to know them. These admirable characteristics are not entirely dead in them, but long ago American injustice and cruelty quenched them to faintly smoldering embers.

To the world they are known as Sioux, but that is both a misnomer and a twisted abbreviation. Their prehistoric enemy, the Chippewa, called them *Nadowe-is-iw,* signifying "adders." To the early French *voyageurs* the word sounded like *Nadouessioux,* and this was abbreviated to *Sioux.*

Their own name was *Ocheti shakowin.* It means "the seven council fires." When they began to call themselves by this name is not known, but its derivation seems to be clear. There were seven main divisions of the Dakota. As enumerated by the authority Swanton [32] they were: "(1) Mdewkanton, (2) Wahpeton, (3) Wahpekute, (4) Sisseton, (5) Yankton, (6) Yanktonai, including (a) Upper Yanktonai, and (b) Lower Yanktonai or Hunkpatina, from whom also the Assiniboine are said to have separated, and (7) Teton, including (a) the Brule (Upper and Lower), (b) Hunkpapa, (c) Miniconjou, (d) Oglala, (e) Oohenonpa or Two Kettle, (f) San Arcs, (g) Sihasapa or Blackfoot."

Seven main council fires . . . and the word *Dakota* signifies "allies" in the Santee dialect. In the dialects of the Yankton and the Assiniboine it is *Nakota.* In the Teton dialect it is *Lakota.* But however it is spelled the meaning is the same—"allies."

The Sioux who lived on the Great Plains were not always Plains Indians. Indeed, they became dependent on the immense buffalo herds of Nebraska and the Dakotas in historical times. Their earliest known home—that is, where the first explorers found them—was in southern Minnesota, northwestern Wisconsin, and northeastern Iowa. However, there is evidence to indicate that at a much earlier period they dwelt farther south, probably in Kentucky, southern Ohio, and Indiana. As recounted previously, Siouan peoples moved in several directions from this central midwestern region, going southeast to the Atlantic Seaboard, southwest to Arkansas, and north to the upper Great Lakes.*

---

* See Parts Three and Five.

Under strong pressures from the Chippewa and other tribes the Northern Sioux spread gradually westward. The *Jesuit Relations* speak of them as being on the upper Mississippi in 1640. (Some of them were still in Minnesota more than two hundred years later.) Yet, not much later they had reached the Northern Plains, and probably early in the eighteenth century they had crossed the Missouri and were continuing to fight their way westward and northward. The exact years of their various migrations remain obscure, but the fact remains that within a very short period they had been transformed from Woodland Indians to Plains Indians, and had achieved domination of an enormous territory reaching from Canada to the Platte River, from Minnesota to the Yellowstone, the Black Hills, and Powder River.

Royal B. Hassrick, an authority on Sioux history, suggests that their transition from woodland customs to nomadic buffalo hunters may have been accomplished within half a century. He adds: [33] "To be sure, the shift from a woodland hunting and gathering economy was far less drastic a change than the transition of the Cheyennes and Crows from agriculture to nomadic hunting. To the Sioux, the new way of life was different in degree, not in kind."

Oddly, although they were spread over a vast area, the bonds of the Sioux as a people strengthened as the years passed, when separation might have been expected to weaken them. They made attempts to meet in council each summer, to settle problems of importance to all of them, to partake in festivals and religious ceremonials, to pledge anew their loyalty to each other. As Hassrick notes, the annual meeting, at which the seven divisions were represented, "symbolized the cohesiveness of the nation. The deliberations and actions of the chief men in council were the epitome of Sioux political thought. The Sun Dance was the ultimate of spiritual expression. Together, at one grand occasion, all the Sioux celebrated." [34]

There could have been nothing more colorful and stirring than the sight of several thousand Sioux in their finest regalia, tanned soft skins painted and decorated, necklaces of bone and shell and elk and grizzly bear teeth, ornaments of copper and obsidian, and perhaps turquoise brought a thousand miles from the Southwest through trade channels, and garments embroidered with quills. The long rows and circles of tall tepees dotted the grassland along some stream, and the columns of smoke from the cooking fires stood up to the sky by day, and by night the flames burned holes in the darkness, and the beat of drums and the cries of the dancers shattered the plains' silence. Feathers should be given special mention in such an imaginary sight. They were not only used as personal decorations. They entered largely into war and into religion. Of all primitive Indian artifacts there was nothing as beautiful as the feathered bonnets of the Plains Indians, and the long Sioux warbonnets were superb beyond compare. They were made of eagle plumes, and the white ones with black tips were the most prized of all, although some warriors would wear only the feathers of the golden eagle. The Sioux also carried fans made of eagle wings as an accessory to costumes worn in certain dances and ceremonies. Eagle feathers were attached to buckskin shirts, and shields were ornamented with them.[35]

If one wonders how men on foot, armed only with lances and bows and arrows, could kill the sharp-eyed wary eagle, it would not be surprising. But the hands were the only weapons employed. An eagle hunter constructed a small pit and covered it with a light frame of poles and brush. On the top he placed a rabbit or prairie dog or some other small animal. Then he concealed himself in the pit. When an eagle alighted to take the bait, he grabbed it by the feet, pulled it down, and wrung its neck.[36]

It was at the summer assembly that the great Sioux leaders, who were selected from the outstanding headmen of each division, met for deliberation. Hassrick [37] states that "theirs was a position of unparalleled honor. Their opinion was paramount, their prestige unsurpassed, their reputation unimpeachable." Among their duties was the forming of national policy, and they "formally approved or disapproved actions taken by the headmen of separate divisions during the past year . . . they endorsed or rejected plans proposed by subordinates. Here they sat in judgment on offenses against national unity and security. They were, in effect, at this one summer session, an exclusive senate with supreme-court authority." [38]

In an excellent study the Sioux character and philosophy are thoroughly and clearly analyzed and explained by Hassrick. He states: "National destiny was paramount, and any device which promised a chance of securing control and dominance of a situation was the prevailing *modus operandi*. Although personal integrity was expected between Sioux and Sioux, for the tribe national integrity involved deceit and treachery. . . . The Sioux also expected treachery and deceit on the part of their neighbors; they assumed that their enemies were as devoted to the cause of tribal power as they were themselves. The Sioux had no illusions on this score. To fail to gain the upper hand was to court defeat and probable death. . . .

"As if to impress upon themselves a constantly positive attitude toward their national fortune, vanity was crystallized in exhibitionism at home and abroad. Risk in battle, to the extreme of overtly courting death, was recognized as among the highest achievements. Such action was accorded high honor and widespread fame. Prestige and influence accrued to the brave in heart. At home, such a man might be given a position of great responsibility. To a neighboring tribe, his name and presence might mean the turning point in battle or the successful accomplishment in treaty-making or trading. Therefore, to assume the boastful attitude, to be self-assertive to the point of overbearance, was the keynote of individual and national survival.

"To exhibitionism was added an aura of violence. . . . To kill an enemy was not enough; often he must be mutilated. To force an enemy tribe into submission was not sufficient; it must be driven from the territory. This violent approach was found within the patterns of in-group adjustment too. The penalties of disfigurement for infidelity,* of tipi and property destruction for infraction of hunting regulations, are examples of the severity of Sioux disposition. . . . As opposed to the quiet of peace-loving men, these were an audacious people for whom boldness was a primary virtue. . . . While it is very true that the Sioux were not mere pompous bluffers, the fact that any people should have to resort to public displays of their fortitude and courage not only indicates an underlying fear that their true merit would not be fully recognized but also shows that through repeated assertions of a fact, an individual as well as a group may remain thoroughly convinced of it. While the Sioux may not have been consciously aware of these factors, their effectiveness sustained the nation for a long period of time. . . . They were a people convinced of their superiority. When that attitude became threatened, they had already developed mechanistic patterns which were quite ample for reassuring themselves." [39]

The Sioux fought their white destroyers as they fought their prehistoric enemies, with courage and determination unsurpassed by any people in the history of the world. Their faith in themselves was never lost. On the battlefield they achieved some notable victories. But there were forces they could not fight. For all their bravery, they could not fight the criminal violations of legal treaties, the wanton disregard of civil rights, the breaking of solemn promises, the starvation inflicted upon them by a corrupt political system and a people who, in the way of a faucet, turned moral standards on and off to serve a desire of the moment.

Omaha: Going Against the Current

Except for minor dialectical differences, the Omaha and the Ponca speak the same language. Yet, the meaning of the word "Ponca" is unknown. The word "Omaha," however, means "those going against the wind or current," and in the sense that it tells much of their early history it is applicable to both tribes.

They belong to the group of the Siouan linguistic family called Dhegiha, the other members being the Kansa, Osage, and Quapaw. All

---

* Such as cutting off the nose of a wayward wife.

lived at one time on the Ohio and Wabash rivers, in northern Kentucky and southern Indiana. In late prehistoric times the Omaha, Ponca, Kansa, and Osage moved northward, *against the current* of the Mississippi. Some time later the Quapaw went *with the current,* down the great river to Arkansas.

On the northward migration the Osage remained on the river that would be given their name. The Kansa continued on up the Missouri. Staying together, the Omaha and the Ponca—with the Iowa tagging along—pushed on northward overland until they had reached the Red Pipestone Quarry in Minnesota.*

The migration of these Siouan peoples probably began about A.D. 1500. It took years to complete, and when the Omaha and Ponca reached the Red Pipestone Quarry area has not been established, but it seems certain that they inhabited it for more than a hundred years, perhaps as late as the third or fourth decade of the seventeenth century.

They lived mainly on game, supplementing this diet with maize and perhaps other vegetables. Their dwellings were similar to those of the Mandan, that is, constructed mainly of earth, but they did not occupy them the year round. In the early spring and late fall they were absent on communal hunts, traveling westward to the plains in quest of buffalo.

The Omaha were the dominant tribe, and their ways generally established the behavior patterns of their allies. They were polygamists, but unlike others who practiced this social custom a man was allowed no more than three wives, no matter how many he might have been able to support. They were ruled by two principal chiefs, having different responsibilities. In addition there was a body called the Council of Seven which deliberated on tribal problems.

While their political structure generally conformed to that of most Plains tribes, in the administration of law the authority of the Council of Seven was unusually great. According to Lowie,[40] it had the "power to order the killing of an unruly and rebellious tribesman. The decree was executed by some trustworthy man with the aid of a poisoned staff. Usually it was customary to give the criminal fair warning † . . . but if he failed to pay heed to this admonition, he himself would suffer the extreme penalty."

The Council of Seven also took action in murder cases. The customary penalty was banishment for four years. During this period "the murderer was obliged to remain on the edge of the camp and hold no

---

* See *Scientific Note—Tobacco and Pipes,* this part.
† By destroying his personal property. After Plains Indians became mounted, the lawbreaker's horses were destroyed.

intercourse with anyone but his immediate family, who might seek him out and furnish him with provisions. The duration of the penalty was in a measure dependent on the sentiments of the mourning kin, for as soon as they relented the exile was allowed to return. That is to say, homicide despite tribal interference ranked after all as a tort: it was not the tribe that exacted punishment but the suffering family, and the council intervened not to exact a condign penalty but to satisfy the private feeling of revenge and prevent civil dissension with consequent weakening of the community." [41]

In Minnesota the Omaha and Ponca (and Iowa) found the pressure from the Dakota too great to be combated, and they retreated westward. At the mouth of White River, South Dakota, they separated, the Ponca continuing westward to the Little Missouri and the Black Hills. The Omaha and the Iowa settled on Bow Creek, Nebraska. This parting probably occurred about the year 1650.[42]

Apparently finding their position in the Black Hills untenable, the Ponca returned, and the three tribes were once more united. Soon thereafter the Iowa crossed the Missouri eastward into the future state of Iowa. The Omaha and the Ponca continued to live west of the Missouri between the Platte and the Niobrara until American farmers decided they were not suitable neighbors. Most of their lands were stolen in a scandalous political maneuver, and the majority were forcibly exiled to the Indian Territory (Oklahoma).

Seduction on Grand River

When explorers and missionaries first reached the lower Missouri River they heard a tale from old Oto chiefs. It must, at least in part, be classed as a tradition, but later scientific research indicates that it is rooted in some reality.

The tale was this: At some period, probably in late prehistoric times, the Winnebago, the Missouri, the Iowa, and the Oto were one tribe. They moved southwestward on a great hunt. At Green Bay, Wisconsin, they decided to separate. The Winnebago remained, but the Missouri, the Iowa, and the Oto moved on toward the southwest and eventually reached the Mississippi at the mouth of the Iowa River. The Missouri and the Oto wished to go on, and the Iowa were left behind.*

Together the Missouri and the Oto pushed on westward until they had come to the confluence of the Missouri and Grand rivers. There a breech was created between them that was never healed. The row occurred, according to the tale, when the son of the Oto chief raped, or at least seduced, the daughter of the Missouri chief.

---

* Later movements, as they are known, have been recounted.

The tribe to which the young seducer belonged was dubbed Oto. It derives from the word *Wat'ota,* meaning "lechers." The Oto chief took his people farther up the Missouri. The tribe had another name for themselves, *Che-wae-rae,* the meaning of which is uncertain, but if they remembered it, others did not, and they were never able to escape the opprobrium fastened upon them by the resentful chief of the Missouri. And so they are known to history—the lechers.

A scientific fact is that the Missouri, the Iowa, and the Oto speak tongues that are almost identical. They comprise the Chiwere Group of the Siouan linguistic family. Their close linguistic relationship to the Winnebago has been established. But whether or not the various separations occurred in the manner and at the places indicated must remain in the realm of conjecture.

The Oto villages consisted of large earthen houses similar to those of the Kansa and Omaha. Although they habitually built permanent dwellings, they apparently were not permanent occupants of them. They were also cultivators, but if their own traditions are to be believed they could not be termed farmers. At least it could not have been one of their major pursuits, for they tell of wandering on long forays and hunts far across both the Northern and Southern Great Plains. To describe them as roamers and hunters seems more appropriate. An event which occurred in early historical times serves as an illustration. In 1680 a contingent of Oto visited La Salle on the Illinois River. They were on foot, but they told him that they had traveled far enough west to get in a fight with men who rode horses, obviously Spaniards in western Nebraska or Colorado.

Crow: the Bird People

Until early historic times the Crow lived with the Hidatsa on the upper Missouri River. The identities of the first white men to find them—

Language Groups in Part Six

NORTHERN GREAT PLAINS

Algonquian:	Arapaho	Siouan:	Assiniboine
	Cheyenne		Crow
			Dakota
Caddoan:	Arikara		Hidatsa
	Pawnee		Kansa
			Mandan
			Omaha
			Oto
			Ponca

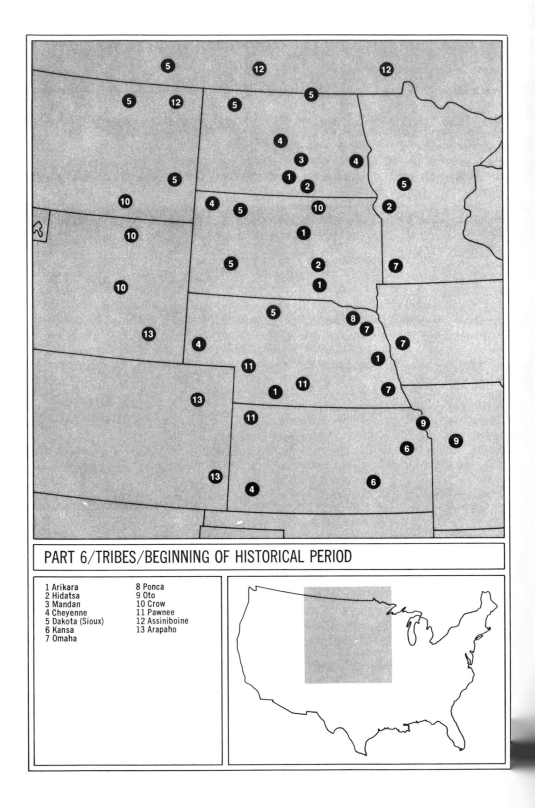

PART 6/TRIBES/BEGINNING OF HISTORICAL PERIOD

1 Arikara
2 Hidatsa
3 Mandan
4 Cheyenne
5 Dakota (Sioux)
6 Kansa
7 Omaha

8 Ponca
9 Oto
10 Crow
11 Pawnee
12 Assiniboine
13 Arapaho

undoubtedly French *voyageurs*—are not known, but whoever they were they heard from both the Hidatsa and the Crow stories of how a bitter quarrel resulted in a permanent separation.

The stories differed in detail, but the ending of each was the same. The Hidatsa said that the disunion was brought about by an argument over a game. The Crow said that it was caused by a dispute between two strong chieftains who were jealous of each other. In any case, the angry Crow migrated westward across the Northern Great Plains until they had reached the Rocky Mountains.

The Crow called themselves *Absaroke,* which means "bird people," but also signifies "crow or sparrow-hawk." Traders came to call the large territory over which they acquired domination Absaroka. It was a beautiful land rolling against the blue and crystal wall of the Big Horns and the towering jagged peaks of the Wind River Mountains. Over the grass ranges that swept away from the Yellowstone, the Big Horn, the Wind, the Powder, the Tongue rivers grazed immense herds of buffalo, deer, antelope, elk. It was a land of grizzlies and cougars and big wolves and coyotes, and it was rich in beaver and otter and other fur-bearing animals.

But it was not a land without enemies. To the north and northeast were the Sitsika (Blackfoot) and the Dakota, and they and other tribes came into it on forays and on hunts, and from the time the Crow entered it no year passed without warfare. They were not always fighting as defenders. They were bold warriors, and they struck back, raiding their neighbors and taking scalps. But they had an advantage: they could retreat if necessary into the mountains, to strongholds virtually impregnable.

It is improbable that any Indian people possessed qualities and characteristics of greater variance, or a more complicated social structure. They were physically strong and morally weak. They were highly intelligent and extremely superstitious.

The Crow were a wandering tribe of hunters and gatherers of wild plant foods. The only crop they cultivated was tobacco, and it played an important part in their religion. They sought to avoid white men, despising them, they were thieves *par excellence* and would plunder them whenever an opportunity arose. They were inordinately vain. The men wore their hair long and took great pride in caring for it. As craftsmen the men ranked with the finest of the Great Plains, showing talent as well as taste in manufacturing their weapons, especially their large bows, some of which were covered with rattlesnake skin or decorated with colorful designs.

A premarital affair might develop into a permanent union, and while such a marriage was not disapproved, in tribal estimation the most honorable way for a warrior to acquire a wife was by purchase. Lovers were not punished, yet chastity in a girl was valued, and a certain ceremonial role could be performed only by a woman who had been a virgin bride and had remained faithful to her husband.[43]

Lowie [44] states that the matrimonial history of a typical Crow might "consist of several love matches and a single orthodox marriage by purchase, which through the sororate often became polygamous. A woman did not become an outcast by associating herself with a man from inclination: she merely fell short of ideal perfection. Indeed, she would not even rouse unfavorable comment unless she frequently changed mates. A handsome or brave man was expected to have an indefinite number of love affairs. . . ."

Besides purchasing a wife, a Crow also might acquire one by inheriting his brother's widow, and he might "enter an alliance of love without payment or legitimately acquire additional spouses through the sororate after purchasing the eldest daughter in the family, or capture an alien woman in an attack on a Dakota camp, or under special conditions legitimately take away a tribesman's wife if she had previously been his mistress." [45]

Among the Crow there was no such thing as an orphan. Indeed, the word itself comprised the greatest insult a Crow could hurl at another. Parentless children were adopted by adults of the sib to which they had been born, and were shown great affection. The Crow were divided into thirteen exogamous mother-sibs, but personal names were in no way connected with sib names. Usually a young person was given a name deriving from a characteristic, an experience, or a deed.

Under Crow law the leader of a successful raid was entitled to all the plunder obtained, yet if he kept it he was publicly condemned for his greed, and he would have difficulty obtaining warriors for another foray.

Corporal punishment was rare or mild among the Crow, but they had a strong psychological deterrent to wrong-doing. It was applied by persons called "joking relatives." A Crow's "joking relative" was either his father's brother's child or his father's male sib mate's child. "Although the accusations leveled by joking relatives against each other were often groundless," states Driver,[46] "the threat of one's protagonist finding real holes in the armor of his personality was always present and served as a deterrent to defiant behavior."

The Crow not only loved their children and cared for them in every possible way, but they guided them with gentleness and intelligence. Rarely were they scolded or criticized in public. The family and sib presented a "united front to the outside and sought to protect and defend their members rather than to ridicule them." [47] Young persons were rewarded with praise for a deed well done, or even when they had tried to succeed in an undertaking but had failed. Blaming a person for an honest mistake or an unavoidable failure was considered inadvisable as well as unbeneficial.

The Crow Tobacco Society was unique, and its rituals were among the most colorful performed by Plains Indians. To the Crow the tobacco plant had a sacred character. Planting and cultivating it was one of their oldest ceremonies, held by them long before they migrated to the western mountains. Both men and women belonged to this sodality, which had numerous chapters, each of which, according to Driver,[48] "originated when an individual experienced a vision and received instructions from a spirit to found a new chapter."

Two kinds of tobacco were raised, one for ordinary smoking and the other, called "medicine tobacco," to be smoked only on special occasions and in religious rites. The observances in the planting of the medicine tobacco included a "solemn march, a foot race among the young men, the planting of seed, the building of a hedge of green branches around the seed bed, a visit to the sweat house, followed by a bath and a solemn smoke, all ending with a feast." [49] The medicine tobacco was nurtured with great care, and the patches were rigorously guarded. When it had ripened, it was harvested with ceremony, the leaves were stored in specially constructed shelters, and the seeds were put into deerskin pouches, to be kept for the next planting season. As a gesture of thankfulness to the patron spirit of the tobacco plant some of the leaves and seeds were cut and crushed into tiny fragments and dropped into a flowing creek—to be carried away to the realm of the gods.

Kansa: Pride and Prejudice

Here is another example (like the Iowa and the Missouri) of a state, a river, cities, and smaller places being given the name of a people who played an unimportant role in Indian history, who were unaggressive, unenterprising, and who were not overburdened with intelligence. Perhaps the most admirable qualities of the Kansa were two in number: (1) They held an unbounded and indestructible pride in themselves. (2) They made uncommon efforts to instill high standards of morality in their young, and, to a greater extent than any other Great Plains people, they guarded the chastity of their women.

The Kansa (also known as the Kaw) belong to the Dhegiha group of the Siouan linguistic family, which also includes the Osage, Quapaw, Omaha, and Ponca.[50] The various prehistoric migrations of these tribes from the Ohio River region has been recounted. The Kansa separated from the "upstream people" of this group at the confluence of the Kansas and Missouri rivers. The parting is believed to have taken place shortly after the beginning of the sixteenth century, but the evidence to support the date is slight. However, it has been established on good authority that in the year 1601 their villages stood on tributaries, if not on the main stream, of the river that would bear their name.* This general region continued to be their homeland until Americans destroyed them.

The significance of the word *kansa* is not known. It may have applied to a subdivision of the tribe. The Spanish called them *Escansaques.* The French simply added an "s" to the word, and this name endured.

The Kansa were conservative and intolerant. They subsisted chiefly by hunting, and had only a casual interest in cultivating the soil. Their military operations were poorly executed, and even though they displayed courage on the battlefield, especially in defending themselves, they were easily defeated by more capable fighters such as the Cheyenne and Pawnee. On their buffalo hunts—vitally necessary to their existence—they often suffered serious losses of life and property at the hands of assailants.

The better to illustrate the nature of the Kansa, it is necessary to speak of them as they were in historical times. They looked with equal contempt on the ways of other Indians and of white men. With the extinction of the buffalo herds in their area, they became desultory farmers, only to avoid starvation. They considered it degrading to adopt any custom of the white man, and when mission schools were built for them they refused to permit their children to be pupils.

Under a treaty with the United States, a reservation was established for them at Council Grove, Kansas. Settlers promptly invaded it, and the government made no effort to remove the illegal intruders. Instead, the reservation was "sold" to white farmers, but the money obtained did not go to the Kansa. It was used to buy other lands for them in Indian Territory. Cheated of their rightful property and defenseless, they were forced to move to Oklahoma. They went, but with no diminution of their prejudices and no loss of pride.

Pawnee: Men of Men

The Pawnee were the only people of the Great Plains to practice human sacrifice. Periodically, but not annually, they took the life of a maiden of their own tribe. The chosen victim was tied to a frame on a platform and killed by arrows. The offering was made to the Morning Star, usually in the late spring at the time corn was planted.

The religious system of the Pawnee was elaborate and complex, their rites were colorful and dramatic, their mythology was remarkably rich in symbolism and poetic fancy. An authority on this tribe, Alice C.

---

* See *Dates to Remember,* this part.

Fletcher, states that Pawnee religious ceremonies "were connected with the cosmic forces and the heavenly bodies. The dominating power was Tirawa, generally spoken of as 'father.' The heavenly bodies, the winds, thunder, lightning, and rain were his messengers. Among the Skidi [branch] the morning and evening stars represented the masculine and feminine elements, and were connected with the advent and the perpetuation on earth of all living forms. A series of ceremonies relative to the bringing of life and its increase began with the first thunder in the spring and culminated at the summer solstice in human sacrifice, but the series did not close until the maize, called 'mother corn,' was harvested. At every stage of the series certain shrines, or 'bundles,' became the center of a ceremony. Each shrine was in charge of an hereditary keeper, but its rituals and ceremonies were in the keeping of a priesthood open to all proper aspirants. Through the sacred and symbolic articles of the shrines and their rituals and ceremonies a medium of communication was believed to be opened between the people and the supernatural powers, by which food, long life, and prosperity were obtained." [51]

The origin of the Pawnee, who were among the greatest raiders and fighters of the Plains tribes, is shrouded in mystery. Not even their own traditions are in agreement. This is understandable, for elements of the language, their customs, and their beliefs can be traced to the Southeast and to the Southwest. Some tribal historians have always maintained that they never lived anywhere but on the Platte River in Nebraska, and that they lived in this region a very long time, perhaps for several millennia, there is no reason to doubt. Indeed, some ethnologists think that the Pawnee reached the Platte Valley from the south so long ago that they encountered Athapascan and Shoshonean groups from Siberia migrating southward. The Pawnee themselves claim to have taken the region by conquest, but they have no names for the people they drove out of it.

The Pawnee belong to the Caddoan linguistic family, and this indicates that they were part of the general northward movement of Caddoan tribes which occurred in remote prehistoric times. There is disagreement between linguists as to the meaning of their name. As interpreted by some it signifies "horn," and derives from the peculiar manner in which Pawnee men dressed their hair. Warriors stiffened the scalp-lock with paint and fat to make it stand erect and curved like a horn. Other scholars maintain that the name means "hunter." However, the Pawnee identify themselves by the unpronounceable name of *Chahiksichahiks*, and they say that it signifies "men of men." For no reason, except to complicate the issue still more, it might be noted that they also applied the appellation "men of men" to other tribes they considered "civilized," and that the Arapaho, Cheyenne, Comanche, and Hidatsa called them "wolf people." Whatever its meaning, Pawnee outlived all the other names, and so they have been designated since the sixteenth century when the first white men are believed to have reached their country.

Actually the Pawnee were a confederation of four Caddoan tribes: the Chaui (Grand Pawnee), the Kithehahki (Republican Pawnee), the Pitahauerat (Tapage Pawnee), and the Skidi Pawnee.[52] The political structure of the tribe was based on village communities, each of which had its hereditary chiefs, its shrine, its priests, and a council of leading men. The chiefs of the various villages comprised a tribal council which rendered final decisions of military and civil problems.

The Pawnee dwelt in large earth lodges, each of which was constructed with elaborate religious ceremonies. The men wore a scarf tied like a turban around their heads, and, according to Fletcher,[53] "Both beard and eyebrows were plucked. . . . The breechcloth and moccasins were the only essential parts of a man's clothing; leggings and robe were worn in cold weather and on gala occasions. Face painting was common, and heraldic designs were frequently painted on tent covers and the robes and shields of men. Women wore the hair in two braids at the back, the parting as well as the face being painted red. Moccasins, leggings and a robe were the ancient dress. . . . Descent was traced through the mother."

The Pawnee are known to have raided as far east as the Missouri, as far south as Texas, north into the Dakotas, where they fought the Sioux and other tribes, and as far west as southern Colorado and New Mexico. They were the scourge of the early Spanish settlements in the Southwest. They fought the Ute and the Navajo, and these tribes retaliated by invading Pawnee territory.

Although they were by nature aggressors and fierce fighters, the Pawnee never went to war against the United States. Although they suffered repeated injustices from the national and territorial governments, they displayed great forbearance, and while patiently waiting for the wrongs done them to be righted, Pawnee scouts faithfully and courageously served with American troops in an effort to bring peace to the Great Plains. Regrettably, American authorities and settlers failed to display a similar deference toward them.

Assiniboine: Lost Glory

Numerous scholars and historians speak of the Assiniboine as being among the finest human specimens of all the aborigines of the Great Plains. They were distinguished not only for their physical prowess but for their cunning, courage, and capabilities as warriors, for their innate intelligence and for their enterprise as producers and traders.

One writer, Michael Stephen Kennedy, described them as "one of the largest, boldest, handsomest, most able buffalo-hunting, gregarious, picturesque, peripatetic and most individualistic and iron-willed of all the northern Great Plains tribes." [54] While in a large measure this praise is merited, they were not so greatly outstanding in all of these respects as to be beyond comparison with their two traditional enemies, the Sioux and the Blackfoot, and their strongest ally, the Cree.

This qualification is supported by the noted artist George Catlin, in a reference to the Assiniboine and several other tribes of the upper Missouri River region he visited in 1832. He stated that they "are undoubtedly the finest-looking, best-equipped, and most beautifully costumed of any on the Continent . . . and they are the most independent and the happiest races of Indians I have met with: they are all in a state of primitive rudeness and wildness, and consequently are picturesque and handsome almost beyond description. Nothing in the world, of its kind, can possibly surpass in beauty and grace, some of their games and amusements—their gambols and parades." [55]

The homeland of the Assiniboine was not on the Northern Plains until shortly before the beginning of the historical period. A Siouan people, originally part of the Yanktonai, they had migrated from the Ohio River in late prehistoric times. It is believed they separated from the Yanktonai in the region of the upper Mississippi River, and continued northward to settle in the vicinity of the Lake of the Woods and Lake Nipigon in the last years of the sixteenth or earliest years of the seventeenth century.

Their alliance with the Cree—which was never abrogated—and their continued northward movement probably was largely due to economic factors. The Assiniboine wanted peaceful access to the early British trading posts on Hudson Bay.* Some of them remained Woodland Indians but the greater number of them eventually became a Plains people. The early traders and missionaries found them spread over an enormous territory reaching from the Arctic Circle to the Missouri River in Montana, and from James Bay on the east to the Rocky Mountains on the west.

In the United States region they were constantly at war with the Dakota and the Blackfoot. Their life as roving hunters without permanent villages also brought them into conflict with other tribes whose territories they invaded. They were universally feared as warriors, and their well-organized and executed forays left no doubt as to their ability as military strategists.

The name by which they identified themselves in prehistoric times

---

* The range to which this work is limited precludes a detailed discussion of the Assiniboine in northern Canada.

is not known. *Assiniboine* derives from the word *u'sin¹* of the Chippewa dialect of the Algonquian language. In the earliest reference to them, the *Jesuit Relations* of 1640, they are called *Assinpour*. Thus, it appears they were known as Assiniboine, or by some variation of the name, before any white man had encountered them. It means "one who cooks by the use of stones."

Mooney and Thomas [56] state that physically "the Assiniboine do not differ materially from the other Sioux. The men dress their hair in various forms; it is seldom cut, but as it grows it is twisted into small locks and tails, and frequently false hair is added to lengthen the twist. It sometimes reaches the ground, but is generally wound in a coil on top of the head. Their dress, tents, and customs generally are similar to those of the Plains Cree, but they observe more decorum in camp and are more cleanly, and their hospitality is noted by most traders who have visited them. Polygamy is common." Regarding their hair style, Kennedy remarks that "some of the vainest Assiniboines actually were competing with the Crows in the great length of their hair." [57]

Brides were purchased. The marriage ceremony was extremely simple. If the price offered by the swain was satisfactory, the parents of the young couple exchanged gifts, and the bride simply moved into the tepee of her husband. An account by the Jesuit missionary De Smet indicates that the Assiniboine revered the dead and that their burial ceremonies were involved: [58] "They bind the bodies with thongs of rawhide between the branches of large trees, and, more frequently, place them on scaffolds, to protect them from the wolves and other wild animals. They are higher than a man can reach. The feet are always turned to the west. There they are left to decay. When the scaffolds or the trees to which the dead are attached fall, through age, the relatives bury all the other bones, and place the skulls in a circle in the plain, with the faces turned toward the center. They preserve these with care, and consider them objects of religious veneration. You will generally find there several bison skulls. In the center stands the medicine poke, about twenty feet high, to which *Wah-Kons* are hung, to guard and protect the sacred deposit. The Indians call the cemetery *the village of the dead*. They visit it at certain seasons of the year, to converse affectionately with their deceased relatives and friends, and always leave some present."

According to the early explorer Alexander Henry,[59] if a death occurred in winter at a distance from the burial ground of the family, "the body was carried along during their journeying and placed on a scaffold, out of reach of dogs and beasts of prey, at their stopping places. Arrived at the burial place, the corpse was deposited in a sitting posture in a circular grave about five feet deep, lined with bark or skins; it was then covered with bark, over which logs were placed, and these in turn were covered with earth." Henry was speaking of an older burial custom than that described by De Smet. In prehistoric times the Assiniboine also cremated the dead.

De Smet notes regarding the Sun Dance that the Assiniboine "often speak of it in the course of a year, and look forward to its immediate arrival with joy, respect and veneration." [60] Unlike other Plains tribes, however, as Kennedy states, the Assiniboine "did not associate self-torture with the Sun Dance. It was used only in preparation for war," and he adds: "Braves who aspired to lead a war party often lay out in the rain or snow for several nights, fasting and praying to the Great Spirit for favorable visions; and some of them gashed their arms and breasts with knives, the more to excite his pity." [61]

Undoubtedly because of their long association with the British the Assiniboine were disposed to favor them with their trade, and they did not welcome efforts of the French to disrupt this old relationship. Nor were they friendly to Americans. After the purchase of the Louisiana Territory by the United States, British agents often succeeded in persuading them to attack American trading companies.

It was not conflict with white men, however, but contact with them that brought about the destruction of the Assiniboine. It was the smallpox, the venereal diseases, and the whiskey of the white men. The first serious smallpox epidemic occurred in 1780 and took a heavy toll. Periodically other epidemics swept through them. One traveler to the upper Missouri in the early eighteen-thirties reported they were almost exterminated. He was not quite correct, but epidemics in the late eighteen-thirties, which took the lives of more than four thousand Assiniboine, completed the destruction.

The liquor and venereal diseases had been present all during these years, contributing in their own fiendish ways to the deterioration of Assiniboine glory.

Arapaho: Traders

Numerous Indians identified themselves by names which included the words "people" or "men," but became known to history by dissimilar names given to them by other tribes. This was the case of the Arapaho. Their own name was *Inuna-ina*, signifying "our people." By the Caddo, Comanche, Shoshoni, Pawnee, Wichita, and Ute (and probably others) they were called "dog eaters." To the Cheyenne and the Dakota they were known as "sky men" and "blue cloud men." The Kiowa called them "men of the worn-out leggings." Linguists are not certain of the meaning of *Arapaho*, but it is believed to have derived from a Pawnee word signifying "traders." How long ago or why it was applied to them are unanswered questions. Nevertheless, it was the name which endured through past centuries to the present day.

NORTHERN GREAT PLAINS

Earliest Population Estimates*

Arikara (1780)	3,000	**Omaha** (1780)	2,800
Mandan (1780)	3,600	**Pawnee** (1780)	10,000
Dakota (1780)	25,000	**Kansa** (1780)	3,000
Oto (1780)	900	**Crow** (1780)	4,000
Ponca (1780)	800	**Arapaho and Atsina**	
Assiniboine (1780)	10,000	(1780)	6,000
Hidatsa (1780)	2,500		
Cheyenne (1780)	3,500	**TOTAL**	75,100

* See Note, Population Table, Part One.

Swanton states that the Arapaho and their close relatives, the Atsina, "constitute the most aberrant group of the Algonquian linguistic stock." [62] Like several other tribes who became Plains Indians, they were once a sedentary people who derived a large part of their subsistence from farming. Their earliest known home was in northern Minnesota in the Red River Valley, where they dwelt in permanent villages.

Forced by stronger people, probably the Sioux, to abandon this way of life, they moved southwest across the Missouri River. It is believed this migration preceded that of the Cheyenne, who were victims of the same enemy. However, as Plains tribes, the Arapaho and the Cheyenne formed a permanent alliance.

Apparently the Arapaho did not hold their relatives, the Atsina, in high regard. Their name for them meant "beggars" or "spongers." * Tradition relates that the Crow drove a wedge between the Arapaho and the Atsina, and that under the pressure the Atsina fled north. For a time they associated themselves with the Sitsika (Blackfoot), but within a few years had passed the point of no return on the road to oblivion.

---

* Mooney states that in the sign language the tribal sign for the Atsina was commonly but incorrectly interpreted as signifying "big bellies" by early French Canadians, whence came their popular name *Gros Ventres,* and they have been erroneously confused with the Hidatsa, or Gros Ventres of the Missouri.[63]

Except in a few respects, the Arapaho proper were a typical Plains tribe. The Sun Dance was their greatest annual religious ceremony, and they attached great importance to visions and dreams. They were expert hunters and courageous warriors, but there was in their nature a tendency to show more kindliness and tolerance than most Plains people. The name "Dog Eaters" was deserved, for they thoroughly enjoyed a repast of canine stew. While some tribes ate dog meat only on special occasions, and some refused to eat it at all, the Arapaho did not associate the dish with a religious or military ceremony. They ate it whenever it appealed to them, and needed no other reason.

SOME INDIAN PLACE NAMES*

Kansas

Pottawatomie, town
Cherokee, county, town
Shawnee, county, town
Powhattan, town
Seneca, town
Oneida, town
Lenapi, town
Ottawa, town
Erie, town
Miami, county
Huron, town
Wyandot, county
Kansas, state, river, town
Arkansas, town
Osage, county, river, town
Iowa, town
Cheyenne, county
Pawnee, county, river
Kiowa, county, town
Comanche, county
Wichita, county, town

North Dakota

Tioga, town
Erie, town
Dakota, state, river

Mandan, town
Sheyenne, river
Lakota, town
Absaraka, town

South Dakota

Senaca, town
Huron, town
Dakota, state, river
Kennebec, town
Iroquois, town
Cheyenne, river
Sioux Falls, town
Ponca, river
Spokane, town

Nebraska

Senaca, town
Nebraska, state
Winnebago, town
Cheyenne, county
Dakota, county, town
Sioux, county, town
Omaha, city
Otoe, county
Pawnee, county
Ponca, town
Arapaho, town

* Tribes and subdivisions.

In historical times the Arapaho slowly divided into two bands. One group, the Northern Arapaho, continued to live in Wyoming on the headwaters of the North Platte River, while the others, who would become known as the Southern Arapaho, drifted southward to the

289

Upper Arkansas River in eastern Colorado. Before the time of the mass migrations of settlers, the Arapaho had made peace with their old foes, the Sioux, the Kiowa, and the Comanche, but they remained at war with the Shoshoni, the Ute, and the Pawnee until they became hungry and hopeless people on reservations in Oklahoma and Wyoming.

Dates to Remember

1541—Coronado, with forty men, reached the Smoky Hill River in central Kansas. These were the first Europeans to look upon the vast buffalo herds and luxuriant grass ranges of the Northern Great Plains. They encountered Wichita and perhaps some Pawnee people. "The people are large," wrote Coronado.[64] "I had some Indians measured and found they were ten spans tall.* The women are comely, with faces more like Moorish than Indian women." The women of the Plains generally were more lean and lithe than the women he had seen in the southwestern pueblos who led sedentary lives. A Coronado chronicler provided the first description of the Kansas country. Jaramillo[65] thought it had a "fine appearance, the like of which I have never seen anywhere in our Spain, in Italy, or in any part of France where I have traveled. . . . It is not a hilly country, but has table lands, plains, and charming rivers with fine waters. . . . I am of the belief that it will be very productive of all sorts of commodities. . . . We found plums, of a variety not exactly red, but shading off from reddish to green. The tree and its fruit are surely Castilian, the plums being of excellent flavor . . . we found a sort of flax growing wild in small clusters some distance apart . . . with little heads of blue flowers. Although small, it is excellent . . . there are grapes of fairly good flavor." Buffalo in countless number, Indian fields of maize, beans, and calabashes, wild fruits. Plenty of good food. But no gold, no great cities. A primitive, half-naked people dwelling in grass houses. Coronado started back, a dispirited man.

1601—Juan de Oñate, governor of the new Spanish province of New Mexico, unceasingly searching for the treasure which everyone felt certain Coronado had missed, reached the country of the Pawnee and the Kansa. He found to his sorrow that Coronado had missed nothing.

1640—The *Jesuit Relations* of this year speak of the Dakota and other people living to the west of the Mississippi River and the northern Great Lakes. The identities of the first *voyageurs* to reach them and to enter the Northern Great Plains region are not known to history. However, long before any of the Frenchmen, pushing westward

---

* Six feet, eight inches.

into Michigan and Wisconsin, had seen the big rivers of the West, they knew of their existence. The Indians spoke of them, one on each side of the great mountains, and sometimes the Indians talked vaguely of a third river that lost itself in the southwestern sky. The Frenchmen long dreamed of seeing them. Unfortunately the first men who gave reality to those dreams kept no written records, and if they orally recounted their exploits and discoveries their reports were forgotten. Yet there seems litle doubt that by the time Marquette and Joliet had seen the Missouri spilling its great flood into the Mississippi (1673) *voyageurs* had penetrated westward to the Red River of the North, or possibly beyond it, and had gazed on the Great Plains. However, the truth about these earliest explorations of the region probably will never be known.

1650–1670—It is probable that within this span of years Spanish traders from New Mexico had traveled northward on the high plains immediately east of the mountains through eastern Colorado to Wyoming.

1706—Spanish traders heard Plains Indians speak of meeting Frenchmen. Captain Juan de Ulibarri was ordered to investigate the reports. With a well-equipped force of one hundred and forty soldiers he set out from Taos in the early summer, traveling over Palo Flechado Pass. It was his plan to follow the old Indian trade trail to the southeastern area of Colorado called El Cuartelejo, but he turned north before reaching Raton Pass when his scouts learned that Comanches were lying there in wait for him. Reaching the upper Purgatoire River by way of another route through the Raton Mountains, he turned northwest, crossing the Apishapa River. To the left rose the magnificent Spanish Peaks. From the Huerfino River, Ulibarri continued on to the Arkansas River, reaching it at the mouth of Fountain Creek. Against the sky toward the northwest a great snow-capped mountain was clearly visible. It would come to be known as Pike's Peak, named for a man who did not discover it.

It may be assumed that inasmuch as Ulibarri's scouts took him directly to the confluence of the Arkansas River and Fountain Creek they had previously been there. If that were not true, then they were following a well-known route. It was up Fountain Creek that a main prehistoric trading trail wound its way toward the junction of the Platte and Laramie rivers in Wyoming. Undoubtedly Spanish traders previously had passed over it, but no Spanish military force ever before had reached a point farther north.

Ulibarri met no Frenchmen, but he made an important discovery. After descending the Arkansas for some distance, he found indisputable evidence that they were not far away. A chief with whom he conferred showed him a new French gun. Inquiries developed the information that it had been purchased from the Pawnee near the place where the Platte River divided into its north and south branches. The newness of the weapon indicated that it could not have been in the possession of the Pawnee for any great length of time. The Platte divided less than three hundred miles from Ulibarri's position on the Arkansas. He returned home satisfied that the rumors of Frenchmen invading the Great Plains were not without foundation.

1710–1712—By this time there were reports, some of them written, that *voyageurs* had ascended the Missouri River for three or four hundred leagues, and had come upon country incredibly rich in furs. Trading had been carried on with people called Omaha, and the locations of the Mandan and Arikara were established. Six hundred leagues from the mouth of the river, said the reports, there were large tribes of nomadic people living in a land filled with immense herds of buffalo and deer, and there were streams swarming with beaver.

1719—Governor Antonio Valverde y Costo made a trip from Santa Fe to southeastern Colorado, where Indians told him that Frenchmen were on the Platte. He could have acquired the same intelligence from traders without leaving his office.

1720—Indeed, Valverde did learn the same thing, but greatly embellished, in the spring of this year. A report reached him in Santa Fe that not only were Frenchmen on the Platte but they were marching up it six thousand strong for the purpose of invading New Mexico.

Either Valverde was gullible or he was ignorant of Plains geography, and perhaps he was both. If France had managed to move an army of six thousand soldiers up the Platte in secrecy—a feat that was utterly impossible—all hope of Spain holding colonies north of Mexico was futile. Yet, if such a miracle had been accomplished, French troops proceeding from the lower Mississippi—the only possible place of origin for a force of this size—hardly would have gone as far north as the Platte, then cut hundreds of miles southwest and struggled through easily defended mountain passes in a campaign to capture Santa Fe.

Whatever Valverde's thought or deductions were in this summer of 1720 they concluded with a decision to send out a scouting party to observe and report on the whereabouts of the invaders. The man chosen for the assignment was Captain Pedro de Villasur, and he set out with forty-three soldiers and sixty Pueblo Indians. In El Cuartelejo, the soldiers painted their faces and bodies and otherwise attempted to disguise themselves as Comanches.

No Frenchmen were found on the Arkansas, and the intrepid Villasur led his men northward. They reached the South Platte early in August and went on to the North Platte. Scouts reported that Indians were gathered at the confluence of the Platte branches. Villasur crossed the North Platte and turned down its left bank. Four days later he camped near the confluence, across the main river from a Pawnee village.

The Pueblo guides sought to arrange a friendly smoke with the Pawnee, but their overtures were rejected. Because of this unpromising situation Villasur moved to the slender tongue of land separating the two streams, believing it to be a safer camping place.

At dawn on August 14 the Pawnee, who had not appreciated the soldiers' attempt to disguise themselves, attacked with such suddenness and fury that Villasur was killed before he could fire his gun. His men fought bravely, taking a heavy toll of the Pawnee, but only nine soldiers and several Pueblos lived to escape.

1731–1732—The great trailbreaker and fur trader, Pierre Gaultier de Varennes, Sieur de la Verendrye, and three of his sons, were at Rainy Lake and the Lake of the Woods, in trade with the Cree and Assiniboine. They heard from Indians, who drew crude maps on the earth, of a great river that ran straight toward the setting sun. La Verendrye's blood raced with excitement, for he believed the river would lead to the Western Sea, the Pacific.

1733—La Verendrye heard of a large nation living on the "River of the West," more than seven hundred miles from the Lake of the Woods. These people dwelt in eight villages and had fields of corn, beans, and pumpkins, besides great quantities of furs. There, said Indians, they could obtain more information as to how to reach the Western Sea.

1738—Other explorations and fur-trading problems had prevented La Verendrye from going south, but in this year he reached the villages of the Mandan, Arikara, and Hidatsa on the upper Missouri.

1742—Although La Verendrye never had an opportunity to go in search of the river that led to the Pacific, he always dreamed of going. At last, in this year, he sent two of his sons, Louis-Joseph and François, to find it. Accompanied by two *voyageurs,* in the heat of summer, they started west on foot. Eventually they were able to obtain horses. They found the Cheyenne, the Sioux, and the Crow. They crossed the Little Missouri, passed through the Bad Lands, and forded a stream that would be called Powder River.

1743—On New Year's Day, Louis-Joseph de la Verendrye, his brother, François, two French *voyageurs,* and a few Indian companions stood on a height in eastern Wyoming and they saw far to the west a great range of mountains—the Big Horns. The Verendryes wanted to go on, believing that from the top of the peaks they would be able to see the Pacific, but the Indians refused and told them of how other white men (Villasur's force) who had ventured up the Platte had been slain. Wrote Louis-Joseph: "All that cooled my ardour considerably for a sea which was already known, nevertheless I should have wished greatly to go there, had it been possible." [66] They turned back, found the Belle Fouche River, circled the Black Hills, and traveled across South Dakota to the Arikara village of Little Cherries on the Missouri. In a hillside they buried a metal plate recording their passage. On it they inscribed the names of the French king and of their father, whom they revered, as well as the names of the two *voyageurs* with them, and the date March 30, 1743. In an Indian village at the site they learned to their astonishment that "three days' journey from where we then were there was a Frenchman who had been settled there for several years." [67] Thus, it may not be said how long before the time of the Verendryes *voyageurs* had been living on the upper Missouri.*

Scientific Note—Tobacco and Pipes

Nothing is more American than tobacco, pipes, cigars, and cigarettes.

The word "tobacco" can be traced back through the Spanish *tabaco* which derived from an Arawak Indian term for cigar. Columbus and his men saw Indians of the Caribbean Islands smoking large cigars, and it was through them that knowledge of the drug, which Indians said had a soothing effect, first reached Europe.

In every Indian language there are words meaning tobacco and tobacco plant. Some forty varieties have been classified, and this makes it plain why prehistoric trading in tobacco was complicated. Blending and mixing were carried on long before the discovery of America. Tastes and preferences existed, and Indians of one region sometimes traveled far to obtain a supply of a certain tobacco that would give smoothness or otherwise change another kind. The most widely used species originated in South America and were brought north, but some varieties are native to western North America.

According to Driver,[68] a "majority of North American Indians mixed other plants with their tobacco . . . mixtures in the eastern United States and Canada were called *kinnikinnik* from an Algonquian word meaning 'that which is mixed.' Two common adulterants in this area were sumac leaves and the inner bark of a species of dogwood." On the Northwest Coast, instead of smoking the Indians mixed tobacco with shell lime and molded the concoction into pellets which were allowed to dissolve in the mouth. In California and Nevada tobacco leaves were ground in a stone mortar with lime and water, and the mixture was swallowed. Everywhere else in the United States region tobacco was smoked in pipes, in cigars, wrapped with tobacco leaves, or in ciga-

---

* The plate was buried where Pierre, the capital of South Dakota, would stand, and it was found by some schoolchildren in February, 1913.

rettes in which the tobacco was wrapped in some other burnable material. Cigarettes and pipes, states Driver, which were made by filling short pieces of cane with tobacco, date from Basketmaker times in the Southwest.[69]

Prehistoric pipes have been recovered in an endless variety of sizes and shapes. The pipe most widely distributed in North America was a straight tube, usually plain on the outside, but occasionally elaborately ornamented. The rudest pipes of this type were made from the legbone of a deer or other animal, and were often reinforced with a piece of rawhide, which, wrapped on wet, contracted in drying and thus aided in preventing the bone from splinting.[70] Pipe bowls ranged in length from three inches to more than a foot. Besides bone, they were made of clay, wood, chlorite, steatite, stalagmite, quarzite, and many other kinds of stone. Some weighed scarcely an ounce, others weighed several pounds. Pipestems were constructed in many forms, round, flat, straight, curved, and twisted. They were adorned with ornaments made of feathers, quills, and hair.

One of the most popular materials for pipes was a red claystone which was obtained from a single quarry in southwestern Minnesota. Holmes [71] described it as a "very handsome stone, the color varying from a pale grayish-red to a dark red, the tints being sometimes so broken and distributed as to give a mottled effect. It is a fine-grained argillaceous sediment, and when freshly quarried is so soft as to be readily carved with stone knives and drilled with primitive hand drills." Indians traveled great distances to barter for it. The stone from the Red Pipestone Quarry was given the name Catlinite because it was first brought to the attention of mineralogists by the famous painter of Indians, George Catlin.

The popular meaning of the word "calumet" is a long pipe smoked by the negotiators of a treaty. That is, a peace pipe. It was much more than that.

"Calumet" is not an Indian word, but derives from a French word meaning "reed" or "tube." [72] It appears in the writings of the earliest French missionaries. Obviously it was in use before the white man penetrated the continent, but a general Indian name for it, if ever known, has not been preserved.

In remote prehistoric times the calumet was not a pipe in which ceremonial or sacred tobacco could be smoked. It was a highly symbolic shaft of reed or wood varying in length from eighteen to forty-eight inches.[73]

There were both male and female calumets. They were perforated to create a pathway for the breath, i.e., the spirit, and they were painted and adorned with symbolic colors and objects. Accessories of the male calumet represented the male procreative power and his physical aids—the fatherhood of nature. The female calumet, with its colors and adornments, represented the productive female power and her aids—the motherhood of nature.

When the tobacco pipe bowl became an altar for the burning of sacred tobacco to the gods the idea was conceived—when or by whom is not known—to unite it with the already highly symbolic calumet shaft. So the calumet-pipe became one of the most profoundly sacred objects.

All calumet-pipes were not made, however, to be used only in religious ceremonies. Some tribes made them for trade. Calumets were also employed by ambassadors and travelers. They were a kind of passport, for they signaled that persons on a journey desired nothing more than a safe passage. Each tribe made a calumet with certain characteristics, and could be identified by it. This identity was achieved by colors, by carvings, by symbols, and by other decorations. Calumets were universally recognized as instruments of harmony and peace.

Calumets invariably figured in negotiations between tribes, in the ratifying of alliances, in sealing pledges of brotherhood and friendship, but they also figured in councils of war. Upon a decision to wage war the feathers adorning a calumet usually were colored red. Trade calumet-pipes, considered less sacred, were used chiefly in dances and on other social occasions. Indeed, some of the early missionaries gave the name "calumet" to both dances and pipes.

Tobacco played an important part in the social, economic, and religious life of every tribe, and to most of them the plant had a sacred character. Almost invariably it was used on solemn occasions, and the rites included appropriate invocations to deities. It was used in ceremonies to cure sickness, to ward off danger, to bring good fortune, to allay fear. The medicine men of some tribes smoked a variety that was highly narcotic and which made them see visions.

In trade, tobacco ranked with the most valuable staples, such as maize and buffalo robes. It was a commodity with a never-failing market. For as well as being a medicine and an article with religious significance it was an instrument of diplomacy. Few intertribal conferences or ceremonies were held without tobacco being smoked or used in some other manner. Treaty negotiations were usually begun and usually concluded with a smoke. Pacts were sealed with the passing of a pipe. Many tribes maintained two stores of tobacco, one to be used in trade and the other to be used only in sacred rites. In many places the planting and harvesting of tobacco were times for both religious observances and social activities.

Tobacco was not a luxury. It was a necessity. It was woven into all the superstitions, all the beliefs, all the thought patterns of the American aborigine.

Southern Great Plains

Midland Minnie

Winds blow fiercely much of the time on the Llano Estacado. This immense, barren, semi-arid area of western Texas and eastern New Mexico is a "remnant of a great alluvial plain which once extended westward to the Rocky Mountains. At present its edges are well marked on three sides by escarpments several hundred feet high." [1] The Pecos River twists along the Llano's western edge, cutting it back with cap rock cliffs. The South Canadian River Valley separates it from the High Plains on the north. Various streams have cut canyons that mark its eastern limits. On the south it slopes gradually to the Edwards Plateau of central Texas. In the hot summer months thunderstorms driven inland by high winds from the Gulf of Mexico slash the Llano Estacado with brief hard rains and not infrequently with hail. In the winter the prevailing south winds change abruptly to the north, and "these northers bring storms and snow, as well as setting off thunder storms when they meet the warm tropical air from the south." [2]

Besides geography and climatology, geology is an important factor in the story of Midland Minnie. In recent years great dust storms have blackened the sky, and sand dunes have moved as the wind dictated, and erosion has cut through the surface, exposing underlying deposits. However, this was nothing new. It was a continuation of the destruction which began far back in prehistoric times. How far back may not be stated with accuracy, but geologists can produce indisputable evidence which presents a picture of a Llano Estacado vastly in contrast to that which has existed for many millennia. Once it was a region carpeted with lush grasses and other vegetation, containing numerous lakes and streams, and inhabited by immense herds of animals long extinct.

And over it, living on the Pleistocene mammals, wandered some of the earliest human hunters to inhabit the Southern Great Plains.

The first part of Midland Minnie was found in a sand blowout on the Scharbauer Ranch near the Texas town for which she has been named. She was not all together. Fortunately for science, her discoverer was a competent amateur archeologist, Keith Glasscock from Pampa, Texas. He had been examining the desolate area, and had discovered several ancient Folsom artifacts. The wind was blowing like hell on the June day in 1953 when he came upon some human bone fragments in the bottom of a sand blowout. They were highly mineralized. Glasscock sensed at once that he had made a major find, which, indeed, was true.

Looking about, he found other skeletal remains, parts of a human skull, a first rib, and two metacarpals. These, which he did not disturb, were "in process of being exposed by wind cutting into a grayish sand in the floor of the blowout." [3] Glasscock picked up some fragments that were in danger of being blown away and shattered, and hurried back to Midland, realizing the necessity of enlisting the aid of specialists. He mailed the bone fragments he had gathered to Dr. Fred Wendorf at the Laboratory of Anthropology in Santa Fe. When Wendorf saw "the degree of fossilation and the presence of a thick calcerous accretion on the skull," he promptly got in touch with the distinguished scientist Alex Kreiger. Accompanied by several prominent archeologists, they visited the site.

Only preliminary examinations were necessary to prove that "for the first time in the United States, human bones had been found in unquestionable association with extinct Pleistocene faunal remains." [4]

In the following months and into the year 1954, the scientists worked slowly and cautiously in excavating not only the blowout in which Glasscock had discovered the first bone fragments but four others in the immediate vicinity. Besides additional human skull pieces, ribs, and another metacarpal, several hearths and bones of extinct species of horse, antelope, and bison were uncovered. Associated with them were found a strange type of projectile point. They were similar in design to the famous Folsom point, but they were *unfluted,* and they were extremely thin and flat, and probably could not have been successfully fluted. According to Wormington,[5] the "number of specimens recovered suggests that the thinness of the points was due to intentional preparation rather than to an accident which prevented the maker from producing a fluted point."

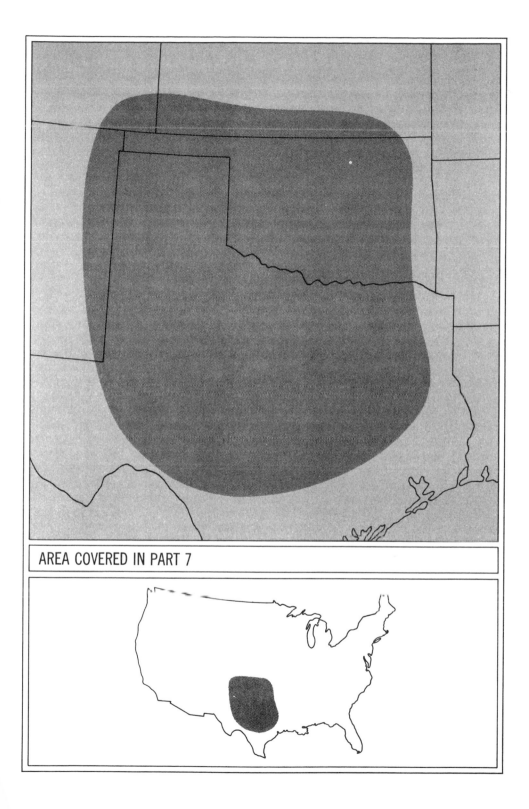

AREA COVERED IN PART 7

A new type of point made in the Ice Age had been found. It was called Midland.

The skeletal remains belonged to a female, who was probably thirty years of age at the time of death. Chemical analyses and geological studies of the formations in which the bones were found left no doubt that Midland Minnie had lived before the end of the Ice Age.

To Dr. T. D. Stewart, curator of physical anthropology at the Smithsonian Institution, fell the difficult task of putting her long-shattered head together. He reported: [6] "Since most of the broken edges were sharp, it was possible to assemble rapidly and without trouble quite a large portion of the vault. Then further progress became slow. Finally, since some warping was evident and parts were missing, I decided to stop short of trying to support with wires a lot of ill-connected pieces. At this point, about sixty pieces of the skull had been assembled and about seventy pieces—many quite small—were left over." Dr. Stewart had some of Minnie's teeth, but her lower jaw was missing. All the recovered teeth belonged to the upper jaw, and "an abnormally placed tooth, either a normal incisor or a supernumerary element, is located in the floor of the left side of the nasal cavity. The malposed tooth has its occlusal edge directed backwards . . ." Clearly Minnie had been in need of a dentist.

"Perhaps the most notable feature of the Midland skull," said Stewart, "is its elongated shape, or dolichocrany. No other American skull with a good claim to antiquity is so relatively longheaded."

Although this was an outstanding characteristic of Midland Minnie's cranium, other comparatively longheaded skulls have been found in Texas. Stewart remarked: "Indeed, few, if any, geographical areas of this size in the New World have yielded so many really longhead skulls. Apparently, too, the type was in existence here for a long time."

How long is the question. Tests by several methods of Minnie's bones and the artifacts found with her have produced various dates. Carbon extracted from caliche stones used in cooking fires yielded a date in excess of twenty thousand years. The Rosholt "uranium clock" technique gave fossils from the blowouts ages ranging from nineteen thousand to fifteen thousand years.

As the scientific reports conclude: [7]

"In its hardness, degree of mineralization, and chemical properties, the human being is just as much a Pleistocene fossil as any of the extinct vertebrates discovered at this site.

"The present age determinations are *ceiling dates.* That is, the true dates cannot be younger but they can be older."

Whether or not Midland Minnie is older, she holds the distinction of being the oldest human yet discovered in the Western Hemisphere, and her remains are the first to be found in unmistakable association with the bones of mammals that lived long before the last of the great glaciers of the Ice Age had vanished from North America.

Hunter's Paradise

Scientific findings indicate that for perhaps thirty millennia great herds of elephants, giant bison, camels, horses, mastodons, sloths, and other species of mammals roamed the vast rich grasslands and gathered about the marshes, streams, and lakes of the region that now comprises the Southern Great Plains of the United States.

Man was there. He survived by hunting and gathering the wild vegetable foods. By 7500 B.C., anthropologists believe, most of the Ice Age animals had become extinct. Not man. He continued to survive by the same means, hunting the smaller animals, the buffalo, the deer, the elk, the antelope, the coyotes, the wolves, the hares that were living there when the New World was discovered by Europeans. He continued to live on the wild foods of the plains and rivers. He steadily improved his weapons. In time he learned to farm and to manufacture utensils and other products. He was there until the white man destroyed the game, took his land away from him, and destroyed him.

A Counter-Clockwise Discovery

For five years archeologists, both professional and amateur, had been poking about the upper reaches of the Trinity River in northern Texas, and numerous artifacts and ancient animal bones had been recovered. It remained, however, for a dragline operator working in a borrow pit in 1956 near Lewisville to make the most important discovery in the area. He uncovered nineteen hearths on which Pleistocene people had cooked their elephant steaks. Archeologists Wilson W. Crook, Jr., and R. K. Harris, and members of the Dallas Archeological Society were soon working at the site.[8]

A Clovis-type projectile point and a large piece of charred wood were found in one hearth. Now, thought the scientists, they may be able to obtain an accurate date for the Clovis point. At the time most archeologists believed that Clovis points were less than eighteen thousand years old. They had a surprise coming.

The charred wood was sent to the Humble Oil Company laboratory to be tested by the Carbon-14 method. The report submitted said: "Too old for us." The range of the laboratory's technique was thirty-seven thousand years![9]

Surely an error had been made. More tests were made. The results were the same.

Archeologists shook their heads in dismay. Never before had there been evidence to indicate that hunters had made chipped stone projectiles so many years ago. The famous Folsom points were scientifically dated as being twelve thousand to ten thousand years old. Admittedly Clovis points were older than that, but not that much older. If the tests were accurate, then man had been manufacturing flaked projectiles for twenty-seven thousand years before the generally accepted age of the Folsom Complex.

The bones of elephants, giant bison, horses, and camels found in association with the Lewisville hearths shed no light on the problem. They lived far back in the Pleistocene, and were obviously contemporaneous with the charcoal. Perhaps, in some way, the Clovis point had been "introduced" into the charcoal. Not possible, said the eminent Alex D. Kreiger. The hearth in which the Clovis point had been found had been carefully examined, and there was not the slightest evidence to show that it had been disturbed before the dragline operator had come upon it. Nor had any of the other eighteen hearths been previously disturbed. Geologists agreed. The hearths lay in an ancient formation created during the Ice Age.

The tests had been made by experts in an excellent laboratory. The chance of great error is remote, indeed nonexistent. Scientists are still striving to unravel the mystery, but they are up against strong material evidence which continues to defeat their best efforts.

No Pleistocene artifacts approaching the age of those found at Lewisville have been discovered in the Southern Great Plains, but this does not preclude the possibility that others recovered may be much older than they are believed to be, or much older than tests have suggested. Many artifacts are not suitable for definitive testing. Ages of more than ten thousand years are commonplace. If guesses mean little or nothing, even scientists cannot exclude wonder and speculation from their minds.

Death Pit

The case of the projectile point now bearing the name Plainview is thought-provoking.

As described by Wormington, Plainview points "are lanceolate in outline and have concave bases. They somewhat resemble Clovis fluted forms, but they are ungrooved. In general, the flaking is rather irregular, but some specimens have parallel flaking at the distal end. Basal edges are smoothed, and there is some basal thinning produced by the removal of vertical flakes." [10]

These details are significant to archeologists, but there are other matters having to do with Plainview points that are of interest to anyone who appreciates a dramatic story. For a number of years points of this distinctive type had been recovered in surface finds. They were called by various names. Their age was debated.

The first step toward a solution was achieved in 1945. Near Plainview, Texas, in a pit from which road material was being taken, E. H. Sellards and archeologists and geologists from the Texas Memorial Museum uncovered an astonishing number of Pleistocene bison bones concentrated in a small area. Among them were a score of the projectile points that thereafter would be identified by the name Plainview.[11]

For the first time these peculiar points were discovered in unmistakable association with extinct Ice Age mammals, that is, *in situ.* It was a find of great importance.

At least a hundred of the ancient giant bison had perished in the pit, apparently within a short period of time. Several educated explanations were proffered by scientists. The animals may have been driven into the depression by a storm. They may have been stampeded by hunters who shot darts at them, have become mired in mud, and slain by their human pursuers.[12] Implements used for cutting meat and dressing hides were found among the bones. However the giant bison got into the pit, there could be no question that many of them, if not all, were dispatched by men. It was the scene of a mass kill.

There is another chapter of great significance to the story of the Plainview points. It begins in the Arctic and ends in Mexico. Plainview points have been recovered in Alaskan muck of Pleistocene origin, in the Northwest Territories, in Ontario, in Alberta. In the United States they have been found in such widely separated areas as Washington State and Florida, as well as in Missouri, Nebraska, South Dakota, New Mexico, Colorado, and numerous places in the Southern Great Plains, notably in Texas. In Mexico they have been found at two sites in Tamaulipas. This immense distribution might reflect upon the migrations of early Pleistocene man. In any case, the hunters who used Plainview points got around.

Minnie's Relatives?

The Abilene region of Texas has been rewarding to archeologists. As long ago as 1929, Cyrus N. Ray found worked flint points at depths which indicated great antiquity.[13] Similar discoveries were made by E. B. Sayles and others. Some of the finds in this area were made in a geological deposit known as Durst Silts, believed to have been formed in the Illinoian Glaciation Age, which preceded the final Ice Age period known as the Wisconsin.

In 1941 Ray and Sayles recovered some distinctive chipped stone implements resembling gouges.[14] One end was a cutting edge and the other was pointed. Oddly shaped projectile points, some stemmed and others stemless and triangular, also were found. Other points discovered in the area were leaf-shaped and crudely flaked. Location and geology suggested these artifacts were at least twenty thousand years old. The points were given the name Abilene, but were not accorded the distinction of being classified as a type.

Ray and Sayles termed the focus Clear Fork Complex. For several years other archeologists disagreed with them as to its age, expressing the belief that it was later than they had estimated.

Then in 1947, J. Charles Kelley found artifacts of the Clear Fork Complex near Austin.[15] Similar discoveries in connection with more recent complexes of the Edwards Plateau region indicated that the Clear Fork Complex had existed over a long period of time, perhaps far back into the Pleistocene.

Change and Method

Through the millennia the climate of the Southern Great Plains underwent drastic transitions. Droughts came and went. Perhaps there were periods when the animals shifted to other areas. If so, they returned in the pluvial periods.

Undoubtedly the people did the same thing, for they were dependent upon the animals for their survival. The hunters who used Plainview points may have been the first in the region. Other types of points, known to be younger, show that different hunters were there at different times, over a great many thousand years. The men who made and used projectiles of the Clovis type were probably there fifteen thousand years ago. Their weapons have been found with mammoth remains near Miami, and a short distance southwest of Abilene, and near Houston, all in Texas.

That the hunters who made and used Folsom points were there ten to twelve thousand years ago there can be no doubt. Important discoveries of their weapons embedded in the bones of Pleistocene mammals had been made at numerous Texas localities, notably in Yellowhorse Draw near Lubbock and in a bison quarry near Lipscomb.

The Lipscomb site is of particular interest for another reason. In an area measuring twelve by twenty feet excavators found fourteen giant bison skeletons overlapping each other and all headed toward the east or southeast.[16] The most logical supposition appears to be that they took refuge in a depression during a blizzard. They stood together, shielding their heads from the "norther." When the storm abated, hunters came upon them and slaughtered them.

Mass kills were not a practice invented by Indian buffalo hunters of historic times. It was followed by hunters of Pleistocene animals, and the evidence leaves no doubt that they were skillful in accomplishing it. They slaughtered animals trapped in depressions, sinks, streams, and which had banded together in storms. But they also engineered stampedes. Fire would have been a most effective weapon. As Wedel states: [17] "The grasslands of the Plains, as is well known from historic records . . . were well suited to the use of fire in hunting. Dry seasons, high, steady winds, and extensive areas of flat unbroken terrain permitted grass fires to sweep for miles across country. Herds of large grazing animals in the path of such fires, if unable to escape, would have left dead and maimed beasts, with survivors perhaps, finding refuge at upland ponds and lakes or in the breaks along a waterway. . . . The headlong flight of the herds might have carried them into ravines or waterholes, where injured and blinded animals could have been easily dispatched. Such kills, like the surrounds and falls of later Plains Indians, may well have exceeded the requirements of the hunters for meat and hides, so that many of the carcasses would have been left unbutchered, their skeletons to endure in more or less complete articulation."

The people were there when the Pleistocene mammals vanished. Most probably they had much to do with exterminating them. They were there when the Paleo-Indian stage gave way to the Early Archaic stage. It is not believed that fluted projectile points were used much after the time of the Folsom Complex, although they may have continued to be common weapons in some areas, for the great Pleistocene mammals did not disappear in all regions at the same time. However, more effective points came into use. And in contemporaneity with them came milling stones and manos. Game was not gone from the Southern Great Plains, but people were learning to depend more on natural vegetable foods, and they were learning how to enjoy them in greater variety. Long before they knew anything of agriculture, how to cultivate and plant and reap, they knew how to pound and grind seeds and roots and nuts, and turn them into palatable dishes. Yet, until long after the coming of the white man hunting was their chief source of sustenance.

Telltale Corn

The Archaic Period began ten thousand years ago. The people who lived in the Southern Great Plains in the early part of this period knew nothing of agriculture. When corn, beans, squash, and other domesticated plants first became known to the Archaic peoples cannot be determined. For various reasons, studies of the matter become lost in confusion.

Much of the region, for example, was not suitable for farming. Even if the people inhabiting such sections as the Llano Estacado, Big Bend, and other semi-arid localities knew about corn, they could not grow it. In parts where it would grow under beneficial conditions, adverse weather might prevent planting or cause crop failures for several successive years.

In the Archaic Period the weather of southern Kansas, Oklahoma, and western and northern Texas was very much the same as it is in this century. Cycles of drought and adequate rainfall occurred throughout prehistoric millennia as they do now. The results four or five thousand years ago, when it is known that agriculture was practiced, were the same as they were during the tragic years of the Dust Bowl, still vivid in the memories of Americans.

Whether they were agriculturists or not, droughts forced the Archaic peoples to move. Game moved in search of grasslands, and the hunters followed them. Wild vegetable foods vanished, and the people migrated in search of areas in which precipitation had been sufficient to sustain the native plants. When the rains returned, they returned and resumed hunting and farming in locations they had previously occupied.

It has been scientifically demonstrated that since the beginning of agriculture on the Southern Great Plains—certainly no less than four or five thousand years ago—Indian farmers suffered from droughts and dust storms.[18]

According to Martin: [19] "The evidence of tree rings and alternate deposits of wind-blown soils and humus layers suggest that the wet-and-dry cycle was in operation long before the White man entered the Plains. The remains of agricultural Indians are found in the humus zones, often buried or separated by sterile zones of wind-blown material. Thus it looks as if the Indian farmers pushed into the Plains during periods of suitable moisture and abandoned them during periods of drought."

The correctness of this postulation has been established. Good examples are the Maravillas Culture of the Big Bend Region and the Bravo Valley Culture. Both appeared in periods of drought, but they were separated in time by several thousand years.

The shifts caused by climatic changes also contributed to the spreading of ideas, customs, and techniques. Archeological sites have been excavated in Oklahoma, Texas, and eastern New Mexico which produced evidence to show that they had been occupied at different times over several millennia by peoples with sharply contrasting customs and in various stages of advancement.

The presence of corn and pottery indicates a chronology, but in the case of the Southern Great Plains it remains indefinite. Apparently the Fumarole Culture arose early, or at least midway, in the Archaic Period in extreme northeastern New Mexico and western Oklahoma.[20] Wedel notes: "Here were found fireplaces, milling slabs with oval-shaped grinding depressions, animal bones, and many percussion-flaked quartzite scrapers, knives, borers, and projectile points. Deer, elk and rabbit bones outnumbered those of bison. Tubular beads, whistles, and a few other artifacts of bone were found. There was no evidence of corn or squash, and the milling stones were presumably used for grinding wild vegetal products." [21]

From caves and rock shelters near Kenton, Oklahoma, in the same area, similar artifacts were recovered, but "from one cave came ears of corn stored in a bag made of prairie dog skin; shelled corn was found inside two bundles of grass. In another cave were found corncobs with sticks inserted in the butts. . . . Circular, flattened cakes made of acorns mixed with wild plums or cherries had been perforated for stringing. . . . Of weapons, the spear-thrower and the foreshaft of a dart were directly indicated, but there was no evidence of the bow and arrow. Bone objects included awls for piercing and basket-making, and also short tubular beads. There were also crude flaked-stone implements and milling stones. . . . No pottery, grooved axes, or other polished stone artifacts have yet been reported from these cave deposits. A possible antiquity of thousands of years has been estimated. . . ." [22]

A comparison of the materials which the two sites yielded points to several conclusions, but it also leaves unanswered a number of questions. The hunting weapons of the Fumarole and Kenton peoples were similar, prompting the suggestion that the cultures overlapped. Yet the Kenton people had corn. Neither had pottery. These facts indicated that the Kenton people entered the region after the Fumarole people, that they were more advanced, at least in the respect that they were farmers, yet in other ways their culture was on a level with the people they found inhabiting the area. It would appear that the Kenton cave dwellers were migrant farmers, but their reasons for leaving their earlier homeland or its location remain to be determined. They may have moved a long distance from the south or southeast, or perhaps they came from no farther away than central or northern Texas. Obviously in the shiftings throughout the Southern Great Plains cultures merged, separated, and were rejoined.

Wedel points out that in central Texas, for example, "there are large accumulations of fire-cracked stones mixed with ashes and cultural material. These, the burned rock middens, have been found on stream terraces, in caves, and in rock shelters, and the deposits sometimes reach a depth of five or six feet. In them are found dart points of various kinds, chipped knives, scrapers, axes, choppers . . . as well as milling stones and handstones. There are some polished stone pendants, occasionally incised, crude boat-shaped weights for spear-throwers, bone awls, antler flaking tools, and perforated shell hoes, *but arrow points,*

pottery remains, or traces of domestic crops or agriculture are absent.
The size of these accumulations indicates that some of the localities
were used over long periods of time. . . ." [23] Archeologists estimate
that this central Texas culture probably arose five thousand years
ago.[24] Agriculture apparently was unknown to it, at least there is no
evidence that it was practiced. Yet, at the same time, corn was being
grown by Indians, not only east of Texas but west of it in New Mexico.

Pottery estimated to be more than four thousand years old has been
found on the Georgia coast.* It came from the south, and is the first
pottery known to have reached the region of the United States. As
stated, no pottery has been found in the archeological sites of the
Southern Great Plains which belong to the Archaic Period. It is not
known that Indians of this area possessed any type of ceramics until
much later, perhaps in most sections not until late prehistoric times.
Then it began to reach the Southern Great Plains from the South, the
Southeast, the Southwest, and even from the Ohio-Illinois-Missouri
area.

The first people of the Southern Great Plains, the Pleistocene hunters, were nomads. Even after agriculture had reached the area, the
people continued a life that was for the most part nomadic, forced by
circumstances and changing conditions to shift in search of food. The
arrival of pottery did little to alter this way of life. Pottery, easily
breakable and difficult to transport, was not practical for general use
as utensils. When the white men invaded the Southern Great Plains
large villages had been established, but few of them were occupied
throughout the year. In them, of course, pottery was useful and practical. In the east parts of the Southern Great Plains farming could be
undertaken with relative assurance that a harvest would be enjoyed.
That was not true on the higher plains and the arid areas along the
western perimeter, for the reasons previously cited.

But there was no deficiency of animals. Some of the greatest buffalo
herds in North America grazed over the Southern Great Plains. On
them, on the inconceivable numbers of deer and antelope and rabbits
and other game, the people lived well. Indeed, it may be said that
through countless millennia, although wild species vanished and were
supplanted by different kinds, the way of life changed little. When the
first Spaniards gazed over the seas of grass and saw the vast herds, they
also saw people whose economy was much the same as it had been since
their earliest ancestors had reached the Southern Great Plains—far
back in the Ice Age.

---

* See Part Two.

Branches from the Main Stem

In late prehistoric times people of Athapascan stock began to move southward from northwestern Canada along the eastern flanks of the Rocky Mountains. It was not a mass migration. They filtered southward on the High Plains in small bands over many years, perhaps over several centuries. Some of the bands may have lived for generations in one region before moving on. Somewhere along the route of their migration, perhaps in southeastern Colorado, their trail branched. Those who found their way into the Southwest through mountains of southern Colorado and northern New Mexico would come to be known as Navajos. Those who continued southward into eastern New Mexico and western Oklahoma and Texas would be given the name Apache.*

Undoubtedly Athapascans were pushing southward in the first millennium of the Christian Era. When they began to reach the southwestern region of the Southern Great Plains, the Llano Estacado and adjacent areas, remains a problem that may never be resolved. However, there is no doubt as to who they were nor about the North American region that was their earlier homeland. The tongue of the Apaches known as Lipans, Jicarillas, and Mescaleros unmistakably identifies them as belonging to the great Athapascan linguistic family of the Canadian Northwest and Alaska.

Because they were nomadic hunters in the Southern Great Plains, almost constantly shifting in pursuit of game, they left few traces of themselves. While almost nothing is known of the early Eastern Apaches archeologically—no sites at all identifiable as Apache have been discovered in Texas—it seems probable, as Newcomb suggests, that sites have been found but have not been recognized as Apache.[25]

Sites discovered farther north, however, have yielded some knowledge of the customs and way of life of these Plains hunters. Archeological discoveries assigned to the Dismal River Culture of Nebraska, which is dated about A.D. 1600, are unquestionably Apache. This places them in the early historical period, but a fact of transcending significance is that the Dismal River Culture did not suddenly spring into full-fledged existence. It is given identity because of certain advances contained in it, but its roots run far back in time. Some archeologists believe that the Dismal River Culture is a direct descendant of much older cultures, dating back as far as A.D. 500.[26] While it seems highly improbable that Athapascans had reached the Southern Great Plains at such an early date, they may well have been on their way.

Lipan derives from *Ipa-n'de*.[27] *Ipa* apparently was a personal name, perhaps that of some ancient leader. The suffix *n'de* means "the peo-

---

* See Part One.

ple." * The Lipan, who were closely related to the Jicarilla, were never a large tribe, but they roamed over an enormous territory. In prehistoric times it is believed they wandered from the Rio Grande in New Mexico as far southeastward as the Gulf of Mexico. At the beginning of the historical period, or shortly thereafter, their range was generally restricted to eastern New Mexico, the Llano Estacado, and far western Oklahoma and Texas.

Nothing certain is known of the origin of the Teyas, but they were on the western Texas stage when the historical curtain went up.

The Indians known as Kiowa Apaches were Athapascans. They spoke a dialect of the Athapascan tongue, but were never otherwise connected with Apache tribes. Their entire known history is synonymous with the Kiowa, who are believed to have been connected with two linguistic stocks, the Tanoan and the Shoshonean. Therefore, although the Kiowa Apaches always retained their identity and spoke their dialect of the Athapascan language, they will be included in the part dealing with the Kiowas.

More is known about the Jicarillas than any of the other Eastern Apache tribes. *Jicarilla* is a Mexican-Spanish word meaning "little basket." According to Swanton,[28] it was given to them because Jicarilla women were expert basketmakers. Their own name for themselves, as might be expected, is very similar to that of their closest relatives, the Lipan. It is *Tinde.*

After migrating to the Southern Great Plains from the Canadian northwest, the Jicarilla chose to establish themselves in northern New Mexico, southeastern Colorado, and the Texas Panhandle, although they frequently ranged far into ajoining areas.

The paucity of archeological material is regrettable, but in the dawn of the recorded history of the United States region Spanish *conquistadores* saw the Eastern Apaches. They met them before the middle of the sixteenth century in eastern New Mexico and the Texas Panhandle, and they wrote accounts of them, detailed and colorful accounts which, fortunately, were preserved in Spanish archives.

There is nothing to negate the postulation that the Eastern Apaches had been living for centuries where they were first encountered by white men. They were then, in every sense of the word, true Plains Indians, in their customs, their characters, their traditions, their economy, indeed, in every way of life. Their culture had not been acquired and developed in a brief span of years. Thus, these earliest reports make it possible, at least, to gain some idea of them as they were in late prehistoric times.

---

* Both the Western Apache tribes and the Navajo called themselves "the people," and still do.

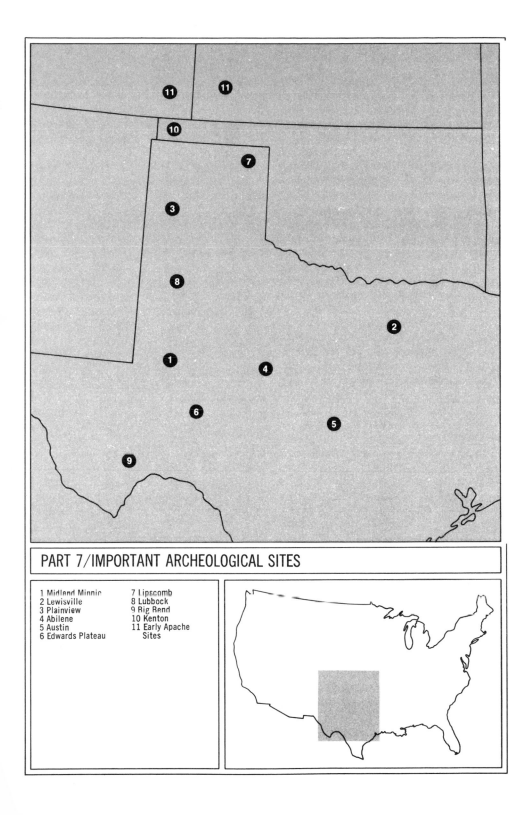

PART 7/IMPORTANT ARCHEOLOGICAL SITES

1 Midland Minnie
2 Lewisville
3 Plainview
4 Abilene
5 Austin
6 Edwards Plateau
7 Lipscomb
8 Lubbock
9 Big Bend
10 Kenton
11 Early Apache Sites

In 1541 Coronado pushed eastward from New Mexico across the Llano Estacado into Texas before turning to the northeast in search of the fabled Province of Quivera. He met Indians whom the chronicler of the expedition, Pedro de Castañeda, called Querechos and Teyas.

The Querechos, who were encountered near the eastern border of New Mexico, have not been definitely connected with an Apache tribe existing in historic times. That they were Apaches, however, is certain. Querecho was the name by which Pueblo Indians called the Apaches of the Southern Great Plains. The eminent ethnologist Adolph Bandelier identified them with the Q'irauash, a name which Keresan pueblo people gave to a wild Plains tribe which had destroyed the Tano villages south of Santa Fe, and had threatened other New Mexico pueblos in prehistoric times.[29] The authority Frederick Webb Hodge states that the Querechos were "most likely the plains Apache, later known by the names Mescaleros, Jicarillas, Faraones, Llaneros, etc.; in short, all the Apache who subsisted on the bison, excepting possibly the Kiowa Apache." The name Vaqueros also would be applied to the Querechos by Spanish explorers.

The origin of the Teyas of the Llano Estacado is obscure. Their name—which would become "Texas"—has always been applied by ethnologists to Caddoan peoples who inhabited the northeastern part of the state of Texas, agriculturists living in permanent villages. The Teyas Coronado found far west on the High Plains, and who obviously were identified by that name to him, were full-fledged Plains people who subsisted almost entirely by hunting buffalo and other game. Had not they been called by a different name they could not have been distinguished from the people known to be Apaches. A difference in language would have meant nothing to the Spaniards, for they understood no Indian tongue, and their guides talked almost entirely with the Indians encountered in the sign language, in which, incidentally, all Plains people could fluently converse.* It has been suggested that the Teyas of the Texas Panhandle were Caddoans who, perhaps centuries earlier, had separated from their people, wandered westward, and had found the hunting life of the plains preferable to a sedentary existence.[30] Not all scientists, however, share this opinion. Some think that despite their name the Panhandle Teyas were Apaches. The differences may never be finally resolved. The Teyas of the far western plains vanished when invaders from the north drove the Apaches from the Southern Great Plains, and their separate identity vanished with them.

"These folks live in tents made of the tanned skins of the cows [buffalo]," Castañeda said of the Querechos.[31] "They travel around

---

* See *Scientific Note,* this part.

near the cows, killing them for food. They did nothing unusual when they saw our army, except to come out of their tents to look at us, after which they came to talk with the advance guard, and asked who we were. . . . That they are very intelligent is evident from the fact that although they conversed by means of signs they made themselves understood so well that there was no need of an interpreter.* They said that there was a very large river over toward where the sun came from, and that one could go along this river through an inhabited region for ninety days without a break from settlement to settlement. . . .[32] These folks started off from here the next day with a lot of dogs which dragged their possessions. For two days, during which the army marched in the same direction . . . that is, between north and east, but more toward the north . . . they saw other roaming Querechos and such great numbers of cows that it already seemed something incredible."

The Querechos and Teyas were not living together when Coronado met them, but Castañeda makes it clear that their customs and mode of life were identical in a passage applying to both tribes. He thought "they have better figures, are better warriors, and are more feared" than the Pueblo Indians of New Mexico. "They travel like Arabs, with their tents and troops of dogs loaded with poles and having Moorish pack-saddles with girths. When the load gets disarranged, the dogs howl, calling someone to fix them right." This was the first known written description of the common dog travois of Plains Indians. The poles were obtained in cedar breaks along the ravines of streams, and were used to support tepees.

And speaking again of both the Querechos and Teyas, he wrote:

"These people eat raw flesh and drink blood. . . . They dry the [buffalo] flesh in the sun, cutting it thin like a leaf, and when dry they grind it like meal to keep it and make a sort of sea soup of it to eat. A handful thrown into a pot swells up so as to increase very much. They season it with fat, which they always try to secure when they kill a cow. [This was Indian pemmican.] They empty a large gut and fill it with blood, and carry this around the neck to drink when they are thirsty. When they open the belly of a cow, they squeeze out the chewed grass and drink the juice that remains behind, because they say that this contains the essence of the stomach. They cut the hide open at the back and pull it off at the joints, using a flint as large as a finger, tied in a little stick, with as much ease as if working with a good iron tool. They give it an edge with their own teeth. The quickness with which they do this is something worth seeing and noting. There are

---

* This statement should be modified with the note that Coronado had with him Plains Indian guides who were expert talkers in the sign language.

very great numbers of wolves on these plains, which go around with the cows. . . . The deer are pied with white. Their skin is loose, so that when they are killed it can be pulled off with the hand while warm, coming off like pigskin."

Castañeda tells of meeting "an Indian girl . . . who was as white as a Castilian lady, except that she had her chin painted like a Moorish woman. In general they all paint themselves in this way . . . and they decorate their eyes." Presumably he was speaking of an albino seen among the Querechos.

The Indians of the New Mexico-Texas plains tanned skins "to take to the settlements in winter to sell . . . some to the settlements at Cicuye, others toward Quivera, and others to the settlements which are situated in the direction of Florida." Cicuye was the great pueblo on the Pecos River, east of the present Santa Fe, New Mexico. Quivera was on the Arkansas River in the state of Kansas. By the term "the direction of Florida," Castañeda undoubtedly means Indian towns on or adjacent to the seacoast of Texas, for all the Gulf of Mexico coastal region in his time was considered a part of "Florida." In this statement he provides evidence to show that trade was carried on between Plains Apaches and other tribes in prehistoric times. Buffalo skins were a prized commodity, and not only were traded to the Pueblo Indians of New Mexico and Arizona, but, as Cabeza de Vaca had written, reached Indians in Mexico.*

Coronado encountered the Teyas northeast of Palo Duro Canyon, perhaps on the headwaters of either the Colorado or Brazos river. Castañeda was impressed with their prowess as buffalo hunters, recording that "a Teya was seen to shoot a bull right through both shoulders with an arrow, which would be a good shot for a musket." He thought the Teyas "very intelligent; the women are well made and modest. They cover their whole body. They wear shoes and buskins made of tanned skin. The women wear cloaks over thier small under petticoats, with sleeves gathered up at the shoulders, all of skin, and some wore something like little *sanbenitos* with a fringe, which reached half-way down the thigh over the petticoat." [33]

In 1598 Governor Juan de Oñate established the first capital of the new province of New Mexico at San Juan on the Rio Grande. The next spring he sent an aide, Vicente de Saldivar Mendoza, with a small company to obtain buffalo fat on the eastern New Mexico plains. Mendoza was not the first Spaniard to meet Eastern Apaches after Coronado—several expeditions had passed through their country in the intervening years—but he was the first man after Coronado's chroniclers to take note of them in a manner extremely valuable to historians. [34]

---

* See Part One.

Mendoza called the Querechos Vaqueros. He first encountered them in the vicinity of Las Vegas, New Mexico, and found them in increasing numbers as he traveled eastward to the watershed of the Canadian River.[35] In the warm days of early summer many Vaquero men were naked, "but some are clothed with skins of buffalo and some with blankets. The women wear a sort of trousers made of buckskin, and shoes or leggings, after their own fashion." [36]

Indian camps or villages were called *rancherias* by the early Spaniards. One Vaquero camp which Mendoza visited consisted of "fifty tents made of tanned hides, very bright red and white in color and bell-shaped, with flaps and openings, and built as skillfully as those of Italy and so large that in most ordinary ones four different mattresses and beds were easily accommodated. The tanning is so fine that although it should rain bucketfuls it will not pass through nor stiffen the hide, but rather upon drying it remains soft and pliable as before. . . ." Mendoza bartered for one of the big tents and took it to his own camp. He and his men were astonished to find that it weighed no more than fifty pounds.

At the time of the founding of the Province of New Mexico, and for many years thereafter, according to various statements, Plains Apache warriors (called by several names) "cut off the hair on the left side of the head even with the top of the ear and allowed the hair on the right side to grow long, sometimes almost reaching the ground. The long hair normally was folded up and tied with string so that it did not fall below the shoulder level. Feathers and trinkets adorned the hair. The left ear was pierced with from six to eight holes, the right with one or more. On dress occasions earrings were worn in all these perforations. The men spent many spare moments plucking out their beard and eyebrows, the ideal masculine face being devoid of hair." [37]

Both red and white pressures combined to drive the Eastern Apaches from their ancestral homelands. Kiowas and Comanches came from the north, and the Spanish pushed their frontier steadily outward from the south and west. On the east there were not only Spanish and French stations but strong Caddo tribes. The Plains Apaches retreated southward into Mexico and southwestward in the vast deserts of southern New Mexico and Arizona.

Speaking of the Lipan Apaches (Querechos and Vaqueros), Swanton states:[38] "In 1757 the San Saba Mission was established for them, but it was broken up by their enemies, the Comanche and Wichita. In 1761–62 the missions of San Lorenzo and Candelaria were organized for the same purpose but met a similar fate in 1767."

"From the proud and independent warriors Coronado met in the sixteenth century," says Newcomb,[39] "they became the skulking, beggardly riffraff of the Texas frontier."

Americans drove the remnants of them into Coahuila, Mexico. At the beginning of the present century no more than a score of them were known to be alive.

Jicarilla: Secure in the Mountains

The Jicarilla were saved from early destruction by alliances and remoteness. Like the Lipan, at some prehistoric period they migrated southward from northwestern Canada. The dialect of the Athapascan language they speak is closest to the tongue of the Mescalero Apaches, but according to their own traditions they have long regarded both the Mescalero and the Navajo as their enemies.

Jicarilla legends indicate that at various periods they dwelt in southeastern Colorado, in the area which Spaniards called the Cuartelejo, and along the upper Arkansas, the Canadian, and the Rio Grande. It is most unlikely they were among the Querechos met by Coronado, as there is no evidence to indicate that they had reached the Southwestern Great Plains at such an early date. It was not long after Coronado's time, however, when they began to appear in western Kansas, Oklahoma, and the Texas Panhandle, and some authorities believe that Coronado "probably" met them.[40]

The Jicarilla also long inhabited the mountain fastnesses of northern New Mexico and southern Colorado, and some of them always claimed that this high region was their original homeland. Although science has refuted this contention, there is documentary proof that they were in this area when the first explorers entered it. Hodge states that their traditions "seem to center about Taos and the heads of the Arkansas River." [41] According to Mooney, "their alliances and blood mixture have been with the Ute and Taos." [42] Under such circumstances the Jicarilla would have enjoyed havens and protection not available to other tribes of Eastern Apaches.

The Jicarilla, like their enemy relatives, the Navajo, were by nature incorrigible and fierce raiders, but they stood below the Navajo on the intellectual scale, and they were, unlike the Navajo, neither progressive nor thrifty. How they were regarded by other Eastern Apaches cannot, of course, be stated, but it seems logical to assume that in prehistoric times they were feared as plunderers, and were antagonists of their own linguistic kindred. The character of a people does not undergo a drastic transition in a short period of time.

From the beginning of the colonization of New Mexico until the Jicarilla were conquered by Americans, whites regarded them as "a worthless people . . . in raids for plunder the worst of the Apache tribes, more treacherous and cruel and less brave and energetic warriors than the Ute, but equally fond of intoxicants. While they sometimes planted on a small scale, they regarded theft as a natural means of support." [43]

There seems to be no question that before the year 1600 Spanish treasure-hunters met the Jicarilla in western Texas, western Oklahoma, and southeastern Colorado, although they did not mention them by a name that definitely can be connected with them. (Actually, these people were not called Jicarilla until early in the eighteenth century.) However, an event took place, purportedly in 1593, which stands as the first recorded conflict between Spaniards and the Jicarilla. If in the sparse account of it that has been preserved they are considered simply as "Plains Indians," there can be little doubt about their true identity, for the bloody clash occurred almost in the heart of their traditional and historic realm.

The story begins in the barren country along the Rio Conchos in northern Mexico. There, in 1593, a small force of cavalry, commanded by Captain Francisco Leyva de Bonilla, had been sent out by the governor of Nueva Viscaya to capture and punish renegade Indians who had been raiding cattle herds. Captain Bonilla had other thoughts in mind. He had schemed with an adventurer named Antonio Gutiérrez de Humana to go to New Mexico in search of the silver mines rumored to exist there.

Unauthorized explorations were forbidden by royal decree, but when Humana joined Bonilla with recruits and servants they set out. A few of the soldiers in Bonilla's command who had not been apprised of the plot before starting on the assignment to hunt cattle thieves refused to participate in it and turned back, but most of them were willing to join in the venture, even though they were aware of the punishment they might suffer.

The Bonilla-Humana expedition pushed down the Conchos to the Rio Grande and turned north. After weeks of hard travel the pueblos of the upper Rio Grande were reached. From Indians in this area the leaders heard about a "fabulously rich province" called Quivera, which lay toward the northeast. It was the same old tale which had lured Coronado, more than half a century before, on his fruitless journey to the buffalo plains. Bonilla and Humana swallowed it, and left with dreams no less exhilarating than those which had been held by all their predecessors.

Only one person would live to tell what happened.

Exactly where the Bonilla-Humana company wandered during the summer of 1593 * is not a matter of historical record, but it is known that they passed the great pueblo of Pecos, and traveled slowly to the buffalo country. Going on toward the northeast, "the farther inland

---

* More probably in the spring of 1594, but accounts are vague on this point.

317

they went, the larger was the number of buffalo they saw." Eventually, after weeks of travel, "they reached two large rivers, and beyond them many [Indian] *rancherias* with a large number of inhabitants. Farther on, in a plain, they came to a very large settlement . . . one of the two large rivers they crossed earlier flowed through this big town . . . in some places between the houses there were fields of corn, calabashes, and beans. The natives were very numerous but received the Spaniards peacefully and furnished them with abundant supplies of food."

Although scholars have been unable to establish the exact route taken to the two large rivers, they agree on one thing. It is that the Bonilla-Humana expedition, after crossing the panhandles of Texas and Oklahoma, had reached the land that would become American Kansas.

In a camp somewhere on the southwestern Great Plains, Bonilla and Humana had a bitter argument. The cause of their discord is not known, but they may have disagreed over the route to be taken. After the quarrel Humana sulked in his tent. At last he sent a soldier to summon Bonilla, "who came dressed in shirt and breeches. Before he reached the tent Humana went out to meet him, drew a knife from his pocket, unsheathed it, and stabbed Captain Bonilla twice, from which he soon afterward died. He was buried at once."

Frightened by the violence, five Indian servants deserted. Four of them would meet death while attempting to make their way back to Mexico. The survivor, known only as Jusepe, would fall into the hands of a band of Apaches. After being held captive for a year, he would escape and reach safety in a pueblo on the upper Rio Grande. Several years later he would recount his experiences to Spaniards, and his story would be recorded.

But Jusepe's account would not be the entire story of the Bonilla-Humana expedition. After murdering his partner, Humana continued the search for the legendary treasures of Quivera. Just where the company went has never been learned. One unconfirmed story said Humana went farther north and east. Another report, equally without proof of its accuracy, said the expedition went west and reached a small stream in southern Colorado close to the present border between that state and New Mexico. One night when they were camped in a pleasant place along this stream Indians set fire to the surrounding grass, and killed every man of the expedition as they attempted to escape through the smoke.

There is good reason to believe that the latter report is true, and that the raiders were Jicarillas, for the location of the massacre was deep within their territory, in the shadow of the mountains, which at the time they jealously controlled.

Years later—so the tale goes—a party of explorers and padres came upon a number of badly rusted Spanish guns and swords in a grove of cottonwoods along the small stream. They gave it the name *El Río de Las Ánimas Perdidas en Purgatorio*—the River of Lost Souls in Purgatory—for they believed the rusted arms belonged to Humana and his men.

The Jicarilla were not exterminated. They still live in northern New Mexico—on a reservation infinitesimal in size compared to the vast domain over which they once ruled.

Comanche: the Conquerors

The Comanche, a name that for nearly two centuries struck fear in the hearts of both red men and white, were not prehistoric inhabitants of the Southern Great Plains. They belong to the Shoshonean linguistic family. Their language is virtually identical with that of the Shoshoni of the northern Rocky Mountains and the Great Basin. Horses were in the possession of northern Indians when the Comanche began migrating southward from Wyoming, and invaded southern Colorado, the western extremities of Kansas, Oklahoma, and Texas, and northern New Mexico.

Their southward movement was in every sense an offensive, although it took place over a long period. Band followed band from the north, until at last, enjoying great numerical strength and being well armed and mounted, they became the indomitable rulers of the Southwest Plains.[44]

The prehistoric culture of the Comanche was that of the Shoshoni, who still live in the north, and, therefore, what little is known of it properly belongs in the story of these Great Basin people.

The Spaniards were the first white men to use the name Comanche in written documents, but until recent years its origin remained a puzzle. It had not derived from any Spanish word. Not until 1943 was the mystery solved. Then the distinguished scientist Marvin K. Opler successfully traced it to the language of the Ute, who also are of Shoshonean stock.[45] It came from the Ute word *Komantcia*, which in its fullest sense means "anyone who wants to fight me all the time." The Ute also applied the same name to other traditional enemies, such as the Arapaho, Cheyenne, and Kiowa. The Spanish got the name Comanche from the Ute. As for the Comanches' name for themselves, it is, like the name by which so many other tribes identify themselves, a variation of a word meaning simply "the people."

Early French explorers heard the Comanches called Padoucas, a name the Sioux had for them, but it is believed to have derived from one band of them, and was not applicable to the entire tribe. However, it endured and was widely used. Lewis and Clark heard of the "great nation of the Padouca" who dwelt between the Platte and Kansas [Arkansas] rivers, but they did not encounter them. As late as 1805 the North Platte was known to frontiersmen as the Padouca Fork.[46] By the time Americans had begun to occupy the Southwest, however, the name had disappeared from common usage.

The exact time of the Comanches' departure from their prehistoric homeland in the northern mountains is open to question, but both traditions of other tribes and historical records say that some of them still lived in Wyoming, and perhaps along the Yellowstone in Montana, in the early sixteen hundreds. According to the Comanches' own traditions, they emerged from the Rocky Mountains, in the area of the Arkansas River headwaters, about the beginning of the eighteenth century. It is definitely known that they were in northern and north-eastern New Mexico as early as 1705, and that for some time previously had been in eastern Colorado and western Kansas.

Several traditional accounts of their separation from the northern Shoshoni attribute the cause to a fight among themselves. One given by an elderly Comanche and recorded in 1933 at the Laboratory of Anthropology in Santa Fe states: [47]

"Two bands were living together in a large camp. One band was on the east side; the other on the west. Each had its own chief.

"Every night the young boys were out playing games. . . . They were having a kicking game. . . . One boy kicked another over the stomach so hard that he died from it. The boy who was killed was from the West camp. He was the son of a chief.

". . . the West camp cried all night. In the East camp it was silent. Next day, they buried that boy.

"The boy's father, the chief, had his crier go around announcing that there would be a big fight to see which camp was best so as to settle the question of his son's death. There was big excitement. Both sides had good warriors. The East camp ran to its horses. 'If they really mean what they say, they will kill us,' they cried.

"The two sides lined up, and the chiefs met in the center. Then an old man from the East camp came up into the center. He wept and told them it wasn't right for them to fight among themselves like that. They took pity on him. Then other old men came out and gathered with him. 'You have plenty of enemies to fight,' they cried. 'These were just boys playing a game. Don't take this thing so seriously. You are setting a bad example for the children. Whatever this chief wants to keep the peace, we'll do it.'

"That chief called it off. He said he did not realize what he was doing. So the East camp brought them horses and other things.

"After that the chief had his announcer tell the people it was time to move camp. 'We have had bad luck here. There has been hard feeling.' While they were still there, smallpox broke out.

"Then they broke up. One group went north; those are the Shoshones. The other group went west."

Although other accounts say the separation resulted from wrangles over how spoils were to be divided—in one case a bear—all maintain that it followed an irreconcilable quarrel. These, of course, are legends. The disputes may have occurred—probably they did—but other pressures known to be indisputable facts were undoubtedly more responsible for the Shoshoni schism than intramural rows.

In historic times major population shifts occurred on the Northern Great Plains. Strong tribes armed with guns obtained from fur traders pushed out from the northeast. People living along the western reaches of the Plains were forced back into the mountains and to retreat toward the south. Flathead tradition says that shortly after this happened the Shoshoni disappeared from the region of the upper Missouri River.[48]

Drifting southward, either through the mountains of Colorado or along the western edge of the Great Plains, the Comanches were among the first Plains Indians to obtain Spanish horses. When they first acquired them cannot be stated precisely, but it was most probably in the middle years of the seventeenth century. Some Comanches must have gone far enough south to steal them from either Indians or Spanish settlements. Two historians express the opinion that "the desire for a more abundant supply of horses was certainly an important motive for moving closer to the source of supply: the Southwest." [49] Another authority does not believe the Comanches were driven into the south, but continued to go there to obtain more horses.[50] Still another scholar terms the Comanche movement a voluntary advance carried out entirely for the purpose of obtaining horses.[51]

Some students of the subject believe that horses were possessed by tribes of the middle Great Plains very early after 1600.[52] The Pawnee, for example, evidently had them in fairly sizable numbers by 1630. At this time Comanches were apparently neighbors of the Pawnee. Whether the Comanche went around the Pawnee or were permitted by them to pass, the fact remains that the Comanche eventually established themselves close to the Spanish frontier, creating what came to be known as the Comanche Barrier and which made numerous northern tribes dependent upon them for the invaluable horses.

Thereafter, the Comanche became the greatest raiders of Spanish settlements, extending their forays far into Mexico. In fierce and sudden attacks they sacked Indian and white communities alike, not infrequently depleting them almost entirely of horses and mules. They were the terror of the Southern Great Plains and adjacent areas for nearly two centuries, although in this time they were constantly the quarry of Spanish, Indian, and American punitive expeditions. Nearly two centuries of continual warfare, until at last they were overwhelmed by natural and human forces—but that story belongs to the period of recorded history—and only one final note seems appropriate here.

In their scholarly work, Professors Wallace and Hoebel have this to say about the final capitulation of the Comanches: "On a sultry summer day in June, 1875, a small band of starving Comanche Indians straggled in to Fort Sill, near the Wichita Mountains in what is now the southwestern part of the State of Oklahoma. They were surrendering to the military authorities. So ended the reign of the Comanches on the Southwestern Frontier. Their horses had been captured and destroyed; the buffalo were gone; most of their tipis had been burned. They had held out to the end, but the end was now upon them. They had come in to submit." [53]

Language Groups in Part Seven

SOUTHERN GREAT PLAINS

Caddoan:	Tawakoni	Athapascan:	Lipan Apache
	Wichita		Kiowa Apache
	Yascani		Jicarilla Apache
	Hasinai Confederacy		
	Kichai	Shoshonean:	Comanche
	Kadohadacho		Kiowa
	Confederacy		(also Tanoan)
	Waco		
	Tawehash		

Kiowa: Proud Wanderers

The Kiowas were supreme egotists. Although never known to be a large tribe, they were haughty and vain. They considered themselves incomparable warriors and raiders, and, indeed, the daring and bravery they often displayed gave substantiation to their claims. Even their name was reflective of their pride in themselves and the prowess as fighters and hunters of which they boasted. It means "principal people."

Yet less dependable information regarding the origin of the Kiowa has been obtained than of any other Indians of the Southern Great Plains. There is evidence to indicate that they are connected linguistically with both the Tanoan and Shoshonean stocks. This discovery, made by John Peabody Harrington,[54] considerably deepened the mystery surrounding them, for previously they had been considered a separate linguistic family.

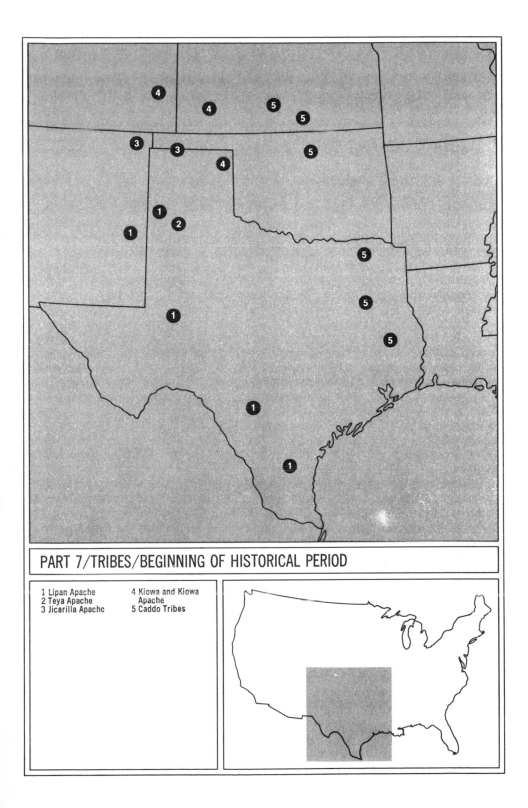

PART 7/TRIBES/BEGINNING OF HISTORICAL PERIOD

1 Lipan Apache
2 Teya Apache
3 Jicarilla Apache
4 Kiowa and Kiowa
  Apache
5 Caddo Tribes

The Tanoans are New Mexico puebloans. The Shoshoni are people of the northern mountains and the Great Basin. It is possible that some prehistoric Tanoans abandoned their sedentary town life, moved eastward to the Plains, and became buffalo hunters. It is equally possible that Plains people of the Shoshonean linguistic family could have migrated to New Mexico and united with Tanoans already living there.[55]

Traditions are in conflict. The Kiowa themselves always maintained that their place of origin was on the headwaters of the Missouri River in southwestern Montana. In late prehistoric times, they assert, they moved out of the high mountains and formed a close alliance with the Crow on the High Plains of the Yellowstone River watershed. The anthropologist Robert H. Lowie disputes the Kiowa claim, stating "that these contacts were peculiarly intimate is demonstrated neither by Crow tradition, which fails to support Kiowa assertions, nor by a comparison of Kiowa with Crow culture." [56]

Some scholars lean toward the belief that the Kiowa wandered far north in prehistoric times but did not long remain there.[57] Swanton expresses the opinion that they were driven southward by the Arapaho and the Cheyenne, and notes that the Dakota (Sioux) claim to have driven them from the Black Hills.[58] There is documentary support for Swanton's assertion. Early accounts show that the Kiowa were in the Black Hills area as late as 1780. A few years later they were encountered between the forks of the Platte River. Soon afterward it is known from records that they had continued the southward trek and had reached the Arkansas in western Kansas and southeastern Colorado. Here they came up against the Comanche Barrier, and a bitter and bloody war ensued. Thus, they were under pressures from both north and south.

It has been established that near the end of the eighteenth century a lasting peace was effected between the Kiowa and the Comanche. Citing the Kiowa authority James Mooney, Newcomb records a Kiowa tradition of how the armistice was reached: ". . . a small party of Kiowas stopped at a house in a Spanish settlement, presumably in New Mexico, unaware that a party of Comanches was already there. Before a battle could break out, the Indians' host, acting as a mediator, proposed that the Kiowas and Comanches come to a peaceful settlement of their differences. After some discussion by both sides, the leader of the Kiowa's party, Wolf-Lying-Down, went with the Comanches so that the matter could be further discussed by a larger and more representative segment of the Comanche tribe. He parted with his fellow Kiowas with the request that they avenge his death if he had not returned by fall. He did return, however, the Comanches having agreed to a cessation of hostilities." [59]

Whether or not the tradition is rooted in truth, the fact remains that at the beginning of the nineteenth century the Kiowa and Comanche were allies, hunting and raiding together, and so they remained until destroyed by Americans.

Whatever their origins, after the amnesty with the Comanche the Kiowa occupied what Swanton terms their "best-known historic location," a large territory that contained contiguous parts of Oklahoma, Kansas, Colorado, New Mexico, and Texas, and there they made their last stand. Their forays, however, were not confined to this region. With Comanches they constantly raided Mexican territory, ranging several hundred miles southward in Mexico as far as Durango. Although fewer in number than the Comanches, they were no less vicious and bold in their attempts to stay the tide of white settlement.

When the Kiowa Apaches separated from their Athapascan kinsmen, the Lipan and Jicarilla, and joined the Kiowa is not certain. Swanton stated that the "first historical mention of the Kiowa Apache is by La Salle in 1681 or 1682, who calls them Gattacka, the term by which they are known to the Pawnee." [60] On this basis it may be assumed that they were with the Kiowa in the north, and came back to their former homeland on the Llano Estacado with them. Other students think the Kiowa Apache became affiliated with the Kiowa after the Comanches had gained control of the Southwestern Great Plains, and that they entered into the alliance to prevent their own destruction. Whatever the case, the Kiowa Apache held "a definite place in the Kiowa camp circle" until their freedom ended, and they shared the same fate as the Kiowa.

Just to add to the confusion about the origins of the Kiowa, I quote two descriptions by men fully qualified to speak on the subject.

Wrote the great painter of Indians, George Catlin, who saw them in 1834: "The Kioways are a much finer looking race of men, than either Camanchees or Pawnees—are tall and erect, with an easy and graceful gait—with long hair, cultivated oftentimes so as to reach nearly to the ground. They have generally the fine and Roman outline of head, that is so frequently found in the North,—and decidedly distinct from that of the Camanchees and Pawnee Picts [Wichitas]." [61]

Wrote the distinguished ethnologist James Mooney, in 1898: "Although brave and warlike, the Kiowa are considered inferior in most respects to the Comanche. In person they are dark and heavily built, forming a marked contrast to the more slender and brighter complexioned prairie tribes farther north." [62]

Whatever their linguistic connection, however they appeared, wherever they came from, it cannot be disputed that the Kiowa and the Kiowa Apaches left an ineradicable trail through the pages of American Indian history.

Caddoans: Old Residents

The ancestry of the Caddoans may not be scientifically traceable back to the first families of the Southern Great Plains, but they had lived there for several thousand years when white men first encountered them.

Their culture was more advanced, and their economy more diversified than any other prehistoric Indians of the vast region. They were both expert game hunters and successful agriculturists. They lived in towns, some of them unusually large. An unfailing food supply, inherent industriousness, and an ability to absorb beneficial practices and new ideas brought them prosperity that endured for countless centuries. Bountiful material assets made it possible for them to maintain relatively dense population centers, gave them security, and provided the opportunity, as Newcomb states, to develop elaborate and complex social institutions that were impossible for tribes struggling to subsist in arid regions to the south and the nomadic Apaches of the High Plains to the west. He adds: "The intricate [Caddoan] cultural structure that grew from this ample subsistence is as fascinating and in many ways as exotic as any known in the Americas." [63]

The remarkable talent of prehistoric Caddoans for creating and maintaining political, social, and military unity gave rise to two powerful confederations in the heart of the Plains region they inhabited, as well as the successful establishment of smaller amalgamations in more remote areas toward the north.

The roots of early Caddo Culture extend in several directions. While they are believed to be direct descendants of earlier inhabitants of the Southern Great Plains and woodland regions adjacent to them on the east, their prehistoric customs, mores, and rituals, as well as their manufactured products, their farming and hunting patterns reflect imported influences. These may be tracked to sources in the southeastern region of the United States, the Caribbean, Mexico, and the Southwest of the Pueblos.

The Caddoan Culture probably reached its highest development shortly before or shortly after the beginning of the Christian Era. It apparently had been in the ascendancy a thousand years earlier. There is ample evidence to indicate that the Caddoans had widespread contacts with other peoples in late prehistoric times. They were among the earliest, if not the earliest, potters, cultivators, and weavers of the Southern Great Plains. Both ceramics and agriculture were introduced into the United States region from Middle America. Pottery first appeared on the Georgia coast about 2500 B.C., and corn of similar antiquity has been found in a New Mexico cave.[64] The Caddo territory was generally equidistant between these points. Pottery undoubtedly reached them from the Southeast, while seeds for domestic plants may have come to them from both the South and West. They engaged in trade with all of these areas long before the discovery of America.

In late prehistoric times influences originating in Mexico and the Circum-Caribbean region began to quicken the development of the Caddoan Culture. Features of the Mississippian Culture also were noticeable among the Caddo way of life. By A.D. 500, as Josephy states, "With a strong agricultural base, population grew, and major ceremonial centers, with large temple-mounds and villages of well-built houses, appeared. Influences now ran the opposite way, and traits from the Caddoan Culture moved eastward." [65] A short time later, bands and tribes began to move northward into Oklahoma and southern Kansas while others pushed westward in Texas from the Caddoan cultural area. Some archeologists think that at least some of the pottery first in wide use among the Anasazi of New Mexico and Arizona reached them from the Caddoans, but other scientists are in sharp disagreement with this opinion. However, there seems to be no doubt that a thousand years before the time of Christ the people of northern Mexico were beginning to transmit influences farther north, providing routes of travel for the spread of agriculture and other traits to northern people, such as those in the Mogollon, Hohokam, and Anasazi cultural areas, and the area of the Caddoan Culture.[66] *

The Kadohadacho, who formed a confederacy comprised of six subdivisions, dwelt in northeastern Texas in permanent towns, but they ranged far west on the buffalo plains to hunt. Their name means "real chiefs." From it came the abbreviation "Caddo," applied by white men to all branches of the tribe, whatever their location, as well as to their language.†

For the Kadohadacho the prehistoric period ended when De Soto and his army, late in 1541, met the Cahinnio, a subdivision of the confederacy, in a province which the Spaniards called Tula. Before departing from Tula a few days later De Soto and his soldiers had come to have a wholesome respect for the bravery and fighting ability of these people.[67]

The Indians of Tula, says the account by the Gentleman of Elvas,[68] were summoned by De Soto, "and as they gathered by fifteen and twenty at a time, they would come to attack the Christians. Finding that they were sharply handled, and that in running the horses would overtake them, they got upon the housetops, where they endeavored to defend themselves with their bows and arrows. When beaten off

---

* See Chapter One.
† The Caddoan linguistic family also includes the Pawnee and the Arikara, an offshoot of the Skidi Pawnee. See Part Six.

from one roof, they would get up on to another; and while the Christians were going after some, others would attack them from an opposite direction."

One soldier had the misfortune to climb into a granary in which five Caddo women had taken refuge from the fighting. Having no desire to shoot or knife them, he sought to back out, but one of his legs broke through the flimsy flooring. Immediately the women sprang upon him, one seizing him by the penis. He was saved by the timely arrival of a comrade who had no compunctions about killing women.[69]

The first battle of Tula "lasted so long that the steeds, becoming tired, could not be made to run. One horse was killed, and others were wounded. Of the Indians fifteen were slain." De Soto withdrew, but three days later returned. He found the town "abandoned, the inhabitants not venturing to remain for him. But no sooner did they know he was in the town, than, at four o'clock on the morning of the first night, they came upon him in two squadrons, from different directions, with bows and arrows and with long staves like pikes. . . . Many of the Indians were killed. Of those made captives, the Governor sent six to the Cacique, their right hands and their noses cut off, with the message, that, if he did not come to him to apologize and render obeisance, he would go in pursuit, and to him, and as many of his as he might find, would he do as he had done to those he sent." The leader of the Caddoans capitulated, and De Soto went on his way.

In 1542, after the death of De Soto, his successor Moscoso and the remnants of the once powerful army pushed southward into Caddo territory in a desperate attempt to save themselves from perishing in the wilderness. Lost, badly in need of supplies, and almost constantly attacked by Indians, they were forced to turn back to the Mississippi. There they constructed boats in which they descended the river and eventually reached safety in Mexico.

Hasinai: Our Own Folk

The Hasinai Confederacy, composed of nearly a score of Caddo bands, spread over a large territory along the upper Trinity and Neches rivers, south and southwest of the area occupied by the Kadohadacho. The Hasinai, whose name signifies "our own folk," were more popularly known as Cenis by early explorers.

After the retreat of Moscoso nearly a century and a half passed before Europeans again entered Caddo Country. Early in 1687 La Salle and several members of his colonizing expedition started on their third attempt to break out of the Texas wilderness. It was their hope at this time, as it had been on the two previous occasions, to reach the Mississippi somewhere north of the Gulf of Mexico, ascend it, and obtain relief for the ill-fated settlement they had left behind them on the south Texas coast. Traveling toward the north and northeast, the first Caddo people they met were the Hasinai, whom they called Cenis. It was near one of the Hasinai towns that La Salle and a loyal Indian aide who had long accompanied him on his explorations were brutally murdered by some of their companions.

Invaluable descriptions of the Caddo and their way of life were written by three members of this party who eventually reached Canada. They were Henri Joutel, a La Salle lieutenant, Father Anastasius Douay, and La Salle's brother, Jean Cavelier, also a priest.[70]

From Douay comes the information that the Cenis had strong ties with the Comanches. On one occasion, as they neared a large town, the inhabitants came out "bearing the calumet ceremoniously. . . . La Salle was received as if in triumph and lodged in the great chief's cabin. There was a great concourse of people, the young men being drawn out and under arms . . . and, besides, loading us with presents and all kinds of provisions."

The population in this immediate area was spread out for a distance of twenty leagues "in hamlets of ten or twelve cabins, forming cantons, each with a different name. Their cabins are fine, forty or fifty feet high, of the shape of beehives. Trees are planted in the ground and united above the branches, which are covered with grass. The beds are arranged around the cabin, three or four feet from the ground; the fire is in the middle. . . .

"We found among the Cenis many things which undoubtedly came from the Spaniards, such as dollars and other pieces of money, silver spoons, lace of every kind, clothes and horses. . . . Horses are common; they gave them to us for an axe; one Cenis offered me one for our cowl, to which he took a fancy.

"They have intercourse with the Spaniards through the Choumans [Comanches], their allies, who are always at war with New Spain. . . . They reckoned themselves six days' journey from the Spaniards,* of whom they gave us so natural a description that we no longer had any doubts on that point, although the Spaniards had not yet undertaken to come to their village, their warriors merely joining the Choumans to go war on New Mexico."

The continued friendliness and hospitality of the Caddo was undoubtedly due in large part, if not entirely, to La Salle's success in convincing them that he and his men also were enemies of the Spanish

---

* Undoubtedly a misunderstanding of signs, for it would have taken a great deal longer than that to have reached the Spanish settlements in Mexico, and even longer to travel to New Mexico.

and his intimation that at a later time he would return and join them in attacks on Spanish settlements.

Each of the accounts remarks frequently on the beauty and lushness of the Caddo Country. Cavelier tells of coming upon Cenis engaged in hunting buffalo: ". . . óne hundred and fifty Indians, all on horseback, armed with lances tipped with sharpened bone . . . each of whom attacked a bull. . . . They made us mount, the more conveniently to witness the close of the bullfight, which seemed to us the most diverting thing imaginable, and I am convinced there is no chase as curious in Europe. When the combat was ended . . . they led us away to their village. Their frank and cordial manners made us follow them without repugnance. . . . They took us straight to the cabin of their great chief, or captain, where they first washed our heads, hands and feet with warm water, after which they presented us boiled and roast meat to eat and an unknown fish, cooked whole, that was six feet long, laid in a dish of its length. It was of a wonderful taste. . . . We bought at this place thirty horses, which mounted us all and carried our baggage. They cost us thirty knives, ten hatchets and six dozen needles."

Joutel wrote that some Caddo cottages were inhabited by fifteen or twenty families, "each of which has its nook or corner, bed and other utensils to itself, but without any partition to separate it from the rest. . . . When they move their dwellings they generally burn the cottages they leave and build new ones on the ground they design to inhabit.

"Their moveables are some bullocks' hides and goats' [?] skins, well cured; some mats, close wove, wherewith they adorn their huts, and some earthen vessels, which they are very skillful at making, and wherein they boil their flesh or roots, or sagamis, which is their pottage. They have also some small baskets made of canes, serving to put in their fruit and other provisions. Their beds are made of canes raised two or three feet above ground, handsomely fitted with mats and skins. . . .

"When they design to till the ground they give one another notice, and very often above a hundred of each sex meet together. When they have tilled that piece of land . . . those the land belongs to give the others to eat, and then they spend the rest of the day in dancing and merrymaking. This same is practiced from canton to canton, and so they till the land all together."

Joutel provided history with the first account of the tattooing commonly practiced by the Caddo. He thought them "generally handsome," but deplored the custom of disfiguring themselves "by making scores or streaks on their faces, from the top of the forehead down the nose to the tip of the chin, which is done by pricking the skin with needles or other sharp instruments till it bleeds, whereon they strew fine powder of charcoal, and that sinks in and mixes with the blood under the skin. They also make, after the same manner, the figures of living creatures, of leaves and flowers, on their shoulders, thighs and other parts of their bodies, and paint themselves with black or red, and sometimes both together."

He composed a vivid picture of Caddo women, declaring "They are generally well shaped, and would not be disagreeable did they adhere to nature, but they disguise themselves as ridiculously as the men, not only with the streak they have like them down their face, but by other figures they put on it, at the corners of their eyes, and on other parts of their bodies, whereof they make more particular show on their bosom, and those who have the most are reckoned the handsomest, though that pricking in that part be extremely painful to them.

"The women wear nothing but a skin, mat, or clout, hanging round them like a petticoat, and reaching down halfway their legs, which hides their nakedness before and behind. . . ."

Northern Relatives

Along the Great Bend of the Arkansas River and southward from this part of Kansas into Oklahoma and northern Texas, long before the beginning of the historical period, dwelt a number of Caddo tribes affiliated in what might be termed a loose confederation. It had no single name, such as Hasinai or Kadohadacho, each of the branches maintaining its own identity, yet they were held in close association by social, religious, economic, and linguistic bonds.

How far back in prehistoric times they reached this heartland of the Southern Great Plains is an archeological mystery. Some of them maintain that they migrated from far to the south with their Nebraska kinsmen, the Pawnee, and if true, that was a very long time ago. Somewhere in the region of the Platte River, according to these traditions, they separated from the Pawnee, and turned back toward the south. The Pawnee remained, and thereafter lived far apart from other Caddoan tribes. Others say that their original homeland was on the lower Red River, and that it was from that region they set out on their northward migration with the Pawnee. There is no scientific evidence to support any of these legends.

The dominant tribe of this loose Plains confederation was the Wichita. Their name, which means simply "man," holds a secure place in history, for they were the Indians of Coronado's legendary Province of Quivera. Other peoples of the Great Plains who came of different stock called them Black Pawnees, and with good reason. Their skins were considerably darker than those of any other Indians of the Great Plains.

The Wichita, as well as most other people of the amalgamation, were tattooed virtually from head to foot. Their decorations excelled those with which other Caddo tribes adorned their bodies in artistry, in variations of design, and in profusion. Newcomb notes that the men were tattooed "on both eyelids, and a short horizontal line extended from the outside corner of the eye." [71] Other parts of the face, the neck, arms, shoulders, the chest, and even the hands bore extravagant designs and marks symbolizing various honors gained in hunting and war. Women were no less tattooed than males, their faces, shoulders, and arms covered with triangles and zigzag lines. They took particular pains in decorating the breasts, including the nipples, which were tattooed "with several short lines, and around them were tatooed three concentric circles, said to prevent pendulous breasts in old age." [72]

The statements by Coronado's chroniclers that the houses of the Indians in the Great Bend of the Arkansas were round and thatched with straw remove all doubts as to their identity. In all the immense region of the Central Great Plains only the Wichita constructed dwellings of this type. In the seventeenth century, the Wichita were forced to move south from Kansas by tribes to the north, notably the Osages, who had begun to obtain European guns from traders.

Other tribes or bands associated with the Wichita in the Southern Great Plains family of the Caddo included:

Tawehash. The meaning of their name is unknown, but the first French explorers called them *Panis Noirs* and *Panis Piques,* undoubtedly synonymous with the appellations Black Pawnee and Speckled Pawnee by which other Plains Indians described them. At the beginning of the historical period the Tawehash are believed to have lived with or close to the Wichita, and they probably were a band of that tribe. The French first met them on the Canadian River north of the headwaters of the Washita, but it is not improbable that Coronado had seen them farther north nearly two centuries earlier. They, too, had been forced to move southward by northern enemies. In 1759 they and their allies defeated a strong Spanish force on the Red River.[73]

Tawakoni. The earliest known home of this tribe, whose name signifies "a river bend among red hills," was in the same area occupied by the Tawehash. They were closely allied to the Wichita, the dialects of the two tribes having only slight differences. Under pressures from Northern Great Plains people, they moved southward from Oklahoma into Texas, settling on the Brazos and Trinity rivers.

Yscani. The history of this small Caddoan band is virtually identical with that of the Tawakoni. The significance of their name has not been discovered.

Waco. An unimportant small group, their origin remains obscure. Some ethnologists think they were part of the Tawakoni. At one time they lived in Oklahoma, but were not identified as a band until their village was found on the site of the bustling Texas city which bears their name. Obviously they had migrated southward with other Caddoan people. It has been suggested that their name derives from *Wehiko,* a corruption of "Mexico," and applied to them because they were continually fighting with Mexicans.[74]

Kichai. The Pawnee called this tribe "water turtles," but in their own dialect the name translates as "going in wet sand." In prehistoric times the Kichai lived north of the Red River, but early in the historical period they were found farther south on the upper waters of the Trinity. When Americans plotted to exterminate them in order to obtain their lands, they fled to Oklahoma and found a haven among the Wichita. They lost their individual identity, and at the end of the nineteenth century the number of Kichai known to be alive could have been counted on the fingers of two hands.[75]

The various tribes of the Caddoan confederacies called each other by a word that meant "friends." It has been variously spelled by early writers as *teyas, tejas, tayshas,* and *techas,* but from it comes the word "Texas."

SOUTHERN GREAT PLAINS

Earliest Population Estimates*

Kiowa (1780)	2,000	Hasinai Confederacy (1690)	4,000
Kiowa Apache (1780)	300		
Tawakoni (1778)	600	Kichai (1690)	500
Waco (1824)	350	Kadohadacho Confederacy (1600)	2,000
Tawehash (1778)	1,100		
Wichita (1778)	3,200	Lipan Apache (1690)	500
Yscani (1782)	360	Jicarilla Apache (1845)	800
Comanche (1690)	7,000	TOTAL	22,710

* See Note, Population Table, Part One.

The Spanish, the Mexicans, an independent republic, and a state gave the name to a vast region that embraced the larger part of the Southern Great Plains, as well as immense areas of coastal plains and wooded uplands. If the constituents of these jurisdictions understood its Indian definition they gave no indication of the fact through more than three centuries. It does not matter now. The red peoples of the

Southern Great Plains, and the last vestiges of their cultures, were long ago irretrievably destroyed. Only a few names remain to mark their earthly passage.

Dates to Remember

1535—Cabeza de Vaca and his three companions crossed the Southern Great Plains in Texas. They were followed much of the time by a throng of Indians, but the identity of these people is unknown. In the Southwestern Plains beyond the Pecos River the four men may have encountered Apaches. See Parts One and Two for other details of their epic journey.

1541—Coronado reached the Arkansas River in Kansas, discovering the Wichita. En route across the plains he had encountered the Lipan, Jicarilla, Mescalero, and Teyas. In October of the same year, De Soto and his army entered the region of the Kadohadacho Confederacy of the Caddo. At one time Coronado and De Soto were no more than three hundred miles apart, but neither knew the whereabouts of the other.

1581—Chamuscado-Rodríguez company met Apaches in the plains of eastern New Mexico.

1583—The Espejo expedition passed through country inhabited by Apaches and other buffalo-hunting tribes.

1593—Bonilla and Humana crossed plains to Kansas, following Coronado's general course from the Texas Panhandle. After Bonilla's murder, Humana and his men were massacred by Indians, probably Jicarilla, in southeastern Colorado.

1599—Mendoza, traveling eastward from the Rio Grande, met Apaches on the plains.

1601—Governor Oñate of the new Spanish Province of New Mexico, searching for treasure, reached Coronado's Province of Quivera in central Kansas.

1686 and 1687—La Salle reached the territory of the Hasinai Confederacy of the Caddo. He was murdered in the area in the latter year.

Scientific Note—Signs, Jargon, and Counting in Prehistoric Trade

The sign language was no less than a wonderful means of communication. In it there were beauty and fluid grace, as well as a high degree of practicality. A conversation between men who were experts in it was poetry in motion. It was a gesture system that hardly fell short of a spoken language.

SOME INDIAN PLACE NAMES*

Oklahoma

Apache, town
Navajoe, town
Alabama, town
Sawokla, town
Mehusuky, town
Pensacola, town
Seminole, county
Chickasha, town
Choctaw, county, town
Hichita, town
Cherokee, county, town
Muskogee, county, town
Shawnee, town
Eufaula, town
Tuskegee, town
Appalachia, town
Tioga, town
Miami, town
Wyandot, town
Pottawatomie, town
Oklahoma, state
Illinois, river
Quapaw, town
Osage, town
Cheyenne, town
Pawnee, county, town
Ponca, town
Kansas, town

Kaw, town
Arapaho, town
Kiowa, town
Comanche, town
Texhoma, town
Caddo, county, town
Keiche, hills
Wichita, mountains

Texas

Copano, bay
Ayish, creek
Texas, state
Apache, mountains
Pecos, county, town, river
Seminole, town
Miami, town
Conoy, town
Osage, town
Cheyenne, town
Omaha, town
Comanche, county, town
Texhoma, town
Caddo, town
Keechi, town, creek
Lipan, town
Waco, town
Wichita, county, town, river

* Tribes and tribal subdivisions.

The origin of the American Indian sign language cannot be traced to any linguistic family. It did not come into usage in a short period of time, but gradually evolved over many centuries, perhaps over millennia. Actually, one might say that the practice of communicating by gestures is as old as mankind. Philologists agree that the sign language's evolution followed the same lines along which human speech developed, that is, in a gradual progress from the representative to the conventional, from the picture to the arbitrary symbol. According to the eminent ethnologist James Mooney, "It may, in fact, be described as a motional equivalent of the Indian pictograph, the conventional sign being usually a close reference to the predominant characteristic of the object in shape, habit or purpose. The signs are made almost entirely with the hands, either one or both. Minor differences exist, like dialects in spoken languages. . . ." [76] Even with these slight dissimilarities, however, Indians from the upper Missouri, for example, had no difficulty communicating in it with Indians from the Southern Great Plains.

While traces of a sign system have been discovered by archeologists among the former tribes of the Eastern Woodlands, northwestern Canada, and Mexico, the sign language reached its highest degree of perfection between the Mississippi River and the Rocky Mountains, and southern Canada and the Rio Grande. Nowhere else among prehistoric peoples did it attain such an extensive vocabulary, nor was it as expressive and complete. And in all of this vast region the tribes of the Great Plains excelled in its usage. It seems never to have extended west of the mountains, but some tribes of the mountain region who made periodic journeys to the Great Plains to hunt or trade—such as the Flathead, the Nez Percé, the Kutenai, and the Shoshoni—were capable, if not fluent, in it. Nor did it attain any high development among the sedentary tribes of the East and Southeast, being superseded in these areas by some mother dialect or trade jargon.

There is no mystery about its high degree of development in the Great Plains. In this immense region, stretching two thousand miles from north to south and several hundred miles in width, there was a constant shifting of peoples of many stocks. They could not understand each other. All lived by hunting, and as they moved in pursuit of buffalo and other animals they were continually brought into either friendly or hostile collision. The demands of this nomadic way of life made mandatory a simple yet efficient means of communication. Sign language filled the need.

As this gesture system evolved, signs became conventionalized. For instance, the sign for "man" was made by "throwing out the hand, back outward, with index finger extended upward, apparently having reference to an old root word in many Indian languages which defines *man* as the erect animal. Woman is indicated by a sweeping downward movement of the hand at the side of the head, with fingers extended toward the hair to denote long flowing hair or the combing of flowing locks." Each tribe was identified by a special sign, usually the equivalent of the common name in various spoken languages, i.e., for Blackfoot a speaker would touch his moccasin, then rub his fingers on something black. The length of a journey might be stated in "sleeps." After signifying "sleep" by inclining the head to one side and placing the open palm against the underside, the speaker would count on his fingers.[77]

The sign language was in every sense a full-fledged means of communication, and persons fluent in it could debate and discuss any subject. They could negotiate treaties, talk about intertribal trading, hunting, warfare, the weather, domestic problems, troublesome wives, illness, and they could tell humorous and tragic tales, recite historical legends, and speak to the gods.

Besides the sign language there were in use in prehistoric times several jargons which also were the outgrowth of an extensive aboriginal system of intertribal trade and travel.

The Chinook jargon was used throughout the Columbia River region and along the Pacific Coast to Alaska. The basis of this trade jargon was the Chinook tongue, interspersed with words from the Nootka, Salish, and other languages. As white men infiltrated this area, corrupted English, French, and Russian words were added.

In the Southwestern Great Plains the Comanche language, or variations of it, was the main spoken trade language, and was more or less understandable to other tribes. However, Indians throughout this area were proficient sign talkers, and needed no common spoken language to understand each other.

The so-called Mobilian trade language was a corrupted Choctaw jargon. Another name for it was Chickasaw trade language. It was used by most tribes from Florida to Louisiana and other peoples living on or near the Mississippi as far north as the Ohio River.

As I stated in my study on pre-Columbian Indian trade prepared for the Southwest Museum, currency as modern man thinks of it did not exist, but there were numerous measures and standards of value.[78]

They were very different. In one area strings of shells of varying length might be used. In another area certain furs or hides. In another, semiprecious stones. In still another, flat baskets that would hold a specific amount of some staple. Among some California tribes bird scalps were used as money, being both a standard of value and a medium of exchange. These measures and standards were known to intertribal traders and were accepted as a basis for barter.

Obviously no trade could be conducted without counting. Most prehistoric Indians used the decimal system. That does not mean they wrote figures in sand or on skins or rock walls or wood. However, they did make marks on some occasions to indicate a number or to keep a record. A few tribes of the United States region employed the vigesimal system—based on the number twenty—which was more widely used in Mexico and Central America. It is interesting to consider that some of the Indians using this system lived in California, and others using it dwelt north of the Columbia River on the Pacific, which suggests that they may have had early contacts with people far to the south in Middle America.

The common Indian method of counting was by denoting the fingers of the left hand. It began with the little finger, and the thumb was fifth, or five. In counting the right hand the order was reversed. The right thumb was six, and the right little finger was ten. There were variations in this method of counting with which intertribal traders had to be familiar. Most Indians bent the fingers inward as they counted them, but some tribes began to count with a clenched hand. Each finger was opened as it was counted. Oddly, the Zuñi, who were noted as traders, had the custom of counting the second ten not on the fingers but on the knuckles.

Words were used, of course, in intertribal commerce, but unless a language was thoroughly understood by both buyer and seller—a situation that probably seldom occurred—hand signals were more efficient and a whole lot safer. A few examples prove the case: the Siouan and Algonquian word for "two" was related to the words for "hands" and "legs." In Athapascan the word for "two" meant "feet." In some languages "three" was expressed by joining the words "two" and "one." To some people the word "four" meant "two times two," or "two and two." That could be "four," but to the uninitiated it might suggest "twenty-two."

In some languages there was a word that signified the fingers of the hand, but it excluded the thumb. Some Indians spoke of "eight" as "two from ten," and "seventeen" as "ten plus five and two." Moreover, in many tongues a word uttered in one way gave it a certain meaning, but different tonal inflection might give it an entirely different meaning.

Prehistoric Indians had no scales. They did not use standard weights. There was no such thing as an ounce, a pound, or a ton. There were types of trade, however, in which measuring was more important than counting.

Virtually every linear and circular measurement was accomplished by using the fingers and the arms. Strangely, the foot was not employed as a standard of linear measure, although surface distances were marked off by paces.

The fingers and arms were used in different ways. Among these were finger widths from one to five, palms and spans. A kind of ruler was the length from the elbow to the tip of the extended middle finger. Another was the length from the middle of the chest to the end of the middle finger. Another was the arm outstretched laterally to a right angle with the body. And still another was the distance between the tip of one middle finger to the tip of the other, with arms outstretched on a level line.

The means were adequate. The sign language made prices unmistakable. Yet shrewdness and trading ability and business sense played their parts, and in those ways prehistoric commerce was no different than the commerce of today.

Northern Mountains and Plateaus

Quandary in Wyoming

The country through which Black's Fork passes in haste to join Green River is high, crossed by sweeping plateaus and bold ridges, barren, windy, and bitterly cold much of each year. Unless climatic conditions were less rigorous in the Paleolithic—and there is reason to believe they were at certain periods—it would hardly be expected that primitive people would have entered the region, and if they did, certainly they would not have stayed any great length of time. Whatever the case, the fact remains that they were there, and a very long time ago.

In four summers' work between the years 1935 and 1939, archeologist E. B. Renaud of the University of Denver recovered thousands of artifacts similar in type to Old World Paleolithic tools of great antiquity.[1] In more than threescore sites he recovered fist axes, choppers, scrapers, and flakes that antedate the pre-projectile point stage of man's existence in the Western Hemisphere.

Under the most conservative estimates Old World artifacts of the Early and Middle Paleolithic are dated far back in the Pleistocene. The trouble was, and it still is, that typological similarities are not acceptable to most archeologists as a basis for final decisions.

The eminent Wormington provides the best analysis of the Black's Fork discoveries that has come to my attention: ". . . most archeologists have been reluctant to place much dependence on these typological resemblances, for a variety of reasons. All the artifacts described by Renaud lay on the surface of the ground, and there is absolutely no geological or paleontological proof of antiquity. Furthermore, work in other parts of Wyoming and Montana indicates that when similar implements were found in excavated sites they were part of comparatively recent complexes. . . . It is true that many of Renaud's artifacts were found on high terraces and showed definite signs of abrasion. If it could be proven that this was the result of water action it might provide some evidence of age, for a considerable length of time has elapsed since water last reached these terraces. However, if the smoothing was due to wind erosion it provides no evidence of real antiquity although the fact that some artifacts are worn while others in the same location are not suggests that there are definite age differences between the worn and unworn specimens." [2]

Renaud asserted that the Black's Fork artifacts, based on typology and patination, made three cultures recognizable. The oldest was represented by tools showing typological similarities to those of Early and Middle Paleolithic cultures of the Old World. Both of the other cultures were pre-ceramic, but of more recent age.

In most areas the pre-projectile point stage ended at least twenty thousand years ago. Its beginning in the United States region still remains to be determined, for scientists continue to turn back the archeological chronometer by developing new methods of dating natural and man-made materials. It should be noted that not a great distance away from Black's Fork, on the Snake River in southern Idaho, have been found remains of extinct animals that show evidence of having been killed by Paleolithic hunters more than thirty thousand years ago.[3]

The quandary created by the Black's Fork artifacts may never be resolved, but one thing is certain—Paleolithic men were in the high, windswept country of southwestern Wyoming.

Mountain Trails

When men using Eden, Clovis, Folsom, and other types of projectiles were hunting the immense Pleistocene mammals on the Great Plains and in the Southeastern Woodlands their counterparts were following a similar type of existence in the Rocky Mountains and in the plateau country between them and the Cascade Ranges. In this enormous region, which includes alpine forests, scrublands, great canyons, wide valleys, big lakes, roaring rivers, and deserts, a culture known as the Old Cordilleran developed and prevailed for thousands of years.

The evidence of their presence is ample, their way of life has been revealed, their tools and utensils have been dated. They migrated southward from Alaska on the west side of the Rocky Mountains no later than eleven thousand years ago, and most probably at a much earlier time. Some of them may have come southward on the eastern slope of the mountains and pushed westward through them. They were hunters, gatherers of wild foods, and fishermen. Groups of these people may not have remained long in the mountain-plateau region, electing to continue on southward, perhaps a very great distance, for, as Josephy points out, "spear points and other objects resembling those of the Old Cordilleran Culture have been found in the Great Basin, southern California, Mexico, and parts of South America." [4] Relics of the Old Cordilleran Culture also have been recovered in the Northwest, enabling archeologists to trace the culture's spread eastward from the Cascades. It may, however, climatic conditions permitting, have reached the mountain-plateau region by more direct trails from the north, for the culture extends far up into Canada above Montana and Idaho.

I see no reason to separate, as some persons prefer to do, the Rocky Mountain and plateau regions. The evidence is clear that for many millennia people passed back and forth across both of them. Throughout the long period of the Old Cordilleran Culture, new ideas, new weapons, new customs were exchanged by shifting peoples. There seems to be little doubt that some of these peoples were the ancestors of the Indians belonging to the Shahaptin, Shoshonean, and Salishan linguistic families living in the region at the beginning of the historical period. Long before the coming of the first white explorers to this area in the eighteenth century, intertribal trade channels ran from the Northern Great Plains, over the mountain passes and on to rivers that were part of the Columbia system. Mountain and plateau tribes went eastward to the Plains to hunt buffalo. Military offensives and raids were carried on in both directions. Traits of the Desert Culture of the Great Basin, of the Great Plains Culture, of the northern Pacific Coast Culture, and of the Mountain and Plateau Culture were fused, and characteristics of each of these cultures had influences on the others.

Archeological sites tell the story, and artifacts dated by various methods, including the Carbon-14, provide a chronological record that runs far back into the Pleistocene.* This is true in various locations distributed between western Montana and eastern Washington and Oregon, and between Canada and the Great Basin.

In a stratified site near Helena, Montana, Richard G. Forbis unearthed three levels of occupation.[5] On the lowest level he found Folsom artifacts, and the other two contained different types. On the highest level were points much more recent and similar to a type found

---

* Some of the Wyoming sites were discussed in Part Six because the types of projectile points found in them were identical with those of the Great Plains and other regions. Thus, it was further demonstrated that contacts existed between widely separated peoples, and that hunters using the same types of weapons were seldom confined to one geographical area.

in Nebraska. Other similar finds have been made in Idaho, Wyoming, and Colorado.

Jumping several hundred miles westward, important sites come into focus in eastern Washington, the Columbia River Basin, and southern and eastern Oregon above the northern perimeter of the Great Basin.

The Cascade Range rises as a great barrier between the area of heavy precipitation along the Pacific Coast and the semi-arid region to the east of the mountains. Seven or eight thousand years ago a number of volcanic eruptions occurred in the Cascades. Thick deposits of pumice covered the area, extending for many miles eastward. In several caves in which stratification was clear, L. S. Cressman and his colleagues have found artifacts below the layers of volcanic pumice. Radiocarbon dating of some of them has shown that Indians were living there at least two thousand years before the eruptions, and that the locations were inhabited in later prehistoric periods. At Odell Lake a campsite was found that was overlain by pumice and extended to underlying glacial till.[6]

In Fort Rock Valley a variety of projectiles and tools were found both below and above the pumice. Most interesting among the earliest artifacts were charred sandals made of shredded bark, and fragments of twined basketry. Radiocarbon dating showed the sandals to be more than nine thousand years old, of much greater age than the pumice above them.

In 1952 archeologists under the direction of Cressman began excavating at Five Mile Rapids on the Oregon side of the Columbia River, a short distance east of The Dalles. They operated under a grant provided by the National Science Foundation, and cooperating with them was the National Park Service. For five years the work was continued, and it resulted in the discovery of some of the most important archeological sites in the plateau province.

In a personal communication to Wormington, Cressman wrote that one site "at the head of the Rapids has shown continuous occupation from probably before ten thousand years ago until white contact." [7]

This site, wrote Cressman, "shows change in technological processes from percussion methods of flaking to the varieties of the magnificent stone work characteristic of the Columbia area. In the earliest stage of occupation elk antlers were used for making various kinds of tools and well-made burins are associated with this industry. Sedimentation by the river occurs in the bottom two meters of the site in which artifacts occur. Toward the end of this period fish bones begin to appear, together with the bones of large birds. Following the period of sedimentation occurs a level of heavy occupation with great numbers of bones of salmon and large birds, an extinct vulture, condor, bald eagle, and other large varieties."

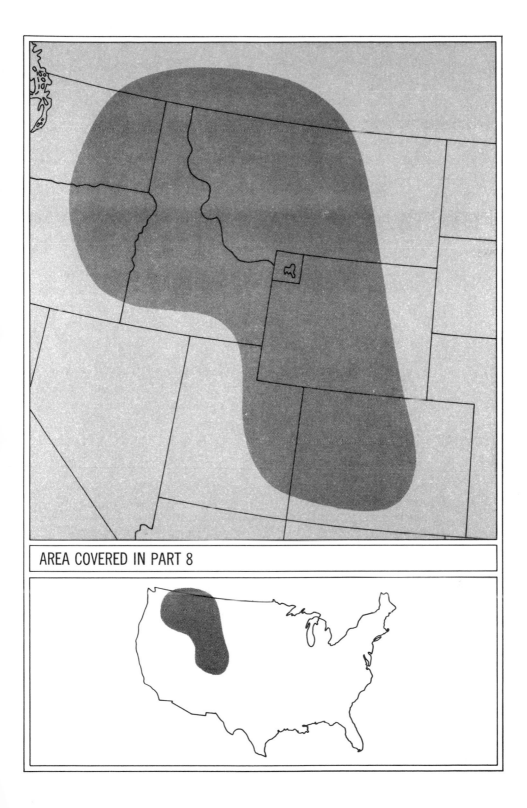

AREA COVERED IN PART 8

In another letter about Five Mile Rapids to archeologist Mark Raymond Harrington, Cressman stated: "The early phase of cultural development . . . fades out about 7,500 years ago. A limited range of artifacts continues until about 6,000 years ago when there is markedly increased activity, followed by the introduction of new types of projectile points probably derived from Great Basin sources. This change is undoubtedly due to in-migration of population." [8]

The Five Mile Rapids site is now covered by U. S. Highway 30 and by the waters behind Dalles Dam.

Lind Coulee in the Columbia Basin plains of Washington was carved by melt waters of Pleistocene glaciers. In 1950 bones of extinct animals and man-made Paleolithic artifacts were found eroding out of the channel walls. Richard D. Daugherty,[9] who directed excavations in the area for two years, wrote that the Lind Coulee Site was situated at the time of occupation at the edge of a sluggish stream or a lake. Some of the material recovered lay under thirteen feet of overburden. Among it were projectile points, some of which were not fluted, chipped stone implements, and large quantities of bones. Daugherty believed, as Wormington records, that the campsite was seasonally occupied, and that the "nature of the deposits, as well as the faunal assemblage, suggests cool moist conditions. Below the bed in which the cultural material was found was a stratum thought to have been formed during the Mankato [glacial] period. Above the artifact-bearing bed was a layer of silt and sand believed to have been deposited by wind during the Altithermal period. It contains lenses and pockets of volcanic ash attributed to a northern Cascade source and equated with a period of volcanic activity which is thought to have occurred some 5,000 or 6,000 years ago." [10]

As in the case of sites farther south, the Lind Coulee artifacts were considerably older than the eruptions. Two Carbon-14 dates obtained from burned bison bones taken from Lind Coulee averaged 8,700 years of age.

Thus, there has been established an incontestable record showing that the mountain and plateau region was occupied by Homo sapiens at least eleven thousand yars ago. Human beings lived continuously in some places through eight, nine, or ten millennia, and were still living in them well into the historical period. But 9000 B.C. is a "safe" date. Archeologists are firmly convinced that men hunted there long before that time, but it is not their way to make unqualified statements on the basis of circumstantial evidence.

A Common Way of Life

Although people of four large linguistic families are known to have occupied the Northern Mountains and Plateaus in prehistoric times, throughout the entire region economic patterns differed only in slight degree. Cultures were characterized by few contrasts and variations. The entire way of life in almost the whole area was virtually the same.

In most sections the winter dwelling was a pit house, dug four to six feet below the surface. Usually it was ten to sixteen feet in diameter—although some prehistoric pit houses were considerably larger—and covered with either a conical or flat roof supported by poles radiating from upright posts. Over the framework were placed cedar planks, a layer of grass and brush, and another layer of earth. An opening in the center of the top was both an entrance and a hole through which smoke escaped.[11]

When warm weather came, people moved into rectangular surface dwellings covered with mats. These houses were customarily about sixteen feet in width and between twenty and sixty feet in length. A smoke opening ran the entire length of an inverted V roof. The main hearth was in the center and was shared by all residents. As many as eight families may have occupied the mat house, each having its own section along one side of the long narrow structure. The mat lodges could be easily dismantled and transported on travois or in canoes to a new location.[12] This often occurred in summer months as people moved in search of vegetable foods, to hunt or to fish.

The prehistoric Indians of the region did not make pottery, but they were expert weavers of grass baskets and clothing, and they fashioned numerous utensils of stone, wood, and horns. Besides bark and grass garments—the usual summer dress of both men and women—they made clothing and leggings of fur and skins. Tribes that crossed the mountains to hunt on the plains possessed quantities of buffalo robes. These were also valuable items of trade, being highly prized by people farther west. From the Pacific via trading trails came the coveted dentalium and olivella shells worn in necklaces and pendants. Jewelry also was manufactured from bones, freshwater clam shells, and wood. Martin notes that a "single pendant of turquoise has come from the region. The nearest known turquoise deposits are in Nevada." [13]

Although several species of roots were used as food, the camas was a staple upon which the people greatly depended. The bulbs, which grew in great profusion on the western slopes of the Rocky Mountains, were dug with a pointed stick, and were cooked by steaming. In the summer large numbers of people gathered on the so-called camas prairies to dig the bulbs and hunt deer. Dr. Walter Hough of the United States National Museum wrote that besides being a staple food throughout the region the camas "was an article of widespread commerce, influenced the migration of tribes, and might have become in time the basis of primitive agriculture, especially in the valley of the Columbia River."

Second only in importance to the camas was the kouse root, from which bread was made. It was dug in April or May, before camas was in season. The kouse was pounded and made into thin cakes, a foot wide and three feet long, which were ribbed from the impression of the poles on which they were laid over the fire to bake.[14]

Another main staple of all tribes of the vast Columbia River Basin was salmon. Even small tributaries of the great watershed teemed with these fish at certain times of the year. They were speared, trapped in weirs, and caught in nets made of Indian hemp cord. Immense quantities were harvested—as well as eels, sturgeon, and various species of trout. The salmon were gutted, split, and hung on drying racks. Sometimes the meat was pounded into a kind of meal. Both the whole dried salmon and the meal were preserved for winter food. The weirs were constructed of wood, rawhide, and hemp. The spears were efficient contraptions with two or three sharp barbed bone heads. Some had detachable heads affixed to the long handle with cord.

The prehistoric peoples of the region were both artists and gamblers. Excellently carved and decorated bone decorations and implements have been recovered. Regarding the art, Martin states that the prevailing type of these regions "was geometric. Implements and ornaments were decorated with incised lines, circle-and-dot designs, and geometric hatched areas. In the Middle Columbia region there existed, in addition, another art type which apparently was the result of a blending of the geometric art of the Plateau with the naturalistic art of the coast. Chief elements of this style were conventionalized human and animal figures, often with accentuated carved ribs, sculptured on stone pipes and mortars, or incised on mortars or bone ornaments." [15]

Beaver teeth, with colored indented dots and stripes, were used as dice.

The Algonquians

There is disagreement among linguists about the Kutenai. The great John Wesley Powell considered them a distinct stock called Kitunahan. Later scholars have expressed the belief they are remote relatives of both the Algonquian and Salishan linguistic families. If the latter verdict is correct, they still are distinct, for they speak a peculiar tongue that is not only difficult to associate with the Algonquian and Salishan languages but is drastically different from the speech of all their neighbors. However, the contention that they originally came of the Algonquian family is growing in favor, for there seems to be little doubt that far back in prehistoric times they dwelt east of the Rocky Mountains north of the Canadian boundary, the early realm of Algonquian peoples.

In the dawn of the historic period they inhabited a large territory in northwestern Montana, northern Idaho, and northeastern Washington. Because of their isolation they were one of the last tribes to be reached by explorers and French and British fur traders.

Kutenai traditions throw little light on the mystery of their origin, and their known history is less illuminating. Even the meaning of their name is unknown. The ethnologist Turney-High believes it derived from the name of one of their bands, the Tunaha, and was first applied to them by the Blackfoot.[16] The Nez Percé and the Salish called them "water people." [17]

After their migration from the Northern Plains, the Kutenai became separated in two general divisions. This situation creates more ethnographic puzzles, for the members of the two divisions differed greatly in their characters and many of their customs. A north-south line drawn through the present little town of Libby, Montana, would serve as a boundary marking the respective habitats of the Upper and Lower Kutenai.[18] Although they lived in mountains west of the Continental Divide, the Upper Kutenai never entirely abandoned their former way of life and journeyed eastward to the Northern Great Plains to hunt buffalo. The Lower Kutenai depended largely on fish, small game, and roots for their subsistence—the way of life of the tribes living farther west on tributaries of the Columbia.

Kutenai traditions recount that they were forced to seek refuge in the Rocky Mountains by powerful Plains tribes. That this claim may have a basis in fact is indicated by their intense hatred for the Blackfoot, their traditional enemies, whom they called Sahantla—"bad people." Their name for the Assiniboine was "cut-throats," and for the Cree "liars."

The Nez Percé and Salish apparently had good reason to speak of the Kutenai as "water people," for the Lower Kutenai, whom they knew best, had long been river and lake Indians. They traveled on the big lakes and rivers of the upper Columbia watershed, as far north as British Columbia, in canoes. O. T. Mason of the United States Museum discovered that the "peculiar bark canoes" of the Lower Kutenai were similar to "some of those used in the Amur region of Asia." [19]

According to Professor Alexander F. Chamberlain of Clark University, the Kutenai generally were well developed physically and ranked among the taller Indians of the region. They were not warlike, and were noteworthy for their morality and kindness. The Lower Kutenai were more primitive than the others, were still using stone hammers

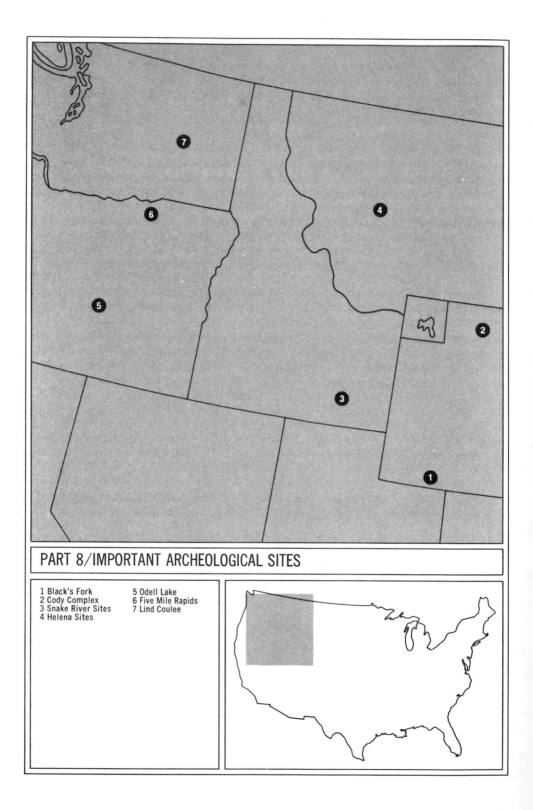

PART 8/IMPORTANT ARCHEOLOGICAL SITES

1 Black's Fork
2 Cody Complex
3 Snake River Sites
4 Helena Sites
5 Odell Lake
6 Five Mile Rapids
7 Lind Coulee

late in the nineteenth century, and were incurably addicted to ancient forms of gambling.

Speaking of the tribe as a whole, however, Chamberlain stated that "more than any other Indians of the country they have avoided drunkenness and lewd intercourse with the whites. They are not excessively given to emotional instability, do not lack a sense of interest, and can concentrate attention when necessary."

The prehistoric social system of the Kutenai is believed to have been quite simple, and no evidence of the existence of totems or secret societies has been found by ethnologists. A chieftainship was hereditary, prisoners of war were enslaved, and relatives were held responsible for the debts of a deceased person. Marriage was polygamous, and adultery was not severely punished. States Chamberlain: "Religion was a sort of sun worship, and the belief in the ensoulment of all things and in reincarnation prevailed. The land of the dead was in the sun, from which at some time all the departed would descend to Lake Pend d'Oreille to meet the Kutenai then living." [20]

One more note to add to the confusion about the Kutenai: most of their cosmogonic legends seem to belong to the Northwest Pacific cycle. Some of their animal tales belong to the cycle of the Rocky Mountain region. Other traditional stories have Siouan and Algonquian aspects. The form of their heads indicates a race mixture.

The international boundary divided the Kutenai between the United States and Canada, as Swanton states, "to the considerable inconvenience of the tribe." [21]

Even less is known of the Atsina than of the Kutenai, and they were never an important tribe, at least not in late prehistoric times or after the arrival of the white man. There seems to be no doubt that originally they were a band or division of the Arapaho,* and lived with them on the Northern Great Plains, possibly in the Red River Country. Swanton states that the languages of both the Arapaho and Atsina "point to the region of the Algonquian tribes northeast of the Plains for their origin." [22] Mooney wrote that the Atsina "in most respects are regarded by the Arapaho proper as inferior to them." [23] This assertion is given support by the name with which the Arapaho identified them. It was *Hitumena,* meaning "beggars" or "spongers."

After the Arapaho migrated across the Missouri to the high Northern Plains the Atsina were cut off from them, possibly by the Crow. The separation probably occurred in the eighteenth century. The Atsina continued northwest to Milk River and ranged northward to the Saskatchewan in Canada. They formed an alliance with the Blackfoot, whose name for them was *Atsena,* which is supposed to mean "gut

---

* See Part Six.

people." Thus, it appears that the Blackfoot gave them the name by which they would be known to history. The Atsina called themselves "white clay people."

Whether warfare or family differences forced the Atsina to leave the Arapaho remains uncertain. Most likely the schism was caused by a combination of pressures. Traditions indicate that the Atsina were not characterized as stable people. They were good hunters but never distinguished for their bravery or prowess in war. There were few of them left by the time Americans had conquered the West.

Since the late years of the prehistoric period the Blackfoot must be classed as both Plains and Mountain Indians, for this enormous confederacy dominated a vast territory spreading between the North Saskatchewan River in Canada, down the eastern flanks of the Rockies, and reaching deep into the mountains beyond the Gallatin, Jefferson, and Madison rivers—the headwaters of the Missouri—in southwestern Montana. The region was not always their homeland. They came, as did other Algonquian tribes, from the woodlands northeast of the Great Plains. The migration must have taken place a long time ago. Ethnologists think that the Blackfoot were the earliest Algonquians to move westward to the Northern Great Plains and the mountains, and that they began their trek long before the discovery of America.

The findings of scientists, however, are contested by Blackfoot traditions. One of the first white men to know them was David Thompson, an educated and inquisitive explorer and fur trader, who spent the winter of 1787–1788 in a Blackfoot camp in Alberta. He sought to determine their origin, and aged warriors invariably declared they had come from the Northwest.[24] So they have continued to maintain ever since.

Swanton calls the Blackfoot speech "the most aberrant of all the well-recognized tongues of the Algonquian linguistic family except Arapaho and Atsina." [25] Noting that Blackfoot "differs most markedly in its word formation from the presumed parent tongue spoken by tribes living in the western Great Lakes region," Ewers suggests that "relative isolation from other Algonkian-speaking peoples, on the one hand, and prolonged tribes speaking alien tongues, on the other, may help to explain the considerable differences between Blackfoot and all other Algonkian dialects." [26]

In a remote period when they were fewer in number—wherever they dwelt—the Blackfoot probably were one tribe, but by the time they had reached their northwestern plains-mountains domain three distinct and politically independent divisions had evolved. Farthest north were the Siksika, or Blackfoot proper. To the south of them were the Kainah, or Blood. The southernmost division, and the largest, was the Piegan, living along the present international border and deep into western

Montana. In these three divisions nearly half a hundred bands are identifiable.

The Blackfoot were polygamists. Before reaching the menopause no woman needed to remain unmarried. A man might marry several sisters. A friend of a deceased warrior would marry his widow. Affluent Blackfoot men frequently had as many as seven wives. Thompson told of a leader who had twenty-two sons and four daughters by five wives.[27]

The Blackfoot were exceeded by few, if any, other northwestern Indians as fighters, hunters, and raiders. They were feared by tribes from Hudson's Bay to the Missouri. Intellectually and physically they ranked high among all American Indians. Mooney states that they were "a restless, aggressive, and predatory people, and were constantly at war with all their neighbors, the Cree, Assiniboine, Sioux, Crows, Flatheads, and Kutenai." Intrusions upon Blackfoot territory were efficiently and viciously repelled. Even though the divisions were politically autonomous, each having its own council and elective leaders, in defending their homeland and in warfare the Blackfoot acted in unqualified unison. According to Mooney, they maintained a military and fraternal organization known as All Comrades, and there were at least twelve other orders to which both men and women could belong.[28]

That the Blackfoot were handsome and colorful is made apparent in the general description of them which Ewers composed from numerous sources. The men were "tall, well-proportioned, and muscular, with manly features and intelligent countenances. Their eyes were large, black, and piercing, their noses full and straight, their teeth white and regular, and their hair long, straight, and black. They plucked the hair from their faces to keep them smooth. The women were known for their good features, and were somewhat hardened by constant exposure to the weather.

"Blackfoot men generally wore their hair loose around their necks, with a long narrow lock falling over the bridge of the nose and cut square at the lower end. Young dandies painted their face in stripes, circles, dots, and other designs in several colors. . . . Red was the preferred color, but the warriors also employed yellow ochre and a glossy lead color obtained from west of the Rockies.

"Men did not wear breechclouts. However, their long skin leggings, which were tied to the belt, may have crossed in front, affording concealment of the privates while leaving the buttocks bare. Skin moccasins, which were lined with buffalo hair in winter, and a buffalo robe completed the man's everyday costume. On dress occasions men wore skin shirts trimmed with locks of their enemies' hair and cut skin fringes, and decorated with porcupine quill embroidery. Some men wore feathers in their hair and necklaces of grizzly bear claws.

"Women wore their hair long and loose. Their principal garment was a sleeveless, skin dress in the form of a slip. Its length fell to the wearer's ankles. The slip was supported by straps over the shoulders. Probably women wore separate skin sleeves in cold weather, held up by skin cords tied at the back of the neck. Cut fringes and porcupine quillwork decorated these dresses." [29] These pictures of the prehistoric Blackfoot are made possible not only through archeological investigations and ethnographic studies, but because some of the first British traders in their country took the trouble to write of them as they were at the very beginning of the historical period.

The significance of the name Piegan is uncertain. It may mean "those who possessed poorly dressed or torn robes," [30] but the origin of this translation is unknown, and if it is correct it seems inappropriate for these proud people. *Kainah* signified "many chiefs." According to one scholar, Prince Maximilian of Wied Neuweid, the name Bloods was given to them when they returned home after massacring a band of Kutenai with the blood of their victims on their faces and hands.[31] Other students think the name may have derived from their custom of coloring their faces and robes blood-red. In any case, the Kainah didn't like the name, preferring to call themselves Many Chiefs.

There is no mystery as to why the entire tribe came to be called Blackfoot. Siksika comes from the word *siksinam,* meaning "black," and *ka* is the root of *ogkatsh,* meaning "foot." The people of all three divisions, the Piegan, the Kainah, and the Siksika, dyed their moccasins black.

The Salishan

Of all the numerous tribes in the Northern Mountain and Plateau Region which belong to the inner division of the large Salishan linguistic family the best known are the people erroneously called Flatheads. Their proper name is Salish, and it means simply "people." It is popularly thought that they were given the name Flatheads by other Indians because they followed the practice of deforming the heads of infants. The opposite is true. They were called Flatheads because, unlike some of their congenitors who lived farther to the west, they left their heads in a normal condition, that is, flat on top, instead of deforming them by pressure to slope toward the crown.

In attempting to write about the prehistoric Salish the historian is left in a quandary. Their earliest known homeland about which there seems to be no dispute was in the mountains of western Montana, extending into western Idaho, southward to some of the headwaters of the Missouri, and centering in the vicinity of Flathead Lake. Their name was originally applied by ethnologists and linguists to the Indians inhabiting this area, but was later extended to include all people speaking dialects of the same language. Therefore, the Salishan family includes tribes spread all the way from the Montana mountains to Puget Sound, southern British Columbia, and the coast of Oregon.

In the region under consideration in this part, besides the Salish proper, there were nine other tribes of some importance in prehistoric times who spoke the Salishan tongue. The culture and economy of all these people, except the Flatheads, were virtually identical. They lived by fishing, hunting, and gathering wild foods, especially the camas and other roots. The main difference between them and the Salish proper of western Montana was that the latter were both mountain and plains Indians, and regularly traveled east of the mountains to hunt buffalo. For them this was a perilous, and sometimes tragic journey, for they were attacked by the Crows, Blackfoot, and other tribes who looked upon them as intruders on their respective hunting domains.

About Pend d'Oreille and Priest lakes and on the lower Clark's Fork were the Kalispel. They hunted as far north as Canada and in the Salmon River Country, and may have ranged even farther in remote times. Their name is believed to mean "camas." The first fur traders to meet them, apparently French-Canadians, called them Pend d'Oreilles because nearly all of them wore large shell earrings.

The Skitswish lived on the upper Spokane River, about Lake Coeur d'Alene, and on the Clearwater River. They still live in the same country. The meaning of their name is unknown, and they have no tradition that might throw light on their origins or early migrations.

The Indian name of the Chelan has never been discovered. They dwelt about the lake that bears the same name. Nothing more is known about them, except that they spoke the same Salishan dialect as the so-called Wenatchee people and may have once been a part of that tribe.

The Sinkiuse lived on the east side of the upper Columbia River from Fort Okanogan to Point Eaton in Washington. Their name is believed to have belonged at one time to people who inhabited the Umatilla Valley. The Nez Percé called them "arrow people." One of their noted leaders was named Moses, and his followers were known as the Moses Band, but his christening undoubtedly took place after the arrival of white men. As some of their most important bands lived along the Columbia, they came to be known to fur traders as the Sinkiuse-Columbia tribe.

The Methow, whose Indian name is unknown, lived on the Methow River, and were closely associated with the Moses Columbia band.

The name of the Okanogan is believed to be derived from some landmark on the Okanogan River near Okanogan Falls. They hunted northward into Canada, where it is thought they fought and drove out people of Athapascan stock. When the international boundary was established they were living on both sides of it.

Although it may appear to be French, Sanspoil is a native Salishan word, but its significance has never been learned. The Sanspoil lived on Sanspoil Creek and the Columbia River below Big Bend. Their dialect places them in close connection with the easternmost tribes of the Salishan family.

Spokan may mean "sun people," but this translation is doubtful. Some ethnologists think the Spokan may be composed of several distinct tribes that became fused over a long period of time, but this, too, remains uncertain. They lived on the streams now spelled Spokane and Little Spokane, and no one knows how that occurred, either, unless it happened that early white men couldn't spell the name correctly or arbitrarily decided it looked better with the appended letter.

Regarding the origins of the Salish proper, or Flatheads, prominent ethnologists are locked—and always have been—in what apparently is hopeless disagreement. Hodge wrote that physically and culturally "the coast and interior Salish belong to different groups, the former being affiliated to some extent with the other coast people to the north, and the interior Salish resembling interior stocks in their own neighborhood." [32] This suggests that both the coast and interior Salish had dwelt in their respective areas for a very long time.

A quote from Swanton,[33] who cites several other authorities, points up the controversy: "According to Teit [34] the Salish once extended farther to the east, and there were related tribes in that region which he calls Sematuse and Tunahe. As Turney-High [35] has pointed out, however, the Tunahe were evidently a Kutenai division; and the Sematuse, if not mythical, seem to have been an alien people in possession of this country before the Salish entered it.

"Teit states that these Salish were driven westward out of the Plains by the Blackfoot, particularly after that tribe obtained guns. Turney-High, on the other hand, regards the Salish as rather late intruders into the Plains from the west. . . . Just how far the Salish retired westward [clear to the Pacific?] may be a matter of argument, nor does it affect the theory of an earlier eastward migration if such a movement can be substantiated on other grounds."

I shall proffer a suggestion that I think is safe. It is that the Salish came originally from Siberia. However, I should not be surprised if some scholar would counter my idea with the postulation that they sprang from several other tribes and originated in western North America.

The Shahaptin

First off, it seems proper to explode another myth. The Nez Percé, the largest and most important tribe of the Shahaptian linguistic family, did not customarily pierce their noses.

Since Lewis and Clark are believed to be the first white men the Nez Percé met, these intrepid explorers are held responsible for the misnomer. Their journal for September, 1805, contains the statement that these Indians "call themselves *Chopunnish* or Pierced Noses." The following spring, again meeting the Nez Percé on their return trip, they wrote that "the ornament of the nose is a single shell of the wampum." [36] The name was erroneously adopted by later explorers and fur traders, many of whom had never seen the Nez Percé, and thereby became popularly and permanently applied to them.

The Nez Percé long have believed—and probably correctly—that the name was applied to them because some early interpreter, most likely a French-Canadian, misunderstood a designation in the sign language.[37] Or it may have been, as Ella E. Clark notes, that "some early white man saw among them a few members of some tribe that did pierce the nose." [38] A missionary who lived with the Nez Percé for many years, Kate McBeth, stated: "The Nez Percé deny that they ever did, as a tribe, pierce their noses. Occasionally one did." [39] How Lewis and Clark made their mistake is not known, but they, too, may have seen some Indians among the Nez Percé with pierced noses, or they may have misunderstood a sign language designation.

Linguists think the *Chopunnish* of Lewis and Clark is a corruption of *Tsutpeli,* one of the names the Nez Percé had for themselves.[40] Ella Clark quotes an aged Nez Percé as saying, "In the old language that died with the old Indians of my childhood, our name was *Choo-pin-it-pa-loo,* meaning 'people of the mountains.' " [41]

It would have been a most appropriate name, for the Nez Percé were largely mountain Indians, in both prehistoric and historic times occupying central and western Idaho, northeastern Oregon, and southeastern Washington. They roamed between the Blue Mountains in Oregon and the Bitter Root Mountains bordering Idaho and Montana, and sometimes on hunting expeditions or forays crossed the Continental Divide to the headwaters of the Missouri River.

Neither ethnographic evidence nor traditions have been obtained to indicate the origins of the Nez Percé or other Shahaptin tribes living westward of them, such as the Palouse, Wallawalla, Wanapam, Yakima, Cayuse, and Umatilla. They can be described only as they were when first encountered by white men in 1805.

Speaking generally of the Shahaptian people, Henry W. Hinshaw of the Bureau of American Ethnology and Dr. Livingston Farrand of

Columbia University state that in customs and habits they were "fairly homogeneous. Family organization was loose and showed no traces of a clan system. Village communities of varying size were the rule, but were prevented from normal development by the seasonal changes of residence necessitated by the character of the food supply. Chiefs were local in authority except in times of emergency. Salmon was the staple article of food, but . . . hunting various kinds of game was common. . . . Roots and berries also were much used as food, but no agriculture was evident.

"The Shahaptian tribes have always had a high reputation for bravery, and, except for certain sporadic outbreaks, have been friendly with the whites." [42]

The Nez Percé had the misfortune to dwell in a country where gold was discovered. White miners and settlers swarmed onto reservation lands granted to them in Oregon and Idaho, yet for several years Nez Percé leaders were able to prevent their people from fighting. The federal government, refusing to punish the white invaders, and repudiating its pledges, ordered the Nez Percé to give up their valuable Oregon lands—which settlers were forcefully taking from them—and agree to confinement on a reservation in northern Idaho.

The Nez Percé, after considerably more than half a century of struggling to obtain justice and to live in peace with Americans, at last violently struck back. The government promptly sent troops to destroy them.

But the valiant fight of the Nez Percé against overwhelming forces, and their masterly retreat toward Canada under the leadership of the famous Chief Joseph, is a story that belongs to the history of warfare between Indians and unconscionable politicians.

The Shoshonean

One easily becomes lost while attempting to follow the prehistoric trails of the Bannock Indians. Their tongue was a dialect of the language spoken by the Northern Paiute, who ranged over a large part of the Great Basin. Apparently they were a detached band of the Northern Paiute, but why, when, or how they separated from these consanguineous relatives, and became established in territory far northeast of the Great Basin are questions that bring sharply conflicting answers.

If traditions of the Bannock are correct, they were at one time potentially among the richest Indians in North America. They claimed as a part of their territory the southwestern Montana area that included the fabulously rich gold mines of Alder Gulch and Virginia City. Swanton thinks it probable they were driven across the mountains into the Salmon River Valley of Idaho at a comparatively recent period.[43]

Some ethnologists believe the Bannock were culturally, linguistically, and politically a distinct tribe. Others hold the opinion that although they speak a Great Basin dialect of the Shoshonean language there are no cultural or political differences between them and their relatives, the Northern Shoshoni, among whom they were living when first encountered by white men.[44]

Language Groups in Part Eight

NORTHERN MOUNTAINS AND PLATEAUS

Shoshonean:	Bannock	Algonquian:	Atsina
	Shoshoni (Northern)		Kutenai
			Siksika (Blackfoot)
Salishan:	Salish (Flatheads)		
	Kalispell	Shahaptin:	Nez Percé
	Skitswish		Palouse
	(Coeur d'Alene)		Wallawalla
	Chelan		Yakima
	Columbia		Cayuse
	Colville		Umatilla
	Methow		
	Okanogan		
	Sanspoil		
	Spokan		

There is no doubt that the large territories inhabited by both people —if they were distinct tribes—overlapped, perhaps for centuries, in eastern Idaho, western Wyoming, and southwestern Montana. Nor is there any doubt that the Bannock and the Northern Shoshoni intermarried, and although each group spoke their own dialect they hunted together, raided together, fought common enemies together, and occupied the same villages. Inasmuch as the Bannock were far fewer in number than the Shoshoni they were gradually absorbed by them. Even so they created a permanent place for themselves in western history, and the memory of them is preserved in place names.

Although the Shoshonean linguistic family is one of the largest in America, linguists have not been able to discover the significance of the word *Shoshoni*. It apparently does not belong to the Shoshonean tongue, or to any of its dialects.

Numerous tribes called the Shoshoni by a name indicating "grass lodges, thatch lodges, grass house people," or by some other variation of the term. In the sign language they were identified by a serpentine motion of the hand with the index finger extended. Early explorers

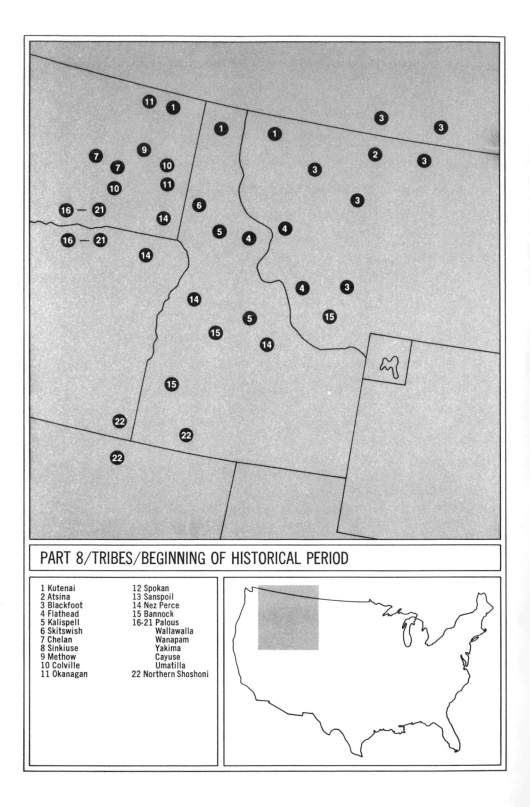

PART 8/TRIBES/BEGINNING OF HISTORICAL PERIOD

1 Kutenai
2 Atsina
3 Blackfoot
4 Flathead
5 Kalispell
6 Skitswish
7 Chelan
8 Sinkiuse
9 Methow
10 Colville
11 Okanagan

12 Spokan
13 Sanspoil
14 Nez Perce
15 Bannock
16-21 Palous
      Wallawalla
      Wanapam
      Yakima
      Cayuse
      Umatilla
22 Northern Shoshoni

and fur hunters and their interpreters thought the gesture meant Snake Indians. Actually, it indicated the method with which they wove their grass and thatch lodges.

NORTHERN MOUNTAINS AND PLATEAUS

Earliest Population Estimates*

Kutenai (1780)	1,200	**Spokan** (1780)	2,000
Atsina (1780)	3,000	**Nez Percé** (1805)	6,000
Blackfoot (1780)	15,000	**Palouse** (1780)	5,000
Flatheads (1800)	3,000(?)	**Wallawalla-Umatilla** (1780)	1,500
Kalispell (1780)	1,200(?)		
Skitswish (1780)	2,000(?)	**Cayuse** (1780)	500
Chelan (unknown)		**Bannock** (1845)	1,000
Columbia-Sinkiuse (1700)	6,000(?)	**Shoshoni** (Northern) (1845)	3,000
Colville (1800)	2,500	**Yakima** (1780)	3,000
Methow (1780)	800	**Wanapam** (1780)	1,800
Okanagan (1780)	2,500		
Sanspoil (1780)	1,600	**TOTAL**	62,600

* See Note, Population Table, Part One.

Dates to Remember

1787–1788—The noted British explorer, cartographer, and fur trader David Thompson spent this winter among Piegan bands of the Blackfoot.

1805—Early in June the expedition of Lewis and Clark neared the Rocky Mountains beyond the Great Falls of the Missouri. This was the country of the Blackfoot. Ahead of them was nearly a thousand miles of wilderness never entered by white men.

1805—In August, the Lewis and Clark company encountered the Shoshoni in eastern Idaho, being the first Americans known to have met any of these people in their northern homeland. Supplied with horses, the expedition went on to discover other tribes of the upper Columbia tributaries.*

---

* The Indians of the Northern Mountain and Plateau Region had long possessed horses when Lewis and Clark reached them. The horses originally had been obtained both by trade and theft from tribes closer to the Spanish settlements of the Southwest.

1806—Under the date of Wednesday, August 11, these words are found in the journals of Lewis and Clark: "At noon they proceeded on about two miles, when they observed a canoe near the shore. They immediately landed, and were equally surprised and pleased at discovering two men by the names of Dickson and Hancock, who had come from the Illinois on a hunting expedition."

The notation was made a short distance below the confluence of the Missouri and Yellowstone rivers, when the first American expedition to break a trail to the Pacific was on its way home.[45] The significance of the meeting with the two trappers stemmed no more from its reality than from its prognostication. The first American Mountain Men had reached the Yellowstone, on the edge of an incredibly immense wilderness which, except for the few eyes of the Lewis and Clark company that had gazed briefly across a fragment of its perimeter, had never been explored.

Little information about Joseph Dickson and Forrest Hancock survived them. In the previous year they had been among the Teton (Sioux) and the Cheyenne, and were eager to visit more remote regions. They spent several days with the expedition, and talked of their plan to remain through the winter on the upper Missouri. The ears of a young man, an accomplished hunter and a conscientious soldier, were attentive to their words. He questioned them, and his apparently sincere interest in their proposal brought an invitation to join them.

The young man's name was John Colter. On August 14 (1806) he made his decision, and the expedition account tells of the event in this way: "In the evening we were applied to by one of our men, Colter, who was desirous of joining the two trappers . . . as he had always performed his duty, and his services might be dispensed with, we agreed that he might go. . . . We, therefore, supplied him, as did his comrades also, with powder and lead, and a variety of articles which might be useful to him, and he left us the next day."

With that military discharge John Colter began a career of adventure and discovery that was to amaze the civilized world and win for him a place among the greatest of all western explorers.

He spent the winter of 1806–1807 with Dickson and Hancock somewhere on the Yellowstone. In the spring he started alone for St. Louis. Near the mouth of the Platte River he met the fur trading expedition of Manuel Lisa. The historian Hiram Martin Chittenden stated: "To this band of adventurers into unknown country the services of a man like Colter, who had spent a winter there and had twice passed entirely through it, could not but be very important. He was persuaded (if persuasion was necessary) to join the [Lisa] expedition and accordingly turned back a second time from his journey towards home." [46]

Lisa established Fort Manuel, the first trading post in the region, at the confluence of the Big Horn and Yellowstone rivers. From this point John Colter set out alone on the perilous and remarkable journey that was to result in the discovery of totally unknown rivers, mountain ranges, geographical phenomena, and Indian peoples—the journey that would bring him fame.

His specific mission was to notify tribes he might encounter of the establishment of the post and to persuade them to come to it with furs to trade. According to Henry Brackenridge, who wrote in 1811, "this man, with a pack of thirty pounds weight, his gun and some ammunition, went upwards of five hundred miles to the Crow nation; gave them information, and proceeded from thence to several other tribes." [47] Colter apparently found the Crows on the Wind River in Wyoming, and induced them to guide him over the great range rising to the west.

How many Crow accompanied Colter is not a matter of record, but in a fight with a band of Blackfoot the Crow were victorious, suggesting that there were a considerable number of them. Nor can Colter's trail be accurately delineated. Indeed, he might have traveled by several routes, and ever since his great venture scholars have quarreled about the matter.[48] But there is no doubt where he went.

In all probability the Crow took him up Wind River, crossed the Wind River Mountains through Togwotee Pass, and saw ahead the splendor of the Teton Range and Snake River sweeping through Jackson Hole. He crossed the Teton Range by Teton Pass, reaching Pierre's Hole in Idaho. There the party was attacked by some Blackfoot, and Colter, "by the necessity of the situation, was compelled to take part with the Crows. He distinguished himself greatly and received a severe wound in the leg. The Blackfeet were defeated, but not until they had seen the pale-faced ally of their enemies, to whom, no doubt, they attributed their discomforture." [49]

After the fight, the Crow, not wishing to give the Blackfoot time to bring up reinforcements, departed for their home, and once again Colter was alone. He recrossed the Tetons to Jackson Hole and turned north, according to Burton Harris,[50] passing Jackson Lake and going on to the West Thumb of Yellowstone Lake. Colter discovered the wonders of the area that today comprises Yellowstone National Park.

After viewing the geysers, boiling springs, bubbling mud pots, and colored terraces in their setting of towering mountains, he may have left the strange region via Cooke Pass. In any case, he saw the immense tar springs at the forks of the Stinkingwater River, which became known to Mountain Men as Colter's Hell.

Colter opened to the world more of the Northern Mountain Region than any other individual explorer. He was the first white man to see the headwaters of the Colorado River of the West, the first to penetrate

Jackson Hole, the Yellowstone National Park, to cross the Wind River and Teton Ranges, to look upon the sources of the Snake River, great tributary of the Columbia.

How much of his journey Colter made on foot and how much on horseback—some students insist he went entirely on foot—is not known, but it is certain that before he returned to Lisa's post at the mouth of the Big Horn he had traveled considerably more than a thousand miles.

SOME INDIAN PLACE NAMES*

Montana

    Potomac, town
    Navajo, town
    Illinois, mountains
    Sioux, pass
    Absarokee, town
    Kootenai, river, mountains
    Flathead, county, lake
    Kalispell, town
    Calispell, mountains
    Chinook, town

Idaho

    Oneida, county, town
    Idaho, state
    Kootenai, river, county, town
    Bannock, county, river, mountains
    Shoshoni, county, town
    Palouse, river
    Spokane, river

Wyoming

    Shawnee, town
    Wyoming, state
    Osage, town
    Absaroka, mountains
    Shoshoni, river, town, mountains
    Cheyenne, town
    Arapaho, town

Colorado

    Yuma, county, town
    Choclawhatchee, river
    Tioga, town
    Erie, town
    Cheraw, town
    Arickaree, town
    Cheyenne, county, mountains
    Pawnee, river, town
    Arapaho, county, mountains, town
    Kiowa, county, town
    Comanche, river
    Ute, town

* Tribes and tribal subdivisions.

Scientific Note—Indian Foods, Medicines, and Plants

Plants domesticated by Indians of North and South America furnish almost half of the world's food supply.

In quantities produced, the leading staples of the world dietary are rice, potatoes, maize, and wheat. Two of these, potatoes and maize, were first domesticated in the New World, and became known to white men only after the voyages of Columbus.

From corn hundreds of products have been derived, including oils, feeds for livestock, meals, flours, starches, mashes, and such widely used dishes as hominy, hominy grits, pone, succotash (corn and lima beans), breads, and muffins.[51]

Two other important food plants developed by Indians are manioc, a staple in Africa, and the sweet potato. In addition, Indians introduced to the white man more than eighty other domesticated plants, among them peanuts, various squashes, peppers, tomatoes, pumpkins, pine-apples, avocados, cacao (for chocolate), chicle (for chewing gum), many types of beans, and other vegetables and fruits well known in countless countries.[52]

The commercial cottons of the world are derived principally from the species and varieties cultivated by American Indians.[53]

All the cotton in the United States is of American Indian origin, as is the long-fiber cotton raised in Egypt and other parts of Africa.[54] Native American varieties of cotton are used in the manufacture of most of the world's clothing.

"If the American Indian had not domesticated any food plants," writes the eminent anthropologist Harold E. Driver, "the world today would have less to eat and population would be smaller. Because each plant grows best in a limited range of soils and climates, Old World domesticated plants would not flourish as well in the regions most suited to New World domesticates. It took centuries to domesticate a plant to the point of high yield of nourishing food, and if the Indians had not achieved this for maize, potatoes, manioc, sweet potatoes, and some other food plants, it is doubtful if Europeans would ever have accomplished it for these species. They would almost certainly have devoted their attention to improving rice, wheat, and other plants familiar to them and would not have recognized the nutritional potential of the scrubby wild relatives of the American domesticates." [55]

Tobacco, which originated in South America, was being cultivated and blended by Indians throughout both South and North America before the discovery of the New World. Within two centuries after 1492 it was being grown around the world. Columbus and his sailors were the first white men to know of it. On the Caribbean islands they saw Indians smoking large cigars made of rolled tobacco leaves.

In today's pharmacology are to be found at least fifty-nine important drugs developed and used by prehistoric American Indians. Best known among them are coca in cocaine and novocaine; curare, a muscle relaxant, used to stop breathing while a rubber tube is inserted into the windpipe during anesthesia; cinchona bark, the source of quinine commonly used throughout the world as a cold and fever remedy; datura, an ingredient of pain-relievers; cascara sagrada in laxatives; ephedra, in nasal remedies; hydrastis, the dried rhizome and roots of a goldenseal used as a bitter tonic, hemostatic, and antiseptic; and jalap, a powdered drug made from a dried purgative root and containing resinous glycosides.[56]

Lotions to prevent sunburn are nothing new in the world. They were used by prehistoric American Indians, especially by those living in the desert regions of the Southwest. Usually they were compounded of red ocher and animal fat. If they were more greasy and malodorous than the so-called suntan concoctions of today, they were no less effective.

The
Great Basin

Between the Wasatch Mountains of Utah and the Sierra Nevada of California, a distance of six hundred miles, lies a geographic phenomenon. From north to south it extends nearly nine hundred miles, beginning in central Oregon and ending in Mexico.

It is a region containing peaks that are mantled with deep snow in winter and burning deserts that are below sea level and in which the annual precipitation frequently measures below two inches. High on the walls of barren ranges can be found the shoreline marks of gigantic bodies of water—long vanished—that were created far back in the Pleistocene, thirty-five to forty thousand years ago, when long tongues of glacial ice began their final retreat. It is a region of vast, sweeping, sage-blanketed valleys, rugged plateaus, dry lake beds as smooth and devoid of vegetation as a cement floor, and towering angular mesas that trace geometric patterns upon the sky. Mount Whitney, the highest peak in the western United States, soars in awesome splendor not far from Death Valley, the lowest place in the Western Hemisphere.

Rivers enter and rivers rise in this gigantic area, but there is no water outlet to the sea.[1]

For countless millennia the Great Basin has been as the first white explorers found it, in its greater part a forbidding land, tortured by alkali, beset by fierce heat and numbing cold, scarred by winds and flash floods, displaying the fantastic wounds inflicted by ages of erosion, arid, desolate, and inspiring in its weirdness and its immensity.

It was not always that way, not always so unfriendly and uninviting.

There were periods in its past when much, if not all, of it was covered with a rich grass carpet, a land jeweled by freshwater lakes and dependable streams, a land over which Pleistocene mammals—camel, bison, horse, mammoth, sloth—roamed in great numbers.

That man was contemporaneous in the Great Basin with these long-extinct animals, that he hunted them and gathered wild plant foods for his subsistence, has been proven by irrefutable evidence unearthed by archeologists during many years of digging—evidence that is still being discovered.

The Years at Tule Springs

"We were heading south out of Tonopah, Nevada, in Frank Bell's old Dodge truck and trailer loaded with camp gear, 40 days grub, a 30-gallon tank for storing drinking water, a small Yukon-type cook stove and several old railroad cross-ties for firewood. . . . We were hoping to make the first collection of Pleistocene mammalian fossils in the little-known Nevada field."

So begins the report of one of the most significant archeological discoveries in America. It was written by Fenley Hunter of Flushing, New York. With him in the battered truck were Frank Bell of Tonopah, and Albert C. Silberling of Harlowton, Montana. All three men were paleontologists assigned to collect bones of extinct animals for the American Museum of Natural History.[2] The year of their expedition was 1932.

A friend who was familiar with the southern Nevada area had advised them to head for Indian Springs, "and visit its only inhabitant, one Tim Harnedy, a long-time resident of the desert." After a week of driving on dirt roads and futile prospecting in numerous places along the way, they reached Harnedy's lonely cabin, and "were soon the recipients of his unbounded hospitality." Harnedy knew nothing about fossils, and eventually confided to Hunter "he had thought our mission a most curious one and he had harbored the opinion we were really looking for silver!"

The old desert-dweller, valuable as a guide, soon came to understand that other treasures were to be found in the bleak uninhabited country. Wrote Hunter: "A week of steady prospecting up and down the main drainage of Las Vegas Valley from Indian Springs yielded an abundance of fossil shells, fragments of bison, camel, horse, and many mammoth bones (52 different mammoth localities in all), so we decided to pitch our tent five miles east of the Tule Springs turnoff from the main highway, on the south side of Las Vegas wash. By this time we had tramped more than two hundred miles in Clark County and were glad to settle down. . . ."

It was December, and the conditions under which they persistently pursued their digging were anything but pleasant, yet the enthusiastic Hunter thought "the wide and rapid variations in temperature, from freezing and below at night to 80 degrees or more at noon on sunny days, was highly stimulating. The arid condition of the desert, with strong winds almost daily, produced sandstorms which would often obscure the sun. Heavy rain storms were not infrequent, but the wind was our worst enemy. To prevent our tent from being carried away by heavy gales coming down off the snow-capped Spring Mountains west of us, we used guy-lines extending fifty feet or more to railroad ties we buried 3 feet in the ground."

Neither cold, heat, snow, rain, nor dismal fog, however, stayed the three men in their work. For, as Hunter recounted, they were determined "to make the first comprehensive collection of Pleistocene fossil in Nevada." They "had not the slightest idea that we were to stumble upon a campsite used by Early Man more than 28,000 years ago!"

Hunter, Bell, and Silberling had found not valuable metal but something far more precious in their eyes—truly an archeological gold mine.

The bones recovered were soon identified as those of Pleistocene mammals which had become extinct in the region probably by 10,000 B.C. How long they had grazed there before they vanished is perhaps a question that will never be answered, but geologists have determined that the country was capable of supporting such mammals at least thirty-five thousand years ago. Whatever the case, Hunter, Bell, and Silberling were delighted with their finds, and they succeeded in making the comprehensive collection that had been their goal.

They were disappointed in one respect. The presence of charcoal in association with burned and split bones indicated that man had been there at the time of the ancient animals and had cooked his meat over campfires. Yet there was no other evidence, no artifacts, to substantiate what they knew to be a fact.

Then, on January 16, 1933, their disappointment turned to joy. As Hunter wrote of the great event, they were working on "two large bison skulls in a short coulee two hundred yards from Las Vegas Wash. We discovered some bone fragments that had been eroded out from a steep slope on the southeast side of the coulee which merited investigation. In quarrying this new bone pocket with pick and shovel to a depth of four or five feet, we had to remove many large chunks of hard grayish matrix which rolled down the slope to the floor of the coulee."

Suddenly the sharp eyes of Silberling, who was gazing down the slope, "noticed an unusual black object on the upturned surface of one of these chunks of matrix." The three men slid down the slope "for a closer look. We found that the black object firmly embedded in the matrix was a worked obsidian flake approximately 1½" long by 1" wide. No other obsidian in any form was found in this region. Also embedded in the same chunk of matrix were many black specks of charcoal and numerous small fragments of bone."

They had found a man-made cutting tool "in immediate association with charcoal and bone fragments."

The entire block of matrix containing the artifact was shellacked, covered in rice paper, and securely bandaged. Scientists who studied and examined it in the laboratory of the American Museum of Natural History were satisfied that man had, beyond any doubt, hunted Pleistocene animals in Nevada.

But how old were the bones, the charcoal, and the obsidian cutting tool? In 1933 science had not found a way to determine with accuracy the age of such materials. Twenty-one years later, the eminent Dr. Mark Raymond Harrington of the Southwest Museum, Los Angeles, would remember those first bits of charcoal found with a man-made artifact at Tule Springs. He urged that they be tested by the Carbon-14 method which had been perfected by Dr. Libby. A few pellets weighing only twelve grams were sent to Dr. Libby's laboratory in Chicago. The result: "More than 23,800 years old."

Meanwhile, during the two decades which had elapsed since the initial discoveries at Tule Springs, Harrington and other archeologists had continued the work begun by Hunter, Bell, and Silberling. Harrington's first expedition to the site was made in October, 1933. Four more artifacts unmistakably manufactured by man were found. The first discovery, Harrington wrote, "was a crude chopper fashioned from a dolomitic limestone cobble and bifacially flaked. For this type of specimen it was a very good artifact. . . . During the days that followed the discovery of this tool, a large uniface scraper of limestone and two bifacially flaked ovoid implements of metaquartzite and orthoquartzite were collected. . . ." [3]

After the discovery and development of the Carbon-14 method of dating, Harrington and Ruth D. Simpson, associate director of the Southwest Museum, went again to Tule Springs for the purpose of obtaining a fresh and larger supply of charcoal to be tested. They were unable to find the main site in which Harrington had obtained specimens nearly twenty years earlier. When they returned to Los Angeles they were dismayed to learn that the material recovered in 1933 could not be located. Not until 1954 were the lost boxes and jars found by Simpson in a locked cupboard in the basement of the museum.

The charcoal was sent to Dr. Libby in Chicago. Tests gave it the same date as that of the charcoal found by Hunter—23,800 years old.

Dr. Libby believed the charcoal was older, but 23,800 years was the maximum age the University of Chicago laboratory was equipped to determine. However, Dr. Libby's suspicions were soon confirmed. Subsequent tests at Lamont Laboratory, Columbia University, established a minimum age of twenty-eight thousand years. This was more than double the oldest archeological date established up to that time.

The noted archeologist Alex D. Krieger visited Tule Springs in 1956. He would write of his investigation: "No sign of a stone projectile point has yet appeared at this locality, nor would one expect such artifacts so long ago. The accounts of the individual sites or features show a certain tendency as follows: where there was fire, the animals identified are mainly camel, horse, or bison; where there was no sign of fire, the animals are mainly mammoth. Is it possible, then, that man could not have killed the mammoths here or anywhere until he had effective weapons such as stone spear points? He naturally would have cut the meat from such animals as bogged in swamps and eventually died, but I have the feeling from the evidence given here that it was the camels which were most often and easily killed by man, and portions roasted at or near the kill sites. One might speculate further that nowhere in the world did man become an effective hunter of the largest animals until he had invented suitable weapons or trapping devices." [4]

It seems apparent that man lived and survived in the Tule Springs region *before* he had invented projectile points and atlatls for throwing spears. That was a very long time ago, when the climate of the area was entirely different from that of today. As Krieger notes: "What impressed me most was the series of silt, sand, and caliche deposits *overlying* the lacustrine clays in which the fire areas and fossils were buried. I thought . . . that the locality had a long and impressive geological history after the time that Pleistocene animals had been killed and roasted around the margins of *pluvial* lakes and swamps. Compared with the present true desert which can be classified as Lower Sonoran, the past environment which supported Pleistocene game represents an enormous difference—as great a change as can be found anywhere in the New World."

In Krieger's view, the radiocarbon date of twenty-eight thousand years "might—if the sample could be completely freed of contaminants —be as much as 33,000 years."

The discoveries made at Tule Springs stand among the most important ever made in America.

Sleuth at Gypsum Cave

When Mark Raymond Harrington was a young archeologist, at the beginning of this century, he was convinced in his own mind that Homo sapiens was contemporaneous in North America with Pleistocene mammals. His conviction was formed after he and other scholars had found evidence of man's presence among ancient animal bones, but the belief was generally discounted by scientists, most of whom maintained that the ancestors of Indians had reached America, at the most, only a few thousand years before the time of Columbus. Harrington was counseled to make no rash statements, lest his budding career suffer serious setbacks.

He was a celebrated archeologist in 1933 when he wrote in a memoir: [5]

"First, last and always the object of archeological research is, or should be, to uncover the real truth about the past, to reveal what actually happened before the days of the written records we call history.

"Unfortunately, however, all archeological work has not been conducted according to this rule. In the earlier days of the science, archeologists frequently first formulated their theory, based on considerations which seemed to them logical and proper, and then sought evidence to support it. Of course, by pursuing this method the temptation was very strong to record only such facts as apparently agreed with the theory and to ignore all evidence of a contrary nature.

"Then the pendulum swung the other way and it became fashionable for the field archeologist simply to record the facts as he found them, but not to venture on any interpretation thereof.

"Apparently it had dawned upon the profession, by that time, that the proper procedure was to gather evidence first and to formulate theories later. . . . In those days archeologists who came forward with interpretations of finds, especially if these were of any unusual character, were frowned upon and their conclusions discounted."

The distinguished professor F. W. Putnam of Harvard, under whom Harrington did his first work for the American Museum of Natural History, had suffered such an experience. Dr. Putnam "made some interpretations of his own on discoveries in California and elsewhere, discoveries which had apparently indicated that man existed in America during the Pleistocene or Ice Age and was associated with various species of animals [then long extinct]." Although Dr. Putnam was one of the leaders of archeology in his day, "his opinions along this line were not generally accepted. . . . I, as his disciple, was cautioned by him against making interpretations as to the age of my archeological finds or the identity of the makers of the artifacts which I unearthed."

Many prominent scholars fought bitterly against the acceptance of any evidence that man dwelt in America in the Pleistocene. Harrington did not agree, but he saw good reason to keep the fact to himself, and "in spite of a secret feeling or impression that man came to America a great deal earlier than was generally believed, I was so influenced by the prevailing opposition that I paid little attention to the accounts appearing from time to time of reputed discoveries along this line. I even hesitated to follow up the clews I found with my own hands."

Gypsum Cave is a large limestone cavern about three hundred feet long, sixteen miles east of Las Vegas, Nevada. It contains five rooms connected by narrow passages. For centuries the Paiute Indians had considered it a sacred place and had deposited offerings in it to their gods. For many years white people, seeking a Sunday afternoon diversion, picnicked at the site and sometimes crawled into its low entrances. In 1924 two amateur archeologists explored the cave briefly and picked up a perfect arrow and some other artifacts which appeared to be fragmentary shafts of darts of a type used with the atlatl, or spear-thrower, by people who had lived in the Southwest before the introduction of the bow and arrow. At the first opportunity, which came in the spring of 1925, Harrington went to the cave accompanied only by a Nevada State Police officer.

The two men made their way up the mountainside to the cave mouth, and down over treacherous rockslides and through low openings into its cavernous depths—opening the gate to one of the most unusual and significant discoveries in the annals of American archeology.

What occurred is best told in Harrington's own words: [6]

"Near the entrance I found a few evidences of relatively modern Indians; in the inner chambers I picked up a few pieces of atlatl darts of Basketmaker type; these were lying on the surface of a deposit which test-holes showed to be dry and fibrous and very much like the layer of dung which accumulates in a neglected stable or barnyard. Later we found unbroken pieces which proved to my satisfaction that the deposit was really dung, but of what animal I could not determine. It seemed too large for horse or burro, and besides I could not see how either animal could have found its way through the low openings into the dark inner chambers.

"I talked the matter over with various local old residents and heard a legend that the cave had been used as a hiding place by a band of Apache from Arizona who had stabled their horses within it; but this did not seem likely in view of the small entrances . . . which appeared to have been in their present condition for a very long time. Others told me that the cave was full of dried seaweed which had accumulated when there was a pool of water in it!"

Harrington was too experienced and competent as an archeological detective to place any credence in such tales. He knew the deposit was dung. But of what animal?

Nearly four years passed before Harrington, because of other commitments, was able to pay a second visit to Gypsum Cave. Now, in 1929, he was convinced more than ever that the strange dung was that of some

Ice Age animal.* Carnivorous animals were ruled out, as the excretions clearly had come from a vegetarian. Harrington asked himself what large extinct herbivorous animal that could crawl into holes had existed in the Pleistocene? By a process of elimination he came to the ground sloths, "great lumbering stupid creatures . . . browsers on trees and bushes and probably inhabitants of caves: at least they were so constructed that they could crawl into caves if they so desired."

His next problem was to confirm his belief with indisputable evidence. He showed the dung to Dr. Jessie L. Nussbaum, archeologist of the Interior Department, and Professor Barnum Brown of the American Museum of Natural History. Both of these eminent scientists agreed with his theory that the dung had come from some species of ground sloth, and urged that the cave be thoroughly explored.

Harrington now sensed that he was on the verge of a major discovery, as, indeed, he was, and in January, 1930, under the auspices of the Southwest Museum—of which the great Frederick W. Hodge was director—he was once more at Gypsum Cave, this time with several competent assistants.

Oddly it was not the scientists who made the first two notable finds, but two women members of the expedition.

Whenever she could escape from her secretarial duties, Mrs. Bertha Pallan devoted her time to exploring the crannies of the cavern. One day late in January (1930) she was poking about in Room Number 3, when "she discovered the skull of a strange animal beneath a slab of rock, in a crevice which was so masked by another slab that it was only by sticking her head under one rock and looking back under the other that she was able to see it." [7] Excavators carefully removed the cranium, which was unlike that of any animal then known to have existed in the Great Basin, and at once took it to Los Angeles for identification.

A few days later, Mrs. Myrtle Evans, the wife of one of the archeologists working at the site, "tiring of watching the excavators, wandered into Room 4 and there scratched about in the dust at the foot of a large stalagmite. Here she turned out some large bones, and this find led to the discovery nearby of a mass of such bones, as well as a quantity of coarse, tawny hair and a huge claw with its horney sheath still intact. . . ." [8]

Now the conviction Harrington had formed, that the dung was that of the giant ground sloth of the Ice Age, *Nothrotherium shastense,* was substantiated by laboratory reports. Mrs. Pallan had found a skull of

---

* By this time the discoveries at Folsom, New Mexico, had left no doubt that men hunted Ice Age game before 8000 B.C. See Part One.

this long-extinct animal, and Mrs. Evans had found bones, hair, and a claw that were identified as belonging to it.

The range of the occupation of Gypsum Cave is great, an indeterminable number of millennia. When, as the Glacial Age came to an end, the animals such as the great ground sloth, llama-like camels, and large and small species of horse entered the area may not be stated. Nor may it be stated when they became extinct. But it can be said that they were there, for their remains have been recovered.

The crude artifacts—darts, scrapers, bone implements, stone axes— are evidence to show that Paleolithic hunters were there at the same time.

After them, through the centuries, came a procession of other peoples, peoples of more advanced cultures. They left evidence of their presence—atlatls, bone tubes, worked sticks, arrows, stone tools, wooden objects with bone prongs, wooden bunts, pottery shards, corn, beans, fragments of woven articles. The people called Basketmakers were there. And with the artifacts they left were the bones of animals and birds that still exist in the West today.

And last, the Paiutes were there, Indians who were living in the Great Basin in late prehistoric times—and still do.

Speleological Puzzles

Caves chart much of the Pleistocene history of the Great Basin, particularly in Nevada and Utah, but it has to be reconciled with the ages of the great lakes, called Bonneville and Lahontan, which were products of the melting glaciers. This is an inescapable requirement which has created numerous unresolved geological and archeological problems. For, as invaluable as they are, modern methods of determining the ages of both man-made and natural materials have produced conflicting dates for Great Basin specimens that continue to baffle scientists.

Bonneville Lake at one time drained an enormous basin in northern and western Utah. The only remnant of it is known as Great Salt Lake. The ancient shoreline of Lake Bonneville may be seen more than a thousand feet above the present level of this body of exceptionally briny water. At the end of the Ice Age, Lake Lahontan spread over an immense part of northwestern Nevada and northeastern California. A few relatively small lakes are all that remain of it.

As previously noted, these two great lakes were probably formed at least thirty-five thousand years ago. In the following millennia, as climatic changes occurred, their levels rose and fell. Studies to determine when these changes took place have opened the door to disagreements, and Carbon-14 tests have varied so greatly in adjacent localities that the problem has become heavily burdened by complications.

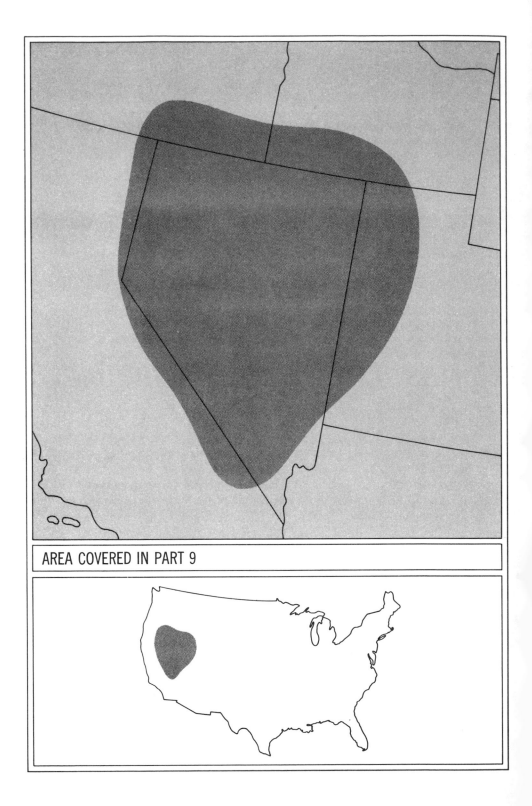

AREA COVERED IN PART 9

Along the shorelines of these lakes, at various altitudes, archeologists have made rich discoveries in caves. Dates of bones and artifacts scientifically determined, however, in numerous cases are in sharp disconformity with dates obtained by geologists in natural materials. The result is a number of questions for which no satisfactory answers have been found. Examples: When did the lakes reach their highest levels? How long ago did they reach levels low enough to drain the caves and make them habitable?

One of the most important sites is Danger Cave, lying at an altitude of about four thousand three hundred feet at the western edge of the Bonneville Salt Flats near Wendover, Utah. In the cave were found pieces of the earliest known basketry in the world, estimated to have been woven ten thousand years ago.

Danger Cave also rewarded excavators directed by Jesse D. Jennings [9] with several thousand artifacts, including chipped stone tools, grinding stones, and objects made of wood, hide, bone, and shell. No bones of extinct Pleistocene mammals were unearthed, but the remains of mountain sheep, deer, and antelope were recovered. Yet, radiocarbon dates obtained from mountain sheep dung and wood objects showed these materials to be more than eleven thousand years old, a period when Ice Age animals existed in the Great Basin. Other artifacts, among them projectile points, found on higher levels produced dates ranging from nine thousand to three thousand years of age. Danger Cave had been occupied—perhaps not continuously—over a very long period of time.

Several other Utah caves have yielded artifacts and animal bones which archeologists have accepted as indications that they were occupied a short time after Lake Bonneville fell low enough to make them habitable. Among them are Black Rock Cave on the south shore of Great Salt Lake, Dead Man Cave, two miles from Black Rock, and Promontory Cave, on the north side of Great Salt Lake. These repositories lie at various altitudes.

In the basin of anicent Lake Lahontan, near Winnemucca, Nevada, seven small caves have been excavated. They were carved by wave action. Fishbone Cave is representative of the group. In it partially burned human bones were found with matting near two large chert choppers which were dated by the Carbon-14 method as being more than eleven thousand years old. Bones of fossil horse and camel, some of them split and burned, were recovered in association with artifacts, indicating that these caves were occupied by Paleolithic hunters. Phil C. Orr of the Santa Barbara Museum of Natural History, who directed the work in Fishbone, reported that radiocarbon dates ranging from ten thousand years to more than eleven thousand years were secured from vegetable matter found in this cave.

375

In the Leonard Rockshelter, a few miles south of Lovelock, Nevada, a complete atlatl dart and thirty Olivella shell beads were recovered. The rockshelter's altitude is more than four thousand feet above sea level. The spear thrower was a weapon used by early Pleistocene hunters. The shells came from the Pacific Ocean, thus showing that the occupants of the cave were in contact with people of the coast. Later work directed by Robert F. Heiser of the University of California resulted in securing a radiocarbon date in excess of eleven thousand years from bat guano found lying on Lake Lahonta gravels.

Projectile points resembling those found in Gypsum Cave were recovered from Etna Cave, near Caliente, Nevada. In association with them were a mano, a worked crystal, an unfinished stone knife, two sandals, several twig effigies, and dung believed to be that of an extinct species of horse.[10]

The evidence is clear that man inhabited these caves at least eleven thousand years ago. Here the picture becomes distorted, creating quandaries with which scientists have struggled for years.

Obviously the caves became dry only after the waters of Lakes Bonneville and Lahontan dropped below their floor levels, but as Wormington states,[11] "there is no indication that the caves were ever inundated after occupation had begun." This fact instead of clarifying the problem only serves to complicate it.

In past years, "glacial and pluvial periods have been thought to coincide, and the expansion and shrinkage of lakes in dry regions have been equated with the expansion and shrinkage of glaciers. It has been believed that the reduction of lake levels below the high strandlines formed during pluvials was a gradual process characterized by minor recessions and readvances and that, after the last pluvial, a considerable period of time elapsed before the water level dropped permanently below such heights as are represented"[12] by the Utah and Nevada caves described.

Perhaps. "Recent studies," continues Wormington, "indicate that the geologic history of pluvial lakes Lahontan and Bonneville is far more complicated than had been thought and that there were some very sudden climatic changes." Some scientists reported that Carbon-14 measurements from fossil tufa and dry cave deposits in the Lake Lahontan area "indicate that the maximum lake level was reached 11,700 years ago, and this was followed by a period of receding lake levels that exposed the caves by 11,200 years ago."[13]

Later studies push these ages farther back. Radiocarbon dates indicate that the Stansbury Beach area of Lake Bonneville had various levels, and that "the climatic minimum, during which the fluctuations occurred that produced these phenomena, lasted from approximately 20,000 to 11,000 years ago."[14] Geologists of the U. S. Geological Survey keep their files on the subject open. Shoreline dates for wave-formed tufas obtained at the Washington laboratory indicate that the history of rising and falling lake states is not only exceedingly complex but largely undeciphered.[15] Tufas from the Provo level of the Bonneville Basin range in age from eleven thousand to more than fourteen thousand. Tufas from the Stansbury shoreline, which lies at a lower elevation than either the Bonneville or Provo levels, range in age from fourteen thousand to eighteen thousand years.

"In view of the stratigraphic evidence," writes Wormington, "it is difficult to believe that these dates can be correct. If they are, all previous interpretations of the terminal history of Lakes Lahontan and Bonneville must be wrong. For archeologists the geological situation is one of complete confusion." [16]

It may be that some Great Basin caves were occupied by Homo sapiens longer ago than is now believed—and it may not. The problem must be resolved by geologists.

One contention, however, with which there is general agreement is that human beings lived in some parts of the Great Basin in the stage termed "pre-projectile," when men had not yet learned to manufacture spear points like those used by Folsom hunters. There probably were not very many of these people, and they were nomadic, their lives affected by climatic changes, seasons in which wild food production was poor, and by shifting animals. Their tools and weapons show that they came into the Great Basin chiefly from the Pacific Coast and the Northwest, and moved on eastward to the Great Plains and to the southeast in their eternal search for richer hunting grounds.

Yet, after the first primitive band reached it, the Great Basin was never without residents. The chronology of their presence is unbroken. Archeologists do not need geological studies to tell them that about 7000 B.C. a Desert Culture arose. It was a way of life more difficult than that in any other part of the United States region. There was little big game in most of the Great Basin, and the people were dependent upon plant foods, small animals, and even insects for their subsistence. There were few running streams, and the remaining waters of the great lakes that once had existed continued to recede, and in many areas vanished, making them uninhabitable.

Yet, the Desert Culture survived for thousands of years, and it flourished long after the first white men had reached the Great Basin.

One Big Family

Every tribe inhabiting the Great Basin in late prehistoric times, with the single exception of the little Washo, spoke a dialect of the Shoshonean language. Tradition suggests that the peoples speaking this tongue originated there, but it seems apparent that they reached the area at some remote period from the north and northwest, probably being pushed southward by stronger tribes. It was long believed by linguists that they constituted a distinct family, but recent studies define Shoshonean as a branch of the larger Utaztecan language group.

Nevertheless, the Great Basin is the earliest identifiable homeland of the Shoshoneans. Long before the dawn of recorded history, however, Shoshonean tribes lived in widely separated localities. In Arizona were the Hopi. In the Rocky Mountains and the Northern Great Plains were the Northern Shoshoni. In the Southern Great Plains were the Comanche.*

The chief tribes or groups which remained in the Great Basin proper from the time they first reached it—whenever that was—until being encountered by white men were the Paiute, Western Shoshoni, Ute, Gosiute, and Koso. The ancestors of the Shoshoneans were the Indians whose cultures were treated in the preceding archeological reports, but who cannot be identified by name or language. Cultural characteristics spread, showing that migrations out of the Great Basin took place, but there is no evidence to indicate a mass exodus at any time. People who left the Great Basin thousands of years ago took their own culture with them, and in each case it was lost through absorption or improved through contact with other cultures. This was not as true for the peoples who made the Great Basin their permanent home. The Great Basin's isolation, its geography, and its climate combined to prevent cultural improvements, and there were few changes during a great many millennia. Indeed, until long after all other regions of the United States territory had been explored, most of the Great Basin remained blank on maps of the West. Well into the nineteenth century explorers were still searching for a great river that was believed to flow through it to the Pacific.

Paiute of the North

Paiute may signify "water Ute" or "true Ute," but there is no certainty about either of these definitions. The people bearing this curious name are divided into two main branches, designated as the Northern and Southern Paiute. Although in prehistoric times the boundaries of their respective territories almost overlapped in Nevada and eastern California, they speak widely varying dialects of the Shoshonean language.

The Northern Paiute ranged over western Nevada, southeastern Oregon, and a part of eastern California in the Great Basin as far south

---

* See Parts One, Six, and Seven.

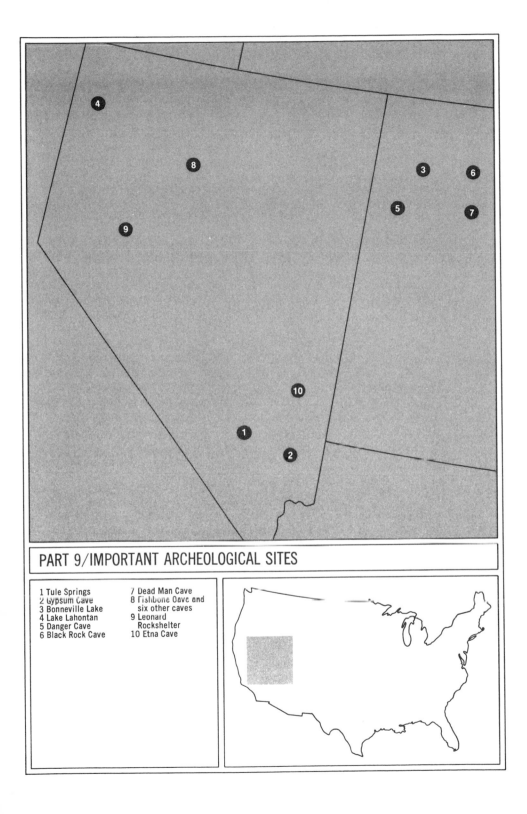

PART 9/IMPORTANT ARCHEOLOGICAL SITES

1 Tule Springs
2 Gypsum Cave
3 Bonneville Lake
4 Lake Lahontan
5 Danger Cave
6 Black Rock Cave

7 Dead Man Cave
8 Fishbone Cave and
  six other caves
9 Leonard
  Rockshelter
10 Etna Cave

as Owens Lake. Some scholars maintain that they were pushed southward from the John Day River region of Oregon by Shahaptian tribes and the Cayuse in the nineteenth century.[17]

The Northern Paiute disagree, contending they lived in their Nevada homeland many centuries ago when red-haired cannibals existed along the Humboldt River. Red hair has been found on human remains in a cave near Lovelock, but scientists declare the hair of these ancient Indians was turned red by chemical changes after death.

While all Shoshoneans of the Great Basin have stories about the red-haired cannibals, the Northern Paiute claim to have destroyed them. According to their legend, as it is recounted by Trenholm and Carley,[18] the red-haired cannibals "would waylay the Indians, then kill and devour them. Not only that, they would come among them and carry away their dead for food. These barbarians, who were considered great fighters, could jump into the air and catch an arrow and hurl it back."

At last, the Northern Paiute concluded that the only way to get rid of them was by a fight to the finish, and they surrounded them "on Humboldt Lake and began killing them as they landed their bulrush boats. One night while the Paiutes were sleeping, the remainder of the barbarians on the lake came ashore and hid in a cave near the mountains. Refusing to come out and agree to live like Indians instead of beasts, they allowed themselves to be trapped in the cave, the Paiutes blocking the entrance with timber. When the barbarians still refused to behave, the Pine Nut Eaters (Paiutes) set fire to the wood and destroyed the tribe, thereby winning for themselves the name *Say-do-carah*, Conquerors."

Because of their remoteness the Northern Paiute were not encountered by white men until a relatively late period, probably not before 1826, when the first American Mountain Men crossed the Great Basin. In the next two decades both British and American fur hunters frequently passed through their territory, for the most part maintaining friendly relations with them. Hostilities were numerous, however, when the great stream of migration occurred, after 1840, but even then the Northern Paiute occupying valleys remote from the main trail of travel were little disturbed by emigrants.[19]

Silver discoveries brought a flood of miners into Northern Paiute territory, and numerous boom towns sprang up. An even greater crisis, writes Swanton,[20] was the introduction of livestock and the establishment of large ranches, with the consequent destruction of native food plants upon which the Indians depended in large part for their subsistence. Piñon trees, from which they obtained nuts, were cut down for fuel. Serious warfare was underway by 1860. By this time the Northern Paiutes were fairly well supplied with horses and guns, and they frequently inflicted severe damage on the white settlers who were stealing and ruining their lands. The federal government established military posts to protect the invaders and destroy any Indians who dared to defend their homes. In 1863 it took the lands of the Northern Paiute "under its authority" without bothering to purchase them or even negotiating for their relinquishment. A few small reservations eventually were established.

The record leaves no doubt that miners and settlers went out of their way to provoke conflicts with the Northern Paiute. The immensity and the forbidding nature of their country probably saved them from early extinction. They were brave and capable warriors, refusing to be confined, and as late as 1878 some of them joined their relatives to the northeast, the Bannock, in an uprising.

Yet the Northern Paiutes, courageous fighters that they were, did not seek war with Americans, did not want it, and often sought to avoid it. They wanted only justice from the civilization that suddenly was forced upon them and threatened to destroy them. Two authorities, Hinshaw and Mooney,[21] state: "As a people the Paiute are peaceable, moral, and industrious, and are highly commended for their good qualities by those who have had the best opportunities for judging. While apparently not as bright in intellect as the prairie tribes, they appear to possess more solidity of character. By their willingness and efficiency as workers they have made themselves necessary to white farmers and have been enabled to supply themselves with good clothing and many of the comforts of life, while on the other hand they have steadily resisted the vices of civilization."

Paiute of the South

Unlike their northern kin, the Southern Paiute were probably the first inhabitants of the Great Basin to meet white men. Although nearly three quarters of the eighteenth century had passed before Utah and Nevada had been penetrated, some scholars believe Spanish explorers came in contact with the Southern Paiute as early as the sixteenth and during the seventeenth centuries.[22] This may be correct, but if so they were called by some other names and cannot be indisputably identified.

The Southern Paiute wandered over a large area reaching from western Utah into northwestern Arizona, southeastern Nevada, and parts of southeastern California. Father Garces passed The Needles on the Colorado River in 1776, traveled westward a short distance in the present state of Nevada, and went on westward across the lower end of the Great Basin. He was the first white man definitely known to have set foot in it, and he may have encountered Southern Paiute.[23]

In July of the same year Fathers Domínguez and Escalante set out from Santa Fe with the hope of discovering a feasible trail to California. They traveled northward to the Colorado River in western Colorado, turned toward the northwest, and discovered Green River. Proceeding almost directly westward they entered the Great Basin in the vicinity of Utah Lake. They learned from Indians of a larger lake to the north which was extremely salty, but they did not see the Great Salt Lake. On their homeward journey they traveled southward through western Utah, into northern Arizona, crossed the Colorado at the famous Crossing of the Fathers, and continued back to Santa Fe. They were the first explorers definitely known to have met Southern Paiutes.* American fur trappers, led by the famed Jedediah Smith, passed through the Great Basin to California in 1826 and 1827.

Language Groups in Part Nine

THE GREAT BASIN

Shoshonean: Northern Paiute, in the Bannock-Northern Paiute Dialectic Group

Southern Paiute, in the Ute-Chemehuevi Dialectic Group

Ute, related closely to Southern Paiute and Chemehuevi

Western Shoshoni, in the Shoshoni-Comanche Dialectic Group

Gosiute, same as Western Shoshoni

Koso, same as Western Shoshoni

Hokan: Washo

It is worth noting that the Southern Paiutes lived in the area of Tule Springs and other sites where remarkable archeological discoveries have been made. How long they had been there, or if they were descendants of the unnamed Paleolithic peoples who inhabited the region, most probably will never be learned.

Although they spoke different dialects, and belonged to two different branches of the Shoshonean linguistic family, in character the Northern and Southern Paiutes are much alike. Their respective histories, with one notable difference, form similar patterns.

With the annexation to the United States of the region encompassing

---

* Other tribes inhabited the part of the Great Basin in extreme southern California, but will be treated under Part Ten, dealing with California, as their history for the most part is associated with that state rather than with the Great Basin proper.

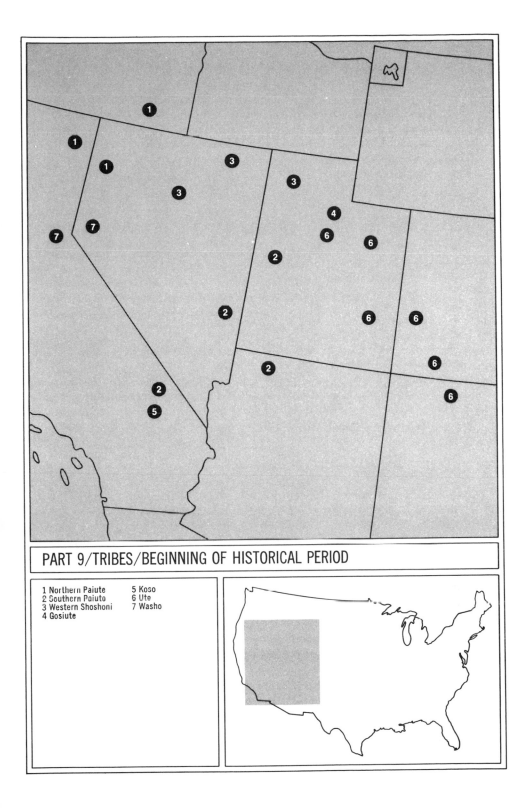

PART 9/TRIBES/BEGINNING OF HISTORICAL PERIOD

1 Northern Paiute   5 Koso
2 Southern Paiuto   6 Ute
3 Western Shoshoni   7 Washo
4 Gosiute

New Mexico, Arizona, and California, the country of the Southern Paiutes was slowly but steadily taken from them. The notable difference between them and their northern kin is that they were less willing to engage in warfare with white invaders. They possessed commendable qualities, but most of them preferred to scatter, to dwell in remote places, than to undertake a stubborn defense of their homeland. There were few bloody clashes between the Southern Paiutes and either the Spanish or American settlers. Some of them moved peacefully onto the small reservations established for them, but by far the greater proportion of them remained widely scattered for many years in Utah, Nevada, and Arizona.

Western Shoshoni

Both the Northern and Western Shoshoni belong to the same dialectic group of the immense Shoshonean linguistic family, but their cultures greatly differ. The Northern Shoshoni,* who at some remote period spread out of the Great Basin to the north and east, possessed the cultures of the Rocky Mountains and the Great Plains. The Western Shoshoni never changed the way of life they had followed for centuries, perhaps for thousands of years. Indeed, dwelling in the arid reaches of the interior Great Basin few changes were possible. Even if they were aware of cultural advances enjoyed by other Indians, they could not have adopted them. Their resources were limited, life was an eternal struggle for existence, and there were few, if any, opportunities for improvement.

Most of the Western Shoshoni lived in northwestern Utah and central and northeastern Nevada, among the most barren and unproductive regions of the entire Great Basin. The Gosiute, a small group of the Western Shoshoni, lived in the vicinity of the Great Salt Lake in northern Utah, enduring what was probably the most wretched existence of any Indians in America. The homeland of another tribe of the Western Shoshoni, the Koso, more popularly known as the Panamint, dwelt in an even drier land, the northern end of Death Valley, but they had the advantage of being able to hunt in the high altitudes of adjacent mountains. The towering Sierra Nevada stood immediately to the west of their homeland, and within its boundaries were other ranges high enough to bear grass for mountain sheep.

The Western Shoshoni owned few horses or guns, for they had nothing to trade for them, the only means by which they might have obtained them from other Indians. They were loosely organized, living

---

* See Part Eight.

mostly in small bands, and having no supreme tribal leaders. Lacking both political and military structures, they rarely engaged in warfare. Moreover, they were by nature a people possessing little prowess as warriors and little inclination to fight. Their greatest battle in life was to survive, to obtain enough seeds and roots, rodents, rabbits, mice, snakes, and insects to keep themselves alive. Even in good years, at the end of winter most of them were on the verge of succumbing to starvation. Yet, through innumerable centuries they won the fight, they survived.

They were known by a variety of names, many of them usually applicable to a single group and denoting a principal type of food in the diet of each band. Examples: Root Eaters, Seed Eaters, Sheep (wild) Eaters, Earth Eaters. They were also called *Shoshoko,* signifying "walkers" or "diggers."

The celebrated scholar and religious, Father Pierre Jean De Smet, was the first missionary to meet Indians of northern Utah. There is some question as to which group he encountered, but they probably were Gosiutes and other Western Shoshoni. He wrote: "There is not, very likely, in all the universe a more miserable, more degraded and poorer people. The French commonly call them *les Dignes de pitié,* or those who deserve to be pitied, and the name suits them admirably. The land they inhabit is a veritable waste. They lodge in crevices of the rocks, or in holes dug in the earth; they have no clothing; their only weapons are a bow, arrows and a pointed stick; they range the barren plains in search of ants and grasshoppers, on which they feed, and they think it a feast when they come upon a few tasteless roots or nauseous grains. . . . They eat the corpses of their kindred, and sometimes even their own children.

"Their number is unknown, for they are seldom seen more than two, three or four together. They are so timid that a stranger would have a good deal of trouble to approach them. . . ." [24]

One work on these people states that when they were driven by hunger to cannibalism the poorest food-producers and drones were victims, and adds: "A girl baby was considered a blessing because the parents knew that someday she would attract a mate who would help the family in its never-ending quest for food." [25]

Many early reports of these Indians were exaggerated, and myths about them were widely circulated. Even the distinguished historian Hubert Howe Bancroft was deceived into writing: "Lying in a state of semi-torpor in holes in the ground during the winter, and in spring, crawling forth and eating grass on their hands and knees, until able to regain their feet; having no clothes, scarcely any cooked food, in many instances no weapons, with merely a few vague imaginings for religion, living in the utmost squalor and filth, putting no bridle on their passions, there is surely room for no missing link between them and the brutes." [26]

Father De Smet described a communal grasshopper hunt. Finding a place where these insects were gathered by myriads, the Indians dug a pit some ten or twelve feet in diameter, and four to five feet in depth, then spread out armed with long branches. They would "surround a field of four or five acres. . . . They stand about twenty feet apart, and their whole work is to beat the ground, so as to frighten up the grasshoppers and make them bound forward. They chase them toward the center by degrees—that is, into the hole. . . . Their number is so considerable that frequently three or four acres furnish grasshoppers sufficient to fill the reservoir." [27]

The grasshoppers were consumed in several ways—in soup, crushed into a paste, dried in the sun, and roasted.

According to Trenholm and Carley, in warm weather "the men wore only a breechcloth and the women a fiber double apron, usually woven from sagebrush which had been pounded into a fringe. . . . Had they been without this necessary shield, they would have violated an old taboo. Those looking upon a woman entirely unclothed would become blind.

"In winter, men and women alike wore a woven garment of strips of rabbitskins. Since it took about forty rabbits for a single robe, one who could boast a complete covering was fortunate. The robe or blanket was the greatest luxury in the basin." [28]

The Koso, southernmost group of the Western Shoshoni, lived in the driest and hottest region of the west, in and adjacent to Death Valley. In describing their diet, the noted anthropologist A. L. Kroeber wrote: "The most important food in the oakless country was the Nevada pine nut, from *Pinua monophylla*. Seeds were gathered by beating . . . *Oryzopsis*, the desert sand grass, perhaps furnished the most abundant supply. Seeds of evening primroses, of *Ephedra*, and of the devil's pincushion cactus were also available. Most of these were ground and then parched with coals in a shallow basket. The mesquite bean, *Prosopis*, was pounded in wooden mortars; the stalks of the common reed, *Pragmites*, were treated similarly and cakes of the flour toasted.

"The 'mescal' of the Southwest hardly penetrates the Koso country, but the tree yucca bud affords a substitute, which has the advantage of being edible after roasting in an open fire, whereas the agave bud or stalk required prolonged steam cooking in an earth-covered pit.

"Prickly pear joints, however, are treated by the Koso in this manner, and then can be kept indefinitely, or are sun-dried and boiled when wanted. The thorns are first rubbed off.

"The leaves and shoots of several varieties of crucifers are eaten.

"In the fertile parts of California, clover and other greens are eaten raw, but the desert vegetation requires repeated boiling, washing, and squeezing to remove the bitter and perhaps deleterious salts.

"Animal food is only occasionally obtainable. Rabbits, jack rabbits, rats, lizards, with some birds, furnish the bulk. Mountain sheep take the place of deer as the chief big game. On the shores of Owens Lake countless grubs of a fly were scooped out of the shallow water and dried for food." [29]

As was the case with the Northern Paiute, the Western Shoshoni suffered greatly from the stampedes of miners and the establishment of immense cattle and sheep ranches in their country, especially in central and northern Nevada. Their age-old vegetable food supplies were greatly depleted by livestock. Because of their primitive manner of existence they were looked upon as animals, and accordingly treated by unconscionable invaders.

By 1860 bloody clashes between whites and Western Shoshoni were frequently taking place. "South of the Great Salt Lake in Utah and in eastern California," states Julian H. Steward,[30] "Shoshoni, especially those known as Gosiute, were commiting depredations against immigrants, raiding the pony express, and attacking the stage line which ran through this territory. . . . For protection, Fort Ruby in Ruby Valley [Nevada] was built in 1862. . . . An Army unit massacred a large number of Shoshoni in Steptoe Valley in 1862, but by 1865 the strife was ended. . . . Shoshoni of central Nevada and of the more remote valleys seem to have kept pretty well out of the conflict."

Once they had resigned themselves to the pressures of civilization, many of the Western Shoshoni, and the Gosiute in particular, demonstrated that they were not as degraded and unintelligent as they had been pictured. Wrote an Indian agent in 1866: "They are peaceable and loyal, striving to obtain their own living by tilling the soil and laboring for the whites whenever an opportunity presents, and producing almost entirely their own living." Reported another agent in 1868: "Many of them are quite industrious, maintaining themselves in good part by herding stock and other labor for settlers." [31]

Ute: Bandits of the Great Basin

Neither legend, history, nor language provides a suggestion as to the meaning of the word *Ute*, or, as it was spelled by some early explorers, *Eutah*. No mystery, however, clouds knowledge of their way of life and their general character.

They were predators, cunning and daring raiders, and fierce and cruel warriors.

They were related to the Southern Paiute of Nevada and the Chemehuevi and Kawaiisu of California, but in themselves constituted an important division of the Shoshonean family. The territory over which they held domination included central and western Colorado, all of eastern Utah, parts of the Salt Lake and Utah valleys, and the upper drainage area of the San Juan River in New Mexico.

The Utes are believed to have been the first tribe to possess horses in any appreciable number in the Great Basin. They began to obtain them shortly after the colonization of New Mexico by the Spanish, which took place at the beginning of the seventeenth century. Some students think that the Utes became fully mounted Indians by 1650, or shortly thereafter. This not only gave them a great advantage over other tribes living both in and outside of the Great Basin, but made possible an accentuation of their inherent warlike nature.

Throughout the Spanish and Mexican regimes they persistently raided ranchos and pueblos, making off with livestock and terrorizing white settlers and New Mexico Indians alike. The Navajos, even more daring and capable as plunderers, usually were able to check them along the northern perimeter of their country, at the San Juan River,* but east of the Rio Grande Ute forays were consistently successful. They had as allies the Jicarilla Apaches, with whom they intermarried, and the two peoples frequently united in an attack. Ute depredations continued for more than three decades after the Mexican War, during which the United States occupied the Southwest.

When the Utes discovered that the Spanish were conducting slave raids against Indians who defied them, such as the Navajo, the Apache, and tribes living on the high plains east of the mountains, they entered the market. They found it easiest to capture their less fortunate relatives, the Western Shoshoni. Raids on these hapless people were carried out mainly in the spring, when the Utes knew they would find them in a weakened condition and unable to escape on foot. They would hold the Western Shoshoni captives—chiefly young men and women—in concentration camps, stuff them with food until they appeared fat and in good health, then take them to the Spanish slave markets in New Mexico and trade them for guns, ammunition, clothing, knives, and other articles. The Utes, however, did not confine their slave raids to the Great Basin, but went beyond it as far as California on the west and the plains in eastern Colorado and western Kansas. After Spanish trading expeditions penetrated the Great Basin they arranged to barter their captives at designated meeting places.[32]

No strong or unified political structure was maintained by the Utes. They were divided into bands, each autonomous. Swanton lists more

---

* See Part One.

than a dozen subdivisions of the tribe.[33] None of the bands is known to have practiced agriculture.

After the Utes obtained horses in sufficient numbers, and began their systematic and far-reaching raiding, however, an elastic military organization was established. Intelligence and plans were exchanged, raids were often joint ventures, and group chieftains were chosen to lead them. At one time in the early historical period, seven Ute subdivisions in Utah reportedly were organized into a confederacy by a chief called Taiwi, but the amalgamation lasted for only a brief time. Very little is known of the Ute social structure. Driver states that the "Arapaho and Cheyenne in the central Plains, and probably also some of the Ute, are the only North American tribes to possess exogamous matridemes." [34]

Treaty negotiations with the Ute comprise a shameful record on the part of the United States. Repeatedly reservations awarded to the various bands were taken away and restored to the public domain, thereby opening them to white settlers.

THE GREAT BASIN
Population Estimates*

Paiute, Northern and Southern (1845)	7,500	**Gosiute** (Aboriginal)	300(?)
		Koso (Aboriginal)	500(?)
Ute (1845)	4,500	**Washo** (1845)	1,000
Shoshoni, Western (1845)	2,500	**TOTAL**	16,300

* See Note, Population Table, Part One.

Washo: a Sad Saga

The story of the Washo is short and tragic. When they were first discovered by white men they lived on the Truckee and Carson rivers, both of which flow from the Sierra Nevada to lose themselves in desert sinks. In the summer they moved to hunt and fish about Lake Tahoe and in other high mountain valleys almost as far north as Honey Lake, California.

They spoke a strange language which had no connection whatsoever with any dialect of the Shoshonean tongue, which was dominant in the Great Basin. At one time scientists regarded them as constituting a distinct linguistic stock. Recent studies, however, showed a relationship with the tongue of some California tribes of the Hokan linguistic family, and they are now placed in that group.

How far back in prehistoric times the Washo, whose name derives from the word *washiu* by which they identify themselves, became a Great Basin tribe, it seems safe to say, will never be known. Nor will their origins be established with any reasonable certainty. Yet, as Kroeber states, "It is tempting to conjecture . . . especially on the basis of their probable Hokan kinship, that they are an ancient California tribe, which has gradually drifted, or been pressed over the Sierra. But there are no concrete grounds other than speech to support such an assumption." [35] Today the situation remains unchanged.

It can be said that the Washo were outstanding weavers of baskets and other articles. In the excellency of their finish and the refinement of their decorative treatment these products reflected traits traceable to expert weavers of central California. They wore garments made of well-tanned and sewn deerskin obtained in the Sierra forests, and of other animals, such as rabbits, foxes, wolves, and coyotes hunted on the lower eastern slopes of the mountain ranges. They used sinew-backed bows and foreshafted arrows. Quivers were made of deerskin with the hair turned in. Rabbit hunts were community affairs. Nets, some with a length of three hundred feet, were hung on stakes or bushes. Rabbits driven into it became entangled in the mesh of the sagging net and were killed with clubs. Seeds and pine nuts were ground in mortars—usually no more than holes found in boulders—with cobblestones. Houses were made of poles joined in an oval dome and thatched with tule mats.[36] Very little more is known of their way of life or their culture.

The undoing of the Washo, a small and militarily weak tribe, began with the western migrations of the eighteen-forties. The tide of settlers following the California Trail, which passed through their homeland, steadily increased each year. The discovery of gold in California brought the mad stampede of the Forty-niners. For more than a decade the Washo suffered at the hands of unscrupulous settlers rushing toward the promised land to get something for nothing, and uncouth, unconscionable fortune-seekers, who regarded all Indians with the utmost contempt, who stole anything they could use or carry away, and who shot anything that moved. They left a trail of devastation through the Washo Country.

But for the Washo the worst was still to come. In 1857 two prospectors discovered silver in the mountains between the present sites of Reno and the Nevada capital, Carson City, but died before recording claims. Two years later Henry T. P. Comstock laid claim to the fabulous lode that would be given his name. Although Comstock would sell his holdings for insignificant sums, the Comstock Lode would turn out to be the richest silver deposit ever known.

The roaring boom town called Virginia City would be the capital of the land of the Washo. Hordes of miners and prospectors swept down upon them. As Indians had no legal standing, and even less standing in the thoughts of the invaders, they were accorded no civil rights. Stockmen followed the miners, establishing ranches on the meadowlands and the ranges adjacent to the cold clear streams flowing from the mountains. The Washo were forcefully driven from the lands they had occupied for centuries, and those who resisted were brutally murdered. Saloons, stores, gambling casinos, and houses of prostitution arose seemingly overnight where a short time before villages of thatch-covered huts had stood.

Adding to their woes, the Northern Paiute, themselves faced with a desperate situation resulting from the influx of settlers, attacked the Washo in a dispute over the use of certain lands. The Paiute won the contest, scattering the Washo, and forbade them thenceforth to own any horses.

In 1865 the cesspool of corruption dignified with the name of Indian Bureau proposed that two reservations be established for the Washo in the Carson and Washoe valleys. An investigation of these areas resulted in the discovery that they were already occupied by white farmers and ranchers, and the plan was abandoned. The Washo were forgotten and left to survive as best they could.

SOME INDIAN PLACE NAMES

Utah	Nevada
Paiute, county	Tuscarora, town, mountains
Utah, state, county	Shoshone, town, river,
Wasatch, mountains	mountains
Uinta, mountains, river	Winnemucca, town
Uintah, county	Gosiute, mountains
Tavaputs, plateau	Washo, county, town, lake,
Shivwits, town	valley
Hovenweep, Nat. Mon.	Mohave, lake
Timpanogas, peak, cave	Owyhee, river
	Pahrump, town
	Tonopah, town

Homeless and helpless, destitute and starving, the Washo had no alternative but to adopt a parasitic way of life. They dwelt in filthy clusters of huts in arid valleys and on the edges of the rapidly growing towns in which millions of dollars poured across the green felt of gaming tables. They begged and they pilfered. They combed the trash heaps for discarded clothing and anything else that might in some small way contribute to their comfort. They subsisted on rabbits and rats and insects, and on the garbage thrown out from cafes and the kitchens of millionaires.

Adding insult to their misery, the politicians and civic leaders who had permitted the wanton destruction of the Washo and had helped to steal their country chose to bestow their name on a county, a beautiful valley, a town, and a lake.

Dates to Remember

1776—In March, Father Garces, exploring for a good route to California, entered the southern edge of the Great Basin in Nevada. In September, Fathers Escalante and Domínguez, also hoping to open a trail to Monterey and San Francisco Bay, reached northern Utah before turning back to Santa Fe. Thereafter, no official Spanish government expeditions were sent into the region, but private parties frequently entered it to trade with the Indians.

1811—Five American Mountain Men were detached from John Jacob Astor's expedition to the Columbia to trap in Idaho. In their wanderings during the next two years they are believed to have entered the Great Basin in northern Utah. They were Joseph Miller, Jacob Reznor, Edward Robinson, John Hoback, and Martin Gass. They trapped along Bear River, which flows into Great Salt Lake, and explored a large territory totally unknown to white men.[37]

1824—The intrepid fur hunter–explorer Jedediah Strong Smith and other trappers of the Rocky Mountain Fur Company entered the northern Great Basin.

1825—Peter Skene Ogden of the Hudson's Bay Company led a party of British trappers into the Utah Valley that would be given his name.

1826—Jedediah Smith crossed Utah and southern Nevada to southern California, the first American Mountain Man to break a trail from the northern Rocky Mountains to the Pacific. He returned in 1827 across the Sierra Nevada and central Nevada to Salt Lake.

1827–1830—Ogden led three expeditions into the Great Basin from Idaho and Oregon.

1844—John Charles Frémont, after virtually circling the vast region between the Wasatch Mountains and the Sierra Nevada, reported that it had no outlet to the sea and gave it the name Great Basin.

Scientific Note—the Name "Indian"

What is perhaps the greatest nomenclatural error of all time was made in 1492 by Christopher Columbus. When he found the islands of the Caribbean (named for the Carib tribe) he thought he had reached the coast of India, and he called the people inhabiting them *los indios*. By the time it was learned that not Asia but a vast previously unknown land mass of two continents had been discovered, the name "Indian" had entered the major languages of the world, irrevocably applied to the aboriginal inhabitants of North and South America.

The famous John Wesley Powell, founder of the Bureau of American Ethnology, urged that "Amerind" be substituted for Indian. Some scientists attacked the suggestion, while others endorsed it, in a debate before the International Congress of Americanists, held in New York in 1902. No final decision was reached, but the term, nevertheless, thereafter appeared in numerous scientific journals.

"Indian" became a legal name, used in statutes, in treaties, in all official documents, as well as in histories and literature. It is the most popular and most widely applied place name in the United States. A geographical dictionary of considerable size would be required to list and locate the thousands of Indian arms, bays, bayous, beaches, bottoms, branches, brooks, camps, coves, creeks, crossings, diggings, fields, fords, gaps, groves, gulches, harbors, heads, hills, islands, lakes, mills, mounds, mountains, necks, orchards, passes, points, ponds, ridges, rivers, rocks, runs, springs, swamps, towns, traces, trails, valleys, villages, and wells.

A few names which have been coupled with the word "Indian" indicate the extraordinary extent of its usage by Americans in identifying plants: [38]

Indian Apple—The May apple or wild mandrake.
Indian Arrow—The burning bush, or wahoo.
Indian Arrow-wood—The flowering dogwood.
Indian Balm—The erect trillium.
Indian Bark—The laurel magnolia.
Indian Bean—The catalpa.
Indian Beard Grass—The bushy beard grass.
Indian Bitters—The cucumber tree.
Indian Black Drink—The ilex.
Indian Boys and Girls—The Dutchman breeches.
Indian Bread—The tuckahoe.
Indian Bread Root—The prairie turnip.
Indian Cedar—The ironwood.
Indian Cherry—The serviceberry.

Indian Chickweed—The carpet weed.

Indian Chief—The American cowslip.

Indian Cigar Tree—The common catalpa.

Indian Corn—Maize.

Indian Cucumber—The cucumber root.

Indian Cup—The common pitcher plant.

Indian Currant—The coral berry.

Indian Dye—The Yellow puccoon, or orange root.

Indian Elm—The slippery elm.

Indian Fig—The prickly pear (cactus).

Indian Fog—The dwarf houseleek.

Indian Hemp—The army root, and swamp milkweed, also
called Indian Mallow.

Indian Hippo—The bowman's root, also called Indian Physic.

Indian Lemonade—The fragrant sumac of California.

Indian Lettuce—The wintergreen.

Indian Millet—The silky oryzopsis.

Indian Moccasin—The lady's slipper.

Indian Mozemize—The dogberry.

Indian Paint—The bloodroot.

Indian Paintbrush—The scarlet painted cup.

Indian Peach—A variety of clingstone peach.

Indian Pear—The serviceberry.

Indian Pine—The loblolly.

Indian Pink—The Carolina pink, and the milkwort.

Indian Pipe—The ghost flower.

Indian Pitcher—The sidesaddle plant.

Indian Plantain—The wild collard.

Indian Poke—The white hellebore.

Indian Posey—The sweet life-everlasting.

Indian Potato—Indiscriminately given to many species of
bulbs.

Indian Red Root—The red root.

Indian Rhubarb—*Saxifraga peltata.*

Indian Root—The spikenard.

Indian Sage—The common thoroughwort.

Indian Shamrock—The ill-scented wake robin.

Indian Soap Plant—The soap berry.

Indian Tea—Various plants, the leaves of which were infused
by Indians, and later by whites, in steeping a
drink.

Indian Tobacco—The wild tobacco.

Indian Turnip—The jack-in-the-pulpit.

Indian Wickiup—The fireweed.

To which might be added:

Indian Bread—Cornbread.
Indian Dad—A batter cake.
Indian File—Single file.
Indian Giver—A repentant giver.
Indian Pudding—A pudding made of cornmeal, molasses, etc.
Indian Sign—Evidence of the recent presence of Indians.
Indian Summer—Pleasant weather in the late fall.

The Pacific Coast

The Calico Hills Gateway

A few miles north of the tiny Mojave Desert waystation of Yermo, in San Bernardino County, California, the pastel ridges of the Calico Mountains rise against a hot azure sky.

On an alluvial fan of this barren range scientists discovered a prehistoric site which the world-famous archeologist Dr. L. S. B. Leakey has called "the first at which positive proof has been obtained of the really early movement into America of early man, and is likely to represent the most important milestone in the whole history of the study of the prehistory of America." [1]

The Calico Gateway has led archeologists to repositories of manmade artifacts at least fifty thousand years of age.

These crude specimens—stone scrapers, knives, hammerstones, and flakes—are the oldest ever recovered in the Western Hemisphere.

The estimates of their great antiquity are not guesswork. They are based on years of geological and archeological studies and on scientific tests. Their discovery has made obsolete the theory that man did not reach North America at such a remote period of the Pleistocene epoch, although some scientists stubbornly adhere to this belief. On the other hand, many accept it, and Dr. Leakey, as one of these, predicts that even older sites will be found.[2] Regarding the ancient tools he has stated: "While the exact age of the deposition on the fan is still a matter of discussion, I think there is no real doubt in the mind of any serious geologist that the age is well over 50,000 years." [3] Some geologists think the Calico Hills Fan may be as much as eighty thousand years old. The artifacts were recovered at varying depths beneath the slope's surface. The principal excavation is twenty-five feet square with a depth of thirteen feet.

Archeologists had long believed, as the result of cursory examinations, that the general area would reward excavators with extraordinary finds. In 1939 Dr. Malcolm Rogers of San Diego's Museum of Man reported that not far from nearby Mannix Station, on the Union Pacific Railroad, "a quarry site exists . . . which is of great magnitude." [4] During the decade of the forties Dr. Gerald A. Smith, president of the San Bernardino Historical Society, and archeologists Ruth D. Simpson, Stuart Peck, and Ritner Sayles, on several trips to the area, collected numerous stone implements on the surface which had been exposed by winds. Field trips were continued between 1950 and 1958, various sites of later dates being found.

Ruth De Ette Simpson, then with the Southwest Museum in Los Angeles, was convinced that major finds would be made in the Calico Hills.* In 1958 she went to England and obtained an audience with Dr. Leakey, who was there on leave from his archeological work in East Africa, which had brought him great renown. She showed him some of the surface artifacts from the Calico Hills. His interest profoundly stirred, he agreed to visit the site as soon as possible, but four years passed before he could make good his promise.

At last, in May, 1963, Miss Simpson took Dr. Leakey on a reconnaissance of the Calico sites. The trip was all he needed, as Belden recounts, to pronounce the surface material representative of an "early workshop area, as there were spots literally paved with crude stone implements and chippings which gave evidence that prehistoric people had either occupied or frequently visited the area in considerable numbers. The workshops were on the surface of an ancient alluvial fan that intrigued the noted visitor." [5] In an old road-cut, several feet below the surface, were found exposed artifacts.

Dr. Leakey recommended that excavations be made "in depth," and that a thorough geological study be undertaken. The project would involve greater expense than the resources of the new San Bernardino County Museum would allow. In a discussion with Dr. Leakey, the museum's director, Dr. Smith, and Miss Simpson, who had been engaged as San Bernardino County archeologist, it was suggested that efforts be made to interest the National Geographic Society. Dr. Leakey offered his services, and en route back to England he presented an application to the Society's officials in Washington. It was accepted.

In May, 1964, with Miss Simpson directing field operations, the

---

* See *The Years at Tule Springs*, Part Nine.

work was begun under the united auspices of the National Geographic Society and the San Bernardino County Museum. The undertaking was conducted without undue fanfare for four years, during which Dr. Leakey interrupted his African work to visit the site at least twice each year, and numerous other noted scientists from all parts of the world came to observe the digging.

Among the archeologists who had long contended that man lived in North America at a much earlier date than most scientists believed were Thomas and Lydia Clements.[6] In 1951, while prospecting on Manley Terrace in Death Valley, they found an assemblage of flaked stone artifacts that were obviously of great age. The terrace marked a level of a Pleistocene lake. It was their belief that the simple uniface tools belonged to the culture of an ancient people to whom projectile points and grinding stones were unknown. Their contentions were not generally accepted in the scientific world, some archeologists suggesting that the Manley Terrace specimens, which were found on the surface, were nothing more than rocks fractured by the elements. The stone tools found in the Calico Mountains undisturbed several feet below the surface support the belief of the Clementses.

The work at Calico, which still continues, has been carried on with the utmost caution and deliberation, but not without interruption by legal troubles. A desert miner named Gunn claimed that the archeologists were excavating within the boundary of a mineral claim to which he held title. He sought to have them evicted, and threatened to destroy the pits they had dug with a bulldozer.[7] The Federal Bureau of Land Management took the stand that under the Federal Antiquities Act the scientists had an "occupancy right," and the irate Gunn postponed his legal actions. The Secretary of the Interior then declared the Gunn claim was invalid, as no evidence had been produced to show it contained minerals of value.

In four years more than twenty thousand cubic feet of soil and rock have been removed and thoroughly examined with tiny picks and trowels, some so small that they make a teaspoon appear large by comparison.[8]

As Dr. Leakey wrote Ruth Simpson, the Calico Mountain finds "will always be pointed out as (1) the turning point in our studies in America, and (2) the demonstration of how sites in a geological context can be dug in an extremely scientific manner." [9]

Some West Coast Treasures

Both the arid and semi-arid areas of southern California have rewarded scientists with discoveries of transcending significance. That man inhabited this region for a great number of millennia—at least fifty—without interruption no longer remains a matter of speculation. The fact has been amply substantiated by the chronological dating of the cultures discovered.

The conclusion seems inescapable that migrants from Siberia entered America in interglacial periods, that is, at times between retreats and advances of the great frozen caps, and that long before the Ice Age had come to an end man went far enough south to escape them. Basing his opinions on recent finds scientifically dated, archeologist George F. Carter is convinced that man could have reached America during the Illinois Glaciation and have penetrated far into the continent before the beginning of the Wisconsin, the final great period of the Ice Age.[10]

On Santa Rosa Island, off the southern California coast, Phil C. Orr of the Santa Barbara Museum of Natural History made an extraordinary discovery. In Pleistocene sediments he found the remains of very small mammoths, some no more than six feet in height.[11] The animals had been butchered and roasted. From burned bones laboratories obtained dates approximately thirty thousand years of age.

Geologists believe that Santa Rosa and other adjacent islands at one time may have been a solid land mass, but, as Wormington notes, "the water between them and the coast is so deep that it is not thought . . . the sea level would have been lowered sufficiently to provide a land bridge to the mainland. However, if the sea were lowered by more than 300 feet, which seems possible, the open water channel would have been only about two miles wide, and no very elaborate water craft would have been required to reach the island." [12] This could account for the presence of Paleolithic Man on the channel islands, but it leaves unanswered the question of how mammoths reached them.

Yet there can be no doubt that man lived, hunted, and died on Santa Rosa Island from at least thirty thousand years ago until well into the historical period. Cemeteries have been found containing some three hundred burials, many of the bodies interred in sitting positions. Red abalone shells—no doubt burial offerings—found in the graves have produced dates in excess of seven thousand years of age. It is possible that islanders were buried on Santa Rosa long before this time, but their graves have not been discovered. At least it is known they were on the island some thirty millennia ago.

In the La Jolla area of San Diego County, Carter, who has been called the chief champion of Interglacial Man in the New World,[13] found stone flakes and a mano in deposits which he believes are dated far back in the Wisconsin Glaciation period. Numerous archeologists dispute him, but he holds the support of others. Whether he is wrong or right, one of the La Jolla specimens he recovered produced a radiocarbon date of 21,500 years.

On a bench at the foot of San Diego's Texas Street, Carter collected

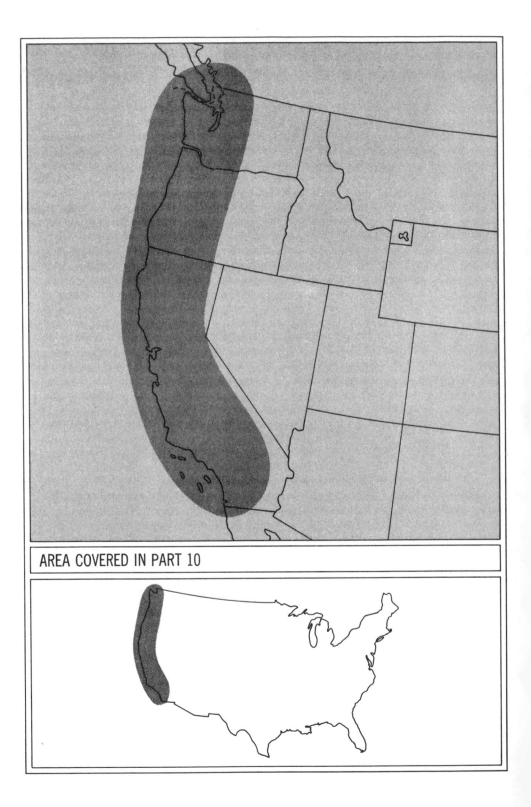

AREA COVERED IN PART 10

more than a hundred quartzite cobbles which he thinks are artifacts. They were found in association with areas of burned earth and rocks of varying sizes which he has identified as hearths. According to his postulations the artifacts and burned areas belong to the Third Interglacial. Two prominent archeologists, John Witthoft and Ruth Simpson, agree that at least some of the specimens were made by human hands, but other equally qualified experts take an opposing view, notwithstanding the date of 21,500 years of age.

Lake Mojave vanished far back in the Pleistocene. Along the former shores of this ancient body of water, archeologists William Campbell and Elizabeth W. Crozer Campbell came upon an important assemblage of man-made objects. Among the stone artifacts recovered both on the surface and some five feet below it by this man-and-wife team of scientists were several types of projectile points, choppers, scrapers, flake knives, drills, and perforators.

The specimens represented a culture considerably younger than that characterized by the discoveries in the Calico Mountains, yet one that predated the metate or milling stone. At one time Lake Mojave was more than twenty miles long and six miles in width. Its waters lay in several basins, two of which, Soda Lake and Silver Lake, figured prominently in the discoveries of the Campbells. The big body of water was fed by a vigorous stream. Eventually the stream dwindled, the waters fell, at last becoming brackish and then vanishing. Few places in the desert now present a more desolate or desiccated appearance.

"Primarily the site was selected," wrote the Campbells, "because shore features remain that had been classed as ancient by competent geologists who had no knowledge of the archeological remains. . . . All specimens recovered from the shores of Lake Mohave suggest great age. . . . Certainly the ancient inhabitants from the widely separated terraces did not walk far out on the playa to procure brackish water from a dwindling puddle. When the river ceased flowing, Silver Lake would have dried first, and then the north end of Soda; yet the finest collections of old flint forms came from the terraces 40 feet above the playa at the north end of Silver Lake and from the spits at the northeast end of Soda playa." [14]

The people who had no grinding stone and who used atlatls in hurling their projectiles at animals dwelt about Lake Mojave when it was a living body of water and overflowing. According to the eminent geologist Ernst Antevs, that was at least fifteen thousand years ago. [15]

Numerous other southern California sites representing differing cultures, and dated from nine thousand to three thousand years of age, have been excavated. Among these are Pinto Basin, Little Lake, and Twenty-Nine Palms region, all of which were investigated by the Campbells. Five sites related to late prehistoric cultures in Los Angeles

County were excavated under the direction of Edwin Francis Walker of the Southwest Museum. They were San Fernando, Malaga Cove, Pasadena, Chatsworth, and Big Tujunga Wash.[16]

Juan Rodríguez Cabrillo commanded the first expedition of white men to reach the coast of southern California. In 1542 he found it heavily populated by Indians. Because of the large number of villages with smoke rising from their fires which encircled Santa Monica Bay he christened the place *La Bahía de los Fumos*. He had no way of learning, of course, that in the region dwelt more Indians than in any comparable area within the limits of the present United States. As Ruth Simpson, Dr. Leakey, Mark R. Harrington, the Campbells, Charles A. Amsden, Edwin Walker, Robert F. Heizer, Ernst Antevs, George Carter, Alex D. Krieger, and all their colleagues have amply demonstrated, man was there a very long time before Cabrillo saw the smoke of the coastal villages.

The recovery of crudely flaked projectile points at several locations in northern California has brought arguments about their age. At Borax Lake—dry most of the year—in Lake County, Mark Raymond Harrington found a variety of the points. They were of several types, some stemmed, and ranging in size from two to four inches in length. With them he also recovered crescentic stone implements, knives, hammerstones, pestles, manos, and mortars. It was his opinion that the site had been visited over considerable time by different groups of people who were attracted to it by adjacent obsidian deposits. Many of the artifacts were made of obsidian.[17]

A later study by Clement W. Meighan brought the opinion that the Borax Lake objects represented a single complex that was widely distributed in the ranges of the Pacific Coast.[18] Robert F. Heizer of the University of California expressed another view. In the Napa Valley, above San Francisco Bay, he found artifacts similar to those from Borax Lake. He stated that the Napa Valley site may be a part of the time period of the Borax Lake location, and pointed out that many of the Borax Lake specimens were similar to artifacts of the Middle Horizon of the Sacramento Valley, dated approximately at 1000 B.C.[19]

Geologists Carl Saur and Ernst Antevs dated the Borax Lake site in a pluvial period which ended about ten thousand years ago. On this basis the artifacts were judged to be of the same age. In a later investigation Antevs knocked about three thousand years off this date.[20] "Evidence from other sites," writes Wormington, "where sound stratigraphic studies can be made, is needed before we can be sure that the fluted points are part of the same complex as the other types found with them. It may be that the fluted points from Borax Lake are pieces picked up locally and brought to a later site by the inhabitants, but, as yet, no fluted points have been found [in California] under conditions suggestive of great antiquity." [21]

If scientists are not in agreement, one significant factor has become clear as a result of the finding of fluted points in northern California. It is that the technique of fluting projectiles, so widely practiced on the Great Plains and in the Southwest, was known to primitive hunters of the Pacific Coast ranges at least before the beginning of the Christian Era, and perhaps seven to ten thousand years ago.

Distribution of artifacts typologically similar is a fascinating and often revealing story, for it reflects on early migrations of peoples and contacts between them. For example, pieces of mammoth bones obviously shaped and polished by men, and used as tools, have been found in California, Oregon, and Washington and are similar to others found in Alaska and the Southwest. Clovis projectile points recovered in New Mexico,* as well as numerous other places, have been found in Washington and Oregon. In Oregon's Willamette Valley, points of the widely distributed Scottsbluff (Nebraska) and Sandia (New Mexico) types have been recovered in association with mammoth remains. Many other similar examples might be cited.

Two important archeological sites are lower and upper Klamath Lakes, the first in extreme northern California and the other some sixty miles north in Oregon. Excavations were directed in both localities by L. S. Cressman. The work established that mammoth and other extinct Pleistocene animals were still living in the area as late as seven thousand years ago.

Several types of stone projectile points were recovered, some of them *in situ* among ancient bones. In one place an obsidian knife and a crude scraper were found in a deposit containing an elephant tusk. A long bone implement with a beveled edge was found in the abdominal area of a skeleton buried in a large midden. In the skull of the same mammoth was a large projectile point with a concave base which had entered the brain through the right eye. This ancient mammal was given a minimum date of seven thousand years. Artifacts were found at a deeper level in the midden, indicating a greater age.

Different types of artifacts were found on five distinct levels of the excavations at upper Klamath Lake. It is apparent that the locality was occupied from the Pleistocene to historic times. Cressman stated, as well, that the work also shows the adaption of the Klamath region culture "from the characteristic Great Basin pattern to one based on the selective exploitation of the ecological resources of the rivers and marshes." [22]

Scientists have long held that the Pacific Coast was one of the great

* See Part One.

"highways of migration" over which the earliest immigrants from Siberia traveled southward in North America. The recent discoveries of archeologists tend to substantiate this belief.

Babel Along the Pacific

In 1891, John Wesley Powell, founder of the Bureau of American Ethnology, published his epochal study of American Indian languages. Taking vocabulary and dictionary as the factors of discrimination, he recognized fifty-eight distinctive linguistic families north of Mexico.

Of this number, twenty-seven were, or had been, represented in the Pacific coastal region of the United States.

Modifications have been made in Powell's enumeration by later scholars. Relationships—some remote, to be sure—have been found between the tongues he classified as distinct. This has led to the practice of combining connected languages under groups or general stocks. However, Powell's work still remains the classic in its field, and no list of languages, nor groups of them, may be considered as final. The study of Indian linguistics still remains far from complete, and the work continues to become more difficult as source materials are exhausted.

A tribe, under Heizer's definition, "comprises a body of people who share in common a group name, a particular speech or dialect, and a common territory." [23] Adhering to these limitations, it has been found that at least one hundred and twenty-five distinct tribes lived immediately on, or adjacent to, the coasts of California, Oregon, and Washington in late prehistoric times. Undoubtedly there were more. Some tribes became extinct so soon after the beginning of the historical period that, even though it is known they existed, their identities are obscure and students had no opportunities to determine their linguistic affiliations.

Yet enough evidence has been accumulated to show that the American Pacific coast was truly a babel of tongues. In California alone, states Heizer, there were "over one hundred dialects, of which perhaps seventy per cent are as mutually unintelligible as Chinese and English. No area of equal size in North America or, according to some, in the entire world, exhibited such a rich variety of native languages." [24] To this number must be added the many dialects spoken by the peoples of Oregon and Washington.

No one can say with certainty when or how any of these tribes reached the region. Investigations indicate that many, if not most, of them were there a very long time ago. Under the present method of grouping languages, at least fourteen basic stocks are represented in the area. At least half of them are also found in other regions of the

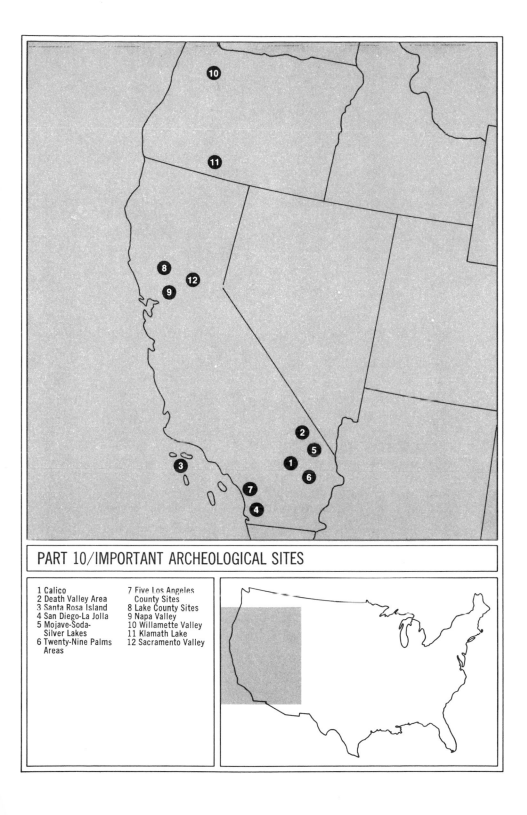

PART 10/IMPORTANT ARCHEOLOGICAL SITES

1 Calico
2 Death Valley Area
3 Santa Rosa Island
4 San Diego-La Jolla
5 Mojave-Soda-
  Silver Lakes
6 Twenty-Nine Palms
  Areas

7 Five Los Angeles
  County Sites
8 Lake County Sites
9 Napa Valley
10 Willamette Valley
11 Klamath Lake
12 Sacramento Valley

Language Groups in Part Ten

THE PACIFIC COAST

Athapascan: Kwalhioqua
Chastacosta
Chetco
Clatskanie
Dakubetede
Mishikhwutmetunne
Tutuni
Umpqua
Bear River
Chilula
Hupa
Lassik
Mattole
Nongatl
Sinkyone
Tolowa
Wailaki
Whilkut
Kato

Chinookan: Cathlamet
Cathlapotle
Chilluckittequaw
Chinook
Skilloot
Wishram
Clackamas
Clatsop
Clowwewalla
Multnomah
Waco
Watlala

Penutian: Costanoan
Maidu
Miwok
Patwin
Wintu
Wintun
Yokuts

Salishan: Chehalis
Clallum
Copalis
Cowlitz
Duwamish
Humptulips
Kwaiailk
Lummi
Muckleshoot
Nisqually
Nooksack
Puyallup
Queets
Quimault
Sahehwamish
Samish
Satsop
Semiahmoo
Skagit
Snohomish
Snoqualmie
Squaxon
Suquamish
Swallah
Swinomish
Siletz
Tillamook

Hokan: Achomawi
Atsugewi
Chimariko
Chumash
Diegueño
Esselen
Karok
Konomihu
Okwanuchu
Pomo
Salinan
Shasta
Yana
Yahi

Kalapooian: Ahantchuyuk
Atfalati
Calapooya
Chelamela
Chepenafa
Luckiamute
Santiam
Yamel
Yoncalla

Shoshonean:	Alliklik	Yakonan:	Alsea
	Cahuilla		Hanis
	Cupeño		Kuitsh
	Fernandiño		Miluk
	Gabrieliño		Siuslaw
	Juaneño		Yaquina
	Kawaiisu		
	Kitanemuk	Algonquian:	Wiyot
	Nicoleño		Yurok
	Serrano		
	Tubatulabal	Chimakuan:	Chimakum
	Vanyume		Hoh
			Quileute
Takilman:	Latgawa		
	Takelma	Yukian:	Huchnom
			Wappo
Wakashan:	Makah		Yuki
	Ozette		
Shapwailutan-Lutuamian-Wailapuan			
	Klickitat		
	Klamath		
	Modoc		
	Molala		
	Tyigh		
	Tenino		

United States territory, some, such as the Shoshonean, Hokan, and Athapascan, reaching out as much as two thousand miles eastward from the Sierra Nevada.

No one knows why the Pacific Coast tribes detached themselves from the main bodies of those speaking their tongues, nor where any of the separations took place. The consensus is that the migrations occurred over a very long period of time, probably both southward along the coast and westward over the mountains. However, that hardly can be true of all of them. Indeed, there is ample evidence suggesting that many West Coast tribes of historic times are direct descendants of Paleolithic people who hunted with the crude stone weapons found in the archeological sites of the Pacific States. There are a great many more indications to substantiate this postulation than there are to disprove it.

The Athapascan

The Navajo have a tradition that says at least a part of them originated on the Pacific Coast. Their language, however, is proof that their earliest known homeland was in northwestern Canada, which they undoubtedly reached from Siberia. Yet the legend cannot be entirely disregarded. It is possible, indeed probable, that some of them

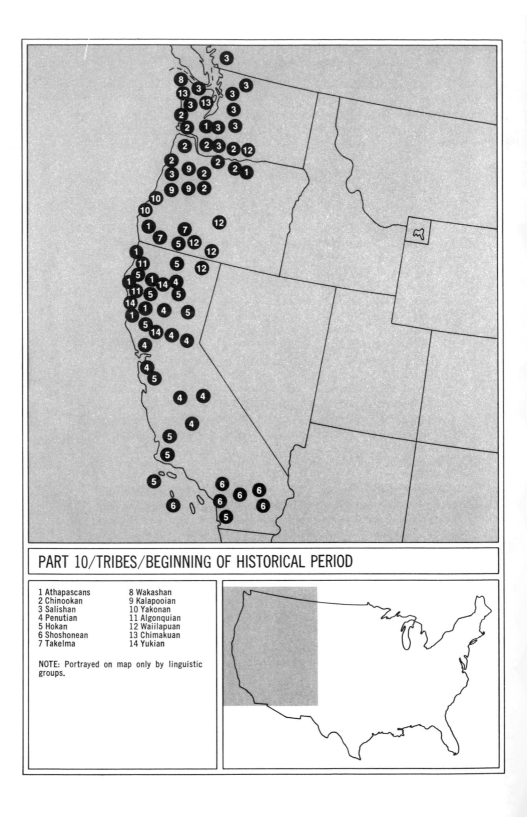

PART 10/TRIBES/BEGINNING OF HISTORICAL PERIOD

1 Athapascans
2 Chinookan
3 Salishan
4 Penutian
5 Hokan
6 Shoshonean
7 Takelma
8 Wakashan
9 Kalapooian
10 Yakonan
11 Algonquian
12 Waiilapuan
13 Chimakuan
14 Yukian

NOTE: Portrayed on map only by linguistic groups.

reached New Mexico from California, while others migrated southward along the eastern side of the Rocky Mountains.

There can, therefore, be no question as to the origin of the Athapascans who chose to terminate their wanderings in the area of the Pacific States. Of the nineteen small Athapascan groups which established themselves in this region only one, the Kwalhioqua, remained in the state of Washington. The Chastacosta, Chetco, Clatskanie, Dakubetede, Mishikhwutmetunne, Tutuni, and Umpqua found suitable homelands in Oregon. The Bear River, Chilula, Hupa, Lassik, Mattole, Nongatl, Sinkyone, Tolowa, Wailaki, Kato, and Whilkut continued on southward, spreading out in northern California.

The Athapascans occupied valleys a few miles inland from the coast, only three of the groups believed to have held small stretches of land touching the sea. They did not move southward in an organized migration, but rather in small bands, and over a period of many centuries. Kroeber states that two things argue against any rapid conquering march: "their assimilation to their linguistically alien neighbors in culture, and in bodily form." [25] Their culture contained many of the customs and beliefs of surrounding tribes, and they were virtually identical in physique to peoples adjacent to the territory they inhabited. "In northwestern California, as in southwestern Oregon," says Kroeber, "a single physical type is the predominant one among the multitudinous tribes: a tallish stature with a round head." Pointing out that these are also the traits of Athapascans in the northwest and the southwest of the continent, he adds: "It is therefore quite possible that the prevalence of this type in the region where California and Oregon join is due to a sustained and abundant infusion of Athapascan blood."

The Athapascans lived in permanent villages, moving about in summer to hunt game and gather wild plant foods. Fish was a staple in their diet, as large rivers in which salmon and other species abounded flowed through their territory. Their normal daily lives deviated little from a traditional pattern, the woman rising first and going to the river for a "complete bath. She then took the burden basket and brought a load of wood for the house fire. She was expected to have finished her bath before the men were astir. The men too were early risers. The dawn was looked upon as a maiden. . . . The men always bathed in the river on rising. A light breakfast was eaten by the family in the house and each went to his day's task. The older men preferred to do most of their work before this meal. In the afternoon, the old men, and the religiously inclined young men, took a sweat in the sweat-house, followed by a plunge in the river. After the bath they sat in the shelter of the sweat-house and sunned themselves. As they sat there they engaged in meditation and prayer. In the evening the principal meal was served. The men ate very slowly, looking about and talking after each spoonful of acorn soup. The women sat in silence without caps and with hidden feet, that they might show great respect to the men. A basket of water was passed after the meal that the men might wash their hands. When they were through they retired to the sweat-house, where they spent several hours in converse." [26]

Unless he met death far from home in war or by accident, an Athapascan man was buried in the village in which he was born. When an Athapascan woman was married she went to live in the village of her husband and usually remained there all her life. Each village had a headman. The position was handed down from father to son. The headman held special hunting and fishing rights, and areas were set aside in which only his women were permitted to gather acorns and seeds. As a result of these privileges most headmen were wealthy, but they were required to furnish food to the villagers in time of need.

The Chinookan

The twelve main tribes of this linguistic family lived on both sides of the lower Columbia, six on the Oregon side and six in Washington, the territory claimed by them reaching from the mouth to The Dalles. In Washington were the Cathlamet, Cathlapotle, Chilluckittequaw, Chinook, Skilloot, and Wishram. In Oregon were the Clackamas, Clatsop, Clowwewalla, Multnomah, Wasco, and Watlala.

Because of their geographical location, Chinookan people were encountered by the first explorers to enter the Columbia. Trading between them and white men had been carried on for several years before the arrival of Lewis and Clark, but their descriptions provide the most authentic picture of them as they were at the beginning of the historic period.

The villages of the Chinookans stood along the banks of the Columbia, usually at the mouths of tributaries, with the larger part of the population dwelling on the right bank. The houses were constructed of wood and were large, often being occupied by three or four families composed of twenty or more individuals.

The rapid development of trade along the Columbia brought affluence and power to the Chinookans that were not enjoyed as early by surrounding tribes. Lewis and Clark found them in possession of guns, clothing, utensils, and gewgaws obtained in trade. Sailors from trading vessels also introduced venereal diseases among them, and the American explorers told of seeing a number of women whose bodies were covered with open sores. As they dominated the commerce of the region, the Chinookan tongue became the basis for the widely used Chinook jargon which was first used as a trade language but developed into a means of communication between tribes from Alaska to California.

Lewis and Clark found the Chinookans exceedingly deceitful and treacherous. They were greedy, demanding, ill-tempered, and menacing, but lacked the courage to carry out most of the threats they made. However, they were expert canoeists, some of their craft being extremely large and hollowed from a single gigantic tree, and as they were intimately acquainted with the rivers they were helpful as guides. They also supplied the expedition with game and fish, but seldom without demanding articles in payment.

These excerpts from the Journals of Lewis and Clark present invaluable pictures of the Chinookans.[27] On November 7, 1805, they reached a village in which the houses were "raised entirely above ground, with the eaves about five feet high and the door at the corner. Near the end, opposite this door, is a single fireplace, round which are the beds, raised four feet from the floor of earth; over the fire are hung the fresh fish, which, when dried, are stowed away with the wappato-roots under the beds . . . the women are clad in a peculiar manner, the robe not reaching lower than the hip, and the body being covered in cold weather by a sort of corset of fur, curiously plaited and reaching from the arms to the hip; added to this is a sort of petticoat, or rather tissue of white cedar bark, bruised or broken into small strands, and woven into a girdle by several cords of the same material. Being tied round the middle, these strands hang down as low as the knee in front, and to the mid-leg behind; they are of sufficient thickness to answer the purpose of concealment whilst the female stands in an erect position, but in any other attitude form but a very ineffectual defense." These people were called Wahkiacum, the name of their leader. They were not a separate tribe, and belonged to the Cathlamet.

Of the Chinook tribe, on January 13, 1806: "The men are low in stature, rather ugly and ill-made, their legs being small and crooked, their feet large, and their heads, like those of the women, flattened in a most disgusting manner. These deformities are in part concealed by robes made of sea-otter, deer, elk, beaver, or fox skins. They also employ in their dress robes of the skin of a cat [wildcat, also called bay lynx] peculiar to the country, and of another animal of the same size, which skin is light and durable, and sold at a high price by the Indians who bring it from above [Canada lynx]. In addition to these are worn blankets, wrappers of red, blue, or spotted cloth, and some old sailor's clothes, which were very highly prized.

"The women have, in general, handsome faces, but are low and disproportioned, with small feet and large legs and thighs, occasioned, probably, by strands of beads, or various strings, drawn so tight above the ankles as to prevent the circulation of the blood. Their dress . . .

consists of a short robe and a tissue of cedar bark. Their hair hangs loosely down the shoulders and back; their ears, neck, and wrists are ornamented with blue beads. Another decoration, which is very highly prized, consists of figures made by puncturing the arm or legs." One squaw had the name "J. Bowman" punctured on an arm, apparently in remembrance of a sailor of whom she had been enamored.

The custom of artificially deforming the head by fronto-occipital pressure was universal among the Chinookan people. They regarded a skull in its natural form as a disgrace.

The Penutian

The seven main tribes of this linguistic family controlled more land area than any other people of the Pacific States, almost half of present California. Yet, only one tribe, the Costanoan, inhabited territory on the coast.

The Maidu, Miwok, Wintun, Patwin, Wintu, and Yokuts dwelt in the great interior valleys between the magnificent Sierra Nevada on the east and the rugged Coast Range on the west. The homeland of the Costanoan reached westward from the Salinas Valley over the high coastal ridges to the sea, extending along the shore from a short distance north of San Francisco Bay southward to Point Sur, below Carmel.

All of this vast empire, which included the immense San Joaquin and Sacramento valleys, was well watered, and all of its many rivers drained into the Pacific through the Golden Gate. There are few regions on earth of the same size—more than four hundred miles in length—endowed with greater diversity of surface, altitude, humidity, soil, and vegetation.[28] The rivers provided easy routes of travel. The contrasting climates of the interior and the coast produced an endless variety of plant foods, of game, and of sea foods. Natural resources differed in each area, making possible the manufacture of many types of articles. The Penutians, in numbers the largest linguistic family in California, not only conducted a constant and heavy commerce among themselves but engaged in extensive trade with adjoining peoples.

There is no reason to doubt that the Penutians occupied central California long before the beginning of the Christian Era, and they may have been there at a much earlier time. While connections between Pleistocene people and the Penutians have not been established to the satisfaction of archeologists, traits in their customs reflect in some respects on characteristics of ancient cultures. Also, it appears that their territory was occupied continuously for many millennia.

Heizer states that "there are strong hints of the presence of man about 8,000 or 9,000 years ago. One of these hints is a long string of

shell beads made from a species native to the coast of central California
and found in a dry cave deposit in Nevada. The age of the beads is
about 9,000 years, and from them we infer the existence in central California, some three hundred miles to the west, of peoples who were
gathering marine shells, fashioning them into beads, and passing them
on by inter-group barter until they reached central Nevada. These
California bead makers . . . we cannot now identify, but we are convinced that their evidences exist. . . ." [29] Artifacts of later cultures have
been recovered in the same area, notably along the Sacramento and
San Joaquin rivers. The last culture of the region, according to Heizer,
"began about A.D. 500 and endured until the Indian culture was destroyed by the Spanish, Mexican and American occupation. It is named
the Late Horizon. . . . Wide-ranging trade relations are evident, and
the culture revealed is clearly that fashioned by the direct ancestors of
the recent Indian tribes. . . ." [30]

Because the Penutians lived at altitudes ranging from sea level to
several thousand feet they built numerous types of dwellings. Some
were of log, others were partly underground and had earth-covered
roofs, while in the mountain areas their houses were conical and constructed mainly of slabs of bark. No permanent settlements were maintained above four thousand feet, but in the summer they made excursions to hunt and gather wild plant foods in the high Sierras. Tattooing
was widely practiced, the women of some tribes decorating their faces.
Others confined the ornamentation to their breasts and stomach.

The Yokuts, who occupied the San Joaquin Valley, were unique
among the Penutians in that they were divided into between forty and
fifty "true tribes." [31] Each of these tribes had a name, a dialect, and a
territory. "Such an array of dialects is unparalleled," says Kroeber,
"and gives to the Yokuts alone nearly one-third of all the different
forms of speech talked in the State. The differences of language from
tribe to tribe were often rather limited; but they are marked enough
to be readily perceptible. . . . Since the total length of the Yokuts area
does not much exceed 250 miles and the breadth nowhere attains to
100, the individual geographical range of these little languages was
exceedingly narrow." [32] Truly there was a linguistic babel along the
San Joaquin River.

The 1848 gold discovery was made in the heart of Penutian territory,
and brought the stampedes which comprise the last chapter of their
story. The Costanoans, dwelling along the coast, were destroyed much
earlier. Seven Franciscan missions were built in their territory, and as
prisoners of religious zealots, forced to face a way of life totally alien
to every concept and instinct they knew, they were soon extinct.

The Salishan

The name of this widely spread linguistic family is derived from the Salish—more popularly and erroneously called Flatheads—a tribe that inhabited far western Montana and parts of eastern Idaho.* Yet, by far the greater number of the people speaking this language, and the many dialects of it, lived in the Puget Sound region and in southern British Columbia. This anomalous situation has been the cause of many disputes between ethnologists, but its explanation probably lies in prehistoric migrations. However, these must have taken place a very long time ago, for the culture of the Salish of Montana is closer to that of mountains and plains people, while the culture of the coastal Salishan people is intrinsically related to that of tribes who dwelt to the north of them. Even the physical characteristics of the upper and lower Salish are drastically different.

Twenty-five of the twenty-seven coastal Salishan tribes held territories in Washington, the other two living in what is now northwestern Oregon. If, in 1592, Juan de Fuca actually entered the great strait named for him, as he claimed, he was the first white man to encounter the Salishans. Other Spanish navigators touched along the coast in Salishan territory in the seventeenth century, but are not known to have been in close contact with them. Very little was known of them until the advent of British and American explorers toward the end of the eighteenth century. However, little reliable information was gained until the arrival of overland fur traders and the expedition of Lewis and Clark. Jurisdiction over their country was long disputed by England and the United States.

One of the greatest annual ceremonies among the Salishan, as it was among other tribes of the northwest coast, was the potlatch. The word came into popular usage from the Chinook jargon, deriving from the Nootka word *patshatl,* meaning "giving" or "gift." According to the distinguished ethnologist Dr. John R. Swanton, "potlatches were mainly marked by the giving away of quantities of goods, commonly blankets. The giver sometimes went so far as to strip himself of nearly every possession except his house, but he obtained an abundant reward, in his own estimation, in the respect with which his fellow townsmen afterward regarded him . . . when others potlatched, he, in turn, received a share of their property with interest, so that potentially he was richer than before." [33] During the potlatches there were singing, dancing, and feasting; the children of prominent men were initiated into secret societies and their ears, noses, and lips were pierced for ornaments.

---

* See Part Eight.

Living in a land that abounded in game, fish, and a great variety of wild plant foods, the Salishans could well afford to indulge in numerous rituals and festivals, some of which lasted for several days without interruption. This pleasant and comfortable way of life was drastically changed by white settlers, and the Salishan were soon disorganized and sent down the road to destruction.

Lewis and Clark included Salishans in a general description of Indians living along the Oregon and Washington coast, stating that "they are commonly of a diminutive stature, badly shaped, and their appearance is by no means prepossessing. They have broad, thick, flat feet, thick ankles and crooked legs; the last of which deformities is to be ascribed, in part, to the universal practice of squatting or sitting on the calves of their legs and heels, and also to the tight bandages of beads and strings worn round the ankles by the women, which prevent the circulation of the blood, and render the legs, of the female particularly, ill-shaped and swollen. The complexion is . . . rather lighter than that of the Indians of the Missouri . . . the mouth is wide and the lips are thick; the nose is of a moderate size, fleshy, wide at the extremity, with large nostrils, and generally low between the eyes . . . the eyes are generally black, though we occasionally see them of a dark yellowish-brown, with a black pupil." [34]

The Americans were appalled and repelled by the Salishan custom of flattening the head, "by which nature is sacrificed to fantastic ideas of beauty." However, they were unstinting in their praise of the skill with which the Salishans of the coast handled canoes, and they marveled at the great size of them, writing that the craft "are upward of fifty feet long, and will carry from 8,000 to 10,000 pounds' weight, or from 20 to 30 persons . . . at each end are pedastles . . . on which are placed strange, grotesque figures of men or animals, rising sometimes to the height of five feet, and composed of small pieces of wood, firmly united with great ingenuity, by inlaying and mortising, without a spike of any kind. . . . When they embark, one Indian sits in the stern and steers with a paddle; the others kneel in pairs in the bottom of the canoe, and, sitting on their heels, paddle over the gunwhale next to them. In this way they ride with perfect safety the highest waves, and venture without the least concern in seas where other boats or seamen could not live an instant." [35]

The Salishan were sharp traders. The customary practice of "getting all the traffic would bear" is aptly illustrated in an anecdote about their last and greatest chief, Seattle. Born in 1790, at the beginning of contact with white traders, he lived through all the tumultuous years of the wrangling over the international border and the influx of settlers who took without regard for justice or human rights the property and lands of his people. He was well along in years when the new town of

Seattle was given his name. Thereupon, he invoked an ancient Salishan belief which said that any mention of a dead man's name disturbed the peaceful repose of his spirit. To compensate for this future annoyance, the old man levied a small monetary tribute on the citizens, collecting the payments in advance.

Seattle erected a monument to him in 1890.

The Shoshonean

One of the most widely extended linguistic stocks in the region of the United States, the Shoshoneans reached the sea in only one area—southern California. It is not believed they have lived there a very long time, perhaps no longer than two thousand years. Other peoples long had been there when they arrived, and they drove between them. Kroeber thinks that "perhaps it would be conservative to allow 1,500 years since the Shoshoneans first began to reach the coast. The languages of the Yuman and Chumash peoples, whom the Shoshoneans have apparently split apart in their ancient shoreward drift, are so extremely different from each other now that this period is certainly the minimum that can be assumed for their separation." [36]

The narrow strip of California that lies east of the Sierra Nevada belongs to the Great Basin. There the Shoshoneans held a frontier six hundred miles in length.* On the coast they occupied hardly a hundred miles of territory. All of them came to California out of the Great Basin, but only one of the thirteen tribes to migrate westward, the Tubatulabal, crossed high ranges at the southern end of the Sierra Nevada. The other twelve tribes followed routes over passes and deserts farther south. Settling on the upper reaches of Kern River, the Tubatulabal were the only Shoshoneans to establish themselves on waters draining into the great interior valley of California, the San Joaquin.

The Shoshoneans reached southern California in successive waves, over many years, band after band moving to reunite with their respective congeners in a region that was warmer in its entirety, and in a large part far more fertile, than the barren and bleak valleys of the Great Basin. Yet only four tribes—the Gabrieliño, Juaneño, Nicoleño, and Luiseño—were able to hold in permanent occupation lands directly on the sea. More than half of this most desirable area of southern California was held by tribes of the Hokan linguistic group. The Shoshonean Alliklik, Cahuilla, Cupeño, Fernandiño, Kawaiisu, Kitanemuk, Serrano, and Vanyume made their homes in various inland locations, extending from the Los Angeles Basin to the San Bernardino and

* See Part Nine.

Tehachapi ranges and to the mountains that tower over the deserts surrounding Palm Springs.

The Shoshoneans, basically desert, hill, and mountain people—which most of them remained—brought their ancient skills with them to southern California, and the way of life they had always known was not greatly modified, except in the respects that they enjoyed more dependable and more plentiful supplies of plant foods and game, that seafoods and by-products of them were obtainable in trade. However, this was not the case for the Gabrieliño, the Nicoleño, the Luiseño, and the Juaneño, who lived on the coast. They were obliged to adjust to an economy entirely alien to them. How many generations this required cannot even be guessed. Undoubtedly succeeding waves of migrants learned from those of their kind who had preceded them, and who had learned from neighboring coastal peoples. That all became expert fishermen, swimmers, and gatherers of shellfish and shells— particularly the highly prized abalone—there can be no question. The sea was the main source of their subsistence. Two of the tribes, the Gabrieliño and Nicoleño, truly became seagoing Indians.

Besides living on the mainland, the Gabrieliño also occupied the islands of Santa Catalina and San Clemente. It is thought they were the most advanced people in southern California, perhaps excepting the Chumash. Kroeber says of them that they "certainly were the wealthiest and most thoughtful of all the Shoshoneans of the state, and dominated these civilizationally wherever contacts occurred. Their influence spread even to alien peoples." [37]

They constructed remarkable boats of planks, there being no trees large enough to be made into dugouts capable of sailing open waters. A student of these Indians, Johnston,[38] writes: "Hard work and great skill were used in the making of these fine craft, with their two prows, and sometimes wing-boards as well. Driftwood logs had to be split into planks with wedges made of bone or antler, and planed with stone scrapers. Drills of stone cut and reamed the holes through which strong cords of fiber were laced. It is said that the planks were buried in wet sand with fires built above them in order to make it possible to bend them into place . . . even after the most thorough caulking with asphalt it was necessary on all extended voyages to take along a youth or two whose duty it was to bail out the inevitable and sometimes formidable seepage. These boats ranged from 12 to 16 feet in length. Having no skeleton, they depended on the keel for strength." The coastal Shoshoneans also used rafts made of logs and rushes for fishing in sheltered waters.

A natural resource that greatly contributed to the wealth of the Gabrieliños was the extensive deposit of soapstone, or steatite, on Santa Catalina Island. From this material could be made utensils far superior to those made of pottery, and they were in great demand by surrounding tribes. Even when a soapstone cooking pot broke after long usage, the pieces "were bored at one corner to allow of the insertion of a stick to handle them by, and utilized as baking slabs or frying pans." [39] Archeologists occasionally have recovered unusually fine soapstone vessels which were used in religious ceremonies. Kroeber reports that they "are shell inlaid and untouched by fire . . . delicately walled, polished, symmetrical, and ornamented. . . ."

On storm-swept, foggy, rocky San Nicolas, the farthest seaward of the Channel Islands, dwelt a small group of Indians known—for want of a more authentic name—as the Nicoleño. Four badly spelled words are all that have survived of their speech. While these prove that it was Shoshonean, they do not establish its dialectic relation.

This is the brief and sad story of the Nicoleño as related by Kroeber: [40]

"Wood was scarce and small on the island. There was enough brush for huts, but most dwellings were reared on a frame of whale ribs and jaws, either covered with sea lion hides or wattled with brush or rushes. Bone implements were very numerous. . . . The island may have afforded sufficient timber for plank canoes, or dugouts may have been burned from drift logs. Steatite was imported from Santa Catalina, but it is represented by small ornaments or charms rather than heavy bowls. Whales must have been very abundant and frequently stranded. . . . Sea otters were to be had in comparative profusion, and, to judge from the habits of other tribes, their furs formed the most prized dress and the chief export in a trade on which the San Nicoleño must have depended for many necessities. Seals, waterbirds, fish, and mollusks were no doubt the principal food, but roots were dug industriously.

"The last handful of the natives, who are said to have suffered previously in quarrels with Aleuts imported by Russian fur hunters, and whose numbers had probably been diminished by drafts to the missions, were taken to the mainland in 1835, soon after secularization [of the California missions]. A woman who at the last moment missed her child was left behind. Eighteen years later, when California was American, she was discovered. Her romantic case aroused the greatest interest, and she was given the best of treatment in her new home at Santa Barbara; but she died in a few months."

The woman was the last survivor of the Nicoleño tribe.

However, very few of the Shoshoneans who dwelt in the Los Angeles Basin, along the coast, and in areas immediately adjacent to it, were still alive when the Nicoleño woman succumbed. Soon thereafter there were almost no survivors. The missions, more than anything else, had brought about their extinction. So successfully had the padres confused and eradicated their identities and destroyed the last vestiges of their cultures that the three main coastal tribes of Shoshoneans became known to history by the names of the missions at which they were forced to live and labor—the Gabrieliño for the Mission San Gabriel, the Luiseño for the Mission San Luis Rey, the Juaneño for the Mission San Juan Capistrano—their native names forgotten. The Fernandiño, long ago totally extinct, who once dwelt along the Los Angeles River and were closely related in dialect to the Gabrieliño, have been given the name of the other mission in Los Angeles County, San Fernando.

The Kalapooian

By the time scientific studies of these Oregon Indians were undertaken they were nearing extinction, and little reliable information about their prehistoric social and political structures could be obtained. All but one of the nine main tribes which comprised the linguistic family dwelt on the Willamette River and its tributaries. However, the odd one, the Yoncalla, inhabited territory not far distant from others of the family on creeks flowing into the Umpqua River.

The meaning of the names of the Willamette Valley tribes—the Ahantchuyuk, Atfalati, Calapooya, Chelamela, Chepenafa, Luckiamute, Santiam, and Yamel—are unknown. Yoncalla is believed to have derived from *Ayankeld*, by which they identified themselves, but it is apparently a place name meaning simply "those living at Ayankeld." The late Livingston Ferrand of Columbia University stated that the Kalapooian language "is sonorous, the verbs excessively complex, few prefixes being used, and the words are distinguished by consonantal endings." [41]

It is possible, but unlikely, that Lewis and Clark saw some of the Kalapooian, although one of the tribes, the Atfalati, is thought to have ranged as far north as the Columbia River in the vicinity of Portland. However, they may have gone there only on trading trips or raids. In any case, Lewis and Clark heard of them, their Journal under date of April 4, 1806, containing the note applying to the Willamette Valley: "As far as the Indians with whom we conversed had ever penetrated that country, it is inhabited by a nation called Calahpoewah, a very numerous people whose villages, nearly 40 in number, are scattered along each side of the Multnomah, which furnishes them with their chief subsistence—fish and roots along its banks." It is not certain whether the explorers were including the Kalapooians in the following passage about the people of the Multnomah [Willamette] Valley: ". . . they are afflicted with the common disease of the Columbia—soreness of the eyes. To whatever [cause] this disorder may be imputed, it is a great national calamity; at all ages their eyes are sore and weak;

the loss of one eye is by no means uncommon; in grown persons total blindness is frequent, and almost universal in old age." [42]

Ferrand stated that Kalapooian territory ended on the north at the falls of the Willamette, and they "seem to have confined themselves" to the valley of that river, although "they were at constant war with the coast peoples." Early traders in the area are said to have considered them indolent and sluggish, yet for countless years they were able to defend themselves successfully against surrounding tribes who attempted to dispossess them.

The Kalapooian suffered severe losses from epidemics—probably measles and smallpox introduced by white men—in the middle eighteen-twenties. In their customs and their way of life they were typical of Indians of the region. They practiced flattening of the forehead.

They suffered greatly at the hands of settlers, who drove them from their lands. They were forced to "cede" all their territory to the United States between 1854 and 1857, and were removed to a reservation. Not many of them were alive at the time, and within a few more years only a few full-blooded Kalapooians still survived.

The Wakashan

The Strait of Juan de Fuca severed the northwest coastal territory occupied by this linguistic family, but approximately five sixths of the population—somewhat more than ten thousand persons—lived in Canada on Vancouver Island and along both sides of Queen Charlotte Sound.

The two tribes inhabiting American territory were the Makah and the Ozette. *Makah* means "cape people," an appropriate name, for they lived on Cape Flattery, the northeast tip of the Olympic Peninsula. Directly to the south of them, on the coast of Washington, were the Ozette, but the meaning of their name is unknown. There is doubt, as well, as to the significance of *Wakashan*. It is derived from the word *waukash*—"good"—which an early explorer heard when he encountered these Indians at Nootka Sound and supposed it to be their tribal name.

The Wakashan were probably the first Indians of the region to be met by white men. The historical period may have begun for them, therefore, in the middle of the sixteenth century. Numerous expeditions anchored in the bays and sounds of their territory, especially on the Canadian side, in later years. In the eighteenth century the demand for sea otter pelts brought an almost constant stream of British and American ships offering goods of all kinds in exchange for them and other valuable furs. The great herds of sea otters were depleted to such an extent by the early nineteenth century that voyages to obtain them were no longer profitable. Thereafter the fur trade was dominated by British and American companies which established permanent posts for the purpose of securing the furs of land animals.

Wakashan dwellings were large structures of huge cedar beams and planks, and stood in a row fronting on the sea. Several families lived in each one, and had separate cooking fires. In the social structure a major difference between the tribes was in their customs of reckoning descent. In the north it was reckoned in the female line, and in the south in the paternal line.

In all America there were no Indians more competent or more daring than the Wakashan. They and some of their close neighbors were the only aborigines known to have pursued and killed whales in the open sea. They constructed large and strong craft in which they performed their deep-water feats. All other Indians of the Pacific Coast were content to obtain meat and oil from dead whales which drifted ashore.

With the taking of their lands by settlers the American Wakashan were placed on a reservation. By this time they had dwindled in numbers to a few hundred. The last Ozette died in 1937, and only a few Makah still survive.

The Yakonan

The people of this small linguistic family were unusually susceptible to tuberculosis. The disease and the inroads of civilization wiped them out.

The six tribes—Alsea, Hanis, Kuitsh, Miluk, Siuslaw, and Yaquina—occupied territory in western Oregon and along the coast in the vicinity of the Yaquina, Umpqua, and Coquille rivers and on Coos Bay. Ethnologists at one time considered the Hanis and Miluk as a separate linguistic family, the Kusan, but studies have indicated it is connected with the Yakonan.

The Yakonan represented the southern limit of a culture exhibited by tribes of the coast of Washington and Vancouver Island. South of them were Athapascan people who were influenced by the cultures of California stocks. Four of the tribes artificially deformed their heads, but the Hanis and Miluk did not indulge in the practice.

Little is known of their social organization. Ferrand wrote that there was "a preference for marriage outside the tribe, though this did not have the force of an exogamous rule, so far as can be learned. The social orders of nobility and common people, peculiar to the northwest coast, obtained, and slavery was an institution in full force until the tribes came under the control of the United States." [43]

The Takilman

The Takilman were almost completely surrounded by Athapascan tribes, yet both their culture and their language endured for many centuries. They themselves perished under the pressures of settlement and the irresistible forces of white men's guns and diseases.

Two tribes composed the linguistic family. The Takelma, who dwelt on the middle course of Rogue River, and the Latgawa, whose villages stood along the upper course of the same stream. They were remotely related to the Shastan stock of northern California. Appropriately, *Takelma* means "those dwelling along the river," and *Latgawa* signifies "those living in the uplands."

The Takilman were few in number, a small island of people speaking a most peculiar language that showed no resemblance in even general morphologic or phonetic traits to either the Athapascan or other tongues spoken by their neighbors. Their way of life, however, was identical with that of the other tribes of southern Oregon and northern California, but their political and social structures were the acme of simplicity.

The Takilman village, usually very small, was the only important sociological unit. Ethnologists have discovered no sign of totemism or clan groupings. Social distinction was based on wealth, and leadership was not inherited. Marriage was outside the village, and brides were purchased. A man could have as many wives as he could support, and the levirate prevailed.

The chief occasions on which ceremonials were held were the appearance of salmon and acorns, which with venison and camas roots comprised the main staples of their diet. The prehistoric Takilman hunted deer by running them into enclosures in which traps had been set. They used a great variety of baskets for cooking, storage, and carrying. Their implements were made of horn, wood, and bone, but, strangely, they made little use of stone, except for projectile points and pestles. Their houses were built partly underground and constructed of hewn timbers. The doorway was raised and reached by a notched ladder.

The Takilman wore scalps of redheaded woodpeckers and basket caps. Their faces were painted red, black, and white. Women tattooed themselves with designs of three parallel stripes, but men used totooing more for practical purposes than ornamentation. On their left arms they placed marks which could be used for measuring strings of dentalium shells—their money.

The Algonquian

The Wiyot lived on Mad River, Humboldt Bay, and Eel River of California. The villages of their kinsmen, the Yurok, were on the lower Klamath River and along the coast north and south of it. Both of these tribes were at one time classified as independent stocks. Later they were combined in a linguistic family which was called Ritwan. Still later ethnologists, notably Edward Sapir and A. L. Kroeber, identified their tongue as belonging to the great Algonquian linguistic family of the eastern United States.[44]

This finding, however, has never met with entire acceptance. If it is correct—and many leading scholars think it is—then a genuine mystery exists. In the northwestern California wilderness dwelt Indians who were separated by some two thousand miles from the nearest members of their linguistic family. When they reached this isolated region, or why they went to it, are questions for which science has no answers.

The culture of the Yurok and adjacent tribes in northwestern California in many aspects attained a higher level than any other in the state. Kroeber wrote that "arts were carried to a distinctive pitch. Manufactured articles were better finished. Many objects which the central and southern Californians fashioned only as bare utility demanded were regularly decorated with carvings in the northwest."[45] Three of the great linguistic families of the continent, the Algonquian, the Hokan, and the Athapascan, border each other in the area, but the innermost core of this civilization is more nearly represented by the Yurok than by any other group.

The principles of Yurok law were sociologically unique, many of them in sharp contrast with concepts and theories held by most other Indian peoples and almost totally strange to social and jurisdictional ideas and practices of other races. Property and rights pertained to the realm of the individual, and the Yurok recognized no public claim and the existence of no community. In the words of Kroeber, the Yurok's world was an aggregation of individuals.[46]

The money of the Yurok was dentalium shells, which they received from tribes living farther north. The main source was Vancouver Island, and it reached the Yurok after passing through numerous hands in intertribal trading. The shells were graded according to length, which determined their value, and kept on strings that reached from the tip of a man's thumb along his outstretched arm to the point of his shoulder.

The Shapwailutan

They were interior people. The 121st Meridian passes through, or close to, the territories occupied by the six main tribes of the Shapwailutan linguistic family, in the states of Washington, Oregon, and California.

The Klickitat, the most northern tribe, dwelt about the confluence of the Klickitat and Columbia rivers. In the Chinook tongue their name signifies "beyond," and refers to the fact that their homeland was east of, or beyond, the Cascade Mountains. Lewis and Clark encountered them in this location, and found them to be extremely friendly. At an earlier time they lived farther to the south.

The Klickitat were enterprising traders. Due to their geographical situation on the Columbia they profited in the capacity of middlemen between the coastal tribes and those living to the east. The agreeableness and hospitality they displayed to Lewis and Clark were not always extended to other tribes. A few years after the passage of the American explorers they demonstrated less commendable qualities in their character. When the tribes of the Willamette Valley were weakened by an epidemic of fever the Klickitat attacked them and carried on a conquest as far south as the valley of the Umpqua River. However, the Willamette tribes soon recovered sufficiently to drive them back to the Columbia.

The Molala participated in the Willamette invasion. According to a tradition of the Cayuse,* they once shared territory with them on the Deschutes River, but the Molala were driven westward by enemies to the Molala and Santiam rivers. Some of them subsequently moved on to the upper waters of the Umpqua and the Rogue rivers.

The Tyigh and Tenino lived in the vicinity of White and Tyigh rivers, the latter being mentioned by Lewis and Clark. Neither tribe figured prominently in the early history of the area.

Both the Klamath and the Modoc, who comprised a dialectical division of the stock, ranged over southern Oregon and northern California. The Klamath dwelt about upper Klamath Lake, Klamath Marsh, and along the Williamson and Sprague rivers. The Modoc villages stood about Little Klamath Lake, Modoc Lake, Tule Lake, in the Lost River Valley, and on Clear Lake in extreme northern California.

"Their cultural position," states Stern,[47] "was at once peripheral and strategic, for they lay at the boundaries of the emergent cultural provinces of the Great Basin, the Plateau, and California, and though they stemmed fundamentally from the Great Basin, they were also subject to influences flowing from California and the Plateau. Consistent

---

* See Part Eight.

with their relative geographical position and ecological resources, the Modoc diverged toward California and the Klamath toward the Plateau; and when in turn the influences of the North Pacific Coast . . . reached them, it was again the Klamath who were somewhat more receptive. Despite their differences, the two peoples retained a substantial common base."

One of the main staple foods of these tribes was wokas. In marshy places these water lilies spread out for miles. The unripe seed pods were picked from canoes. After being sun-dried, the seeds were pounded out. They were cooked in various ways.

The Klamath and the Modoc called themselves *maklaks,* meaning simply "people." When necessary to distinguish themselves they did so by geographical designations. Both were competent and brave in battle, and fought fiercely in defense of their homelands. The Modoc were among the last Indians of the West to succumb to the pressures of settlement and the vastly superior power of the American military.

The Chimakuan

The tongue of this tiny linguistic family is one of the most peculiar of all Indian languages. The three small tribes speaking it—the Chimakum, the Hoh, and the Quileute—dwelt in northwest Washington. It is a question, however, whether they should be remembered for the strangeness of their speech or their warlike natures. Both gave them distinction.

The Chimakum lived on the peninsula between Hood's Canal and Port Townsend. The home of the Hoh was on the river given their name and on the Washington coast. The territory of the Quileute was on the river which is misspelled as Quilayute.

At the beginning of the historical period the population of the three tribes was probably less than a thousand persons. Constant fighting with stronger neighbors was probably responsible for their depletion to this small number. Ethnologists believe that in earlier centuries they were much more powerful and may have occupied the entire region to the south of the Strait of Juan de Fuca, but there is little evidence to support the opinion. Long ago they were driven out of this area by stronger tribes.

The culture of the Chimakuan was typical of the Northwest Coast tribes. They were expert fishermen, and may have been whalers.

Studies of the Chimakuan tongue were undertaken too late to produce dependable results. In 1890 the noted ethnologist Boas could find only three individuals of the Chimakum tribe who could speak the language, and then but imperfectly.[48] A few more Hoh and Quileute survived at the time, but their dialects swiftly suffered adulterations after they were placed on reservations with people speaking other tongues. However, some scholars contend they have detected morphologic and phonetic relations to the Salish and Wakashan languages.

Although the Chimakuan were noted among other Indians for their belligerency, they seldom displayed the same tendency toward white men, a factor which did little to delay their destruction.

The Yukian

The tribes speaking dialects of the Yukian language dwelt in both the inland valleys of northern California and along the coast. There were notable differences between both their cultures and their physical appearances.

The aboriginal name of the tribe called Wappo is in doubt, if it is known at all. *Wappo* is an Americanization of the Spanish *guapo,* signifying "brave." Kroeber states they earned the sobriquet in the California mission period by their stubborn resistance "to the military adjuncts of the Franciscan establishments." [49]

The Wappo lived on the headwaters of the Napa River and Pope and Putah creeks, and on a small part of Russian River.[50] Not only their refusal to become missionized and their fierce fighting against Spanish troops distinguished them. Their language was exceedingly different from that of their congeners, the Yuki and the Huchnom; according to Kroeber, differing more than Spanish from Italian or German from Norwegian and perhaps almost as widely as German from English. He believes that on the basis of such comparisons, "a thousand years would be a short lapse to allow for the degree of divergence. On the other hand, the Wappo were a small people and wholly surrounded by half a dozen nationalities of entirely distinct language. Under such conditions of abundant and enforced alien contact a tongue changes with unusual rapidity. . . ." [51]

The Yukian Huchnom lived in the valley of South Eel River from Hullville nearly to its mouth. Their name is believed to signify "mountain people," and they called themselves by it. Adjoining them were the so-called Coast Yuki, whose own name was *Ukhotno'm,* meaning "ocean people." They lived along the Pacific from Cleone to a point halfway between Rockport and Usal, and inland to the divide between the coast streams and Eel River.

The Yuki proper, from whom the name of the stock derives, inhabited all land lying in the drainage of Eel River above the North Fork, except for a part of South Eel River where their relatives, the Huchnom, were situated.

The position of the Yukian family, in Kroeber's opinion, is somewhat like that of the Basque in Europe, "and the people speaking

Yukian dialects, or some of their ancestors, must accordingly be regarded as having had a long separate career.

"As with the Basques, a peculiar physical type tends to accompany distinctive speech in the case of the Yukian family. The northern tribes of the family possess probably the longest heads in California, and are unusually short of stature." [52] This physical type is found also among adjacent non-Yukian people. The southern Yukians, however, depart from it, and resemble "their broader-headed and taller-bodied neighbors." Kroeber takes the position that this situation "is easily intelligible as a consequence of gradual intermarriage and the shifting of populations from their former seats; in other words, a secondary phenomenon." He adds that the "essential fact remains that the Yukian speech and the Yukian anatomy are both distinctive and both not definitely connectable with any other group. In this sense, the Yuki may fairly be spoken of as coming nearer . . . to being autochthonous Californians than any other of the modern natives of the State."

In their mode of life, habits, and beliefs the Yukian generally resemble the better-known Pomo, although the Yuki proper show the closest specific cultural resemblances to the neighboring Athapascan Wailaki. The Huchnom affiliated with the Pomo, and resembled these more nearly in their habits and practices than they did the Yuki proper.

Yuki women tattooed their faces on the cheeks and chin. One of the important Yuki ceremonies was conducted by a secret society the members of which represented spirits of the dead. The Yukians believed that the world was created by a "being," human in shape, called Taikomol, meaning "he who travels alone."

Aside from the facts that the Yukians were independent and dangerous adversaries in battle, the Spanish learned little about them. That was probably all they cared to know. The Yukians were scarcely known to any other white persons, and least of all to scholars, when the discovery of gold flooded California with miners and settlers. They fought the intruders as best they could, displaying all the bravery they had shown against the Franciscans and the Spanish military, but they were slaughtered by Americans and destroyed.

The Hokan

To the Yahi, one of the small tribes of the widely spread Hokan linguistic family, belongs the most famous story in all the history of the American aborigines. It is the story of Ishi, the last wild Indian in North America.

I can conceive of no better way to conclude this work than by recounting it in small part. First, however, a few brief tasks remain to be accomplished.

The fourteen tribes which comprise the Hokan group of the Pacific region extended in a number of islands from extreme southern Oregon into Mexico. In the north were seven tribes loosely designated as the Shastan Group:

The Achomawi: In the drainage area of Pit River from near Montgomery Creek to Goose Lake. They suffered from slave raids made by the Modoc and Klamath, who sold Achomawi captives on the great intertribal slave market at The Dalles in Oregon. The Achomawi were not overly aggressive. Kroeber says of them that they "had the usual Californian point of view: a stranger would usually be killed on principle because he was a stranger, and a neighbor would be attacked when he had given grievance. But war for the fun of the game, or for gain, was foreign to their ideas, so that they would be actuated to retaliate against the Modoc only by revenge; and as they scarcely even made the attempt, it is likely that fear tempered their desire for revenge." They were hunters, fishermen, and gatherers of wild plant foods. Acorns, a staple for many tribes, were scarce, and most of those they ate were obtained in trade.

The Atsugewi: On three streams draining northward into Pit River, Burney Creek, Hat Creek, and Dixie Valley or Horse Creek. Their way of life was practically identical with that of the Achomawi.

The Chimariko: They occupied one of the smallest areas, if not the smallest, of any tribe in America. It was twenty miles in length, entirely within the canyon of the Trinity River from above the mouth of South Fork to French Creek. The Chimariko carried on bitter fighting with the white gold seekers, which was the chief cause of their rapid diminution and eventual extinction.

The Karok: On the middle course of Klamath River. Although they spoke a totally different language, they were culturally assimilated with their neighbors, the Algonquian Yurok. "Except for a few transient bands of Hudson Bay Company *voyageurs,*" says Kroeber, "the Karok knew nothing of the existence of white men until a swarm of miners and packers burst in upon them in 1850 and 1851." The usual ambushing and slaughtering of the "pesky redskins" followed.

The Konomihu: Their location was territory about the forks of Salmon River. Their culture was closer to that of the Shasta tribe than to the Karok. They wore fringed and painted buckskin clothes and leggings. They, too, were destroyed by miners who occupied the Salmon River Country in 1850—and still occupy it in places.

The Okwanuchu: On the upper Sacramento and the McCloud rivers. Very little is known about them, except that they were a small tribe inhabiting a high mountain fastness and spoke a peculiar dialect. They have long been extinct.

The Shasta: Their name is believed to have been derived from that

of an ancient chief called Sasti. They controlled a mountain and plateau country containing the great extinct volcano and other peaks
that were snow-covered a large part of the year. Their territory extended along Klamath River from a point between Indian and Thompson creeks to a few miles above the mouth of Fall Creek; also a tract
on the north side of the Siskiyou Range in Oregon on the affluents of
Rogue River known as Stewart River and Little Butte Creek. The
Shasta carried on an extensive trade with the Karok and some other
tribes. From them they received dentalium shells—which came all the
way from the north Pacific Coast—salt, seaweed, baskets, tan-oak
acorns, and canoes. In return they gave obsidian for arrow points, deerskins, and sugar-pine nuts. Regarding their culture, Kroeber states that
the "Shasta civilization is a pallid, simplified copy of that of the Yurok
and Karok, as befits a poorer people of more easily contented aspira-
tions. There are some evidences of eastern influences from the Columbia River and Great Basin. . . . In many features there is an approach
to the customs typical of central California: not to the complex institutions of the Sacramento Valley, but to the cultural background of
the peripheral hill tribes, such as the Yana, the mountain Maidu, the
southern Athabascans, and the adjacent Wintun." The Shasta Culture
disintegrated rapidly after the beginning of mining and settlement.

   The Yana and the Yahi: Once thought to be an independent linguistic stock, they are now placed in the large Hokan family. Their
territory extended from Pit River to Rock Creek, and from the edge
of the upper Sacramento Valley to the headwaters of the eastern tributaries of the Sacramento River.[53] Much of this region is still mountain
wilderness.

   The Yana were reputed to be exceptionally fierce and competent
warriors, and they offered strong resistance to both red and white intruders. They cannot be described, however, as a superior stock. As
Kroeber notes, whether the cause of their warlike attitude "was actually
a superior energy and courage or an unusual exasperation aided by
a rough, still thinly populated, and easily defensible habitat is more
doubtful. That they were feared by certain of their neighbors argues
them a hungering body of mountaineers. . . . The hill dweller has less
to lose by fighting than the wealthy lowlander. He is also less exposed,
and in time of need has better and more numerous refuges available. . . . However hardy the Yana may have been, it is clear that they
did not rank high among the natives of California. . . . Mythology, symbolism, ritual, social customs, the uses of wealth, are all of the plainest,
most straightforward, and simplest character." [54]

   Yana speech presents a linguistic phenomenon: The talk of men
and women differed. Men spoke the women's forms when conversing
with them, but women always spoke in female forms. Usually a suffix

THE PACIFIC COAST

Earliest Population Estimates*

Cathlamet (1780)	450	Suquamish		
Cathlapotle (1780)	1,300	(in Duwamish)		
Chehalis (1780)	1,000	Swallah		
Chilluckittequaw		(no information)		
(1780)	3,000	Swinomish (in Skagit)		
Chimakum (1780)	400	Taidnapam (in Klickitat)		
Chinook (1780)	800	Twana (in Squaxon)		
Clallum (1780)	2,000	Wishram (1780)	1,500	
Copalis (1805)	200	Ahantchuyuk		
Cowlitz (in Chehalis)		(in Calapooya)		
Duwamish (1780)	1,200	Alsea (1780) (entire		
Hoh (1780)	500	Yakonan stock)	6,000	
Humptulips (in Chehalis)		Atfalati (in Calapooya)		
Klickitat (1780)	600	Calapooya (1780)		
Kwaiailk (1855)	216	(entire Kala-		
Kwalhioqua (1780)	200	pooian stock)	3,000	
Lummi (1780)	1,000	Chastacosta (1780)	5,600	
Makah (1780)	2,000	Chelamela		
Muckleshoot		(in Calapooya)		
(in Nisqually)		Chepenafa		
Nisqually (1780)	3,600	(in Calapooya)		
Nooksack (in Lummi)		Chetco (in Chastacosta)		
Ozette (in Makah)		Clackamas (1780)	2,500	
Puyallup (in Nisqually)		Clatskanie (1780)	1,600	
Queets (1805)	250	Clatsop (1780)	300	
Quileute (in Hoh)		Clowwewalla (1805)	650	
Quimault (1780)	1,500	Dakubetede (1780)	3,200	
Sahehwamish (1780)	1,200	Hanis (1780)	2,000	
Samish (in Lummi)		Klamath (1780)	1,200	
Semiahmoo (1843)	300	Kuitsh (in Alsea)		
Skagit (1780)	1,200	Latgawa (in Takelma)		
Skilloot (1780)	3,250	Luckiamute		
Snohomish (1780)	1,200	(in Calapooya)		
Snoqualmie		Miluk (in Hanis)		
(in Snohomish)		Mishikhwutmetunne		
		(in Chastacosta)		
Squaxon (1780)	1,000	Modoc (1780)	800	
		Molala (1780)	500	

Multnomah (1780)	3,600	**Kawaiisu** (aboriginal)	500
Santiam (in Calapooya)		**Kitanemuk** (in Alliklik)	
Siletz (in Tillamook)		**Konomihu** (1770)	1,000
Siuslaw (in Alsea)		**Lassik** (1770)	2,000
Takelma (1780)	500	**Luiseño** (1770)	4,000
Tenino (with Tyigh and		**Maidu** (1770)	9,000
other bands)	3,600	**Mattole** (1770)	500
Tillamook (1805)	2,200	**Miwok** (1770)	11,000
Tutuni (in Chastacosta)		**Nicoleño** (in Gabrieliño)	
Tyigh (see Tenino)		**Nongatl** (1770)	2,000
Umpqua		**Okwanuchu**	
(in Dakubetede)		(in Konomihu)	
Wasco (1822)	900	**Patwin** (in Wintun)	
Watlala (1780)	2,300	**Pomo** (1770)	8,000
Yamel (in Calapooya)		**Salinan** (1770)	3,000
Yaquina (in Alsea)		**Serrano** (aboriginal)	1,500
Yoncalla (in Calapooya)		**Shasta** (1770)	2,000
Achomawi (1770)	3,000	**Sinkyone** (in Lassik)	
Alliklik (1770)	3,500	**Tolowa** (1770)	450
Atsugewi (in Achomawi)		**Tubatulabal** (1770)	1,000
Bear River (in Nongatl)		**Vanyume** (in Alliklik)	
Cahuilla (1770)	2,500	**Wailaki** (1770)	1,000
Chilula (aboriginal)	600	**Wappo** (1770)	1,000
Chimariko		**Whilkut** (aboriginal)	500
(in Konomihuh)		**Wintu** (in Wintun)	
Chumash (1770)	10,000	**Wintun** (1770)	12,000
Costanoan (1770)	7,000	**Wiyot** (1770)	1,000
Cupeño (1770)	500	**Yana** (1770)	1,500
Diegueño (1770)	3,000	**Yahi** (in Yana)	
Esselen (1770)	500	**Yokuts** (1770)	18,000
Fernandiño		**Yuki and Coast Yuki**	
(in Gabrieliño)		(1770)	2,500
Gabrieliño (1770)	5,000	**Yurok** (1770)	2,500
Huchnom (1770)	500	**Kato** (1770)	500
Hupa (1770)	1,000		
Juaneño (1770)	1,000	**TOTAL**	196,300
Karok (1770)	1,500		

* See Note, Population Table, Part One.

was clipped by women from the full male form. Example: *Yana,* meaning "person," became *ya* in the mouth of a woman.[55]

The Yahi, who probably never numbered more than three hundred persons, were believed to be extinct for more than forty years when suddenly it was discovered that a few of them were still living.

Dwelling in a remote area of northern California they seldom—if at all—came into contact with white men until more than a decade after the discovery of gold and the influx of the Forty-niners. As Kroeber recounts, they inhabited "a region of endless long ridges and cliff-walled canyons, of no great elevation but very rough, and covered with scrub rather than timber. The canyons contain patches in which the brush is almost impenetrable, and the faces of the hills are full of caves. There are a hundred hiding places; but there are no minerals, no marketable timber, no rich bottom lands to draw the American. . . . Everything, therefore, united to provide the Yahi with a retreat from which they could conveniently raid. Only definite and concerted action could rout them out.

"Of course, this action inevitably came. After numerous skirmishes with small parties of Americans, and at least one disastrous fight or slaughter, practically the whole remnant of the group was surrounded and exterminated in an early morning surprise attack by a self-organized body of settlers. This seems to have happened about 1865. If there were known to be survivors, they were so few and so terrified that they were obviously harmless; and no further attention was paid to them. General opinion reckoned the tribe as extinct. After a time, at intervals of years, a cattleman or hunter would report meeting a wild and naked Indian who fled like a deer. A few of the local mountaineers were convinced that a handful of Indians still remained at large, but the farmers in the valley and the townspeople were inclined to scoff at their stories."

The last printed reference to Indians of Yahi territory was that of a man named Powers. He related that about 1872 a hunter had encountered two men, two women, and a child, who quickly vanished into the brush. As later events would show, these were the last survivors of the Yahi.

"At length," continues Kroeber, "in 1908, a party of surveyors half-way up the side of Deer Creek Canyon . . . not more than fifteen miles from a trunk railroad, ran their line almost into a hidden camp in which skulked four middle-aged and elderly Indians who fled. There was no doubt that they were untamed and living the aboriginal existence. Arrows, implements, baskets, the stored food, the huts, were purely native. . . . It was clear that for 43 years this household, remnant of what was once a nation, had maintained itself in this or similarly sheltered spots, smothering their camp smoke, crawling under the brush to leave no trail, obliterating their very footsteps, and running like animals at the approach of a human being . . . the ingenuity of the Indians was almost as marvelous as the secret of their long concealment.

"The discovery broke up the existence into which the little band had settled. They had lost most of their tools; they feared to remain in the vicinity; their food supply became irregular. A year or two later the huts were found still standing, but abandoned. One after another the handful died."

Thus, the stage is set for the story of Ishi.

The Pomo: A large tribe, they were an isolated group of the Hokan linguistic family. Their territory included almost the entire drainage area of the Russian River. The nearest Hokan tribes to the south were about two hundred miles distant, and it was a hundred miles to the Shasta group in the north. Their closest relatives were the Yana, but the southern limits of their lands were fifty miles away, across the Sacramento Valley, from the extreme northeastern lands of the Pomo, and between these two areas dwelt people speaking different tongues.

Prehistoric Pomo men went naked or wrapped a skin about the hips. Women wore a double skirt. Usually it was made of either shredded inner redwood bark, willow bark, or tule rush, varying in the locales in which these materials were most available. Where deer were plentiful it might be made of their skin. Both men and women wore moccasins with soft soles, and sandals and leggings made from tules. Because the Pomo were spread over a region of divergent altitudes and climates their dwellings were of numerous types. On the coast the houses were built of slabs of redwood bark erected to form a cone ten to fifteen feet in diameter. Farther inland frameworks of poles were set up and covered with thatch. Brush shelters were used by those living in the hot interior valley.

The Pomo were famed for their basketry, some archeologists considering it the finest made by any primitive people in the world. Basket-making was not a utilitarian routine to them, it was an art with unlimited possibilities. Describing some of the finest Pomo baskets as "splendidly showy," Kroeber states: "Black, wavy quail plumes may be scattered over the surface . . . or fine bits of scarlet from the woodpecker's scalp worked into a soft brilliant down over the whole of a coiled receptacle. . . . The height of display is reached in the basket whose entire exterior is a mass of feathers, perhaps with patterns in two or three lustrous colors." Some of the most magnificent baskets had edges of beads and fringe of evenly cut haliotis shells. To the Pomo these served as gifts and treasures. No higher use could be made of them than to destroy them in honor of the dead.[56]

The Esselen: The meaning of the name *Esselen* is unknown. This small Hokan tribe lived on the upper course of Carmel River, Sur River, and on the coast from Point Lopez almost to Point Sur. They were the first Indians of California to become extinct. Almost nothing is known of their culture, a few words of their tongue having been preserved to give them a vague linguistic connection. *Esselen* may have been the name of one of their villages on the Carmel River, and hearing it early explorers, following the usual custom, applied it to the entire group.

The Salinan: They occupied the upper Salinas Valley and reached the coast immediately south of the Esselen. They were discovered by the Portola expedition of 1769. They were forcefully brought under the jurisdiction of the missions, their culture was lost, and they rapidly decreased in number. Only two distinctive peculiarities are known of their rude civilization. They used a kind of musical rasp, notched sticks rhythmically rubbed against each other. And according to an authoritative report from the Franciscans of Mission San Miguel, they lent each other shell money at one hundred percent interest per day. Usury is contrary to all the known customs of California Indians.[57]

The Chumash: In 1592 Cabrillo saw the prehistoric civilization of the Chumash. The first Spaniard to sail along the southern California coast and to land on the Channel Islands, he found a large population concentrated along the balmy shore from Malibu to Point Conception. The Chumash, who were more nearly maritime in their habits than any other California Indians, also held the three large northern islands of the Santa Barbara archipelago, and their villages reached northward from Point Conception to Estero Bay.

The Chumash dwellings were large, sometimes as much as fifty feet in diameter, and were made by planting poles in a circle and bending and tying them together at the top. The walls were laced with sticks over which mats and thatch were fastened. Some structures housed as many as fifty persons. The Chumash were one of few tribes who constructed true beds, and divided their dwellings into rooms with hanging mats. This custom was not followed by those living on the islands. They slept crowded together on the ground. Canoes of various sizes were used, some being large enough to carry twenty sailors. They were constructed of planks laboriously split from logs, and caulked with asphalt, which abounded on the beaches. The Chumash were excellent weavers, and their work surpasses that of the neighboring Shoshoneans. They did not make pottery, but possessed steatite utensils, many of which were obtained in trade. Their money was the clam shell disk bead, and they were the "bankers" dealing in this currency, probably furnishing the bulk of the supply for the southern half of California.

Five missions were established in Chumash territory, but none of the missionaries or other Spaniards took the trouble to write in detail about their culture. As Kroeber remarks, ". . . when California was long enough American for ethnologists to survey it, the old life of the Chumash was a dimming memory. The result is that there exist more impressions than information. There is no group in the state that once held the importance of the Chumash concerning which we know so little."

According to Kroeber, the Chumash surpassed the adjacent Shoshoneans (Gabrieliño and Luiseño) "in their industries, in the arts that accompany ease of life, possibly in the organization of society. . . . Chumash culture presents the appearance of a higher development on the material, technological, and economic side than on the religious, but we cannot be altogether certain. . . ."

The Spanish settlers, the owners of large land grants, and the Franciscan missionaries were far more interested in destroying the Indian way of life than preserving or writing about it. In their endeavors they were eminently successful.

The Diegueño: The Diegueño belong to the Yuman division of the Hokan stock, and are, therefore, linguistically related to tribes of the deserts bordering the lower Colorado River. They dwelt along both the coast and in the interior of San Diego County, and held some territory in Baja California. They were the first Indians encountered by Spanish explorers on the American Pacific Coast.

The Diegueño may have called themselves *Ipai,* meaning "people," but they have come down through history carrying the name of the first mission established in California, a name they hated and a religious institution they resented and tried to destroy.

Their way of life reflected traits of their cultural affinities, but it was strongly influenced by their coastal environment and by adjoining people of other linguistic families. In some ways it was unique. They were, for example, the only California tribe who possessed a color-direction symbolism. East was white, south was green-blue, west was black, and north was red. The Diegueño were divided into exogamous patrilineal clans. The system was vestigial. The totemic moieties of more northerly nations were lacking, as were the totemic names of the cognate Yuman tribes to the east.

Diegueño men habitually went naked. Women wore a two-piece skirt. In thorny areas sandals made of agave fiber were worn. Both sexes wore their hair long. The males bunched it on top of the head, but the women let it hang loose, and trimmed the front at the eyebrows. At times women wore coiled basketry caps. The Diegueño houses were constructed of a framework of poles over which layers of mat brush were laid, then plastered with a layer of soil. They made pottery, but did not practice agriculture. They were both fishermen and gatherers

435

of wild foods, baked mescal being a staple in the diet of those living inland toward the arid areas.

Unlike most other California Indians, the Diegueño refused to submit to the missions. The early Spanish found them "proud, rancourous, boastful, covetous, given to jests and quarrels, passionately devoted to the customs of their fathers, and hard to handle." Kroeber states that although they were "not especially formidable as foes, they at least did not shrink from warlike attempts. Within a month of the founding of the mission (1769) an attack was made for plunder. In its seventh year, the mission, moved to its present site, was definitely attacked, partly burned, and three Spaniards, including one of the priests, killed."

The padre was the only Franciscan to meet martyrdom in the history of the California missions. In the first five years of the mission's existence less than a hundred neophytes were enrolled. Subsequently progress improved, but in the opinion of Kroeber, "the very success of the priests appears to have been the stimulus that drove the unconverted into hostility. There can be little doubt that this un-Californian attitude can be ascribed to a participation by the Diegueño in the spirit of independence characteristic of the other Yuman tribes." *

Dates to Remember

1542—Juan Rodríguez Cabrillo, a Portuguese in the Spanish service, discovered the California coast, sailing along it as far north as Point Arena.

1543—After Cabrillo was accidentally killed on San Miguel Island, off Santa Barbara, his chief pilot, Bartholome Ferrer, sailed farther north than Cabrillo had gone, possibly as far as the present California-Oregon border, before turning back to Mexico.

1565—An Augustinian friar and pilot, Andrés de Urdaneta, touched the southern California coast on a return voyage from the Philippines.

1579—The British pirate Sir Francis Drake, after sailing north perhaps as far as the Olympic Peninsula, almost to Puget Sound, turned back south and landed to repair his ship in a bay just north of the Golden Gate.

1584—Homeward bound to Mexico from the Philippines, Francisco Gali reached the California coast just south of San Francisco Bay.

1587—Also en route to Mexico from the Far East, Pedro de Unamuno anchored in Morro Bay, California. With a small company of soldiers he marched inland to the vicinity of San Luis Obispo. This is the first

---

* The Kamia and the Washo also occupied areas of California, and belonged to the Hokan linguistic family, but as their territories lay mainly within the Great Basin they have been considered under Part Nine.

SOME INDIAN PLACE NAMES

Washington

Sauk, town
Sanspoil, river
Palouse, town, river
Spokane, county, city, river
Okanogan, county, town, river
Walla Walla, county, river, town
Methow, river, town
Yakima, county, town, river
Wahkiakum, county
Chehalis, town, river
Chinook, town
Clallam, county, river
Seattle, city
Duwamish, town
Hoh, river
Humptulips, river
Klickitat, county
Lummi, river
Nisqually, river
Nooksack, river, town
Puyallup, river
Queets, river
Quillayute, town
Quinalt, river
Samish, river
Satsop, river
Skagit, county, river
Snohomish, county, town, river
Snoqualmie, town, river

Oregon

Seneca, town
Oregon, state
Illinois, river
Cayuse, town
Umatilla, county, river, town
Alsea, river
Calapooya, river, mountains
Chetco, river
Clackamas, county, river, town
Clatsop, county, town
Klamath, county, lake, river
Molalla, river
Multnomah, county

Santian, river
Siletz, river
Siuslaw, river
Siskiyou, mountains
Tillamook, county, town
Umpqua, river
Wasco, county
Yaquina, river

California

Chemehuevi, valley
Mohave, river, desert, town
Miami, town
Huron, town
Wyandot, town
Iowa, town
Shoshone, town
Klamath, town, river
Modoc, county
Shasta, county, mountain
Mono, lake, county
Piute, peak
Tuolumne, county
Mokelumne, river, peak
Cossumnes, river
Kaweah, river
Anacapa, island
Chowchilla, town
Coloma, town
Colusa, town
Cucamonga, town
Cuyamaca, peak
Hoopa, town
Inyo, county
Lompoc, town
Malibu, town
Pacoima, town
Panamint, mountains
Pismo, beach, town
Saticoy, town
Simi, town
Siskiyou, county
Suisun, town
Tehachapi, town, mountains
Tehame, town
Temecula, town
Yolo, county
Yuma, county, town, river

known *entrada* of the California mainland from the sea. It resulted in fighting with Indians in which men on both sides were killed.

1592—A Greek pilot, who called himself Juan de Fuca, claimed in 1596 that in 1592, operating under the Spanish flag, he had sailed northward in the Pacific from Mexico and had found a great strait between 47 and 48 degrees north latitude. Eventually the passage that leads to Seattle and other large cities was given his name, but it is improbable that he ever saw it.

1595—Directed to explore the northwest coast of North America, Sebastián Rodríguez Cermeno, sailing from the Philippines, sighted the rough shore off Point Saint George, in extreme northern California. Storms drove him south, and he landed in what he thought to be a safe harbor. He had entered the *ensenada* that would come to be known as Drake's Bay, named for the famous raider who may or may not have anchored in it. There Cermeno's ship was destroyed by a gale. He and his sailors eventually reached Mexico in an open launch, on the way touching at several places and meeting numerous natives along the California coast.

1602—A sea expedition commanded by Sebastián Vizcaíno charted a large part of the California coast, and made several landings. Monterey Bay was recommended as a suitable location for a permanent Spanish colony. However, more than a hundred and fifty years would pass before the Spanish again gave their attention to establishing bases in California.

1769—Land and sea expeditions to colonize California united on San Diego Bay. The first mission was established there by Father Junipero Serra. Twenty others would be built. The chain, which reached from San Diego to San Francisco, comprised the first organized penal system in the region of the United States. Probably sixty thousand Indians, who were no more than a step out of the Stone Age, were forced into these concentration camps during the sixty-five years of their operation. They were compelled to labor at building not only the beautiful shrines but in the fields and at trades. Discipline was rigid. For failing to perform assigned duties adequately, and for minor infractions, they were denied food. For being absent from church, or even tardiness at a service, they suffered corporal punishment and solitary confinement. Women as well as men were suspended by their hands and lashed. Attempts to escape—and there were many—were usually futile. The runaways were pursued by soldiers and brought back to suffer severe penalties, which included beatings and days of starvation. In 1834 the Mexican government secularized the missions, but long before that time thousands of "mission Indians" had died of broken spirits, unable to cope with the demands of a religion incomprehensible to them. Under secularization the lands of each mission were divided among the Indians attached to it, but they derived few benefits from their freedom. Within a short time all had been deprived of their property through illegal processes or had sold it for pittances to Spanish ranchers. A few managed to return to their homelands, but most of the survivors were driven to struggling under hopeless conditions. American settlers and miners finished the job of destroying them.

1778—Captain James Cook touched along the northwest coast.

1792—An American, Captain Robert Gray, discovered and entered the mouth of the Columbia. Later in the same year, an Englishman, Captain George Vancouver, sailed into the great river.

1805—Lewis and Clark, journeying overland from the Missouri, descended the Columbia to the Pacific.

Scientific Note—Ishi in Two Worlds

Early on the morning of August 29, 1911, barking dogs aroused butchers from their sleep in a slaughterhouse near the little northern California town of Oroville. Looking out in the dawn light they saw a man at bay in a corral. Except for a ragged scrap of ancient covered-wagon canvas thrown over his shoulders like a poncho, he was naked. They called off the dogs, and then telephoned the sheriff to say that they were holding a wild man and would he please come and get him. The sheriff, J. B. Webber, and several deputies responded quickly, entering the corral with drawn guns. But the wild man made no attempt to resist capture, quietly allowing himself to be handcuffed. He obviously could understand nothing that was said to him, and he was taken to the jail in Oroville and locked up in the cell for the insane.

This scene is the beginning of Theodora Kroeber's story of the last wild Indian in North America, *Ishi in Two Worlds*, a biographical study that ranks with the outstanding anthropological works on primitive man.[58]

"The wild man," she continues, "was emaciated to starvation, his hair was burned off close to his head. . . . He was a man of middle height, the long bones, painfully apparent, were straight, strong, and not heavy, the skin color somewhat paler in tone than the full copper characteristic of most Indians. The black eyes were wary and guarded now, and were set wide in a broad face, the mouth was generous and agreeably molded." [59]

Sheriff Webber was being neither stupid nor brutal in locking up the man. He was attempting to protect him. Word of the capture had spread rapidly and residents from near and far were pouring in to gaze through the bars at the wild man. The sheriff at last forced them out of the jail.

Sometime later, says Mrs. Kroeber, "Ishi spoke with some diffidence

439

of this, his first contact with white men. He said that he was put up in a fine house where he was kindly treated and well fed by a big chief. That he would eat nothing and drink nothing during his first days of captivity Ishi did not say. Such was the case; nor did he allow himself to sleep at first. Quite possibly it was a time of such strain and terror that he suppressed all memory of it. Or he may have felt that it was unkind to recall his suspicions which proved in the event groundless, for Ishi expected in those first days to be put to death. He knew of white men only that they were the murderers of his own people. It was natural that he should expect, once in their power, to be shot or hanged or killed by poisoning." [60]

Striving to learn something about his prisoner, the sheriff called in local Indians, halfbreeds, Mexicans, and Spaniards to speak to Ishi in a number of languages. His efforts were in vain. When Ishi spoke it was in a tongue totally unintelligible to his questioners.

Lurid stories about the capture of a wild Indian were printed in San Francisco newspapers. They held the rapt attention of two men who were among the few in the country equipped to understand Ishi's dilemma and his personality. They were T. T. Waterman and Alfred L. Kroeber, professors of anthropology at the University of California in Berkeley. Professor Kroeber was Theodora Kroeber's husband.

Three years earlier, in 1908, some surveyors working in the wilderness north of Oroville had come suddenly upon several Indians who had fled, leaving their meager belongings behind them. With two guides Waterman had gone to the area and had spent several weeks in an unsuccessful search for them. Now the scientists thought that the captured wild man might be one of these. Kroeber wired Sheriff Webber to hold the Indian until the arrival of Waterman, "who will take charge and be responsible for him. Matter important because of aboriginal history." The anthropologists knew that Oroville was close to country formerly inhabited by Yana Indians. They guessed—correctly as it turned out—that the wild man might be a Yana, possibly from the southernmost branch of the tribe, the Yahi, believed to be extinct. They had recorded two vocabularies of Central and Northern Yana dialects obtained from elderly members of the tribe.

Waterman went to Oroville on August 31, only three days after Ishi had been locked up. He sat down beside Ishi in the cell, and with his phonetically transcribed list of Yana words before him "began to read from it, repeating each word, pronouncing it as well as he knew how. Ishi was attentive but unresponding until, discouragingly far down the list, Waterman said *siwini* which means yellow pine. . . . Recognition lighted up the Indian's face. Waterman said the magic word again; Ishi repeated it after him, correcting his pronunciation, and for the next few moments the two of them banged at the wood of the cot, telling each other over and over, *siwini, siwini!"*

Recognition of other words followed. Waterman was learning that the unknown dialect Ishi spoke differed, but not completely unintelligibly, from the Northern and Central Yana. Ishi was a Yahi, the last of his people.

Ishi and Waterman had other profitable talks before they left for San Francisco. Mrs. Kroeber tells of the day Ishi walked out of his cell into the world of the white man:

"Side by side, Ishi and Waterman walked from the jail to the railroad station. Women and children peered discreetly from windows or over picket fences to catch a glimpse of the Wild Man, and there were several men and older boys waiting on the platform to see him. They kept their distance, and they were quiet. . . ." The train came, rushing toward the platform, "pouring out clouds of sparks and smoke, and filling the ears with its hollow, moaning voice. Mill Creek and Deer Creek [Ishi's wilderness home] were within range of the sound of that voice; twice a day Ishi had heard it ever since he could remember, and he had watched the train hundreds of times as it snaked along below him, bellowing and belching. His mother had reassured him as a small boy when he was afraid of it, telling him that it was a Demon who followed white men wherever they went, but that Indians need have no fear of it; it never bothered them. Today, Ishi wondered . . . Would the Demon know that he was an Indian? He was wearing white men's clothes. . . ."

Ishi decided it might be well to watch from a distance, and he moved to stand behind an adjacent tree. When he felt certain the train would stay on its own tracks, and he saw people getting on and off, he rejoined Waterman and they boarded. "During the trip, Ishi sat very quiet. He found the speed of the train exciting. . . . He averted his eyes from the strangers in the car. . . ." The Carquinez Straits was crossed on a ferry, and Waterman explained to him that two big rivers united, flowed into San Francisco Bay and out the Golden Gate to the ocean. "Like all Indians, Ishi knew that such was the destination of the creeks and rivers of his home, but . . . he was vague about how the river journey was accomplished, for his informants had known of it only traditionally. . . .

"He was sorry to leave the train at the Oakland Mole, but ahead lay further wonders—another ferry trip, this time across the bay to San Francisco, and after that, a long ride in a trolley car to the Museum of Anthropology.

"Arrived at the museum, Ishi had gone a longer way than the miles which separated him from Deer Creek Canyon. It was eleven o'clock in the evening of Labor Day, September 4, 1911, when Ishi the Yahi completed a trip out of the Stone Age into the clang and glare of the Iron Age. . . ."

Living quarters were maintained in the museum for caretakers—bedrooms, bath, kitchen—and Ishi was given a comfortable home. Other Indians, friends of Professor Kroeber and his colleagues, often came to the museum. A room had been set aside for their use, and they occupied it sometimes for several weeks. They would help Ishi become accustomed to his strange surroundings.

Kroeber met Ishi the morning after he arrived. They would become close and dear friends. Kroeber's first impression of Ishi "was of his gentleness, and of a timidity and fear kept under severe control." It was Kroeber who gave him the name of Ishi, meaning "man" in Yahi. Rarely would a California Indian speak his own tribal name, and never in response to a direct question. Ishi steadfastly followed the custom. He never revealed his own private Yahi name. He "accepted the new name, answering to it unreluctantly. But once it was bestowed it took on enough of his true name's mystic identification with himself, his soul, whatever inner essence of a man it is which a name shares, that he was never again heard to pronounce it."

Mrs. Kroeber writes: "Deeper than shyness and fear was Ishi's awareness that he was alone, not as the unfriendly or too introverted or misanthropic are alone, for he was none of these. To be sure, he would sit, unbored, dreamy, and withdrawn into his own mystic center, but only if there was nothing to do, no one to talk to or to work with. He much preferred companionship, and he smiled readily. . . . He was interested, concerned, amused, or delighted, as the case might be, with everything and everyone he knew and understood.

"His aloneness was not that of temperament but of cultural change, and one early evidence of his sophisticated intelligence was his awareness of this. He felt himself so different, so distinct, that to regard himself or to have others regard him as 'one of them' was not to be thought of. 'I am one; you are others; this is in the inevitable nature of things,' is an English approximation of his judgment on himself. It was a harsh judgment, arousing in his friends compassion, then respect. He was fearful and timid at first, but never unobservant, nor did his fear paralyze his thinking. . . . He faced the areas of his total ignorance, of the disparity of content between Yahi culture and white, and the knowledge that he could not begin from so far behind to come abreast. He would not try to. He would and did adapt as one of goodwill and breeding must adapt to one's host in dress, in forms of greeting and leavetaking, in the use of knife and fork at table; these and other conventions of simple etiquette. Judgment and decisions he left to those who knew better than he could hope or presume to know.

"Meanwhile, he remained himself—a well-born Yahi, never unmindful of the code his mother and uncle had taught him . . . Ishi had kept his morale through grief and an absolute solitariness; the impact of civilization could not budge it."

Ishi enjoyed being with youngsters. Mrs. Kroeber relates an anecdote not in her great work. Now and then Ishi would sneak away with several boys and girls of the neighborhood with whom he had made friends, and who were devoted to him. In time it was discovered that he had taught them to make snares and had taken them on poaching trips to Golden Gate Park.

Physicians estimated that Ishi had been born between 1860 and 1862, making him between fifty-one and forty-nine years of age when he went to live in his museum quarters. From the first he cooperated willingly and tirelessly with scientists in providing them with information. He made field trips with them. He opened cultural gates that were thought to have been forever closed.

It has long been known to the medical world that persons who have lived a primitive existence until middle age, or even fewer years, have little natural resistance with which to combat the diseases of the white man's world, that to survive civilization early immunization to it is required. Ishi was no exception to the rule. Shortly after reaching San Francisco he was afflicted with the first cold and the first pneumonia of his life. In December, 1914, suffering from a respiratory infection, he was taken to a hospital. He was thought to have recovered in late January, 1915, and was taken home. By spring he was more seriously ill, and this time hospital physicians obtained a positive reaction to the tuberculin test. Two months later it was believed the progress of the disease had been arrested, and he was released.

During the summer he tired quickly and lost his appetite. An exhibit was removed from the museum so that he might have a large and sunny room with a wide view of the eucalyptus trees of Sutro Forest. He was given the finest nursing and medical care, day and night.

"Ishi lived on with good days and bad," recounts Mrs. Kroeber, "stoical, uncomplaining, interested in whatever went on, affectionate and responsive, until the spring. He died on March 25, 1916. Death came at noon, in the time of the year when new clover was painting his native hills and when Deer Creek and Mill Creek were swollen with the rush of the spring salmon run."

Less than five and a half years after he had been found cringing, naked, and starving in a slaughterhouse corral, the last wild Indian in America was gone.

Notes

PART ONE

Southwestern Deserts and Mesa Lands

1 The Colorado (now Denver) Museum of Natural History annual report for 1926: "Through the kindness of Messrs. Fred Howarth and Carl Schwachheim of Raton, New Mexico, information was obtained that led to the uncovering of a highly interesting deposit of fossilized remains of an extinct race of Bison. . . . While this material has had only partial study, there appears to be no reason for doubting that it is of a race quite new to science, and since artifacts were found associated with it . . . it will doubtless have a strong bearing upon the question of man's antiquity in America. The finding of these artifacts associated with fossil Bison remains . . . prompted an invitation being extended to Dr. Oliver P. Hay to collaborate in its study with the honorary curator of the department, Mr. Harold J. Cook—this for the purpose of avoiding all possible question regarding the geological age to which the bison belongs, as well as to remove all doubt as to its specific determination: Dr. Hay being the best informed upon this group of fossil mammals."

2 Wormington (1957) gives the most detailed account of the Folsom discoveries. She names the scientists who responded to the 1927 telegrams as Barnum Brown of the American Museum of Natural History; Frank H. H. Roberts of the Smithsonian Institution, and A. V. Kidder of Phillips Academy.

3 The 1928 excavations were conducted by a joint expedition of the Colorado Museum of Natural History and the American Museum of Natural History.

4 Notable discoveries of man's early presence in the Southwest also have been made in New Mexico at Blackwater Draw (Clovis), Burnett Cave, Lucy, West Leggett, Manzano Cave, Milnes, and at sites along the Rio Grande and San Juan; in Arizona at Ventana Cave, Lehner Ranch, Naco, and various sites of the Cochise Complex in the southern part of the state; in Nevada at Gypsum Cave. Artifacts uncovered in these diggings were both younger and older than Folsom.

5 See *Scientific Note,* at the end of this part.

6 Martin, Quimby, and Collier (1947); Wormington (1957); Haury (1950); Sayles and Antevs in Wormington (1941).

7 Wormington (1957).

8 Martin *et al.* (1947).

9 Terrell (1967).

10 Harrington and Simpson (1961).

11 Haury (1950).

12 Harrington and Simpson (1961).

13 Howard (1935); Cotter (1937); Sellards (1952); Antevs (in Wormington, 1941).

14 Wormington (1957): "This [Antevs' theory] seems unlikely in view of the fact that significant faunal and artifact changes may be recognized in the strata separated by the disconformities. Furthermore, geologic studies at the Scharbauer Site in Texas suggest that periods marked by wind erosion and a major drought preceded the Altithermal. Similar conditions probably prevailed in this area [Clovis Complex] which lies only about 200 miles away."

15 Harrington and Simpson (1961): "A Carbon-14 date of approximately 20,000 years has been reported for the fossil ivory found in this [Sandia] de-

445

posit, but it is possible that it was fossilized before being associated with Man."

16 Josephy (1968): "Since Hibben's initial discovery, other points of the same type and perhaps the same age have been found elsewhere in the Southwest and in such widely separated areas as Alberta and the Eastern Seaboard."

17 Archeologist Alex D. Krieger, cited by Josephy (1968).

18 Hibben (1969).

19 Strangely, the horses developed on the western plains migrated to Asia by way of Bering Strait Land Bridge, and finally reached Europe. The earliest Indians slaughtered them for their hides and meat. The American horse became extinct in North America soon after the end of the Ice Age. Eventually, within historical times the horse was domesticated in the Middle East and was taken into Europe. Not until the Spaniards reached North America, after 1492, were horses again in the Western Hemisphere. Thus, the American horse moved around the world. Both camels and ground sloths originated in South America, and moved north. The great ground sloth weighed as much as an elephant. Toward the end of the Ice Age it was common in North America. It became extinct there, as did the camel, but in South America the camel survived. The llama is a true camel, and it was llama-like camels that were killed by early southwestern hunters. (Hibben, 1960.)

20 Mangelsdorf and Smith (1949); Mangelsdorf and Reeves (1939). Also in 1948 corn of the same age was found in La Perra Cave in northeastern Mexico, and research by archeologist Richard MacNeish in the region "revealed an initial stage of experimentation with plant cultivation (bottle gourds, pumpkins, peppers, runner beans) 9,500 to 7,500 years ago . . . common beans were being grown in the area some 5,000 to 6,000 years ago; a pod-pop type of corn about 4,500 years ago . . ." Josephy (1968). Coon (1962) traces the history of numerous agricultural products cultivated by early American Indians.

21 This was not the oldest pottery to be discovered in the area of the United States. See Part Three.

22 Martin et al. (1947).

23 Martin et al. (1947).

24 Sayles (1936); Nesbit (1931); Haury (1936).

25 Martin et al. (1947); Josephy (1968).

26 Chard (1940).

27 Gladwin et al. (1937).

28 Schroeder (1965 and 1966); Haury (1945).

29 Josephy (1968).

30 Sayles (1936); Martin et al. (1947).

31 Douglas (1935).

32 Terrell (1970-A).

33 An excellent study of this subject appears in Martin et al. (1947).

34 Bandelier (1890-A); Colton and Hargrave (1933); Colton and Baxter (1932); Dale (1949); Fewekes (1911); Hendron (1940); Hooton (1930); Jeancon (1923); McGregor (1941); Martin (1936).

35 Kroeber (1925).

36 Hodge (1907). In the diary of his desert journey in 1775–1776, Fray Francisco Garces states that the Chemehuevi wore Apache moccasins, antelope-skin shirts, and a white headdress like a cap, ornamented with the crest feathers of a bird, probably the road runner. They were then a very long way from Apache Country. See Coues (1900).

37 Ives (1861) speaks of the Chemehuevi as a wandering people.

38 Swanton (1952).

39 Martin et al. (1947); Hodge (1907); Swanton (1952).

40 Coues (1900).

41 Josephy (1968).

42 Swanton (1952) states that Fray Garces may have met the Havasupai in 1776, but definite notices of them seem to be lacking until about the middle of the nineteenth century. Leroux (1888); Hodge (1907); Josephy (1968); Martin et al. (1947).

43 Martin et al. (1947).

44 Kroeber (1902 and 1925); Swanton (1952); Hodge (1907); Waters (1946); Forbes (1965).

45 Kniffen (1932); Forbes (1965).

46 Gifford (1931); Heintzelman (1857); Swanton (1952); Hodge (1907).

47 Di Peso (1956); Forbes (1965); Hodge (1907). Di Peso expresses the opinion that the Ootam (Pima and Papago) may already have been established in southern Arizona when the Hohokam intruded from Mexico. He also suggests that the Ootam Culture was derived from the Cochise Culture. Not all archeologists agree with him.

48 The Sobaipuri, who lived in the Santa Cruz and San Pedro river valleys, were a part of the Papago. The Pima called them Rsarsavina, meaning "spotted." They suffered greatly from attacks by Apaches, and finally abandoned their ancient homeland and moved westward among the Papago.

49 Kino (1916); Bolton (1936); Swanton (1952); Hodge (1907); Forbes (1965).

50 Driver (1951).

51 Hodge (1907).
52 Among the Hopi is a little island on which the inhabitants have for nearly three centuries retained their own identity. It is the town of Hano on the First Mesa. Its occupants are descendants of early Tewa Indians who lived near Abiquiu or Santa Clara, New Mexico, and who migrated to their present home late in the seventeenth century, perhaps to escape the vengeance of Spaniards, perhaps at the invitation of the Hopi who needed help in defending themselves against Ute or Navajo raiders. Although the people of Hano have absorbed the Hopi culture, they still speak of themselves as Tewa and they still speak the Tewa language.
53 Parsons (1939); Sterling (1942); Titiev (1944); White (1932, 1932-A, 1935, 1942); Hodge (1907); Swanton (1952); Martin et al. (1947).
54 Cushing (1883, 1895, 1896); Bandelier (1892); Hodge (1937).
55 Bandelier (1881, 1890-A); Hodge (1907); Swanton (1952); Bancroft (1886).
56 Benavides (1965); Bandelier (1881, 1890-A); Hodge (1907); Swanton (1952); Winship (1896).
57 The ruins of Rito de los Frijoles and numerous others are now protected in Bandelier National Monument, named for the distinguished Swiss-American ethnologist Adolph F. A. Bandelier, who spent years late in the last century studying the Pueblo Indians. Besides many scientific works, he wrote an ethno-historical novel, The Delight Makers, in which he sought to picture Frijoles Canyon as it was in prehistoric times.
58 Terrell (1970-A); Kluckhohn and Leighton (1946); Hodge (1895 and 1907); Amsden (1932); Bandelier and Bandelier (1937); Benavides (1965); Dittert (1961); Hall (1944); Hester (1962); Lummis (1900); O'Bryan (1956); Reichard (1950); Underhill (1956); Young (1961).
59 See listings in Note 58; Hodge (1907); Swanton (1952).
60 Núñez Cabeza de Vaca (1542); Smith (1851); Fanny Bandelier (1905); Terrell (1962). When he reached Pueblo de los Corazones, in northern Mexico, Núñez Cabeza de Vaca found cotton shawls he considered "better than those of New Spain." The textiles probably came down the trade trail from the Hopis, who were the outstanding cotton weavers. He also reported seeing "fine turquoises that came from the north."
61 Castañeda in Winship (1896).
62 Bolton (1949); Terrell (1968-C).
63 Terrell (1966); Bolton (1949).
64 Winship (1896); Bolton (1949).
65 Winship (1896).
66 See Note 61.
67 Forbes (1958); Sykes (1927 and 1937); R. Ives (1936 and 1959); Terrell (1966 and 1970-B); Bolton (1949); Hammond and Rey (1940).
68 Hopkins (1967); Wormington (1957).
69 Driver (1961).
70 Coon (1962).
71 Wormington (1957).
72 Terrell (1968).
73 Driver (1961).
74 Martin et al. (1947).

PART TWO

Gulf Coasts and Tidal Swamps

1 Wormington (1957).
2 Ibid.
3 Sellards (1941); Newcomb (1961); Wormington (1957).
4 Gidley (1929 and 1930); Sellards (1917); Wormington (1957).
5 Gidley and Loomis (1926).
6 Rouse (1950).
7 Wormington (1957).
8 Hrdlicka (1907 and 1937).
9 Wormington (1957).
10 Driver (1961).
11 Driver and Massey (1957).
12 Coon (1962).
13 Josephy (1968).
14 Josephy (1968).
15 Martin et al. (1947); Coon (1962); Driver (1961); Josephy (1968).
16 Driver (1961); Martin et al. (1947).
17 Martin et al. (1947).
18 Driver (1961).
19 Martin et al. (1947).
20 Swanton (1952).
21 Driver (1961); Martin et al. (1947); Hodge (1907); Josephy (1968).
22 Driver (1961).
23 Membre (1691); Shea (1853); Cox (1905); Terrell (1968-A).
24 Parkman (1879), quoting Tonty and Membre.

25 Margry (1876). This is an invaluable collection of documents pertaining to French explorations in America. The first three volumes relate almost entirely to La Salle and the accounts of his associates. Also printed are papers of Jean Baptiste Le Moyne, Sieur de Bienville, and Pierre Le Moyne d'Iberville.
26 Newcomb (1961).
27 Swanton (1952).
28 Newcomb (1961, quoting Dyer [1917]).
29 Newcomb (1961).
30 Hodge (1907); Newcomb (1961).
31 Swanton (1952); Hodge (1907); Newcomb (1961).
32 Newcomb (1961).
33 Forbes (1965); Swanton (1952); Newcomb (1961).

34 Newcomb (1961).
35 Swanton (1952).
36 Oviedo (1852); Lowery (1901); Díaz (1927); Casas (1656, 1699, 1674); Brebner (1933); Terrell (1962).
37 See listings Note 36.
38 The primary source of the account of the Narváez expedition is Núñez Cabeza de Vaca's *Relación* (1542). See also Hodge (1959); Smith (1851); Fanny Bandelier (1958); Hallenbeck (1940); Terrell (1962).
39 Lewis (1959).
40 Terrell (1968-C); Smith (1851); Fanny Bandelier (1958).
41 B. Smith (1851).
42 Wormington (1957).
43 Martin *et al.* (1947).
44 Driver (1961).
45 Wormington (1957).

Southeastern Woodlands

1 Wormington (1957).
2 Baity (1968).
3 Kneberg (1952).
4 Soday (1954).
5 Webb (1951).
6 David Thompson (1954).
7 Faulkner (1967 and 1968); Faulkner and Graham (1966); Graham (1964).
8 McCary (1954 and 1956).
9 Coe (1952).
10 Faulkner (1967).
11 Driver (1961).
12 DeJarnette (n.d.)
13 Driver (1961).
14 Cotterill (1954).
15 Driver (1961).
16 Lawson (1860).
17 Swanton (1952).
18 Grace Woodward (1963).
19 This tradition is preserved in the famous Walum Olum (history of the Lenni Lenape, or Delaware). See Brinton (1882).
20 Grace Woodward (1963).
21 Swanton (1952).
22 Speck (1920 and 1951).
23 Woodward (1963) citing Speck.
24 The brilliant Cherokee leader Sequoya invented an alphabet of his native tongue. This is the only case of the adoption of a system of writing by a tribe without white assistance in American Indian history.
25 Spelman (1907).
26 John Smith (1884).
27 Mooney in Hodge (1907).

28 Swanton (1952).
29 Mooney in Hodge (1907).
30 Swanton (1952); Hodge (1907).
31 Swanton (1952); Hodge (1907); Driver (1961).
32 Cotterill (1954).
33 *Ibid.*
34 *Ibid.*
35 Picket (1851).
36 Lewis in Hodge (1959).
37 Lawson (1860).
38 Bartram (1853).
39 Lewis in Hodge (1959).
40 Driver (1961).
41 *Ibid.*
42 Swanton (1946).
43 Cotterill (1954).
44 Swanton (1928-A, 1922, and 1946).
45 Gatchet in Hodge (1907).
46 J. Gravier in Shea (1861).
47 Shea (1853); Cox (1905); La Harpe (1831); Swanton (1952).
48 Debo (1934); Swanton (1931).
49 Swanton (1931) cited by Debo (1934).
50 *Ibid.*
51 Swanton (1931).
52 Debo (1934).
53 Hodge (1907); Swanton (1931); Debo (1934).
54 Debo (1934).
55 Swanton in Hodge (1907).
56 Debo (1934).
57 Swanton (1952).
58 *Ibid.*
59 *Ibid.*
60 *Ibid.*

61 Lewis (1959). B. Smith translation of 1866.
62 Swanton (1952).

63 The Gentleman of Elvas, in Lewis (1959); B. Smith translation of 1866.

PART FOUR

Northeastern Woodlands

1 Byers (1956).
2 *Ibid.*
3 Wormington (1957); Byers (1956).
4 Wormington (1957).
5 Byers (1956 and 1955).
6 Byers (1956).
7 Turner (1920); Billington (1949).
8 Witthoft (1952).
9 Wormington (1957).
10 Wormington (1957).
11 Ritchie (1957).
12 Willey and Phillips (1955).
13 Fowler (1954); Ritchie (1957).
14 Witthoft (1965).
15 Josephy (1968).
16 Martin *et al.* (1947); Hodge 1907); Ritchie (1966); Shetrone (1930); Moorehead (1922); Mills (1902); Fowke (1902); Josephy (1968).
17 Mooney in Hodge (1907).
18 Swanton (1952).
19 Cook (1887).
20 De Forest (1851).
21 Mooney in Hodge (1907).
22 Bliss (1885); De Schweinits (1870).
23 Hewitt in Hodge (1907).
24 See *Algonquian Family* in Hodge (1907).
25 Swanton (1952).

26 Mooney in Hodge (1907).
27 Squier (1851).
28 Brinton (1882).
29 Swanton (1952).
30 John Smith (1884); Swanton (1952).
31 Hewitt in Hodge (1907).
32 Hewitt, *Hanbook of American Indians*, Hodge (1907).
33 *Ibid.*
34 Jesuit Relations (1637), edited by Thwaites (1896); Driver (1961), quoting from Thwaites.
35 Hewitt in Hodge (1907).
36 Champlain (1930).
37 Thwaites (1896).
38 *Ibid.*
39 Ritchie (1965).
40 *Ibid.*
41 Hodge (1907); Josephy (1968).
42 Hewitt in Hodge (1907).
43 Jogues in Thwaites (1896).
44 Shea (1853); Terrell (1968-A); Cox (1905); Parkman (1879).
45 *Ibid.*
46 Terrell (1967).
47 Colton (1941); Brand (1935 and 1938); Terrell (1967); Courville (1963); Tower (1945); Woodward (1965); Joseph D. McGuire in Hodge (1907).

PART FIVE

Central Prairies and Woodlands

1 Jenks (1936 and 1937); Wormington (1957).
2 E. Johnson (1969); Jenks (1936); Wormington (1957).
3 Koch (1839 and 1860); Wormington (1957); Gross (1951).
4 Allison (1926); Nelson (1933); Wormington (1957).
5 Shippee (1948); Coe (1952).
6 Logan (1952); Shippee (1955); Wormington (1957).
7 Koch (1860); Williams (1957); Wormington (1957).
8 E. Johnson (1969); Jenks (1937).
9 E. Johnson (1969).

10 Bryan, Retzek, and McCann (1938); E. Johnson (1969).
11 E. Johnson (1969).
12 Wormington (1957); Leverett and Sardeson (1932).
13 Fowler and Winters (1956); Wormington (1957).
14 McKusick (1964); Wormington (1957).
15 For the convenience of readers who may wish to inquire more into the subject of cultures of the Central Prairies and Woodlands area I list the following, running from late prehistoric to the beginning of the Archaic

Period: Middle Mississippi, Tampico, Fisher, Mille Lacs, Kashena, Clam River, Azatlan, Oneota, Effigy Mound, Wisconsin Hopewell, Laurel, Illinois Hopewell, Lewis, Baumer, Red Ocher, Morton, Old Copper, Brown's Valley, Faulkner.

16 Josephy (1968); Terrell (1967); Holms in Hodge (1907); Boas (1895); McKern (1942).
17 Brackenridge (1814); Bushnell (1904); Moorehead (1922); Shetrone (1930).
18 Martin et al. (1947); Dellinger (1936).
19 Griffin (1952); Hyde (1962).
20 Hyde 1962).
21 Martin et al (1947).
22 Swanton (1952); James Mooney, Cyrus Thomas in Hodge (1907).
23 Swanton (1952).
24 Father Zenobius Membre in Cox (1905).
25 Hodge (1907); Terrell (1968-A); Swanton (1952).
26 Father Marquette and Dablon in Shea (1853).
27 Berry (1938); Swanton (1952); Dorsey and Thomas in Hodge (1907); J. Dorsey (1897).
28 Mathews (1961).
29 Swanton (1952); Hodge (1907).
30 Mathews (1961).

31 J. Dorsey (1897).
32 See notes 28 to 31.
33 Swanton (1952); J. Dorsey (1897); Thwaites (1900).
34 Swanton (1952).
35 Pond (1773).
36 Bulletin 30, Bureau of American Ethnology (1907).
37 Hodge (1907).
38 Charlevoix (1744).
39 Lahontan (1703).
40 Gibson (1963); Mooney and Jones in Hodge (1907); Blair (1911); Jones (1915); Thwaites (1896).
41 Swanton (1952).
42 Mooney and Thomas in Hodge (1907).
43 Hoffman (1896); Jenks (1900).
44 See Nicolet in Jesuit Relations; Thwaites (1896); Champlain (1930).
45 Carver (1778).
46 Radin (1923); Dorsey and Radin in Hodge (1907); Swanton (1952).
47 Warren (1885); Schoolcraft (1851); Thwaites (1896); Swanton (1952); Mooney and Thomas in Hodge (1907).
48 Mooney and Thomas in Hodge (1907).
49 Bourne (1904); Swanton (1952).
50 Terrell (1967).

PART SIX

Northern Great Plains

1 They were Judge C. C. Coffin, Major R. G. Coffin, and the judge's son, A. L. Coffin.
2 Wormington (1957); Harrington and Simpson (1961); Roberts (1935).
3 Wormington (1957).
4 Harrington and Simpson (1961).
5 Ibid.
6 Wormington (1957).
7 Ibid.
8 Ibid.; Figgins (1933).
9 Howard, Satterthwaite, and Bache (1941); Wormington (1957); Howard (1943); Hack (1943).
10 Barbour and Schultz (1932).
11 Howells (1938); Wormington (1957).
12 Wormington (1957).
13 Hughes (1949); Wormington (1957).
14 Wormington (1957).
15 Ibid.
16 Jepson (1951 and 1953); Wormington (1957).
17 Wormington (1957).
18 Ibid.
19 Driver (1961).

20 This is the recording made by Lewis and Clark in 1804. See their journals.
21 Driver (1961).
22 Lowie (1961).
23 Driver (1961).
24 Alice C. Fletcher, James Mooney, J. Owen Dorsey, Cyrus Thomas in Hodge (1907); Swanton (1952).
25 Mooney (1907).
26 Grinnell (1915).
27 Ibid.
28 George A. Dorsey, Field Museum of Natural History, in Hodge (1907).
29 Ibid.
30 Driver (1961).
31 Ibid.
32 Swanton (1952).
33 Hassrick (1964).
34 Ibid.
35 Terrell (1967).
36 Driver (1961).
37 Hassrick (1964).
38 Ibid.
39 Ibid.
40 Lowie (1961).

41 *Ibid.* from Fletcher (1911).
42 Swanton (1952).
43 Driver (1961).
44 Lowie (1961).
45 *Ibid.*
46 Driver (1961).
47 *Ibid.*
48 *Ibid.*
49 McGuire in Hodge (1907).
50 J. O. Dorsey (1897); Swanton (1952).
51 Fletcher in Hodge (1907).
52 Swanton (1952).
53 Fletcher in Hodge (1907).
54 Kennedy (1961).
55 Catlin (1844).
56 James Mooney and Cyrus Thomas of Bureau of American Ethnology (1906).

57 Kennedy (1961).
58 De Smet (1905); Terrell (1964).
59 Henry (1897).
60 De Smet (1905).
61 Kennedy (1961).
62 Swanton (1952).
63 Mooney in Hodge (1907).
64 Bolton (1949).
65 Hammond and Rey (1940).
66 Brebner (1933).
67 *Ibid.*
68 Driver (1961).
69 *Ibid.*
70 McGuire (1897).
71 William H. Holmes in Hodge (1907).
72 Driver (1961).
73 Terrell (1967); McGuire (1897).

Southern Great Plains

1 Wendorf *et al.* (1955).
2 *Ibid.*
3 *Ibid.*
4 Harrington and Simpson (1961).
5 Wormington (1957).
6 In Wendorf *et al.* (1955).
7 *Ibid.*
8 Crook (1957).
9 Wormington (1957).
10 *Ibid.*
11 Sellards *et al.* (1947).
12 Wedel (1961).
13 Ray (1934).
14 Ray and Sayles (1941).
15 Kelley (1947).
16 Schultz (1943).
17 Wedel (1961).
18 *Ibid.*
19 Martin *et al.* (1947).
20 Renaud (1930).
21 Wedel (1961).
22 *Ibid.*
23 *Ibid.*
24 Krieger (1962).
25 Newcomb (1961).
26 Martin *et al.* (1947).
27 Swanton (1952).
28 *Ibid.*
29 Hodge (1907).
30 Newcomb (1961).
31 Winship (1896).
32 These Querechos probably were telling Coronado of the lower Arkansas River, hundreds of miles away.
33 In his work, *Voyage into Nova Hispania,* published in 1555, Robert Tomson described a San Benito as a short garment "with a hole to put in a mans

head in the middest, and cast over a mans head: both flaps hang one before and another behinde . . ." Quoted by Winship (1896) from Richard Hakluyt's *Voyages* (1598).
34 Bolton (1916).
35 Newcomb (1961).
36 Bolton (1916).
37 Newcomb (1961).
38 Swanton (1952).
39 Newcomb (1961).
40 Swanton (1952).
41 Hodge (1907).
42 Mooney (1898) cited in Hodge (1907).
43 Hodge (1907).
44 Wallace and Hoebel (1952).
45 Opler (1943).
46 Swanton (1952).
47 Quoted by Wallace and Hoebel (1952).
48 Wallace and Hoebel (1952).
49 *Ibid.*
50 Richardson (1933).
51 Dobie (1952).
52 Roe (1955).
53 Wallace and Hoebel (1952).
54 Harrington (1910).
55 Newcomb (1961).
56 Lowie (1953), cited by Newcomb (1961).
57 Newcomb (1961).
58 Swanton (1952).
59 Mooney (1898) in Newcomb (1961).
60 Swanton (1952).
61 Catlin (1844), quoted in Newcomb (1961).
62 Mooney in Hodge (1907).
63 Newcomb (1961).

64 Josephy (1968).
65 *Ibid.*
66 *Ibid.*
67 Swanton (1952).
68 Buckingham Smith (1886). See Hodge (1959).
69 Varner (1951), cited by Newcomb (1961).
70 Cox (1905); Parkman (1879).

71 Newcomb (1961).
72 *Ibid.* See G. A. Dorsey (1904).
73 Swanton (1952).
74 Lesser and Weltfish (1932).
75 Swanton (1952).
76 Mooney in Hodge (1907).
77 *Ibid.*
78 Terrell (1967).

Northern Mountains and Plateaus

1 Renaud (1940); Wormington (1957).
2 Wormington (1957).
3 Josephy (1968).
4 *Ibid.*
5 Forbis and Sperry (1952).
6 Cressman (1948).
7 Wormington (1957).
8 Harrington and Simpson (1961).
9 Daugherty (1956).
10 Wormington (1957).
11 Martin *et al.* (1947).
12 *Ibid.*
13 *Ibid.*
14 Hough in Hodge (1907).
15 Martin *et al.* (1947).
16 Turney-High (1941).
17 *Ibid.*
18 Swanton (1952).
19 Mason cited by Hodge (1907).
20 Alexander F. Chamberlain in Hodge (1907).
21 Swanton (1952).
22 *Ibid.*
23 Mooney in Hodge (1907).
24 Ewers (1958).
25 Swanton (1952).
26 Ewers (1958).
27 David Thompson (1916).
28 Mooney in Hodge (1907).
29 Ewers (1958).

30 *Ibid.*
31 Maximilian (1843).
32 Hodge (1907).
33 Swanton (1952).
34 Teit (1930).
35 Turney-High (1937).
36 Lewis and Clark, Coues edition (1904).
37 Ella Clark (1966).
38 *Ibid.*
39 McBeth (1908) cited by Ella Clark
40 Swanton (1952).
41 Ella Clark (1966).
42 Hinshaw and Farrand in Hodge (1907).
43 Swanton (1952).
44 Ella Clark (1966).
45 Terrell, *Six Turnings* (1968).
46 Chittenden (1902).
47 Brackenridge (1814).
48 Sprague (1964).
49 Chittenden (1902).
50 Harris (1952).
51 Driver (1961).
52 Josephy (1968).
53 Driver (1961).
54 Anderson (1952).
55 Driver (1961).
56 *Ibid.*; Hrdlicka in Hodge (1907).

The Great Basin

1 An excellent detailed geographical description of the Great Basin is in Cline (1963). For the Pleistocene history of the area see Antevs (1925).
2 Hunter's account is contained in Harrington and Simpson (1961).
3 Harrington and Simpson (1961).
4 Krieger's comments are in a Fore-word to Harrington and Simpson (1961).
5 Harrington (1933).
6 *Ibid.*
7 *Ibid.*
8 *Ibid.*
9 Jennings (1957).
10 Wormington (1957).

11 *Ibid.*
12 *Ibid.*
13 Broecker (1956) cited by Wormington (1957).
14 Eardly (1956).
15 U.S. Geological Survey Report by J. H. Feth and Meyer Rubin (1957) in Wormington (1957).
16 Wormington (1957).
17 Swanton (1952).
18 Trenholm and Carley (1964), citing Hopkins (1883).
19 Swanton (1952).
20 *Ibid.*
21 Hinshaw and Mooney in Hodge (1907).
22 Swanton (1952).
23 *Ibid.* See also Trenholm and Carley (1964).

24 Chittenden and Richardson (1905). See also Terrell (1964).
25 Trenholm and Carley (1964).
26 Bancroft: *Native Races* cited by Trenholm and Carley (1964).
27 De Smet quoted in Trenholm and Carley (1964).
28 Trenholm and Carley (1964).
29 A. L. Kroeber (1925).
30 Steward (1938).
31 Hodge (1907).
32 Bailey (1966); Trenholm and Carley (1964).
33 Swanton (1952).
34 Driver (1961).
35 A. L. Kroeber (1925).
36 *Ibid.*
37 Terrell (1963).
38 Alexander F. Chamberlain in Hodge (1907).

PART TEN

The Pacific Coast

1 Letter from Dr. Leakey to Ruth Simpson quoted by Belden (1968).
2 *Ibid.*
3 *Ibid.*
4 Belden (1968).
5 *Ibid.*
6 Clements (1953).
7 Belden (1968).
8 *Ibid.*
9 See Note 1.
10 Carter (1954).
11 Orr (1956).
12 Wormington (1957).
13 *Ibid.*
14 Campbell *et al.* (1937).
15 In Campbell *et al.* (1937).
16 Walker (1951).
17 Mark Harrington (1948); Wormington (1957).
18 Meighan (1955).
19 Heizer (1953); Wormington (1957).
20 Antevs (1952)
21 Wormington (1957).
22 Cressman (1956); quote from Wormington (1957).
23 Heizer (1962).
24 *Ibid.*
25 A. L. Kroeber (1925). This remains the classic work on California Indians. It was reprinted without change in 1967. Kroeber spent seventeen years accumulating material for the great work.
26 *Ibid.*
27 Coues Edition (1893).
28 A. L. Kroeber (1925).

29 Heizer (1962).
30 *Ibid.*
31 A. L. Kroeber (1925).
32 *Ibid.*
33 Swanton in Hodge (1907).
34 Coues Edition (1893).
35 *Ibid.*
36 A. L. Kroeber (1925).
37 *Ibid.*
38 Bernice Johnston (1962).
39 A. L. Kroeber (1925).
40 *Ibid.*
41 Ferrand in Hodge (1907).
42 Coues Edition (1893).
43 Ferrand in Hodge (1907).
44 Sapir (1913); A. L. Kroeber (1925).
45 A. L. Kroeber (1925).
46 For those interested in the subject, Kroeber provides a brilliant analysis of the standards by which the Yurok regulated their conduct toward one another.
47 Stern (1965).
48 Swanton (1952).
49 A. L. Kroeber (1925).
50 Swanton (1952).
51 A. L. Kroeber (1925).
52 *Ibid.*
53 Swanton (1952).
54 A. L. Kroeber (1925).
55 *Ibid.*
56 *Ibid.*
57 *Ibid.*
58 T. Kroeber (1961).
59 *Ibid.*
60 *Ibid.*

A Selected Bibliography

ALLISON, VERNON C. *The Antiquity of the Deposits in Jacob's Cavern.* American Museum of Natural History, New York, 1926.

AMSDEN, CHARLES AVERY. *Prehistoric Southwesterners from Basketmaker to Pueblo.* Southwest Museum, Los Angeles, 1949.

——"Navajo Origins." *New Mexico Historical Review,* Santa Fe, 1932.

ANDERSON, EDGAR. *Plants, Man and Life.* Boston, 1952.

ANTEVS, ERNST. *On the Pleistocene History of the Great Basin.* Carnegie Institution, Washington, 1925.

——*Geology of the Clovis Sites.* See Wormington (1957).

——*Climatic History and the Antiquity of Man in California.* University of California, Berkeley, 1952.

ASCHMANN, HOMER H. *Great Basin Climates, etc.* University of California, Berkeley, 1958.

BAILEY, L. R. *Indian Slave Trade in the Southwest.* Los Angeles, 1966.

BAITY, ELIZABETH CHESLEY. *Americans Before Columbus.* New York, 1968.

BAKER, PAUL E. *The Forgotten Kutenai.* Boise, 1955.

BANCROFT, HUBERT HOWE. *Native Races,* Vols. 1–5. San Francisco, 1886–90.

——*History of Arizona and New Mexico 1530–1888,* San Francisco, 1889.

——*History of the North American States and Texas,* 2 Vols. San Francisco, 1884.

BANDELIER, ADOLPH F. A. *The Delight Makers.* New York, 1890.

——*Contributions to the History of the Southwestern United States.* Cambridge, Mass., 1890.

——*Final Report of Investigations Among the Indians of the Southwestern United States,* 2 Vols. Cambridge, 1890.

——*Historical Introduction to Studies Among the Sedentary Indians of New Mexico.* Cambridge, 1881.

——*Documentary History of the Zuñi Tribe.* Boston, 1892.

——*Final Report of Investigations Among the Indians of the Southwestern United States.* Cambridge, 1890-A.

——and FANNY BANDELIER. *Historical Documents Relating to New Mexico.* Carnegie Institution, Washington, 1937.

BANDELIER, FANNY. *The Journey of Álvar Núñez Cabeza de Vaca and His Companions from Florida to the Pacific, 1528–1536,* translated from the 1542 edition of Cabeza de Vaca's *Relación.* New York, 1905.

BARBOUR, E. H., and C. BERTRAND SCHULTZ. *Scottsbluff Bison Quarry etc.* Nebraska State Museum, Lincoln, 1932.

BARNWELL, COL. JOHN. "Tuscarora Expedition." *South Carolina Historical and Genealogical Magazine,* Columbia, S. C., 1908.

BARTRAM, WILLIAM. *Observations on the Creek and Cherokee Indians.* American Ethnological Society, Philadelphia, 1853.

——*Travels Through North and South Carolina.* London, 1792.

BEAUCHAMP, WILLIAM M. *History of New York Iroquois.* New York State Museum, Albany, 1905.

A SELECTED BIBLIOGRAPHY

BELDEN, L. BURR. "50,000 Years Ago." *Desert Magazine*, Palm Desert, California, 1968.

BENAVIDES, ALONSO DE. *Memorial*. Albuquerque, 1965.

BERRY, BREWTON, *ET AL. Archeological Investigations in Boone County*. Columbia, Missouri, 1938.

BERTHONG, DONALD J. *The Southern Cheyennes*. Norman, 1963.

BILLINTON, RAY ALLEN. *Westward Expansion*. New York, 1949.

BISHOP, MORRIS. *The Odyssey of Cabeza de Vaca*. New York, 1933.

BLAIR, EMMA H. *The Indian Tribes of the Upper Mississippi Valley and the Region of the Great Lakes*. Cleveland, 1911.

BLISS, EUGENE F. (Editor). *Diary of David Zeisberger*. Cincinnati, 1885.

BOAS, FRANZ. *Race, Language and Culture*. New York, 1949.

—*Human Faculty as Determined by Race*. Salem, Massachusetts, 1895.

BOLTON, HERBERT EUGENE. *The Spanish Borderlands*. New Haven, 1921.

—*Coronado*. New York, 1949.

—*Spanish Exploration in the Southwest*. New York, 1916.

—*Pageant in the Wilderness: The Story of the Escalante Expedition to the Interior Basin*. Salt Lake City, 1950.

—*Rim of Christendom*. New York, 1936.

BOURNE, EDWARD G. *Narratives of the Career of Hernando de Soto*. New York, 1904.

BRACKENRIDGE, H. M. *Views of Louisiana*. Pittsburgh, 1814.

BRANCH, E. DOUGLAS. *The Hunting of the Buffalo*. New York, 1929.

BRAND, DONALD. "Prehistoric Trade in the Southwest." *New Mexico Business Review*, Vol. 4, Albuquerque, 1935.

—"Aboriginal Trade Routes for Sea Shells in the Southwest." *Association of Pacific Coast Geographers Yearbook*, Cheney, Washington, 1938.

BREBNER, J. B. *Explorers in North America*. London, 1933.

BRINTON, DANIEL G. (Editor). *Library of Aboriginal American Literature*, Vol. 5. Philadelphia, 1882–1885.

BROECKER, W. S., and P. C. ORR. *Late Wisconsin History of Lake Lahontan*. Geological Society of America, Washington, 1956.

BRYAN, ALAN LYLE. *Paleo-American Prehistory*. Idaho State University Museum, Pocatello, 1965.

BRYAN, KIRK, HENRY RETZEK, and FRANKLIN T. McCANN. *Discovery of Sauk Valley Man in Minnesota*. Abilene, Texas, 1938.

BUSHNELL, D. L., JR. *Cahokia and Surrounding Mound Groups*. Cambridge, 1904.

BYERS, DOUGLAS S. "Ipswich B. C." *Essex Institute Quarterly*, Salem, Massachusetts, July, 1956.

—*Bull Brook, Massachusetts*, American Antiquity, 1955.

CABEZA DE VACA: *see* NÚÑEZ CABEZA DE VACA.

CAMPBELL, ELIZABETH W. CROZER, and WILLIAM H. CAMPBELL. *An Archeological Survey of the Twenty-Nine Palms Region*. Southwest Museum, Los Angeles, 1931.

—and WILLIAM H. CAMPBELL, *ET AL. The Archeology of Pleistocene* Los Angeles, 1935.

—and WILLIAM H. CAMPBELL, *ET AL. The Archeology of Pleistocene Lake Mojave: A Symposium*. Southwest Museum, Los Angeles, 1937.

CARTER, GEORGE F. *Pleistocene Man at San Diego*. The Johns Hopkins Press, Baltimore, 1957.

—*More Evidence of Interglacial Man in America*. London, 1954.

CARVER, JONATHAN. *Travels Through the Interior Parts of North America in the Years 1776, 1767 and 1768*. London, 1778.

CASAS, BARTOLOME DE LAS. *Historia de las Indias*. Madrid, 1674.

—*Relation of First Voyages Made by Spaniards*. London, 1699.

—*Tears of the Indians*. London, 1656.

CATLIN, GEORGE. *Letters and Notes on the Manners, Customs and Conditions of the North American Indians*, 2 Vols. New York and London, 1844.

A SELECTED BIBLIOGRAPHY

CHAMPLAIN, SAMUEL DE. *Works of,* 6 Vols. Toronto, 1930.

CHARD, C. S. *New World Migration Routes.* University of Alaska, 1958.

—*Distribution and Significance of Ball Courts in the Southwest.* Excavators' Club, Cambridge, Massachusetts, 1940.

CHARLEVOIX, PIERRE F. X. DE. *Historie et Description Générale de la Nouvelle France.* Paris, 1744. Translated by John Gilmary Shea, New York, 1866.

CHITTENDEN, HIRAM MARTIN. *History of the American Fur Trade of the Far West.* New York, 1902.

—and ALBERT TALBOT RICHARDSON. *The Life, Letters and Travels of Father Pierre-Jean De Smet, S. J.* New York, 1905.

CLARK, ELLA ELIZABETH. *Indian Legends from the Northern Rockies.* Norman, 1966.

CLAVIJERO, FRANCISCO XAVIER. *History of Lower California.* Translated by Sara E. Lake and A. A. Gray, Palo Alto, 1937.

CLEMENTS, THOMAS and LYDIA. *Evidence of Pleistocene Man in Death Valley.* Geological Society of North America, Baltimore, 1953.

CLINE, GLORIA GRIFFEN. *Exploring the Great Basin.* Norman, 1963.

COE, JOFFRE L. *Cultural Sequence of the Carolina Piedmont in Archaeology.* Chicago, 1952.

COLORADO MUSEUM OF NATURAL HISTORY. *Annual Report for 1926.* Denver, 1927.

COLSON, ELIZABETH. *The Makah Indians.* University of Minnesota, St. Paul, 1953.

COLTON, HAROLD S. "Prehistoric Trade in the Southwest." *Scientific Monthly,* New York, 1941.

—and F. C. BAXTER. *Days in the Painted Desert.* Museum of Northern Arizona, Flagstaff, 1932.

—and L. L. HARGRAVE. "Pueblo II in the San Francisco Mountains." Museum of Northern Arizona, *Bulletin* No. 4, 1933.

COOK, FREDERICK. *Journals of the Military Expedition of Major General John Sullivan.* Auburn, New York, 1887.

COON, CARLETON S. *The Story of Man.* New York, 1962.

CORKRAN, DAVID H. *The Creek Frontier.* Norman, 1962.

CORLE, EDWIN. *The Gila, River of the Southwest.* New York, 1851.

COTTER, JOHN LAMBERT. *The Occurrence of Flints and Extinct Animals in Pluvial Deposits Near Clovis, New Mexico: Report on the Excavation of the Gravel Pit in 1936.* Philadelphia Academy of Natural Sciences, 1937.

COTTERILL, R. S. *The Southern Indians.* Norman, 1954.

COUES, ELLIOTT (Editor). *On the Trail of a Spanish Pioneer: The Diary and Itinerary of Francisco Garces,* 2 Vols. New York, 1900.

COURVILLE, CYRIL B. *Trade Tomahawks.* Southwest Museum, Los Angeles, 1963.

COX, ISAAC JOSLIN. *The Journals of La Salle and His Companions* (Contains translations of accounts of La Salle's companions). New York, 1905.

CRANE, H. R. "Antiquity of Sandia Culture: Carbon 14 Measurements," *Science Magazine,* 1955.

CRESSMAN, L. S. *Klamath Prehistory.* Philadelphia, 1956.

—"Odell Lake Site: A New Paleo-Indian Campsite in Oregon." *American Antiquity,* 1948.

—and HOWELL WILLIAMS and ALEX D. KRIEGER. *Early Man in Oregon.* University of Oregon, Eugene, 1940.

CROOK, WILSON W., JR., and R. K. HARRIS. *Hearths and Artifacts of Early Man Near Lewisville, Texas.* Texas Archeological Society, Austin, 1957.

CUSHING, F. H. *Zuñi Fetiches.* Bureau of American Ethnology, 2nd Report, Washington, 1883.

—*Outlines of Zuñi Creation Myths.* Bureau of American Ethnology, 13th Report, Washington, 1896.

—*A Study of Zuñi Pottery as Illustrative of Zuñi Cultural Growth.* Bureau of American Ethnology, 4th Report, 1895.

DALE, EDWARD E. *The Indians of the Southwest.* Norman, 1949.

457

DAUGHERTY, RICHARD D. *Early Man in the Columbia Intermontane Province.* Salt Lake City, 1956.

DAY, A. GROVE. *Coronado's Quest: The Discovery of the Southwestern States.* Berkeley, 1940.

DEBO, ANGIE. *The Rise and Fall of the Choctaw Republic.* Norman, 1934.

DE FOREST, JOHN W. *History of the Indians of Connecticut from the Earliest Known Period to 1850.* Hartford, 1851.

DE JARNETTE, DAVID L. (Curator). *Moundville: A Prehistoric Cultural Center.* Moundsville, Alabama (no date).

DELLENBAUGH, FREDERICK S. *The Romance of the Colorado River.* New York, 1902.

DELLINGER, S. C. *Baby Cradles of the Ozark Bluff Dwellers.* Menasha, Wisconsin, 1936.

DENIG, EDWIN T. *Five Indian Tribes of the Upper Missouri.* Norman, 1961.

DENSMORE, FRANCES. *The American Indians and Their Music.* New York, 1926.

DE SCHWEINITS, EDMUND. *The Life and Times of David Zeisberger.* Philadelphia, 1870.

DE SMET, P. J. *See* Chittenden.

DIAZ DEL CASTILLO, BERNAL. *True History of the Conquest of New Spain.* New York, 1927.

DI PESO, CHARLES G. *The Upper Pimas of San Gayetano del Tumacacori.* Amerind Foundation, Dragoon, Arizona, 1956.

DITTERT, ALFRED E., JR., JIM J. HESTER, and FRANK W. EDDY. *An Archeological Survey of the Navajo Reservoir District.* Museum of New Mexico, Santa Fe, 1961.

DIXON, R. B. *Feathers.* American Museum of Natural History, New York, 1905.

DOBIE, J. FRANK. *The Mustangs.* Boston, 1952.

DORSEY, GEORGE A. *The Mythology of the Wichita.* Washington, 1904.

DORSEY, J. OWEN. *Siouan Sociology.* Bureau of American Ethnology, 15th Annual Report, Washington, 1897.

DOUGLAS, A. E. *Dating Pueblo Bonito and Other Ruins in the Southwest.* National Geographical Society, Washington, 1935.

DRIVER, HAROLD E. *Indians of North America.* Chicago, 1961.

——and WILLIAM C. MASSEY. *Comparative Studies of North American Indians.* Philadelphia, 1957.

DRUCKER, PHILIP. *Indians of the Northwest Coast.* New York, 1955.

DYER, JOSEPH O. *The Lake Charles Atakapas Cannibals.* Galveston, 1917.

EARDLY, A. J. *Basin Expansions and Stability in Levels of Lake Bonneville.* Geological Society of America, Washington, 1956.

EWERS, JOHN C. *The Blackfeet—Raiders of the Northwestern Plains.* Norman, 1958.

FAGES, PEDRO. *The Colorado River Campaign, 1781–1782: Diary of Pedro Fages,* edited by Herbert I. Priestly. Berkeley, 1913.

FAULKNER, CHARLES H. *The Excavation and Interpretation of the Old Stone Fort, Coffee County, Tennessee.* Knoxville, 1967.

——(Editor). *Archeological Investigations in Tims Ford Reservoir.* University of Tennessee, Knoxville, 1968.

——and J. B. GRAHAM. *Highway Salvage in the Nickajack Reservoir.* University of Tennessee, Knoxville, 1966.

FEWKES, J. W. *Antiquities of Mesa Verde National Park: Cliff Palace.* Bureau of American Ethnology, Washington, 1911.

FIGGINS, JESSE DADE. "The Antiquity of Man in America." *Natural History Magazine,* Vol. XXVII, No. 3, 1927.

——*New World Man.* Colorado Museum of Natural History, Denver, 1935.

——*A Further Contribution to the Antiquity of Man in America.* Colorado Museum of Natural History, Denver, 1933.

——*An Additional Discovery of the Association of a Folsom Artifact and Fossil Mammal Remains.* Colorado Museum of Natural History, Denver, 1931.

FLETCHER, ALICE C., and FRANCIS LA FLESCHE. *The Omaha Tribe*. Bureau of American Ethnology, Washington, 1911.

FLINT, RICHARD F. *Glacial Geology and the Pleistocene Epoch*. New York, 1953.

FORBES, JACK D. *Warriors of the Colorado: The Yumas of the Quechan Nation and Their Neighbors*. Norman, 1965.

——"Melchior Díaz and the Discovery of Alta California." *Pacific Historical Review*, November, 1958.

FORBIS, RICHARD G., and JOHN D. SPERRY. "An Early Man Site in Montana." *American Antiquity*, Vol. XXIII, No. 2, 1952.

FOREMAN, GRANT. *The Five Civilized Tribes*. Norman, 1934.

FOWKE, GERARD. *Archeological History of Ohio*. Columbus, 1902.

FOWLER, MELVIN L. *Some Fluted Projectile Points from Illinois*. Springfield, 1954.

——and HOWARD WINTERS. *Modoc Rock Shelter*. Illinois State Museum, Springfield, 1956.

FOWLER, WILLIAM S. *Massachusetts Fluted Points*. Massachusetts Archeological Society, Boston, 1954.

FREEMAN, LEWIS R. *The Conquistadores*. New York, 1933.

GIBSON, A. M. *The Kickapoos*. Norman, 1963.

GIDLEY, JAMES W. *Further Study of the Problem of Early Man in Florida*. Smithsonian Institution, Washington, 1929.

——*Investigations of Early Man in Florida*. Smithsonian Institution, Washington, 1930.

——and FREDERICK B. LOOMIS. "Fossil Man in Florida." *American Journal of Science*, 1926.

GIDOLINGO, J. L., JR. "Denbigh Flint Complex." *American Antiquity*, Vol. XXII, 1951.

GIFFORD, E. W. *The Kamia of Imperial Valley*. Bureau of American Ethnology, Washington, 1931.

GLADWIN, HAROLD S., E. W. HENRY, E. B. SAYLES, and NORA GLADWIN. *Excavation at Snaketown: Material Culture*. Gila Pueblo Medallion Papers, No. 25, Globe, Arizona, 1937.

GRAHAM, J. B. *Archeological Investigation of Moccasin Bend*. University of Tennessee, Knoxville, 1964.

GRIFFIN, JAMES B. (Editor). *Archeology of Eastern United States*. Chicago, 1952.

GRINNELL, GEORGE BIRD. *The Fighting Cheyennes*. New York, 1915.

GROSS, HUGO. *Mastodon, Mammoth and Man in America*. Lubbock, Texas, 1951.

HACK, JOHN T. "Antiquity of the Finley Site." *American Antiquity*, Vol. XIII, No. 3, 1943.

HAGAN, WILLIAM T. *The Sac and Fox Indians*. Norman, 1958.

——*American Indians*. University of Chicago, 1961.

HALL, E. T. "Recent Clues to Athapascan Pre-History in the Southwest." *American Anthropologist*, Vol. XLVI, No. 1, 1944.

HALLENBECK, CLEVE. *Journey and Route of Cabeza de Vaca*. Glendale, California, 1940.

——and JUANITA H. WILLIAMS. *La Jornada del Muerto, Legends of the Spanish Southwest*. Glendale, 1938.

HAMMOND, GEORGE P. *Coronado's Seven Cities*. Albuquerque, 1940.

——and AGAPITO REY. *The Narratives of the Coronado Expedition*. Albuquerque, 1940.

——and EDGAR F. GOOD. *The Adventures of Don Francisco Vásquez de Coronado*. Albuquerque, 1938.

HARRINGTON, JOHN PEABODY. *On Phonetic and Lexic Resemblances Between Kiowan and Tanoan*. Archeological Institute of America, Washington, 1910.

HARRINGTON, MARK RAYMOND. *A Pinto Site at Little Lake, California*. Southwest Museum, 1957.

——*An Ancient Site at Borax Lake, California*. Southwest Museum, 1948.

——*Gypsum Cave, Nevada*. Southwest Museum, 1933.

——*Man's Oldest Date in America*. American Museum of Natural History, New York, 1955.
——and RUTH DE ETTE SIMPSON. *Tule Springs, Nevada, with Other Evidence of Pleistocene Man in North America*. Southwest Museum Papers, No. 18, Los Angeles, 1961.
HARRIS, BURTON. *John Colter*. New York, 1952.
HASSRICK, ROYAL B. *The Sioux—Life and Customs of a Warrior Society*. In collaboration with Dorothy Maxwell and Cile M. Bach. Norman, 1964.
HAURY, EMIL W. *The Stratigraphy and Archeology of Ventana Cave*. Albuquerque, 1950.
——*The Excavation of Los Muertos and Neighboring Ruins in the Salt River Valley*. Peabody Museum, 1945.
——*The Mogollon Culture of Southwestern New Mexico*. Gila Pueblo Medallion Papers, No. 20, Globe, Arizona, 1936.
——"Artifacts, etc.—Naco, Arizona." *American Antiquity*, Vol. XIX, 1953.
——and E. B. SAYLES and WILLIAM W. WASLEY. "Lehner Mammoth Site, Arizona." *American Antiquity*, Vol. 25, No. 1, 1959.
HEINZELMAN, S. P. *Indian Affairs on the Pacific*. House of Representatives' Executive Document 76, 34th Congress, 3rd Session, 1857.
HEIZER, ROBERT F. "The California Indians." *California Historical Society Quarterly* (San Francisco), March, 1962.
——"California Indians." *California Historical Society Quarterly* (Los Angeles), March, 1962.
——*The Archeology of the Napa Region*. Berkeley, 1953.
HENDRON, J. W. *Prehistory of El Rito de los Frijoles, Bandelier National Monument*. Coolidge, Arizona, 1940.
HENRY, ALEXANDER, and DAVID THOMPSON. *New Light on the Early History of the Greater Northwest*. New York, 1897.
HESTER, JAMES J. *Early Navajo Migrations and Acculturation in the Southwest*. Museum of New Mexico, Santa Fe, 1962.
HIBBEN, FRANK C. "Association of Man with Pleistocene Mammals in the Sandia Mountains." *American Antiquity*, Vol. XI, 1937.
——*Evidences of Early Occupation in Sandia Cave, New Mexico*. Smithsonian Institution, 1941.
——*Digging Up America*. New York, 1960.
——"Was Ice Age Man a Game Hog?" *Denver Post*, August 10, 1969.
HODGE, FREDERICK W. (Editor). *Handbook of Indians North of Mexico*. Bureau of American Ethnology, Washington, 1907.
——*History of Hawikuh*. Southwest Museum, Los Angeles, 1937.
——"The Early Navajos and Apaches." *American Anthropologist*, 1895.
——*Spanish Explorers in the Southern United States*. New York, 1907; reprinted 1959 (contains the Smith [q.v.] translation of the Cabeza de Vaca *Relación*, the Winship [q.v.] translation of the Castañeda narrative, and the Smith translation of the De Soto Account by the Gentleman of Elvas).
——and THEODORE H. LEWIS. *Spanish Explorers in the Eastern United States*. New York, 1907.
HOEBEL, E. ADAMSON. *The Cheyenne Indians of the Great Plains*. New York, 1960.
HOFFMAN, WALTER J. *The Menominee Indians*. Bureau of American Ethnology, Washington, 1896.
HOOTON, E. A. *Indians of Pecos Pueblo*. Phillips Academy, New Haven, 1930.
HOPKINS, DAVID M. (Editor). *The Bering Land Bridge*. Stanford, 1967.
HOPKINS, SARAH WINNEMUCCA. *Life Among the Paiutes*. Boston, 1883.
HOWARD, EDGAR B. *Occurrence of Flints and Extinct Animals in Pluvial Deposits Near Clovis, New Mexico*. Philadelphia Academy of Natural Science, 1935.
——"The Finley Site: Discovery of Yuma Points in Situ Near Eden, Wyoming." *American Antiquity*, Vol. XIII, 1943.
——LINTON SATTERTHWAITE, JR., and CHARLES BACHE. "Preliminary

Report on a Buried Yuma Site in Wyoming." *American Antiquity,* Vol. VII, 1941.

HOWELLS, W. W. *Crania from Wyoming.* New York, 1938.

HRDLICKA, ALES. *Skeletal Remains Suggesting or Attributed to Early Man in North America.* Bureau of American Ethnology, Washington, 1907.

——*Early Man in America.* Philadelphia, 1937.

HUGHES, JACK T. "Investigation in Western South Dakota and Northeastern Wyoming." *American Antiquity,* Vol. XIV, 1949.

HYDE, GEORGE E. *Spotted Tail's Folk: Brule Sioux.* Norman, 1961.

——*Indians of the Woodlands.* University of Oklahoma, 1962.

——*Red Cloud's Folk.* Norman, 1957.

——*Indians of the High Plains.* Norman, 1959.

IVES, JOSEPH C. *Report upon the Colorado River of the West.* House of Representatives' Executive Document 90, 36th Congress, 1st Session, 1861.

IVES, RONALD R. "The Grave of Melchior Díaz: A Problem in Historical Sleuthing." *The Kiva Magazine,* 1959.

——"Melchior Díaz, the Forgotten Explorer." *Hispanic-American Historical Review,* February, 1936.

JEANCON, J. A. *Excavations in Chama Valley.* Bureau of American Ethnology, Washington, 1923.

JENKS, ALBERT ERNEST. *The Wild Rice Gatherers of the Upper Lakes.* Bureau of American Ethnology, Washington, 1900.

——*Pleistocence Man in Minnesota.* University of Minnesota, Minneapolis, 1936.

——*Minnesota's Brown Valley Man and Associated Burial Artifacts.* American Anthropological Association, Menasha, Wisconsin, 1937.

JENNINGS, JESSE D. *Danger Cave, Utah.* University of Utah, Salt Lake City, 1957.

——and EDWARD NORBECK. "Great Basin Prehistory." *American Antiquarian,* Vol. 21, No. 1, 1955.

——and EDWARD NORBECK. *Prehistoric Man in the New World.* University of Chicago, 1964.

JEPSON, GLENN L. *Ancient Buffalo Hunters of Wyoming.* Archeological Society of New Jersey. Trenton, 1951.

——*Ancient Buffalo Hunters.* Princeton, 1953.

JESUIT RELATIONS. See Thwaites.

JOHNSON, ELDEN. *Prehistoric Peoples of Minnesota.* St. Paul, 1969.

JOHNSON, FREDERICK. *The Boylston Street Fishweir.* Phillips Academy, Andover, Massachusetts, 1942.

JOHNSTON, BERNICE EASTMAN. *California's Gabrieliño Indians.* Southwest Museum, Los Angeles, 1962.

JONES, WILLIAM (Editor). *Kickapoo Tales.* American Ethnological Society, New York, 1915.

JOSEPHY, ALVIN M., JR. *The Indian Heritage of America.* New York, 1968.

KELLEY, J. CHARLES. "The Cultural Affinities and Chronological Position of the Clear Fork Focus." *American Antiquity,* Vol. VIII, 1947.

KENNEDY, MICHAEL STEPHEN (Editor). *The Assiniboines: From the Accounts of the Old Ones Told to First Boy (James Larpenteur Long).* Norman, 1961.

KINO, EUSEBIA FRANCISCO. *Historical Memoir of Pimeria Alta.* Cleveland, 1916.

KLUCKHOHN, CLYDE, and DOROTHEA LEIGHTON. *The Navajo.* Cambridge, Massachusetts, 1946.

KNEBERG, MADELINE. *The Tennessee Area in Archeology.* Chicago, 1952.

KNIFFEN, FRED B. *The Natural Landscape of the Colorado Delta.* University of California, Berkeley, 1932.

KOCH, ALBERT C. *Evidence of the Contemporaneous Existence of Man with Mastodon in Missouri.* St. Louis, 1839 and 1860.

KOEHLER, THOMAS HUME. *Archeological Excavation of the Womack Mound.* University of Mississippi, 1966.

KRIEGER, A. D. "Earliest Cultures in Western United States." *American Antiquities,* 1962.

461

A SELECTED BIBLIOGRAPHY

KROEBER, A. L. *Handbook of the Indians of California.* Bureau of American Ethnology, Washington, 1925.
——"Preliminary Sketch of the Mojave Indians." *American Anthropology,* Vol. 4, 1902.
KROEBER, THEODORA. *Ishi in Two Worlds.* Berkeley, 1961.
LA HARPE, BERNARD DE. *Journal Historique de L'Establissement des Français à la Louisiane.* New Orleans, 1831.
LAHONTAN, ARMAND L. DE D. *Nouveaux Voyages de Mr. le Baron Lahontan, dans L'Amérique Septentrionale.* France, 1703. (English translation, London, 1703 and 1735.)
LANDBURG, LEIF C. W. *The Chumash Indians of Southern California.* Southwest Museum, Los Angeles, 1965.
LAS CASAS, BARTOLEME DE. *Historia de las Indias.* Madrid, 1875.
LAWSON, JOHN. *History of Carolina.* Raleigh, 1860.
LEACH, DOUGLAS E. *The Northern Colonial Frontier 1607–1763.* New York, 1966.
LEROUX, JOSEPH. *Le Medaillier du Canada.* Montreal, 1888.
LESSER, ALEXANDER, and GENE WELTFISH. *Composition of the Caddoan Linguistic Stock.* Washington, 1932.
LEVERETT, FRANK, and F. W. SARDESON. *Quaternary Geology of Minnesota.* United States Geological Survey, Washington, 1932.
LEWIS, MERIWETHER, and WILLIAM CLARK. *Journals.* Edited by Elliott Coues. New York, 1893.
LEWIS, T. HAYES (Editor). *The Narrative of the Expedition of Hernando de Soto by the Gentleman of Elvas.* (In *Spanish Explorers in the Southern United States*), New York, 1959.
LIBBY, WILLARD J. *Radiocarbon Dating.* University of Chicago Press, 1955.
LOGAN, WILFRED D. *Graham Cave.* Columbia, Missouri, 1952.
LOWERY, WOODBURY. *The Spanish Settlements Within the Present Limits of the United States 1513–1561.* New York, 1901.
LOWIE, ROBERT H. *The Crow Indians.* New York, 1935.
——"Alleged Kiowa-Crow Affinities." *Southwestern Journal of Anthropology,* Albuquerque, 1953.
——*Primitive Society.* New York, 1961.
——*Indians of the Plains.* New York, 1954.
LUMMIS, CHARLES F. *The Spanish Pioneers.* Chicago, 1893.
——"Fray Zarate Salmeron's Relation." *Land of Sunshine Magazine,* Vols. XI and XII, Los Angeles, 1897–1898.
MACGOWAN, KENNETH, and JOSEPH A. HESTER, JR. *Early Man in the New World.* Garden City, New York, 1962.
MCBETH, KATE. *The Nez Percés Since Lewis and Clark.* New York, 1908.
MCCARY, BEN C. *Survey of Virginian Fluted Points.* Charlottesville, 1954 and 1956.
MCGREGOR, JOHN C. *Southwestern Archeology.* New York, 1941.
MCGUIRE, J. D. *Pipes and Smoking Customs of American Aborigines.* United States National Museum, Washington, 1897.
MCKERN, W. C. *The First Settlers of Wisconsin.* Madison, 1942.
MCKUSICK, MARSHALL. *Men of Ancient Iowa.* Iowa State University, Ames, 1964.
MCREYNOLDS, EDWIN C. *The Seminoles.* Norman, 1957.
MANGELSDORF, P. C., and R. G. REEVES. *The Origin of Corn.* Botanical Museum Leaflets, Vol. 18, Nos. 7–10, Cambridge, Massachusetts, 1959.
——*The Origin of Indian Corn and Its Relatives.* College Station, Texas, 1939.
——and C. EARLE SMITH, JR. *New Archeological Evidence on Evolution in Maize.* Cambridge, Massachusetts, 1949.
MARGRY, PIERRE. *Découvertes et Etablissements des Français dans l'ouest et dans le sud de l'Amérique Septentrionale, 1614–1754,* 6 Vols. Paris, 1876–86.
MARTIN, PAUL S. "Lowry Ruin in Southwest Colorado." *Kansas University of Science Bulletin,* 1936.
——GEORGE I. QUIMBY, and DONALD COLLIER. *Indians Before Columbus.* Chicago, 1947.

A SELECTED BIBLIOGRAPHY

MATHEWS, JOHN JOSEPH. *The Osages.* Norman, 1961.

MAXIMILIAN, ALEXANDER PHILIP, PRINCE OF WIED NEUWIED. *Travels in the Interior of North America.* London, 1843.

MAYHALL, MILDRED P. *The Kiowas.* Norman, 1962.

MEIGHAN, CLEMENT W. *Archeology of the North Coast Ranges, California.* Berkeley, 1955.

MEMBRE, ZENOBE. *Narrative of La Salle's Voyage Down the Mississippi.* Paris, France, 1691.

MILLER, CARL F. "Life 8000 Years Ago—Alabama Cave." *National Geographic Magazine,* Vol. CX, No. 4, 1956.

MILLS, W. C. "Explorations of Mounds." *Ohio Archeological and Historical Quarterly,* Jan.-Mar., 1902.

MOONEY, JAMES. *Calendar History of the Kiowa Indians.* Washington, 1898.

——*The Cheyenne Indians.* American Anthropological Association, Lancaster, Pennsylvania, 1907.

——*The Aboriginal Population of America North of Mexico.* Washington, 1928.

MOOREHEAD, W. K. *The Hopewell Mound Group of Ohio.* Field Museum of Natural History, Chicago, 1922.

MORGAN, DALE L. *Jedediah Smith and the Opening of the West.* Indianapolis, 1953.

MORGAN, LEWIS H. *League of Ho-de-no-sau-nee, or Iroquois.* New York, 1904.

MOSS, JOHN H. *Early Man in Eden Valley.* University of Pennsylvania Museum, Philadelphia, 1951.

NELSON, N. C. *The Antiquity of Man in America.* Toronto, 1933.

NESBIT, PAUL H. *The Ancient Mimbreños, New Mexico.* Logan Museum, Beloit, Wisconsin, 1931.

NEWCOMB, W. W., JR. *The Indians of Texas.* Austin, 1961.

NÚÑEZ CABEZA DE VACA, ÁLVAR. *Relación.* Zamora, Spain, 1542.

O'BRYAN, A. *The Dine: Origin Myths of the Navajo Indians.* Bureau of American Anthropology, Washington, 1956.

O'KANE, WALTER COLLINS. *The Hopis.* Norman, 1953.

OPLER, MARVIN K. "The Origins of Comanche and Ute." *American Anthropologist,* Vol. XLV, 1943.

ORR, PHIL C. *Report on Santa Rosa Island.* Santa Barbara Museum of Natural History, 1952.

——*Radiocarbon Dates Santa Rosa Island.* Santa Barbara Museum of Natural History, 1956.

PARKMAN, FRANCIS. *La Salle and the Discovery of the Great West.* Boston, 1879.

PARSONS, ELSIE CLEWS. *Pueblo Indian Religion,* 2 Vols. University of Chicago, 1939.

——*Notes on the Caddo.* Menasha, Wisconsin, 1941.

PEARCE, R. H. *Savages of America.* The Johns Hopkins University Press, 1953.

PICKETT, ALBERT J. *History of Alabama.* Charlestown, 1851.

POND, PETER. *The Journal of Peter Pond, 1773-1775.* Wisconsin Historical Society, Madison, 1902.

QUIMBY, GEORGE I. *Indian Life in the Upper Great Lakes.* Chicago, 1960.

RADIN, PAUL. *The Winnebago Tribe.* Bureau of American Ethnology, Washington, 1923.

——*The Story of the North American Indian.* New York, 1957.

RAU, CHARLES. *Ancient Aboriginal Trade in North America.* Smithsonian Institution, Washington, 1873.

RAY, CYRUS N. *Flint Cultures of Early Man in Texas.* Abilene, 1934.

——and E. B. SAYLES. *An Agreement on Abilene Terminology.* Abilene, 1941.

REICHARD, GLADYS A. *Navajo Religion,* 2 Vols. New York, 1950.

RENAUD, E. B. *The Black's Fork Culture of Southwest Wyoming.* Denver, 1940.

——*Prehistoric Cultures of the Cimarron Valley, Northeastern New Mexico and Western Oklahoma.* Denver, 1930.

RICHARDSON, RUPERT NORVAL. *The Comanche Barrier to South Plains Settlement*. Glendale, California, 1933.
RITCHIE, WILLIAM A. *Traces of Early Man in the Northeast*. New York State Museum, Albany, 1957.
——*The Archeology of New York State*. Garden City, 1965.
——*Pre-Iroquoian Cultures*. New York State Museum, Albany, 1966.
ROBERTS, FRANK H. H., JR. *A Folsom Complex*. Washington, 1935.
ROE, FRANK GILBERT. *The Indian and the Horse*. Norman, 1955.
ROGERS, MALCOLM J. *Ancient Hunters of the Far West*. San Diego, 1963.
ROUSE, IRVING. *Vero and Melbourne Man*. New York Academy of Sciences, 1950.
SAPIR, EDWARD. "Wiyot and Yurok, Algonkin Languages of California." *American Anthropologist*, Vol. XV, 1913.
SAYLES, E. B. *An Archeological Survey of Chihuahua, Mexico*. Gila Pueblo Medallion Papers, No. 22, Globe, Arizona, 1936.
——and ERNST ANTEVS. *The Cochise Culture*. Gila Pueblo Medallion Papers, No. 24, Globe, Arizona, 1941.
SCHOOLCRAFT, HENRY R. *Historical and Statistical Information Respecting the History, Condition and Prospects of the Indians of the United States*. Philadelphia, 1851.
SCHROEDER, ALBERT H. "Unregulated Diffusion from Mexico into the Southwest Prior to A.D. 700." *American Antiquity*, Vol. XXX, 1965.
——"Pattern Diffusion from Mexico into the Southwest After A.D. 600." *American Antiquity*, Vol. XXXI, 1966.
SCHULTZ, C. B. "Some Artifact Sites of Early Man in the Great Plains and Adjacent Areas." *American Antiquity*, Vol. IX, 1943.
SELLARDS, ELIAS H. *Early Man in America*. Texas Memorial Museum, Austin, 1952.
——"Stone Images from Henderson County, Texas." *American Antiquity*, Vol. VII, 1941.
——"On the Association of Human Remains and Extinct Vertebrates at Vero, Florida." *Journal of Geology*, 1917.
——and GLEN L. EVANS, GRAYSON A. MEADE, and ALEX D. KRIEGER. *Fossil Bison and Associated Artifacts from Plainview, Texas*. Geological Society of America, Vol. 58, 1947.
SERVICE, E. R. *Primitive Social Organization*. New York, 1962.
——*Profiles in Ethnology*. New York, 1963.
——*The Hunters*. New York, 1966.
SHEA, JOHN GILMARY. *Discovery and Exploration of the Mississippi Valley*. New York, 1853. Contains translation of Membre (1691).
——*Early Voyages Up and Down the Mississippi*. Albany, 1861.
SHETRONE, H. C. *The Mound Builders*. New York, 1930.
SHIPPEE, J. M. *Nebo Hill*. Menasha, Wisconsin, 1948.
——*Cave Investigations*. Columbia, Missouri, 1955.
SIMPSON, JAMES HERVEY. *Coronado's March in Search of the Seven Cities of Cibola*. Smithsonian Institution, Washington, 1871.
SINCLAIR, WILLIAM J. *Exploration of Potter Creek Cave, California*. University of California, Berkeley, 1907.
SMITH, BUCKINGHAM. *The Career of Hernando de Soto in the Conquest of Florida*. English translation of the Narrative of the Gentleman of Elvas. New York, 1886.
——*Relación of Álvar Núñez Cabeza de Vaca*, translated from the 1555 edition. Washington, 1851.
SMITH, G. HUBERT. "Trade Among the Dakota." *Minnesota Archeologist*, Vol. 13, 1947.
SMITH, JOHN. *Works*. Edited by Edward Arbor. Birmingham, England, 1884.
SODAY, FRANK J. "The Quad Site: A Paleo-Indian Village in Northern Alabama." *The Tennessee Archeologist*, Knoxville, 1954.

SPECK, FRANK G. *Decorative Art and Basketry of the Cherokees*. Milwaukee, 1920.
—LEONARD BROOM and W. W. LONG. *Cherokee Dance and Drama*. Berkeley, 1951.

SPELMAN, HENRY. *Powhatan*. Bureau of American Ethnology, Washington, 1907.

SPRAGUE, MARSHALL. *The Great Gates*. Boston, 1964.

SQUIER, E. G. *Antiquities of the State of New York*. Buffalo, 1851.

STERLING, M. W. *Original Myth of Acoma and Other Records*. Bureau of American Ethnology, Washington, 1942.

STERN, THEODORE. *The Klamath Tribe*. Seattle, 1965.

STEVENSON, M. C. *Zuñi Indians*. Bureau of American Ethnology, Washington, 1901.

STEWARD, JULIAN H. *Basin-Plateau Aboriginal Sociopolitical Groups*. Bureau of American Ethnology, Washington, 1938.

SUHM, D. A., A. D. KRIEGER, and E. B. JELKS. *An Introductory Handbook of Texas Archeology*. Austin, 1954.

SWADISH, MORRIS. "Linguistic Relations Across Bering Strait." *American Anthropology*, Vol. LXIV, No. 6, 1962.

SWANTON, JOHN R. *The Indians of the Southeastern United States*. Bureau of American Ethnology, Washington, 1946.
—*Source Material and Ethnology of the Caddo Indians*. Washington, 1942.
—*Early History of the Creek Indians and Their Neighbors*. Bureau of American Ethnology, Washington, 1922.
—*Social Organization and Social Usages of the Indians of the Creek Confederacy*. Bureau of American Ethnology, Washington, 1928–A.
—*Religious Beliefs and Medical Practices of the Creek Indians*. Bureau of American Ethnology, Washington, 1924.
—*Source Material for the Social and Ceremonial Life of the Choctaw Indians*. Bureau of American Ethnology, Bulletin 103, Washington, 1931.
—*The Indian Tribes of North America*. Bureau of American Ethnology, Bulletin 145, Washington, 1952.

SYKES, GODFREY G. *The Colorado Delta*. Washington, 1937.
—*The Camino del Diablo*. New York, 1927.

TEIT, JAMES A. *The Salishan Tribes*. Bureau of American Ethnology, 45th Annual Report, Washington, 1930.

TERRELL, JOHN UPTON. *Traders of the Western Morning: Aboriginal Commerce in Pre-Columbian America*. Southwest Museum, Los Angeles, 1967.
—*La Salle: The Life and Times of an Explorer*. New York, 1968–A.
—*Black Robe*. New York, 1964.
—*The Six Turnings*. Glendale, California, 1968–B.
—*The Navajos*. New York, 1970–A.
—*The Discovery of California*. New York, 1970–B.
—*Furs by Astor*. New York, 1963.
—*Journey into Darkness*. New York, 1962.
—*Pueblo de los Corazones*. Palm Desert, California, 1966.
—*Estevancio the Black*. Los Angeles, 1968–C.

THOMPSON, DAVID. *David Thompson's Narrative of His Explorations in Western America* (J. B. Tyrrell, Editor). Toronto, 1916.

THOMPSON, RAYMOND H. *Archaic Culture in Kentucky*. Archeological Society of North Carolina, Chapel Hill, 1954.

THWAITES, REUBEN GOLD (Editor). *Jesuit Relations and Allied Documents, 1610–1791*, 73 Vols. Cleveland, 1896–1901.

TITIEV, MISCHA. *Old Oraibi: A Study of the Hopi Indians of the Third Mesa*. Peabody Museum, Cambridge, 1944.

TOWER, DONALD B. *The Use of Marine Mollusca and Their Value in Reconstructing Prehistoric Trade Routes in the American Southwest*. Excavators' Club, Cambridge, 1945.

TREGANZA, A. E., and A. BIERMAN. "Topanga Culture." *University of California Anthropological Records*, Vol. 20, No. 2, Berkeley, 1958.

TRENHOLM, VIRGINIA COLE, and MAURINE CARLEY. *The Shoshonis.* Norman, 1964.

TURNER, FREDERICK JACKSON. *The Frontier in American History.* New York, 1920.

TURNEY-HIGH, HARRY HOLBERT. "Ethnology of the Kutenai." *American Anthropologist,* Vol. 43, No. 2, 1941.
—*The Flathead Indians of Montana.* Missoula, 1937.

TWITCHELL, RALPH E. *Leading Facts of New Mexican History,* 5 Vols. Cedar Rapids, Iowa, 1911.

UNDERHILL, RUTH. *The Navajos.* Norman, 1956.
—*Red Man's America.* University of Chicago, 1953.
—*Red Man's Religion.* University of Chicago, 1965.

VANEGAS, MIGUEL. *Natural and Civil History of California,* 2 Vols. London, 1759.

VARNER, JOHN GRIER, and JEANNETTE JOHNSON VARNER. *The Florida of the Inca.* Austin, 1951.

VERENDRYE, PIERRE G. DE V. *Journals.* Toronto, 1907.

VETROMILE, EUGENE. *The Abnakis.* New York, 1866.

WAGNER, HENRY R. *California Voyages 1539–1541.* San Francisco, 1925.
—"The Voyage of Hernando de Alarcón." *California Historical Society Quarterly,* Vol. III, December, 1924.
—*Spanish Voyages to the Northwest Coast of America.* San Francisco, 1929.
—*Juan Rodríguez Cabrillo.* California Historical Society, San Francisco, 1941.

WALKER, EDWIN FRANCIS. *Five Prehistoric Archeological Sites in Los Angeles County.* Southwest Museum, 1951.

WALLACE, ERNEST, and E. ADAMSON HOEBEL. *The Comanches,* Norman, 1952.

WALLACE, PAUL A. W. *Indians in Pennsylvania.* Harrisburg, 1961.

WARREN, WILLIAM W. *History of the Ojibways Based Upon Traditions and Oral Statements.* Minnesota Historical Society, St. Paul, 1885.

WATERS, FRANK. *The Colorado.* New York, 1946.
—*The Book of Hopi.* New York, 1963.

WEBB, WILLIAM S. *The Parrish Village Site.* University of Kentucky, Lexington, 1951.

WEDEL, WALDO. *Prehistoric Man on the Great Plains.* Norman, 1961.
—*Environment and Native Subsistent Economics in the Central Great Plains.* Washington, 1941.

WENDORF, FRED, ALEX D. KRIEGER, CLAUDE C. ALBRITTON, and T. D. STEWART. *The Midland Discovery.* University of Texas, 1955.
—and ALEX D. KRIEGER, *ET AL.* "New Light on Midland Discovery." *American Antiquity,* 1959.

WHITE, LESLIE A. *The Acoma Indians.* Bureau of American Ethnology, Washington, 1932.
—*Pueblo of San Felipe,* 1932–A.
—*Pueblo of Santo Domingo, New Mexico,* 1935.
—*Pueblo of Santa Ana, New Mexico,* 1942. American Anthropological Association, Menasha, Wisconsin.

WILLEY, GORDON R., and PHILIP PHILLIPS. "Method and Theory in American Archeology." *American Anthropologist,* Vol. 57, No. 4, 1955.

WINSHIP, GEORGE PARKER (Translator). *The Narrative of the Expedition of Coronado by Castañeda.* Bureau of American Ethnology, Washington, 1896.

WITTHOFT, JOHN. *A Paleo-Indian Site in Eastern Pennsylvania: An Early Hunting Culture.* American Philosophical Society, Philadelphia, 1952.
—*Indian Prehistory of Pennsylvania.* Harrisburg, 1965.

WOODWARD, ARTHUR. *Indian Trade Goods.* Portland, Oregon, 1965.

WOODWARD, GRACE STEELE. *The Cherokees.* Norman, 1963.

WORMINGTON, H. M. *Ancient Man in North America.* Denver, 1941 and 1957.

YOUNG, ROBERT W. *The Navajo Yearbook.* Window Rock, Arizona, 1961.

Glossary
of Names and Terms

Southwestern Deserts and Mesa Lands

Anasazi Culture: an extremely progressive civilization in the Southwest that is known particularly for its impressive weaving, pottery, and masonry techniques. Its five-hundred-year Golden Age began circa A.D. 1000. Its customs and techniques were adopted by the Mogollon Culture (q.v.) and others.

Apache: a tribe related to the Navajo (q.v.) whose members called themselves *Dineh* ("the people"). The Zuñi word for enemy, *apachu*, gave them their current appellation. They settled in southeastern New Mexico and western Texas after their migrations from Canada. The Apache were nomadic and warlike.

Arroyo: a dry gully.

Bat Cave: site of the first discovery of maize in North America. Located in New Mexico, the cave was opened up in 1948 and found to contain six-thousand-year-old agricultural specimens.

Blackwater Draw: New Mexico site that yielded the first Clovis points, projectile points slightly older than Folsom points (q.v.).

Cabeza de Vaca, Álvar Núñez: early Spanish explorer who reached the Southwest in the sixteenth century. His travels are recounted in his journal. He was originally part of the expedition to Florida led by Pánfilo de Narváez.

Cacique: a town or pueblo chieftain.

Casa Grande: a site of the Salado Culture (q.v.) in Arizona that is now protected by the National Park Service. Its walls are forty feet high and originally enclosed sixteen rooms.

Chemehuevi: a tribe of the true Paiute, Shoshonean.

Chiricahua: the stage of the Cochise Complex (q.v.) that existed between 8000 and 3000 B.C. in the area of the Chiricahua Mountains in Arizona.

Clovis fluted points: polished, tapering, cylindrical spearheads first located near Clovis, New Mexico. They were first used circa 10,000 B.C.

Cochise: a cultural complex situated in southeastern Arizona and southwestern New Mexico. The name originates with a nineteenth-century Indian chief. The complex spans the period 13,000 to 500 B.C.

Cocopa Culture: a division of the Yuman Culture located in California's Mohave Desert region.

Dendrochronology: the science of dating wood by tree growth rings.

Estevanico the Black: a Moroccan slave with Cabeza de Vaca (q.v.) from the Narváez expedition who was killed by the Zuñi after having discovered Arizona and New Mexico for Spain.

Folsom points: flaked, grooved, and lanceolate pieces of flint that were used as weapon tips in prehistoric times. They are named for the site where they were first discovered, Folsom, New Mexico.

Gentes: tribal divisions, similar to Scottish clans. Each of these had its own special ceremonies.

Halchidhoma: a Yuman tribe, connected with Maricopa.

Harquebusier: a soldier armed with a harquebus, a matchlock weapon.

Havasupai: a small isolated Arizona tribe that was almost the last to be found by white men. They are part of the Yuman Culture and practice rituals similar to those of the Hopi.

Hogan: Navajo dwelling.

Hohokam Culture: a civilization characterized significantly by canal irrigation techniques. It was located near the Salt and Gila rivers in Arizona and flourished until historical times. The name means "those who have gone" in the Pima language—members of this culture are considered the ancestors of the modern Pima Indians.

Hopi Culture: a Shoshonean-speaking Pueblo civilization located in New Mexico and Arizona. The name of the people, derived from *Hopitu,* means "the peaceful ones." A thriving modern tribe, the Hopi are today still renowned for their weaving and pottery.

Jemez: a Pueblo tribe of New Mexico.

Keresan: a well-known and still-active Pueblo tribe that first settled in New Mexico around the twelfth century and built cliff-dwellings along the Rito de los Frijoles (Bean Creek).

Kiva: a subterranean shelter used for sacred rites and usually restricted to men.

Maricopa: a tribe known best in historical times as coexistent with the Pima (q.v.). They called themselves *Pipatsje* but were given the name *Maricopa* by the Pima.

Metate: a shallow stone basin used for grinding grain. The grinding is done with a mano, a polished stone held in the hand.

Mimbres: name given to a river and the culture found along it in southwestern New Mexico. The Mimbreños were skilled artisans and agriculturalists. Pueblo influence, particularly in agriculture, is marked. The culture disappeared suddenly circa A.D. 1200.

Mogollon Culture: the Arizona–New Mexico direct descendant of the Cochise Complex. It included agriculture, pottery-making, and hunting, and flourished between A.D. 500 and 900.

Mohave: the most populous and most hostile of the Yuman tribes, located in southwestern Arizona and southern California. Their name for themselves was *Tzina-ma-a* and they lived in widely scattered small settlements with mud-and-thatch houses.

Navajo: the name given by the Spanish to a tribe that originated in northern Canada. These people, who call themselves *Dineh* (meaning "the people"), have a particularly colorful mythological tradition and began their settlements in the Southwest around A.D. 1000. By raiding Pueblo settlements, they learned Pueblo traditions and practices and soon dominated the entire Southwest.

Pecos: a New Mexico Pueblo tribe whose members dwelt in three-hundred-room buildings along the Pecos River. They were closely related to the Jemez.

Pima Culture: a canal-building culture like the Hohokam that was originally established in the Salt River Valley. The Pimans called themselves *A-a'tam* (meaning "people") but were later given the name *Pima* (meaning "no") by missionaries.

Piro: a large Pueblo tribe inhabiting eastern New Mexico.

Pleistocene Age: geological era that ended circa 9000 B.C.

Pluvial Period: climatic era characterized by rains that followed the close of the Pleistocene Age.

Projectile point. *See* Folsom points; Clovis fluted points; Sandia points.

Pueblo: a Spanish word used to designate Indians who lived in permanent stone or adobe dwellings. Also, the name for such a dwelling. The Pueblo Culture is actually a rather loose grouping of peoples of four linguistic stocks. Although these peoples have general similarities in mores, they are widely scattered across the Southwest and evince innumerable regional differences in their customary traits. The Anasazi Culture (q.v.) was the highest Pueblo-type civilization.

Salado Culture: a civilization marked by sedentary people resident in multi-storied apartments built around plazas and surrounded by protective walls—traits indicating Anasazi influence. The Saladoans began to coexist peacefully with the Hohokam in the fourteenth century, as the Sinaguans (q.v.) had previously, but the Saladoans managed to retain their cultural independence.

Salinas: salt marshes.

San Pedro Period: a stage of the Cochise Complex dating from 3000 to 500 B.C. Named for the San Pedro River in Arizona, it is characterized by the earliest findings of corn pollen in the United States.

Sandia points: flaked projectile points, first found near Sandia, New Mexico, that may date as far back as 20,000 B.C.

Seven Cities of Cibola: a legendary treasure trove sought by early Spanish explorers in the Southwest. The cities were actually a group of ancient Zuñi pueblos. Cibola (Zuñi-land) was the locale of the murders of many of the early explorers.

Sinagua Culture: a small southwestern agricultural grouping that was peacefully absorbed into the Hohokam Culture (q.v.) in the thirteenth century.

Sulphur Spring: earliest stage of the Cochise Complex, centered around Arizona's now-arid Sulphur Spring Valley. Evidence exists that rainfall was once plentiful in the area, although cultural attributes were scarce.

Tewa: a well-organized and well-ruled tribe whose northern and southern divisions extended from central Colorado to northern New Mexico. Their name means "moccasins."

Tiwa: a tribe of New Mexico and Texas whose best-known pueblo is Taos. Taos was an important trade center even in prehistoric times.

Tufa: a porous rock formed as a deposit from streams.

Ventana Cave: site of the recovery of Folsom points and extinct horse and sloth bones, near Tucson, Arizona. It was occupied continuously for more than thirteen thousand years.

Yuma Culture: a civilization found in the Southwest as well as in Baja California. Distinguished by their superior physical prowess and their trading ability (particularly pottery and shells), they called themselves *Kwichana*.

Zuñi: a New Mexico Pueblo tribe with traditions based on those of the Yuma and the Pima. The Zuñi are today particularly known for their artistry in jewelry-making.

PART TWO

Gulf Coasts and Tidal Swamps

Ais: a tribe, Muskhogean stock.

Álvarez de Piñeda, Alonso: discoverer of the Mississippi River, in 1519. He actually sighted it before De Soto.

Apalachee: a large, extremely hostile tribe of the Gulf Coast region. They were successful in routing the ill-fated expedition of Pánfilo de Narváez (q.v.) that was seeking the wonderful kingdom of Apalachen, in truth no more than a dirty village.

Atakapa: a word that means "man-eater" and designates a Texas-Louisiana Indian hunter tribe. Their own name for themselves was *Yuk'hiti ishak*.

Calusa: a Florida tribe known for exquisitely carved jewelry and weapons. They lived in thatch houses near water sources. They are thought to have been cannibalistic—they were certainly fierce warriors and brigands.

Carob: an evergreen tree bearing edible pods.

Coahuiltecan Culture: a civilization that prospered for thousands of years in the hostile climate of arid south Texas. Their linguistic origins have been traced by some scholars to California, although this matter is highly controversial.

Death Cult. *See* Southern Death Cult.

Fountain of Youth: the subject of an ancient Indian legend originating in the West Indies. It was the object of a futile search by Juan Ponce de León in the early sixteenth century. Ponce de León was eventually killed by the Calusa (q.v.).

Karankawa: a Gulf coastal nomadic tribe whose name means "people walking on the water." Although they were cannibalistic, they seem to have restricted the practice to religious ceremonies. Exotic body decorations were de rigueur for warriors and married women.

La Salle, Rene Robert Cavelier, Sieur de: the greatest French explorer of the lower Mississippi. He made early contacts with Natchez Indians.

Narváez, Pánfilo de: leader of a sixteenth-century Spanish expedition that sought to find gold and settle Florida. He was eventually lost at sea after many setbacks. Two of the four survivors of his group were Álvar Núñez Cabeza de Vaca and Estevanico the Black (*see* Part One references, above).

Natchesan Culture: a Mississippi-Louisiana culture that included the Taensa, the Avoyel, and the Natchez tribes. Natchez traditions were chronicled in the seventeenth century by La Salle (q.v). An elaborate social system marked this civilization.

Natchez pelvis: human bones found among Pleistocene animal bones in 1846 near Natchez, Mississippi. They were dated to at least 5000 B.C.

Pensacola: a word meaning "hair people." Florida's Pensacola Indians hold the distinction of having nearly killed Pánfilo de Narváez after warmly welcoming his expedition's stragglers.

Poverty Point Culture: a Meso-American-influenced culture in Louisiana that can be dated as far back as 1500 B.C. Extensive earthworks characterize this civilization.

Southern Death Cult: a tradition that occurred throughout the Gulf coastal region after about A.D. 1200. It was marked by human sacrifices, an influence from Meso-America. Ritual jewelry, of copper, gold, stone, or shell, was widespread and intricately fashioned.

Stallings Island: the site in Georgia where pottery was first discovered in the Southeast. Stallings Island ware has South American characteristics and even some ancient Japanese traits.

Takesta: the earliest Indian tribe known to have dwelt on the site of Miami, Florida.

Temple Mound Culture: a culture emanating from the American heartland that reached the lower Mississippi circa A.D. 700. This culture is marked by tall pyramidal mounds around which extensive settlements were built. Divine rulers led this most advanced and final prehistoric civilization.

Timucua: a tribal and linguistic group scattered over Georgia and northern Florida. The Timucuans were prominent in driving Ponce de León from Florida.

Tonkawa: a tribe consisting of perhaps twenty autonomous groupings spread out over east and central Texas. Nomadic and warlike, they were cannibalistic like many other southeastern tribes. Strangely, their name means "they all stay together."

Utina: *See* Timucua.

PART THREE

Southeastern Woodlands

Atlatl weights: ancient throwing-stick weights.

Cherokee: an extremely large tribal group whose origins may lie in the northern Great Lakes region but whose traditional homeland is the Appalachian highlands. The origin of their name is unknown, but they are part of the Iroquoian linguistic group.

Chert: a dark, flintlike rock.

Chickasaw: a southeastern tribe of raiders and warriors. They were at one time a single tribe with the Choctaw, a comparatively peaceful and sedentary tribe, but migrations and outside influences caused a lasting schism. By absorbing conquered tribes, they eventually became a mixed-blood group and true Chickasaws went out of existence.

Choctaw: although of the same origin as the Chickasaw, the Chocktaw developed a wholly different culture. They were called *têtes plates* (meaning "flatheads") by early French explorers because they customarily flattened the sides of infants' heads. They were peace-loving but competent in defensive battles.

Creek: the more common tribal name of the Muskogee Indians. Their prehistoric location is unknown, but before the Spaniards arrived they had settled in Georgia and Alabama. Their body-painting and tattooing was well-known and their communistic-democratic form of government seems to have been more operable than most modern governments.

Cusabo: a South Carolina tribe of which there were about ten subtribes. They were the first southeastern Indians to be enslaved, having first been subjected to European settlement among them.

De Soto, Hernando: Spanish explorer of wilderness areas from Georgia to Oklahoma. He was probably the first to cross the Mississippi River.

Middle Mississippi Culture: a highly advanced archeological complex derived from sources ranging from the Great Lakes to Mexico. It first appeared circa A.D. 700 and the rulers of its states eventually controlled much of the Southeast. Stone sculpture and pottery-making were well-developed practices.

Moiety: an anthropological term for one part of a two-part tribal subdivision.

Moundville: a Middle Mississippi *(q.v.)* site in Alabama that contains thirty-five ceremonial mounds covering an area of 160 acres. More than three thousand burials were located there.

Muskogee. *See* Creek.

Old Stone Fort: a Tennessee site consisting of a well-constructed enclosure of unknown origin and purpose. It may have been built about A.D. 30.

Powhatan: a small Algonquian tribe whose name is historically significant in Virginia and means "falls in a current of water." The powerful Powhatan Confederacy consisted of at least thirty subtribes. Pocahontas, the Indian maiden, was a Powhatan Indian.

Projectile Points. *See* Part One reference, above, and *Scientific Note—Projectile Points.*

Russell Cave: site in Alabama where artifacts more than eight thousand years old have been discovered. A hinged fishhook and a primitive lamp fueled by animal fat were in this stratum. Later-era human bones were also found.

Shawnee: a far-ranging Algonquian tribe whose name means "southerners." Although their early movements were all over the eastern United States, they eventually settled down in Oklahoma, but not until after the beginning of the historical period. Their renown is as woodsmen, hunters, warriors, and as guides for European explorers.

Sioux: a tribal grouping that includes, for example, tribes as disparate as the Winnebago and the Catawba. Their origin seems to have been in Kentucky or southern Ohio, whence they dispersed, dividing into northern and southern systems. Reports on southeastern Sioux indicate that they were regarded with intertribal animosity due to rather barbaric habits. They finally died out, emigrated, or were absorbed into other tribes in the Southeast while the northern branch continued to flourish in the Midwest.

Stallings Island ware. *See* Part Two reference, above.

Temple Mound Culture. *See* Part Two reference, above.

Tunica: a tribal and linguistic group name that means "those who are the people." The Tunica inhabited Mississippi and Louisiana forest areas and were industrious workers and traders.

Tuscarora: a North Carolina tribe that probably had its origin in the Northeast. The Tuscarora were known in the Southeast by the name "hemp-gatherers," because they skillfully collected and made use of Indian hemp. They were abused by the white explorers and eventually made their way to the Northeast.

Northeastern Woodlands

Abnaki: an Algonquian tribe in New Hampshire and Maine. They may originally have come from the Southwest. They eventually fled before the white man to Canada.

Adena Culture: an early Ohio high civilization that was superseded by the Hopewell Culture (q.v.).

Algonquian: a large linguistic and tribal grouping whose adherents dwelt from Maine to the Great Lakes, with isolated settlements even as far west as California.

Bull Brook: Massachusetts archeological site that yielded more than three thousand prehistoric artifacts, including more than one hundred Clovis fluted points (*see* Part One reference, above).

Delaware: the English name for an eastern coastal tribe whose people called themselves *Lenni Lenape* (meaning "true men").

Erie: an Iroquois name meaning "long tail." It refers to one of the largest tribes in the Eastern Woodlands. Engaged in fratricidal battle with their Seneca (Iroquois) neighbors in the seventeenth century, the Erie were defeated and absorbed into the Iroquois nation.

Hopewell Culture: an Ohio-based culture that had its Golden Age circa A.D. 500. Through trade patterns, its customs and influence were disseminated all over North America. The artistry of its people was unsurpassed and they had the first craft unions.

Huron. *See* Wyandot.

Iroquois: an immense tribal grouping (and linguistic grouping) made up of Canadian and New York prehistoric peoples. They were among the fiercest of northeastern peoples and were perhaps the most chronicled by missionaries and explorers. Their political organization in historical times, the League of Five Nations (q.v.), was without equal, and their domination extended to Lake Michigan in the west, the Ottawa River in the north, and the Tennessee River in the south.

League of Five Nations: the Iroquois confederation that consisted of the Cayuga, the Mohawk, the Oneida, the Onondaga, and the Seneca tribes.

Lenni Lenape. *See* Delaware.

Manito: an Algonquian name for a nature god.

Ottawa: a Great Lakes Algonquian tribe whose members were known for their bartering prowess. Tribal lore relates that they were once one tribe with the Chippewa and the Potawatomi, having migrated from the Northwest.

Potawatomi: an Algonquian tribe of the Great Lakes region. Their name means "peoples of the place of the fire," and they were perhaps the most peace-loving of Great Lakes tribes. The eventual historical homeland of the Potawatomi, like many other midwestern groups, was Oklahoma.

Raccoon Creek: a spectacular Hopewell (q.v.) site in Ohio that included four square miles of enclosures and elaborate moats and mounds.

Shoop Site: a Paleo-Indian (eight thousand to eighteen thousand years old) site in Pennsylvania that yielded many Clovis fluted points and many tools made of Onondaga chert, a material found more than two hundred miles away.

Susquehanna: Pennsylvania-Maryland Iroquois tribe. Intertribal warfare so depleted their numbers that they ceased existing in the eighteenth century.

Walum Olum: the tribal history of the Delaware Indians. It was first printed in 1836.

Wampumpeage: the original term used by northeast Algonquian Indians to mean "money"; it actually meant "measure of value." It was shortened to "wampum" by colonists. Wampum consisted of shells.

Wyandot: a Canadian tribe to which the name *Huron* was applied by the French. In historical times, they were pushed westward by the Iroquois and settled in parts of Ohio, Michigan, Illinois, and Wisconsin.

PART FIVE

Central Prairies and Woodlands

Brown's Valley: a Minnesota site that yielded what may have been twelve-thousand-year-old human bones.

Cahokia Mound: a one-hundred-foot-high prehistoric earthwork that covered about sixteen acres in Illinois near the Mississippi River. It was built in the thirteenth century with the aid of about a thousand laborers.

Chippewa: a barbarous tribe that was, in prehistoric times, probably the largest individual North American tribe. They are presumed to have originated in Canada and migrated south to Wisconsin by historic times. They are also known by the name *Ojibway*.

Fox: an Algonquian tribe that lived in Michigan's lower peninsula in prehistoric times and was driven into Wisconsin by eastern Indians shortly before the white man arrived. Their name for themselves was *Meshkwakihug*, meaning "red earth people." Although following the same migratory pattern as the Sauk (q.v.) the Fox were hostile and deceitful. They were particularly renowned for their elaborate warpaint.

Graham Cave: a Missouri site that yielded ten-thousand-year-old man-made stone implements.

Illinois: a rather weak, untrustworthy Algonquian tribal confederation located in Illinois, Missouri, and Arkansas. They were largely decimated by the Iroquois soon after explorers entered the Midwest.

Indian Knoll Culture: the ancestors of the midwestern Siouan tribes. They reached the Midwest from Kentucky and settled along riverbanks where they constructed twelve-foot-high shell middens.

Iowa: an undistinguished Siouan tribe that originated somewhere east of the Mississippi and eventually settled in the state of Iowa. Their name for themselves was *Pahodja*, meaning "dusty noses." The Dakota called them *Ayuhwa*, meaning "sleepy ones."

Kickapoo: an Algonquian name meaning "he moves about." Fierce and cunning warriors, the Kickapoo rank with the Apache and the Navajo as raiders. Their forays ranged through about twenty of our modern-day states. By historical times they had moved steadily southward to settle in southern Illinois. Their descendants today live in Mexico—the last stop on their migratory journeys.

Manito. *See* Part Four reference, above.

Menominee: a tribe that probably had its homeland in Michigan's lower peninsula. Their name, meaning "wild rice men," stems from their existence in Wisconsin and the upper peninsula of Michigan in historical times. Their descendants still live in Wisconsin.

Miami: a hunting (buffalo) and agriculture (corn) tribe that originated around Green Bay, Wisconsin. They settled in Illinois and eventually ended up in Ohio.

Missouri: an Algonquian word for a Siouan tribe—it means "people having dugout canoes." They probably originated around Green Bay, Wisconsin, and moved south, after feuding with neighbors, to the area that is now Missouri.

Nebo Hill points: long, narrow, and thick projectile points that have been unearthed near Kansas City, Missouri, and may be eight thousand years old.

473

Ojibway. *See* Chippewa.

Old Copper Culture: a singular Wisconsin and upper Michigan culture that developed around the independent discovery of copper-working techniques. Metal ornaments and implements were traded to far-distant peoples and perhaps as far as Mexico.

Osage: a Siouan tribe best known for its extensive traditions and folklore. Their traditional homeland is along the lower Ohio River, but they migrated shortly before the historical period, to Missouri.

Pleistocene. *See* Part One reference, above.

Quapaw: a Siouan tribal group of which one subtribe was named Arkansas. Arkansas later became the name of the entire group, courtesy of the Illinois. They were probably descendants of the Indian Knoll Culture (q.v.). The name *Quapaw* means "those going with the current."

Sachem: a chieftain.

Sauk: an Algonquian tribe, from Michigan's lower peninsula, that was closely related to the Fox (q.v.). Their name for themselves was *Osa'kiwug,* meaning "people of the yellow earth." They were considered honest, fierce in battle, and enterprising, and maintained a complex social structure. The famous war chieftain Black Hawk was a Sauk Indian.

Temple Mound Culture. *See* Part Two reference, above.

Varve: in geology, a layer of silt deposit.

Winnebago: an intelligent, peace-loving though courageous Siouan tribe that settled around Green Bay, Wisconsin, in prehistoric times. The name means "people of the filthy water" in Algonquian—the rationale behind it is unknown. Their name for themselves was *Hotcangara,* meaning "people of the big speech."

PART SIX

Northern Great Plains

Agate Basin: a Wyoming site that yielded projectile points among bison bones. Points of this unique type have also been found in Saskatchewan.

Angostura: a South Dakota site in which were found Angostura points, nine thousand-year-old weapons. Other examples of this type have been located as far distant as Alaska's Seward Peninsula.

Arapaho: an Algonquian tribe whose name for themselves was *Inuna-ina,* meaning "our people." Other tribes variously called them "dog eaters" and "sky men." Their original home was probably northern Minnesota. Their migration to the Plains region was similar to that of the Cheyenne (q.v.) and the two tribes were staunch allies.

Arikara: a Caddoan term meaning "horns." It refers to the Arikara headdress, consisting of two pieces of bone placed hornlike in the hair. Maize held a prominent place in their existence—they referred to it as "Mother." The Arikara dwelt along the upper Missouri River.

Assiniboine: a Siouan tribe whose people were distinguished for their handsome bearing and hunting prowess. Living in the Ozarks in historical times, they originated in the Ohio River region. Their name means "one who cooks by the use of stones." They were avid traders and ranged as far afield as Hudson Bay in Canada. They were eventually obliterated by smallpox epidemics.

Cheyenne: a large, well-organized Algonquian tribe that originated in Minnesota, moved to North Dakota, and then was driven into the Northern Great Plains along the Missouri River. Their societal organization almost resembled that of Sparta, with requisites of strict obedience and enormous courage. War was the main goal of the men, while the women participated in buffalo hunts and helped the men in other ways.

Crow: a tribe that coexisted with the Hidatsa (q.v.) along the upper Missouri River until a feud divided them. Their name for themselves was *Absaroke*, meaning "bird people." They were fierce warriors, and hunter-gatherers, but they also cultivated tobacco, an item significant for tribal religious rituals.

Dakota. *See* Sioux.

Dent: a Colorado site that yielded eleven-thousand-year-old projectile points and bones of twelve mammoths from the Pleistocene Age (*see* Part One reference, above).

Eden: a Wyoming site that yielded long, narrow projectile points—termed Eden points. Eden points are thought to have been brought from Canada and Alaska during the Pleistocene.

Hidatsa: once of the same tribe as the Crow (q.v.), the Hidatsa dwelt along the Missouri River. Their ancestral home was said to be in North Dakota. They were a sedentary people who were pushed toward extinction by a smallpox epidemic brought by the white man.

Kansa: an insignificant Siouan tribe whose origin was in the Ohio River area. They probably settled in Kansas in the sixteenth century.

Lindenmeier Site: the Colorado location of the most impressive Great Plains Folsom remains. Extinct animal bones and artifacts provided rich clues to the Folsom tradition in the Great Plains region, but no human remains were found.

Mandan: a tribe whose origin is in the upper Great Lakes region. By the historical period, they had migrated to North Dakota. Although their language is related to the Winnebago (Siouan), their appearance was not: they were rather fair-skinned, with long, thin noses, and were termed "white Indians" by the explorers. Smallpox extinguished the population early in the historical period.

Omaha: a tribal name meaning "those going against the current." The name refers to their prehistoric migrations from the Ohio and Wabash river valleys against the current of the Mississippi, into Minnesota, and from there to Nebraska. Throughout most of their wanderings, the Omaha were accompanied by a smaller tribe, the Ponca, and although the Ponca settled briefly in South Dakota, they eventually continued on to Omaha territory.

Oto: a Missouri River tribe that originated northeast of Green Bay, Wisconsin. Traditionally they were a single tribe with the Winnebago, the Missouri, and the Iowa (*see* Part Five references, above), but after a split the Oto and the Missouri went southwestward to settle along the Missouri and Grand Rivers. Their name for themselves was *Che-wae-rae*.

Pawnee: the only Great Plains tribe that practiced human sacrifice, though it was usually only as a fertility rite. They seem to have arrived in Nebraska very early, perhaps a few thousand years prior to the historical period. Aggressive raiders, they called themselves *Chahiksichahiks*, meaning "men of men." Pawnee served as guides for the American army.

Pleistocene. *See* Part One reference, above.

Pluvial Period. *See* Part One reference, above.

Scottsbluff: a Nebraska site at which were found Scottsbluff points, similar to Eden (q.v.) points, dating back ten thousand years.

Sioux: a historical-period Great Plains tribe that had made its way from Kentucky or Ohio to Minnesota and Wisconsin and then westward. (*See* Part Three reference, above.) Their name for themselves was *Ocheti shakowin*, meaning "the seven council fires." There were seven subtribes of the Northern Sioux, and they all gathered for an annual problem-solving and ceremonial meeting. The Sioux were colorful and efficient warriors and were deservedly feared in the Great Plains.

Southern Great Plains

Caddoans: a very early Southern Great Plains tribal grouping whose origins seem to be rooted in Mexico and the Caribbean. The name *Caddo* is a shortened form of *Kadohadacho,* meaning "real chiefs." Small Caddoan tribes scattered throughout the Southern Great Plains include: Tawehash, Tawakoni, Yscani, Waco, and Kichai. Most lived in Texas and Oklahoma and have passed out of existence.

Comanche: a Shoshonean tribe whose name means "anyone who wants to fight me all the time." They called themselves "the people." Their homeland is Wyoming, but by historical times they ranged throughout Kansas, Colorado, Texas, and New Mexico. Acquisitive of horses, they conducted frequent raids long into early historical times in the Southern Plains.

Fumarole Culture: a New Mexico–Oklahoma culture characterized by hunting artifacts and no evidence of agriculture or pottery.

Hasinai: a Caddoan (q.v.) tribal confederacy that included about twenty separate groups. Their name means "our own folk," but they were termed *Cenis* by the first white men. They were closely allied with the Comanche.

Jicarilla: an Eastern Apache tribe that originated in northwestern Canada. They settled in Colorado, Texas, and New Mexico and were fierce raiders. Their name, dating from Spanish times, means "little basket," and connotes the basketmaking skill of the women. Their own name for themselves was *Tinde,* meaning "the people." Their descendants still live in New Mexico.

Kenton: an Oklahoma site that yielded evidence of early agriculture—corncobs. No pottery was found.

Kiowa: a Great Plains tribe whose origins remain ambiguous. Their name means "principal people." Their language has both Shoshonean and Tanoan influences. They were joined by the Kiowa Apache at some point in historical times, probably as a defensive measure. Descriptions of their physical appearance likewise are ambiguous.

Lewisville: Texas site consisting of nineteen Pleistocene-era hearths. Clovis-type points were uncovered in charcoal nearly forty thousand years old, signifying that the points may be up to twenty-five thousand years older than their traditional dates.

Plainview points: a unique type of point named after a Texas site but found in areas that range from Ontario to Florida and from Alaska to Mexico.

Scharbauer Ranch: Texas site of first North American discovery of Pleistocene human bones with extinct animal bones. Other finds at the site were Clovis fluted points and unfluted points similar to the Clovis type but now known as Midland points.

Wichita: a Caddoan (q.v.) tribe of unknown origins whose name means "man." They were the darkest-skinned Indians of the Great Plains and were referred to as Black Pawnees, in part because tribal legend alludes to one-time connections with the Pawnee. Their main settlements were at the Great Bend of the Arkansas River, in Kansas.

Northern Mountains and Plateaus

Atsina: a rather insignificant Algonquian tribe that may once have been part of the Arapaho (*see* Part Six reference, above). The Arapaho referred to them as *Hitumena,* "beggars." Their name means "gut people" in the Blackfoot language.

Bannock: a Shoshonean tribe related to the Northern Paiute of the Great Basin (*see* Part Nine reference, below). They were in Montana in prehistoric times and probably moved to Idaho in the historical period. They are closely related to the Shoshoni (q.v.).

Blackfoot: an Algonquian tribe whose traditions hold to a northwest origin, although they probably came from the Canadian woods. Actually a confederacy, Blackfoot people can be divided into three main groups, the Siksika, the Kainah, and the Piegan. Their territory ranged from western Montana to deep into Canada. Their martial prowess was well known and feared. Their name came from the fact that they dyed their moccasins black.

Black's Fork: a southwestern Wyoming region, investigated during the 1930s, that was found to include at least three types of projectile points, the oldest of which were similar to Old World styles of more than twenty thousand years ago.

Burin: a pointed flint implement used for engraving.

Camas: a starchy root used in prehistoric times as a staple food item.

Five Mile Rapids: an Oregon site that gave evidence of having been continuously inhabited from ten thousand years ago until the beginning of the historical period. A number of types of projectile points were uncovered. The site has now been inundated by a damsite.

Kouse: a root used for making bread.

Kutenai: a tribe whose origins are unknown. At one time they may have dwelt in the Algonquian homeland in Canada. By the historical period they were settled in Idaho, Montana, and Washington. They were referred to as "water people" by neighboring tribes in the Columbia River region.

Lind Coulee: a site in Washington. Burned bison bones nearly nine thousand years old were found there.

Nez Percé: a tribe whose French name is actually a misnomer: it means "pierced nose," but there is no evidence to indicate they practiced nose-piercing as a tribal trait. Their name for themselves was *Tsutpeli,* meaning "people of the mountains." They were located in Idaho, Oregon, and Washington by historical times, but their original homeland is unknown. They were eventually driven into Canada by American soldiers.

Salish: a tribe whose name means "people." They were frequently termed "flatheads" because their heads were allowed to remain flat rather than deformed in infancy. Their earliest known homeland was in Montana and Idaho, although they may originally have come from Siberia. They are the people whose name was given to the Salishan linguistic family, a grouping that extends from Montana to Oregon and into Canada. Some tribes within this linguistic family include the Kalispel, the Skitswish, the Chelan, the Sinkiuse, the Methow, the Okanagon, the Sanspoil, and the Spokan.

Shoshoni: a tribe whose name is not yet deciphered. Names given them by neighboring tribes were "grass lodges" and "grass-house people." They gradually absorbed the Bannock (q.v.) tribe.

The Great Basin

Danger Cave: a Utah site that yielded examples of the world's earliest known basketry, dating from circa 8000 B.C. Thousands of artifacts were also found there.

Gypsum Cave: a Nevada site of five rooms that yielded remains of the extinct giant sloth as well as a wide variety of artifacts of many epochs.

Paiute, Northern: a Great Basin Shoshonean tribe that settled in Nevada, Oregon, and California. They are thought to have moved southward from an Oregon homeland, although tribal tradition holds to Nevada as their prehistoric homeland. They were relatively peaceful and industrious—and were ultimately ousted from their territory by silver miners despite a valiant defensive effort.

Paiute, Southern: a Great Basin tribe whose territory extended from Arizona to Utah and into Nevada and California. White men met little resistance when they wanted to move the Southern Paiute onto reservations—their defense was usually submission or flight.

Shoshoni, Western: a Great Basin tribal group whose way of life remained always on the subsistence level, or even below it. They settled in the most desolate parts of Utah and Nevada with few resources. Their territory included Death Valley. Groups within the tribe were the Gosiute and the Koso (or Panamint). They were termed *Dignes de pitié,* "those who deserve to be pitied," by the French.

Tule Springs: an important Nevada site that yielded charcoal that was dated to twenty-eight thousand years ago. Embedded with scrapers and other artifacts were bison, camel, horse, and mammoth bones.

Ute: a tribe whose territory included areas of Colorado, Utah, and New Mexico. They were prodigious raiders, making good use of horses that they had stolen. Their only equals as bandits seem to have been the Navajo (*see* Part One reference, above). They even stooped to slave raids, capturing Western Shoshoni and selling them to eager Spaniards.

Washo: a small Nevada tribe of unknown origin whose finest trait was highly skilled basketry. Their language is related to California Hokan (*see* Part Ten reference, below) dialects. They were ultimately decimated and scattered by miners in the historical period.

The Pacific Coast

Algonquian: Two Pacific Coast tribes, the Wiyot and the Yurok, seem to be isolated offshoots from the Algonquian linguistic group (*see* Part Four reference, above). They both were settled in northern California. The Yurok have been extensively studied due to their lack of communal laws—they have been termed "an aggregation of individuals."

Athapascan: a Pacific Coast linguistic group whose adherents originally came from Siberia, via Canada. Nineteen tribes are found in Washington, Oregon, and California. The Navajo and Apache (*see* Part One reference, above) are also Athapascan.

Borax Lake: a California site whose cultural influences have been noted throughout the Pacific coastal region. Many of the artifacts, including mortars and pestles, knives, and projectile points, were about eight thousand years old.

Calico Hills: a California site at which the Western Hemisphere's oldest man-made artifacts have been located. The crude tools found there are thought to be from fifty thousand to eighty thousand years old.

Camas. *See* Part Eight reference, above.

Chimakuan: a linguistic group of three tribes in northwestern Washington. They were the Chimakum, the Hoh, and the Quileute, and their language has been the object of considerable inquiry, as its origins are mysterious and its style is unique.

Chinookan: a linguistic group consisting of twelve tribes that settled in Washington and Oregon, along the banks of the Columbia River. Their trading ability brought the coastal trading jargon—a variation of the Chinook language—into existence. Chinookans served as guides for the Lewis and Clark expedition in the nineteenth century.

Hokan: a large linguistic grouping whose fourteen tribes were found in clusters in the coastal region from Oregon to Mexico. Seven tribes known as the Shastan Group lived in southern Oregon and northern California. Farther south, and slightly west, were the Yana and the Yahi. A four-man remnant of the latter tribe was discovered still living a primitive existence in the twentieth century. The large Pomo tribe was isolated from other Hokan tribes and inhabited the Russian River area near the coast. Other Hokan tribes, farther south in California, were the Esselen, the Salinan, the Chumash, and the Diegueño.

Kalapooian: a linguistic group of nine tribes, most of whose members lived in the Willamette River area of Oregon.

Klamath Lakes, Lower and Upper: sites in California and Oregon that yielded bones of extinct animals that dated from as recently as 5000 B.C.

Lake Mojave: a fifteen-thousand-year-old California site whose earliest occupants left a large supply of stone artifacts. The lake is now dry.

Penutian: a large linguistic group of seven tribes that controlled more than half of the territory of California. They may be in a direct line from Pleistocene inhabitants of the region. One tribe, the Yokut of the San Joaquin Valley, has been subdivided into about forty-five different tribes speaking distinct dialects.

Powell, John Wesley: founder of the Bureau of American Ethnology and author of *Indian Linguistic Families North of Mexico,* published in 1891. He was also the first to navigate the Grand Canyon of the Colorado River. Nearly half of the fifty-eight linguistic groups outlined by Powell in his treatise could be found along the Pacific Coast.

Salishan: a linguistic group of twenty-seven tribes whose name is derived from that of the Salish of the Northern Mountains and Plateaus (*see* Part Eight reference, above). The Salishan settled in Oregon and Washington. The city of Seattle was named after the last Salishan chief.

Santa Rosa Island: a California site in which burned mammoth bones and evidence of man's presence have been found. It may date to thirty thousand years ago.

Shapwailutan: a linguistic group of six tribes inhabiting Washington, Oregon, and California. One Shapwailutan tribe, the Modoc, may have been the last to succumb to the white man's incursion in the West.

Shoshonean: a thirteen-tribe linguistic group whose members reached California from their homeland in the Great Basin region beginning around A.D. 400. The coast-dwellers gained a reputation as efficient boatbuilders, and the Gabrieliños were known for their artistry in soapstone.

Takilman: a language group composed of two tribes, the Latgawa and the Takelma. Both dwelt along Oregon's Rogue River.

Tule: a type of bulrush.

Wakashan: most tribes of this language grouping were settled in Canada. There were two Pacific Coast tribes, the Makah and the Ozette. Both were located in northern Washington by historical times. Their name is thought to come from *waukash,* meaning "good." The Wakashan were known for their courageous feats of whale-hunting on the open sea.

479

Wokas: water lilies whose seeds were used as a staple by Shapwailutan (q.v.) tribes.

Yakonan: a small and little-studied linguistic group of six tribes in Oregon.

Yukian: a linguistic grouping whose tribes evidence widespread cultural and dialectical divergences. They settled in the valleys and coastal areas in northern California, and may actually be aboriginal inhabitants of the region. They were eventually massacred by Americans, as were so many other Pacific Coast Indians.

Index